GOINGPLACES
paragraph to essay

CANADIAN EDITION

Richard E. Bailey

Henry Ford Community College

Linda Denstaedt

Oakland Writing Project, University of Michigan

Therese Gormley Hirmer

Seneca College and University of Guelph

**McGraw-Hill
Ryerson**
Connect. Learn. Succeed.

Going Places: Paragraph to Essay
Canadian Edition

Copyright © 2013 by McGraw-Hill Ryerson Limited, a Subsidiary of The McGraw-Hill Companies. Copyright © 2010 by The McGraw-Hill Companies Inc. All rights reserved. No part of this publication may be reproduced or transmitted in any form or by any means, or stored in a data base or retrieval system, without the prior written permission of McGraw-Hill Ryerson Limited, or in the case of photocopying or other reprographic copying, a licence from The Canadian Copyright Licensing Agency (Access Copyright). For an Access Copyright licence, visit www.accesscopyright.ca or call toll-free to 1-800-893-5777.

The Internet addresses listed in the text were accurate at the time of publication. The inclusion of a website does not indicate an endorsement by the authors or McGraw-Hill Ryerson, and McGraw-Hill Ryerson does not guarantee the accuracy of information presented at these sites.

ISBN-13: 978-0-07-105672-4
ISBN-10: 0-07-105672-6

1 2 3 4 5 6 7 8 9 0 WEB 1 9 8 7 6 5 4 3

Printed and bound in Canada

Care has been taken to trace ownership of copyright material contained in this text; however, the publisher will welcome any information that enables it to rectify any reference or credit for subsequent editions.

Editorial Director: *Rhondda McNabb*
Publisher: *Kim Brewster*
Sponsoring Editor: *Karen Krahn*
Marketing Manager: *Margaret Janzen*
Senior Developmental Editor: *Sara Braithwaite*
Supervising Editor: *Cathy Biribauer*
Photo/Permissions Researcher: *Cindy Howard*
Senior Editorial Associate: *Marina Seguin*
*i*learning Sales Specialist: *Lisa Gillman*
Copy Editor: *Colleen Ste. Marie*
Production Coordinator: *Lena Keating*
Cover and Interior Design: *Peter Papayanakis*
Composition: *Laserwords Private Limited*
Cover Photo: *©Miguel Navarro/Getty Images*
Printer: *Webcom Ltd.*

Library and Archives Canada Cataloguing in Publication Data

Going places: paragraph to essay/Richard E. Bailey . . . [et al.].
—Canadian ed.

Includes index.

ISBN 978-0-07-105672-4

1. English language—Paragraphs—Problems, exercises, etc. 2. Report writing—Problems, exercises, etc. 3. College readers. 4. Critical thinking. I. Bailey, Richard E., 1952–

PE1439.G64 2013   808'.042076   C2012-905297-3

Brief Table of Contents

CONTENTS

PART 2 Paragraph Writing and Patterns of Thinking

4 Description 62

5 Example 79

PART 3 ❯ Going to the Next Level: Essay Writing and Patterns of Thinking

25 ⟩ Punctuation   457

26 ⟩ Mechanics   474

PART 5 — Reading and Thinking Critically

27 ⟩ Critical Reading, Thinking, and Writing   497

Our authors believe that whatever the destination, effective writing and critical thinking will make a fundamental difference in each student's journey. *Going Places: Paragraph to Essay,* first Canadian edition, offers a process-oriented introduction to paragraph and essay writing. The clear step-by-step instructions are enhanced by a wealth of student and professional writing samples, a contemporary visual design, and engaging exercises. Recognizing that every student's journey is unique, a variety of program-specific examples and exercises have been included throughout. *Going Places* not only offers writing frameworks, it also provides instruction and opportunity for students to develop their critical reading and thinking skills.

FEATURES

Dynamic Design: The innovative design is visually appealing, highly readable, and engaging. By avoiding a text-heavy format, the content is made more memorable and digestible for students.

Program-Specific Content: The Canadian edition of this textbook incorporates exercises and examples from a variety of program disciplines.

Student Models: Throughout Part 2, readers follow a "Going Places" student through each step of the writing process. Annotations highlight the decisions made as the student writes. These models help readers understand writing as a *decision-making* process.

Professional Readings: The last chapter of this text contains ten Canadian professional readings that help students connect critical reading to the writing process. Each reading is followed by comprehension and discussion questions as well as a list of writing assignments.

PEDAGOGY

Interactive visual chapter openers with "Think First" writing prompts kick-start each chapter and get students ready to write.

Chapter-opening exercises in Parts 1–3 invite students to connect writing activities with their personal, school, and work lives and to develop these connections by brainstorming and discussing their ideas with classmates.

"At a Glance" annotated student writing samples in each chapter of Parts 2 and 3 point out important elements of effective writing, such as thesis statements, topic sentences, supporting details, unity, and coherence.

"A Professional's Take" reading selections written by professional writers in each chapter of Part 2 show how the experts effectively use the same patterns of organization in real-world settings.

"_____ **Thinking**" sections in each chapter of Part 2, such as "Description Thinking" or "Narration Thinking," help students focus and develop their thoughts in relation to the chapter's main concepts.

"_____ **in Process**" sections in each chapter of Part 2, such as "Classification in Process" or "Cause and Effect in Process," walk students through the steps of the writing process. Students discover which forms of prewriting work best for them, what challenges they may encounter when drafting and revising, and which errors might need special attention as they edit.

Checkpoints help students stay on point throughout the chapter and connect each chapter's ideas to their own habits, beliefs, and goals:

"Ask Yourself" for critical thinking, self-reflection, and personal analysis

"Talk about it" for sharing ideas with peers

"A Writer's Response" for low-pressure writing practice

McGraw-Hill Connect™ is a web-based assignment and assessment platform that gives students the means to better connect with their coursework, with their instructors, and with the important concepts that they will need to know for success now and in the future.

With Connect, instructors can deliver assignments, quizzes and tests online and integrate grade reports easily with Learning Management Systems (LMS) such as WebCT and Blackboard. By choosing Connect, instructors are providing their students with a powerful tool for improving academic performance and truly mastering course material. Connect allows students to practise important skills at their own pace and on their own schedule. Importantly, students' assessment results and instructors' feedback are all saved online—so students can continually review their progress and plot their course to success.

Connect English helps students improve their writing and grammar skills through comprehensive and reliable instruction, practice material, and more!

Talk to your iLearning Sales Specialist today!

The Online Learning Centre (www.mcgrawhill.ca/olc/Bailey) will contain the instructor's manual and PowerPoint slides to aid in teaching.

SUPERIOR SERVICE

The McGraw-Hill Ryerson team is ready to help you assess and integrate any of our products, technology, and services into your course for optimal teaching and learning performance. Whether it's helping your students improve their grades, or putting your entire course online, the McGraw-Hill Ryerson team is here to help you do it. Contact your iLearning Sales Specialist today to learn how to maximize all of McGraw-Hill Ryerson's resources!

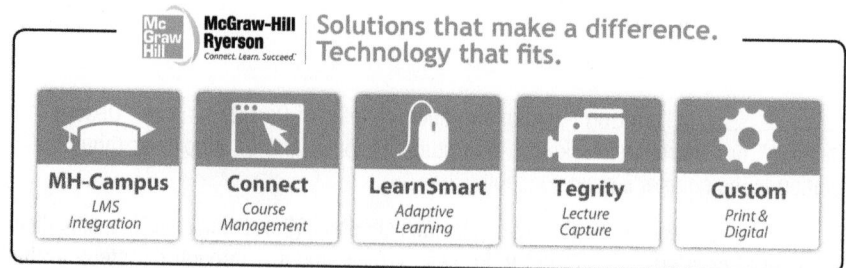

McGraw-Hill Ryerson | Solutions that make a difference. Technology that fits.

MH-Campus — LMS Integration
Connect — Course Management
LearnSmart — Adaptive Learning
Tegrity — Lecture Capture
Custom — Print & Digital

For more information on the latest technology and Learning Solutions offered by McGraw-Hill Ryerson and its partners, please visit us online: **www.mcgrawhill.ca/he/solutions.**

ACKNOWLEDGEMENTS

Writing a textbook is a collaborative effort and I would like to extend sincere gratitude to the team at McGraw-Hill Ryerson for their expert guidance. In particular, I am indebted to Karen Krahn, humanities sponsoring editor, and Sara Braithwaite, senior developmental editor, for their patience and professional advice. I would also like to thank Lisa Gillman, iLearning sales specialist, higher education; Cathy Biribauer, supervising editor; and Colleen Ste. Marie for her careful handling of the copy editing.

My colleagues and students at Seneca College and The University of Guelph, Centre for Open Learning and Educational Support, supplied comments and feedback that were an inspiration for writing this text.

The reviewers also deserve recognition since they provided constructive suggestions, which were incorporated into the text.

Sara Beck, *St. Lawrence College*
Barbara Buetter, *Niagara College*
Bill Bunn, *Mount Royal University*
Paula Crooks, *Conestoga College*
Angela Garmaise, *Seneca College*
Susan Hesemeier, *Grant McEwan University*
Andrea Jacobs, *Centennial College*
Sean McNabney, *Sheridan Institute of Technology*
Cyndy Reimer, *Douglas College*
Curtis Runions, *St. Lawrence College, Saint Laurent*
Prita Sethuram, *Centennial College*
Sandra Slade, *Langara College*
Lesley Watts, *North Island College*
Dagmar Vavrusa, *Centennial College*

Finally, I thank my husband and family for their encouragement and unconditional support during this project.

Therese Gormley Hirmer

Meeting the Demands of College and University Writing

CHAPTER OVERVIEW

- ☐ Writing for Post-Secondary Study
- ☐ Purpose and Form
- ☐ Focus and Content
- ☐ Improve Word Choice
- ☐ Critical Reading and Thinking
- ☐ Set Goals

THINK FIRST

Does learning involve pleasure, hard work, or both? What makes learning fun? Recall a positive and a negative experience you had in school. Think about these two experiences and write down what you remember. Be specific about the time, place, subject, and people involved.

Getting to Know Yourself

Most of us have ideas and beliefs we do not think about or question. Maybe you love art. Perhaps you are concerned about the environment. When you write about these topics, you may be surprised by what you discover. Writing is actually a great way to learn about yourself. Although it may be challenging at first, it is worth the effort to learn how to write well.

BRAINSTORM

Brainstorm a list of subjects you really care about. Then select the two or three most important ones. When did these subjects become important? Has their importance to you changed over time? What caused that change?

The "Write" Audience

Whenever you write, ask yourself who your reader is. Just as you shift gears when you stop talking to a friend outside of class and address an instructor instead, when you write for different readers you need to adjust (1) how you write, (2) what you choose to say, and (3) what words you use. If you write an assignment for an instructor and then email a friend, you are writing for two very different readers. Being sensitive to your tone and language, professionally and personally, will help you communicate more effectively. You will learn more about tone later in this chapter.

DISCUSSION

Who is the person you find it easiest to talk to? Why? Who do you find it most difficult to talk to? Why? Turn and talk to a classmate about these two people, and describe what it feels like to talk to them.

Get Ahead: Moving Toward Successful Writing

Knowing what you want to say (subject and focus), why you are saying it (purpose), how you will say it (form), and who you are saying it to (reader/audience) will give you a head start on any writing project. If you take the time to reflect on and explore your ideas, you will make the writing process less frustrating and the end result more successful. By becoming a successful writer in post-secondary studies, you will be prepared for almost any career.

DISCUSSION

Brainstorm for a minute or two, recalling times in school or at home that you had to write. Recall the subject, purpose, form, and audience. Then turn and talk to a classmate, describing one of these writing experiences.

Writing for Post-Secondary Study

Take out a piece of paper and a pen. In post-secondary studies your writing will often begin with an assignment. Assignments have a purpose. In some cases, you will write to explore ideas and make connections between one idea and another or between classroom learning and the real world. More often, you will write to convey information or to demonstrate what you know about course content. Finally, you will sometimes write to persuade: to change your reader's mind and possibly to motivate someone to act. More often than not, the reader of your writing will be the instructor who provides you with a subject. The form of your writing will vary, from journal entry to summary, from paragraph to essay, from short-answer and essay test to report and term paper.

Purpose and Form in Writing

The reason you write is your **purpose**. You write to reflect, to inform, or to persuade. Purpose will often determine the way you present your message or the **form** your writing takes—in other words, the way it is organized and presented. For example, when you write to figure something out, you do not write a memo to yourself; you keep your thoughts and words flowing in a journal entry. In contrast, when you write to inform or to persuade, you do so with a reader in mind. Readers of academic writing look for organization, supporting detail, and correct use of language. Readers of workplace writing look for the same things.

In school, you will often write paragraphs and essays; in the workplace, you will often write memos and reports. When writing to inform or persuade, your writing will be more effective if you select an appropriate presentation or form for your ideas. You can begin by asking yourself these questions in any order:

What is this writing supposed to look like?

Why am I writing?

What do I want to say?

Who am I writing for?

Moreover, in most academic writing, keep in mind these guidelines when considering word choice and style:

1. Minimize your use of first-person pronouns: *I, my, me.*
2. Minimize your use of contractions: *isn't, don't, won't.*
3. Avoid slang and the kind of informal language you use in casual conversation.
4. Use gender neutral, politically correct words.

EXERCISE 1-1 **Purpose in Home and Work Writing**

Directions: *Select the **purpose** that best relates to each of the forms of writing listed. For each form of writing, indicate the subject (what it is about) and who will read it. Some forms of writing may have more than one purpose. The first one has been done for you.*

PURPOSE

A. **Think on paper:** Explore your thoughts, ideas, feelings, and beliefs.

B. **Convey information:** Share what you know and what you have learned.

C. **Persuade your reader:** Change your reader's mind, motivate your reader to do something.

Exercise 1-1	How will you write it? FORM	Why are you writing?			What do you want to say?	Who are you writing for?
		PURPOSE			SUBJECT & FOCUS	READER or AUDIENCE
		A. Think on paper	B. Convey information	C. Persuade your reader		
Example 1	Shopping list		✓		Things to buy at store	Me
Example 2	Email					
Example 3	Diary					
Example 4	Notes to family					
Example 5	Writing at work					
Example 6	Application form					

EXERCISE 1-2 Purpose in Post-Secondary Studies Writing

Directions: *Select the purpose that best relates to each of the forms of post-secondary writing listed below. (Some forms of writing will have more than one purpose.) Indicate possible subjects and readers for each form of writing. The first one has been done as an example.*

Exercise 1-2	How will you write it? FORM	Why are you writing?			What do you want to say?	Who are you writing for?
		PURPOSE			SUBJECT & FOCUS	READER or AUDIENCE
		A. Think on paper	B. Convey information	C. Persuade your reader		
Example 1	Journal entry	✓			Personal writing, class notes, assignments	Me, instructor
Example 2	Summary					
Example 3	Paragraph					
Example 4	Essay					
Example 5	Short-answer test					
Example 6	Lab report					

EXERCISE 1-3 Purpose in Your Own Writing

Directions: *Review your responses in Exercises 1-1 and 1-2 and write short answers to the following questions. Explain your thinking.*

1. What is the most common purpose in your personal writing?

_____

2. What is the most common purpose in your college or university writing to this point?

_____

3. What is the biggest difference between personal and post-secondary writing?

_____

4. In what forms of writing are spelling and grammatical correctness most important?

_____

Focus and Content

The focus of your writing will vary according to your purpose for writing. In assignments asking you to think on paper (journal writing, for example), the content may be personal. As you explore ideas or think on paper, the focus is on you, the writer, and the subject you are writing about. You do not worry about your reader's reaction. You are the primary audience.

However, in writing assignments in school, you are asked to convey information and show your understanding of course material. The content is academic in reports, short-answer tests, papers, and exams so that you can demonstrate your knowledge to a professor. The focus is on the subject and the reader.

Through argument and persuasion, you demonstrate your knowledge to a professor by stating and supporting an opinion. The focus is on the writer, the subject, and the reader. There is a subject—for example, "Should the legal drinking age be lowered?" There is an audience—a reader who is not convinced it is a good idea. Along with the evidence you present, you will include your personal knowledge of the subject to influence the reader's thinking.

The following samples of student writing illustrate the relationship between focus and writing content.

A. Unedited Student Journal Entry

FOCUS: The writer

What is so great about drinking? I do not get enjoyment, pleasure, or satisfaction from it. It seems like everyone my age is drinking just to get drunk and stupid. People drink to be more social and or to enhance life. Life would be boring without alcohol right? Not in my opinon. I like to talk to and aproach people, I can act goofy and stupid, and I can enjoy myself. People have found it hard to believe that I do not enjoy drinking. I suppose it is odd, considering most 18-year-olds pass the weekends with getting hammered and wasted at parties. Ive been there and done that. Ive had a good time too. People get hurt physically and mentally when drinking. People will say things they do not mean or do things they would not do when they were sober. I imagine this is another reason why so many people do drink: A temporary solution to life's problems.

FORM AND PURPOSE
The journal entry focuses on the writer's experiences, thoughts, and beliefs.

FOCUS
The writer is the audience. He is not worried about who might read his journal. The use of *I* is acceptable in this form of writing. Spelling and grammatical correctness are not big issues because this writing is not for an outside audience.

How will you write it?	Why are you writing?			What do you want to say?
FORM	PURPOSE			SUBJECT & FOCUS
	A. Think on paper	B. Convey information	C. Persuade your reader	
Journal	✓			Writer

B. Report on Workplace Visit for Physics Class

FOCUS: The subject and the reader

This facility was doing tests on truck frames, with the goal of making trucks lighter by reducing the mass of the frame. The manufacturer needs to be sure the truck frame is strong enough to be safe in normal operation. A number of tests were devised to obtain data. Technicians outfitted a vehicle with instrumentation and took it to an appropriate site so data could be collected and recorded. Test situations included travel over rough terrain, ordinary highway mileage, and sudden shocks such as those caused by potholes. After data were recorded, the vehicle was then returned to the test facility, where the recorded data were, in effect, played over and over. In a few weeks' time, the vehicle was subjected to a lifetime of road wear. Engineers analyzed the results.

FORM AND PURPOSE
This report focuses on the subject, explaining the test process. The writer provides detailed observations and tries to answer questions the reader might have about the workplace.

FOCUS
The focus here is also on the reader. This report was written for a supervisor or other professional in the field, so spelling and grammatical correctness are very important.

How will you write it?	Why are you writing?			What do you want to say?
FORM	PURPOSE			SUBJECT & FOCUS
	A. Think on paper	B. Convey information	C. Persuade your reader	
Report		✓		Subject, reader

C. Response to Discussion Question in Literature Textbook

FOCUS: The writer, the subject, and the reader

Young Maya Angelou was ashamed that Mama could show off her ignorance in the presence of a woman as great as Mrs. Flowers. To Angelou the way Mama used incorrect grammar in front of a gentlewoman was a sign of ignorance. She did not understand why Mama could not remember her verbs. Why did Mama always say "is" when she talked about more than two people? Why did Mama insist on calling her "Sister Flowers"? Why did Mama have to embarrass her so much? To Angelou, Mrs. Flowers was the

FORM AND PURPOSE
This response focuses on detailed knowledge of a reading assignment. Although we aren't given the question, the content shows that the writer is familiar with the reading. The writer quotes the essay by Maya Angelou and provides a thorough response.

definition of elegance. Angelou felt that Mrs. Flowers deserved a proper greeting. Mama's improper speech never bothered Mrs. Flowers. She understood the difference between ignorance and poor education. Mama had her own intelligence even if she did not use proper English. They spoke easily with each other. Mrs. Flowers and Mama were bound together by how they were alike in a prejudiced and sexist society. They both understood that money and appearance were not what make a person great. What seemed like a strange relationship at the time was really a relationship of respect. She discovered years later that a formal education was all that separated them.

FOCUS
The focus is also on the reader. The careful writing, use of quotations, and detailed explanations show that this writer knows what the professor wants. The content and careful writing persuade the reader that the writer is disciplined, informed, and capable of critical thinking. The writer avoids first-person pronouns and slang.

How will you write it?	Why are you writing?			What do you want to say?
	PURPOSE			
FORM	**A. Think on paper**	**B. Convey information**	**C. Persuade your reader**	**SUBJECT & FOCUS**
Essay			✓	*Subject, reader*

EXERCISE 1-4 **Form, Purpose, and Focus**

Directions: *After reading the following passages, select the form, purpose, and focus that best describe each writing sample, and fill out the chart for each passage. (The chart appears at the end of the passages.)*

1.

All of a sudden, rock music is getting way too popular. More and more young people are forming their own bands. They are even changing their appearance. Kids who always had short hair are coming out with "college hair." Kids who used to be all but invisible are dying their hair green and sporting chained wallets. Even the ones who used to sell drugs want to become rock stars as their next source of income. The competition is suddenly so steep that the odds of being successful have declined. In addition, the sound is uniform. It is all hardcore bandwagon noise. Where is the originality? They just follow the crowd. The popularity of rock, and the idea that anyone can play, means everything sounds the same—and bad, at that.

2.

Vehicle 33 arrived at the scene of the accident at 2:25 p.m. Scene was the southwest corner of Canfield and Beck. Two-car collision. Driver of one car, middle-aged male, was unconscious, breathing 25 bpm, bleeding from the mouth. Trauma to the head and face. Situation called for airway management. C-collar was applied. Patient was boarded, oxygen administered high flow, transported by paramedics. Driver of the other car, 18-yr-old female, was sitting on the curb, responsive. Quick survey indicated possible fracture of ulna, right arm; lacerations. Fracture was splinted. Patient was stable when transported to emergency.

3.

I worked on your campaign last year in the Cold Lake area. Your stance on water quality and Alberta's participation in the oil sands mining was very important to me. In fact, that issue sold me on your candidacy.

For that reason, I urge you to alter your stated position on future funding for the mining industry. I know you are a participant in the Oil Sands Advisory Panel, and I know you are a man of conscience and vision. Environment Canada regulations have been important factors in preventing environmental damage. Cutting funding will diminish the ability to regulate the disposal of mine tailings which will have long-term and, I fear, negative effects on monitoring groundwater and surface water quality, one of Alberta's greatest natural resources.

4.

In Walter E. Williams's article "Making a Case for Corporal Punishment," Williams expresses his opinion on this controversial subject. He states that the old-fashioned way of whipping misbehaved children produces more civilized young people. Parents today do not discipline their kids the way they used to. Children in today's society are hostile and disrespectful toward adults. Williams believes that whipping these children, as a form of punishment, would make them as respectful as the children of yesterday. By disciplining children, parents and other figures of authority would have more control over the children of today.

5.

FROM: sadsoul22@omni.com
DATE: Sun, 13 Dec 2012 19:44:29 EDT
SUBJECT: Your 2B
TO: Professor Safer
Sorry i did not turn in my essay! i'll take care of it, as soon as i can. the past week has been tough, my kids have a serious case of ear infection and

the flu for two weeks now, so it has been pretty challenging for me. and on top of that we left to ottawa friday and i just got back two hours ago. I'm done with my most of the work and i'm working as hard as i can. so sorry for the delay. is tomorrow ok?

your student, Sue

How will you write it?	Why are you writing?			What do you want to say?
	PURPOSE			
FORM	**A. Think on paper**	**B. Convey information**	**C. Persuade your reader**	**SUBJECT & FOCUS**
1				
2				
3				
4				
5				

Improve Word Choice

To improve your writing, you need to use appropriate academic vocabulary. Using a thesaurus and a dictionary is one way to increase your vocabulary. Another way to improve your writing is by paying close attention to **diction**, or word choice. Carefully choosing words helps a writer create a specific mental picture for a reader. To improve word choice, use precise nouns and verbs, select words to create a tone, and monitor your choices of words to make sure they are appropriate for your purpose. As you become more conscious of how and why you are using specific words, your vocabulary will also expand.

PRECISE NOUNS AND VERBS

Powerful writing begins with use of precise nouns and verbs. You can move your writing from general, everyday conversation-style diction into precisely written diction by replacing vague or overused nouns and verbs with more specific words that fit the context of your writing.

Read the following sentence:

The high winds caused the hiker to pull his **jacket** closed as he **walked** up the mountain.

In this sentence, the boldfaced words are too general to create a specific image in the mind of the reader. To improve the diction, the general noun *jacket* could be replaced with a more precise noun such as *anorak, cardigan, bomber jacket, pea coat,* or *parka*. Similarly, the vague word *walked* could be replaced with a more precise verb such as *traipsed, trekked, marched, wandered, trudged,* or *strolled*.

Here is one way the writer could effectively revise the sentence:

The high winds caused the hiker to pull his **parka** closed as he **trudged** up the mountain.

In the revised sentence, the writer helps readers visualize the hiker struggling in high winds. The word *jacket* is replaced by *parka,* a specific type of coat designed to withstand difficult weather. The verb *trudged* replaces the general word *walked* and is more effective in conveying the difficulty of the climb.

You can also use more precise language when you are writing about some research you have done. Rather than use an expression such as "The author goes on about . . ." try "The author discusses. . . ." The verb *discuss* is more precise and academic than "goes on about."

TONE

The words you use in your writing give what is often referred to as the *tone* of your writing. When writers choose specific words, they also can express an attitude, or tone, in their writing, in much the same way that a speaker does with facial expressions or tone of voice. Writing can be formal or informal, positive or negative. A tone can also be angry or serious, or reflect any emotion, so in selecting their words, writers should consider an audience.

Academic essays are written for a single reader, your professor. In college or university writing, the style is generally formal, and your words are chosen to express a view or attitude toward an academic subject. You might explain the destructive consequences of a historical event or examine the positive influences of an effective strategy for businesses.

For example, in conversation, you might say, "This majorly affects the outcome of our study." To convey this idea academically, you might write, "This has a significant impact on the outcome."

Look at the photograph here and read the sentences related to it that reflect basic tones in writing. Words chosen to create the tone are underlined in each sentence.

- **Formal Tone:** A formal tone may be objective, clinical, instructive, factual, or informative. The following sentence illustrates a factual tone.

  Landscape <u>designers</u> use <u>garden statues</u> as <u>focal points</u> to express the personality of the homeowner.

- **Informal Tone:** An informal tone may be sentimental, emotional, nostalgic, or sarcastic. The following sentence illustrates a sarcastic tone.

  <u>Pot-bellied</u> ceramic gnomes <u>scattered</u> around a lawn are an <u>eyesore</u>, not landscaping.

- **Positive Tone:** A positive tone may be hopeful, enthusiastic, appreciative, confident, or optimistic. The following sentence illustrates an appreciative tone.

  Garden gnomes create a <u>playful element</u> in any garden and suggest the homeowner <u>loves fun</u>.

- **Negative Tone:** A negative tone may be angry, accusing, scornful, or critical. The following sentence illustrates an angry tone.

> There should be a neighbourhood watch initiated to remove all <u>unsightly</u> and ridiculous lawn art, and the garden gnome should be the first item <u>thrown</u> in the <u>trash</u>.

DENOTATION AND CONNOTATION

Effective word choice not only improves and clarifies your writing, but also helps you create a tone that matches your purpose. Words have two types of meaning: denotative and connotative.

Denotation is the exact dictionary definition of a word. Words can have a variety of dictionary meanings or denotations.

> **lift** (verb) 1. the act of raising something; 2. the act of stealing; 3. the beginning of flight as in *lift off*; (noun) 1. a ride; 2. an elevator; 3. a machine designed to raise something.

Connotation is the implied meaning of a word that conveys an emotion and creates an emotional response in a reader. The word *lift* denotes the act of raising something up or moving something from one place to another. It can also suggest or connote power, change, or growth. In the sentence that follows, *lift* means "to raise the level" of morale. However, it also has a positive connotation and suggests power and improvement.

> The management team planned to restructure expectations and **lift** morale.

As you select words, consider both the denotation (dictionary meaning) and connotation (implied or suggested meaning). Use a dictionary or thesaurus to aid you.

APPROPRIATE WORD CHOICE

When you are thinking about which word to use in a given writing situation, ask yourself, "Who is my audience?" For most of your academic papers you will be writing for your instructor or professor, who will expect you to use formal English. You should avoid using informal language, such as jargon, idioms, slang, and clichés. You should also avoid sexist or insensitive language.

1. Avoid **jargon**, which is specialized or technical language used by professionals and other groups. It is not always familiar to a general audience. Here is an example from the business world:

> Money market accounts offer <u>competitive yields</u> and easy access to cash.

Here, the phrase "competitive yields" means the account offers competitive interest rates. If you are writing an assignment for a business course, you could expect to use this term and have your reader understand it. However, for a general audience, it would be more effective to avoid jargon and use simpler words that any reader could understand.

> Money market accounts offer <u>the opportunity to earn interest</u> and to access cash easily.

Ask Yourself

Which type of informal language will be hardest for you to remove from your writing? Why?

2. Avoid **idioms**, which are commonly used phrases that mean something different from their literal meanings. For example, a person might say his aunt "kicked the bucket" (meaning she died) or your friend might say she needs to "burn the midnight oil" in order to finish a project (meaning she needs to stay up late). Although idioms are commonly used in speech, you should avoid using them in formal academic writing.

3. Avoid **slang**, which is informal, casual language used in everyday speech. It is acceptable to use within your circle of friends or daily life but is too informal for academic writing.

   My friend looks like an <u>airhead</u> because she <u>parties</u> constantly, then pulls <u>all-nighters</u> to <u>cram</u> for tests.

   In the sentence above, slang is used to create a colourful description of a friend. Here is the sentence written in formal English.

   My friend's behaviour shows she is <u>not a serious student</u> because she <u>goes to parties</u> constantly and <u>stays up all night</u> to <u>study</u> just before a test.

4. Avoid **clichés**, which are overused expressions that are no longer surprising or interesting. Everyone can complete these phrases: busy as a (bee); selling like (hotcakes); light as a (feather). What other clichés can you think of? If you want to make your writing fresh and interesting, avoid clichés.

<u>COMMON CLICHÉS</u>

better late than never	playing with fire
beyond a shadow of a doubt	sink or swim
blind as a bat	starting at the bottom of the ladder
cool as a cucumber	the bottom line
crystal clear	tried and true
hard as a rock	water under the bridge
last but not least	what comes around goes around
like a bull in a china shop	white as a ghost

5. Avoid **sexist language**, which can directly or indirectly stereotype men or women. Sometimes it is easy to recognize; for example, calling a woman "a babe" is sexist. However, it might not be so clear that referring to a nurse or doctor as a "male nurse" or a "lady doc" is also sexist. In these examples, the suggestion is that nurses are usually female, and doctors are typically male. Use gender-neutral language. See the box for examples.

GENDER NEUTRAL LANGUAGE

Sexist Terms	Gender-Neutral Terms
actor, actress	actor
anchorman, anchorwoman	anchor

chairman	chairperson, chair
clergyman	member of the clergy, pastor
fireman, policeman	firefighter, police officer
foreman	supervisor
mailman	mail carrier, letter carrier
salesman	sales associate, sales clerk
stewardess, steward	flight attendant
woman engineer	engineer

6. Use politically correct language. Besides avoiding sexist terms, good writers should try to write so that their message is not insulting to anyone. By carefully selecting words, you can avoid having an unintended negative undertone. Here are some examples. You may be familiar with other ones.

POLITICALLY CORRECT LANGUAGE

Offensive Term	Neutral Term
handicapped	person with special needs; someone who is physically or mentally challenged
retarded	developmentally challenged
gifted	advanced learner
race	ethnicity or nationality
Indian	First Peoples, First Nations

EXERCISE 1-5 **Appropriate Word Choice**

Directions: *Read each sentence below and identify any informal (jargon, idioms, slang, or clichés), sexist, or offensive language. Underline the inappropriate word or phrase. In the space provided, identify the kind of informal language being used, and then rewrite the sentence using a more precise word or phrase. An example is shown.*

EXAMPLE

The sales associate happily offered assistance to the hunk trying to coordinate a shirt and tie.

(sexist language) The sales associate happily offered assistance to the

customer trying to coordinate a shirt and tie.

1. The student realized he was nervous when he felt butterflies in his stomach.

_____

2. The firewoman quickly climbed the extension ladder to rescue the children trapped in a third-floor bedroom.

_____

3. Scientists are engaged in gender research to solve the battle of the sexes.

_____

4. Electronic surveillance of the Internet practices of employees borders on invasion of privacy.

_____

5. It was awesome to be chosen student representative for the college, which was a big deal for her.

_____

Critical Reading and Thinking

Good writers become better writers by becoming critical readers. Because of the volume of reading required in post-secondary studies, your academic survival will depend on your ability to become a critical reader. You need to identify your purpose for reading, apply strategies to help you read effectively, and monitor your comprehension. See Chapter 27 for a more detailed discussion of critical reading.

FIVE STRATEGIES FOR READING AND THINKING CRITICALLY

These five strategies will help you develop your critical reading and thinking skills. Apply these strategies before, during, and after reading materials for your classes. You can also apply these strategies to essays written by your peers. Remember to refer to a dictionary to look up unfamiliar words. This will help you truly understand what you are reading as well as expand your vocabulary.

1. Read with a pen.
2. Ask questions.
3. Make personal connections.
4. Determine important information and ideas.
5. Draw inferences.

1. Read with a Pen

Reading with a pen helps you interact with and work on what you are reading. With a highlighter, you can cover too much, so you may not always select the most important information. Instead, as you read each page, use a pen or pencil to underline the most important ideas, jot notes in the margins, circle key terms, and trace connections across the page.

2. Ask Questions

In this chapter, you have started to ask questions about writing: What is the form being used? What are the purpose and focus of a particular piece of writing? *Ask these questions about everything you read*. This will help you become a critical reader. Ask yourself: What is the writer's main idea? What supporting details does the writer provide? Does the writer use words with certain connotations? Why did the writer select a particularly precise word? The questions you ask are like an imagined conversation with the writer. As you work through the chapters in Part Two of this text and learn about different patterns of organization, you will ask more questions about the organization of what you read. For example, does it tell a story? Does it compare and contrast two items or points of view? Does it explain the steps in a process?

3. Make Personal Connections

The meaning of what you read comes from both the page and from you: you bring some knowledge to the page. What you read might remind you of people, events, ideas, and opinions you are familiar with or have thought about. Use a pen or pencil to briefly note these personal connections in the margin or in your notebook. Make connections with similar things you have previously read, too. When you read, you create a web of meaning that consists of what you know, what you have read, and what you are currently reading. However, sometimes personal connections can lead you astray, so monitor your thinking to stay connected to the subject of the material.

Talk about it

Which strategies do you already use? How do they help you?

4. Determine Important Information and Ideas

Everything you read is not of equal importance: some ideas are more important than others. You can get an idea of what is important by reading titles and headings and the first and last sentences of paragraphs, by looking for bold and italicized type, and by checking for marginal notes and boxes. If you are reading a textbook, first survey each chapter and look for review sections and anything that specifically announces what is important. Do the same in other types of reading, and look for ideas that appear in more than one place. Anything repeated is likely important.

5. Draw Inferences

Critical reading involves *drawing inferences*. You want to be able to point to the facts. But you also want to *read between the lines*. When you make an **inference**, you use facts and information in the text to make an informed guess about what the author is saying. For instance, earlier in this chapter, in the response to a question about a reading, the writer asserts, "Mrs. Flowers and Mama were bound together by how they were alike in a prejudiced and sexist society." The writer has put two and two together. She has made a connection between separate statements of fact and come to a conclusion. The conclusion is not explicitly stated, but given the facts, the inference makes sense.

Now notice how the reader of the following excerpt has read with a pen and has underlined ideas from the text.

from "On Baking"
by RICHARD SENNETT

A year or so ago, I went back to the Boston bakery where twenty-five years ago, in researching *The Hidden Injuries of Class*, I had interviewed a group of bakers. Back then, the bakers worried about <u>upward social mobility</u> among themselves; they feared their children would lose their Greek roots in becoming more American. And the bakers were certain Boston's white Anglo-Saxon Protestants looked down on immigrant Americans like themselves—perhaps a realistic assessment.

Work in the bakery bound the workers self-consciously together. The bakery was <u>filled with noise</u>; the smell of yeast mingled with human sweat in the hot rooms; the bakers' hands were constantly plunged into flour and water; the men used their noses as well as their eyes to judge when the bread was done. <u>Craft pride</u> was strong, but the men said they did not enjoy their work, and I believed them. The ovens often burned them; the primitive dough beater pulled human muscles; and it was night work, which meant these men, so family-centered, <u>seldom saw their families</u> during the week.

But it seemed to me, watching them struggle, that the ethnic solidarity of being Greek made possible their <u>solidarity</u> in this difficult labor—good worker meant good Greek. The equation of <u>good work and good Greek</u> made sense in the concrete, rather than the abstract. The bakers needed to cooperate intimately in order to coordinate the varied tasks of the bakery. When two of the bakers, brothers who were both alcoholic, showed up plastered on the job, others would <u>berate</u> them by referring to the mess they were making of their families and the loss of prestige of their families in the community where all the Greeks lived. <u>Not being a good Greek was a potent tool of shame</u>, and thus of work discipline. When I returned to the bakery years later, I was amazed at how much had changed.

The reader uses all the strategies we have mentioned as he reads this essay with a pen. He underlines important details. He makes personal connections to himself and to other classes he has taken. Although his comment about loving the smell of bread may not be relevant to understanding Sennett's purpose, it demonstrates he is personally engaged in the reading. Plus, he makes an inference about the pressures these bakers face by connecting his thinking about prejudice to the inference in the third paragraph. Finally, he also asks and answers a question to define a difficult but important word.

EXERCISE 1-6 **Reading Critically**

Directions: *Read the following excerpt and try out the strategies for critical reading we have detailed above. Read with a pen. Place a P in the margin and write a word or two about the personal connection you make with the reading. Underline one or two sentences that seem important. Place a Q in the margin and ask a question. Place a C in the margin where you make a connection between what is said in different places in the reading.*

from "Mother Tongue"
by AMY TAN

Writer's Response

Tell the class about a time you helped a parent solve a problem.

Lately, I have been giving more thought to the kind of English my mother speaks. Like others, I have described it to people as "broken" or "fractured" English. But I wince when I say that. It has always bothered me that I can think of no way to describe it other than "broken," as if it were damaged and needed to be fixed, as if it lacked a certain wholeness and soundness. I have heard other terms used, "limited English," for example. But they seem just as bad, as if everything is limited, including the people's perceptions of the limited English speaker.

I know this for a fact, because when I was growing up, my mother's "limited" English limited my perception of her. I was ashamed of her English. I believed that her English reflected the quality of what she had to say. That is, because she expressed them imperfectly her thoughts were imperfect. And I had plenty of empirical evidence to support me: the fact that people in department stores, at banks, and at restaurants did not take her seriously, did not give her good service, pretended not to understand her, or even acted as if they did not hear her.

My mother has long realized the limitations of her English as well. When I was fifteen, she used to have me call people on the phone to pretend I was she. In this guise, I was forced to ask for information or even to complain and yell at people who had been rude to her. One time it was a call to her stockbroker in New York. She had cashed out her small portfolio and it just so happened we were going to go to New York the next week, our very first trip outside California. I had to get on the phone and say in an adolescent voice that was not very convincing, "This is Mrs. Tan."

And my mother was standing in the back whispering loudly, "Why he did not send me check, already two weeks late. So mad he lie to me, losing me money."

And then I said in perfect English, "Yes, I'm getting rather concerned. You had agreed to send the check two weeks ago, but it has not arrived."

EXERCISE 1-7 **Form, Purpose, and Focus**

Directions: *Select the form of writing, focus, and purpose that best describe the passage from Amy Tan's essay, "Mother Tongue," and complete the following chart.*

How is it written?	Why was it written?			What does the author want to say?
	PURPOSE			
FORM	**A. Think on paper**	**B. Convey information**	**C. Persuade the reader**	**SUBJECT & FOCUS**

Set Goals and Become a Reflective Student

Improving your writing will depend on your awareness of your own strengths and weaknesses. To monitor your progress, keep track of the skills you need to improve. Reflect on your work and set goals for improving your writing. Doing so will help you become a better writer and a more effective student.

REFLECTIVE WRITING

Reflective writing helps you examine your attitudes about issues, explore your feelings about events in your life, and recognize your achievements. Reflective writing is most effective when you write regularly, which enables you to reread your thoughts, identify your strengths, and set goals. Over time you can recognize how your thinking and writing have changed.

1. *Keep a journal to capture your personal experience of learning to write.* Reread your journal regularly. Journalling enables you to see trends that might help you solve a writing problem or identify a successful strategy. You can write in a traditional paper notebook or keep a journal on your computer.

Ask Yourself

Do you write every day to improve your writing? Why or why not?

2. *Write every day.* Establish a place and time when you can write every day or, at least, regularly to explore topics that are important to you. Write for a minimum of ten minutes. Aim for quantity in your writing. Try to write a little more each time. Use your writing to apply what you are learning about the sentence, the paragraph, and the essay. Try to do new things with your writing.

EXERCISE 1-8 Setting Goals and Applying What You Have Learned

Directions: *Answer the following questions to help you explore your previous writing experiences and to help you set goals for improvement.*

1. What kinds of assignments do you like to write?

_____

2. Who taught you to write your first successful assignment? What made the assignment good? What was the form of the writing? The purpose? The subject and focus?

_____

3. What kinds of assignments do you *not* like to write?

_____

4. Describe one assignment in particular that was very difficult for you. What made it so difficult? What was the form of the writing? The purpose? The subject and topic?

_____

5. What do you like about writing, and what do you believe you do well?

_____

6. According to your analysis in these exercises, what do you need to work on to be more effective as a college or university writer?

_____

CHAPTER REVIEW

Recall what you have learned in this chapter about academic writing in a post-secondary setting:

☐ Purpose and form
  • *How will you write it?*
  • *Why are you writing?*
☐ Focus, subject, content, and audience
☐ Improve word choice
  • *Precise nouns and verbs*
  • *Appropriate tone*
  • *Denotation and connotation*
  • *Appropriate word choices*
☐ Critical reading and thinking
  • *Five strategies*
☐ Set goals and reflect

THINK FIRST

Many students seek post-secondary diplomas or degrees to help them build a future. In that future, they see meaningful work that also earns them a good living. Describe the work environment you see in the photograph. What kind of work do you think the man does? What do you think his co-workers are like?

Prewrite: Think Through Ideas

You may be surprised by how much you know about a wide range of topics. Freewriting in your journal or a notebook, brainstorming, or even just talking ideas through with a friend will help you discover what you know now and what your attitudes are on a subject. When you sit down to write, you will not be starting from scratch. That alone will make your first draft more successful.

BRAINSTORM

Think about a complex task you do with confidence, such as preparing for a trip, planning a party, or purchasing something important. How do you prepare? What are the steps you take to get ready? Brainstorm for five minutes, recording as many ideas and details as you can.

Revise and Get Organized

Revising a paper is a lot like reviewing your wardrobe. What works and what does not? Can you get that jacket to look good, or should you just get rid of it? Are those ripped jeans okay, or do they give people the wrong impression of you? When revising a paper, you ask similar questions. Can a passage be altered to be more persuasive, or should you just delete it? Is colloquial language appropriate, or should you be formal? Are you using accurate, academic vocabulary? Is the paper's structure sound? Do you have details to support your point? It takes a careful eye to revise a paper. You rethink your ideas and conclusions based on information and insights you gain during the writing process.

DISCUSSION

Turn and talk to a classmate about the writing process. What do you like best about it? What do you like least? What do you think you need to work on the most to become a better writer? What points did you each write down about preparing for a task in the previous brainstorming exercise?

From Good Editing to Getting a Job

When applying for a job, be sure to edit your resumé and cover letter. Potential employers view errors in your application as signs of carelessness. Incorrect grammar and spelling will contradict the message you convey about your talents. Your employer has good reason to be picky; in the workplace, the ability to express yourself reflects not only on you but also on your employer. Good editing will give you a better shot at getting—and keeping—a job.

BRAINSTORM

Good editing often depends on having another person look at your writing. Who would you trust to read and comment on your writing? Make a list of at least three people. When no one is available to look over your writing, you should take a break and come back to your assignment later so that you can look at it with a fresh view. Alternatively, read your writing out loud to yourself—you might "hear" an error that you couldn't see.

The Writing Process

"I use a three-step approach to writing papers: (1) read the assignment, (2) write the paper, (3) turn it in." If this sentence describes your approach to writing, thinking of writing as a process will be a big shift for you. There are several reasons why you should change your approach to writing. First, a process approach allows you to relax and begin writing to get your ideas on paper. Good writers know that what they write at the beginning of the process may not appear in the final draft. Second, writing takes time and energy. Good writers want to be efficient, but they also know that taking time to write a first draft will result in a better final copy. Third, you need strategies to make writing decisions. Knowledge of the process helps you make good decisions as you write.

The writing process is rarely a neat step-by-step process, and you may go back and forth between steps. Following is a five-step model that may help you get your ideas on paper, save you time and energy, and lead to efficient completion of your writing assignments. Remember, though, that you may return to some steps several times before you finish your writing assignment.

> *Step 1—Prewrite:* This step involves thinking, making preliminary notes, and doing exploratory writing. In the prewriting and drafting stages of the process, you experiment with various responses to an assignment. If these attempts do not work, you can try again. This experimental attitude enables many writers to do their best work. There are several strategies you can use during this step that are described later in this chapter.
>
> *Step 2—Draft:* After prewriting, you put pen to paper. You write sentences and paragraphs to express what was in sketchy form or unclear in your prewriting. When you draft, you flesh out your ideas. Once you have a first draft, it is a good idea to have someone read it and respond. This feedback gives you ideas for improving your writing at an early stage.
>
> *Step 3—Revise:* During revision, you move, cut, and add content to your writing. You organize it logically to make your points more forcefully. Even at this stage, nothing is written in stone; you can make changes. Writing involves revision at every step of the process. You revise your prewriting when you draft. You revise your first draft when you write a second draft. Even when you edit, you may review everything you have written and make meaningful changes in your writing.
>
> *Step 4—Edit:* After revising, you edit your work. You fix grammar, spelling, punctuation, capitalization, and anything else that will distract a reader. When you edit, you also fine-tune word choice and style, so your writing is appropriate for an academic audience or suitable for its purpose.
>
> *Step 5—Reflect:* The edited revision is your best effort. At this point, it is good to reflect on what you have done, noticing those parts of the writing you like and those that are still challenging and need improvement.

REVISION IN ACTION
Watch for these boxes throughout the chapter. They indicate the importance of revision at various points in the writing process. Writing is recursive: you constantly look back before moving forward. Revision in Action reminds you to look back and improve on good writing you have already done.

Prewrite: Write Before You Write

How do I get started? All writers begin by facing a blank page. It can be intimidating. A positive approach and an experimental attitude are essential. Prewriting generates thinking and ideas on a topic.

Prewriting is thinking and writing *before* you write. You explore what you know before you begin to draft. **Talking** to someone about your ideas can be useful because it is fast and interactive. You find out what your ideas are and get ideas from the person you talk to. **Clustering** is another form of prewriting. You jot down ideas and draw their connections to related ideas and details. **Brainstorming** is listing everything you can think of related to your topic. You accept everything that comes to mind. **Questioning** is another method to prewrite. Finally, **freewriting** is continuous writing to explore your topic; it is your thoughts written down. Before you begin a draft, take 10 or 15 minutes to prewrite on your subject.

TALKING

Talking is relaxed and natural. It does not require you to make a commitment the same way writing does. As you talk to someone about your topic, you explore your thinking and respond to the listener, who helps you by adding ideas or personal experiences that develop your topic further. The conversation can help you generate ideas.

EXERCISE 2-1 Talking to Find a Topic

Directions: *Have a conversation with another student to prepare for the writing exercise that follows. Briefly describe a childhood leisure activity, something you especially enjoyed. You might talk about playing a sport, picnicking with your family, going to a relative's house, drawing at the kitchen table, or going to the park.*

- *Take turns talking for five minutes.*
- *Begin by discussing the childhood activity of your choice, but allow the conversation to remind you of other activities.*
- *As you recall events, include facts, details, examples, and the exact words you used or heard.*

EXERCISE 2-2 Writing about Your Conversation

Directions: *Write for five to ten minutes about your conversation with your classmate. Begin by writing a sentence that introduces your topic. Review the following list of sentences that might introduce the topic of drawing at the kitchen table. Then write a similar sentence to introduce your topic.*

- *Love of art began with a box of crayons and a colouring book.*
- *In order to foster creativity, burn colouring books.*
- *Crayons, scissors, glue, and paper make hours of fun and memories.*

CLUSTERING

If you are a visual thinker, clustering will help you picture a subject. You begin with a key term from your writing assignment and branch out to possible topics, related ideas, and supporting details. For each new idea, you add additional lines and ovals as you extend your thinking. When you cluster, push for at least four or five topic chains. You can use different-coloured highlighters to mark related ideas in each chain. This is experimental work, so you want to be flexible and open to new thinking.

In a matter of minutes, clustering can help you see potential relationships between your ideas and supporting details. Clustering also helps you be specific. Each time you add new links to the chain, you are narrowing the subject, making it smaller, more detailed, and focused, or you are imagining a new idea that might lead to a whole set of different details.

If you can't think of a precise word to use, perhaps your partner can help you.

If you don't know how to express a thought, leave a blank or make a quick drawing to remind you of your idea. You can consult a dictionary later.

Writer's Response

Who is the most important person in your life? Why? Has this person always been the most important person to you?

Here is an example of clustering on the topic of taking a vacation.

```
          ┌──────────────┐
          │ Shopping at the │
          │ West Edmonton   │
          │  Mall with Mom  │
          └──────────────┘
       ┌──────────┐
       │ We actually │
       │  saw some   │
       │    bears    │
       └──────────┘
  ┌─────────┐
  │  Banff   │
  │ National │
  │   Park   │
  └─────────┘
      ┌──────────┐        ┌──────────┐     ┌────────────┐
      │ I'd rather │      │ Fishing with │   │ Cleaning the │
      │  be hiking │      │   Grandpa    │   │    catch     │
      └──────────┘        └──────────┘     └────────────┘
                                                ┌──────────────┐
                                                │ Slime and scale │
                                                │   and guts      │
                                                └──────────────┘
  ┌──────────┐       ┌────────────┐
  │ Mom takes  │      │ Begin here:  │
  │  pictures  │      │  vacation    │
  └──────────┘       └────────────┘
                                  ┌──────────────┐
  ┌──────────┐                    │   Grandpa     │      ┌──────────────┐
  │ "Smile,"   │                   │ tries hard, but │    │ I'll probably   │
  │ she says   │                   │   he's sad     │    │ teach my kids   │
  └──────────┘                    └──────────────┘     │ those songs     │
                     ┌──────────────┐                   └──────────────┘
                     │ First vacation │
                     │ since Grandma  │
                     │    died        │
                     └──────────────┘
  ┌──────────┐    ┌──────────────┐               ┌──────────────┐
  │ Fake smile │   │  Fishing w/    │             │  She taught     │
  └──────────┘    │  Grandma on    │             │ us songs while  │
                  │   the lake     │             │   we fished     │
                  └──────────────┘               └──────────────┘
       ┌──────────┐        ┌──────────────┐
       │  Grandpa   │       │  We caught     │
       │  loves it  │       │   four fish    │
       └──────────┘        └──────────────┘
```

EXERCISE 2-3 **Clustering to Find a Topic**

Directions: *Use the clustering diagram as a model for generating possible topics. Examine the photograph "Boy Fishing" to further prompt your thinking on the topic of childhood. As you look at it, think about how this photograph connects to you. What does it remind you of? What view of childhood does it suggest to you? Now, you can practise clustering on a separate sheet of paper.*

BRAINSTORMING

Brainstorming is clustering without the ovals and lines. It can be as simple as randomly listing as many ideas about a topic as you can think of. It can also involve *piggybacking*. In this case, you review your random list and find categories of ideas to explore further. More is better in brainstorming. Following is an example of brainstorming on the topic of childhood:

Boy Fishing

Random Listing

flashlight tag	sharing a bedroom
reading groups	my first bike
Spiderman comics	food fights
Halloween	raking leaves

Boy Scouts	Willard, my dog
my first fish	making cookies for
soccer games	a bake sale
my friend Billy	pickup road hockey
moving away	mowing lawns
my secret ring	schoolyard games
the Santa Claus lie	hating dance lessons

Here is an example of piggybacking. The writer has chosen three categories of ideas to explore further: firsts, holiday traditions, and jobs.

Firsts

fish

fishing pole that broke the first time I used it

girlfriend—Lucy in grade 6 who was 30 cm taller than me

two-wheeled bike

time I broke a window playing ball

Holiday Traditions

time I got caught soaping windows on Halloween

making cookies—cornflake wreaths and gingerbread people

cutting out pumpkins—I got to dig out the insides and draw the faces

volunteering at the retirement home

going to Grandma's for the holidays

Jobs

manning the bake sale table with my friend Billy who ate many of the cookies

raking leaves in the neighbourhood

mowing the Petersons' lawn—my first business

taking out the garbage and discovering maggots in the trash can

EXERCISE 2-4 **Brainstorming to Find a Topic**

Directions: *Brainstorm a list of your childhood memories on a separate sheet of paper. Use the lists above as models for brainstorming on your own.*

QUESTIONING

One way to get ideas is to ask questions about the topic; the answers will give you a direction to take when writing about it. Ask questions using who, what, why, when, where, and how. You can form many possible questions with various answers using this method.

EXERCISE 2-5 **Questioning to Find a Topic**

Directions: *Look at the example; the topic is sports. Then pick your own topic and ask questions to generate ideas for your topic.*

	POSSIBLE QUESTIONS	POSSIBLE ANSWERS
Who?	**Who** plays sports?	Children play sports.
	Who watches sports?	Many people watch professional sports teams.
What?	**What** sport should I write about?	Hockey; soccer
	What equipment do you need for this sport?	Ice skates and a helmet; soccer shoes and shin pads
Why?	**Why** should people play sports?	Participating in sports is good for one's health.
	Why are sports popular?	Playing sports is a fun social activity.
When?	**When** are the games played?	After school; in winter; in summer
	When is a good age to learn sports?	Between 6 to 12 years of age
Where?	**Where** can you learn how to play?	At the local arena; through a local soccer organization
	Where can you watch?	On television; at an arena; at a soccer field
How?	**How** are sports funded?	Parents pay for their children's sports.
	How are the rules of the game enforced?	Most sports have official rule guides.

FREEWRITING

The key to freewriting is staying relaxed. Keep your hand moving. When you talk, you do not stop to correct your grammar; you allow lapses in grammar and thinking. Freewriting is the same. You do not need to worry about spelling and grammar because freewriting is not for an audience; it is just for you.

Be messy. It is fine to jump around when you freewrite. There is no real logic to it. Change subjects and look for new directions. Freewriting enables you to recall forgotten memories, uncover ideas that have personal value, and understand attitudes in a new or deeper way. Following is an example of freewriting by a student, Christina.

Christina's Freewrite

I could talk with my family and friends forever. Me standup in front of people and tell a speech, no way! I become extremely nervous I feel my heart pounding, I cannot take a breath while my face turns red. I took speech it did not help. My eyes are always focused on the paper, I cannot make eye contact, and I do not know what to do. Last semester in my history class, I experienced all the symptoms one can go through. I also gave a speech in Spanish and could not maintain eye contact. If the instructor decides to ask me a question or read what I wrote sitting down I am fine. Stand in front of the class? Forget it. I volunteer to give speeches. I want to improve. They keep getting worse. I do extensive research on all my speeches and almost memorize the whole thing. Still nervous. I write very little on my notecards, which forces me to keep eye contact. Find a focal point and fix my eyesight on it. Which is a little better. They see my face and not just the top of my forehead.

Childhood entertainment.

Talk about it 》》》

Which prewriting strategy is new, familiar, helpful, or difficult?

EXERCISE 2-6 **Freewriting to Find a Topic**

Directions: *Examine the photo of the children playing video games to prompt memories of childhood. Then freewrite on a separate sheet of paper for five to ten minutes without stopping. Allow your thinking and writing to wander. As you do so, you may discover memories or ideas that surprise you.*

REVIEW YOUR PREWRITING AND DEFINE YOUR TOPIC

Prewriting is the beginning. It is not a first draft. Take a few minutes and review the ideas and memories generated about childhood in your prewriting from the previous exercise. Use the following exercises to help you define a topic. You'll find additional information about refining your topic sentence in Chapter 3.

EXERCISE 2-7 **Defining Your Topic**

Directions: *List some possible topics you generated from talking, clustering, brainstorming, questioning, and freewriting. Two topics have been provided as models for you.*

- *Write a phrase or two to describe each possible topic.*
- *Indicate which prewriting strategy you used to discover each topic.*
- *Then use the questions that follow to select the topic you will use to write a paragraph.*

Possible Topics   *Prewriting Strategy*

Example: pet ownership   freewriting

Example: media influences on children   clustering

1. _____

2. _____

3. _____

4. _____

5. _____

Look over your answers and try to discover which prewriting strategy works best to help you to define your topic.

Which topic interests you the most? _____

_____

Which topic generated the most interesting ideas? _____

_____

Which topic generated the most interesting details or examples? _____

_____

Which topic seems most clearly organized on paper? _____

_____

The topic I will explore further is _____

_____

Select the prewriting strategy that is most effective for you, and use it in the future. Some students use two or more strategies to explore a topic. Maintain an experimental attitude, trying other forms of prewriting from time to time. You may discover that particular forms of prewriting are best suited to specific topics or writing assignments.

EXERCISE 2-8 **Choosing a Prewriting Strategy that Works Best for You**

Directions: *Review your prewriting work, and answer the following questions to determine which strategy is most effective for you.*

1. Which strategy is easiest for you to use? Why? _____

_____

2. Which strategy generates the deepest thinking? Why? _____

_____

3. Which activity generates the most interesting topic or the most interesting details or examples and ideas? Why? _____

_____

4. Which activity allows you to most clearly organize your ideas on paper?_____

_____

5. Which strategy would you like to use again? Why? Would you combine strategies? _____

_____

Draft: Focus and Organize

What do I want to say? Who will read this paragraph? Drafting organizes your prewriting ideas into readable text. Your job in the first draft is to identify your main point, organize your prewriting into a logical structure, and shape it to meet a reader's expectations. At this point you define your topic, formulate a topic sentence, select and explain supporting details, and end with a convincing concluding sentence.

Remember, you will probably write multiple drafts of a paper. You will read peers' papers, and they will read yours. Peer review will give you more ideas. Most writers make substantial changes as they write and rewrite. Drafting enables you to improve your writing to the point where it satisfies both you and your audience. In this chapter you will follow the multiple steps used for a sample student paragraph from prewrite to final draft. Your writing may follow a similar process.

CONSIDER YOUR READER OR AUDIENCE

When you draft, you shift from writing for yourself to writing for your audience. In prewriting, you did not have to worry about what is acceptable for

Writing multiple drafts is not an indication of poor writing skills. Writing multiple drafts indicates you are following a good revision process.

an audience; now you do. In Chapter 1, you explored possible readers as the focus of your writing. This means you may need to change your draft from using the first person (*I, me*) to using the third person (*children, they*) if appropriate for the assignment. In drafting, you provide specific details, such as names of people and places that are obvious to you but that your audience may not know. You provide careful descriptions, such as sensory detail and exact dates and times that you know all about but that your audience does not. Finally, you consider any specific knowledge you have of your subject that your audience might not have.

At this stage of the process, you also start to eliminate slang and make your language more formal. For example, you write, "I was going to," not "I was gonna." Remember that by paying careful attention to your language and your word choice, you convey respect for your audience and yourself.

Ask questions like these when considering your audience:

- Who will read this paragraph, and what do they expect?
- How much do they know about my topic?
- How much do they need to know about my topic to understand the point I want to make?
- How might they react to what I have to say?

EXERCISE 2-9 Determining What You Want to Say

Directions: *Read your prewriting for the topic you chose previously. Gather together all the ideas and details you generated about it. You may want to do additional brainstorming, freewriting, clustering, questioning, or talking about the topic. Then respond to the prompts below. Remember to be specific enough so your audience understands the point you are making.*

Topic: _____

A. Write a topic sentence that states the point you want your audience to understand.

_____

_____

B. List five to seven details, examples, or reasons from your prewriting that explain your topic sentence. Circle the two or three most convincing details, examples, or reasons.

_____

_____

FOCUS YOUR TOPIC SENTENCE

Focus is essential to good writing, and it begins with your topic sentence. The topic sentence states the main idea of a paragraph and is often the first sentence. Think about your assignment. You have a topic and something to say about it, so your topic sentence should focus on topic and point. Develop this **1 (topic) + 1 (point)** approach. Getting this sentence focused will also focus the paragraph. Use only one topic for each paragraph. Another way of looking at topic sentences is to think of the topic plus your controlling idea about that topic.

Take a few minutes to step back and analyze your first sentence. Are you specific enough? You may have used questioning while you were pre-writing, but you can ask questions again to focus your topic sentence. An easy way to narrow your topic is by asking who, what, when, where, why, and how.

Academic writing in college or university may be different from how you have previously written. Although you may not be accustomed to beginning with a strong or direct point, it is expected in academic writing.

First Draft of Topic Sentence

(topic)   (point)

Vacations in a cramped car and equally small tent created an unbreakable family bond.

1   +   1

Focusing Questions

Who went on vacation? Me, my brother, and the dog

What vacation? The vacation we took the year my brother left for college

When? When I was in grade 6

Where? Beaver Glen

Why did we go on vacation? To spend time together before he left for college

How did we camp? He and I slept in a small pup tent together. It was crowded.

Second Draft of Topic Sentence

(topic)   (point)

Two brothers and a dog in a pup tent created laughter and a bond of love.

1   +   1

EXERCISE 2-10   **Focusing Your Topic Sentence**

Directions: *Rewrite and focus your topic sentence from the previous exercise, making sure to clearly state your topic and the point you want to make about it or your controlling idea about the topic.*

_____

_____

ORGANIZE AND CONNECT IDEAS AND DETAILS

Paragraph **unity** means every idea and detail support the topic sentence. In your paragraph, all the supporting details need to relate to the paragraph's topic sentence. Furthermore, there should be a *reason* why you present details in the order that you do. When the order makes sense, your draft is coherent. Paragraph **coherence** means there is a clear, smooth flow of ideas in the paragraph, brought about by careful organization and the use of appropriate transition words and phrases, otherwise known as "signal words."

Drafting your paper involves transforming your prewriting and making significant changes in the content of your paragraph to make it logical. The

Stay on the topic; do not digress or the reader will be confused. If you have other points, you can write about them in other paragraphs.

organization of your draft cannot be random. The order in which ideas and details occur has an impact on your audience, and the content has to make sense.

Depending on your focus and purpose, you can use one of the following methods to organize your paragraph. These methods of organizing supporting details will also be discussed in Chapter 3.

- *Spatial:* Describing an object or place from top to bottom, back to front, left to right, and so on.
- *Chronological:* Describing events or the steps in a process in the order in which they occur.
- *Order of importance:* Describing either the most important or the least important details first.
- *Simple to complex:* Describing the simple details first and working toward more complex ones.

For example, here are some different ways you could organize details related to the topic of casino gambling:

Topic: The pleasures of casino gambling

Spatial
The pool and gardens—from right to left
The lobby and rooms—from downstairs to upstairs
The casino gambling area—from front to back

Chronological
First visit, 2008, Casino Rama
Second visit, 2009, Casino Rama again
Third visit, 2012, Casino Niagara

Order of Importance
Get some rest
Eat some good food
See a couple shows

Simple to Complex
Play the games and come home with some money
People watching
Different places to eat (reasonable prices)
The games

Ask Yourself

What transitions do you already use? Will you try to add a variety of other transitions in your writing?

Transitions

Transition words signal the connections you make between ideas and details in your writing. They give your paragraph coherence and help the reader see how everything fits together. This table shows some commonly used transition words. You can add more transitions to the list as you learn to use them. Bookmark this page to refer back to when you write your assignments.

Additional Detail	Contrast	Sequence	Logical Connectors	Time
consequently	however	first	consequently	after
furthermore	but	second	therefore	as soon as
and	yet	third	thus	at first
in addition	nevertheless	generally	hence	then
moreover	on the contrary	furthermore	in conclusion	at last
also	on the other	finally	indeed	finally
in the same way	hand	in the first place	in the final	before
		also	analysis	later
		last		next
				soon
				in the first place
				in the meantime

EXERCISE 2-11   **Ordering the Details in Your Paragraph**

Directions: *Using the key details, ideas, and examples you generated to support your topic sentence in Exercise 2-9, create a logical order for the details in your paragraph. Try using spatial order, chronological order, order of importance, or simple to complex order. Indicate the transition words you think will be most useful.*

_____

_____

_____

Transition Words: _____

Here is an example of a first draft of Christina's writing.

Christina's First Draft

Giving a speech is a nerve-wracking challenge for most people. There are few things folks are more afraid of. The signs and symptoms of nerves are totally obvious to see. The speaker's cheeks turn bright read. Her voice starts to quiver and crack. Even in college courses, some speakers sound like teenagers going through puberty. Another symptom is the struggle to maintain eye contact. Some speakers stare off into space. Most keep their eyes down, focused on their papers or notecards. Then there are those rockers and tappers, the ones who go completely nuts. Some speakers rock back and forth without knowing it, fidgeting and fiddling, making it totally distracting to watch them. Others are all wound up, so full of nervous energy, they tap pencils or pens like crazy, distracting the reader even more. Then there is the "statue." This poor guy is petrified. He does not move a muscle through the whole speech.

REVISION IN ACTION
Christina changes her focus, details, and organization in the first draft.

FOCUS
In this draft, Christina leaves behind the first-person focus of her prewriting. This is an important step in adapting her ideas to an academic audience.

SUPPORTING DETAILS
Her supporting details describe how some speakers display their nervousness during a speech.

UNITY AND COHERENCE
She uses transition terms to show she is adding detail and to create a coherent paragraph. Plus, she stays on the subject, making her paragraph unified. However, her paragraph seems inconclusive because she has no concluding sentence.

Revise: Read Critically, then Rewrite

Will a reader understand what I know about my topic? How can I get a good grade? A draft is your beginning, but there is more to do. Experienced writers often say the end product is not at all what they thought they would write when they began. Revision means rethinking. Give yourself plenty of time to do this important step as it helps improve the quality of your writing.

As you revise, read critically. Look for evidence that you have achieved your purpose. Identify what you did well and where your paper is weak. Listen to the views of other readers. Ask yourself these questions:

- Did I keep my readers' interest?
- Were my readers confused? What can I do to reduce their confusion?
- Can I try something new? What do other writers in my class do that I could try? What do professional writers do that I could try?

As you revise, be open to adding, cutting, or reorganizing your writing. College and university students often say too little about their subjects, so be prepared to add details and explanations that support the controlling idea about your topic. To have unity in your paragraph means you may need to cut information that is not relevant to your topic. Finally, by moving around ideas and details in your draft, you often see new possibilities. Here are three useful strategies for revising your work.

REVISE STRATEGICALLY

Strategy 1: Add

Add new details, examples, and explanations that answer questions raised by your readers. Add sentences that connect or relate one part of your paper to another. To ensure a more coherent paragraph, add appropriate transitions.

Strategy 2: Cut

Cut details, examples, and explanations that your readers did not understand or that did not connect directly to the topic. Do not be afraid to cut deeply. If you need to, you can always put something back in. Cutting from and adding to your draft will help you see your writing in a new light.

Strategy 3: Reorganize

Reorganize your work so that it looks, feels, and reads differently. Sometimes what you write at the end of a paragraph or paper works better if it's moved to the beginning. Reorganizing may help you discover appropriate transition words and phrases so that you produce a more coherent paragraph.

READ CRITICALLY

Critically reading the works of published writers will help you improve your writing. Look closely at their writing styles and try to apply to your writing what they do in theirs. As you read, ask these questions:

- How does the writer present information?
- What does the writer do that I admire?

- How does the writer solve a problem that I have in my writing?
- Is there a technique in professional writing that I can try?

EXERCISE 2-12 **Reading Critically**

Directions: *Read the paragraph from "Growing Up Game" three times, following the instructions below.*

1. *First reading:* Read without a pen or pencil. Simply try to understand the author's subject and purpose. Then, in a sentence or two, write your view of the author's purpose.

2. *Second reading:* Underline two sentences that express Peterson's subject and purpose. Circle the details that support or explain her purpose as you read the rest of the paragraph. If you don't want to write in your text, you can use sticky notes or write on a separate piece of paper.

3. *Third reading:* Place a checkmark in the margin next to a sentence or two that you admire. Label what the writer is doing.

4. *Rethinking after a close reading:* In a sentence or two, write your view of the author's purpose.

from "Growing Up Game"
by BRENDA PETERSON

This hunting trip was the first time I remember eating game as a conscious act. My father and Buddy Earl shot a big doe and she lay with me in the back of the tarp-draped station wagon all the way home. It was not the smell I minded; it was the glazed great, dark eyes and the way that head flopped around crazily on what I knew was once a graceful neck. I found myself petting this doe, murmuring all those graces we had been taught long ago as children. Thank you for the sacrifice, thank you for letting us be like you so that we can grow up strong as game. But there was an uneasiness in me that night as I bounced along in the back of the car with the deer.

USE RESPONSE GROUPS

A real audience tells you if your writing says what you think it says. In a response group of your peers, you are both a writer and a reader. Response groups work most effectively when readers avoid focusing on problems in the writing or on trying to fix them. Effective groups discuss the strengths as well as weaknesses of the writing.

You can form a response group with three to four members of your class. Here are some guidelines for how to make effective use of a response group:

Guidelines for an Effective Response Group

As a Writer

- Distribute copies of your work to group members.
- After you read your work aloud, listen quietly and take notes as the group members talk to you about their responses to your writing.

Do not feel uncomfortable getting feedback from your peers. They can provide good insights and offer you another point of view.

- When members are done talking, ask for clarification of any comments you did not understand. Also ask for advice on specific problems you are having with your writing (topic sentence, including enough relevant details, etc.) or ask for ideas to expand your paragraph.
- Thank the group for their comments.
- Collect the copies so you can use their notes or comments for your revision.

As a Reader and Listener

- Identify the point or purpose of the paragraph or essay.
- Identify the topic sentence and key words that state the purpose. Does the topic sentence grab your interest?
- Discuss key details, examples, or reasons. Notice the details or examples that grab your interest. Are they connected?
- Notice places where the writing is confusing, inconsistent, or underdeveloped.
- Identify the conclusion. What does the writer emphasize in the conclusion?

EXERCISE 2-13 **Forming a Peer Response Group**

Directions: *Form a response group with three or four members of your class. Using the guidelines listed above, take turns sharing your writing and listening to the group respond to your work.*

REVISE WITH A PLAN

Here is Christina's revision plan and revised first draft. In her revised paragraph, added text is in bold font. Text she deleted from her first draft is crossed out.

REVISION IN ACTION
Christina takes control of her paragraph structure. She cuts and adds to create unity and coherence. She changes her (a) topic sentence, (b) informal language, (c) transition terms, and (d) concluding sentence.

Christina's Revision Plan: Focus my paragraph's purpose

1. Rewrite my topic sentence to clarify my purpose.
2. Add transition terms to connect my points and create coherence.
3. Cut informal language not appropriate for academic writing.

TOPIC SENTENCE
Christina replaces vague words with specific ones to focus her topic sentence and purpose.

Christina's Revised Paragraph

Giving a speech ~~is a~~ **can be** nerve-wracking ~~challenge~~ for **both the speaker and the audience** ~~most people~~. **In fact,** there are few things folks are more afraid of. The signs and symptoms of nerves are ~~totally~~ obvious to see. **For instance,** ~~The~~ a speaker's cheeks often turn bright **red** ~~read~~. **and** Her voice ~~starts to~~ quivers and cracks. ~~Even in college courses,~~ Some speakers sound like teenagers going through puberty. Another symptom is the struggle to maintain eye contact. ~~Some speakers~~ **There are those who** stare off into space, **and those who** ~~Most~~ keep their eyes down, focused on their papers or notecards. Then there are **the** ~~those~~ rockers and tappers, ~~the ones who go completely nuts. Some speakers rock back and forth without knowing it,~~ **who** fidget~~ing~~ and fiddl~~ing~~, making it ~~totally~~ distracting to watch them. ~~Others are all wound up, so full of nervous energy, they tap pencils or pens like crazy, distracting the reader even more. Then there is~~ **Finally, we come to** the "statue." This ~~poor guy~~ **speaker** is petrified. He does not move a muscle through the whole speech. **It can be agonizing for some speakers to make even a three-minute speech, and it is just as agonizing for the audience, especially during an in-class presentation. Students know their turn might be next.**

TRANSITION TERMS
She adds transition words and phrases. She also repeats "those who" to make the supporting details fit together, enhancing the coherence of the paragraph.

INFORMAL LANGUAGE
She cuts "totally" and "Poor guy," which are informal and not appropriate for academic writing.

EXERCISE 2-14 Revising Your Draft

Directions: *Review the peer feedback and your own assessment of your writing. Add, cut, and reorganize to clarify your paragraph's meaning and purpose.*

Edit

I am terrible with grammar. Is there no quick way to edit?

Too often, students simply scan their papers before turning them in for a grade. If they see errors, they correct them, but as they look over their writing, students may not be specifically searching for errors. Good editing is a focused, systematic search. To edit effectively, you need to anticipate the errors you make, search for those errors, and correct them.

ELIMINATE YOUR USUAL ERRORS

It is important to know what mistakes you consistently make. This is easier than it sounds. You may already know, for example, that your spelling is weak. When your instructors return work to you, they will alert you to errors that appear in your papers. Keep a tally or log of errors and search for them when you edit your work. The following seven editing strategies will help you do a thorough job when you edit your work.

Strategy 1: Use a Checklist

Your instructors may provide you with an editing checklist for papers; in the meantime, use the following universal checklist to look where you can improve the quality of the writing of your assignment. Using a checklist like this one to edit your writing means your writing will be more academic, and this can lead to better marks.

YOUR EDITING CHECKLIST

Words

_____ I removed unnecessary contractions.

_____ I removed informal language.

_____ I checked my capitalization.

_____ I corrected all spelling errors by consulting a dictionary, a peer editor, or my computer spell-check, being sure to look for words my computer spell-check missed.

Sentences

_____ I checked all end punctuation marks.

_____ I used complete sentences with subjects and verbs.

_____ I proofread all my sentences so their meaning is clear.

_____ I removed sentence fragments.

Paragraphs

_____ I indented all new paragraphs.

EXERCISE 2-15 **Editing Your Paragraph**

Directions: _Use the preceding checklist to review your paragraph._

Strategy 2: Eliminate One Error at a Time

Read your paper several times using the following guidelines. Concentrate on one error at a time.

- _Read each sentence individually or read your paragraph backward, from the last sentence to the first, so you read each sentence in isolation._

- _Look for spots that signal a consistent error._ If you know you have trouble with punctuation, look at those sentences that might require commas, semicolons, colons, or apostrophes.

Strategy 3: Read Your Work Aloud

Use one of the following approaches:

- _Read aloud slowly._ Listen and look closely at each sentence. Watch for missing words, words missed by spell-check, and confusing language.

- _Read aloud to a classmate._ If you have difficulty reading certain parts of your writing, those parts probably need editing. Often you will find problems with sentence structure and grammatical errors.

Strategy 4: Highlight Signal Words

Highlight words that signal punctuation. For example, highlight all the coordinating conjunctions and then use the rules for items in a series or compound sentences to determine the need for commas. (See Chapter 25 for tips on comma use.)

Strategy 5: Use Computer Aids—Spell-Check and Grammar-Check

Your computer's grammar-check alerts you to confusing or grammatically incorrect sentences. Use it as an aid. If the computer questions your sentences, you should, too. However, like spell-check, grammar-check can be unreliable. To the computer, "I would hope in the back" is just as correct as "I would hop in the back." It takes a human reader to know the difference and to select the correct words and spelling. Computer aids do not

FOCUS ON ONE COMMON ERROR
Use the lessons and activities in The Writer's Guidebook (Part 4 of this text) to practise proofreading for a specific error that recurs in your writing. Read your work carefully with this single error in mind.

replace careful proofreading and knowing how to make good decisions about grammar.

Strategy 6: Use Proofreading Peers

Proofread your paper with someone who has an objective eye. Tell this person about the errors you are inclined to make. Read your paper aloud, or ask your proofreading peer to do so, and search for your errors. Proofreading works best with two sets of eyes.

Strategy 7: Double-Check Your Work

If you are writing for an academic assignment, reread the instructions. Check for specific directions that define length, content, typing format, or other requirements. If you are writing for your job, be sure you know what your boss's expectations are before you turn in your work.

Here is Christina's edited paragraph. Added text is in bold font. Text she deleted from her first draft is crossed out.

Christina's Edited Paragraph

Giving a speech can be nerve-wracking for both the speaker and the audience. In fact, there are few things people are more afraid of. The signs and symptoms of nerves are obvious ~~to see~~. For instance, ~~a~~ **the** speaker's cheeks ~~often~~ turn bright red, and her voice quivers and cracks. Some speakers sound like teenagers going through puberty. Another symptom is the struggle to maintain eye contact. There are ~~those~~ **speakers** who stare off into space, ~~those~~ **speakers** who keep their eyes down, focused on their papers or notecards. ~~Then there are the rockers and tappers,~~ **and speakers** who fidget and fiddle, making it ~~totally~~ **almost completely** distracting to watch them. Finally, we come to the "statue." This speaker is petrified. He does not move a muscle through the whole speech. It can be agonizing for some speakers to make even a three-minute speech, and it is just as agonizing for the audience, especially during an in-class presentation **because** students know their turn might be next.

EXERCISE 2-16 **Final Editing of Your Paragraph**

Directions: *Use at least two of the editing strategies listed above to produce a final edited draft of your paragraph.*

Christina's Final Draft

Giving a speech can be nerve-wracking for both the speaker and the audience. In fact, there are few things people are more afraid of. The signs and symptoms of nerves are obvious. For instance, the speaker's cheeks turn bright red, and her voice quivers and cracks. Some speakers sound like teenagers going through puberty. Another symptom is the struggle to

---

maintain eye contact. There are speakers who stare off into space; speakers who keep their eyes down, focusing on their papers or notecards; and speakers who fidget and fiddle, making it almost completely distracting to watch them. Finally, there is the "statue." This speaker is petrified. He does not move a muscle through the whole speech. It can be agonizing for some speakers to make even a three-minute speech, and it is just as agonizing for the audience, especially during an in-class presentation because students know their turn might be next.

Reflect

Successful students are reflective. They think about what they did, what worked, and what did not work so they can make good decisions the next time around. For that reason, at the end of the writing process, you will be asked to think about the work you did, the decisions you made, what you learned, and what challenges you still face.

IDENTIFY SUCCESSES

Remember what you do well and what you enjoy. Becoming a good writer involves recognizing and using your strengths.

EXERCISE 2-17 Reflecting on Your Success

Directions: *Take a few minutes to reflect on your successes. Write one or two sentences that explain two things you have learned from this chapter and how you successfully applied them to your writing. Use a specific example from your work to support what you say.*

_____

_____

Locate the writing support centres on your campus. Find out available days and hours. Some provide workshops or online support that you may want to use.

SET GOALS

As you move forward, set realistic goals. Use your successes to identify changes in your writing. Become aware of breakthroughs in your use of skills and strategies and strive to create additional breakthroughs. Remember that small achievements add up to large gains.

EXERCISE 2-18 Identifying Your Writing Challenges

Directions: *Now that you have examined your successes, determine what challenges lie ahead. Rate yourself using the following scale: 1 indicates a task that you consider a challenge most of the time, and 5 indicates a task for which you have the required skills and strategies. What will you do to make your writing challenges easier for you?*

PREWRITING

_____ 1. I prewrite to explore my ideas and think more deeply about a topic.

DRAFTING

_____ 2. I check that the form, or how I will write, fits the assignment requirements.

_____ 3. I focus my paragraphs with a clear purpose in the topic sentences.

_____ 4. I consider the audience, use formal language and appropriate academic vocabulary.

_____ 5. I organize my ideas and connect them.

_____ 6. I insert details, examples, and reasons to explain my thinking.

_____ 7. I eliminate irrelevant details to enhance the unity of my writing.

_____ 8. I use transition words and phrases to provide coherence.

_____ 9. I eliminate first-person focus.

REVISING

_____ 10. I read critically to identify and use the successful techniques of other writers.

_____ 11. I identify the strengths and weaknesses in my papers.

_____ 12. I apply specific revision strategies to my papers.

_____ 13. I am flexible and willing to make changes in my writing.

Editing

_____ 14. I employ all or some of the following editing strategies:

    _____ Use a checklist.

    _____ Eliminate one error at a time.

    _____ Read my work aloud.

    _____ Highlight transition words.

    _____ Use spell-check or grammar-check on my computer.

    _____ Use a proofreading peer.

    _____ Double-check the assignment and expectations.

Reflecting

_____ 15. After submitting an assignment, I think about what I have learned, and what I would do differently on the next assignment.

CHAPTER REVIEW

Recall what you have learned in this chapter about the writing process:

☐ Prewriting techniques to generate ideas

  • _Talking, thinking, clustering, brainstorming, questioning, freewriting_

☐ Draft your paragraph

  • _Consider audience_

  • _Define and focus topic sentence: 1 topic + 1 point_

  • _Organization: connect ideas and details_

  • _Unity, coherence (organizational pattern), and transitions_

  • _Follow instructions_

☐ Revise strategically and rewrite; read critically

  • _Add, cut, reorganize_

☐ Edit your words, sentences, and paragraphs.

  • _Editing checklist_

☐ Reflect

  • _Successes and goals_

CHAPTER
3

Writing Paragraphs in College and University

CHAPTER OVERVIEW

- [ ] Paragraph Structure
- [ ] Assignments and Topics
- [ ] Supporting Details
- [ ] Concluding Sentence
- [ ] Paragraph Organization

THINK FIRST

To start thinking about ideas for paragraphs you might write, describe what you see in this photo. After you write a careful description, consider these questions: What does the photo remind you of? What issues or ideas would you like to explore in connection with the photo?

Be Specific: Details Matter

"I will have the stuffed-crust pan pizza with extra cheese, ham, and pineapple." "One venti double nonfat caramel latte, please." When you place an order, you do not just say simply "pizza" or "coffee." You need to be specific to get what you want. Similarly, when developing a paragraph, you need to be specific to get the response you want from your reader. Vague, unsupported statements—like vague orders—will not make your point.

DISCUSSION

Turn and talk to a classmate about something you are picky about, such as the food you eat, how you listen to music, the way you want a closet or drawer arranged, or something else. Provide as much specific detail as you can.

Your Opener

Whether you are preparing an oral presentation or writing a paragraph, nothing hooks an audience like a great first sentence. Whether structured deductively (stating your point right away) or inductively (beginning with your evidence), what you say first makes an impact; it establishes purpose and direction. You may not think of a great opening sentence as soon as you start to write. In fact, the best hooks are often discovered at later stages of the writing process. As discussed in Chapter 2, as you move through the steps of the writing process, you will often go back and change content or the order of your sentences during revisions.

DISCUSSION

Television commercials need to have a hook to catch viewers' attention. Next time you watch TV, focus on the commercials. Look for two or three examples of good hooks that grab the viewer's attention. Be prepared to tell the class about what you saw and how the commercial introduced its topic.

Writing on the Job

In the working world, you will often carry a project through from the idea stage to the completed project. Let's say, for example, that an assistant at a nonprofit agency is given his boss's vague notes from a meeting and asked to write a grant letter. He might ask his boss some questions and do additional research to make sure the information in the letter is accurate, the arguments are persuasive, and the tone is confident. Or suppose a parent writes a brief proposal about how to raise test scores in her child's school; if the school board approves her plan, the school will have to follow the proposal to see that the initiatives and programs she suggested are created and carried through.

DISCUSSION

Turn and talk to a classmate about a project idea that you would like to see through to completion. What is it? Who would be involved? When and where? What is the project's purpose? What potential difficulties do you see?

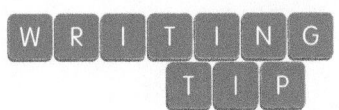
Paragraph Structure

A paragraph explores a clearly focused topic in a number of related sentences. The main idea—the main point an author wants to make about the topic—is stated in the **topic sentence**. Sentences following the topic sentence explore and explain the main idea. They provide **supporting details** that relate directly to the paragraph's specific focus. Supporting details come in a variety of forms, such as examples, facts, and stories. The type of support you provide depends on your purpose for writing. A **conclusion sentence** restates the main point or comments on the paragraph's main idea.

EXERCISE 3-1 **Paragraph Structure**

Directions: *Read the two paragraphs below and answer the questions that follow.*

PARAGRAPH A

> Many people go to stores because they have great deals. Some stores carry items for 30 percent less than the price at other places. I bought dress clothes from The Bay until I found out that I could get the same suits, shirts, ties, and shoes from local stores for a third less. What about the stores that do not have bargains? When I am walking by a store and see something I like, I walk in. Stores display products in windows that get customers' attention. The store changes as it gets in new products so customers have to keep looking. Merchandising executives decide how they want everything set up for a reason. They want to maintain the company's image, which could be hip and fashionable or just young and contemporary. It is the visual manager's job to set up the store using those guidelines, and it is the associate's job to organize and colour-coordinate all the products. This creates a pleasing and welcoming look for the store which will keep you coming back.

PARAGRAPH B

> Seeing a movie in the theatre has its advantages. One advantage of going to a theatre to watch a movie is the extremely large movie screen. Also the sound in a theatre is loud and dynamic. The big screen and sound can be a huge advantage when watching battle scenes in an action movie, such as *The Avengers*. The viewer experiences action scenes on the largest scale possible. Another advantage is refreshments. A bag of popcorn and a pop go with a movie much like peanut butter goes with jelly. For people who do not like to wait to see a movie, the biggest advantage to going out is seeing a movie as soon as it is released. Then again, there are a few disadvantages. You miss part of the movie if you go to the bathroom. If you sit

near talkers or hear cellphones ring, it is hard not to be upset. Then there is everybody's favourite: being kicked in the back of your chair by the antsy kid sitting behind you. Finally, there is cost. A movie experience can easily cost 30 dollars or more. For these reasons, it may be best to go to the theatre only on rare occasions, mainly for big spectacle movies.

1. Which of the two paragraphs seems better organized? List and explain two or three things the writer does to organize her content.

   _____

   _____

2. Briefly explain what makes the other paragraph seem confusing and poorly organized.

   _____

   _____

Assignments and Topics

College and university writing usually begin with an assignment, either provided by the instructor or that you choose from the textbook. Your job as a writer is to respond to that assignment. You generate a topic and then provide your reader with a focused, detailed discussion of that topic. You may recall from Chapter 2 that you should approach a paragraph as one topic and one point.

Here is everybody's favourite high school assignment: *What did you do last summer?* Maybe you worked at an amusement park. If you did, your work at the amusement park becomes your topic. Your reader expects you to say something focused and detailed about this topic.

In many classes, especially for disciplines other than English, your assignment will be specific. It will be designed to produce writing that shows what you have learned. Here are some examples of focused assignments:

*   Name and describe the four major food groups as they contribute to the maintenance of health and growth in early childhood.
*   Discuss the domestic and international impact of the North American Free Trade Agreement.
*   Describe two or three approaches to determining level of consciousness in initial patient assessment.

These assignments include key terms ("four major food groups," "domestic and international impact," "approaches, level of consciousness, patient assessment") that define the topic.

However, if you are faced with a less specific assignment, generating a topic is more challenging. Suppose your assignment is to write about stress. Your first task is to identify a specific topic related to stress. For example, you could begin by listing specific causes of stress in a person's life. Then you could select one—the stress of being a single parent, for instance—and narrow it down by asking, "What makes being a single parent so stressful?"

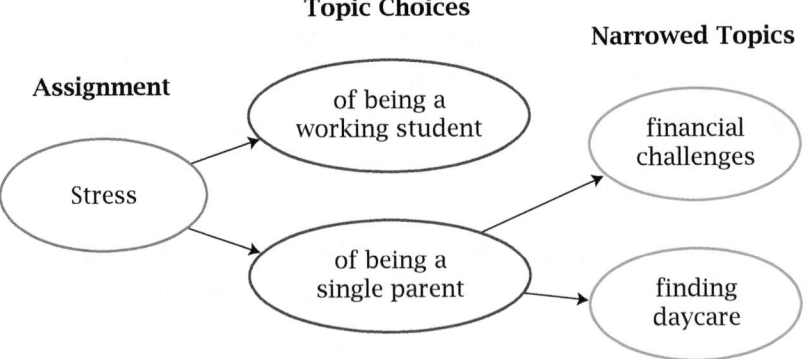

Topic Choices

Narrowed Topics

Assignment

Stress → of being a working student

Stress → of being a single parent → financial challenges

of being a single parent → finding daycare

Assignment: Stress

Specific Topic: Single parents stress over finding daycare for their children.

THE TOPIC SENTENCE

A good topic sentence makes a specific point about a topic. It establishes the position you are taking on the topic or your controlling idea about the topic. It prepares the reader for what you are going to write about. If you are given a focused assignment, often your topic sentence will use key terms from the assignment.

> **Assignment:** What evidence do you see of help for people with disabilities on this campus?
>
> **Topic Sentence:** There is considerable evidence of help for people with physical challenges on this campus.
>
> *In the rest of your paragraph, you would support this topic sentence by writing about the accommodations your campus offers.*

> **Assignment:** What kind of an impact does television have on the lives of young people?
>
> **Topic Sentence:** Television has a very definite impact on the lives of young people, mostly negative.
>
> *Here, in the sentences that follow your topic sentence, you would then describe some of the negative effects of television on young viewers.*

With general assignments, you have the challenge to generate and narrow down a topic yourself. In these cases, try to avoid a vague topic sentence that lacks focus and is too broad to discuss in a paragraph, or a specific topic sentence that is so limited there is nothing to say about it. Look at these examples of vague, too specific, and focused topic sentences to see the differences.

> **Assignment:** Stress
>
> **Topic Sentences**   **Vague:** Single parents have lots of things to worry about.
>
> **Too Specific:** My daughter caught a cold at daycare last week.
>
> **Focused:** Finding quality daycare for their children is a real source of stress for single parents.

Writer's Response

Describe something that causes stress for you.

Assignment: Travel

Topic Sentences   **Vague:** Airport security is simply maddening these days.

Too Specific: Last week I stood in line for an hour-and-a-half while airport security officials searched older women.

Focused: Airport security procedures have slowed down travel, especially at the check-in stage.

EXERCISE 3-2   **Vague Versus Specific Topic Sentences**

Directions: *Read the following topic sentences and evaluate them. Place a V for vague next to those topic sentences that are not adequately focused. Place an S next to topic sentences that are too specific.*

_____ 1. When teens think of marriage, they want someone with that certain something.

_____ 2. Many teenaged girls start smoking at 14.

_____ 3. Saturday morning television is a wasteland.

_____ 4. Liquid crystal display monitors are affected by cold temperatures.

_____ 5. A mechanic knows a lot about cars.

_____ 6. Organized sports are what is wrong with high school; end of conversation.

_____ 7. To lie under a shade tree on a warm summer day and take a long nap is a treat.

_____ 8. What people call "flu" is actually a virus.

_____ 9. Last fall, a Holland Marsh farmer grew the largest pumpkin in York Region.

_____ 10. Women: can't live with them, can't live without them.

Focus Your Topic Sentence

To write a focused topic sentence, develop the habit of asking yourself, *What exactly am I saying about my topic? What do I want the reader to understand?* As mentioned in Chapter 2, you can ask questions to focus your topic sentence. Form questions with *who, what, where, when, why,* and *how.* Look at these examples:

Ask Yourself

Are you usually too general or too specific when you write?

Vague: Championship wrestling is really cool.

"Really cool" does not direct the reader's attention to anything specific about championship wrestling. Ask yourself a question like *What makes championship wrestling cool?*

Focused: Championship wrestling has <u>continuous action</u>, which makes it <u>very entertaining.</u>

"Continuous action" focuses the reader's attention on a specific dimension of wrestling and connects that aspect of wrestling to its entertainment value.

Too Specific: Last week, the patient lost 1.5 kilograms.

This sentence states a fact but does not focus the reader's attention on a subject. There are few additional details you can add to create a meaningful paragraph. Ask yourself a question like *How did the patient lose the weight?*

Focused: Losing weight is possible only when a person makes hard choices many times a day.

"Losing weight" is the subject; "hard choices many times a day" focuses the reader's attention on a specific dimension of the subject.

To visualize the process of narrowing your topic, it might help to use a graphic like this one.

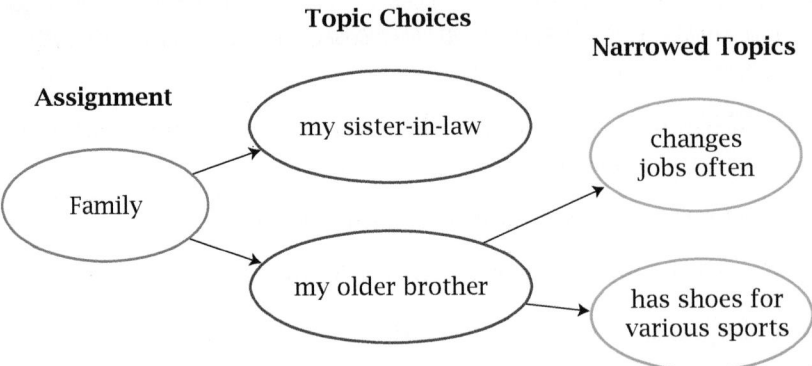

From the ideas in your graphic, you can generate a good topic sentence:

Topic Sentence: My brother has a special pair of shoes for each sport he plays.

To make the topic sentence even better, you could use the third person focus:

Revised Topic Sentence: My brother, like many high school athletes, has special pairs of shoes for each sport he plays.

TOPIC SENTENCES:
Not too vague or too broad

Not too specific or too limited

Focused with one controlling idea

EXERCISE 3-3 **Writing Focused Topic Sentences**

Directions: *For each of the following topics, use a graphic like the one above to narrow the topic. Then write a focused topic sentence that makes a specific point about the topic. Underline the terms that direct the reader's attention to the topic's specific focus.*

1. Swimming

_____

2. Textbooks

_____

3. Musical instruments

_____

4. Household chores

_____

5. Old age

_____

6. Insects

_____

7. Bottled water

_____

8. Mountains

_____

9. Jewellery

_____

10. Counterfeiting

_____

From Prewriting to Topic Sentence

In Chapter 2, you saw that prewriting is a way of exploring what you know about your topic. Prewriting is also a way of narrowing and focusing your topic. After talking, clustering, brainstorming, questioning, and free-writing, you will likely end up with a focused topic sentence about your assignment and the specific details you need to develop your paragraph's main idea.

Here is an illustration of a student using clustering and freewriting to explore what he knows about his topic. A focused topic sentence is the end product of his work.

Assignment: Write a paragraph that explains how people can get into debt. Your focus will be on the causes of debt.

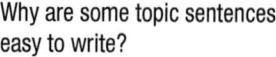

Talk about it

Why are some topic sentences easy to write?

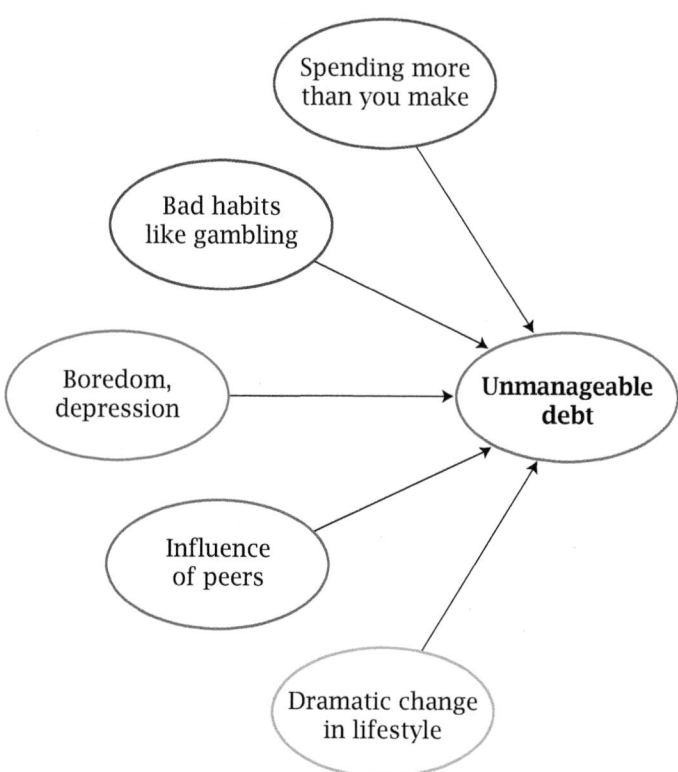

Freewrite

How can you not be in debt when you spend your money foolishly? I have friends who love those casinos. Once or twice a month they go. They drop a lot of cash. One guy says, "I always say I am up a few hundred, even if I am down a grand." Down a grand! I can't imagine those words ever coming out of my mouth. Other friends bet on sports. They have bookies they call. They place bets. Then Saturday comes. They win and lose. Over time maybe it evens out but some get in debt up to their ears. It's kind of a club. They gamble. Their peers gamble. Some get cash against credit cards. One guy I know went to a casino near the college he attended. By November all his money was gone. Bad decisions. These are bad decisions about how to have fun.

Topic Sentence: Problems with debt are often caused by bad decisions about how to have fun.

Prewriting is an act of discovery. In the process of exploring what he knows about his topic (problems with debt), this student discovers the point he wants to make: they are caused by bad decisions. He states this point in his focused topic sentence.

EXERCISE 3-4 **Finding Topic Sentences in Your Prewriting**

Directions: *Choose two of the following topics. On a separate sheet of paper, explore each topic using two methods of prewriting (talking, clustering, brainstorming, questioning, freewriting). Then, for each topic, formulate a focused topic sentence for a paragraph you could write about it.*

1. Difficult classes

Topic Sentence: _____

_____

2. Television

Topic Sentence: _____

_____

3. Athletics

Topic Sentence: _____

_____

4. Poverty

Topic Sentence: _____

_____

5. ·Goals

Topic Sentence: _____

_____

Supporting Details

Be specific. This is one of the most common demands made of writers in college and university. Readers want to see detailed content. The details you provide support the focused topic sentence in your paragraph, and they will vary according to your paragraph's purpose. You might use description, examples, narrative, facts, or statistics. You might talk about the steps in the process of carrying out a lab experiment or the causes or effects of inflation. The chapters in Part 2 of this book give you extensive practice at developing and organizing various kinds of supporting details depending on the pattern of writing you select for your assignment.

A useful way to picture the supporting details in your paragraph is to write an outline of the **major details** you plan to include. Identifying the major details helps you to keep your paragraph's focus. Organizing the major details in an outline helps you to put them in a logical order.

Topic Sentence: My brother has a special pair of shoes for each sport he plays.

A. Walking shoes, usually found by the back door

B. Two pairs of running shoes in the garage, always muddy

C. Baseball cleats that he does not use anymore

D. Three pairs of Converse Allstars, his basketball shoes

Topic Sentence: The secret to a good homemade pizza is getting the crust just right.

A. Buy raw dough at the local Italian market.

B. Roll it out on a cookie sheet—very thin.

C. Bake it twice.

D. High temperature (the key detail!).

In the first illustration, the writer outlines the major *examples* she will use to support her topic sentence; in the second, the writer outlines the *process* of making the crust for a pizza. In both topic sentences, the writers state what they want the reader to understand about their focused topics. In the outlines of major supporting details, the writers make decisions about the specific content of their paragraphs.

EXERCISE 3-5 **Outlines and Major Supporting Details**

Directions: *Fill in the outlines below with major supporting details that would provide specific content for each topic sentence.*

1. A fun and entertaining vacation requires specific planning beforehand.

   A. _____

   B. _____

   C. _____

   D. _____

2. Saturday morning television can have negative consequences for children.

   A. _____

   B. _____

   C. _____

   D. _____

3. Even though fast food is not healthy, there are a few places where students just cannot resist eating.

   A. _____

   B. _____

   C. _____

   D. _____

4. The cost of operating a car can keep a young person very busy earning money.

   A. _____

   B. _____

   C. _____

   D. _____

5. Quality leisure time has to satisfy a few specific needs in a person's life.

   A. _____

   B. _____

   C. _____

   D. _____

ELABORATE ON YOUR MAJOR SUPPORTING DETAILS

The most common shortcoming in post-secondary writing is that students do not give enough details. They do not elaborate sufficiently, and they do not explain thoroughly. When you write, you need to be specific and tell the reader what you know. For each major supporting detail, you can often add one, two, or even three sentences of explanation, called **minor details**. As you try to think of minor details, refer to a dictionary or thesaurus to help you choose precise words.

Recall the previous example, and look at how the writer added details and explanations to the first outline. The writer might add two or three sentences of explanation (minor details) for each major detail as outlined below:

Topic Sentence: My brother has a special pair of shoes for each sport he plays.

A. **Major Detail:** He has two pairs of walking shoes, usually found by the back door.
   1. **Minor Detail:** He leaves them in the same place my dad takes off his work boots.
   2. **Minor Detail:** This means there is always a huge pile of shoes right by the door.
   3. **Minor Detail:** It really makes my mother angry.

B. **Major Detail:** He also has two pairs of running shoes in the garage, always muddy.
   1. **Minor Detail:** He runs every morning, rain or shine.
   2. **Minor Detail:** When it rains, his shoes pick up mud.
   3. **Minor Detail:** He tracks the mud in on his shoes, getting mud all over the garage.

C. **Major Detail:** Then there are the baseball cleats, which he does not use anymore.
   1. **Minor Detail:** He played baseball in high school and in a league for a year or two after high school.
   2. **Minor Detail:** That was two or three years ago, but he still has those cleats, in the heap by the back door.

D. **Major Detail:** Finally, there are the three pairs of Converse Allstars, his basketball shoes.
   1. **Minor Detail:** One pair is worn down to nothing.
   2. **Minor Detail:** Another pair is brand new.
   3. **Minor Detail:** Then there is the pair his friends autographed when he graduated from high school.

In this illustration, the writer provides additional visual details (pile of muddy shoes by the back door), more information about her brother's running habits and background, and some proper names (Converse Allstars). The writer maintains equal emphasis, providing a similar amount of elaboration for each detail. The writer also moves from using point form in the first outline to full sentences in the more detailed outline.

EXERCISE 3-6 **Elaborating**

Directions: *Choose an outline you wrote for Exercise 3-5 and elaborate on the supporting details you provided. For each detail, write two or three sentences of elaboration.*

Topic Sentence: _____

  A. **Major Detail:** _____

    Minor Details

     1. _____

     2. _____

     3. _____

     4. _____

  B. **Major Detail:** _____

    Minor Details

     1. _____

     2. _____

     3. _____

     4. _____

  C. **Major Detail:** _____

    Minor Details

     1. _____

     2. _____

     3. _____

     4. _____

  D. **Major Detail:** _____

    Minor Details

     1. _____

     2. _____

     3. _____

     4. _____

BE SPECIFIC

You may need to work with a dictionary or thesaurus for help in providing good word choices for the specific details.

As we've discussed, your reader needs specific details to fully understand your point. For example, it is not enough to say your brother has lots of shoes. From the extended outline in the previous section, the reader now knows about at least eight pairs of shoes and the specific brand name of some. Effective writers are specific about places and times, dimensions and sizes, and proper names. Look at the difference between vague and specific details below:

Vague Details	*Specific Details*
a big house	a two-story, four-bedroom house with a three-car garage
last year	the long weekend in October, for Thanksgiving
my high school biology teacher	Mr. Perry, my high school biology teacher
a bad smell	the stench of burning rubber

a short vacation somewhere nice	three nights at the Lynx Tundra Lodge
expensive clothes	a black leather YSL belt that cost $59

Specifying Details

Directions: *Transform each of the vague details below into a specific detail. Keep place and time, dimensions and sizes, and proper names in mind when you work.*

1. A snack

_____

2. Older people

_____

3. The newspaper

_____

4. Electronic devices

_____

5. Clutter

_____

Concluding Sentence

Your paragraph's point is stated in the topic sentence and then backed up with the supporting details. Finish your paragraph with a sentence that comments on the main idea. The concluding sentence emphasizes the point of the topic sentence but uses different words. Sometimes, it also makes a transition to the next paragraph's main idea. Like the topic sentence, the concluding sentence helps remind the reader what your paragraph is about and your purpose for writing it. As you try to restate your topic sentence, you may find it useful to refer to a dictionary or thesaurus to find synonyms and keep your writing more interesting.

Analyzing Paragraphs

Directions: *Read each paragraph, underline the topic sentence, and number the major details. Then answer the questions that follow.*

People go to tanning booths for a variety reasons. Some people start going to tanning booths at a young age, in high school, for example. They say they like the way they look when they have a nice tan. They spend a lot of time and money keeping themselves tan. They cannot just go once in a while. They have to go all the time, or their tan will fade. Looks are not the only reason they do this. Some individuals go right before vacation to get some colour. That way when they get to the beach, their tan is already started, and nature can then take over. Finally, there are those people who are simply addicted to tanning. Some women go so often that their skin gets discoloured and blotchy. They know they should take a break, but they do not listen. Their skin is already wrinkled, and sometimes these women are still quite young. It is important to them that they look tanned year-round. Going to a tanning booth once in a while, maybe before a vacation, might be acceptable, but compulsive tanning is just plain dangerous.

1. What is the topic of the paragraph?

_____

2. What is the focus of the topic sentence?

_____

3. What kind of supporting detail is used?

_____

4. What is the purpose of the paragraph?

_____

5. Does the concluding sentence comment on the main idea?

_____

Increasing the amount of fish in a person's daily diet has health benefits. First, fish is easier to digest than red meat. Eating more fish improves digestion and reduces colon problems. In addition, seafood contains little or no fat. Consequently, people in cultures where fish is a significant part of the diet have a lower incidence of obesity. Plus, the fats found in fish actually have a positive effect on consumer's health. For example, fish oil can lower an individual's cholesterol. Research shows that the omega-3 fatty acids found in fish benefit the heart and vascular system. There may even be favourable effects for those suffering from autism, Alzheimer's disease, and attention deficit disorder. Researchers claim that people who eat fish live longer.

1. What is the topic of the paragraph?

_____

2. What is the focus of the topic sentence?

_____

3. What kind of supporting details are used?

_____

4. What is the purpose of the paragraph?

_____

5. Does the concluding sentence comment on the main idea?

_____

> Video games can be educational in a positive way. The first time I saw a video game, I knew I had to play. I was around four years old. Some of my relatives were playing "Super Mario Brothers" for the Nintendo Entertainment System (NES) at my grandparents' house. I did not play that day, but I knew I would. Soon after, when I got that NES as a gift, I was a happy boy. I sat and played games all day, every day. As often as I could, I would go to the video store and rent a new game. Once, when I was five, I rented a role-playing game. It required a whole lot of reading. That was not something I could do too well, but I had fun anyway. In fact, that game inspired me to start learning to read. The first words I can remember figuring out were _continue_ and _game over._ Knowing the difference between those words helped a lot. I also learned a little math from remembering my high scores. I have been playing video games ever since I got that NES. I would like to think that I learn a little something from every new game that I play. It may not be that important, but I learn something.

1. What is the topic of the paragraph?

_____

Ask Yourself

Have you identified your personal or preferred style of writing?

2. What is the focus of the topic sentence?

_____

3. What kind of supporting details are used?

_____

4. What is the purpose of the paragraph?

_____

5. Does the concluding sentence comment on the main idea?

_____

Paragraph Organization

Where should the writer place the topic sentence? It is common to place it at the beginning of a paragraph to send a clear message to the reader: *This is the topic that will be discussed in this paragraph.* When a paragraph begins with a topic sentence, the writer is using **deductive order** by stating her point right away.

Learn a variety of ways to organize a paragraph. Examine each pattern to determine when it is appropriate to use it.

Topic: Math in daily life

People use math all the time in daily life. When a customer goes shopping, she adds up the prices of her items before she gets to the checkout line to avoid overspending. At least once a month, people have to balance their chequing accounts. Sometimes a consumer will have to figure out loan terms (when buying a new car, for example) and which approaches to financing the purchase will be most economical. In my own case, when I work at the family store all summer, I balance a cash box every day. Every month, I write out a budget and pay bills online. I rarely use a calculator for these routine chores, and I believe my mind is sharper for it.

However, there are times when it makes sense to place the topic sentence at the end of a paragraph. When you begin with your supporting details, you "hook" your reader and create interest in your topic. When it comes at the end of a paragraph, your topic sentence states the main idea as a conclusion. Beginning with details and ending a paragraph with a topic sentence is called **inductive order**.

Topic: Knitting

Details come first in this paragraph.

When I was 13 years old, I came down with the flu. I was stuck in the house for a week. My grandmother came to visit me to see how I was feeling. She had a crazy idea that she would teach me how to knit. She thought that it might help pass time. Well, bless her heart, she tried. She brought me yards of pretty blue yarn and two knitting needles. My mom and grandma sat on the couch with me, trying to explain the concept of "knit one, pearl two." It just did not work. I practised and practised. The most that I could come up with was an odd-shaped potholder. My grandmother and my mother gave me the impression any woman could knit. They had me convinced that I would have an afghan in no time. They were right, if you want to call an odd-shaped potholder an afghan. Every once in a while, I pick up my mom's needles and give it a try. Those horrible memories come back. I remember: I cannot do this, and furthermore, I do not like it. Knitting is one of those "woman things" I just do not get.

TOPIC SENTENCE:
In this example, the topic sentence comes at the end of the paragraph.

EXERCISE 3-9 **Deductive and Inductive Order**

Directions: *Underline the sentence that works best as a topic sentence for each of the following lists. To make a unified paragraph, cross out those detail sentences that do not* *support the topic sentence. On a separate piece of paper, rewrite the sentences to form a paragraph, organizing the detail sentences so they logically support the topic sentence. Use either a deductive or inductive order for each list.*

EXAMPLE

1. He puts a lot of thought into the art he gets.

2. The first time I looked in the mirror and saw a 30-something mom looking back at me, I thought of getting a tattoo.

3. His tattoos are a collection of significant and meaningful things in his life.

4. He is able to display his devotion on his skin for all to see.

5. <u>Skeptics who do not understand another's love for living art have to look at the fan of body art.</u>

6. Therefore, anyone can understand the man by studying his tattoos.

7. The fan of body art has sentimental feelings about tattoos.

Deductive order: 5, 7, 1, 3, 4, 6. Delete 2.

Skeptics who do not understand another's love for living art have to look at the fan of body art. The fan of body art has sentimental feelings about tattoos. He puts a lot of thought into the art he gets. His tattoos are a collection of significant and meaningful things in his life. He is able to display his devotion on his skin for all to see. By studying his tattoos, one begins to understand him.

PARAGRAPH A

1. Late fees are ridiculous.

2. If customers pay with credit cards, they have to pay later, which can be a hassle.

3. Credit cards are not for everyone.

4. If consumers are not careful, it can take forever to pay off their bills.

5. Credit cards can be a big hassle.

6. Not all businesses take credit cards, like fast-food places.

7. Some people end up using them for petty things like gas and food, and before they know it they owe more money than they ever imagined.

8. The interest rates can go through the roof.

9. Sometimes the card gets bent or scratched, and it will not work.

10. There can be problems if one gets behind on a credit card bill.

11. There is nothing more to pay.

12. When a customer buys things with cash, on the other hand, it is a done deal.

13. That can be a hassle, but it is when the card works that the real trouble starts.

Ask Yourself

Do you generally use deductive or inductive order for your paragraphs?

PARAGRAPH B

1. Teams get together often for pizza parties after games or practices.

2. A good soccer player controls the ball with his head up high and his eyes on the field, not on the ball.

3. In high school, soccer games are two 40-minute periods.

4. It is a great place to meet nice people and make friends.

5. There is a lot of practice involved in learning to dribble down the field.

6. Soccer teaches the value of control and endurance.

7. Soccer players need endurance to stay ahead in the game.

8. It is definitely a game of coordination, body position, and skill.

9. The main skill is running back and forth down the field, trying to manoeuvre around opponents, and still having the soccer ball under control.

10. Spending lots of time together both on and off the field improves performance as a team.

11. Sometimes players playing defense will not get a break until halftime comes, and then they go back on the field for the second half.

12. Faced with physical and mental challenges in every game, team members learn to trust and depend on one another.

PARAGRAPH C

1. They seek to change or influence the listeners' attitudes or behaviour.

2. These presenters use vivid language and relevant examples to captivate their audience.

3. The most common example of an informative speech is a classroom lecture where a knowledgeable instructor acquaints the students with something they wish to learn about.

4. A presentation can inform the audience, persuade the listeners, or simply entertain them.

5. Presenters who are enthusiastic about their subject often have a dramatic flair to keep the attention of the audience.

6. Many politicians give persuasive speeches close to election time.

7. Sometimes speakers wish to persuade their listeners.

8. A third purpose for a speech can be to entertain an audience.

9. Politicians talk about reasons people should vote for them.

10. In planning a speech, one should first decide on the main purpose of the presentation.

11. Giving oral presentations is one kind of academic assignment that students must complete.

12. As well, many employers often ask employees to present ideas to their co-workers.

13. These are three general purposes for presentations, and many effective speeches will combine some or all of these purposes.

14. The purpose of one kind of speech is to give new information to the listener.

15. Once the purpose of a presentation is clear, the next step is to organize the speech logically.

ORDER YOUR DETAILS

How you present your supporting details matters a great deal. It is not enough to simply list them in the order you thought of them. There has to be a reason for the order. In Chapter 2, you saw different ways to organize content details. Here is a review; your choice will depend on your focus and purpose.

In description writing, **spatial order** makes sense. When you use spatial order, you might describe an object or place by beginning outside, then moving inside, working from left to right, or moving from top to bottom.

Details may be presented in **chronological order.** This means they are organized in the order in which they happened. In a narrative paragraph, you begin at the beginning of the story and tell what happens next. This is true in process paragraphs as well.

In persuasive writing, **order of importance** gives maximum impact to your details. You often save the most important, most persuasive detail for last.

In writing about causes and effects, or in comparison and contrast writing, it is useful to organize details from **simple to complex.** You begin by explaining relatively simple details; then you transition to more complicated details and ideas.

Be sure to use transition words and phrases to signal the order of your details and enhance the coherence of your paragraph. Refer back to the list of commonly used transition words and phrases listed in Chapter 2.

ORDER OF DETAILS
Spatial order
Chronological order
Order of importance
Simple to complex order

UNITY AND COHERENCE

In a well-written paragraph, the main idea is stated in the topic sentence, and all the supporting details relate to that one main idea, forming a **unified** paragraph. When you go off topic in a paragraph, introducing new and unrelated ideas, your writing lacks unity. Further, in a well-written paragraph, the details have a clear, logical relationship that fit together and *work together,* forming a **coherent** paragraph. When you do not indicate connections between the details in your paragraph, your writing lacks coherence. A good writer determines the order of the sentences in each paragraph to make sure that the sentences flow logically from one to the other. Depending on your purpose, there are different ways that you can order your sentences, which was discussed in the previous section. However, each sentence should still maintain the focus of the topic sentence, which ensures the paragraph has unity, or discusses only one topic.

Let's look at and analyze a paragraph that lacks unity and coherence.

Some of my most enjoyable memories are of my grandparents. I am sure most children are spoiled by their grandparents as I was by mine. When I would feel sick and had to stay home, I would go over to my grandma's and be pampered like a prince. She would give me a bell to ring to be answered on every waking call. As a society we have many prejudices, which lead to the separation of young and elderly people and the prevention of communities coming closer together. We should take various steps to control these prejudices and create a better environment for older people. Many are locked up in nursing homes and are never seen by the rest of society. Some of us have prejudices because we never take the time to get to know older people. We tend to only see their flaws and do not appreciate the contributions they have made.

This writer has two important topics in his paragraph: (1) memories of his grandparents and (2) the poor treatment of elderly people in our society. One topic, the first one, is personal and specific; the other is impersonal and general. Given proper focus, either would be a suitable topic for a paragraph or an essay. In this paragraph, however, the writer fails to do justice to either topic.

Here is a revision of the above paragraph where the writer focuses on the more general topic. Not only is this paragraph now unified around the main idea, "elderly people can make a contribution," it is also a coherent paragraph because of the writer's use of transition words and phrases. Notice how the concluding sentence restates the idea of the beginning topic sentence but uses different words to do so.

Given half a chance, elderly people can make an important contribution to our society. **For example**, these days it is common to find a senior citizen working as a greeter in a department store. They are friendly and helpful, pointing a shopper in the direction of linens or plumbing supplies. **Seniors are also** visible in schools these days. In the local school in my community, **they stand** at crosswalks and help young children across the street. **They work** in the cafeterias and supervise on playgrounds. Some are in the classroom in lower grades, reading to students and, at times, helping little children learn to read. Some seniors get involved in health care **as well. They drive** patients to appointments, work in blood drives, and make a real difference in people's lives. **A final contribution is they remember** what life was like in the past. They can recall what it was like to live through a world war or what it was like coming to this country. **They remember** fashions and fads and the funny and tragic parts of life. If we do not listen, we lose what they know forever. No one wants to be locked away. Seniors are too important to push aside: in so many ways, they can make our lives richer and better.

PART 1 Writing in College and University

Writing with Unity and Coherence

Directions: *Following the steps of the writing process from Chapter 2, write a short paragraph in response to the following assignments. After drafting your topic sentence, determine the best order of your details while considering your purpose in writing. Survey the list of transition words and phrases in Chapter 2, and select the transitions you need to enhance the coherence of your writing.*

1. Write a short paragraph about your first job. Describe the process of learning to do the job well. Begin with a topic sentence that states the main idea of your paragraph. Use transition words relating to sequence to organize the details of your paragraph.

2. Write a short paragraph about a disappointing trip you took. Begin with a topic sentence that states the main idea of your paragraph. Be specific about where and when you took the trip. Tell what happened. Use transition words relating to time to organize the details of your paragraph.

3. Write a short paragraph about a goal you have set for yourself, why it is important, and what benefits you will have by achieving your goal. Begin with a topic sentence that states the main idea of your paragraph. Use transition words relating to additional detail to organize the details of your paragraph.

CHAPTER REVIEW

Recall what you have learned in this chapter about paragraph structure:

☐ Assignments and topics
  - *Focused topic sentences, not vague or too specific*
  - *Key terms from assignment*

☐ Supporting details
  - *Outlines, major details, minor details, specific details*

☐ Concluding sentences
  - *Comments on main idea of topic sentence*
  - *Synonyms for key ideas*

☐ Paragraph organization
  - *Deductive and inductive order*
  - *Order of details*
  - *Unity and coherence*

CHAPTER 4

Description

THINK FIRST

Write a description of what you see in this photograph. Begin with a sentence that states the general impression you get. Then use your senses to describe what you see in the scene. Get the details down. Make your description a word painting, so that if you read it to someone over the phone, the other person would see exactly what you see.

Seeing Is Believing

"That man outside looks odd." *Odd* seems like a descriptive word, when in fact it is not. What is odd to one person might not be odd to another. To explain *odd,* you need concrete, specific details. Look again: "He is tugging a lock of brown hair on the side of his head. He is dressed in a black, three-piece suit with a pink tie. He is in his late fifties. If you get close enough to him, you can smell pipe tobacco and hear him talking about mathematical equations." Description takes the reader to the scene. There is odd, and then there is odd. Careful description matters in order to give precise information to our readers.

DISCUSSION

Turn and talk with a classmate to answer the following questions: Do you know someone who seems odd? Remember where you saw that person. Describe the person. Think about appearance, actions, and conversations. Use several senses to describe this "odd" person.

What I Mean Is . . .

In the paragraphs and essays you write in an academic or work setting, good description will always make a significant difference to the quality of your writing. Whether you are looking through a microscope or conducting a physics experiment, careful observation and description will help your reader understand exactly what you observed. If you report on a music performance, it will not be enough to say, "It was a big band in a big room." What is big? Are 8 instruments a big band? Are 43 instruments a big band? Is a big room one that seats 200 or 2000? In art appreciation, describing a painting as "a colourful country scene" will be just the beginning. You will need to mention the three yellow haystacks and the wooden barn with its red door half open. Detailed description is a writer's basic tool to paint an image with words in the mind of the reader.

BRAINSTORM

Think about your favourite place. Why do you like it? For example, you might make a statement about a restaurant. You might write, "The Purple Pickle Restaurant is a place with a really good atmosphere." You would then illustrate what you mean by atmosphere *with specific descriptions of the restaurant, the food, or the customers. As you brainstorm, list examples and details that explain why you like it.*

Details Matter

On the job, careful observation is essential. A health-care employee needs to assess a patient's symptoms and convey them clearly to other practitioners. A police officer on the scene of an accident notes traffic conditions, weather, damage, and the names and contact information of individuals involved. In food service, recipes depend on exact descriptions of ingredients. For example, if a recipe calls for cheese, the cook needs to know if the cheese is sliced, shredded, or grated and if the recipe requires Parmesan or Gorgonzola. Precise detail can make a critical difference. Description is dependent on specific word choice.

RESUMÉ BUILDER

Any job requires you to learn precise vocabulary. Words are one tool necessary to do a good job. Think about your job. What specific language do you use just at work? Make a list of ten precise words that are necessary for you to do a good job. Then write a sentence or two to explain why using these words is essential to doing your job well. Consider whether someone outside your work would understand the words. Once you determine who you are writing for, you can choose the appropriate vocabulary.

At a Glance

Like all paragraphs, a description paragraph has three basic parts: a topic sentence, supporting details, and a concluding sentence. Recall from Chapters 2 and 3 that the topic sentence states the topic plus your point, which in a description paragraph is the dominant impression about the topic. A description uses words that appeal to the five senses: sight, sound, smell, touch, or taste. The paragraph support provides concrete, sensory details to make a vivid impression on the reader. These details combine to convey the writer's purpose. The concluding sentence restates or emphasizes the dominant impression.

The Description Paragraph at a Glance

Here is an example using description to answer an assignment.

ASSIGNMENT   Write about a region, city, neighbourhood, or building, and describe the living conditions of the people who live in it. Describe this place using details that convey a dominant impression.

TOPIC SENTENCE
The writer uses key words from the assignment and states the dominant impression.

SUPPORTING DETAILS
The writer uses multiple senses to describe the slum: (1) sight—description of the homes; (2) touch—description of the water; (3) sound and smell—description of the area where the slums are built.

ORDER AND TRANSITIONS
The writer uses a list to describe the slum in three ways. He begins with "in these slums" and adds a second description and a final description of the place.

CONCLUDING SENTENCE
The writer emphasizes the dominant impression and impact of this impression on the people who live there.

Mumbai, a famous city in India, has slum areas where poor people live in the worst conditions possible. (1) **In these slums**, people barely make it through the day. There, the homes are built out of scrap materials found in the garbage. People use pieces of metal or cardboard for roofs. Walls are built like a camper tent since bricks are impossible to afford. These homes keep the residents sheltered but not warm or safe from the weather. Often these make-shift homes do not survive severe weather conditions and have to be rebuilt. (2) **In addition**, the biggest problem people face is getting water. Each morning, they wake up before the sun rises to line up near a government-provided water pump. These impoverished people have to carry enough water to last them the rest of the day. The water is always cold since it is expensive to heat, so daily bathing is unpleasant. (3) **Finally**, the make-shift dwellings are usually built near sewage areas, garbage dumps, railroad tracks, or even runways for airplanes. Slum residents have to live with the stench of human excrement, spoiled food, and the roaring noise of trains and planes. Sewers get backed up causing water to overflow, increasing the risk of disease. Moreover, rats also reside in these slums, and they carry contagious diseases. These destitute slum conditions make everyday life for the unfortunate people living there extremely difficult.

1. Can you identify the supporting detail that best illustrates the dominant impression stated in the topic sentence?

2. Why is it effective?

Thinking
DESCRIPTION THINKING

As you noticed in the example paragraph about Mumbai, effective descriptions make a point by creating a dominant impression using sensory details and comparisons, which are the basic elements of description. Recall the exercises from Chapter 3 that encouraged you to provide additional specific details to your supporting points. This will also apply to descriptive writing.

Elements of Description

How does description thinking work? Below is a brief summary of the elements you should keep in mind when writing a description paragraph because this will help you choose appropriate descriptive words. You may also use description in other patterns of paragraph writing.

- *Dominant impression:* The topic sentence states your impression of the person, place, or object being described. It states your attitude or feeling about it. A slum, for example, is a depressing place.

- *Sensory description:* Effective sensory description consists of specific details gathered through the five senses: sight, sound, smell, taste, and touch. In the sample paragraph, the writer provides vivid detail to capture what living in a slum is like. Through the details, we can imagine how shocking taking a shower in cold water is or how disgusting human excrement smells.

- *Comparisons:* Sometimes supporting details are hard to describe. For this reason, writers use comparisons to indicate what something is similar to or like. There are two kinds of descriptive comparisons used in writing. These are called "figures of speech." One uses *like* and is called a simile. For example, in the sentence "Taxi cabs hum around the street corners like bees looking for honey," the writer is comparing taxi cabs to honey bees, using *like*. Look back at the paragraph about Mumbai for another example of a simile. Another kind of literary comparison is called a metaphor; this comparison doesn't use *like*, but implies a comparison between two dissimilar things. Here's an example of a metaphor from Exercise 4-3, found later in this chapter, which compares a city to a weather pattern: " Vancouver is a whirlwind of energy . . ." Keep an eye out for the use of metaphors when you're reading to see how writers use comparisons to clarify what they are trying to describe.

Get Started

The details in good description need to work together to create a dominant impression. Good description consists of both general observations and specific concrete details.

Notice in the following example how a student has brainstormed a list of general observations and the specific details that illustrate them in preparation for writing a description paragraph about a coffee shop she visits.

The Coffee Shop

General Detail	*Concrete Detail*
nice atmosphere	classical music piped in (esp. piano and classical guitar)
	just enough noise to drown out surrounding conversation
	like a bookstore but better: more sociable, yet private
good smells	fresh bagels
	grilled sandwiches prepared for lunch
spacious	18 to 20 tables—plenty of room to be alone to read and sip coffee
courteous help	May, fiftyish, brown hair. "Want a mug today, hon?" "Take all the time you want"
good light	track lighting, ochre walls, lots of windows

Good description depends on the use of precise language. To find the best word for a precise description, refer to a dictionary or thesaurus. In this student's work, when she mentions track lighting and ochre walls, you get a much more vivid impression of the coffee shop's interior than from the term "good light." Notice the writer includes a comparison detail, too: "like a bookstore but better: more sociable, yet private." In this exploration, all the details add up to a vivid description of the coffee shop. In addition to helping the student get to the concrete details, the general observations help her formulate a topic sentence.

Topic Sentence: The coffee shop, because of its inviting atmosphere and friendly employees, is a great place to pass time.

Directions: *Go to a public place where you can sit undisturbed. Decide on a focal point—a person, a place, or an object. Make as many observations as you can and record them as notes. Try to cover as many of the senses as you can in these observations. If it is useful, make comparisons as well. When you have finished, review your notes and write a couple of sentences that sum up your impression.*

Writer's Response

Are you a people watcher? Why or why not? What details do you notice about people?

Organize Your Thinking

Good description comes more easily if you think systematically about your subject. If you describe an object or place, organize your thinking by scanning the object or place from top to bottom, front to back, or left to right.

A graphic organizer can help you think in an organized way. You can make a table using the five senses as headings to inspire you. Alternatively, you can draw a diagram of the place you are describing or make a sketch of the object or location. This gives you a visual sense of what you are describing; you can use this diagram to organize your description and suggest additional descriptive details.

Figure 4-1 is the diagram the student made of the coffee shop she described as "a great place to pass time"; it includes the notes the student made.

If you describe people, organize your thinking by listing their physical characteristics or personality traits. A t-chart can be helpful. Figure 4-2 is a t-chart a student used to list the physical and personality traits of a close friend.

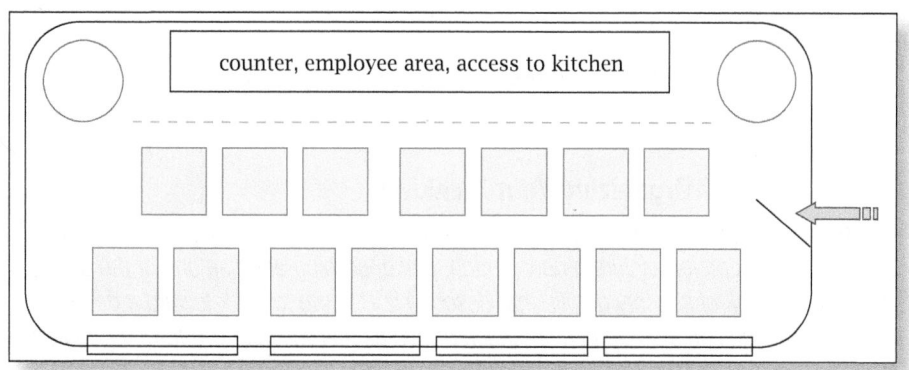

counter, employee area, access to kitchen

FIGURE 4-1 Student Diagram of Coffee Shop

I forgot about the comfortable chairs (the circles)! You can really relax in this place. The coffee shop is long. It is deep. Seating along the windows on the left of the entrance is the best. Booths on the right, tables on the left, along the windows. Art work on the walls I forgot that too. A photo of a man with a giant piece of bread!

On a t-chart, try to include both **concrete details**, which you see on the left in the "Physical Characteristics" column of this illustration, and general observations, which you see on the right under "Personality Traits". This column will be especially useful for finding the words to describe your dominant impression, which leads to your topic sentence.

Physical Characteristics	Personality Traits
Clothes—always khakis or shorts. A brown braided belt that is too big, hangs down like a dog's tongue. T-shirt with "dogshirt" written on the front. (Get close and he smells like a dog!)	Sloppy, but good sloppy. Really easy to be with. A dog lover.
Dark hair, almost black. Parted on the left. Long hair, over the ears, full in the back. Usually looks like he is just out of bed. Sticky-up hair, esp. in the back. Matted hair.	The most laid-back person in the world. Capable of sleeping long hours.
Terrible shoes. Canvas sports shoes with the toes ripped open. Muddy shoes, shoes practically falling off his feet. Do not get too close, they smell bad!	Known him for years. When we were kids, if there was a puddle, he walked through it. Seemed like he was always wet.
Powerful legs. You can tell this guy is a jock. Angry red scar on his forearm from a recent surgery.	He may be laid-back, he may seem lazy, but on the football field, he is an animal. Naturally, he loves the mud on the football field.

FIGURE 4-2 T-Chart Showing Physical and Personality Traits

EXERCISE 4-2 Organizing Your Thinking

Directions: *Use one of the graphic organizers shown to organize the work you generated for Exercise 4-1. If you prefer, picture a new person, place, or thing and use one of the graphics to help you think of sensory details that describe it. Be sure to work toward a dominant impression that you can sum up in a sentence or two as this will help you form a good topic sentence.*

Comparisons and Description Thinking

In ordinary conversation, we naturally compare one thing to another. For example, your father's overcooked hamburger looks like a hockey puck on a bun. When your grandfather pulls into the driveway, his big old car reminds you of a parade float. The tiny hat your grandmother wears looks like two scoops of vanilla ice cream. Comparisons help us see things clearly. Comparisons convey a sense of what we are describing.

EXERCISE 4-3 Using Comparisons in Description

Directions: *Read the description paragraph that follows. Underline the comparisons you see. Then answer the questions that follow.*

New York City is bustling and alive. The streets are filled with multicoloured cabs zipping up the streets and honking. They buzz around corners like bees in search of honey, stopping to pick up a fare, and then buzzing away. A delivery truck blocks traffic as the driver unloads slim envelopes and stacks of brown boxes before he disappears into a building. Every corner has a food vendor. The smell of onions and peppers draws a lunch-hour crowd to stainless-steel carts selling hot dogs, coffee, and drinks. The sidewalks are filled with people weaving in and out of traffic like professional dancers on a dance floor. Small children tug on their mothers' hands and shout over honking horns. Tourists wander and point as they open a map and fight the wind to keep it steady as they check their location. New York is a whirlwind of energy 24 hours a day.

DISCUSSION QUESTIONS

1. How many comparisons did you find in this description?

2. How do the comparisons contribute to the overall description?

3. Reread the paragraph looking for sensory detail. Which of the senses does the writer appeal to? Which sensory details do you like best? Why?

Process

DESCRIPTION IN PROCESS

Good description writing benefits from using the writing process: prewriting, drafting, revising, and editing.

Select an Assignment

In a post-secondary setting and in the workplace, you will be asked to write descriptions in a variety of contexts and assignments. In these cases, you must respond directly to the assignment. Your description will be most effective if you provide your reader with plenty of specific detail.

These steps of the writing process can be easily done on a computer or tablet with a word-processing program, and you can cut, paste, and move your changes.

EXERCISE 4-4 Selecting an Assignment for a Description Paragraph

Directions: *Review the assignments that follow. Choose the one you know the most about and think is best suited for an effective description paragraph.*

1. Describe a person, place, or thing that has value to you or to society.

2. Recall a place you visited that made you feel uneasy or even frightened. Describe the place in detail.

3. Think about the advantages of being a young, middle-aged, or older person. Describe a person you know who really lives those advantages.

4. Working conditions contribute positively or negatively to the work you do. Describe the working conditions of a workplace you know well. Create a positive or negative dominant impression that reveals your attitude toward this workplace.

5. Technology is everywhere in modern Canadian education. Describe a technology that really makes a difference in your learning in a particular subject or discipline.

6. Select a photograph from a magazine or newspaper that has a powerful impact on the viewer. State the impression and describe what in the photograph conveys this impression to a reader. Attach the photograph to your paragraph.

7. Describe a fashion fad that you like or dislike.

8. Describe a classroom with an atmosphere that contributes positively or negatively to learning.

9. Describe an animal you find to be odd, funny, or threatening.

10. Choose your own topic.

<table>
<tr><td>

PREWRITE
- Talk
- Think
- Cluster
- Brainstorm
- Question
- Freewrite

</td></tr>
</table>

Prewrite: Write Before You Write By Brainstorming and Freewriting

When you describe, you are building a word picture for your reader. As mentioned earlier, to ensure you include all the relevant details, it helps to be systematic about your work. Take nothing for granted. Imagine that your reader has never seen what you are describing. Use plenty of sensory details—including specifics of size, colour, texture, and shape—and comparisons with familiar objects, places, or people. Even the smallest details are important in description.

For description, you can combine two prewriting strategies: brainstorming and freewriting.

EXERCISE 4-5 **Brainstorming**

Directions: *On a separate sheet of paper, brainstorm for ten minutes on the assignment that you chose in Exercise 4-4. Write the assignment at the top of the page. Then list as many description details as you can (use all your senses), as well as details of items you could compare to your subject. Include ideas about your topic as well as descriptive details.*

EXERCISE 4-6 **Focused Freewriting**

Directions: *On a separate sheet of paper, freewrite for ten minutes on the assignment that you chose in Exercise 4-4. You might start with a detail from your brainstorming but focus on* *your attitude toward your subject and the dominant impression you aim to create. Ask yourself, "What is my attitude toward this topic? What does it mean to me?" Focused freewriting should expand your current thinking about your topic or subject.*

Draft: Focus and Organize

DRAFT
- Consider your audience
- Formulate your topic sentence
- Outline for unity and coherence
- Write a concluding sentence
- Compose your first draft

After prewriting, you usually have a hunch about what you want to include in your paragraph. You can point to three or four concrete details you really like. This will lead you to the dominant impression you wish to explore in your topic sentence.

CONSIDER YOUR AUDIENCE

In Chapter 1, we discussed the importance of knowing whom you are writing for. Before you draft, you need to consider your reader. Begin by rereading the assignment and identifying the key words. What kind of description is the reader expecting? Think about how to organize your paragraph so your reader can make sense of the description and understand why you are describing the topic in this way. Use the following questions to consider how to convey your dominant impression to an audience:

- Why is my topic important?
- What do I want my readers to understand or what is my purpose in writing?
- What details will help them understand and connect to my perspective?

EXERCISE 4-7 **Considering Your Audience**

Directions: *Use the questions above to think critically about which specific details to include in your paragraph and how you will use them to convey your dominant impression to an audience. Talk with a classmate to clarify your purpose and decide on the descriptive details you will use. Take notes on this conversation and add them to your prewriting.*

FORMULATE YOUR TOPIC SENTENCE

To begin, write a clear topic sentence that echoes the key words from the assignment. If you are not sure of your dominant impression, relax. Often it only becomes clear after you have written a first draft. Remember, revision can happen as you write, so you can always state the dominant impression in the conclusion, rewrite the topic sentence as you are drafting or when you have finished your first draft.

Ask Yourself

Do you relax or get tense when you write a paragraph or essay?

OUTLINE FOR UNITY AND COHERENCE

Your paragraph should be unified around one main idea. That means all the descriptive details relate to that idea. Be careful not to go off the subject. Remember, too, that your details need to fit together to form a coherent, logically organized paragraph.

Description is often organized using spatial order. For example, a room can be described by moving from front to back, left to right, or by the placement of furniture to the left or right of an important focal point. You may want to try some commonly used transition terms based on spatial order.

TRANSITIONS BASED ON SPATIAL ORDER	
to the right	below
to the left	in front
close by	in back
above	in the centre

Bookmark this page so you can easily refer back to the transitions as you write.

Many writers mix spatial order transitions with other types of transition terms. Transitions based on priority and importance can be used to emphasize key details. The following is a list of commonly used transition terms based on priority and importance.

TRANSITIONS BASED ON PRIORITY OR IMPORTANCE	
To Show Priority	**To Show Importance**
always	most
certainly	equally
definitely	absolutely
never	
obviously	

Adjectives and Adverbs

One further way to add descriptive detail to your writing is using adjectives and adverbs. Consider adding a quality adjective to the nouns in your sentences as well as adding a quality adverb to the verbs in your sentences. For example, in the earlier paragraph about Mumbai, the writer adds the adjective *roaring* to the noun *noise* to describe the sounds of the trains and planes. Look for adverbs in professional writing to see how they clarify the verbs they describe. The adverb in the sentence "He walked briskly toward the subway platform" gives the reader a different impression than the sentence "He walked reluctantly toward the subway car." Chapter 24 gives you more information about using adjectives and adverbs effectively.

WRITE A CONCLUDING SENTENCE

Remember, a concluding sentence reflects the idea of the topic sentence. Before writing your conclusion, carefully reread your paragraph to be clear about what your dominant impression is. Do your details support that dominant impression? What point would you like to emphasize in the last sentence of the paragraph? See "Supporting Details" in Chapter 3 for detailed explanation of outlining.

EXERCISE 4-8 **Planning Your First Draft**

Directions: *On a separate sheet of paper, write a topic sentence that echoes the key words from the assignment topic you selected and states the dominant impression you want to convey. Make a short outline to organize your descriptive details.*

COMPOSE YOUR FIRST DRAFT

You have chosen your topic, decided on the dominant impression you want to convey, and organized your description details. Now, it is time to write a first draft of your paragraph. As you write, you may think of details that are not in your brainstorming and freewriting. As you draft, make use of any new ideas and details that are important and relevant.

EXERCISE 4-9 **Writing Your First Draft**

Directions: *Write a draft of your paragraph. Using the first-draft checklist from the inside back cover as a guide, be sure to include enough sensory details to help a reader picture your descriptions. Also, check that your choice of transitions organizes your description by spatial order, by priority, or by importance.*

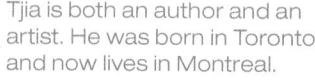

A PROFESSIONAL'S TAKE

Here is a description by Sherwin Sully Tjia, in an excerpt from his essay "Of Lemons & Lemonade":

I can, however, tell you about concrete, steel, tar and glass, and go on endlessly about the myriad uses of bricks. Of these, the structures and lines remain rigid in my visual vocabulary; these I can envision with clarity. Though disgracefully ignorant about the natural world, this is my world, this world of malls and lawns and faceless houses, generic streets and measured sidewalks and parks where one can see the other side by standing at one end. And while sometimes one grows strangely nostalgic for a world one's never really seen, except through a movie lens or the inscribed word, for what experience would I leave my familiar gridiron of Scarborough, Ontario? Would I leave it for a world of limitless lands, unscarred sunsets and fields? In a second. What kind of fields? I don't care; fields of wheat, grain, weeping willow leaves—fields of anything but shorn green grass and playgrounds. But I've never been to those places, so let me tell you about what I can see.

I can tell you about skinning bare knees on the coarse school-yard lot, and getting up bleeding and crying with pebbles still embedded like shrapnel around one's wicked-looking wound. I can tell you about the tremendous impetus the fixed playground was for our imaginations. When every recess game had to be new, the jungle gym becomes an island, a base, a prison, a fortress. The angular teeter-totters become skyward-gazing missile silos; the swings jet planes, or catapults; the sand pit the Middle East, the baseball cage an enemy wall to be climbed—everything was something. The playground was a proving ground.

Tjia is both an author and an artist. He was born in Toronto and now lives in Montreal.

Directions: *Using the first-draft checklist from the inside back cover as your guide, identify the elements of an effective description paragraph in A Professional's Take. Next, compare the elements the author used in this excerpt with the ones that you used in your first draft. Do you need to add more vivid descriptive details to your paragraph?*

Revise: Read Critically, then Rewrite

What if your reader does not "get it"? In description, writers often assume the reader can see the person, place, or object they are describing. As a result, they leave out critical descriptive details. It helps if you have someone read and talk with you about your writing. The comments you receive can help you to formulate a revision plan.

REVISE
- Read critically
- Develop a revision plan

REVISION IN ACTION

Revision is rethinking a draft and making decisions to improve the quality of the writing. You read critically, plan your revision, and revise the writing. Here is an example of revision by a student named Martin. Examine the differences between his first and revised drafts.

Assignment: Describe a person, place, or thing you value highly.

TOPIC SENTENCE
Martin states the thing he will describe.

SUPPORTING DETAILS
He describes (1) the physical appearance of the watch, (2) how it works, and (3) the cost.

ORDER AND TRANSITIONS
He begins with order of importance, but continues with a list.

CONCLUDING SENTENCE
Martin makes a comment that states his attitude toward the watch.

Martin focuses his revision on improving the dominant impression. He also decides to make the writing more appropriate for an academic audience by removing the first-person pronouns.

Martin's First Draft

All the world is digital, but I have an analogue Timex wristwatch. (1) **First and most important**, the analogue wristwatch is simple and beautiful. The face of the watch is round. There are black Arabic numerals. There are thin black stems for hands. There is no month, no date, or day of the week. It just gives me the time of day. (2) **In addition to being beautiful**, this watch is environmentally friendly. There are no batteries to replace because it has to be wound. The tiny machine inside works based on a mainspring that has tension. I pinch the stem between my thumb and forefinger and turn it back and forth. I often find myself winding it. This does make it noisy. When I hold it to my ear, it ticks. When it is lying by my bed at night, I can hear it. (3) **Last**, the watch is cheap. If I lose it, I buy another one. No matter what other people think, I still like my simple analogue watch.

Revision Plan: Revise the topic sentence to connect to the assignment and clarify the dominant impression. Reorder, cut, and add details to support the dominant impression. Change the paragraph to objective description by removing first-person pronouns.

TOPIC SENTENCE
Martin revises his topic sentence by inserting the dominant impression.

SUPPORTING DETAILS
He cuts irrelevant description and adds details to describe why a simple watch has value.

ORDER AND TRANSITIONS
He uses spatial order to clarify the description.

CONCLUDING SENTENCE
The conclusion now emphasizes the key words from the assignment.

Martin's Revised Draft

All the world is digital, but a simple Timex wristwatch still has value. **The insides** of an analogue Timex watch might be the most valuable because it is a tiny machine. It works by creating tension on a mainspring, so it does not use a battery. Therefore, it has to be wound to keep tension on the mainspring and the watch ticking. This reminds its wearer that time matters. **The outside** of a Timex wristwatch is simplified beauty. This watch has a round white face and black Arabic numerals. The hands are thin, black stems. There is no month, no date, or day of the week to clutter the simple face. No matter what other people think, a Timex is a simple reminder to value time.

DISCUSSION QUESTIONS Which changes in the revision most improve Martin's paragraph? Why?

LEARN TO READ CRITICALLY

Pay attention to how other writers craft their paragraphs to guide you with what you are trying to write. It helps if you read your peers' papers so you can compare your work to theirs. Do their paragraphs have a dominant impression that makes sense to a reader? Do they provide enough descriptive details so a reader can understand the dominant impression? Revision gives you a chance to improve the clarity of your description.

EXERCISE 4-11 **Reading Peer Papers**

Directions: *Exchange papers with another student. Be a critical reader and make suggestions you think will improve your classmate's first draft. Also identify what your classmate did well. Make notes in the margin as you read to remember your suggestions. After you read, discuss your suggestions. Use the guidelines in the revision checklist from the inside back cover.*

REVISE WITH A PLAN

Always reread your assignment before revising to make sure you are doing what is required. Some description paragraphs can be written in first person, but most require an objective description, which requires a shift to third-person pronouns.

EXERCISE 4-12 **Revising Your Draft**

Directions: *Develop a revision plan and revise the draft of the paragraph you wrote for Exercise 4-9.*

Edit

To make your description more professional, edit for careless punctuation and grammar, which can annoy your reader. Work to make your writing as perfect as possible. In any class, not just for an English course, and in all jobs, your instructors and bosses want to see that you care about your work. In

EDIT
- Search and correct
- Self-edit

Chapter 2, you set goals for your writing and identified your individual challenges. Now focus on editing your writing by keeping those goals in mind.

EXERCISE 4-13 **Revising and Editing Practice**

Directions: *Read the following paragraph that was written in response to the assignment below. The paragraph contains errors that require revising and editing. Then answer the questions that follow. The questions will give you practice in the kind of revising and editing you should do with your writing assignments.*

Talk about it

Which do you use more in your descriptions, comparisons or sensory details?

Assignment: Write about a region, city, neighbourhood, or building, and describe the living conditions of the people who live in it. Describe this place using details that convey a dominant impression.

(1) _____ (2) People and noise are everywhere. (3) Driving in the city is more than unpleasant! (4) Rush hour is unbearable. (5) Cars are backed up bumper to bumper. (6) Everyone constantly honks their horns. (7) Once traffic starts moving, drivers cut in and out of traffic, racing to the next red light. (8) They cannot seem to go fast enough. (9) Few people remember how to be courteous behind the wheel. (10) _____ neighbours can be a nuisance. (11) The houses are so close that everything a family does in their home can be heard by their neighbours. (12) If you looked in a neighbour's window you would see they are watching the same show, and you are just one big family. (13) Even the backyards are not very peaceful, because of the barking dogs plus summer brings the personal problems outside. (14) Children argue over games, and teen's shout and fight, but the domestic arguments are the most unpleasant. (15) A couple shouting insults across the front lawn as if they are in the privacy of their kitchen is embarrassing. (16) Cities are crowded and unpleasant places where living is rarely peaceful, and privacy does not exist.

REVISING

_____ 1. Which sentence should be inserted in blank 1? The sentence would state the dominant impression and serve as the topic sentence.

    a. Privacy is not possible in a city.

    b. City living is unpleasant.

    c. City living has its downside, but I love it anyway.

    d. You cannot get away from noise and people in the city.

_____ 2. Select the order of sentences 5, 6, 7, 8, and 9 that provides the most logical sequence of ideas and supporting details. If appropriate, choose "no change is necessary."

    a. 5, 9, 6, 7, 8   c. 5, 7, 8, 6, 9

    b. 9, 5, 6, 7, 8   d. No change is necessary.

_____ 3. Which word or phrase should be inserted in blank 10? The word or phrase would serve as a clear transition between the writer's two ideas in this paragraph.

    a. Next   c. In addition

    b. Also   d. Even more unpleasant

_____ 4. Which sentence should be cut to improve the focus of the paragraph?

    a. Sentence 12   c. Sentence 16

    b. Sentence 13   d. No change is necessary.

EDITING

_____ 1. Choose the option that corrects the error in sentence 6.

    a. Everyone is honking their horn.

    b. Everyone honks at the driver in front of them.

    c. Up and down the road, horns make a terrible racket.

    d. No change is necessary.

_____ 2. Choose the option that corrects the error in sentence 11.

    a. are so close and everything

    b. are so close; everything

    c. are so close: everything

    d. No change is necessary.

_____ 3. Choose the option that corrects the error in sentence 13.

    a. dogs, plus summer

    b. dogs, moreover, summer

    c. dogs. Plus, summer

    d. No change is necessary.

    4. Proofread for an apostrophe error in the paragraph and correct the error.

EXERCISE 4-14 **Searching and Correcting**

Directions: _Exchange papers with a proofreading peer and proofread each other's work. In addition to spelling, punctuation, and capitalization, find out what other errors your classmate often makes; tell your classmate what errors you often make._

EXERCISE 4-15 **Self-Editing**

Directions: _Carefully rewrite your paper, correcting the errors you and your classmate found. Give yourself time to set aside the finished paper for a while. Then come back to it and read your final draft one last time, using the editing checklist at the back of this text as a guide._

CHAPTER REVIEW

Recall what you have learned about descriptive writing:

■ **DESCRIPTIVE THINKING**

☐ Elements of description

- *Dominant impressions in topic sentences*
- *Sensory descriptions*
- *Comparisons, simile, metaphor*

☐ Organize your thinking

- *Organize by spatial order, by priority, or by importance*
- *Graphics and diagrams or T-charts*
- *General details/concrete details*

☐ Comparisons and description thinking

- *Simile and metaphor*

■ **DESCRIPTION IN PROCESS**

☐ Select assignment

☐ Prewrite

☐ Draft

- *Consider the reader*
- *Transitions, adjectives, adverbs*

☐ Revise with a plan

☐ Edit and read critically

- *Peer editing and self-editing*
- *Checklists*

☐ Reflect

- *Strengths and weaknesses and writing goals*

Reflect

Take a moment and reflect on what you have learned. Identify your strengths and set goals for future writing assignments.

EXERCISE 4-16 **Identifying Strengths and Setting Goals**

Directions: *Review your writing and your writing process. On a separate sheet of paper, write answers to these questions:*

- *What did you do well in the paragraph you wrote?*
- *What did you enjoy working on in this chapter?*
- *What have you learned that you will apply in future writing assignments?*
- *Do you find checklists helpful to improve your first draft?*

Your answers to these questions will increase your awareness of your particular strengths and weaknesses. For your next writing assignment, you can focus on improving your weaknesses.

Example

THINK FIRST

Turn and talk to a classmate about this photo. How do you pay for things that you buy? What is money for? What problems does it cause? How do you spend money? How often do you use cash? Do you use debit or credit cards? After your conversation, write a short paragraph that states your attitude toward money and spending. Include several examples that illustrate how you feel about this.

For Example . . .

One of the first rules of good communication is to be specific. General statements like "My brother is annoying" or "My boss is the greatest" might convey the speaker's main idea, but they do not have much impact on the listener or reader. Real communicative power comes in the form of specific examples: "My brother refuses to take phone messages for me, he teases me relentlessly about my taste in clothes, and he sold my CD collection." "My boss mentors me, pays me well, and she gave me her tickets to the baseball game tonight." Specific examples provide weight and strength to any point you may make. You should use them often in your writing.

DISCUSSION

Turn and talk with a classmate to answer the following questions: Who is annoying to you? Or who is a great influence in your life? Give several specific examples to illustrate just how annoying or great this person is.

Drawing In Your Reader

While logic is the foundation of all academic writing, the strongest piece of writing is more than that. Your work also needs to be *engaging*. The surest way to capture your reader's attention is by using examples that, in addition to providing the basic evidence for your writing, also evoke laughter, sympathy, anger, or fear. Whether you choose to focus on a historical land battle, the migratory patterns of birds, or an interpretation of a Jane Urquhart poem, your writing will receive greater attention if readers can find something to latch on to.

BRAINSTORM

College and university instructors want specifics in your work. Brainstorm a list of assignments you have had that asked you to provide specific examples.

The Lessons of the Past

In the business world, practicality comes first. Theories about efficiency and philosophies of customer relations have their place, but the usual questions of the business world are more mundane: How many boxes can we ship to Winnipeg by Thursday? What are Anna's job responsibilities? How much will it cost to develop a new product, and how much revenue will it generate? Hence, in a business setting, your ability to draw effectively on real-world events and facts by using examples is essential. For instance, if you want to convince your boss to take a risk on a new product, you will need to demonstrate how similar products have fared in the past or how many paying customers would be interested. The more specifically you can support your claims, the more credibility your ideas will have.

RESUMÉ BUILDER

Think about your current job. What is your job title? What are your responsibilities? List two or three specific examples to illustrate how you are an effective and efficient employee.

At a Glance

THE EXAMPLE PARAGRAPH AT A GLANCE

The topic sentence is usually the first sentence in an example paragraph followed by the major supporting details, which consist of one or more examples. These examples are supported and explained through facts and specific details that make the examples clear and interesting. The concluding sentence emphasizes the point of the paragraph.

The Example Paragraph at a Glance

ASSIGNMENT   Some of the individuals we have studied this semester have left interesting legacies for Canadians. Write a paragraph discussing two or three examples.

Some of the individuals we studied this semester still influence Canadians today. (1) **For example,** one interesting Canadian is Georgina Pope, who grew up in a privileged family in Prince Edward Island. She bucked traditions of the time and trained as a nurse in a school established by Florence Nightingale in New York. Pope nursed wounded soldiers for several years during the Boer War in South Africa. After her return to Canada, she developed the first training programs for military nurses. The Canadian army was the first in the world to grant the nurses from her program officer status, a distinguished recognition of Pope's work. (2) **Another example** of someone whose life has left a legacy for Canadians was a British immigrant named Archibald Belaney. He masqueraded as an Aboriginal person named Grey Owl and wrote articles describing Canadian animals and forests. His views on the cruelty of trapping and the importance of environmental conservation established him as one of the first in this country to be concerned with animal welfare and forest preservation. (3) **A final example** is Terry Fox, who received a diagnosis of bone cancer resulting in the amputation of his right leg above the knee. He resolved to raise money to advance awareness and cures for cancer. He began his "Marathon of Hope" on the Atlantic coast with the goal of running across the entire country. Unfortunately, the disease returned, and he died in 1981 before he reached the Pacific coast. However, every year Fox's heroic efforts are remembered with runs in many communities that continue to raise significant funds for cancer

TOPIC SENTENCE
The writer repeats the key words from the assignment and then adds her opinion about interesting Canadians.

EXAMPLES AND DETAILS
The writer provides examples of three people who did interesting things. Each example gives facts and details to show how the individual's life work has had a lasting effect on Canadians.

ORDER AND TRANSITIONS
The examples are organized in a list. Each transition introduces the "next" example.

CONCLUDING SENTENCE
The writer restates the topic
sentence by rephrasing it.

research. <u>The life paths chosen by these three people have left a legacy for current Canadians in the areas of military nursing, animal cruelty prevention, and cancer research.</u>

DISCUSSION QUESTIONS

1. Identify the specific, minor details in each example that help make the example's point.

2. Which of these facts and details do you find most effective?

Thinking

EXAMPLE THINKING

You use examples in every aspect of your life. When you tell friends about your busy weekend, you use specific examples to convince them you are exhausted. You might say you worked eight hours at the laundry folding shirts and unbuttoning buttons, wrote a three-page essay on conditions of poverty in the 1920s, and studied angles and formulas for a geometry test. Whether you write for college, university, or your workplace, you will use examples to explore a topic, explain a concept, or support an argument.

Elements of Example

Typically, an example paragraph includes a main point and has specific examples, facts, or details to support that main point. Below is a brief description of the elements you should keep in mind when writing an example paragraph.

*   *Point:* A topic sentence makes a point. It states your main idea and what you want a reader to understand about your subject's controlling idea. In the example on the previous page, the writer makes a point about perseverance and success by using examples of three interesting individuals who left legacies in Canada in the fields of military nursing, wildlife protection, and cancer research. The point is stated at the beginning of the paragraph. The examples and details that follow help the reader understand the point.

*   *Examples:* Using examples helps to illustrate and explain the point made in the topic sentence. Examples should be fresh, interesting, and relevant. Readers will immediately connect good examples to their own experience and to the topic. On the previous page, the reader can connect with the examples because the writer provides the

proper names of actual people and makes specific remarks about these historical examples.

- *Facts and details:* Specific facts and details help you elaborate and develop your examples. You want the reader to understand how the examples illustrate your point. It is not enough simply to cite the example; you also need to help the reader see the example the way you see it. The example paragraph doesn't just name Georgina Pope, but details how she pursued a career against her family's wishes, gained valuable experiences overseas, returned to Canada, and taught other nurses what she had learned.

Get Started

Examples explain what you mean. They help you think more clearly about the point you would like to make; they also help your reader begin to grasp your meaning. The sooner you get specific by using examples, the sooner you begin to make progress in your writing.

Suppose you are taking a course in health studies, and on the first day of class, you are asked to write a paragraph on your formula for maintaining good health. Experienced students learn to "think in threes." An experienced student asks herself, "What are the three most important things a person does to maintain good health?" She divides her subject into three manageable subtopics, or three examples of what she knows about healthy living. Then she gets specific. This process of thinking about how three examples can move you from an assigned topic to manageable subtopics can be pictured in this visual outline:

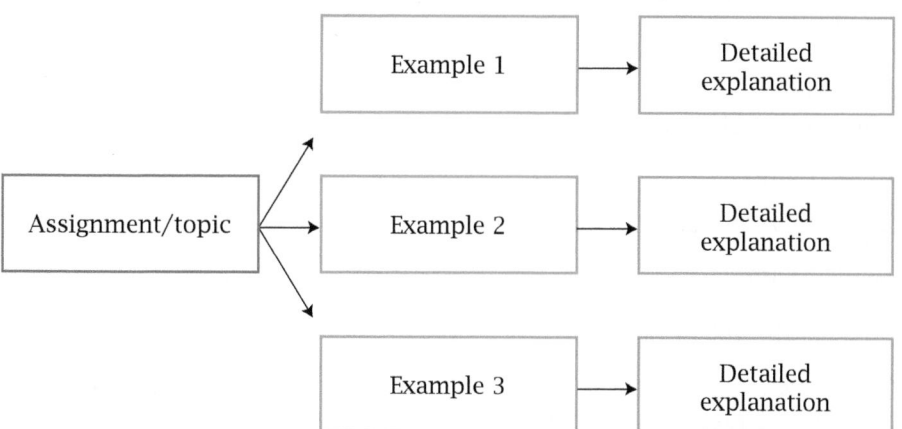

Learning to divide your topic like this is the beginning of effective example thinking. Is three the magic number? Of course not. You might think of two important approaches, or four, or even five. The important thing is to narrow your thinking, and move from general to specific. Effective students actually make two moves: first from topic to examples, and then from examples to details, as shown in the diagram above. You can adjust your visual outline to reflect how many examples and detailed explanations you wish to use.

GENERAL TO SPECIFIC

We now know that an effective example paragraph moves from a general topic to a more specific one, followed by detailed examples that support the specific topic. Notice in this example how the writer gets specific to explain a healthy lifestyle:

Topic Sentence: <u>Good health</u> is built each day by making healthy lifestyle choices.

Example 1: Choose a healthy diet by using Canada's Food Guide for the <u>four basic food groups</u>.

Details: Eat a variety of <u>fruits, vegetables; bread or grains; dairy products or cheese; and meat, fish, or protein</u> every day.

Example 2: Forget the gym. Start a <u>daily exercise program</u> that can fit easily into a busy schedule.

Details: Allocate 15 to 30 minutes at lunch. <u>Walking or climbing the stairs</u> provides an aerobic exercise that improves heart and lung health. <u>Yoga, tai chi, or stretching at your desk</u> will reduce stress and tone muscles.

Example 3: Go to bed on time. Good health is more likely if you get <u>plenty of rest</u>.

Details: Studies have shown there is a connection between good rest and a person's resistance to illness. <u>Less rest means lower resistance.</u> Those who do not make sure they sleep well and long enough are more likely to get sick.

EXERCISE 5-1 **General to Specific**

Directions: *For each of the general topics and topic sentences below write three specific examples that could support them.*

1. **General:** Children

Topic Sentence: Watching violent television shows can have a lasting impact on children.

Specific Example 1: _____

Specific Example 2: _____

Specific Example 3: _____

2. **General:** Education

Topic Sentence: Practical skills such as budgeting and managing money should be taught at school.

Specific Example 1: _____

Specific Example 2: _____

Specific Example 3: _____

3. **General:** Employment

Topic Sentence: Teenagers with part-time jobs gain valuable work experience.

Specific Example 1: _____

Specific Example 2: _____

Specific Example 3: _____

Types of Examples

You can use different types of examples or cite multiple examples to support your topic sentence. Examples can be related to each other, or they can be contrasting. Sometimes, you will find that only one extended, or longer, example serves your purpose best.

RELATED EXAMPLES

Examples build support and convince readers to adopt your point of view. While writers vary the number of examples they use, they are careful to connect them. Sometimes writers connect similar examples; sometimes they connect contrasting examples.

Ask Yourself

Do you examine your examples to connect them with transitional words for a reader?

Topic Sentence: Success comes from being creative.

Similar Examples

- The McCain family in Florenceville, New Brunswick, has made millions selling frozen French fries and oven-ready frozen food products.
- Similarly, Bill Gates is expanding his billion-dollar business in computers to online banking and interactive TV.

Contrasting Examples

- Madonna makes millions because she creatively changes her music to keep up with trends and shocks audiences.
- In contrast, Oprah Winfrey invents creative ways she and others can give away millions of dollars to help underprivileged people.

EXERCISE 5-2 **Similar and Contrasting Examples**

Directions: *Refer to your own experiences, television advertisements, magazines, or newspapers to find examples to support the topic sentences below. Provide two similar examples and one contrasting example for each topic sentence.*

1. **Topic Sentence:** Credit cards can be the road to financial ruin.

Example: _____

Similar Example: _____

Contrasting Example: _____

2. **Topic Sentence:** Athletes serve as role models to the world.

Example: _____

Similar Example: _____

Contrasting Example: _____

3. **Topic Sentence:** Good study habits are the key to success in college and university.

Example: _____

Similar Example: _____

Contrasting Example: _____

EXTENDED EXAMPLES

A single, extended example can adequately support a point or claim. Students use this approach when they have one convincing example and can elaborate that one example with facts and details. Sometimes, writers can use a narrative that illustrates their point. For example, you might tell the story of a disastrous haircut to illustrate that communication is important.

To extend a single example, a writer will provide additional information by answering the six basic questions: *who, what, when, where, why,* and *how*. Here is a paragraph in which one extended example is used to illustrate the writer's point.

TOPIC SENTENCE
Who: A 12-year-old girl.
What: She wished for nylons to feel grown-up.
When: It was her twelfth birthday.
Where: She rode her bike around the neighbourhood wearing her nylons.
Why: She did not realize nylons were not for riding bikes.
How: She ruined her nylons riding her bike.

CONCLUDING SENTENCE

Sometimes people wish for things before they are ready for them. I will always remember my cousin turning 12. She wanted to be a grown-up, so she wished for a pair of pantyhose. She was not disappointed. She got a pair of Hanes that looked like a second pair of legs when she took them out of the box to put them on. For that birthday, she also received a blue-and-silver three-speed bike with a black seat and thin black tires. After breakfast the day after her birthday, wearing her pantyhose, of course, she raced out of the house to meet her best friend, Connie. They met on the sidewalk, got their bikes, and rode around the neighbourhood showing their friends. Just before she left for home, my cousin remembered the pantyhose, but they were ruined. They hung in shreds on her legs. At that moment, she realized that even though she wanted to be a grown-up at 12 by wearing pantyhose, some clothing just wasn't suitable for sports activities.

EXERCISE 5-3 **Writing an Extended Example**

Directions: *Choose one of the topic sentences below and write a paragraph using an extended example to develop the main idea. Do your work on a separate sheet of paper.*

1. A good teacher can make all the difference in the world.

2. A bad teacher can make all the difference in the world.

3. Co-workers can make a bad job tolerable.

4. Co-workers can make a good job intolerable.

EXAMPLES AS PROOF

An example paragraph can provide proof of a point or claim. When used in this way, it is best to state the point in the topic sentence. Then you can decide if you will use multiple examples or a single extended example to prove your point.

EXERCISE 5-4 **Examples as Proof**

Directions: *"People have to find an approach to fitness that works best for them." Write a paragraph in which you use either a number of related examples or an extended example to prove this claim.*

PART 2 Paragraph Writing and Patterns of Thinking

Elaborate on Examples

Citing an example is just the beginning. For your example to really function in your writing, you need to explain what the example means and what you want your reader to understand. This explanation is called *elaboration*. Note the contrast between the following simple examples and the elaborated versions of them that follow:

Simple Examples

The small town often felt the force of nature. For example, there was a river that flowed through the town. Also, because the town was located in the snowbelt, it was not unusual for five to ten inches of snow to fall in a few hours' time.

Here the writer cites two examples to develop the main idea in the topic sentence. Neither example is elaborated on.

Elaborated Examples

The small town often felt the force of nature. For example, there was a river that flowed through the town. Every spring, if there was heavy rain, the river would rise, overflow its banks, and tear through people's backyards, carrying away swing sets, overturning doghouses, and leaving a sea of mud on lawns. Also, because the town was located in the snowbelt, it was not unusual to have five to ten inches of snow fall in a few hours' time. One year, it snowed for three days, accumulating five feet of snow. Schools and businesses closed. People stayed home from work and climbed up on their roofs to shovel off snow. Some roofs collapsed under the weight of the snow.

Here the writer elaborates on the two examples. He shows how the river was a force of nature and the impact that snow had on the community. The impact of flooding and heavy snow helps the reader appreciate what the writer means by "felt the force of nature."

Elaboration ensures that your reader connects your example to the main idea. It drives home your point.

EXERCISE 5-5 **Elaborating on Your Examples**

Directions: *Provide an example that supports the main idea of each of the following topic sentences. Then provide additional details that explain and support the example. In the examples below, notice how the transitional word signals the beginning of the next example.*

EXAMPLE

Topic Sentence: Divorce can have a lasting impact on children.

Example 1: Losing one parent and the security of the family unit can cause loneliness and insecurity in elementary-age children.

_____

Details: Young children understand the sadness of having one parent leave the house. However, they cannot explain their feelings or express them. As a result, young children may have feelings of resentment or embarrassment that never get resolved and affect other relationships.

Example 2: In addition, living in a single-parent home puts pressure on teens, who often take on the responsibilities of the missing parent.

_____

Details: Teens may take on child care of younger siblings or increase duties to maintain the house. These added responsibilities reduce their relationships with friends and push them into adulthood too early.

1. **Topic Sentence:** Reading is an essential life skill.
Example 1: _____

_____

Details: _____

_____

Example 2: Moreover, _____

_____

Details: _____

_____

2. **Topic Sentence:** A global economy impacts jobs and employment.
Example 1: _____

_____

Details: _____

_____

Example 2: Furthermore, _____

_____

Details: _____

_____

Organize Your Examples

If you use more than one example to make a point, be sure to think about the order in which you present those examples. How you organize your ideas and details can affect, either negatively or positively, the impact you have on a reader. Two common ways of organizing your examples are chronological order and order of importance.

In chronological order, you begin in the past and move to the present, or vice versa.

> **Topic Sentence:** Blake always had a hard time learning French.
>
> **Example 1:** In Madame Bidwell's class last semester, he struggled with verb tenses.
>
> **Example 2:** In elementary school French, the only French word he could really pronounce was the name that Madame Vey gave him, Benois.
>
> **Example 3:** He learned to count in French by watching television when he was very young, but counting and speaking are two different things.

The order used in this sentence outline begins in the present and moves to the past. In fact, the impact on the reader might be stronger if the student reversed the order, beginning with the example of counting and finishing with his recent experience of trying to learn French verbs.

When using order of importance, writers often save the best for last. The idea is that the last example makes the greatest impact on the reader. The opposite approach, however, can also be effective. You can begin with your most persuasive example to convince the reader of the importance of your main idea, using the example to pull in the reader.

> **Topic Sentence:** Studies show that young drivers are at considerable risk on the road.
>
> **Example 1:** They tend to drive fast and overestimate their reaction times and ability to control their vehicles.
>
> **Example 2:** They are often listening to music, probably played at high volume, or talking on cellphones, which distracts them from the road.
>
> **Example 3:** They frequently have friends in the car with them, creating distractions that significantly enhance the risk of accident and injury.

The three examples here each explain a risk young drivers face. Which is the most important? The answer may be determined by interpretation, by personal experience, or by the data from the studies. Whatever the order, writers should use transitions to indicate their thinking about importance. In this case, transitions related to impact would be appropriate.

Writer's Response

Which form of organization do you use most, chronological order or order of importance?

> **Topic Sentence:** Studies show that young drivers are at considerable risk on the road.
>
> **For example,** they are often listening to music, probably played at high volume, or talking on cellphones, which distracts them from the road.
>
> **More importantly,** they tend to drive fast and overestimate their reaction times and ability to control their vehicles.
>
> **Finally, the most important reason** young drivers are at risk is that they frequently have friends in the car with them, creating distractions that significantly enhance risk of accident and injury.

EXERCISE 5-6 **Organizing Your Thinking**

Directions: *For each topic sentence, indicate the order in which you would present the following examples. In the space provided, indicate whether you recommend chronological order or order of importance. Briefly explain the reasons for your choices.*

Topic Sentence: Although high school sports may distract students' attention from their studies, there are definite benefits from these programs.

_2_ The students learn about teamwork.

_1_ The students have to manage their time effectively.

_3_ The students' spare time is organized around physical activity.

Order of importance. Because so many young people are now overweight,

I think the physical fitness aspect of sports is the most important.

1. **Topic Sentence:** A good school is vital to an inner-city community.

_____ A school that sets high standards will encourage positive behaviours that help children in the long run.

_____ A good school provides students with role models.

_____ A good school is vital to a community if it offers children a safe place to be and a chance to do constructive activities after school.

_____

2. **Topic Sentence:** The options available on cars these days make use of the latest technology.

_____ New models have GPS systems, sensors to indicate the distance of the car from curbs and other cars, and, of course, amazing sound systems.

_____ Twenty years ago, a car had an AM radio, and that was it.

_____ Then came FM radios, cassette players, CD players, and, ultimately, Bluetooth-enabled devices.

_____ The sound systems in some cars can even be synchronized with the driver's iPod and cellphone.

_____

3. **Topic Sentence:** Many academic subjects have immediate practical applications in everyday life.

_____ A course in nutrition will identify issues and lifestyle decisions that have far-reaching consequences for a student's health.

_____ Mathematics is useful in the grocery store, at the car dealership, and at the bank.

_____ Psychology gives a person the skills to size up other people, read their motives, and understand their behaviour.

_____

Process

EXAMPLE IN PROCESS

For producing good example writing, you can benefit from using the steps in the writing process: prewriting, drafting, revising, and editing.

Select an Assignment

In college and university, you will be asked to write a variety of assignments. Most of them will require you to find an example to illustrate your point. Sometimes the examples will come from your experience. Other times the examples will come from the reading and research you are doing for the course.

EXERCISE 5-7 **Selecting an Assignment for an Example Paragraph**

Directions: *Review the assignments listed below. Choose the one you know the most about and believe is best suited for you to develop into an effective example paragraph.*

1. Explain the advantages of organized sports in school.

2. Explain the disadvantages of organized sports in school.

3. Provide examples of the challenges of being a teenager today.

4. Explain the advantages of being married (or being single).

5. Provide strategies for saving money.

6. Give some tips for getting good grades.

7. List some strategies for getting a good work reference.

8. Name an important person in your life.

9. Describe some approaches for staying thin or gaining weight.

10. Respond to the following quote by Alexander Graham Bell: "When one door closes another door opens; but we so often look so long and so regretfully upon the closed door, that we do not see the ones which open for us."

Prewrite: Write Before You Write

Perhaps the two most important words in post-secondary writing are "for example." However, your examples are only as good as the details that follow because examples do not explain themselves. That is the writer's job.

Before you start writing, do some prewriting to discover the specific details that will really make your examples work. Look at the margin note here to help you remember the variety of prewriting techniques to choose

PREWRITE
- Talk
- Think
- Cluster
- Brainstorm
- Question
- Freewrite

from. For the example mode of writing, you can focus on brainstorming and freewriting.

EXERCISE 5-8 **Brainstorming**

Directions: *Brainstorm on your topic for about ten minutes. Try "thinking in threes" if it helps. List three examples and specific details that go with each example. Then find three different examples with specific details. After you find the breakdown of your topic that you like best, analyze your examples and details, assessing their connection to your assignment. What is your point? Will the examples help you make your point clear?*

EXERCISE 5-9 **Freewriting**

Directions: *Freewrite on your topic from the previous exercise for ten minutes. Explore as many examples as you can think of. Try to provide several sentences of explanation for each example. To get additional details for each example, ask the six basic questions: who, what, when, where, why, and how.*

Draft: Focus and Organize

Prewriting helps you see your subject more clearly. Then you can select what interests you and build on that. In the next phase of the writing process, you add content. However, you also think more about what the writing means and the point you want to make. You analyze the content to decide what examples and details will be most effective.

CONSIDER YOUR AUDIENCE

Read the assignment instructions again. Think about who will read your paragraph. If you had a conversation with your audience about this topic, they could pull information out of you and ask for clarification. What questions would your audience ask? What do you know that they do not know?

Your paragraph will have to stand on its own and speak for itself. As you think about your topic and your audience, consider these questions:

* Why is my topic important?
* What do I want my reader to understand?
* Which examples will most effectively illustrate my point?
* Which examples will need some explanation?

EXERCISE 5-10 **Considering Your Audience**

Directions: *Use the questions above to think critically about the point, examples, and details you want to include in your paragraph. Talk with a classmate to explore what you know and want to say. Test your examples and details on this classmate. Take notes on this conversation and add them to your prewriting.*

FORMULATE YOUR TOPIC SENTENCE

Writers often write and rewrite topic sentences as they work on revisions to their writing. At this point in the writing process, think of your topic sentence as a work in progress. A clear topic sentence will state your point, echo the assignment, and help organize the details from your prewriting. Compose a topic sentence for now, but don't be afraid to improve it later.

DRAFT
* Consider your audience
* Formulate your topic sentence
* Outline for unity and coherence
* Write a concluding sentence
* Compose your first draft

OUTLINE FOR UNITY AND COHERENCE

Paragraphs with examples have a cumulative effect. The evidence adds up. When you draft your paragraph, think about the case you are building. Examine your examples and details, and be alert to those details that might lead readers astray. You will want to delete off-topic details.

You want your paragraph to be unified—clearly focused on one idea. Remember, too, that your readers want to feel that you are in control of the discussion. The best way to create this impression is by using appropriate transitions to make connections, which create coherent text. In example writing, transitions related to examples and priority help your reader follow your thinking.

TRANSITIONS BASED ON EXAMPLE	
for example	in this case
a second (and third) example	to illustrate
for instance	

TRANSITIONS BASED ON PRIORITY OR IMPORTANCE	
however	in particular
more important	specifically
equally important	of course
better	certainly
worse	in fact

WRITE A CONCLUDING SENTENCE

Plan your concluding sentence, which summarizes the point of the paragraph. Sometimes it does this by referring back to the most important example; at other times it restates the main idea expressed in the topic sentence.

EXERCISE 5-11 **Planning Your First Draft**

Directions: *On a separate sheet of paper, write a topic sentence that echoes the key words from the assignment topic you selected. Then organize and outline your details.*

See "Supporting Details" in Chapter 3 for a detailed explanation of outlining.

COMPOSE YOUR FIRST DRAFT

Think of your outline as a roadmap. If you follow it, you will reach your destination, which, at this point, is a rough draft of your paragraph. As you work toward this goal of a first draft, however, pay attention to what your writing is telling you. If you have difficulty developing and explaining an example, that might be a reason to cut it from your draft. If you find that you have a great detail to add about another example, that might be an indication that your paragraph could be developed with an extended example, rather than with multiple examples.

As they draft, writers often go back and revise their outlines. If you decide to do that, it is probably the right thing to do. After all, there is more than one way to get to your destination.

EXERCISE 5-12 **Writing Your First Draft**

Directions: *Write a draft of your paragraph using the outline you created in Exercise 5-11. Also, refer to the first draft checklist on the inside back cover as a guide.*

A PROFESSIONAL'S TAKE

Here is Yann Martel's use of examples, from his book
Life of Pi:

In the literature can be found legions of examples of animals that could escape but did not, or did and returned. There is the case of the chimpanzee whose cage door was left unlocked and had swung open. Increasingly anxious, the chimp began to shriek and to slam the door shut repeatedly—with a deafening clang each time—until the keeper, notified by a visitor, hurried over to remedy the situation. A herd of roe-deer in a European zoo stepped out of their corral when the gate was left open. Frightened by visitors, the deer bolted for the nearby forest, which had its own herd of wild roe-deer and could support more. Nonetheless, the zoo roe-deer quickly returned to their corral. In another zoo a worker was walking to his work site at an early hour, carrying planks of wood, when, to his horror, a bear emerged from the morning mist, heading straight for him at a confident pace. The man dropped the planks and ran for his life. The zoo staff immediately started searching for the escaped bear. They found it back in its enclosure, having climbed down into its pit the way it had climbed out, by way of a tree that had fallen over. It was thought that the noise of the planks of wood falling to the ground had frightened it.

EXERCISE 5-13 **A PROFESSIONAL'S TAKE**

Directions: *Using the first draft checklist on the inside back cover as your guide, identify the effectiveness of the elements of an example paragraph found in Yann Martel's paragraph. Next, compare the elements the author used in this excerpt with the ones that you used in your first draft. Did you include enough effective examples and details in your paragraph?*

Revise: Read Critically, then Rewrite

Sometimes an example is not as effective as you hoped it would be. Sometimes you forget to explain a critical detail. It helps if you have someone read and talk with you about your writing and if you read your peers' papers so you can compare your work to theirs. Do their paragraphs make a clear point? Is their point expressed in a topic sentence? Do their examples connect the support to their point? Can you identify transition terms that help the reader make connections? Revision gives you a chance to get things right.

REVISE
- Read critically
- Develop a revision plan

REVISION IN ACTION

As you know, revision is rethinking your draft and making decisions to improve the quality of your writing. You read critically, plan your revision, and then revise the writing. Here is an example of revision by a student named Theresa.

Assignment: Write about a person who was important in your life. Provide examples that illustrate why that person was important.

Theresa's First Draft

<u>My mother taught me the importance of family fun.</u> Family is the focus of my mother's life. She is always happy and works hard to keep the whole family together. And not just on holidays and birthdays. We make time for family fun during the week. (1) **For example,** one of her favourite family events is movie night. She likes to do family movie nights. Instead of going out, we download a movie and pop popcorn. **Even though** we are a lot older and a lot bigger, we all climb onto the sofa and eat out of the same huge bowl filled with buttered popcorn. She likes to select a comedy so we all laugh together. **These days,** movie night is a double-feature. We rotate who gets to pick the second movie. Another family fun event is game night. She likes to play games. (2) **After dinner,** we do the dishes and pull out the board games. She especially likes to play cards. Rummy is our favourite game. **We laugh** a lot more than we win because everyone cheats. **We love** the competition, and **we argue** over who is cheating because we all cheat. It is like a war between us. I think cheating and getting away with cheating are more important than winning the game. I have gotten really good at looking innocent. Sometimes we play until 2:00 in the morning. <u>Family fun nights taught me how important a family is and how special my mother is as well.</u>

TOPIC SENTENCE
Theresa chooses key words from the assignment: *person* and *important* to write a 1 + 1 topic sentence.

SUPPORTING DETAILS
She explains why family fun is important and provides two examples. Each example has minor details that describe the activity and why it is fun.

ORDER AND TRANSITIONS
Theresa uses a variety of transitions. She uses example ("for example"), comparison ("even though"), and time ("these days," "after dinner") word or phrase transitions. She also uses repetition ("we laugh," "we love," "we argue").

CONCLUDING SENTENCE
Theresa adds a comment that restates the topic sentence.

Revision Plan: Revise the topic sentence to clearly state the purpose of the paragvtails to focus the paragraph on the two examples and the new point in the topic sentence.

Theresa's Revised Draft

Family values are important, and my mother has taught me this with weekly family events. **Movie night is one of her favourite family events.** Instead of going out, we download a movie and pop popcorn. Even though we are a lot older and a lot bigger, we all climb onto the sofa and eat out of the same huge bowl filled with buttered popcorn. She always selects a comedy so we can all laugh together. Crowding together to laugh and relax has made our family close. **Game night is another family fun event.** After dinner, we do the dishes together and pull out the board games. She especially likes to play cards. Rummy is our favourite game. We laugh a lot more than we win because everyone cheats. She loves the competition, so we argue over who is cheating. Sometimes we play until after midnight, but it is not hard to get up the next day because family fun helps us all relax. Family fun nights have taught me the importance of family, and how special my mother is as well.

DISCUSSION QUESTIONS Which changes in the revision most improve Theresa's paragraph? Why? Are you able to critically read your own drafts to make similar revisions?

READ CRITICALLY

Half the task of revising well is reading well. Critical reading is a search for the characteristics of effective writing: topic sentence, supporting examples and details, transitions, and concluding sentence. Critical reading involves making careful comparisons between your writing and that of successful writers. Pay attention to how other writers craft their sentences using examples, like you are trying to do.

EXERCISE 5-14 **Reading Peer Papers**

Directions: *Exchange papers with another student. Be a critical reader and make suggestions to improve and clarify your classmate's first draft. Identify what your classmate does well. Make notes in the margin as you read to remember the suggestions. Discuss your suggestions with each other. Use the same guidelines you used from earlier in the chapter for your draft.*

REVISE WITH A PLAN

Effective example paragraphs are focused and specific. As you review the comments from your classmate, consider whether your paragraph is adequately focused. Look for the point you are making in your topic sentence. Is it clear? Look at your examples. Do they prove your point? Do you include enough details to explain your examples?

EXERCISE 5-15 **Revising Your Draft**

Directions: *Based on the feedback you receive, write a revision plan and use it to revise the first draft of the paragraph you wrote for Exercise 5-12.*

Edit

The ideas in your work matter, but if your content is expressed in language that contains careless errors, readers may focus on the errors and miss your point. Once you have revised your writing, you must invest time in getting your work as close to perfect as possible. Be aware of the particular errors you tend to make. You can focus your editing using the editing checklist at the back of the book.

EDIT
- Search and correct
- Self-edit

EXERCISE 5-16 **Revising and Editing Practice**

Directions: *Read the following paragraph that was written in response to the assignment below; it contains errors that require revising and editing. Then answer the questions that follow.*

Assignment: Television shows compete for viewers. What makes a hit show? Write an example paragraph to discuss a single show or several shows you love or hate.

(1) Reality television provides totally unimaginative, brain-numbing entertainment. (2) *Survivor* was the first big hit with a simple concept. (3) Sixteen strangers flew to a remote island, formed tribes, ate bugs, faced challenges like making fire and voted each other off the island. (4) It seemed like a totally ridiculous show. (5) Unfortunately, it clicked with viewers and remained popular. (6) _____, television producers imagined new scenarios in which people win, lose, cry, and look foolish. (7) Love became the next hot competition in *the Bachelor*. (8) Women flocked to their televisions to watch competitors engage in a fairy tale romance. (9) _____, they created twists to the love story. (10) In *Battle of the Blades,* two very different styles of skaters come together when hockey players are paired with figure skaters to perform a pairs skating routine. (11) Eventually, producers invent more terrible reality television to make millions of viewers sit on the edge of their couches. *The Amazing Race, canadian Idol,* and *Top Chef* all drew big ratings. (12) It seems that we are getting more and more terrible reality programming. (13) Critics recently predicted the end of reality television. (14) _____.

REVISING

_____ 1. Which transition word or phrase should be inserted in blank 6?

    a. To my surprise   c. In addition

    b. As a result   d. Furthermore

_____ 2. Which word or phrase should be inserted in blank 9? The word or phrase would serve as the best transition between the writer's ideas in this paragraph.

    a. Next   c. Eventually

    b. Soon   d. No transition is necessary.

_____ 3. Which sentence should be cut to improve the focus and reduce repetition in the paragraph?

    a. Sentence 11   c. Sentence 13

    b. Sentence 12   d. No change is necessary.

Talk about it ▶▶

Is repetition a good or bad thing? Why or why not?

_____ 4. Which sentence should be inserted in blank 14? The sentence would serve as the concluding sentence.

    a. However, I counted five new reality shows this fall.

    b. In conclusion, _Dancing with the Stars_ is one more horrible example to prove my point.

    c. Obviously, reality television is not dead because brain-numbing shows draw viewers and make money.

    d. No conclusion is necessary.

EDITING

_____ 1. Choose the option that corrects the error in sentence 3.

    a. faced challenges, like making fire, and voted

    b. faced challenges like making fire, and voted

    c. faced challenges, like making fire; and voted

    d. No change is necessary.

_____ 2. Choose the option that corrects the pronoun reference error in sentence 9.

    a. women   c. producers

    b. viewers   d. No change is necessary.

Ask Yourself ▶▶

Do you know what an antecedent is? You can check Chapter 23 for help.

_____ 3. Choose the option that corrects the error in sentence 11.

    a. producers are inventing more terrible reality television

    b. producers invented more terrible reality television

    c. producers had invented more terrible reality television

    d. No change is necessary.

_____ 4. Proofread the paragraph for a capitalization error and correct the error.

EXERCISE 5-17 **Searching and Correcting**

Directions: _Exchange papers with a classmate and proofread each other's work. In addition to spelling, punctuation, and capitalization, find out what other errors your classmate often makes; tell your classmate what errors you often make._

EXERCISE 5-18 **Self-Editing**

Directions: _Carefully rewrite your paper, correcting errors you and your classmate found. Give yourself time to set aside the finished paper. Then come back to it and read your final draft one last time, using the editing checklist at the back of the text as a guide. This will help you find errors you may have overlooked earlier._

Reflect

Take a moment and reflect on what you have learned about using examples in paragraphs.

REFLECT
- Identify your strengths.
- Set goals to improve your writing.

EXERCISE 5-19 **Identifying Strengths and Setting Goals**

Directions: *Review your writing and the example writing process. On a separate sheet of paper, write answers to these questions:*

- *What did you do well in the paragraph you wrote?*
- *What did you enjoy working on in this chapter?*
- *What have you learned that you will apply in future writing assignments?*

Your answers to these questions will increase your awareness of your particular strengths and weaknesses. For your next writing assignment, you can focus on those areas that need improvement.

CHAPTER REVIEW

Recall what you have learned about using examples in your writing:

■ EXAMPLE THINKING

☐ Elements of example
- *Main point with examples; facts or details to elaborate*

☐ Get started
- *Think in threes; general to specific*

☐ Types of examples
- *Related, similar, and contrasting examples, or one expanded example; examples as proof*

☐ Elaborate on examples
- *Extended explanations, support, and additional details*

☐ Organize your examples
- *Chronological or order of importance; transitions*

■ EXAMPLE IN PROCESS

☐ Select an assignment
- *Examples: experience; reading and research*

☐ Prewrite: Brainstorm, freewrite

☐ Draft
- *Audience; topic sentence; unity, transitions, and coherence; concluding sentence*

☐ Revise
- *Read critically; plan revision*

☐ Edit
- *Spelling, punctuation, capitalization, word choice, sentence errors*

☐ Reflect
- *Examples in your assignments*

CHAPTER

6

Narration

THINK FIRST

Think of an event that involved winning or losing. Write a paragraph describing the event so a reader can picture it and understand who was involved, the actions that took place, the event's outcome, and your point.

Once Upon a Time . . .

Is there any phrase in the English language more arresting than "once upon a time"? We have all heard it a thousand times, but it still evokes a simple-hearted enthusiasm, an anticipation of what is to come. In almost any context and at any age, we enjoy hearing stories. Mastering the skills of narration will benefit you in many contexts. Wherever you are and whatever you are doing, it is often advantageous to be able to tell a good story.

DISCUSSION

Turn and talk with a classmate to answer the following questions: What recent movie have you seen that is particularly memorable? Can you describe a specific scene or event in the movie and explain why it is memorable?

The Story

There are many ways to structure a paragraph or an essay, but from a reader's point of view perhaps the most interesting is narration. Think of your writing as a story: Who (or what) are the main "characters"? What does your reader need to know about them for them to seem convincing? What happens to them? What kind of conclusion is the story building toward? The next time you write about a physics lab, think about the ways that you can transform your writing into more than just a recitation of facts; try to make those facts into a coherent report or narration.

BRAINSTORM

For which courses or assignments might you be expected to write a narration? Brainstorm a list of when you would write a narration to make a point or to engage a reader.

The Story of Your Life

Like everyone else, people in the business world are interested in stories. Keep this in mind as you put together your resumé—think of it as a story of your working life. Following proper formatting guidelines, shape your resumé so it presents a snapshot of your career and of you as a person. Similarly, in a job interview, do not restrict yourself to yes and no answers; rather, treat the interview as an opportunity to reveal something about yourself. Interviewers are looking for someone they want to see five days a week, so present yourself as interesting and captivating.

RESUMÉ BUILDER

Prior experience is a powerful tool for convincing someone to hire you. Think of a job you would like. What experience have you had that might convince an interviewer that you are perfect for the job? Write the story of this experience on a sheet of paper. You may have learned skills that can transfer to the different context of another job.

At a Glance

Like most paragraphs, a narration paragraph has three basic parts: a topic sentence, supporting details, and a concluding sentence or sentences. The topic sentence can be found at the beginning or end of the paragraph. The supporting details provide specific information about the scene, the actors, the action, and the outcome. These details are most often organized in chronological order. The conclusion may be several sentences long, and its purpose is to convey the event's impact and illustrate the claim the writer is making. Often, a narration paragraph is used as an essay's introductory paragraph.

The Narration Paragraph at a Glance

ASSIGNMENT   Life experiences teach us lessons. Tell a story that relates to something you believe to be true. Consider experiences that taught you a lesson or changed your view of something in some way.

TOPIC SENTENCE
The writer uses key words from the assignment.

SUPPORTING DETAILS
1. The writer describes the scene and the actors. The relationship between Mike and the writer helps a reader make sense of the actions that follow.
2–5. The writer describes actions and thoughts related to the competition.
6–7. The writer describes the competition's outcome.

ORDER AND TRANSITIONS
The writer uses time order to tell the story of an important lesson. The last transitions emphasize the final event.

CONCLUDING SENTENCES
The writer states two lessons and makes two points: one about foolishness and the other about fear.

Fear is often the best teacher, and it taught me a lesson about foolishness. (1) **One hot day** in July, Mike and I were bored, so we started the challenge-wars. Soon it was obvious that he could spit farther and run faster than I could. Then he challenged me to climb the corkscrew tree in my backyard. The tree was huge. It seemed to shade the entire block. It had all the right branches in all the right spots, so it was great for climbing. (2) **Immediately**, I leaped into the tree. I knew this tree and was sure I could climb to the top and finally beat Mike at something. (3) **Before long**, I was halfway up the tree, and I was winning. The branches were getting smaller. That is when I stopped and thought, "This is stupid" but I did not listen to my fears. I climbed higher. (4) **When I got to the top**, the wind was strong, and the branches swayed back and forth. I froze and was afraid to climb down. (5) **Soon**, Mike got frightened and climbed down. He knew I was in trouble and tried to talk me down, but I was too afraid, **so** he called the fire department. I clung to the branches as I swayed in the wind. I thought about how stupid I had been to climb so high. (6) **Finally**, the fire truck arrived, and they raised the ladder and helped me down. The whole neighbourhood gathered to watch the rescue. (7) **Worse**, one neighbour called my mother, who blew her top when she arrived home and found me sitting on the porch with a firefighter. That day I learned that I will do foolish things to win. More importantly, I also learned that fear is a good thing, and I should listen to it.

1. Identify the supporting detail that best illustrates the point of the topic sentence.

2. How many sentences does the writer use to describe this detail?

3. Why is it effective?

Thinking

NARRATION THINKING

In conversation, it is natural for us to tell stories. In writing, however, effective narrations are carefully constructed, using these basic elements: scene, actors, actions, and outcome. A writer combines these elements to make a point. You tell a story for a reason.

Elements of Narration

Effective narration takes the reader to the scene of an event, and introduces the actors, participants, or important people. The narration shows these people in action and reveals the outcome.

- *Scene:* Details about scene tell where and when an event took place—for example, in the corkscrew tree in the writer's backyard.

- *Actors:* Details about the actors in a narration tell who is important and who had an impact on the event's outcome. The writer climbed the tree because of a challenge game with his friend, Mike.

- *Actions:* Details about action are the heart of effective narration. A writer decides which actions are crucial to the point of the narration. Once the writer reached the top of the tree, he could not climb down.

- *Outcome:* Details about outcome provide an ending, but they also emphasize the point. The reader wants to know what happened. In academic writing, the reader wants to know why the story is important. The writer learned a valuable lesson about listening to his inner voice of fear the day he was stuck at the top of a tree.

Get Started

An effective narration paragraph contains a clear point stated in the topic sentence, narration elements to illustrate the story, and a clear conclusion to state the event's impact. In the clustering diagram, you can see how a student pieced together a narration response to a specific assignment in a science class.

> **Assignment:** Describe a breakthrough in your learning about physics this semester.

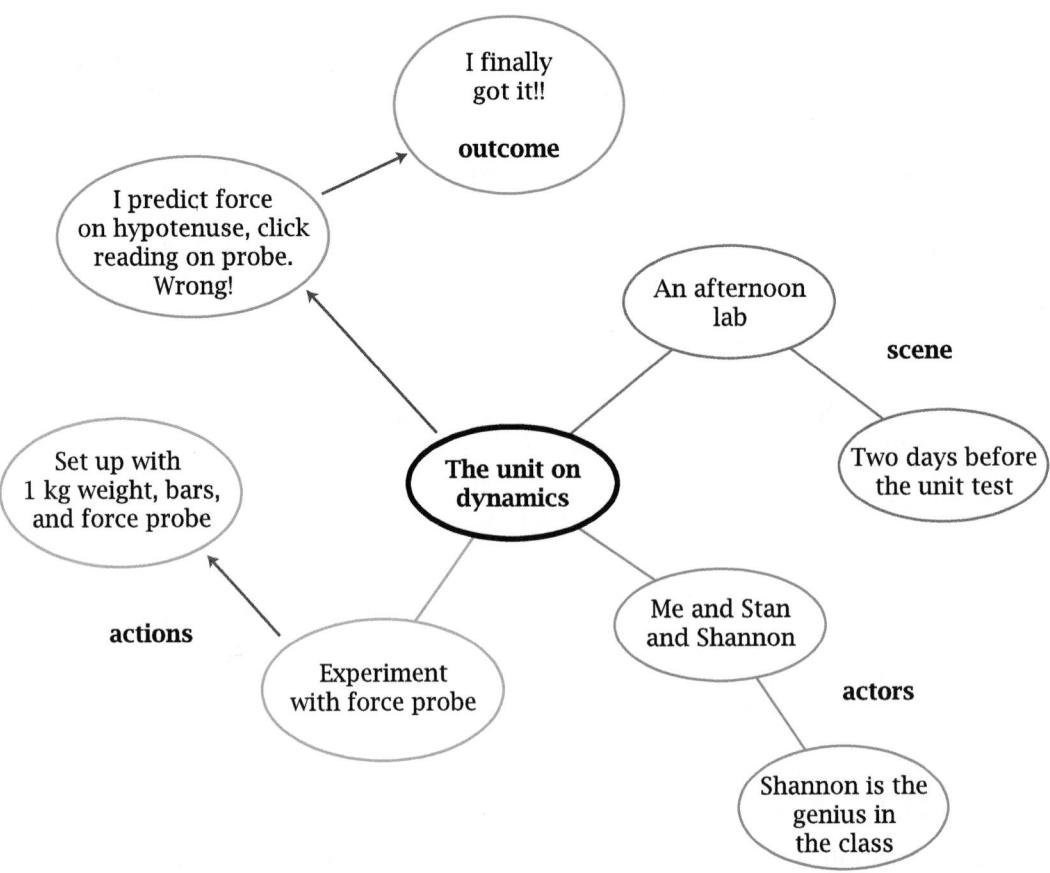

When you pay attention to all the elements of narration, the story will make its point more effectively. In this clustering exercise, the student covers all the details, scene, actors, actions, and outcome. He notes that Shannon is the genius in the class. He indicates the specific experiment the students ran and when it happened in relation to the unit exam. These narration details provide the skeleton for the story the student will tell in the paragraph's final version. At this point, the student can formulate a topic sentence that incorporates the assignment's key terms and points to the paragraph's important content.

Topic Sentence: My breakthrough in physics learning came during a study session a few days before the unit test on dynamics.

EXERCISE 6-1 **Elements of Narration**

Directions: *Pick two of the topics listed below and use the four elements of effective narration to plan a story that would support each one of your choices. To find details for each element, cluster on a separate sheet of paper.*

EXAMPLE

Topic: Sometimes just a little extra effort can make all the difference in the world.

Scene: Fort McMurray, Alberta. The construction site, "The Gold Camp," where Juan worked as a labourer for Fisher Plumbing

Actors: Kenny, the owner; Bill, the foreman; the other labourers on the job

Actions: (1) Juan is ordered to do a difficult job. (2) He spends a long afternoon digging underneath a footing full of rocks. (3) Kenny tells Bill to get the backhoe.

Outcome: Juan impressed the owner by not giving up on a really hard job. As a result, Kenny liked Juan's attitude and gave him a chance to do some better jobs.

Talk about it

Actions relate to the point of a story. What is the point here?

1. **Topic:** Making mistakes is an essential part of learning.

Scene: _____

Actors: _____

Actions: _____

_____

Outcome: _____

_____

2. **Topic:** Money spent quickly is not always spent wisely.

Scene: _____

Actors: _____

Actions: _____

_____

Outcome: _____

_____

3. **Topic:** In times of crisis, people show their true colours.

Scene: _____

Actors: _____

Actions: _____

_____

Outcome: _____

_____

Narration and Specific Detail

As we have discussed, the elements of narration are scene, actors, actions, and outcome. The real content, however, is in the details you provide. For each of these elements, think about what your reader needs to know for your narration to make sense. In some cases, you may not need to elaborate on all the elements of your narration. Focus on only those elements that provide essential support for the point you wish to make. When a narration paragraph is used as the introduction to an essay, the narration grabs readers' attention and leads them into the rest of the essay.

Scene

Actors

Actions

Outcome

In your narration, which of these elements is most important? Which requires elaboration and explanation?

When the student responding to his physics assignment examined the elements of his narration, he decided to provide additional details about the actors and actions involved.

Elements	Details	Elaboration
Scene	afternoon lab two days before the test	
Actors	Shannon and Stan	Shannon is the brain. Taking the course for refresher. A future teacher. Makes me do all the work. Asks me to explain my thinking as I do it.
Actions	We set up the exp. 1 kg weight, bars, force probe	I don't understand why the force on the long bar (hypotenuse) is not the same as the short one. We set it up. I predict. Click the force probe. Wrong! We draw a couple triangles and do the addition. I finally get it.
Outcome	I get it.	What I now understand is the experiment is a practical instance of the vector addition problems we have been doing in the book.

Part of your thinking task here is to elaborate only on those details that are relevant to the point you wish to make and that are essential to your reader's understanding. Doing so will ultimately improve your paragraph's unity.

Narration Detail

Directions: *Choose one of the topics from Exercise 6-1 and elaborate on the key details you provided for the elements of narration. Choose only those details most relevant to the point you want to make with your narration.*

Scene: _____

Key Detail: _____

Elaboration: _____

_____

Actors: _____

Key Detail: _____

Elaboration: _____

_____

Actions: _____

Key Detail: _____

Elaboration: _____

_____

Outcome: _____

Key Detail: _____

Elaboration: _____

_____

Ask Yourself

Elaboration helps a reader see action more clearly. Do you elaborate on key details when you write a narrative?

Make Connections

Good narration helps the reader see the connections between details. Transition words and phrases make these connections explicit. In the narration paragraph at the beginning of this chapter, for example, the writer uses the following transition words and phrases: *one hot day, immediately, before long, when I got to the top, soon, so, finally, worse,* and *that day.* These transitions help the writer use chronological order to organize his details. They make the story coherent.

Making Connections

Directions: *Read the paragraph below and underline the transition words and phrases. In the margin, note the elements of narration as they appear in the paragraph: scene, actors, actions, and outcome.*

Canada Day is family day. My family gathers at Uncle Mark's cottage on the lake. My father cooks four or five slabs of ribs. Aunt Jill brings her famous potato salad and apple strudel, and everyone contributes food or entertainment. This year Uncle Mark added an unusual contribution to the picnic: his new fiancée whom he met on the Internet. Uncle Mark has trouble finding girlfriends, so we were all eager to meet her. We were disappointed when he showed up by himself. He said she would be along a little later. About an hour later, Mark, my dad, my brother-in-law Stan, and I were playing horseshoes and teasing Uncle Mark about his computer fiancée. Just then a blue Ford Focus drove up and parked. It was the girlfriend. My dad said, "What is that on the side of her car?" We all stared, and then blinked to be sure we were seeing correctly. Hanging from the side of her car was the handle and hose of a gas pump. She had driven off with the whole thing and did not even know. It was the funniest thing I ever saw. We just could not stop laughing. Later, even Uncle Mark continually broke into laughter as he introduced Kim to the family. She was very embarrassed, but we made her feel like part of the family and shared our own ridiculous stories. Eventually, she did not feel like a total fool. However, we did take pictures of her car. From now on, every Canada Day we will tell that story. That is what happens in a big family. If you do something funny, everyone hears about it, and no one forgets. After all, laughter is the glue that holds a big family together.

DISCUSSION QUESTIONS

1. Where is the topic sentence in this paragraph?
2. What details in the story best demonstrate the point of the paragraph?

Process

NARRATION IN PROCESS

In order to write effective narration, it helps to remember the steps in the writing process. In this section you will use a process approach to write a single paragraph that tells a story and supports a claim.

Select an Assignment

In post-secondary studies, you will be asked to write assignments on a variety of topics. For some, narration will be a useful way to explore a topic. Before you tell a story, however, be sure the point of the story relates to the assignment's purpose. Some of your stories will be in the first person, but other times, you can use the third person. You may be asked to write third-person narration paragraphs at your job to describe an incident with a customer, a fellow employee, a patient, or a supplier.

EXERCISE 6-4 **Selecting an Assignment for a Narration Paragraph**

Directions: *Review the assignments listed below. Choose the one you know the most about and think is best suited for an effective narration paragraph.*

1. Getting help in school at just the right time can be critical for success. Recall a time when you, or someone you know, sought help and it made an important difference to the outcome.

2. Consider the value of punishment or the damage it can do. Tell a story about a time someone you know was punished properly or improperly.

3. Good employees make an important difference in the workplace. Tell a story about a good (or bad) employee, explaining what this person did (or did not do) at work.

4. Being surprised can be both pleasant and unpleasant, depending on the people and circumstances involved. Recall a pleasant or unpleasant surprise and explain its positive or negative impact.

5. Being disappointed or frightened can teach a valuable lesson. Write about a lesson you, or someone you know, learned from such an experience.

6. Write a story about playing a sport.

7. Tell a story about how you learned to manage money.

8. Recall a time when you changed your mind about something or someone and write about that experience.

9. Relate a story about a trip you took.

10. Choose your own topic.

Writer's Response

Good writing can come from trouble. Write about a troubling event you have seen.

Prewrite: Write Before You Write

When you tell a story, it is easy to overlook important details. Your reader will want to know about everything: where and when the story took place, who was involved, what happened, and what the outcome was. Before you start writing, do some prewriting to make sure you touch on all the important elements of narration. Prewriting will help you discover what you have to say. You have a variety of prewriting techniques to choose from, and clustering and talking are especially helpful when you use the narrative form of writing. You can also make a table like the one earlier in the chapter with headings for elements, details, and elaboration to guide your prewriting.

PREWRITE
- Talk
- Think
- Cluster
- Brainstorm
- Question
- Freewrite

EXERCISE 6-5 Clustering

Directions: *Cluster on your assignment for ten minutes. Include details relating to the elements of the narration: actors, scene (place and time), actions, and outcome. List as many narration details as you can. Later, you may decide not to use them all.*

EXERCISE 6-6 Talking about the Assignment with a Peer

Directions: *Turn to your neighbour in class and tell this person the story you focused on in your clustering. Be specific about important information. Include details about scene, actors, actions, and outcome. Then be a critical listener of your neighbour's story. Listen without interrupting. When the speaker finishes, ask questions or offer suggestions. Identify to each other what was clear and what was not clear.*

Draft: Focus and Organize

DRAFT
- Consider your audience
- Formulate your topic sentence
- Outline for unity and coherence
- Write a concluding sentence
- Compose your first draft

Prewriting helps you get your ideas and details down on paper. Now, you may have more to say than you did before. You may also have a better idea about the point your narration paragraph will make.

CONSIDER YOUR AUDIENCE

Now that you have selected your topic, consider who will read your paragraph. Chances are your reader was not at work with you when your co-worker came in late or in the class when a student was caught cheating. Your reader does not know any of the specifics about your story. When telling a story, you might neglect to mention information that is obvious to you. However, your reader needs this information in order to understand the story's point. Use the following questions to consider how to convey your point to an audience:

- What special meaning does this topic have for me?
- What do I want my audience to understand about this story?
- What details relating to time, place, people, and actions are important to help my audience understand my meaning?

EXERCISE 6-7 Considering Your Audience

Directions: *Use the questions above to think critically about the specific details to include in your paragraph and how you will use them to convey your point to an audience. Talk with a classmate to clarify your purpose and the details that will convey your point. Take notes on this conversation and add them to your prewriting.*

FORMULATE YOUR TOPIC SENTENCE

In a narration paragraph, the topic sentence might not be the paragraph's first sentence. As you write, decide on the best place for your topic sentence.

OUTLINE FOR UNITY AND COHERENCE

Your narration should be focused on a specific point you wish to make. As you work, watch for details that go off topic so you can eliminate them from your writing. For your paragraph to be unified, all the details should relate to the paragraph's main idea.

Narration is typically organized by chronological order. The story is told in sequence from the first action to the last action or outcome. By using transition terms indicating chronological order, a writer helps the reader follow the story. Here are some transitional words you can use to improve your paragraph's coherence.

TRANSITIONS BASED ON CHRONOLOGICAL ORDER

first	then
second	soon
third	moreover
to begin with	to conclude
next	eventually
in addition	finally

Narration paragraphs can also be organized by priority or importance. To do this, the writer emphasizes key actions using transition terms that show impact and create emphasis. Following are examples of some transitions. You may add others to this list.

TRANSITIONS BASED ON PRIORITY OR IMPORTANCE

also	likewise
another	plus
as a result	worse than that
at the same time	better yet
consequently	thus
equally important	most importantly

EXERCISE 6-8 **Transitions and Chronological Order**

Directions: *This narration is written in chronological order. Write an appropriate transition term in each line to introduce each action. Use both types of transition terms, choosing from the above tables.*

Sometimes nosy neighbours can be a good thing. One rainy night in October, my mom and I could not sleep. We watched a movie and folded laundry until after midnight. (1) _____ Mom shoved a last load in the dryer, we tried to wait for it to finish, but we were too exhausted. I went to bed, and Mom fell asleep on the couch. (2) _____ I heard someone beating on the front door. It sounded like they were trying to break in. (3) _____ I thought I was dreaming, but when I opened my eyes, the pounding was still there. I sat straight up in bed and looked at the clock. It was 1:13 a.m., and I had only been asleep a little while. (4) _____ I heard Mom open the door. Our neighbours were shouting that the house was on fire. I raced down the stairs and out onto the lawn. (5) For ten minutes we watched the house, but there were no flames. (6) _____ we realized the smoke was from the dryer vent. Our neighbours were frightened over nothing. At first, my mother and I were irritated, but later we were grateful for our nosy neighbours who wanted to keep us safe.

DISCUSSION QUESTIONS

1. Which actions did you emphasize by using transitions based on impact?

2. Why did you choose these actions?

WRITE A CONCLUDING SENTENCE

Plan your concluding sentence. Try to avoid ending your narration paragraph with the last thing that happened. Go one step farther and state the meaning or point of the narration.

EXERCISE 6-9 Planning Your First Draft

Directions: *On a separate sheet of paper, write a topic sentence that echoes the key words from the assignment topic you selected. Then organize and outline your details. See "Supporting Details" in Chapter 3 for a detailed explanation of outlining.*

COMPOSE YOUR FIRST DRAFT

Now that you have chosen your topic, decided on the point you want to make, and selected the details you will use to support your claim, you are ready to write your paragraph's first draft. Most writers say too little in their first draft. As you write, you may think of details to add that were not in your clustering. It is better to write too much than too little: you can always cut back later. Make sure your paragraph also has a lot of sensory detail and description.

EXERCISE 6-10 Writing Your First Draft

Directions: *Write a draft of your paragraph. Use the first draft checklist on the inside back cover as a guide.*

A PROFESSIONAL'S TAKE

Here is Drew Hayden Taylor's use of narration from the prologue to his book *The Night Wanderer, a Native Gothic Novel.*

One day, down by a slow-flowing river, an ancient Anishinabe (Ojibwa) man was sitting under a tree, teaching his beloved grandchildren about the ways of life. He said, "Inside of me, a fight is going on. It is a terrible fight between two wolves. One wolf is evil—he is fear, anger, envy, sorrow, regret, greed, arrogance, self-pity, guilt, resentment, inferiority, lies, false pride, competition, superiority, and ego. The other wolf is good—he is joy, peace, love, hope, sharing, serenity, humility, kindness, benevolence, wisdom, friendship, empathy, generosity, caring, truth, compassion, and faith. The same fight is going on inside you and inside every other person too." His grandchildren thought about the story for a few moments, then one child asked, "Grandfather, which wolf will win? Which one is stronger?" The old man smiled and said, "The one you feed."

EXERCISE 6-11 **A PROFESSIONAL'S TAKE**

Directions: *Using the first draft checklist from the inside back cover as your guide, identify the elements of an effective narration paragraph in the excerpt above. Next, compare the elements the author used in this excerpt with the ones that you used in your first draft. Are all the elements of narration in your paragraph?*

Revise: Read Critically, then Rewrite

> **REVISE**
> - Read critically
> - Develop a revision plan

What if your reader doesn't "get it"? Narration paragraphs can have two common problems. One is assuming readers understand something they do not; therefore, you leave out a critical detail. Adding the missing detail will help readers understand the narration and your point. A second problem is failing to sufficiently focus the paragraph. Maybe you include too many people or places or try to tell too much of the story. If you identify the narration's most important or exciting part and expand on just that, you will help readers better understand your point.

REVISION IN ACTION

Revision is about rethinking a draft and making decisions to improve your writing. You read critically, plan your revision, and revise your writing. Here is an example of revision by a student named Sara.

Assignment: Not everyone relaxes in exactly the same way. Tell about a time when you found that you did not agree with your friends on how to relax.

Sara's First Draft

My friends and I disagree about what makes a good night out. Just the other night, I went to Rocco's Club with some friends. It was a **Saturday night**, and the place was packed with people. There were no empty tables. I love hip-hop music, but the noise totally killed it. My friends did not seem to mind. I found an empty chair. They immediately started to dance. **To make matters worse**, all the cute guys had their girlfriends with them. The few single guys there all seemed to have attitude problems. Most of them looked like they had had too much to drink already. I joined my friends on the dance floor. I was having fun after a few songs, and the band did not seem so loud. **Even** that was short-lived. Some strange guy came over, and he started dancing with me. I enjoyed myself **at first**. It was actually fun until he put his hands on my waist and pulled me close. I love to dance, but I hate even the smallest physical contact with a stranger. I quickly walked off the floor. **Luckily** he got the point and did not follow me. **Before long** the place got more crowded and very smoky. The air was so bad it was hardly possible to breathe. My friends were having a great time, but I was not. That is when I realized that maybe nightclubs are not fun to me anymore.

TOPIC SENTENCE
Sara connects to the assignment by stating she disagrees with friends and identifies a specific way to relax—*a good night out.*

SUPPORTING DETAILS
She tells the story of a good night for her friends and a bad night for her to illustrate the topic sentence. She uses many minor details to make her point clear.

ORDER AND TRANSITIONS
The story is told in chronological order. Her transitions indicate time and impact.

CONCLUDING SENTENCE
She states the different views of the evening to emphasize the point of her topic sentence.

Revision Plan: Revise my topic sentence and purpose. Focus on the major details and actions. Cut irrelevant personal details. Cut informal language to sound sophisticated and thoughtful. Although my assignment is a personal narrative, to make it more academic, I will start fewer sentences with "I."

Sara's Revised Draft

Fun is a personal thing: what is fun for one person is not always fun for someone else. Like my girlfriends, I love hip-hop music, so we planned a night of fun at Rocco's Club. However, **after 15 minutes** of crowds, smoke, and head-splitting noise, they were having fun, but I was not. "Check out the men," Lisa said. **In fact**, the men were a big part of the problem. All the cute men had girlfriends hanging all over

TOPIC SENTENCE
Sara revises her topic sentence to clearly state an idea about fun—*it is a personal thing.*

them. The few dateless men seemed to have attitude problems. **After 15 more minutes**, a tall, athletic guy asked me to dance. It was actually fun until he put his hands on my waist and pulled me close. **After all**, he was just a sweaty stranger. **As soon as the song was over**, I quickly walked off the floor, found my girlfriends, and said, "Let's leave." They looked shocked; they were enjoying the smoke, loud music, and sweaty strangers. **Two hours of torture** went by as I watched my friends dance with one guy after another. **Finally**, they reluctantly agreed to leave. On a Saturday night, at a smoky club packed with sweaty men, I learned what fun is not.

SUPPORTING DETAILS
Sara focuses on 30 minutes. She focuses on the action and stops starting sentences with "I." She cuts irrelevant details about her experience and adds details to focus on the differences between her view and her friends' view.

ORDER AND TRANSITIONS
Sara uses time and impact to focus the narrative and the point.

CONCLUDING SENTENCE
Sara restates and makes a comment on her experience.

DISCUSSION QUESTIONS Which changes in the revision most improve Sara's paragraph? Why?

READ CRITICALLY

Critical reading is a search for the characteristics of effective writing: topic sentence, supporting details, transitions, and concluding sentence. Critical reading also involves careful analysis of the content. Are there sufficient details? Are some irrelevant? Is the narration focused? Keep these basic, essential questions in mind as you read peer papers.

EXERCISE 6-12 **Reading Peer Papers**

Directions: *Exchange papers with another student. Be a critical reader as you make suggestions to improve your peer's first draft. Also, identify what your classmate did well. Make notes in the margin as you read to remember your suggestions. After you read, you will discuss your suggestions. Refer to the guidelines from the revision checklist at the back of the text.*

REVISE WITH A PLAN

Before you revise your paragraph, reread your assignment. Some narrations can be written in first person. If your assignment indicates that third person is preferable, you need to prepare your writing for an academic audience using the revision checklist.

EXERCISE 6-13 **Revising Your Draft**

Directions: *After you have developed a revision plan, revise the first draft of the paragraph you wrote for Exercise 6-10, keeping in mind what you noted in your plan. Always reread the assignment instructions before revising to make sure you are doing what is required.*

Edit

The ideas in your work matter, but if your content is expressed in language that contains careless errors, readers may focus on the errors and miss your point. Invest time in getting your work as close to perfect as possible.

EDIT
- Search and correct
- Self-edit

Directions: *Read the following paragraph that was written in response to the assignment below; it contains errors that require revising and editing. Then answer the questions that follow.*

Assignment: Life experiences teach us lessons. Tell a story that states something you believe to be true. Consider experiences that taught you a lesson or changed your view of something in some way.

(1) The only true "punishment" I can remember was when I was in High School. (2) After working all summer, I had saved enough money to buy myself an MP3 player. (3) It had earphones. (4) Before that I had a CD player, but I wanted to get rid of it. (5) In January, semester report cards were handed out and I did not do so well, my grades were terrible. (6) I have always disliked science, and I have never done very well in it. (7) At first, I tried to hide my report card, but my parents caught on after 2 weeks and demanded to see it. (8) Before giving it to them, I edited the grades that I earned. (9) _____, my mother was not fooled, and she grounds me until my dad comes home from work that evening. (10) He chose to take away my brand-new prized possession, but there was a catch. (11) He did not want the entire component. (12) he took only the electrical charger. (13) He thought that looking at the device would be a constant reminder of my wrongdoing. (14) I was forced to look at my brand-new MP3 without being able to listen to it for a week since it couldn't be recharged. (15) I never did anything like that again.

REVISING

_____ 1. Which sentence below would work best as a topic sentence for the paragraph?

　　a. An effective punishment can change a person's behaviour.

　　b. Never lie about your report card.

　　c. My father really knew how to punish me.

　　d. Who wears the pants in your family?

_____ 2. The first sentence is not always the topic sentence of a narration. In this paragraph, where would you place the topic sentence you selected in question 1?

　　a. Replace sentence 1　　　　c. Replace sentence 14

　　b. After sentence 1　　　　　d. After sentence 15

_____ 3. Which sentences should be cut to improve the focus of the paragraph and reduce irrelevant details?

　　a. Sentences 3, 4, 6, and 7

　　b. Sentences 3, 4, and 6

   c. Sentences 3, 4, 6, and 14

   d. No change is necessary.

_____ 4. Which word or phrase should be inserted in blank 9? The word or phrase would serve as a clear transition between the writer's ideas in this paragraph.

   a. However   c. Next

   b. Without hesitation   d. Since

EDITING

_____ 1. Choose the option that corrects the capitalization error in sentence 1.

   a. High school   c. Highschool

   b. high school   d. No change is necessary.

_____ 2. Choose the option that best edits sentence 5.

   a. In January, semester report cards were handed out. I did not do well.

   b. In January, semester report cards were handed out, in which I did not do so well. My grades were terrible.

   c. In January, semester report cards were handed out, I did not do so well. My grades were terrible.

   d. In January, when semester report cards were handed out, and I did not do so well, my grades were terrible.

_____ 3. Choose the option that corrects the error in sentence 9.

   a. she grounded me until my dad comes home from work that evening.

   b. she grounded me until my dad came home from work that evening.

   c. she grounds me until my dad came home from work that evening.

   d. No change is necessary.

4. Proofread the paragraph for an error in how numbers are written and correct the error.

EXERCISE 6-15 **Searching and Correcting**

Directions: *Exchange papers with a classmate and proofread each other's work. In addition to spelling, punctuation, and capitalization, find out what other errors your classmate has made; tell your classmate what kinds of errors you often make.*

EXERCISE 6-16 **Self-Editing**

Directions: *Rewrite your assignment, correcting the errors you and your classmate found. Give yourself enough time to set aside the finished paragraph. Then come back to it later, and read your final draft one last time, using the editing checklist on the inside back cover as a guide.*

Talk about it

Where are your strengths as a narration writer?

Reflect

Take a moment and reflect on what you have learned about writing narration paragraphs.

EXERCISE 6-17 **Identifying Strengths and Setting Goals**

Directions: *Review your writing and your writing process. On a separate sheet of paper, write answers to these questions:*

- *What did you do well in the narration paragraph you wrote?*
- *What did you enjoy working on in this chapter?*
- *What have you learned that you will apply in future writing assignments?*

Your answers to these questions will increase your awareness of your particular strengths and weaknesses. For your next writing assignment, focus on reaching your writing goals.

CHAPTER REVIEW

Recall what you have learned about narration paragraphs:

■ NARRATION THINKING

☐ Elements of narration

- *Topic, scene, actors, actions, outcome (conclusion)*

☐ Narration and specific detail

- *Most important details: elaborate and explain*

☐ Make connections

- *Coherence: transitions*

■ NARRATION IN PROCESS

☐ Select an assignment

☐ Prewrite

- *Cluster and talk; focus and organize; select audience*

☐ Draft

- *Checklist*

☐ Revise

- *Reading critically; revision plan; concluding sentence*

☐ Edit

- *Peer and self-editing: relevant supporting details*

☐ Reflect

- *Narration paragraphs as introductions to essays*

THINK FIRST

Process writing explains how to do something. Having a dinner for friends is a process that takes planning and organization. Consider the steps you take to arrange a successful dinner. What will you do before, during, and after the dinner? Make a list of three other activities you do every day that involve following a process. Select one and write a paragraph describing the steps in the process.

Thinking in Terms of a Process

Some tasks can be done in a moment, without much thought. It does not take a lot of preparation and concentration to make a sandwich or fill the car with gas. Then again, other tasks are more complicated, and can require a great deal of thought and effort. How, for example, does one graduate from a program of studies, or maintain a successful relationship, or find the right job? Tasks like these require you to think in terms of a process. Graduating with a diploma or a degree requires a series of small accomplishments achieved over two to four years—classes attended, readings done, quizzes taken, and so on. By turning your attention to the immediate task at hand, you can more easily and effectively fulfill your master goal.

DISCUSSION

Turn and talk with a classmate to describe a process you have used to achieve a goal. For example, how did you find your current job? How do you achieve good grades? How do you balance work, school, and home responsibilities? List the steps you use to achieve one of these tasks.

Writing as a Process

Writing a paragraph or an essay is a process. If you feel dizzy trying to imagine how you are going to get from an empty sheet of paper to a great grade on a finished assignment, try breaking the process down into manageable steps like these ones: brainstorming, freewriting, talking with friends to figure out what you want to write about; narrowing your topic and roughing out a topic sentence or a thesis; writing a first, rough draft; redrafting and rewriting; editing for mistakes and spelling; and then handing in your finished essay. If you think of writing as a series of steps, instead of being daunted by the entire process of writing, you should be able to face any assignment.

BRAINSTORM

Reflect on your writing process by reviewing the list of steps in the Chapter Overview at the beginning of this chapter. Select two steps in the process you use to write assignments for courses other than English. Explain why these steps are helpful to you.

Big Goals, Small Steps

The first day on a new job is never easy. In addition to adjusting to a new work environment, new co-workers, and possibly a new city, you need to learn *how to do your job.* The change from rookie to reliable veteran does not happen overnight. You gradually learn what your colleagues know, such as terminology, computer programs, the basics of how your new workplace operates. Then you begin to acquire more complex skills and, eventually, become knowledgeable about your position and field. By concentrating on learning one new task at a time and discovering how multitasking itself is a process, you can become a dependable and effective employee.

RESUMÉ BUILDER

One difference between novices and experts is their ability to identify and solve problems. Experts identify problems and connect them to past experience to determine solutions. What problems do you face at work? How does your ability to solve them show you are, to some degree, an expert? Write about how you solved a problem at work.

At a Glance

THE PROCESS PARAGRAPH AT A GLANCE

The topic sentence of a process paragraph states the purpose or end result of the process. There are two kinds of process writing. Some paragraphs describe a process or explain how something works through analysis; the purpose is to give precise information. This kind of writing shares elements with descriptive writing. It is written in third person and you don't expect the reader to be able to duplicate what you are describing. For example, one step in the water cycle might explain, "The sun evaporates water from a pond." Other process paragraphs may explain how something can be improved. In that case, a writer identifies the key details that explain how something works well or poorly and suggests improvements. A second kind of process writing gives readers steps or directions about how to perform a process, such as how to insert a contact lens. This second pattern uses second person imperative during steps of the procedure, such as, "Place the contact lens on the tip of your finger." The reader is expected to be able to follow the steps for the intended outcome. The supporting details usually explain the steps in chronological order. Transition terms establish and highlight the coherence of the details. The conclusion states the effects or impact of the process on the work, the product, or the people involved or the outcome of the procedure. Process writing is often found in technical reports.

Review how to write the "command" forms (imperatives) used in process writing; with this verb form, make sure to omit the subject pronoun "you."

The Process Paragraph at a Glance

ASSIGNMENT Describe or explain a process that explains how to do something.

How to Escape from a Sinking Vehicle

Every year, ten percent of accidental drownings in Canada happen in submerged vehicles. Professor Gordon Giesbrecht from the University of Manitoba conducted studies where vehicles were submerged in lakes in controlled conditions, and volunteers attempted to escape the sinking automobiles. Based on his findings, Giesbrecht developed <u>the following recommendations that will increase your chances of surviving should you happen to be trapped in a sinking car.</u> Unlike dramatizations in movies or on television of actors waiting until an automobile has fully submerged, people actually have to act extremely fast. (1) **First of all**, Giesbrecht stresses that you shouldn't attempt to use a cellphone. Vehicles will float for less than a minute, and you need all that time to get out. Using a phone will take up valuable escape time. (2) **Secondly**, remember to release your

TOPIC SENTENCE
The writer responds directly to the assignment and clearly states the point of the paragraph.

SUPPORTING DETAILS
The steps in the process are sequenced in chronological order. Some steps have additional explanation (steps 1 and 3).

seat belt and help other passengers, especially children, to do the same. When people panic, it's easy to forget to do this. (3) **Next**, if the windows of the vehicle are not yet under water, open the windows and climb out. However, if the windows are already totally submerged, you won't be able to open the windows or the doors because of the pressure from the surrounding water. You will need to break the glass by kicking it with all your strength at the weakest area of the window, near the hinge of the door. (4) **Alternatively**, Giesbrecht recommends buying a small centre-punch from a hardware store and hanging this gadget from the rear-view window so you can find it right away. This centre-punch tool easily smashes the window. (5) **Most importantly**, with the glass shattered, you will be able to move out through the smashed window opening, despite the force of water flowing into the car. **Lastly**, grab any other passengers, like children in the back seat, push them out the window ahead of you, and swim towards the surface of the water. (6) **Of course**, the professor acknowledges that everyone will panic in such a critical scenario, so it's good to be aware of an effective escape procedure ahead of time. Finally, the best strategy to help you remember the steps to escape from a sinking vehicle is to remember these four words: seat belts, children, windows, out.

ORDER AND TRANSITIONS
The steps are organized by chronological order and introduced by transitions. The concluding sentence uses a transition to emphasize the final comment.

CONCLUDING SENTENCE
The writer comments on remembering the steps to get out of a sinking car.

DISCUSSION QUESTIONS

1. This paragraph is organized chronologically. Has the writer indicated the most important step or key detail in the process?

2. If you think the most important step is indicated, what is it? If not, what do you think it is? Why?

Thinking

PROCESS THINKING

Like narration, process description is common in conversation. You tell someone how to download a game from the Internet. You explain how to change the setting on a car's digital clock. Sometimes you evaluate a process, describe the best way to prepare for running a marathon, or give tips to avoid difficulty when enrolling for classes online.

In academic writing, you want to build on this skill you have already used in conversation. However, as is the case with all post-secondary writing, you have to think about an academic audience that looks for precise detail and careful use of language. Recall from Chapter 1 that good writers consider the purpose for writing as well as the focus and content, and the reader or audience.

Elements of Process

The elements of process are (1) purpose or end result, (2) the participants and materials involved in arriving at the result, (3) the order in which steps occur, and (4) the key details involved in the process.

- *Purpose:* The purpose of the process is often stated in the topic sentence as a "how to . . ." statement.
- *Participants and materials:* In processes involving people, discussing the participants is useful. For example, in the previous illustration, consider how many people might be passengers in a vehicle. In processes involving materials, such as equipment, tools, ingredients, components, facts, and information, detailed explanations of each can be helpful for the reader.
- *Steps and order:* Process thinking takes a complex activity and reduces it to steps that are manageable to discuss. For example, when a car plunges into a lake or river the driver must make a rapid series of decisions and take distinct actions. In a paragraph discussion of the process, however, those actions are covered in three or four steps. Organization is important in this area of process thinking, too. The supporting details (which are the steps in the process) and the transition words and phrases are key to clearly communicating how a process works.
- *Key details:* When you evaluate a process, critical thinking comes into play. Not everyone has the same approach to a process. Experience teaches us special ways of doing things that ensure a better outcome. Often there is a key detail you need to emphasize in your paragraph. Without this detail, the process might fail.

Get Started

Effective process writing explains a process in a detailed, organized manner. In the topic sentence, you identify the process in question, then proceed to discuss it in clear language, paying attention to detail and order of steps, and providing any specialized information a reader might need to fully understand the process. In the brainstorming exercise shown here, you can see a student's initial exploration of an important process: making a good cup of coffee. Many retail coffee shops depend on their staff's ability to accurately follow the steps of this ubiquitous task.

Writer's Response

What gets you started in the morning? Do you follow a routine each day?

Purpose	Participants and Materials
What is the purpose of coffee?	What participants? Do it by yourself.
Wakes you up.	Type of pots: stovetop, perk, drip, espresso, pots with timers.
Goes great after a meal.	

(continued)

Purpose	Participants and Materials
Needed for conversation, like with friends in a coffee shop.	Instant coffee too (yuck).
Keeps you awake studying.	Grind your own, buy it ground.
	Flavoured coffees (yuck).
	You need a good cup.
	Styrofoam cup, the worst.
	Stiff paper cup, less worse.
	China cup, too delicate.
	Gimme a mug heavy enough to knock someone out.
	Cream and sugar.
	Whiskey (Irish coffee).

Steps or Order	Key Detail(s)
Fill the pot with water (has to be cold water).	Easy pot, like one with a timer.
Put in the coffee.	Convenient!
Turn it on.	Good coffee.
Wait. Wait. I hate to wait.	Good mug.
If the coffee sits in the pot and gets old, it smells.	A timer pot means you have coffee when you wake up in the morning.
Drink it.	
Clean up.	
Before—decide on kind of coffee.	
During—how to fix it up (two sugars).	
Continuous stirring (put spoon in materials list), love the clang.	
Maybe choose something to eat with it.	

Your goal in your early thinking or brainstorming about your subject is to be as thorough as possible. Include everything you can think of that is related to your topic. Later in the thinking process, you will use some of these ideas and details and reject others. In the exploration shown here, the student moves systematically through the process of making coffee. He knows a lot. He specifies what he does not like: instant coffee, flavoured coffee, Styrofoam cups. He specifies what he does like: a mug. He mentions the pot with the timer twice and underlines "I hate to wait," suggesting a possible point of interest to him.

As you think about your topic and get ideas down on paper, you will probably develop a feel for a possible focus for your paragraph. However, as you get started, be inclusive. Here is this student's tentative topic sentence:

Topic Sentence: Good coffee is necessary to get going in the morning, and the key is the right pot.

EXERCISE 7-1 Elements of Process

Directions: *Choose one of the processes listed below and brainstorm to get started thinking about the topic. Look at all four elements of process thinking: purpose, participants and materials, steps or order, and key details. When you finish, formulate a tentative topic sentence on the process.*

- *Learning how to find journal articles on a library database*
- *Selecting a suitable daycare facility for a child*
- *Breaking a bad habit*

Purpose: _____

Participants and Materials: _____

_____

Steps and Order: _____

_____

Key Detail(s): _____

_____

Topic Sentence: _____

_____

Organize Your Details

A common challenge in process writing is reducing many actions to a few steps. Remember, a reader of academic writing does not want to read about the 18 steps involved in the process you have chosen. Not only do you risk losing your reader (and getting a low grade), but you also lose an opportunity to provide the kind of detail your academic reader values. Your job is to reduce the 18 steps to a manageable number. For this reason, you may need to group steps into categories or stages, making transitions from one stage of the process to another.

Consider the coffee example from earlier in this chapter. Here are all the steps based on the student's brainstorming:

1. Decide on the type of coffee.
2. Fill the pot with water.
3. Put the coffee in the basket.
4. Pack it.
5. Plug in the coffeemaker or put it on the stove.
6. Take the basket out of the pot.
7. Fix the coffee (cream, sugar, etc.).
8. Choose something to eat with the coffee.
9. Drink it.
10. Stir continuously.

Returning to this list, this student organizes his details, cutting and adding as he works.

Step 1: Get the right materials:

a. Coffee pot

b. Coffee

     Make it easy on yourself. Get one of those pots you can program to turn on by itself. No waiting in the morning.

c. Cup or take-it-with-you mug

Step 2: Program the machine the night before:

a. Fill the reservoir with water.

b. Put one of those cartridges in the basket.

c. Go to bed.

Step 3: Wake up and smell the coffee (I hate waiting!):

    a. Pour the coffee, add two sugars.

    b. Turn on the TV, listen to traffic updates, drink the coffee, and wake up.

    c. Fill your road mug and head for school.

    d. Cleanup is a snap with those prepared cartridges.

This student has reduced the process of making coffee to three main steps. In the process of organizing his details, his thinking has become more focused, causing him to select specific details from his initial exploration. He shifts his focus to convenience. This shift means that some of his initial thoughts—about types of pots and different grinds of coffee, for example— are no longer relevant. His new purpose is explaining how to get good coffee in the morning in the most convenient way.

EXERCISE 7-2 **Organizing Your Details**

Directions: *Return to the brainstorming you did in Exercise 7-1. Organize your process details into three or four major steps. In the space below, outline the process and draft a topic sentence stating your purpose in explaining the process.*

See "Supporting Details" in Chapter 3 for a detailed explanation of outlining.

Step 1

    a. _____

    b. _____

    c. _____

Step 2

    a. _____

    b. _____

    c. _____

Step 3

    a. _____

    b. _____

    c. _____

Step 4

    a. _____

    b. _____

    c. _____

Purpose: _____

_____

Talk about it

Are you a big idea or a detail person? Is it challenging to limit yourself to only four steps?

Identify Key Details

Processes run smoothly (or poorly) because of where they occur, who helps (or does not help), environmental factors, quality of the materials, and the level of experience of those involved. Whether you are writing about how to do something or how to improve a procedure, process thinking becomes critical thinking when you notice the key details involved and explain why they are essential.

EXERCISE 7-3 **Identifying Key Details**

Directions: *Read the following paragraph. With a classmate, answer the discussion questions that follow.*

PURPOSE
The topic sentence states the purpose of the paragraph: what steps to take to wake up to a good cup of coffee.

MATERIALS
Materials include the following: programmable coffeemaker, automatic shut-off, coffee filter packs, coffee mug and travel mug.

STEPS AND ORDER
The supporting details explain the steps of the process. The writer uses three transitions to indicate the paragraph's steps and emphasis.

IMPACT
The concluding sentence comments on the effects of the process.

> Waking up to a good cup of coffee requires having the right machine and planning ahead. (1) The most important step in the process is buying the right equipment. Look for a programmable coffeemaker. This enables you to set your coffeemaker the way you set your alarm and wake up to the smell of coffee already brewed. Mr. Coffee offers an inexpensive model that is easy to use. Slightly more expensive is the Krups Programmable Coffee Maker, "the coffee is ready when you are." The Krups comes with an automatic shut-off so you do not have to remember to turn it off as you rush out the door. Once you have all the right equipment, a daily three-step routine delivers great morning coffee. (2) To start, set up the pot before you go to bed. Make this simpler by purchasing coffee in filter packs. This decision will make coffee-making effortless and reduce cleanup as well. (3) Next, set out a cup for your first cup of the day and your travel mug. (4) Lastly, wake up to fresh coffee. The smell will urge you out of bed. Waking up to fresh brewed coffee improves a coffee-lover's attitude toward the day to come.

DISCUSSION QUESTIONS

1. What is the key detail in this paragraph?
2. What transition words or phrases does the student use?

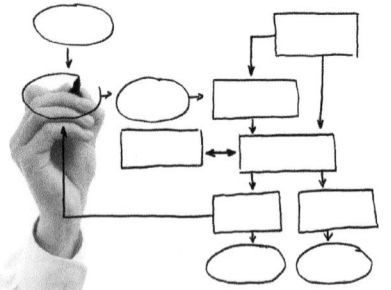

Process

PROCESS IN PROCESS

Writing about a process can help you understand it and then clearly communicate that understanding to others. As mentioned earlier in the chapter, process writing can also focus on improving a procedure. In academic writing, you will use process description and analysis in a variety of courses: in science labs, in writing accompanying calculations in mathematics, in criminal justice, and in hospitality programs.

In this section, you will use a process approach to write a single paragraph that describes or explains a process.

Select an Assignment

When you write about a process in a post-secondary course, your primary concerns are how the process works, why it is important, and what can be done to improve it.

EXERCISE 7-4 **Selecting an Assignment for a Process Paragraph**

Directions: *Review the assignments listed below. Choose the one you know the most about and think is best suited to an effective process paragraph.*

1. Explain how to search for information on the Internet.

2. Describe the process of getting registered for college or university classes.

3. Outline the steps involved in taking out a loan.

4. Describe how to handle a customer complaint at work.

5. Describe how to compose secure computer passwords.

6. Explain how to buy a used car.

7. Explain how to avoid identity theft.

8. Describe how to prepare for a job interview.

9. Explain the process of disease prevention or a process used to manage a disease.

10. Choose your own topic.

Prewrite: Write Before You Write

When you write a process paragraph, you have a specific purpose in mind. You want a reader to understand the process; in addition, you may want to explain how the steps impact the people and work involved. To get started, you might try these two prewriting strategies: talking and brainstorming.

PREWRITE
- Talk
- Think
- Cluster
- Brainstorm
- Question
- Freewrite

EXERCISE 7-5 **Talking about It**

Directions: *Turn to a classmate or find an interested listener to gain other perspectives that can help clarify your thinking. Describe your process: its purpose, participants and materials, steps, and key detail(s). Be specific and include details so your listener understands your process. Then be a critical listener to your partner's process thinking. Listen without interrupting. When your partner finishes, ask questions or offer suggestions. Identify what was clear and what was not. Take notes on this conversation and add the new ideas and details to your prewriting.*

EXERCISE 7-6 **Brainstorming**

Directions: *On a separate sheet of paper, brainstorm for ten minutes on the assignment you chose in Exercise 7-5. List the elements of the process and include as many details as possible. Then identify the key detail(s) and consider the impact of the detail(s) on the people* *or process. Remember the elements of process writing: purpose, participants and materials, steps and order, and key detail(s). Ask yourself, "What do I know about this process? What does the reader need to know to understand it?" Jot down as many ideas and details as you can think of.*

DRAFT

- Consider your audience
- Think critically about the key terms, participants and materials, essential steps, and specific details
- Formulate your topic sentence
- Outline for unity and coherence
- Write a conclusion sentence
- Compose your first draft

Draft: Focus and Organize

After prewriting, you probably have a feel for what you want to include in your paragraph. You can identify your purpose for explaining the process and list the participants and materials, the steps in the process, and the key detail(s).

CONSIDER YOUR AUDIENCE

Before you draft, consider your readers' background. What do they know about this process? What terms will be new to them? Identifying and defining new information and key terms will help readers follow your train of thought. No two people complete a process in the same way. What is the most important step in the process from your perspective? Use these questions to consider how best to convey the process you are explaining to an audience:

- What terms do I need to define to explain the process?
- What essential steps and methods do I need to include?
- What do I want my audience to understand about this process?

FORMULATE YOUR TOPIC SENTENCE

To begin, write a clear topic sentence that echoes the key words from the assignment and states the purpose of your paragraph, in other words, the outcome of the process.

OUTLINE FOR UNITY AND COHERENCE

Since your goal is a unified paragraph, all the details you include should be relevant to your main point. Do not go off the subject, and refrain from including details that are interesting to you but not directly related to the discussion at hand.

Steps in a process are typically organized by sequence or chronological order. Your careful use of transition words and phrases will enhance your paragraph's coherence.

TRANSITIONS BASED ON CHRONOLOGICAL ORDER	
first	then
second	soon
third	afterward
finally	simultaneously
next	

Some students use transitions based on priority or importance to indicate the key steps in a process.

Ask Yourself

Which transitions do you always use? Look at the list of transitions in the tables on this page and the next. Are there some new ones you could use? As you read and come across other transitions, add them to the table for future reference.

TRANSITIONS BASED ON PRIORITY OR IMPORTANCE	
most	certainly
equally	definitely
absolutely	never
always	obviously

WRITE A CONCLUDING SENTENCE

A concluding sentence states the importance of the process. Often, it underscores the point your paragraph makes about improving the process or discusses the end product or result.

EXERCISE 7-7 Planning Your First Draft

Directions: *Decide on the purpose of your process paragraph. Then write a topic sentence that echoes the key words from the assignment and states your paragraph's purpose. Make a short outline to organize the paragraph. Write a concluding sentence that comments on the process.*

See "Supporting Details" in Chapter 3 for a detailed explanation of outlining.

COMPOSE YOUR FIRST DRAFT

Write a first draft of your paragraph and select only the relevant ideas and details from your brainstorming or outlining. It may be helpful at this point to reconsider the order of what you have written and the transition terms you plan to use. Look for the details that seem most important for readers so they can understand your purpose. Be sure to provide adequate explanation of these details.

EXERCISE 7-8 Writing Your First Draft

Directions: *Write a draft of your paragraph. Be sure to divide the process into three or four steps. Provide enough detail related to time, place, material, and people involved in the process to explain the steps. Are there effective transitions to show the relationship between the steps and details?*

A PROFESSIONAL'S TAKE

Here is Mark Caldwell's use of process in a short *Discover Magazine* article entitled "Polly Want a PhD?"

It's not just what the parrots say that makes them seem eerily human; it's the level of intelligence they easily demonstrate. Consider Griffin's [a parrot] performance on a test Pepperberg [a researcher] devised to see whether the birds could use a mirror image of an object to manipulate it. Children don't typically master that skill until they're 3 years old. In the experiment, a nut is concealed underneath the lid of a box. The nut is attached to a wire that runs up through a slit in the lid and connects to a paper clip for the parrot to yank. The slit branches out into three tracks, each of which ends in a hole through which the nut can be pulled. The trick is that two of the three slits are blocked by obstructions that can only be seen by looking in a mirror that reflects a backward view of what's inside the box. Most humans who try to solve the puzzle are baffled, but Griffin, watching intently from his perch on the lab counter, will demand to be brought over, peer into the mirror for perhaps half a second, triumphantly zip the nut down the right track, jerk it up through the opening, and grab it.

 **EXERCISE 7-9**   **A PROFESSIONAL'S TAKE**

Directions: *Using the first draft checklist found on the inside back cover as your guide, identify the elements of an effective process paragraph in the excerpt.*

Revise: Read Critically, then Rewrite

REVISE
- Read critically
- Develop a revision plan

Process analysis is complex. Revision in process writing means rethinking and evaluating your explanation of steps in the process. Ask yourself a few questions as you reread your first draft. What is your purpose? Are you explaining how something works or how a process can be improved (both process analyses), or are you explaining how to perform a process (a directional process)? Do you provide all the essential steps and necessary explanation? Is there any unnecessary detail you could cut? Revision gives you a chance to read critically and to reorganize, clarify, or cut.

REVISION IN ACTION

Revision is rethinking a draft and making decisions to improve the quality of your writing. You read critically, plan your revision, and revise the writing. Here is an example of revision by a student named Deidre.

> **Assignment:** Describe, explain, or analyze a process that you know well.

TOPIC SENTENCE
Deidre states the process and the focus of the process paragraph in her topic sentence.

SUPPORTING DETAILS
She explains the process step by step. She lists the steps using technical language.

ORDER AND TRANSITIONS
Deidre inserts transitions for some steps in the process that emphasize the point in her topic sentence—*getting the process right.*

Deidre's First Draft

Providing CPR can save a person's life; the important thing is starting CPR early and getting the process right. CPR consists of alternating breathing and compressions to provide a patient with oxygen. The **first important step** is to assess the patient. Not every unconscious person needs CPR. I look, listen, and feel for breathing, heartbeat, and pulse. If all three are negative, I proceed with CPR. I use universal precautions, such as gloves and a mask. **It is best** to move the patient to a hard, flat surface so compressions have maximum effect. I learned that CPR consists of breathing and compressions. Recent guideline changes place an emphasis on high quality chest compressions, so the next step is that rescuers should begin with chest compressions right away. To help a patient breathe I tilt her head back to open her airway. **Then** I apply the mask and give one long breath, until the diaphragm rises. **At this point**, I start CPR. Give another breath and start chest compressions, 30 compressions for every two breaths, two breaths a minute. If I have a buddy responder, it is a good idea to change positions, one doing breathing and maintaining airway, the other doing compressions. **Every so often**, I stop and check for respiration and heartbeat. <u>Doing CPR is hard work, but when I save a life, it is definitely worth it.</u>

Revision Plan: Revise my topic sentence to focus on my purpose: to explain how a process can be effective. Adjust organization to emphasize effectiveness, especially placing emphasis on the key detail in the process. Add another important detail: CALL 911! Revise my concluding sentence to comment on my topic sentence. <u>Shift to third person.</u>

Deidre's Revised Draft

<u>Cardiopulmonary Resuscitation (CPR) is hard work, but knowledgeable responders save lives.</u> CPR consists of alternating breathing and compressions to provide an unconscious patient with oxygen. Responders must know the correct procedures thoroughly, so their responses are automatic. The **first important step** is to assess the patient. Not every unconscious person needs CPR. Responders should look, listen, and feel for breathing, heartbeat, and pulse. If all three are negative, they should have someone call 911 and prepare for CPR. **It is best** to move a patient to a hard, flat surface so compressions have maximum effect. **However**, responders should check for serious back or neck injuries before moving the patient. Recent guideline changes place an emphasis on high quality chest compressions, so the **next step** is that rescuers should begin with chest compressions immediately. **In addition**, responders should use universal precautions, such as wearing gloves and a mask, to protect themselves and the patient from infection. **Next**, responders should tip a patient's head back to open his or her airway. They should apply a mask and give one long breath, until the patient's diaphragm rises. Responders should then give another breath and start chest compressions, 30 compressions for every two breaths. Chest compressions involve placing both hands, the heel of one hand, the other on top of that, between the patient's nipples. A compression should be at least two inches deep. Giving compressions is hard work. If there is another person available, it is a good idea to change positions at five-minute intervals, with one person doing breathing and maintaining the airway and the other doing compressions. **Every so often**, it is important to stop and check for respiration and heartbeat. <u>Providing CPR can save a person's life; the important thing is starting CPR early and getting the process right.</u>

TOPIC SENTENCE
In her revised draft, Deidre uses formal language and emphasizes that saving a life requires specific skills. She adds a second sentence to explain why knowledge can make a difference.

SUPPORTING DETAILS
She adds significant detail to her explanation, particularly about how to give chest compressions.

ORDER AND TRANSITIONS
Deidre divides the paragraph into two major parts: (1) steps before CPR, and (2) steps during CPR. She rearranges the order of her minor details to connect all the steps that are done before and during CPR. She also uses two kinds of transitions: importance and time. This emphasizes her point in the topic sentence that knowledge can save a life.

CONCLUDING SENTENCE
Deidre revises her conclusion sentence to emphasize the key detail—*starting early and doing it correctly.*

DISCUSSION QUESTIONS Which changes in the revision most improved Deidre's paragraph? Why?

READ CRITICALLY

Critical reading is a search for the characteristics of effective process writing: topic sentence, supporting details, transitions, concluding sentence. It is also a search for clarity of purpose, participants and materials, steps and order, and key detail(s).

EXERCISE 7-10 Reading Peer Papers

Directions: *Exchange papers with another student. Be a critical reader and make suggestions to improve your peer's first draft. Also identify what your classmate did well. Make notes in the margin as you read to remember your suggestions. After you read, discuss your suggestions. Use the guidelines from the first draft checklist found at the back of the text.*

REVISE WITH A PLAN

As you review your classmate's comments, consider how focusing on chronological order might make your paragraph more effective. As you develop your revision plan, remember that time controls the order and transitions in a process paragraph. Look at the details you have included. Do they explain the process? Are they relevant?

EXERCISE 7-11 Revising Your Draft

Directions: *Develop a revision plan and revise the first draft of the paragraph you wrote for Exercise 7-8. Be sure to check the assignment instructions once again to make sure you are doing what is required.*

Edit

EDIT
• Search and correct
• Self-edit

EXERCISE 7-12 Revising and Editing Practice

Directions: *Read the following paragraph that was written in response to the assignment below; it contains errors that require revising and editing. Then answer the questions that follow.*

Assignment: Explain a process you use at home, school, or work. State the impact of the process and support your point with specific details.

(1) Making enemies out of your neighbours, should never be a difficult task. (2) Following three easy steps will send Mr. Johnson through the roof. (3) The first rule of thumb is to always show disrespect. (4) Begin responding to hello with a menacing glare. (5) Follow this up by responding with the term "Yo!" (6) This will send Mr. Johnsons mind meandering through corridors of shock. (7) With some neighbours this will be enough. (8) _____. (9) You may need to create more animosity in the air using sound waves. (10) Arrange a playlist of grind core metal to disrupt the still of the night. (11) Begin your social gathering at midnight. (12) Plan a large gathering on a business day. (13) If it

begins earlier you may risk Mr. Johnson still being awake. (14) The most important piece of the puzzle is to be sure that everyone stays all night. (15) _____, the climactic moment is upon you. (16) The day after the party, in the mid-afternoon, Mr. Johnson will knock on your door, keep your wits about you because he is certain to be upset. (17) When he blames you for not being able to rest the night before. (18) Smile and slam the door. (19) If you have the nerve to follow these instructions you can easily make enemies with your neighbours.

REVISING

_____ 1. Is sentence 2 relevant?

     a. Yes   b. No

_____ 2. Which sentence should be inserted into blank 8 to provide a transition?

     a. For others, however, more effort will be required.

     b. Mr. Johnson's mind is easy to disturb.

     c. Making enemies is not advised for good neighbourhood relations.

     d. No transition is necessary.

_____ 3. Select the order of sentences 10, 11, 12, and 13 to provide the most logical sequence of ideas and supporting details.

     a. 10, 13, 11, 12   c. 10, 12, 11, 13

     b. 12, 10, 11, 13   d. No change is necessary.

_____ 4. Which word or phrase should be inserted in blank 15?

     a. Therefore   c. Finally

     b. Once in a while   d. Indeed

EDITING

_____ 1. Choose the option that corrects the error in sentence 1.

     a. Making enemies out of your neighbours should never be a difficult task.

     b. Making enemies, out of your neighbours, should never be a difficult task.

     c. Making an enemy out of your neighbour, should never be a difficult task.

     d. No change is necessary.

_____ 2. Choose the option that corrects the error in sentence 6.

     a. This will send Mr. Johnsons' mind meandering through corridors of shock.

     b. This will send Mr. Johnson mind meandering through corridors of shock.

Ask Yourself

Do you insert commas where you would take a breath when reading what you wrote? What does Chapter 25 tell you about commas?

c. This will send Mr. Johnson's mind meandering through corridors of shock.

d. No change is necessary.

_____ 3. Choose the option that corrects the error in sentence 16.

a. The day after the party, in the mid-afternoon, Mr. Johnson will knock on your door, keep your wits about you, because he is certain to be upset.

b. The day after the party, in the mid-afternoon, Mr. Johnson will knock on your door. Keep your wits about you because he is certain to be upset.

c. The day after the party, in the mid-afternoon; Mr. Johnson will knock on your door, keep your wits about you because he is certain to be upset.

d. No change is necessary.

4. Proofread the paragraph for a sentence fragment and correct the error.

EXERCISE 7-13 **Searching and Correcting**

Directions: *Exchange your first draft with a peer and proofread each other's work. In addition to spelling, punctuation, and capitalization, notice what other kinds of errors your classmate has made; tell your classmate what kinds of errors you often make. This will raise your awareness of common errors that you need to look out for in your writing.*

EXERCISE 7-14 **Self-Editing**

Directions: *Carefully rewrite your paper, correcting any errors you and your classmate found. After setting aside the finished paper for a short time, come back to it and read your final draft once more, using the editing checklist on the inside back cover as a guide.*

Reflect

Take a moment and reflect on what you have learned about writing effective process paragraphs.

EXERCISE 7-15 **Identifying Strengths and Setting Goals**

Directions: *Review your writing and your writing process. Then, write answers to these questions:*

- *What did you do well in the process paragraph you wrote?*
- *What did you enjoy working on in this chapter?*
- *What have you learned about process writing that you will apply in future writing assignments?*

Your answers will increase your awareness of this style of writing, as well as your particular strengths and weaknesses when writing about a process.

REFLECT
- Identify strengths
- Set goals

CHAPTER REVIEW

Recall what you have learned about process writing:

■ PROCESS THINKING

☐ Elements of process
- *Purpose, audience, participants/materials, steps/order, key details, outcome*

☐ Organize your details
- *Manageable steps*

☐ Identify key details
- *Focus, unity, transitions, and coherence*

■ PROCESS IN PROCESS

☐ Select an assignment

☐ Prewrite
- *Talk and brainstorm*

☐ Draft
- *Focus; organize; consider reader*

☐ Revise
- *Unity and coherence: transitions; concluding sentence*

☐ Edit
- *Critical reading; peer/self-editing; use checklists*

☐ Reflect
- *Strengths and writing goals*

Classification

THINK FIRST

Many people are getting tattoos these days. Why? Brainstorm to develop a list of all the people you can think of with tattoos. Sort the individuals on your list into categories based on their reasons for getting a tattoo. Then write a paragraph in which you describe the various types of people who are getting tattoos.

Organizing Your World

That is not where that goes! We make sense of the world by organizing it—by sorting things, people, events, and ideas. Think of a kitchen cupboard. Open the doors and most likely you will see objects stored according to their size, use, and materials: glasses on the first shelf; on the shelf above, dinner plates, salad plates, and dessert dishes. Think about movies. There are comedies, action movies, romance movies, and horror movies. This is classification. It serves a purpose. It answers a need. The philosopher William James said the world is a "humming-buzzing confusion" until we organize it through experience. James says this work of organizing goes on continuously; it is never complete. So, we create categories, and they work—for a while. For example, at one time, our category for CEO meant a white male boss. Then we re-created our categories, making them more inclusive. A CEO could be any gender, from any ethnic background. How we organize the world and understand our place in it is a work in progress. Classification is at the heart of this work.

DISCUSSION

Talk with a classmate to answer the following questions: How do you find your way around a grocery store, electronics store, or home repair store? How does a place like that use classification to make shopping quick and easy for its customers?

Your Program of Study

Are you studying in health care? That field of study is divided into different categories: nursing, X-ray technology, dental assistance, or emergency response. How about business? The business field is divided into a number of categories: accounting and finance, marketing and advertising, and administration and human resources. These distinct fields focus on money, on sales, and on the management of personnel and operations. A student going into business might also consider whether her future is in corporate work, small business, a family business, or a limited partnership. These broader categories are determined by the operation's size. For each category, your post-secondary curriculum helps you build a knowledge base and develop skills in math, science, social science, and humanities that are relevant to optimum job performance. College or university curricula provide countless examples of classification at work.

BRAINSTORM

Think about the career you are interested in. Create several lists to help you explore what this career possibility might mean. Consider the type of education required, the different types of work environments, the various types of responsibilities, and the kinds of people with whom you might interact.

Job Description

In the workplace, classification defines an employee's responsibilities and pay scale. For years we have distinguished between white-collar and blue-collar employees, between those who make a salary and those who make an hourly wage, between those who work with their minds and those who work with their hands. This division of the workforce allows us to see the big picture and describe work in broad strokes. However, a closer look changes the picture. Blue-collar employees can be classified as skilled or unskilled, and, on the job, skilled workers use sophisticated technology, exhibit high levels of expertise, and demonstrate important critical-thinking skills. The classification "those who work with their hands" just does not fit the facts. New classifications are necessary, such as "knowledge workers," for example. What colour are their collars?

RESUMÉ BUILDER

Use classification to examine what makes you an effective and efficient worker. Identify two or three job categories at your place of work. Then list the characteristics or requirements of each job. Where are you currently in the organization? What would you have to do to move to a more responsible position?

At a Glance

THE CLASSIFICATION PARAGRAPH AT A GLANCE

The topic sentence of a classification paragraph serves multiple purposes. It states the key words from the assignment, names the topic to be discussed, and lists the categories to be described. The supporting details in the body of the paragraph consist of examples that describe and illustrate each category. The concluding sentence may restate the topic sentence or make a comment about the categories included in the paragraph.

The Classification Paragraph at a Glance

ASSIGNMENT Discuss the types of personalities you might encounter at work or in school.

People have individual conflict styles, but in their book *Conflict Is for the Birds: Understanding Your Conflict Management Style,* authors G.W. Oudeh and N. Oedeh have <u>classified five distinct approaches to conflict that bear comparison to different kinds of bird behaviour.</u> **The first conflict management style** is the woodpecker. A person using the woodpecker behaviour is assertive and aggressively addresses issues. **A second way** to handle disagreements is the parakeet style. A parakeet is someone who seeks to maintain friendships and is excellent at avoiding conflict. **Another approach** is that of the owl. An owl reaches decisions only after receiving all the facts and deliberating wisely. **Then** there are people with an ostrich conflict-management style. These people like to work in secluded environments and they strive to avoid hostile situations. **However,** ostriches can stand their ground in arguments. **One last category** is the hummingbird. This group includes energetic people who make snap decisions, can quickly change their minds, and are willing to negotiate. The authors point out the importance of both understanding why people can disagree and learning how to handle various conflict scenarios. No matter what bird personality one has—the woodpecker, parakeet, owl, ostrich, or hummingbird—a balanced approach to a conflict is one that can separate an issue from the personalities involved. **Above all**, <u>maintaining the flexibility to use more than one conflict management style can help everyone to understand multiple perspectives and resolve disagreements.</u>

TOPIC SENTENCE
The student's topic sentence states there are five different types of conflict management styles.

SUPPORTING DETAILS
For each style of conflict management she discusses, the student provides a label and an explanation.

ORDER AND TRANSITIONS
Transitions from descriptions of one type to the next are clearly stated.

CONCLUDING SENTENCE
In the concluding sentences, the student reiterates the five categories and connects them to an important idea: "resolve disagreements."

1. What reasons can you suggest for presenting human conflict styles that parallel bird behaviour?

2. Suppose the assignment was to write about different kinds of banking accounts. How would you classify them? Why?

Thinking

CLASSIFICATION THINKING

We divide complex things into easier to understand categories. For example, the medical field is divided into specialties, including gerontology, pediatrics, and obstetrics. The divisions are distinct and avoid overlap so that something can be placed in only one division. Like division, classification breaks things into more easily understood groups. However, classification includes recognizing difference or ranking those groups. Rating, or ranking, the groups involves careful observation, which in turn leads to careful thinking. When you classify, you make a complex topic more focused and easier to understand. For instance, think of classifying first-, second-, and third-degree burns. The injuries are divided into groups, but also ranked depending on the burn's severity. Classifying things helps the reader see the subject in a new way. Because it's possible to classify a subject in more than one way, classification draws on other kinds of writing. You may want to give your own definitions for the criteria for placing things in each division. You'll also use descriptions or examples to illustrate your categories of division or classification.

Elements of Classification

The important elements of classification thinking are purpose, basis for classification, categories, and examples.

- *Purpose:* Classification serves a purpose. It imposes order on information to meet your needs or your readers' needs. For example, you notice different types of conflict management styles and begin to think critically about how people handle disagreements.

- *Basis for classification:* To impose order on information, you need a basis for classification. In the case of conflict styles, you consider what could be the basis of classification to distinguish among different people. Always provide at least three categories. With only two categories, the basis for classification will appear to be a comparison or contrast rather than a classification.

- *Categories:* From purpose and a basis for classification come the categories you will use. In the case of conflict styles, you might identify styles used within a family, in relationships with friends, or in business settings.

- *Examples:* Within the categories, examples provide the specific details in classification thinking. You discuss, in this example, specific characteristics of different conflict styles, or you provide descriptive detail to elaborate on each category.

Get Started

Classification thinking moves from general to specific. You begin with a topic, divide it into general categories, and then move toward specific examples that illustrate each category. How you divide your topic depends on your purpose, which then leads to the basis for classification.

Take a general subject like popular music. There are many possibilities for classification. One student might be interested in guitar music; another, in instrumental music. Their different purposes result in different bases for classification.

Topic	Interest/Purpose	Basis for Classification
Popular Music	To explore the influence of the electric guitar	Types of music in which electric guitar is used
	To discuss the pleasures of nonvocal, instrumental music	Types of popular nonvocal, instrumental music

The importance of the electric guitar and the pleasures of instrumental music are two different purposes for classifying popular music. Approaching classification with these purposes in mind, one student would focus his topic sentence on different types of music in which the electric guitar is prominent, using categories such as blues, rock, and jazz. Another student would focus her topic sentence on different types of instrumental music—categories such as jazz, orchestral, techno—that people find enjoyable. These different approaches to classification would lead to topic sentences that reflect the specific focus and purpose for each writer's classification:

The influence of the electric guitar can be heard in many categories of popular music.

A rich variety of instrumental music is available in popular music today for the enjoyment of the interested listener.

Directions: *For each topic, state two different interests you have that are related to the subject. Then explain how each interest provides you with a basis for classification.*

EXAMPLE

Topic: Reading materials

A.   I'm interested in reducing the amount of clutter in my house. I will classify reading materials based on whether I plan to keep them or get rid of them.

B.   I'm interested in planning what I will read over the next few months. I'll classify reading materials based on whether they are something I really enjoy or something I read for personal improvement.

1. **Topic:** Hobbies/pastimes

A. _____

_____

B. _____

_____

2. **Topic:** Students

A. _____

_____

B. _____

_____

3. **Topic:** Shoppers

A. _____

_____

B. _____

_____

Provide Examples of Categories

Classification serves a purpose. You decide on categories because doing so helps you explore what interests you about your topic. Your next task is to be specific—to cite and discuss specific examples in your categories.

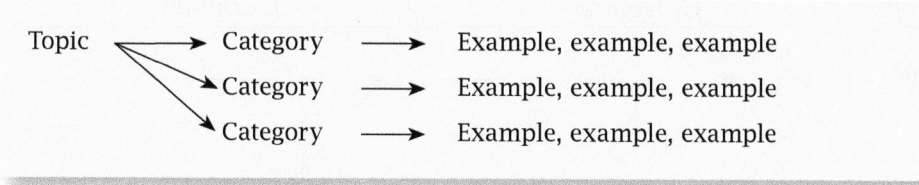

For instance, the student who explores the influence of the electric guitar in popular music would cite specific examples, as shown here:

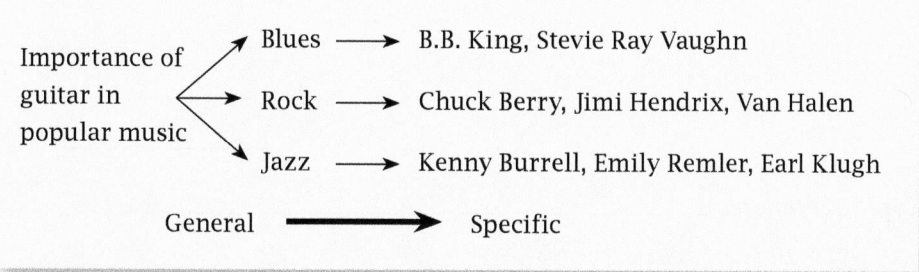

Examples, of course, are always more complex than their categories. Jimi Hendrix was not only a rock musician. His style of play also drew upon the blues category. A student examining popular music with a different purpose would have different categories and arrive at many different specific examples. The important thing in using classification is to be clear about your purpose, focus, and reason for classification.

EXERCISE 8-2 **Topics, Categories, and Examples**

Directions: *Using the model below as a guide, divide each topic into at least three categories. Be sure your categories reflect a clear purpose and basis for classification. This basis should be consistent and exclusive. Once your categories are in place, provide specific examples for each category. Then write a topic sentence that states the topic and purpose for the classification. For practice, you can add topics to this exercise and use the diagram format to determine the basis for classification of each topic and then provide examples.*

Talk about it

Cite an example of thinking from general to specific.

EXAMPLE

Topic: Parents

Basis for Classification: Approaches to discipline

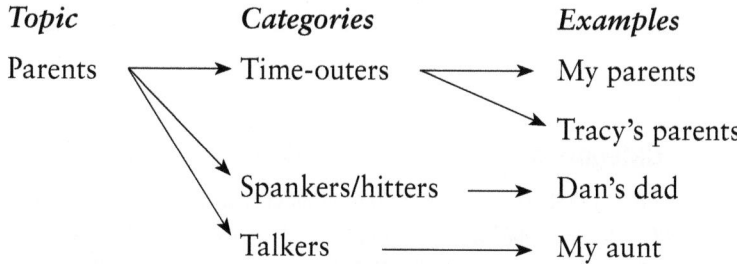

Topic Sentence: Not all parents have exactly the same approach to disciplining their children.

Topic: Friends

Basis for Classification: _____

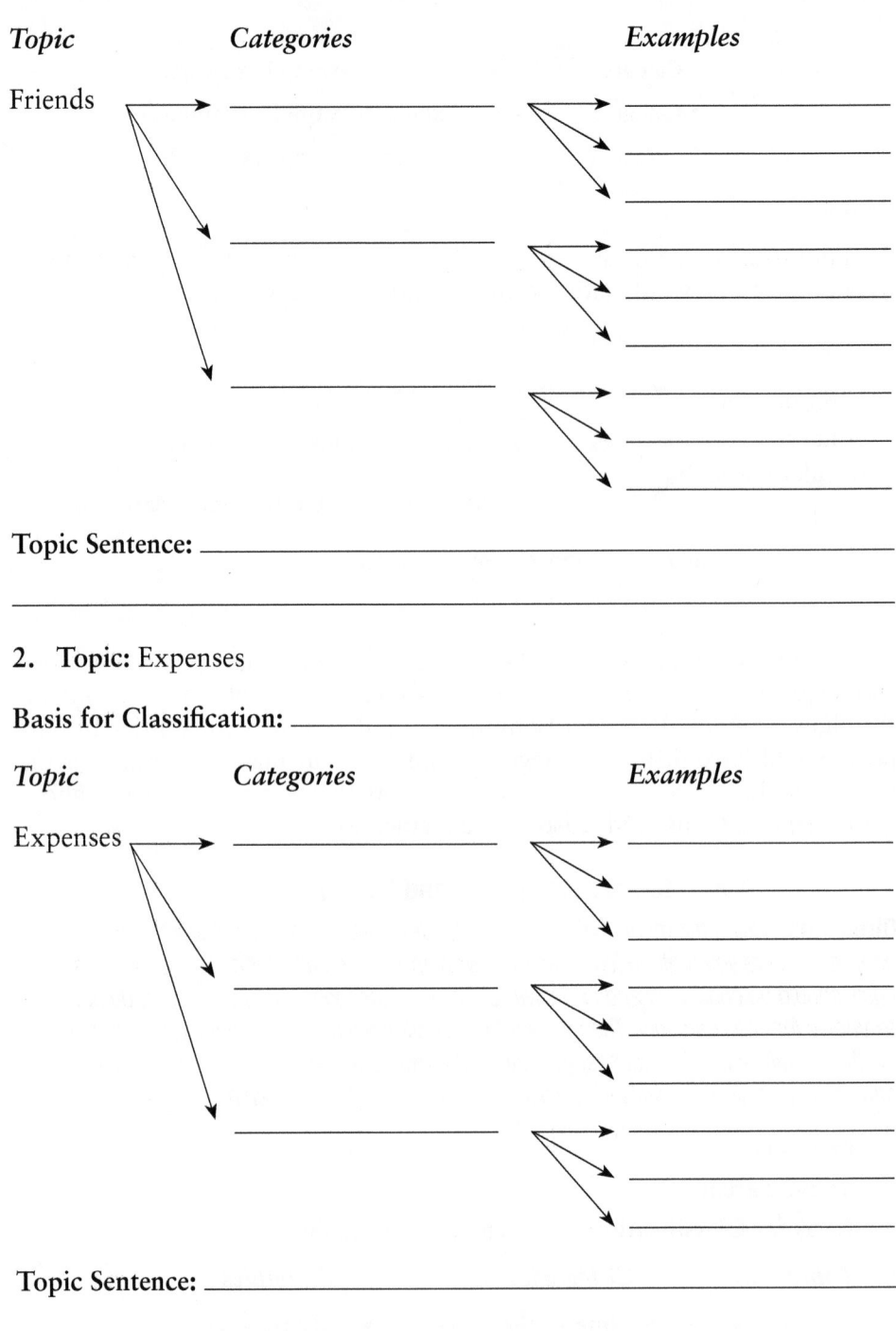

Topic	Categories	Examples
Friends	_____	_____
		_____
		_____
	_____	_____
		_____
		_____
	_____	_____
		_____
		_____

Topic Sentence: _____

_____

2. **Topic:** Expenses

Basis for Classification: _____

Topic	Categories	Examples
Expenses	_____	_____
		_____
		_____
	_____	_____
		_____
		_____
	_____	_____
		_____
		_____

Topic Sentence: _____

_____

EXERCISE 8-3 **Categories and Examples Working Together**

Directions: *Good examples persuade the reader that a category is accurate. Also, examples help a reader understand why classification is a helpful way of thinking about a subject. To further explore the relationship of categories and examples, provide one example to explain how each category below relates to the general topic and supports the topic sentence.*

EXAMPLE

Topic: Fashion fad

Topic Sentence: Fads often emphasize an antisocial or subversive effect of fashion.

Category A: Tattoos and piercings <u>Tattoos and piercings have shock value. For example, pierced eyebrows and nostrils are visible and shocking to some people. It is impossible to look at a person and not see a pierced eyebrow or nostril. When the piercings are recent, they look red, angry, and painful.</u>

Category B: Low-cut tanks and shirts <u>Low-cut tanks and shirts also have shock value. For example, it is common to see young women showing both belly and cleavage. It is brash. It says, I'll uncover myself if I want to. When these articles of clothing are combined with jeans worn low on the hips, maximum exposure is the result.</u>

Category C: Gothic style <u>Wearing all black clothing and pale makeup with dramatic black eyeliner and even black lipstick can have a shocking effect. For example, dark clothes, black leather boots, and fishnet stockings are worn as a protest against colourful pastels and serve as a reminder of the Victorian era cult of mourning.</u>

1. **Topic:** Part-time jobs

   Topic Sentence: A part-time job can be categorized in three ways: a mindless and for-the-money-only job, an opportunity to learn something directly connected to your career goal, or volunteering for community service.

   Category A: A mindless part-time job for money only _____

   _____

   Category B: A part-time job that provides a chance to learn something

   _____

   Category C: A volunteer job that provides a chance to meet people in one's community

   _____

2. **Topic:** Extracurricular activities

   Topic Sentence: Some extracurricular activities are strictly related to socializing and having fun, whereas others are related to classroom learning and skill development, or volunteer community service activities.

   Category A: Activities that are strictly related to socializing and having fun

   _____

Category B: Activities related to classroom learning and skill development

_____

Category C: Activities related to community service _____

_____

3. **Topic:** Stress

Topic Sentence: Stress comes in various forms—for instance, family-related stress, work-related stress, money-related stress.

Category A: Family-related stress _____

_____

Category B: Work-related stress _____

_____

Category C: Money-related stress _____

_____

Avoid Stereotyping

Stereotyping occurs when you categorize someone or something using oversimplified and possibly biased criteria. Often, good classification thinking occurs in response to a stereotype. You realize, "Not all female bosses are pushy." "Not all men are chauvinist pigs."

Because individuals vary, stereotypes always distort the truth. Consequently, when considering a group, you need to develop broad categories that will include the range of different types of individuals in that group. Once you have established categories, you can think more critically and classify the individuals that fall within your categories. For example, you might analyze female bosses as follows:

Female bosses bring a variety of personal characteristics to the workplace.

1. Some are hard-driving bosses who demand commitment and professional competence.
2. Others quietly delegate work.
3. Others are good at bringing people together and building consensus.

Classifying like this enables you to avoid stereotyping. These three broad categories provide room for individual differences, and you avoid the overgeneralization of saying all individuals in one category are alike. In your analysis, you do not want to oversimplify or distort the truth.

Process

CLASSIFICATION IN PROCESS

Good classification writing is an invitation to think critically about your subject. When you think carefully, you typically revise and refine your ideas. Like all writing, then, classification writing benefits from the writing process: prewriting, drafting, revising, editing, and reflecting.

Select an Assignment

In this section, you will write a single paragraph that uses classification to define categories. You will also provide specific examples to explain those categories.

EXERCISE 8-4 **Selecting an Assignment for a Classification Paragraph**

Directions: *Select a topic from the list below. Choose the one you know the most about and think is best suited for writing an effective classification paragraph.*

1. For most people, free time is a valuable commodity. Briefly discuss different ways to make valuable use of free time.

2. Not all parents are the same. Describe different approaches to parenting.

3. Educators talk about different kinds of learning styles. What are some different kinds of teaching styles you have observed this semester or in past classes?

4. A good budget is essential to effective money management. What types of expenses should a person keep track of to be an effective money manager?

5. Careless eating habits contribute to a rapidly expanding waistline. What types of eating should a weight-conscious person be on the lookout for?

6. Talents

7. Service from cellphone providers

8. Automobile insurance

9. Illnesses

10. A topic from your other courses

> **Ask Yourself**
>
> How do you focus an assignment so it leads to a specific classification paragraph?

Prewrite: Write Before You Write

When writing a classification paragraph, you begin by thinking about your purpose and the basis for classifying your topic. Once you know how you will classify your topic, you can generate useful categories and examples through focused exploration. For this kind of writing, try brainstorming and clustering as methods of exploring the various elements of classification.

> **PREWRITNG**
> - Talk
> - Think
> - Cluster
> - Brainstorm
> - Question
> - Freewrite

EXERCISE 8-5 Brainstorming

Directions: *Brainstorm to come up with several different ways you could break your topic into divisions or categories. Choose the most useful basis of classification of your topic for your purpose, and use it to brainstorm a list of at least three categories to use in your paragraph.*

EXERCISE 8-6 Clustering

Directions: *Cluster for ten minutes on the categories you identified in Exercise 8-5 to come up with examples that illustrate or explain them. You may find it useful to use the diagram outline with topics, categories, and examples from earlier in this chapter.*

Draft: Focus and Organize

> **DRAFT**
> - Consider your audience
> - Formulate your topic sentence
> - Outline for unity and coherence
> - Write a concluding sentence
> - Compose your first draft

In classification writing, focus is essential. You want to be sure your categories are useful, easily recognizable, and serve your purpose for classifying the topic in the way you have. You also must ensure that your examples fit the categories and are not stereotypes. So as you draft, you focus and organize your prewriting to double-check your thinking.

CONSIDER YOUR AUDIENCE

Read the assignment again. Think about your audience. Your classification system should provide your reader with a useful way of looking at your topic. Keep in mind these questions as you consider your audience:

- Why is this topic important?
- What do I want my reader to understand about my topic?
- Why is classification helpful in a discussion of this topic?

EXERCISE 8-7 Considering Your Audience

Directions: *Talk with a classmate about your topic. Use the previous three questions to think critically about the key terms and specific details to include as you explain your classification to an audience. Take notes on this conversation and add new ideas and details to your prewriting. If possible, talk to a different classmate to gain another perspective and clarify your thinking.*

FORMULATE YOUR TOPIC SENTENCE

The topic sentence of a classification paragraph links the topic and the categories you will explore.

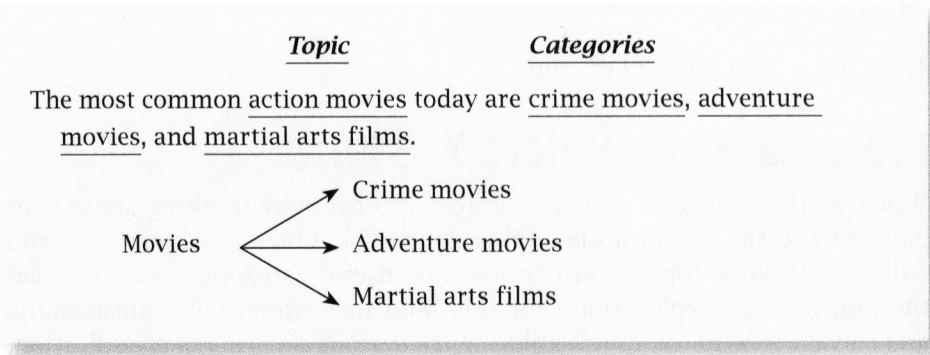

Topic	*Categories*

The most common <u>action movies</u> today are <u>crime movies, adventure movies</u>, and <u>martial arts films</u>.

Movies → Crime movies
→ Adventure movies
→ Martial arts films

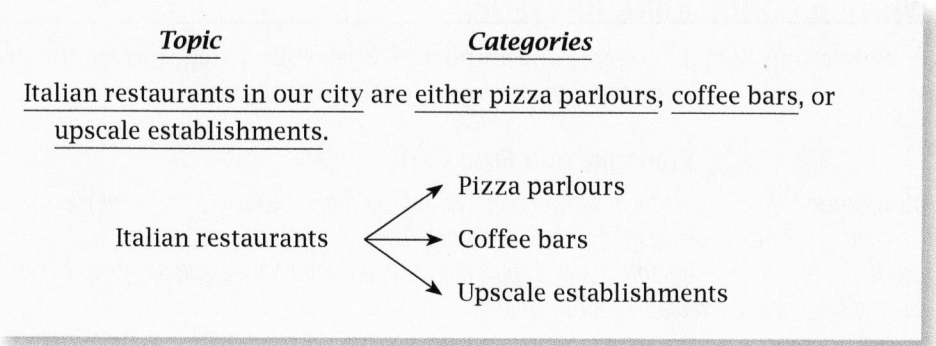

Topic	Categories

Italian restaurants in our city are either pizza parlours, coffee bars, or upscale establishments.

Italian restaurants
- Pizza parlours
- Coffee bars
- Upscale establishments

Effective topic sentences in classification paragraphs use **parallelism**, which means the terms describing the categories are related in meaning and use the same parts of speech, usually nouns, adverbs, adjectives, or phrases. In the examples above, the categories are expressed with parallel nouns: *movies* and *films; parlours, bars,* and *establishments.* In addition, each noun is preceded by an adjective: *crime* movies, *adventure* movies, and *martial arts* films; *pizza* parlours, *coffee* bars, and *upscale* establishments.

OUTLINE FOR UNITY AND COHERENCE

Before you draft, outline your paragraph and check your details. To plan a unified paragraph, make sure everything in your paragraph relates to your topic sentence. Choose transitions that make the relationship between your examples visible to a reader. Transitions also emphasize examples.

TRANSITIONS TO EXPRESS CONTRAST

yet	on the contrary
in contrast	however
nevertheless	notwithstanding
though	nonetheless
on the other hand	otherwise
after all	at the same time

TRANSITIONS FOR EXAMPLES

for example	furthermore
moreover	too
also	in the second place
again	in addition
even	more
next	further
last	lastly
finally	besides
first	secondly

WRITE A CONCLUDING SENTENCE

A concluding sentence states the importance of your categories or underscores the point your paragraph makes about your subject.

EXERCISE 8-8 **Planning Your First Draft**

See "Supporting Details" in Chapter 3 for a detailed explanation of outlining.

Directions: *Write a clear topic sentence that states the main idea and purpose of your classification paragraph. Following your topic sentence, list the categories and examples you will use to develop your paragraph. Make a short outline to organize the paragraph. Write a concluding sentence that restates your main idea.*

COMPOSE YOUR FIRST DRAFT

Review your prewriting and check your outline. Then write a first draft of your paragraph, refining your sentences and rethinking your organization and details. Keep in mind emphasis. As you develop your ideas and explain categories and examples, use a similar amount of detail in each category.

EXERCISE 8-9 **Writing Your First Draft**

Directions: *Write a first draft of your paragraph. At this stage, it is better to write too much than too little. You can always cut back on content later. Include sufficient details, explanations, and appropriate transitions so that a reader will understand how the examples fit with the categories you established. Use the first draft checklist at the back of the text as a guide. Be sure that the topic sentence states the categories you will use. Your transitions should make the categories easy to recognize.*

A PROFESSIONAL'S TAKE

Classification is used in the following adaptation of part of an article by Lynge Nielsen of the International Monetary Fund called "Classifications of Countries Based on Their Level of Development: How It Is Done and How It Could Be Done".

HOW COUNTRIES IN THE WORLD ARE CLASSIFIED

Governments and businesses often need accurate information about the many countries around the world so that they can develop public policies or plan business strategies. To make the information useful to the people who need it, researchers can classify countries in several ways. The first way we think about classifying countries is by geography, regions, or climate, so often countries are grouped by the continents they are located on. For example, some countries are often grouped as belonging to Africa, Europe or Asia. Another instance is that some analysts include Canada, the United States of America, Greenland, and the islands of Saint Pierre and Miquelon (the overseas territory of France) as countries in North America. However, there are people who believe that

Mexico is also part of North America. Others would argue that Mexico should be part of the Latin American and Caribbean countries. This illustrates a difficulty in classifying countries geographically, so many people prefer to group countries by the languages or culture of the inhabitants. In fact, Australia groups countries by the level of English proficiency of the immigrants from those countries, in the hopes of selecting future immigrants who are most likely to have success getting settled into English-speaking Australia. Insurance com-

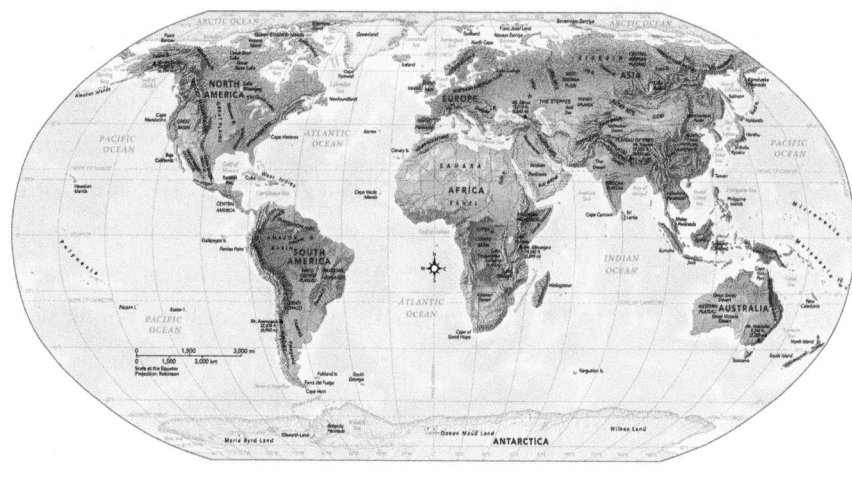

panies may classify countries by the life expectancies of the male and female populations while health organizations might divide areas according to disease outbreaks, such as malaria or AIDS. Moreover, educators use statistics about the literacy levels of people around the world. Tradition-ally, economists have grouped countries as either developed or developing countries, but there has been no universally accepted agreement for the definition of a developing country. Should the basis of classification be based on income levels, standards of living, levels of education achieved, or some other benchmark such as happiness? In selecting a basis of classification, the needs of the end user of the information play a large role. Clearly, researchers and the policy makers should determine a basis of classification that not only suits their purposes, but is also easy to under-stand and avoids confusion by using more than two categories.

● **EXERCISE 8-10** **A PROFESSIONAL'S TAKE**

Directions: *Using the first draft checklist at the back of the text as your guide, identify the effectiveness of the elements of the classification found in A Professional's Take. Next, com-pare the elements the author used in this excerpt with the ones that you used in your first draft. Did you include exclusive categories with enough examples and details in your para-graph draft?*

Revise: Read Critically, then Rewrite

Few writers get things perfect in one draft. Now that you have a first draft, you need to read it critically and revise. Ask yourself, "Is my purpose clear? Do my categories make sense? Do the examples I have included adequately explain my categories?" Revision gives you a chance to rethink, to add and cut content, and to more accurately focus on your intended purpose.

REVISE
- Read critically
- Develop a revision plan

REVISION IN ACTION

Revision is rethinking a draft. You read critically, plan your revision, and revise the writing. Quality revision will also improve your future writing. Here is an example of revision by a student named Denny.

> **Assignment:** Every summer, thousands of Canadians flock to amusement parks. Write a paragraph about the different types of people who go to amusement parks.

Every weekend during the summer, the usual maniacs, family fun seekers, and shade seekers crowd into Canada's amusement parks, hoping to find a good time. **To begin with,** we have the maniacs. These are usually young people in T-shirts, shorts, and flip-flops, screaming at their friends at the top of their lungs. The maniacs go on the highest roller coaster as many times as possible. **Along with** the roller-coaster maniacs, we have the game idiots who throw hoops at pop bottles and darts at balloons, hoping to win a stuffed animal the size of an adult bear. These maniacs and idiots are joined by the junk food fools who stuff their faces with hot dogs, popcorn, and cotton candy, eating until they puke all over their feet. Now that is what I call fun. **A second category** of fun seeker is the average Canadian family. We're talking little kids on rides that move at walking speed. Kids love animals. They love amusement parks. They tire out their parents, but hey, weren't the parents little kids once, too? Oh, and do not forget those cameras. The family fun seekers take pictures all day long. **A final category** is the shade seekers. These are usually grandparents who have escaped from the rest of the family. They want shade, they want quiet. Good luck! Sometimes these grandparents have little kids sleeping on blankets in the shade. It is kinda cute. Also in the shade, you just might find one of the junk food fools cleaning you know what off his feet. It takes all kinds. Amusement parks are for the slightly crazy and those, like those grandparents, with little or no choice in the matter.

TOPIC SENTENCE
Denny lists three types of people who go to amusement parks.

SUPPORTING DETAILS
He describes the categories of park-goers and provides specific details to illustrate the ways they have a good time.

ORDER AND TRANSITIONS
His transitions list the types: "to begin," "second category," "final category." He adds the word "category" to connect the examples to the assignment.

Revision Plan: Create an academic tone by eliminating informal language and minimize use of "I" and "you." Make the transitions similar. Cut extra details that are interesting but not essential to the description of the three categories of park-goers.

Denny edits word choice in this draft and uses third person. This makes the paragraph more appropriate for an academic audience.

Denny's Revised Draft

Every weekend during the summer the usual maniacs, family fun seekers, and shade seekers crowd into Canada's amusement parks. The maniacs, **the largest category of park-goers,** are usually young people in T-shirts, shorts, and flip-flops. They race from one ride to another and scream wildly as they ride the highest roller coaster as many times as possible. They never get tired. **In addition to** the roller-coaster maniacs, there are the game maniacs, who play games all day. They throw hoops at pop bottles and darts at balloons, hoping to win that special

TOPIC SENTENCE
Denny shortens his topic sentence to focus on the categories of park-goers.

stuffed animal. Then there are the average **families in the second category:** typical moms and dads with little children on rides that move at walking speed. **Occasionally,** the dads (or moms) slip away to go on an adult ride. **Generally,** the family fun seekers take pictures, eat hot dogs and cotton candy, and buy identical T-shirts as souvenirs. **The quietest category** is made up of shade seekers. These are usually grandparents who have escaped from the rest of the family. They want peace and quiet. **Sometimes,** the shade seekers sleep next to little children on blankets in the shade. Amusement parks try to offer something for everyone; as long as they do not run out of roller coasters, games of chance, fast food, children's rides, benches and shade, most people will probably be happy with their visits to the amusement parks.

SUPPORTING DETAILS
He cuts one example from the maniacs category and adds details to the average Canadian family and shade seeker categories.

ORDER AND TRANSITIONS
Denny's decision to cut and focus impacts his transitions. He uses three parallel transitions that name each category. He also uses transitions to connect the details in each category.

CONCLUDING SENTENCE
Denny comments on and lists the things that draw people to amusement parks.

DISCUSSION QUESTIONS Which changes in the revision most improved Denny's paragraph? Why?

READ CRITICALLY

When you read a peer's paper, you can get insights into your own writing. Beginning with the topic sentence, read with classification in mind. Notice if the writer uses sufficient examples and details to explain distinct categories. Pay attention to how other writers accomplish classification writing so you can improve what you are trying to do.

EXERCISE 8-11 **Reading Peer Papers**

Directions: *Exchange papers with another student. Consider the significant changes that Denny made between his first draft and his revision. Be a critical reader and make suggestions to improve and clarify your peer's first draft. Make notes in the margin as you read. After you read, discuss your suggestions.*

REVISE WITH A PLAN

Before you revise your paragraph, reread your assignment. Be sure that you provide a detailed response to the assignment. As you revise, prepare your writing for an academic audience by changing to the third person and substituting more formal words for slang.

EXERCISE 8-12 **Revising Your Draft**

Directions: *Develop a revision plan and revise the first draft for the paragraph you wrote for Exercise 8-9.*

Edit

The ideas in your work count and content matters, but you must use standard punctuation. Classification paragraphs often use specific types of punctuation: colons and semicolons. Check out how to use them correctly in Chapter 25. Also, be sure to list the categories using parallelism. Focus your editing by using the editing checklist at the back of the text.

EDIT
- Search and correct
- Self-edit

Directions: *Read the following paragraph that was written in response to the assignment; it contains errors that require revising and editing. Then answer the questions that follow.*

Check that you use parallelism for your categories.

Assignment: Examine a current trend. Identify the types of people that engage in this trend. Use specific examples to explain the categories.

(1) Cosmetic procedures can be classified as beauty maintenance, age reduction, or obsessive reconstruction. (2) Cosmetic surgery is not just for the rich and famous. (3) Every day across the country, cosmetic surgeons performed procedures that range from simple injections to major reconstruction. (4) Beauty maintenance is accomplished in the office on a lunch-hour. (5) Botox is the most popular procedure. (6)_____. (7) Injection's of Botox are quick, fairly inexpensive, and instantly improve appearance. (8) Age reduction generally requires reconstructive surgery and a hospital stay which include tummy tucks, liposuction, eyelid surgery, and partial or full face-lifts are the most common and they can remove 10, 20, or 30 years. (9) Unfortunately, cosmetic surgery becomes a crazed obsession for a few individuals. (10) They completely reconstruct their faces. (11) And mould their bodies with repeated surgeries. (12) At the appearance of the smallest wrinkle, they panic and schedule another surgery. (13) Michael Jackson is a perfect example of the obsessive use of cosmetic surgery. (14)_____.

REVISING

_____ 1. The topic sentence does not have to be the first sentence in a paragraph. Identify the topic sentence. Then select the best order for sentences 1, 2, and 3 to establish the topic and clarify the purpose of the paragraph.

  a. 2, 3, 1   c. 3, 2, 1

  b. 3, 1, 2   d. No change is necessary.

_____ 2. Which sentence should be inserted into blank 6? The sentence would provide the best specific details to support the topic sentence.

  a. Botox reduces or removes frown lines for people 18 to 65.

  b. Surgeons treat medical procedures like spa services.

  c. However, laser hair removal, chemical peels, and microdermabrasion top the list as well.

  d. Compared to a facelift, Botox is a walk in the park!

_____ 3. Which sentence should be cut to improve the paragraph's focus?

  a. Sentence 2   c. Sentence 13

  b. Sentence 12   d. No change is necessary.

_____ 4. Which sentence should be inserted into blank 14? The sentence would provide a concluding sentence that restates the topic and makes a comment.

    a. These days, anyone can be young and beautiful for a price.

    b. Beauty is big business, and there is a cosmetic surgeon willing to serve any category of patient.

    c. In my opinion, any cosmetic surgery is a waste of money.

    d. In conclusion, cosmetic surgeons perform procedures on men and women every day.

EDITING

_____ 1. Choose the option that corrects the error in sentence 3.

    a. Every day across the country, cosmetic surgeons perform procedures that range from simple injections to major reconstruction.

    b. Every day across the country, cosmetic surgeons performed a procedure that range from simple injections to major reconstruction.

    c. Every day across the country, cosmetic surgeons have performed procedures that range from simple injections to major reconstruction.

    d. No change is necessary.

_____ 2. Choose the option that corrects the error in sentence 8.

    a. Age reduction generally requiring reconstructive surgery and a hospital stay. Tummy tucks, liposuction, eyelid surgery, and partial or full face-lifts are the most common and they can remove 10, 20, or 30 years.

    b. Age reduction generally requiring reconstructive surgery and a hospital stay, which include tummy tucks, liposuction, eyelid surgery, and partial or full face-lifts, are the most common. They can remove 10, 20, or 30 years.

    c. Age reduction, which includes tummy tucks, liposuction, eyelid surgery, and partial or full face-lifts, generally requires reconstructive surgery and a hospital stay. These surgeries can remove 10, 20, or 30 years.

    d. No change is necessary.

_____ 3. Choose the option that corrects the error in sentence 11.

    a. Delete sentence 11.

    b. Combine sentence 10 with sentence 11.

    c. Combine sentence 11 with sentence 12.

    d. No change is necessary.

4. Proofread the paragraph for an apostrophe error, and correct the error.

> **Writer's Response**
>
> Find two short sentences in your paragraph and combine them in two different ways. Using sentence variety can make your writing more interesting to read.

Searching and Correcting

Directions: *Exchange papers with a peer and proofread each other's work. In addition to spelling, punctuation, and capitalization, find out what other errors your classmate has made; tell your classmate what errors you often make.*

Self-Editing

Directions: *Carefully rewrite your paper, correcting the errors you and your classmate found. After setting aside the finished paper for a short time, come back to it and read your final draft once more, using the editing checklist on the inside back cover as a guide.*

REFLECT
- Identify strengths
- Set goals

Reflect

Take a moment and reflect on what you have learned about writing classification paragraphs.

Identifying Strengths and Setting Goals

Directions: *Review your writing and your writing process. Write answers to these questions:*

- *What did you do well in the classification paragraph you wrote?*
- *What did you enjoy working on in this chapter?*
- *What have you learned that you will apply in future classification writing assignments?*

As you answer these questions, think about your particular strengths and weaknesses. For your next writing assignment, you can focus on reaching your personal writing goals. When you read assignments for your classes, notice how often classification is used.

CHAPTER REVIEW

Recall what you have learned about classification writing.

- ■ CLASSIFICATION THINKING
  - *General to specific; complex to clear*
- ☐ Elements of classification
  - *Purpose, basis, categories, examples*
- ☐ Provide examples of categories
- ☐ Avoid stereotyping
- ■ CLASSIFICATION IN PROCESS
- ☐ Select an assignment
- ☐ Prewrite
  - *Brainstorm, cluster*
- ☐ Draft
  - *Focus, outline, organize*
- ☐ Revise
  - *Unity, coherence, critical reading, plan*
- ☐ Edit
  - *Peer and self-editing; checklists*
- ☐ Reflect
  - *Strengths and writing goals*

Cause and Effect

THINK FIRST

Poverty and homelessness are not simple problems. What are the causes and the effects? Write a paragraph in which you examine a cause or an effect of poverty or homelessness.

Targeting Cause, Gauging Effect

1. The king died, and then the queen died.

2. The king died, and then the queen died of grief.

The difference between these two sentences involves only two words but a whole world of meaning. Every day, we exercise a basic component of critical thinking: asking ourselves why something happened. If you like what happened—let's say, you managed to talk a police officer out of giving you a speeding ticket—you might ask yourself how you can get it to happen again, by examining the chain of cause and effect that led up to the event. Where were you driving? Exactly how fast were you going? Why were you speeding? What did you say to the officer when you were stopped? On the other hand, if you do not like what happened—let's say you got the ticket and a hefty fine—you will need to follow the chain of events back far enough so that you can keep it from happening again.

BRAINSTORM

Identify an important event in your life. Brainstorm the causes and the effects of it. List as many as you can.

Making Your Case in Class

You will often find yourself arguing about cause and effect in papers and in classroom discussion. Every statement you make about "what caused what" is, in fact, a claim and implies an argument. What were the causes of the 1917 Halifax explosion? Why do so few Canadians vote in elections? Why didn't the photocopy machine work? Why did the mixture of two chemicals form a noxious gas? Arguing convincingly for the cause (or causes) you think is (are) most relevant will make the difference between persuading your audience and leaving them doubting your conclusions.

DISCUSSION

Turn and talk with a classmate about a time when you explained the causes or effects of an event. Did you deal primarily with causes or effects? How do you know?

Working It Out

Cause and effect analysis is a skill you need in virtually any job. You may assemble data on consumer buying patterns or changes in the way you market a product. In the medical field, you may note physical symptoms carefully, consider the patient's history, and perform the necessary tests before making a proper judgment as to causes of a condition. Understanding causes or effects in analyzing a situation can make the difference between success and failure in your chosen career.

RESUMÉ BUILDER

Interviewers love to ask job applicants to talk about something they did that they are proud of. They also want to know what caused them to do it. What would your answer be in this situation?

At a Glance

THE CAUSE AND EFFECT PARAGRAPH AT A GLANCE

In cause and effect analysis, students use evidence to explain how or why something happened (causes) or the consequences (effects) of certain actions or events. For example, when asked to analyze the causes of a traffic accident, your knowledge about other accidents will help you identify the probable causes. You also might want to examine the facts, make diagrams of the accident scene, interview witnesses, and review the accident's effects in order to determine the actual cause or causes.

In a cause and effect paragraph, the topic sentence frequently states the problem or situation and the paragraph's focus. The supporting details provide examples, facts, or reasons to illustrate and explain the point of the topic sentence. The concluding sentence comments on the issue or emphasizes a key cause or effect related to it. Although essays might deal with both causes and effects of some event, to maintain unity, a paragraph usually focuses on only causes *or* effects.

There are three typical paragraph structures: one cause and one effect, multiple causes and one effect, and one cause followed by multiple effects. Some causes or effects can be described as chain events, i.e., the first cause or effect must happen before the second cause or effect, which leads to the third cause or effect, and so on.

ONE CAUSE & ONE EFFECT

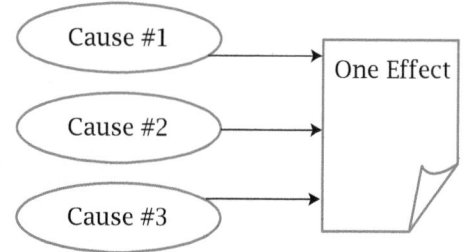

MULTIPLE CAUSES & ONE EFFECT

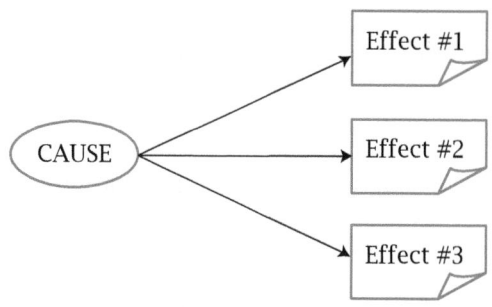

ONE CAUSE & MULTIPLE EFFECTS

ONE CAUSE & CHAIN OF EFFECTS

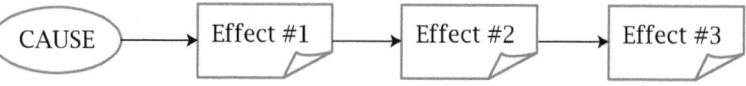

The Cause and Effect Paragraph at a Glance

ONE CAUSE, ONE EFFECT

ASSIGNMENT   Examine an environmental factor's cause and effect on learning.

TOPIC SENTENCE
The writer uses a key word from the assignment—"learning"—and states a specific environmental factor—"lead paint."

SUPPORTING DETAILS
The writer uses details about laws and studies to support his point.

ORDER AND TRANSITIONS
The writer's first transition ("Even though") suggests changes in laws have not corrected this problem. Then he uses two parallel transitions ("Studies show" and "Studies link") to repeat key words from the topic sentence.

CONCLUDING SENTENCE
The writer restates the topic sentence.

Studies show that lead absorption can reduce a young child's ability to learn. (1) **Even though** laws were passed in Canada in 2005 to ban lead use in paints, lead poisoning is still a major threat to young children who are exposed to consumer products manufactured with lead. In the past, lead paint has been the primary cause of lead poisoning in young children. For example, the paint used in housing built prior to 1960 and older school buildings contained potentially dangerous levels of lead. (2) **Studies show** children living in housing that is old and deteriorating are most susceptible to lead poisoning from the flaking paint, and children who play with toys containing lead are also exposed to unsafe amounts of lead. Children from birth to age five are the most likely to put objects in their mouths and, if they are contaminated with lead, this increases their risk for developing learning difficulties. (3) **Studies link** lead poisoning to children's reading difficulties and problems with attention. These problems have a singular effect: young children exposed to lead paint may sustain serious damage that affects their ability to learn.

ONE CAUSE, MULTIPLE EFFECTS

ASSIGNMENT   Write a cause and effect paragraph to illustrate the following quote: "If you think you can do a thing or think you can't do a thing, you're right."—*Henry Ford*

TOPIC SENTENCE
The student cites the quotation from the assignment.

SUPPORTING DETAILS
The details all relate to a single individual: multiple effects of can-do thinking in the life of a father.

ORDER AND TRANSITIONS
The student's repeated use of *think* makes connections between details in the paragraph. The term *also* contributes to the paragraph's coherence.

CONCLUDING SENTENCE
The student makes a connection with the assignment and reiterates that his father confirms the truth of Henry Ford's belief.

Henry Ford said, "If you think you can do a thing or think you can't do a thing, you're right." This statement, in my experience, is very true. My father is a good example. He **thinks** he can do something, and he is right. He proposed greatly expanding operations in his work. When he met with the district manager of the company he worked for, the manager asked: "Can you do this?" My father answered, "I **think** I can." The manager pressed him. "I don't want to know if you **think** you can. I want to know if you can do it." "I can do it," my father said, and he did it. He **also** thought he could tear the kitchen out of our house and install a brand-new one. He planned, he studied, and he drew diagrams. Then he ordered a custom-designed kitchen. When it was delivered to the house, he and I had already done the demolition of the old one. In a weekend, he installed the new kitchen, floor to ceiling. I thought he was crazy to attempt it, but he thought he could do it, and he was right. His can-do attitude causes him to attempt all sorts of things he might not do if he did not think he could. In my father's case, Henry Ford was definitely right.

MULTIPLE CAUSES, ONE EFFECT

ASSIGNMENT Examine the causes or effects of sibling rivalry.

Birth order, gender, and family dynamics can cause sibling rivalry. (1) **An unavoidable cause** of sibling fights is position in the family. For example, the eldest child is inevitably given more responsibility or freedom. Younger sisters or brothers may feel jealous, and a fight will break out, but no one is the winner in this fight. (2) **Another predictable cause** of sibling rivalry is gender. Parents may not notice that they expect boys to do outdoor chores and girls to do housecleaning. They may not see that their attitudes create stereotypical roles and problems between the siblings. (3) **Yet another common cause** of sibling rivalry is parents playing favourites. Parents may not even realize they treat the child who does his homework without whining in a special way. Consequently, parental favouritism causes tension and fights between the siblings. To a certain extent, sibling rivalry is probably an inevitable and normal condition in families with more than one child.

TOPIC SENTENCE
The writer focuses the topic sentence on one effect (sibling rivalry) and three causes.

SUPPORTING DETAILS
The writer explains three causes of sibling rivalry: position in the family, gender, and favouritism.

ORDER AND TRANSITIONS
The writer lists the three causes. The transitions identify each cause.

CONCLUDING SENTENCE
The writer comments on sibling rivalry.

DISCUSSION QUESTIONS

1. These three paragraphs illustrate cause and effect thinking. What situations, problems, or issues in your life came to mind when you were reading them?

2. Discuss an issue you recall with a classmate. Is it an example of one cause and one effect, one cause and multiple effects, or multiple causes and one effect?

Thinking
CAUSE AND EFFECT THINKING

Cause and effect analysis begins with a situation, problem, or event. The car will not start. Your co-worker gets a raise that you expected to get. You are not working up to your potential in school. The doctor tells your mother that her cholesterol is too high. These situations have causes. They also have effects that are the result of the causes. In addition, these effects can have further consequences. It's important to look beyond the obvious causes or effects and delve into hidden or secondary causes.

The complex relationship of causes and effects can be pictured in this diagram. The pollution in a nearby lake has specific causes; further, there are consequences of the effects of the pollution.

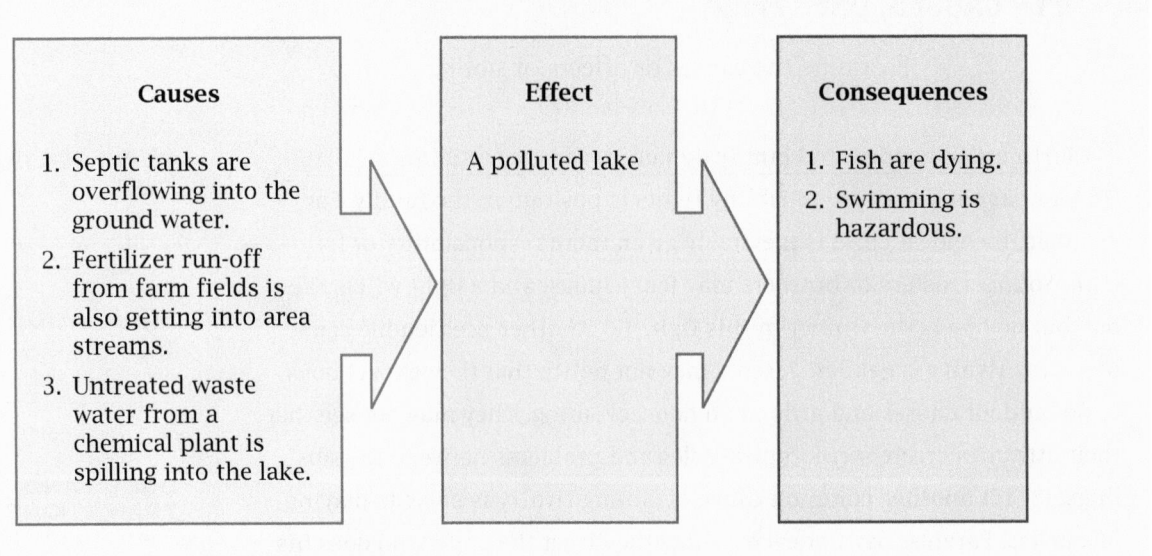

Elements of Cause and Effect

To get started, consider these elements of cause and effect thinking.

- *Problem, situation, or event:* The topic sentence states the problem, situation, or event and establishes the paragraph's focus. A paragraph usually focuses on either cause or effect, not both.

- *Causes:* Causes are the reasons, circumstances, or conditions that bring about a problem or situation. Supporting details for a paragraph focusing on causes examine and explain these reasons, circumstances, or conditions. For example, lead paint causes learning problems in children. How does this happen? Supporting details elaborate on the cause.

- *Effects:* Effects are the outcomes or consequences of a problem or situation. A paragraph's supporting details focusing on effects should examine and explain these outcomes or consequences. Sibling rivalry, for example, is the effect or result of various family dynamics.

Get Started

Time is an important aspect of cause and effect thinking. Causes occur prior to a situation, problem, or event; effects occur afterward. In the illustration shown here, a student uses a graphic organizer to analyze her situation in a math class.

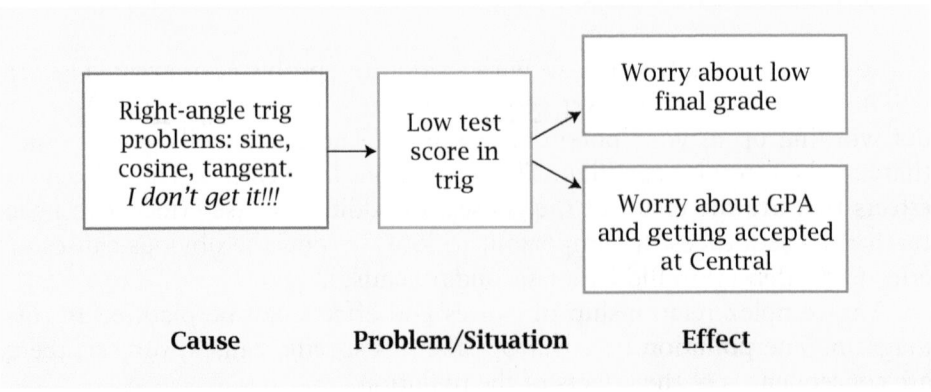

The diagram provides a snapshot of a problem the student faces. The immediate situation is a low test score. She has diagnosed the cause of the problem: she is having trouble with right-angle trig problems. She has also identified two effects of the problem: that her final grade in the class may suffer because of the low test score and, as a result of a lower average, she might not get accepted into the post-secondary institute of her choice.

Cause and effect analysis like this invites critical thinking. In her next move, the student can decide to examine either the cause or the effects of the problem in more detail. The decision she makes focuses her thinking further and determines her paragraph's content.

> **Topic Sentence:** Because of my low grade on the most recent math test, my final grade in the course could be a C, and that may affect my application to Central.

EXERCISE 9-1 Getting Started

Directions: *Use a graphic organizer to analyze two of the following situations. (Use the student sample above as a model.) Indicate multiple causes and multiple effects as needed. Beneath the graphic organizer, write a topic sentence indicating your decision to focus on the cause(s) or effect(s).*

- *Satisfaction (or dissatisfaction) with your current job*
- *Progress (or lack of progress) toward your career goal*
- *Success (or difficulty) you are currently having in a course*

Cause and Effect Details

For the sake of unity and focus, it is usually best to focus on either causes or effects. Being clear about your focus helps you think systematically about the situation or problem you have chosen as your topic. To identify relevant details, you need to carefully analyze the problem.

In this diagram, the student having trouble in her math class focuses on the reasons, circumstances, and conditions that brought about her low test score.

Notice that these details are in the past tense. They focus on circumstances and

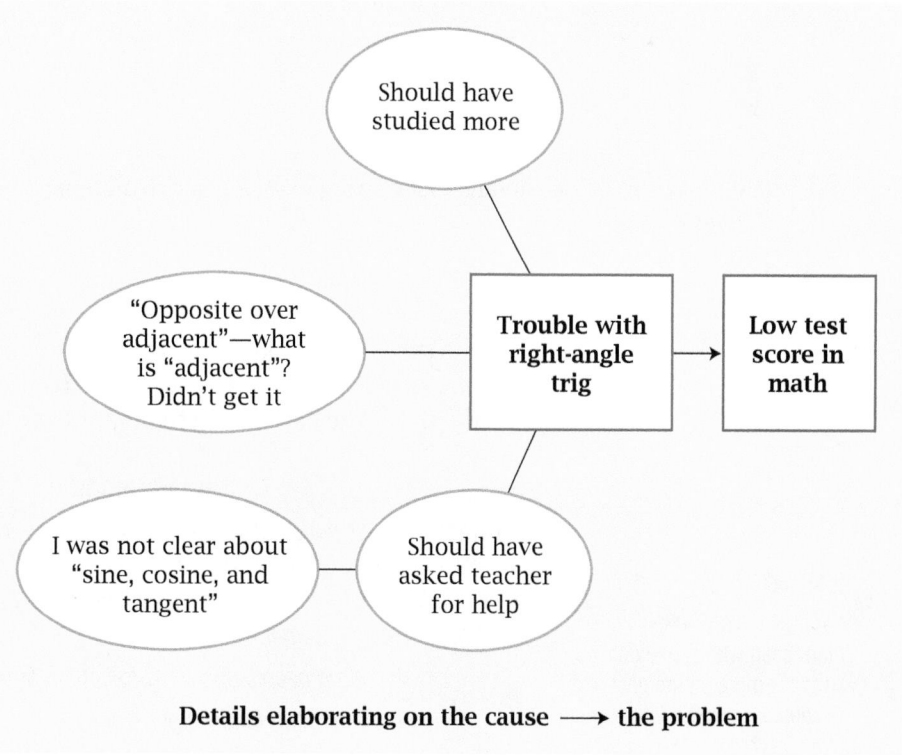

Details elaborating on the cause ⟶ the problem

conditions that preceded the student's poor performance on her test. The analysis is valuable to the student because she can now address the causes and possibly rectify the problem.

If this student decided to focus on effects, she would elaborate on the problem's consequences.

When the student elaborates on effects, the emphasis is more on what happens next. The verbs would usually be in present or future tenses.

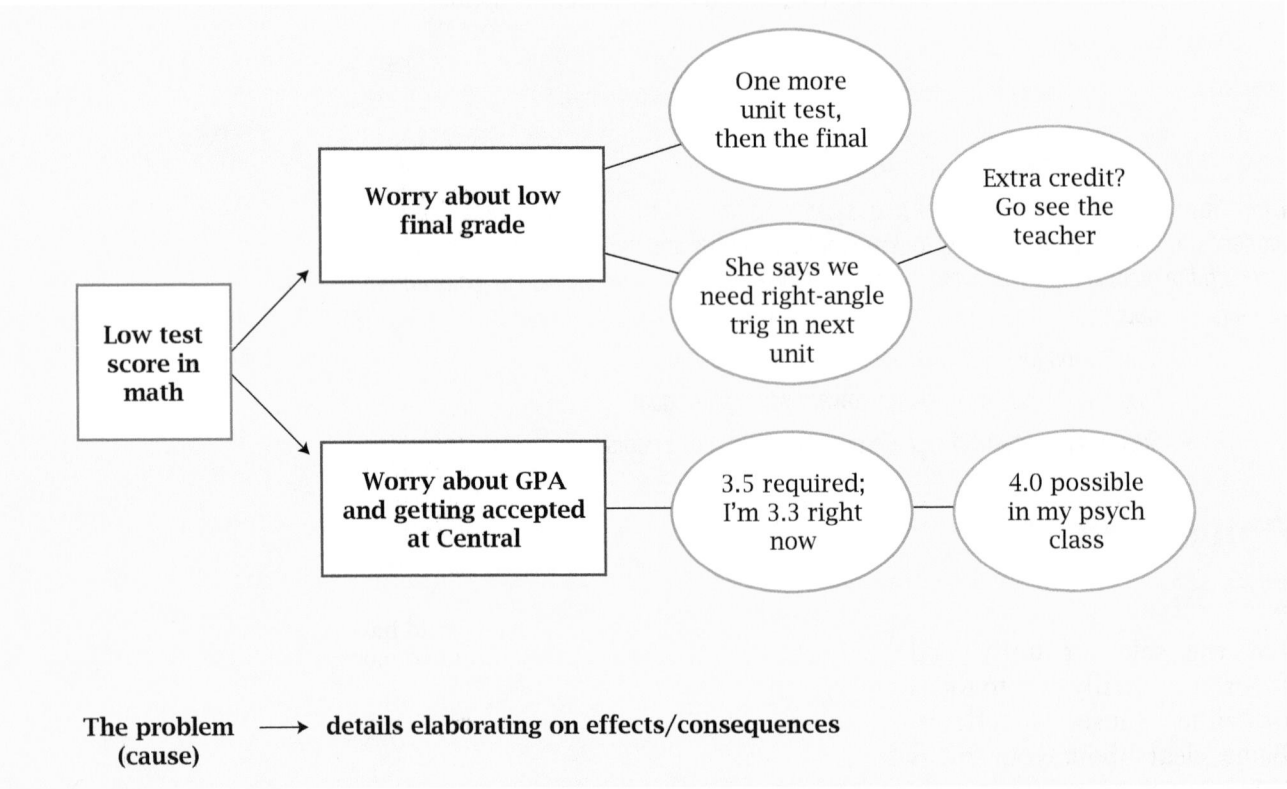

The problem   ⟶   details elaborating on effects/consequences
(cause)

After your initial reflection on your topic in cause and effect analysis, focus on either causes or effects. To keep unity in your paragraph, write only about the causes or effects, not both.

EXERCISE 9-2   **Getting Focused on Causes or Effects**

Directions: *Use a graphic organizer to examine either causes or effects related to one of the following topics. Look for supporting details that explain the reasons, circumstances, or conditions that led up to the problem (causes) or that illustrate the outcomes and consequences (effects) resulting from it.*

- *Young people spending too much time texting on their cellphones*
- *A recurring family argument*
- *A bad habit*

Talk about it

When faced with a challenge, do you focus more on the past and the causes or on the future and the effects?

Organize Your Thinking

How you organize your cause and effect thinking may be influenced by either the importance of the events or when they happened (time). All cause and effect details are not necessarily equal. Consequently, you may organize your thinking by proceeding from the least important to the most important detail. On the other hand, multiple causes or effects might not occur simultaneously, in which case it makes sense to organize them according to when they happened. In this illustration, the student uses order of importance to organize her details. You may notice that you will need to use clear descriptions to identify how one event leads to the other.

Low Test Score in Math

Cause

  3   "Opposite over adjacent"—what does that mean?

  4   Not clear about what sine, cosine, and tangent are

  2   Should have asked instructor for help

  1   Should have studied more

Notes: It makes sense to organize my details by order of importance. First of all, I should have studied more. I knew I was not "getting" the problems in right-angle trig, but I did not apply myself. Second, and even more important, in addition to studying, I should have gone to see the instructor right away. I knew what the problem areas were—I did not get "opposite over adjacent" or exactly what sine, cosine, and tangent are. How can I figure out answers to questions when I do not even know what the terms mean?

The student's notes reflect her thinking as she fits the pieces together in her analysis of the causes of her low grade. Here is the same student's analysis of the effects of receiving a low test grade. In this instance, she relies on chronological order.

Effects

  1   Worry about low final grade

    C   One more unit test, then the final

    B   She says we need right-angle trig for next unit

    A   Go see instructor about extra credit

  2   Worry about GPA and getting accepted at Central

    A   3.5 required; I am 3.3 right now

Notes: It makes sense to order these details chronologically. The short-term consequence of doing poorly on the test is that I might get a low grade in the class. The long-term effect is that I might not get into Central. I need to go see the instructor. I do not understand right-angle trig. She said everything we do after this involves right-angle trig so I need to know that. If I ace the next unit test and do really well on the final, maybe I can do well in the class and keep my GPA where I want it.

Organizing Your Details

Directions: *The following topic has multiple possible causes and effects. In the spaces provided, indicate how you would organize these details. Write a short paragraph explaining whether you used order of importance or chronological order and the reasons for your choice.*

Topic: Bullying in school

Causes

_____ Not conforming to groups

_____ Peer pressure

_____ Influence of certain students

_____ Hard for school administrators to detect

_____ No culture of respect

_____ Pressure tactics at school or in cyberspace

_____ Relationships in the home

_____ Anti-social behaviour

_____ Self-esteem issues

Form of organization: _____

_____

Effects

_____ Social isolation

_____ Social exclusion

_____ Depression

_____ Loss of concentration in school

_____ Lack of effort in friendships

_____ Need for increased involvement of parents and teachers

_____ Desire to skip school or certain classes where bullies are

_____ Physical and emotional health problems

Form of organization: _____

_____

> **Writer's Response**
>
> What are some causes and effects of bullying in your school or at your workplace?

Process

CAUSE AND EFFECT IN PROCESS

As previously mentioned, you analyze an idea, event, or problem with cause and effect writing. A focused, organized paragraph helps your reader understand your topic's complexities. To make your points clear and simple, provide detailed explanations of causes and effects.

Select an Assignment

When asked to write about causes and effects in college or university, you will often analyze ideas, events, or problems to determine a focus for your paragraph. This may require research or outside reading. Keep track of the sources of your information as academic writing requires that you list where your ideas come from. More about citation and referencing can be found in Chapter 16.

EXERCISE 9-4 **Selecting an Assignment for a Cause and Effect Paragraph**

Directions: *Choose from one of the topics below as a topic for a cause or effect paragraph.*

1. Explain the impact of a scientific or technological development on education, health, or daily life.

2. Describe the effect of a strong Canadian dollar on the Canadian economy.

3. Provide advantages of having GPS systems in automobiles or on cellphones.

4. Explain the negative effects of posting too much personal information on social networking sites.

5. Relate the effects of consenting to an organ donation.

6. Explain how miscommunication can lead to a problem between an instructor and a student.

7. Give the consequences of refusing to allow genetically modified crops to be planted.

8. Explain why post-secondary institutions are vigilant about plagiarism.

9. Explain the consequences of building more gambling casinos as tourist destinations.

10. What are some of the most common causes of anxiety in students?

Prewrite: Write Before You Write

PREWRITE
- Talk
- Think
- Cluster
- Brainstorm
- Question
- Freewrite

To reduce your topic to manageable terms, allow yourself to explore your subject before you write. Careful analysis involves thinking and rethinking. You may find it productive to cluster and talk in order to organize and focus your topic. Clustering enables you to see how ideas and details connect and relate to one another. You can use clustering to think about the sequence of causes and effects in a particular situation. You may also wish to freewrite or brainstorm examples, reasons, and facts that explain and illustrate the subject's causes and effects.

EXERCISE 9-5   Clustering and Talking about It

Directions: *First, cluster on your assignment for a few minutes. List as many causes and effects as you can. Next, turn to your neighbour in class and show this person your clustering work and talk about the causes or effects you have analyzed related to your topic. Be specific about important information. Include examples, facts, and reasons. Then be a critical listener of your neighbour's topic. Listen without interrupting. When the speaker finishes, ask questions or offer suggestions. Identify to each other what was clear and what was not clear. When you combine talking with clustering, you take your thinking deeper. Capture your new ideas on paper after you finish talking.*

Draft: Focus and Organize

DRAFT
- Consider your audience
- Formulate your topic sentence
- Outline for unity and coherence
- Write a concluding sentence
- Compose your first draft

In cause and effect thinking, you must be clear about your focus. Are you talking mainly about causes or effects? For example, a storm came through town and downed power lines. The cause of no power is obvious and simple. What if you focused on the storm's effects? As you prepare to write, be clear about your focus.

CONSIDER YOUR AUDIENCE

Read the assignment again and think about who will read your paper. Your instructor is interested in analytical thinking. Use the following questions to consider how to focus your paragraph on causes or effects and how you will support your thinking for your audience.

- What does my reader expect of my paragraph?
- Is my paragraph about causes or effects?
- What do I want a reader to understand about my topic?

Then ask these questions:

- What supporting details do I have to develop my ideas?
- Why are these supporting details important? Do I need to explain any of them to my reader?

EXERCISE 9-6   Considering Your Audience

Directions: *Use the questions above to think critically about your focus and the supporting details you will use to explain your analysis in your paragraph. Talk with a classmate to clarify your focus, examples, facts, and reasons. Take notes on this conversation and add them to your prewriting.*

FORMULATE YOUR TOPIC SENTENCE

Students often revise and refine their topic sentences as they work through the writing process. In cause and effect writing, your topic sentence controls the rest of the paragraph. Be sure you clearly state whether the paragraph will deal with causes or effects; you can even alert the reader to exactly what you are analyzing. Some paragraphs may require a second sentence that explains the topic or hooks a reader with an interesting fact.

OUTLINE FOR UNITY AND COHERENCE

Is your paragraph primarily about causes or effects? To write a unified paragraph, focus on one or the other and include relevant details. Transitions between details will link sentences, making your paragraph coherent.

Cause and effect paragraphs are typically organized using transitions based on causes or effects. These transitions act as markers to alert readers of the connection between the event and the cause or effect the writer is discussing. Additionally, writers use transition terms so readers can easily shift their attention to the next cause or effect in the paragraph.

In some cases, however, you may want to use transitions based on importance or chronological order.

TRANSITIONS RELATED TO CAUSES AND EFFECTS

Causes

the first (second, third) cause	the first (second, third) reason
yet another factor	because
is caused by	results from

Effects

one important effect	a first (second, third) outcome
then	next
therefore	thus
so	however
consequently	as a result
hence	therefore

TRANSITIONS BASED ON IMPORTANCE OR CHRONOLOGICAL ORDER

To Show Importance

more important	equally important	better
worse	in particular	specifically
of course	certainly	in fact

To Show Chronological Order

to begin with	first of all	next
second	in addition	moreover
then	third	finally

WRITE A CONCLUDING SENTENCE

A concluding sentence comments on the idea, event, or problem after you have analyzed it. It also restates the causes or effects related to your analysis. You may find this easier to do after you reread your first draft.

WRITE A FIRST DRAFT

Next, review your prewriting and check your outline. Then write a first draft of your paragraph. Writers often reconsider the order of what they have written and the transition terms they use; they add additional examples, facts, or reasons. Look for the details that seem most important for readers to notice so they can understand your purpose.

EXERCISE 9-7 **Planning and Writing Your First Draft**

Directions: *First, write a topic sentence that echoes the key words from the assignment topic you selected and focuses your paragraph on causes or effects. Then organize and outline your paragraph and supporting details. Write a concluding sentence that comments on your cause or effect paragraph. See "Supporting Details" in Chapter 3 for detailed explanation of outlining.*

Now, write a first draft of your paragraph. Then use the first draft checklist on the inside back cover as a guide to make sure you have included all the elements of cause and effect writing.

A PROFESSIONAL'S TAKE

Here is Laurence Steinberg's use of cause and effect, from a short article in *Psychology Today:*

My own studies point to early adolescence—the years from ten to thirteen—as a period of special strain between parents and children. But more intriguing, perhaps, is that these studies reveal that puberty plays a central role in triggering parent-adolescent conflict. Specifically, as youngsters develop toward physical maturity, bickering and squabbling with parents increase. If puberty comes early, so does the arguing and bickering; if it is late, the period of heightened tension is delayed. Although many other aspects of adolescent behavior reflect the intertwined influences of biological and social factors, this aspect seems to be directly connected to the biological event of puberty; something about normal physical maturing sets off parent-adolescent fighting. It's no surprise that they argue about overflowing trash cans, trails of dirty laundry, and blaring stereos. But why should teenagers going through puberty fight with their parents more often than youngsters of the same age whose physical development is slower? More to the point, if puberty is inevitable, does this mean that parent-child conflict is, too?

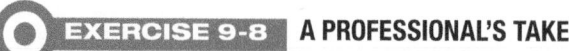

Directions: *Using the first draft checklist from the inside back cover as your guide, identify the effectiveness of the elements of the cause and effect paragraph in A Professional's Take. Next, compare the elements the author used with the ones that you used in your first draft. Did you include clear transitions to identify the causes and effects in your paragraph?*

Revise: Read Critically, then Rewrite

Revision means rethinking. Ask yourself a few questions as you reread your first draft. Is your problem, situation, or event clearly stated? Is your focus on causes or effects? Are you explaining either a combination of causes, or the effects and impact on people or situations? Revision gives you a chance to read critically and then cut, reorder, or clarify the information in your paragraph.

> **REVISE**
> - Read critically
> - Develop a revision plan

REVISION IN ACTION

Revision is rethinking a draft through a series of actions and decisions to improve the quality of your writing: read critically, plan revision, and revise the writing. Here is an example of revision by a student named Roberto.

> **Assignment:** Write a cause or effect paragraph that explains how people can get into debt.

Roberto's First Draft

Three problems can cause unmanageable debt. Possibly, **the most difficult problem** to face is losing a job. This situation changes people's lifestyle. With a steady job and paycheque, people are sure they can make the mortgage, car, and living expenses. They might have a budget, but they always have extra money to spend. Life is easier when people have a steady job. Without a job they struggle to pay the bills, and they start paying for rent, groceries, and utilities with credit cards. This leads to growing debt. Sometimes this debt might even keep people from getting another job because an employer will see they have bad credit. **However, the most common problem** is spending habits. It is simple: people spend more money than they make. People spend money because they are bored or they are trying to keep up with friends who have more money. Credit cards make money easy to spend until people hit their limit and cannot pay their monthly bills. This problem leads to increasing debt. Debt like this can cause depression and then more spending until the debt is unmanageable. **Finally, another problem** is gambling. Gambling is a bad habit that leaves many people in extreme debt. Gamblers believe they will win the next time. So they spend their paycheques and then get cash advances in the hopes of winning back the lost paycheque. In the end, they lose everything. Although they can pay off credit cards with minimum payments,

TOPIC SENTENCE
Roberto focuses his paragraph on three problems.

SUPPORTING DETAILS
He provides details on each problem. His details explain how each problem causes unmanageable debt.

CONCLUDING SENTENCE
Roberto restates the topic sentence, including the key term "causes."

they still owe money for years to come. Plus, gamblers must always fight the hope that they might win it all back. <u>These are a few causes of unmanageable debt that should be avoided.</u>

Revision Plan: Narrow my topic to focus only on credit card debt. I'll focus my paragraph so a reader can understand the causes of unmanageable credit card debt. Cut irrelevant details and insert specific, relevant details. Focus on causes and state the effect in the topic sentence.

TOPIC SENTENCE
Roberto uses key words from the assignment and clearly states the effect (unmanageable credit card debt) as well as the three causes he will explain in his paragraph. *Notice the use of parallelism in this topic sentence.*

SUPPORTING DETAILS
Roberto does not discuss effects in his revision. Instead, Roberto includes facts about credit card debt to explain the causes.

ORDER AND TRANSITIONS
Roberto uses transitions based on importance or priority. He begins with the most significant cause but ends with the most damaging cause.

CONCLUDING SENTENCE
He comments on the effects of credit cards.

Roberto's Revised Draft

<u>Unmanageable credit card debt has three causes: overspending, misusing credit, and carrying debt on the card.</u> Probably, the **most significant cause** is overspending. People can use plastic to buy anything they want, even if they do not have the money to pay for it. Credit card companies suggest that easy credit causes people to spend 12 to 18 percent more on purchases than they would if they paid cash. **However**, misusing credit causes as much debt as overspending. Many people use credit to pay for emergencies or special purchases. This debt can be paid off quickly. The trouble starts when people use credit to pay for basic needs like groceries, medical expenses, rent, or utilities. **The most damaging cause** is carrying credit card debt. With 14 to 18 percent interest on the unpaid balance, it can take years to pay off the outstanding balance. Plus, the interest will cost more than the original charge. <u>These days credit cards make purchases easy, but using them requires self-control and money management skills; otherwise, major debt is a likely outcome.</u>

DISCUSSION QUESTIONS Which changes did Roberto make in his revision that most radically improved his paragraph? Why?

READ CRITICALLY

Critical reading is a search for the characteristics of effective writing: topic sentence, supporting details, transitions, concluding sentence. It is also a search for clarity of purpose.

EXERCISE 9-9 **Reading Peer Papers**

Directions: *Exchange papers with another student. Consider the significant changes that Roberto made between his first draft and his revision. Be a critical reader and note if the* *writer focuses on causes or effects, but not both. Then make suggestions to improve your peer's first draft. Also, identify what your classmate did well. Make notes in the margin as you read. After you read, discuss your suggestions with each other. Use the guidelines from the revision checklist at the back of the text.*

REVISE WITH A PLAN

Reread the instructions from your assignment before revising. Some assignments may require you to focus on causes, while others may require a focus on effects. Be sure your focus matches the assignment. In addition, simplify your paragraph: narrow your topic and cut irrelevant details.

Cause and effect paragraphs are complex. This can cause a writer to include more information than is necessary. Reread your paragraph and the notes from your peer conference. Where can you narrow the focus or cut out irrelevant details? After you cut, where do you need to add relevant details?

EXERCISE 9-10 **Revising Your Draft**

Directions: *Develop a revision plan and revise the paragraph you wrote for Exercise 9-7.*

Edit

To ensure your cause or effect paragraph is clearly written and grammatically correct, after your revisions, you will need to edit your work. Focus your editing using the editing checklist at the back of the text. Also, check that your work reflects a focus on an academic audience by using academic vocabulary and third person.

> **EDIT**
> • Search and correct
> • Self-edit

EXERCISE 9-11 **Revising and Editing Practice**

Directions: *Read the following paragraph that was written in response to the assignment below; it contains errors that require revising and editing. Then answer the questions that follow.*

Assignment: Write a paragraph to examine the causes and effects of technology on the ways people meet, date, or communicate.

(1) Since 1993 Internet communication has created opportunities and problems. (2) Today, Facebook is one of the hottest sites online to meet young people; however, it is also a supermarket for predators. (3) Young people flock to the site, posting photos and real personal information and search for new friends. (4) However, a predator can also simply search, click, and connect to a young victim. (5) Why is it so easy? (6) First, Facebook does not require verification of a persons identity. (7) This makes the online Community open to a wide range of users. (8) Unfortunately, users can create a fake identity, age, address, email, and photograph. (9)_____, predators can exchange messages with complete anonymity. (10)_____, these Web sites cannot legally kick registered sex offenders off the sites. (11) Moreover, if social networking Web sites tried to remove registered sex offenders, they could only remove the ones

that provide a real name. (12) Last, even if Facebook removed sex offenders, they can go to a dozen other sites like YouTube or Twitter, so the problem is not really solved. (13) eBay had similar problems with fraud when it first started. (14) Obviously, the problem will not be resolved by sites, therefore, Internet users must use caution when communicating online.

REVISING

_____ 1. Which sentence(s) should be deleted to focus the topic sentence and the opening of this paragraph?

   a. 1   c. 1 and 5

   b. 1 and 4   d. No change is necessary.

_____ 2. Which word or phrase should be inserted in blank 9? The word or phrase would serve as the best transition between the specific details the writer is using to support his point.

   a. Next   c. In addition

   b. As a result   d. In fact

_____ 3. Which word or phrase should be inserted in blank 10? The word or phrase would serve as the best transition between the writer's major points in the paragraph.

   a. Second   c. In addition

   b. As a result   d. Unfortunately

_____ 4. Which sentence should be cut to improve the focus of the paragraph?

   a. Sentence 9   c. Sentence 13

   b. Sentence 11   d. No change is necessary.

EDITING

_____ 1. Choose the option that corrects the error in sentence 3.

   a. Young people flock to the site, posting photos and very personal information and searching for new friends.

   b. Young people flock to the site, posting photos and real personal information and search for new friends.

   c. Young people flock to the site and post photos and real personal information and search for new friends.

   d. No change is necessary.

_____ 2. Choose the option that corrects the error in sentence 6.

   a. First Facebook does not require verification of a persons' identity.

   b. First, Facebook does not require verification of a person's identity.

c. First, Facebook doesn't require verification of a persons identity.

d. No change is necessary.

_____ 3. Choose the option that corrects the capitalization error in sentence 7.

a. Online Community

b. online community

c. Online community

d. No change is necessary.

_____ 4. Proofread the paragraph for a comma splice error and correct the error.

EXERCISE 9-12 **Searching and Correcting**

Directions: *Exchange papers with a proofreading peer and proofread each other's work. In addition to spelling, punctuation, and capitalization, determine what other errors your classmate made; tell your classmate what errors you often make.*

EXERCISE 9-13 **Self-Editing**

Directions: *Carefully rewrite your paper, correcting errors you and your classmate found. Set aside the finished paper for a short time, then come back to it and read your final draft one last time, using the editing checklist on the inside back cover as a guide.*

Reflect

Take a moment and reflect on what you have learned about writing cause and effect paragraphs.

EXERCISE 9-14 **Identifying Strengths and Setting Goals**

Directions: *Review your writing and your writing process. Then, write answers to these questions:*

- *What did you do well in the paragraph you wrote?*
- *What did you enjoy working on in this chapter?*
- *What have you learned about cause and effect that you will apply in future writing assignments?*

As you answer these questions, think about your particular strengths and weaknesses. For your next writing assignment, you can focus on reaching your personal writing goals.

REFLECT
- Identify strengths
- Set goals

CHAPTER REVIEW

Recall what you have learned about the cause and effect paragraph.

■ CAUSE AND EFFECT THINKING

☐ Elements of cause and effect
- *Problem, situation, or event: causes and effects*

☐ Cause and effect details
- *Reasons, circumstances, or conditions (causes); explanations of outcomes or consequences (effects)*

☐ Organize your thinking
- *Order of importance or chronological order*

■ CAUSE AND EFFECT IN PROCESS

☐ Select an assignment
- *Research to determine a focus*

☐ Prewrite
- *Cluster, talk*

☐ Draft
- *Focus, organize; consider the reader*

☐ Revise
- *Unity, coherence, transitions*

☐ Edit
- *Critical reading; peer and self-editing; checklists*

☐ Reflect
- *Strengths and writing goals*

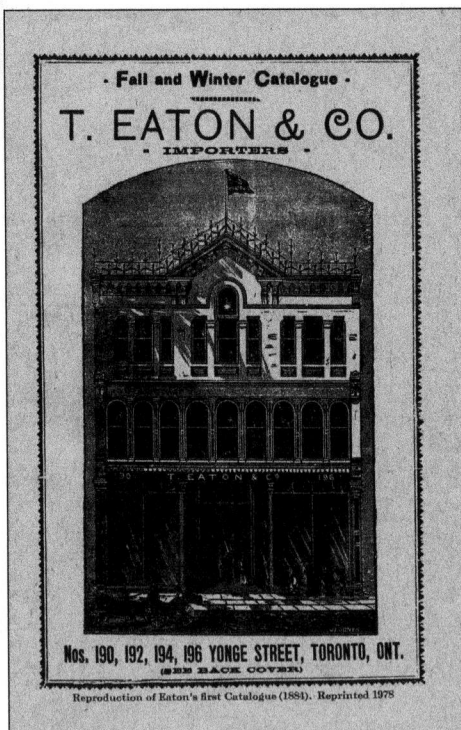

THINK FIRST

Write a paragraph describing how these two photographs offer options of how people have been able to shop from home. Focus on how shopping online is alike or different from shopping from a catalogue.

Making Daily Decisions

Think about the last time you made a purchase—say you were looking for running shoes. In order to decide what to buy, you almost certainly compared different brands according to the qualities that were important to you—for example, sole construction, support and cushioning, ventilation, price, and looks. You looked to see how various brands were similar or if one pair had a feature that the other did not. You did this more or less automatically, without thinking explicitly about choosing the criteria.

What is the value of learning about comparison and contrast? It is important to become fully conscious of what you are doing when you compare and contrast things in order to apply these same skills to more complicated situations. Imagine that you are trying to persuade someone to see one movie over another. To do this effectively, you have to be aware of the criteria that matter to that other person and present the two movies accordingly.

BRAINSTORM

Choose a movie that you have seen and really liked. Then brainstorm a list of other movies that are similar. What elements or qualities do they have that make them similar?

On the Other Hand . . .

Comparing or contrasting for a particular purpose is an important aspect of critical thinking and of writing. You might draft a proposal for a solution to a social problem like homelessness and present two alternatives (one of which you favour), or you might present two methods of performing an experiment, explaining why you chose one over the other. In order to make the best case for your position, you will need to have relevant information to make fair comparisons or contrasts.

DISCUSSION

Talk with a classmate to answer the following questions: What is your favourite course? What is your least favourite course? Compare and contrast these two courses. What makes your responses to these courses different?

Which One Would You Choose?

If you are involved in purchasing anything for your business—from office supplies to next season's clothing—you are required to choose from among a number of options, and you have to base your decision on specific criteria, such as cost, quality, availability, and variety. Comparison and contrast are not just useful for buying things, of course. A mechanic compares different repair jobs in order to prioritize them, while a dental assistant compares a patient's X-rays between visits to determine whether treatment is required. The more practice you have in comparing and contrasting effectively, the better you will be at your job. Knowing how to use comparison/contrast writing will enable you to justify decisions you reach.

RESUMÉ BUILDER

Think about a job you want. To prepare for an interview, you might think about the similarities and differences between your current job and one you want. What skills do you need to change jobs? List two or three. What skills do you currently use that you might also apply in your new job? List specific skills that are similar in both jobs.

Comparison and contrast analysis begins when you have to make a decision about two situations, ideas, or objects. An effective paragraph can compare two things that have something in common. You use contrast for two things that appear similar but that, in your opinion, have important differences. For example, you want a job, but you cannot decide which one will provide the best opportunities. You would compare what the two jobs have in common, but use contrast to show where the two jobs are different. To think critically, make lists of points to consider as the criteria to use in your analysis. In the job example, your points might include commuting time to get to work, benefits available to you, and potential for advancement.

For a paragraph, you would select three points from a list you make, and use these points to examine the common and contrasting characteristics between the two situations, ideas, or objects. You must give equal consideration to each alternative using the points of comparison or contrast you selected. You cannot just describe one alternative and merely state that the other is "different" or "similar." You must show that you are giving equal consideration to both, using the same evaluative criteria. Based on your analysis, you can then reach a decision.

In comparison and contrast paragraphs, the topic sentence states the two alternatives to be compared or contrasted and the writer's position on the similarities or differences. The supporting details provide specific examples, reasons, or details to explain the points of similarity or difference. These details are examined in a balanced way with both of the items that are being compared or being contrasted. A final sentence not only restates the criteria for the points of comparison or contrast, but also draws a conclusion or makes a comment about one of the items over the other.

Comparison and contrast paragraphs can be structured in two ways. The first is subject by subject, or the block method, and the second is the point-by-point method. In **subject-by-subject organization**, you take turns focusing on each subject, including all the points about one subject and then discussing all the points about the other subject in the same order as the first one. In **point-by-point organization**, you focus the discussion on each point. First, you state a point and then include details about both of the items being compared or contrasted. You proceed through the other points in the same way.

You may wonder what the difference is between comparison and contrast writing. Generally, since a paragraph is a relatively short piece of writing, you **compare** two items or issues that at first appear to be quite different in order to show what they may have in common. You would **contrast** two items that initially appear quite similar to uncover what is unique about each. For a paragraph assignment, you would probably decide to compare *or* contrast the two alternatives, rather than compare *and* contrast.

However, you could also list several points that two items have in common and one point where there is an important, but decisive, difference between the two.

For a longer assignment, such as an essay, you could develop your analysis in multiple paragraphs and compare the items in one paragraph and contrast them in another. Take care not to be confused since sometimes people will talk about only "comparing" two items when they really mean comparing/contrasting them.

Ask Yourself

What factors do you consider when you compare two courses or two co-workers?

The Comparison/Contrast Paragraph at a Glance

BLOCK METHOD: SUBJECT-BY-SUBJECT ORGANIZATION

ASSIGNMENT Compare or contrast two approaches to a recreational activity and show why one approach is superior. Making an outline will help you organize your ideas.

Subject by Subject

Topic Sentence: Pools have advantages that lakes cannot provide.

First—Subject A: Pools

    Point 1: Accommodations

    Point 2: Recreational options

    Point 3: Water quality

Next—Subject B: Lakes

    Point 1: Accommodations

    Point 2: Recreational options

    Point 3: Water quality

(Subject A) Pools have advantages that lakes cannot provide. (Point 1) **For one thing**, the *accommodations* are almost always more comfortable at a pool. Pool-goers walk on a cement deck. **Moreover**, the pool supplies comfortable chairs, tables, and umbrellas. Nearby, a snack bar offers convenient access to drinks and accessories such as tanning lotion or batteries. (Point 2) **An added** benefit is the *recreational options*. Pools almost always have diving boards, slides, and fountains. There is often a hot tub as well. (Point 3) **Most importantly**, the water quality is predictable. At a well-run facility, the water is usually very clean. There are no leaves floating on the surface and no bacteria waiting to infect the swimmer. (Subject B) **On the other hand, consider a lake.** (Point 1) **First**, the *accommodations* are natural. There are sand, waves, and sun. Beach-goers lie on towels in the sand. The wind blows sand in their faces. Snack bars are not within walking distance or even on the beach itself. (Point 2) **In addition**,

TOPIC SENTENCE
The writer states his purpose: to show that pools have advantages. He will contrast pools and lakes to do this.

CONTRAST POINTS
The writer contrasts a pool and a beach by focusing on three points of contrast: accommodations, recreational options, and water quality.

ORDER AND TRANSITIONS
The writer discusses the three points in connection to pools, using transition terms to list and state importance. When he shifts to the discussion of lakes, he uses a transition showing contrast ("on the other hand"). He uses transition terms to list the same three points.

waves are the only *recreational option.* (Point 3) **Lastly**, because a lake is natural, the *water quality* is unpredictable. Swimmers might find dead fish floating next to them. A hot summer day can increase growth of bacteria in the water, so swimming there is actually a health hazard. <u>Unless you are a nature-lover or a risk-taker, a pool offers a relaxing day in the sun without health hazards.</u>

POINT-BY-POINT ORGANIZATION

ASSIGNMENT   Compare or contrast two approaches to a recreational activity and show why one approach is superior.

Point by Point

Topic Sentence: Pools have advantages that lakes cannot provide.

First—Point 1: Accommodations

> Subject A: Pools
>
> Subject B: Lakes

Second—Point 2: Recreational options

> Subject A: Pools
>
> Subject B: Lakes

Next—Point 3: Water quality

> Subject A: Pools
>
> Subject B: Lakes

<u>Pools have advantages that lakes cannot provide.</u> (Point 1, Subject A) **For one thing**, the *accommodations* are almost always more comfortable at a pool. Pool-goers walk on a cement deck. **Moreover**, the pool supplies comfortable chairs, tables, and umbrellas. Nearby, a snack bar offers convenient access to drinks and accessories such as tanning lotion or batteries. (Point 1, Subject B) **On the other hand, consider a lake. First**, the *accommodations* are natural. There are sand, waves, and sun. Beach-goers lie on towels in the sand. The wind blows sand in their faces. Snack bars are not within walking distance or even on the beach itself. (Point 2, Subject A) **An added** benefit with pools is the *recreational options.* Pools almost always have diving boards, slides, and fountains. There is often a hot tub as well. (Point 2, Subject B) **In contrast**, at a lake, waves are the only *recreational option.* (Point 3, Subject A) **Most importantly**, the water quality in a pool is predictable. At a well-run facility, the water is usually very clean. There are no leaves floating on the surface and no bacteria waiting to infect the swimmer. (Point 3, Subject B) **However**, because a lake is natural, the *water quality* is unpredictable. Swimmers might find dead fish floating next to them. A hot summer day can increase growth of bacteria in the water, so swimming there is actually a health hazard. Therefore, <u>unless you are a nature-lover or a risk-taker, a pool offers a relaxing day in the sun without health hazards.</u>

1. Which paragraph is easier to follow? Why?

2. Which paragraph makes greater use of transition words and phrases?

3. When you compare and contrast, which form of organization are you more likely to use?

Thinking

COMPARISON/CONTRAST THINKING

When you compare and contrast, you look for similarities and differences in two people, places, ideas, or items. You compare and contrast to make a point. A compare/contrast paragraph includes three elements: a focus on similarities or differences; points of comparison or contrast; and details, reasons, or examples to support those points.

Elements of Comparison/Contrast

These are the basic elements of effective comparison and contrast paragraphs.

- *Purpose of your comparison/contrast:* The topic sentence identifies the two alternatives being discussed and indicates the purpose of the discussion, such as choosing between two different cellphones.

- *Points of comparison/contrast:* The middle section of the paragraph states the points by which the items will be compared or contrasted and examines each one using these points. In the case of cellphones, points of comparison or contrast might be features, price, and the billing packages that come with the phones. You are trying to decide how similar or how different the cellphones are so you can make a wise choice about which one to purchase or recommend.

- *Details, reasons, and examples:* These elaborate on each point and provide support for the main idea of the paragraph. It is not enough simply to say "features." You need to provide some explanation of what this means by providing details that explain the points you selected.

Get Started

To answer the questions of how your work environment has changed since the new manager took charge, you would contrast the work environment with your old manager to the current environment with the new manager. To decide which of the two teams in the Stanley Cup final is most likely to win, you would compare the two teams. To decide why you prefer one instructor over another, you might contrast their teaching styles.

A clear statement of purpose focuses your inquiry. Here are three topic sentences that state the purpose of comparison and contrast paragraphs written on the topics just mentioned:

- *Work environment:* Several important changes have occurred since the new manager started.
- *Stanley Cup finals:* Because of the skills of their superior goaltenders, the team's ability to play under pressure, and the accuracy of their shots on net, the Edmonton Oilers are likely to beat the Montreal Canadiens in the National Hockey League Stanley Cup final game.
- *Instructor preference:* Mr. Gruber's use of visual aids, his clear explanations, and his sense of humour make his class much more interesting than Dr. Koll's economics class.

EXERCISE 10-1 Thinking about Purpose

Directions: *For each of the following topics, write a topic sentence stating the purpose of comparing and contrasting them.*

EXAMPLE

Buying clothes online and buying them in a store: <u>For the consumer who</u> <u>is difficult to fit, buying clothes in a store is much better than buying</u> <u>them online.</u>

1. Used cars and new cars: _____

_____

2. Female and male shopping habits: _____

_____

3. Parents' attitudes toward something (spending money, leisure time) versus their children's attitudes: _____

_____

4. Television 25 years ago and television today: _____

_____

5. Working with a group and working individually: _____

_____

Points of Comparison/Contrast

The focus of comparison/contrast thinking is finding points of similarities or differences between two ideas, places, objects, or people and the details that help you explain these points. Once you have an idea of your purpose, you might take two different approaches to get started.

BEGIN WITH POINTS OF COMPARISON OR CONTRAST

Sometimes you begin comparison/contrast thinking with a clear idea of your points of comparison or contrast. For example, you want to compare/contrast the attraction of two destination cities for spring break. In this case, your points to consider are (1) how easy the destinations are to reach, (2) their climate, and (3) what there is to do when you get there. In this case, you can proceed to list and explore details.

The side-by-side diagram in Figure 10-1 displays this thinking process. The student begins with her points of comparison and works back and forth across columns, filling in details that relate to each point. The purpose of her thinking process is to explore why one destination city is better than another.

BEGIN WITH DETAILS AND DISCOVER POINTS OF COMPARISON/ CONTRAST

What if you do not know what your points of comparison are? In this case, you begin by brainstorming and listing details. Examine the subject you know the most about first, listing all the details you can think of, then turning to the second subject.

The side-by-side diagram in Figure 10-2 illustrates the thinking process of a student who compares and contrasts exercising at home to exercising in a gym. He fills in details in the exercise-at-home category first; then he moves to exercising at a gym, using the details in the left column to generate details in the right column. When he finishes, he examines his list and notes possible points of comparison and contrast. The purpose of his thinking process is to determine which place will produce the best exercise results. The points of comparison/contrast for this student seem to be ease of access, variety of exercises, and other people's impact on the process.

City #1	City #2
Point 1: How easy is it to get to 12 hours by car	**Point 1: How easy is it to get to** 18 hours by car
Point 2: Climate 24–27 degrees, little chance of rain	**Point 2: Climate** 27–32 degrees, never rains, higher humidity
Point 3: What to do there Beach, sunbathing and body surfing, parasailing, great clubs at night	**Point 3: What to do there** Beach, sunbathing and body surfing, parasailing, great clubs at night, visit family friends (they know all the latest places to eat and cool places to go at night)

FIGURE 10-1 Listing and Exploring Details

Working Out at Home	Working Out at a Gym
Less emphasis on machinery 1 2 Weights	State-of-the-art machines
	Elliptical, weight machines
NordicTrack machine	Stairmaster, rowing machines
Working out in the laundry room	Working out in public
Walking and jogging outside	Always inside
Weather can be a factor	Any kind of weather
Can't be as noisy (listen to TV loud)	No choice over music or TV station
No need to have fancy clothes	Want to look good

FIGURE 10-2 Listing Details for the Subject You Know Best

EXERCISE 10-2 **Points of Comparison/Contrast**

Directions: *Choose two of the following subjects and fill in the charts with details related to them.*

- *If you know what points you will be comparing or contrasting, number them, write them in the columns provided, and list your supporting details under each point (see Figure 10-1).*

- *If you do not know what your points of comparison or contrast will be, list details in the column for the subject you know best. Use this list to generate details for the other column, and then note possible points of comparison or contrast in the space provided. Circle or highlight the points you select to use. Then decide if you will be comparing or contrasting the items.*

When you are finished, write a sentence or two stating what your points of comparison or contrast are (see Figure 10-2).

1. Tests

Essay Tests   *Multiple-Choice Tests*

_____   _____

_____   _____

_____   _____

_____   _____

_____   _____

_____   _____

_____   _____

Points of Comparison or Contrast: _____

_____

2. Where to do homework

Doing Homework at School   *Doing Homework at Home*

_____   _____

_____   _____

_____   _____

_____   _____

_____   _____

_____   _____

_____   _____

Points of Comparison or Contrast: _____

_____

3. Types of class

Face-to-Face Classes   *Online Classes*

_____   _____

_____   _____

_____   _____

_____   _____

_____   _____

_____   _____

_____   _____

Points of Comparison or Contrast: _____

_____

Select and Elaborate on Details

As you explore your subject in comparison/contrast thinking, you will generate a lot of details—far more than you can use in a paragraph. Consequently, choose only those details that are most significant and helpful in explaining similarity in a comparison paragraph or the differences in a contrast paragraph. Two or three good details are probably better than six or seven details that you simply list. Using only three clear points of comparison/contrast makes it easier for your reader to understand your purpose, which is presented in a more persuasive manner.

Here are details selected by the student comparing home and gym workouts.

Topic Sentence: Although working out at home is more convenient, the advantages of exercising in a gym outweigh mere convenience.

Working Out at Home	Working Out at the Gym
Point 1: Ease of access Always open. Go downstairs or step outside.	**Point 1: Ease of access** Have to leave the house. Collect clothes, shoes, get in the car, drive.
Point 2: Variety of exercises Home loses here. Cannot compete with the gym.	**Point 2: Variety of exercises** Gym has greater variety: elliptical, weight machines, stair machines, rowing machines, pool, track, sauna, massage.
Point 3: Influence of other people Have to be quiet, so do not disturb the family. Home loses here, too.	**Point 3: Influence of other people** Everyone is in the same boat.

EXERCISE 10-3 **Selecting and Elaborating on Your Details**

Directions: *Choose a topic from Exercise 10-2 and, in the space below, write a topic sentence for it. Then use the side-by-side chart to fill in points of comparison and contrast, along with the most important details related to each point.*

Talk about it ▶▶▶

Which comparison/contrast approach do you prefer: subject-by-subject or point-by-point? Why?

Topic Sentence: _____

_____

Subject 1	*Subject 2*
Point 1: _____ _____ _____ _____	Point 1: _____ _____ _____ _____

Point 2: _____   Point 2: _____

_____   _____

_____   _____

_____   _____

Point 3: _____   Point 3: _____

_____   _____

_____   _____

_____   _____

Process

COMPARISON/CONTRAST IN PROCESS

Effective comparison/contrast writing systematically examines a topic. You determine the purpose of your writing, establish points of comparison or contrast, then identify and elaborate on supporting details. Ultimately, you reach a conclusion about the two topics you have been examining.

Select an Assignment

In your post-secondary courses, comparison/contrast writing calls for attention to detail and meticulous organization. This challenging thinking and writing activity cuts across all disciplines and is also often used at work to guide decision making between two possible courses of action.

EXERCISE 10-4 **Selecting an Assignment for a Comparison/Contrast Paragraph**

Directions: *Review the assignments listed below. Choose the one you know the most about and think is best suited to either a comparison or contrast paragraph.*

1. Compare or contrast an expensive hobby and an inexpensive hobby.

2. Compare or contrast putting children in daycare or having one parent stay home.

3. Compare or contrast driving a car or taking public transportation.

4. Compare or contrast two vocations or careers.

5. Compare or contrast using hand tools or power tools.

6. Compare or contrast why it is better or worse to be the boss rather than the worker.

7. Compare or contrast which job is better—a desk job or a manual labour job.

8. Compare or contrast two ideas, events, people, or objects you recently studied.

9. Compare or contrast two people you know who have made a difference in the community.

10. Compare or contrast two different approaches to solving the same problem in your community.

Prewrite: Write Before You Write

PREWRITE
- Talk
- Think
- Cluster
- Brainstorm
- Question
- Freewrite

You have a lot to keep track of in comparison/contrast writing, which is all the more reason to take full advantage of the writing process. Talk to classmates and others about your ideas. Use brainstorming to get your ideas and details down on paper so you are clear about your thinking. A side-by-side chart can also help organize your ideas.

EXERCISE 10-5 **Talking about It**

Directions: *Turn to a classmate or an interested listener. Explore the two subjects you wish to compare or contrast. Be sure to consider your paragraph's purpose and the points of comparison or contrast you have in mind. Be specific and include details. Then be a critical listener of your neighbour's comparison or contrast thinking. Do not interrupt. When the speaker finishes, ask questions or offer suggestions. Identify what was clear and what was not.*

EXERCISE 10-6 **Brainstorming**

Directions: *Brainstorm for ten minutes on the assignment that you chose in Exercise 10-4. At the top of a sheet of paper, write a sentence expressing your tentative purpose. Then use the side-by-side approach to list the points of comparison and contrast. When you finish, identify which of your points are comparison and which ones are contrasts. If you are unsure, list as many details as you can, review your brainstorming, and look for two to three points that organize your thinking.*

Draft: Focus and Organize

After prewriting, you should have a sense of your paragraph's purpose. In addition, you can list your points of comparison or contrast, and you have generated a number of details to provide the substance of your paragraph. Your next step is to focus, organize, and draft your paragraph.

DRAFT
- Consider your audience
- Formulate your topic sentence
- Outline for unity and coherence
- Write a concluding sentence
- Compose your first draft

CONSIDER YOUR AUDIENCE

Reread your assignment. Look for key words, and make sure you incorporate the words and ideas into your plan for your paragraph. As you consider your audience, keep these questions in mind:

- Why is this topic important?

- What do I want my reader to understand about it?

- What special knowledge about this subject do I have that might require explanation for a reader to understand?

Directions: *Use the questions above to think critically about your paragraph's purpose and the points and details to include in it. Talk with a classmate to try out your thinking on an audience. Take notes on this conversation and add any new ideas and details to your prewriting.*

FORMULATE YOUR TOPIC SENTENCE

The topic sentence in a comparison/contrast paragraph identifies the two things being compared or contrasted and states the paragraph's main idea. Review your prewriting, especially anything you wrote relating to purpose and points of comparison or contrast. Feel free to reconsider and revise your thinking.

OUTLINE FOR UNITY AND COHERENCE

Planning well will help you write a unified paragraph. Know what your points of comparison or contrast are and which details are needed to explain those points. Eliminate those details that do not relate to these points. Then, think about the order in which you present your points of comparison or contrast. Lead off with an important point, or perhaps you want to save the best for last. Changing the order of your ideas can help you understand something about your topic that eluded you before.

In your comparison or contrast paragraph, you will make extensive use of transition words and phrases because you are discussing two subjects at the same time. These transitions will also help you to handle multiple ideas and details. In addition, you will have two or three points of comparison or contrast, along with supporting details relating to these points.

TRANSITIONS BASED ON COMPARISON

again	as well as	likewise
both	in the same way	similarly
in addition	also	

TRANSITIONS BASED ON CONTRAST

although	but	however
in contrast	moreover	on the contrary
on the other hand	opposite of	

WRITE A CONCLUDING SENTENCE

Plan your concluding sentence, which makes a comment on the position stated in the topic sentence. It can also restate the paragraph's purpose.

See "Supporting Details" in Chapter 3 for a detailed explanation of outlining.

EXERCISE 10-8 **Planning Your First Draft**

Directions: *Write a topic sentence that echoes the key words from your assignment topic. Then organize and outline your details. Look back to earlier in this chapter for help with planning point-by-point or subject-by-subject structure.*

COMPOSE YOUR FIRST DRAFT

Now that you have chosen your topic, decided on your position, and selected examples and details, you can write a first draft of your paragraph. At this point, it is better to write too much than too little: you can always cut back later. Make sure your paragraph has sufficient detail and explanation so a reader understands your position.

EXERCISE 10-9 **Writing Your First Draft**

Directions: *Write a draft of your paragraph. Refer to the side-by-side chart you made, and also use the first draft checklist at the back of the book as a guide.*

A PROFESSIONAL'S TAKE

Here is Monte Hummel's use of comparison and contrast, from his essay *A Passion for the Environment: Two Accounts:*

On a sunny day in August 1959, my honey-coloured spaniel Roxy and I went fishing. At the time, my family lived in a hydro camp at White Dog Falls, north of Kenora in northwestern Ontario. Roxy and I scrambled over familiar rocks along the river bank, caught frogs for bait, shared a sandwich for lunch, landed a couple of medium-sized pike out of dark swirling pools below the rapids, and rested looking up through pines at osprey who were also fishing these northern waters. Two men noticed us, and asked if I would show them where I caught the fish, which I was pleased to do if they would let me fillet anything they caught at 25 cents each. It was truly a Huck Finn kind of upbringing, and deeply formative of "a passion for the environment."

On a sunny day in August 1969, I returned to visit my home river of those halcyon boyhood days, with the ink barely dry on a university degree. Memories welled up as I picked my way down to the shore to see what a small sign said, posted right by the water. "Fish for Fun Only." This message was screened against the background of a skull and crossbones, by authority of the Government of Ontario. The English-Wabigoon river system had become tragically contaminated by mercury from an upstream chlor-alkali plant associated with the pulp and paper industry. The fish were no longer fit to eat. The Ojibway kids I went to school with had lost their commercial whitefish fishery and jobs guiding sport anglers, so the economic base of their reserve was in tatters. So was my Huck Finn upbringing. On that day, "a passion for the environment" came crisply into focus.

EXERCISE 10-10 **A PROFESSIONAL'S TAKE**

Directions: *Using the first draft checklist at the back of this book as your guide, identify the effective comparison/contrast elements in A Professional's Take. Next, compare the elements the author used in this excerpt with the ones that you used in your first draft. Did you clearly use subject-by-subject or point-by-point organization in your paragraph?*

Revise: Read Critically, then Rewrite

Revision gives you a chance to get things right. Even if you have carefully analyzed, focused, and planned your first draft, you have done this work alone. You will always benefit from having an outside reader.

REVISE
- Read critically
- Develop a revision plan

REVISION IN ACTION

Revision is rethinking a draft to improve the quality of your writing: you read critically, plan your revision, and revise your writing. Quality revision will also improve your future writing. Here is an example of revision by a student named Barbara.

> **Assignment:** Examine an important dietary issue in our country today, such as the use of food supplements, the availability of genetically modified food, or the demand for organic foods in the marketplace.

Barbara's First Draft

The wide variety of food in local grocery stores can often confuse Canadian consumers as they decide whether to purchase organic or genetically modified food. **The first consideration is the cost.** Since farmers of organic produce spend more time controlling pests and weeds and they have lower crop yields, their products are more expensive. The typical famer is interested in keeping his production costs low. With genetically modified crops, the original DNA structure of the plant has been changed to produce certain qualities in the plant, such as resistance to herbicides. This means the farmer can spray his soybean or corn fields with herbicides to kill competing weeds, without affecting his herbicide resistant crops. The farmer spends less time removing the weeds and gets a more bountiful crop, leading to lower prices for his crop in the grocery store. I like to buy cheap fruits and vegetables. Healthy food choices are **a second concern** for consumers. Most consumers have faith that the agricultural industry is monitored by the Canadian Food Inspection Agency to ensure that high standards are maintained in Canada's food supply. These consumers believe that they can get the vitamins and minerals from the regularly available produce in their grocery stores. However, other consumers are worried about the lack of long-term studies on the effects on people or animals that eat genetically modified food. You might be worried that the bacteria and viruses used to alter the plants' DNA may be harmful to the good bacteria in your digestive tract. **Most importantly**, consumers need to be aware of where the food they are eating actually comes from. Recently, there has been a trend to buy food that is locally produced and in season. Many restaurants advertise that they prepare food grown on farms located within a reasonable distance of the community. Since most people care for the environment around their neighbourhoods, they can become supporters of

TOPIC SENTENCE
Barbara repeats key words from the assignment and states the two subjects that she is comparing.

SUPPORTING DETAILS
She uses examples, facts, and reasons to support each point, stating why consumers can feel the food supply is affordable, safe, and healthy.

ORDER AND TRANSITIONS
She uses a point-by-point order contrasting regular produce with buying organic food. She uses a combination of enumeration and contrast transitions.

their local farmers by buying what these farms are producing. Of course, fresh food is healthy and tasty. In Canada, manufacturers of processed food are not required to indicate whether their ingredients contain genetically modified products. Thus, some consumers have already been eating prepared foods that contain genetically modified ingredients for many years without adverse health affects. <u>Buying reasonably priced, fresh food that is locally grown will ensure consumers' nutritional requirements are met.</u>

Revision Plan: The content is clearly organized in a point-by-point pattern. Add more details and transitions. Eliminate first-person and second-person pronouns.

Barbara's Revised Draft

As Canadian consumers choose from the wide variety of food in their local grocery stores, they need to decide whether to purchase organic or genetically modified food. **The first consideration is the cost.** Since farmers of organic produce spend more time controlling pests and weeds and they have lower crop yields, their products are more expensive. Organic produce is often more than double the cost of regular fruit and vegetables. Consumers on tight budgets cannot often see the value in paying so much more for a bag of carrots, for example. **In contrast**, the typical famer is interested in keeping his production costs low. With genetically modified crops, the original DNA structure of the plant has been changed to produce certain qualities in the plant, such as resistance to herbicides. This means the farmer can spray his soybean or cornfields with herbicides to kill competing weeds, without affecting his herbicide-resistant crops. The farmer spends less time removing the weeds and also gets a more bountiful crop, leading to lower prices for his produce in the grocery store. The majority of shoppers like to buy these reasonably priced fruits and vegetables. Healthy food choices are **a second concern** for consumers. Most Canadians have faith that the agricultural industry is sufficiently monitored by the Canadian Food Inspection Agency to ensure that high standards are maintained in Canada's food supply. These consumers believe that they can get their vitamins and minerals from the regularly available produce in their grocery stores. **On the other hand**, other consumers are worried about the lack of long-term studies on the effects on people or animals that eat genetically modified food. They might be worried that the bacteria and viruses used to alter the plants' DNA may be harmful to the good bacteria in the digestive tract. However, there is no conclusive evidence for their fears. **Most importantly,** consumers need to be aware of where the food they are actually eating comes from. Rather than purchasing food from another continent, recently, there has been a trend to buy food that is locally produced and in season—the 100-mile diet. Many restaurants advertise that they prepare food grown on farms located within a short distance of the community. Local produce does not travel very far before reaching the consumer, which saves on transportation costs and pollution. Since most people care for the environment around their neighbourhoods, they can support their local farmers by buying what these farms are producing as the crops are harvested. Of course, fresh food is always healthy and tasty. **Moreover,** in Canada, manufacturers of processed food are not required to indicate whether their ingredients contain genetically modified products. For example, a Canadian sugar company in Alberta has been processing genetically engineered sugar beets since 2008 and this sugar is used in many products such as canned goods, baked goods, and chocolate bars. Thus, some consumers have already been eating foods prepared with genetically modified ingredients for many years without adverse health affects. <u>**In conclusion,** buying reasonably priced, fresh food that is locally grown will ensure consumers' nutritional requirements are met.</u>

CONCLUDING SENTENCE
She comments on the benefits of local traditional products.

DISCUSSION QUESTIONS What changes did Barbara make in her revision to improve her paragraph? Why?

READ CRITICALLY

Half the task of revising well is reading well. Critical reading is a search for the characteristics of effective writing: topic sentence, supporting examples and details, transitions, and concluding sentence. In comparison/contrast writing, the reader must pay attention to a writer's approach to organization. Is it point by point or subject by subject? Also, note how effective the supporting details are. Watch for repetition and lists. Does the writer elaborate and explain details?

EXERCISE 10-11 **Reading Peer Papers**

Directions: *Exchange papers with another student. Consider the significant changes that Barbara made between writing her first draft and her revision. Be a critical reader and make suggestions to improve your peer's first draft. Also identify what your classmate did well. Make notes in the margin to remember your suggestions.*

REVISE WITH A PLAN

Reread your assignment before revising. Be sure the paragraph you have drafted is an appropriate response to the assignment. Also, review everything you have written, including prewriting. If you need to add to your paragraph, your prewriting may contain ideas and details that you can revise and improve on. If you need to cut parts from your paragraph, think about how those cuts will enhance the unity of your paragraph.

EXERCISE 10-12 **Revising Your Draft**

Directions: *Develop a revision plan and revise the paragraph you wrote for Exercise 10-9.*

EDIT
- Search and correct
- Self-edit

Edit

The ideas in your work count. The content matters. Focus your editing using a personalized checklist that focuses on strengthening your writing. In comparison/contrast writing, you particularly need to proofread for correct comparative and superlative forms. For example, with the word *sensitive*, the comparative form is *more sensitive* and the superlative form is *most sensitive*.

To have your writing clearly state what you mean to write, note that there is a distinction between the use of some determiners, or limiting words that come before some nouns. Consider these examples:

For items that are *countable* (*12* exam booklets):

a few: A few exam booklets lay on the desk. (This means there are some, but not many, exam booklets, probably enough for our needs.)

few: Few exam booklets lay on the desk. (This means there aren't enough exam booklets or hardly any. We need to get more booklets.)

For items that are too small to count, belong to a group or mass, or are considered a collective noun, you should use:

a little: A little understanding was shown to the student who arrived late for the test. (This means that the teacher was sympathetic with the student.)

little: Little understanding was shown to the student who arrived late for the test. (This means no excuse was accepted from the student for being late.)

For more information about determiners, consult a dictionary or grammar book. Chapter 24 gives you more information about using comparative adjectives.

EXERCISE 10-13 **Revising and Editing Practice**

Directions: *Read the following paragraph that was written in response to the assignment below; it contains errors that require revising and editing. Then answer the questions that follow.*

Assignment: Write a comparison or contrast paragraph to examine two approaches to organizing your home, work, or school life.

(1) _____. (2) First, many people think a handheld smart phone is better because it is a mini-computer. (3) They can connect a smart phone to their computer at work and at home to synchronize items on their personal and work calendars. (4) A smart phone makes it easy for a person to keep track of appointments and contact information. (5) In addition, they have access to the Internet, and some

even have word processors and spreadsheets. (6) What anyone does with a spreadsheet is beyond me. (7)_____, there are some disadvantages. (8) For one thing, the keyboards and displays are small and hard to read in addition, it can be irritating to constantly recharge the device. (9) Some users do not like the fact that they rely on it and when they need it, the battery is dead. (10) On the other hand, a paper day planner may be more convenient for work and personal appointments. (11) There is no computer to boot up at work or at home, no synchronization process to go through, and no batteries to charge. (12) _____. (13) The smart phone is fine for some people but definitely not without it's problems.

REVISING

_____ 1. Which sentence should be inserted in blank 1? The sentence would include key words from the assignment and state the paragraph's purpose.

    a. Smart phones are not all they are cracked up to be; nevertheless, people love these devices.

    b. Handheld devices are replacing day planners, but are they all they are cracked up to be?

    c. There are many differences between a day planner and a smart phone.

    d. If you compare a day planner and a smart phone, you will choose the one right for you.

_____ 2. Which word or phrase should be inserted in blank 7? The word or phrase would serve as a best transition between points that describe a smart phone.

    a. Also   c. In addition

    b. Nevertheless   d. Surprisingly

_____ 3. Which sentence should be cut to improve the paragraph's focus?

    a. Sentence 4   c. Sentence 9

    b. Sentence 6   d. No change is necessary.

_____ 4. Which sentence, if any, should be inserted in blank 12? The sentence would provide the best specific details to support sentence 10.

    a. Making changes simply requires erasing.

    b. Plus, who needs an electronic device to write down an appointment?

    c. In addition, planners have space for contact information in the back.

    d. No sentence should be inserted.

_____ 1. Choose the option that corrects the error in sentence 5.

    a. In addition, they have access to the Internet, and some smart phones even have word processors and spreadsheets.

    b. In addition, a smart phone have access to the Internet, and some even have word processors and spreadsheets.

    c. In addition, a smart phone has access to the Internet, and some even have word processors and spreadsheets.

    d. No change is necessary.

_____ 2. Choose the option that corrects the error in sentence 8.

    a. For one thing, the keyboards and displays are small and hard to read, in addition, it can be irritating to constantly charge the batteries.

    b. For one thing, the keyboards and displays are small and hard to read, additionally, it can be irritating to constantly charge the batteries.

    c. For one thing, the keyboards and displays are small and hard to read; in addition, it can be irritating to constantly charge the batteries.

    d. No change is necessary.

Writer's Response

What kinds of technology have improved your life? How has it been improved?

_____ 3. Choose the option that corrects the punctuation error in sentence 9.

    a. Some users do not like the fact that they rely on it, and when they need it, the battery is dead.

    b. Some users do not like the fact that they rely on it and, when they need it, the battery is dead.

    c. Some users do not like the fact that they rely on it. And when they need it the battery is dead.

    d. No change is necessary.

4. Proofread the paragraph for an error with a commonly confused word and correct the error.

EXERCISE 10-14 **Searching and Correcting**

Directions: _Exchange papers with a peer and proofread each other's work. In addition to spelling, punctuation, and capitalization, find out what other errors your classmate has made; tell your classmate what errors you often make._

EXERCISE 10-15 **Self-Editing**

Directions: _Carefully rewrite your paper, correcting errors you and your classmate found. Set aside the finished paper. Then come back to it later and read your final draft one last time, using the editing checklist on the inside back cover as a guide._

Reflect

Take a moment and reflect on what you have learned about writing comparison and contrast paragraphs.

EXERCISE 10-16 **Identifying Strengths and Setting Goals**

Directions: *Review your writing and your writing process. Write answers to these questions:*

- *What did you do well in the paragraph you wrote?*
- *What did you enjoy working on in this chapter?*
- *What have you learned about comparison/contrast that you will apply in future writing assignments?*

Your answers to these questions will increase your awareness of your particular strengths and weaknesses in using comparison/contrast. Set writing goals for yourself and in your next writing assignment, you can focus on reaching these goals.

REFLECT
- Identify strengths
- Set goals

CHAPTER REVIEW

Recall what you have learned about comparison and contrast writing.

- ■ **COMPARISON/CONTRAST THINKING**
- ☐ Elements of comparison and contrast
  - *Two alternatives; three points of comparison or contrast; details; conclusion*
- ☐ Points of comparison or contrast
  - *Begin with points of comparison and contrast*
  - *Begin with details and discover points of comparison and contrast*
- ☐ Select and elaborate on details
  - *Balance details for both topics*
- ■ **COMPARISON/CONTRAST IN PROCESS**
- ☐ Select an assignment
- ☐ Prewrite
  - *Brainstorm; chart; compare or contrast*
- ☐ Draft
  - *Focus and organization; clear purpose; audience*
- ☐ Revise
  - *Plan; order of points; unity/cohesion: transitions; concluding sentence: decision*
- ☐ Edit
  - *Critical reading; peer and self-editing: grammar; comparative adjectives*
- ☐ Reflect
  - *Writing goals*

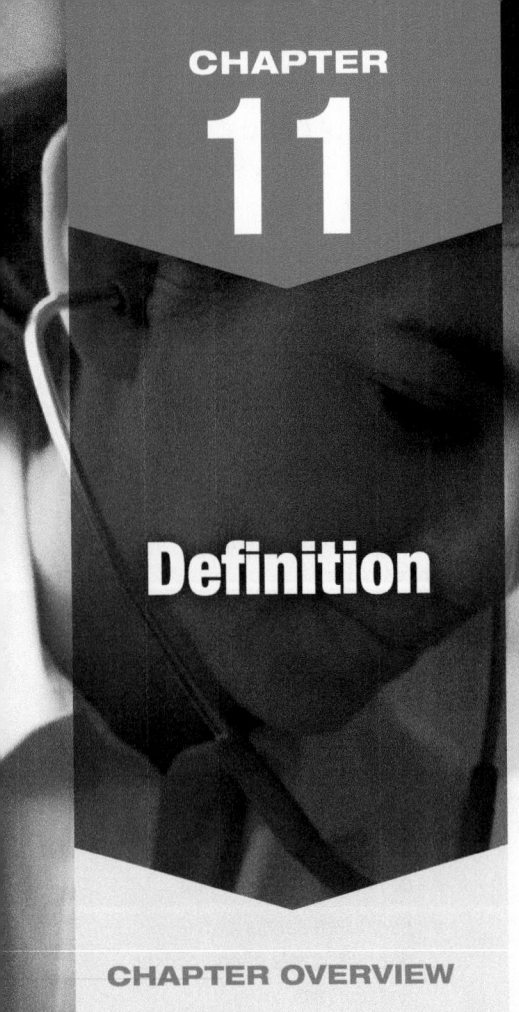

CHAPTER
11

Definition

CHAPTER OVERVIEW

THINK FIRST

Write a paragraph in which you define what health means to you. Elaborate on your ideas, explaining your definition in detail.

What Did You Say Again?

Imagine you are describing a movie you just saw to one of your friends. If you were to say, "It's a screwball comedy, but a little on the dark side," you might hear this response: "What's a 'screwball comedy'? And what do you mean by the 'dark side'?" Your friend is asking you to define your terms, and, in order for the conversation to move forward, you will have to do so. Definition, then, is one way of establishing a basis for an intelligent discussion since everyone in the conversation will benefit from a shared understanding of the terms. You may also find that your notion of a word's meaning will change after talking about it with others.

BRAINSTORM

Brainstorm a list of words you use with your close friends or colleagues that your family members might not understand.

Definition: A Basis for Argument

In class discussion, you will need to carefully define your terms. Suppose you are discussing assisted suicide. At the outset, you might say, "In referring to 'assisted suicide,' I am limiting this discussion to cases in which terminally ill patients—as opposed to physically healthy persons—are aided by others in ending their life." Limiting the argument by defining your terms clarifies an unmanageably large topic.

DISCUSSION

Talk with a classmate to define the following terms: hack, spam, phishing, floss, earjacking, *and* subwoofing. *See if you both define them in the same way.*

Definition on the Job

Definition is obviously key to classroom teaching—"an isosceles triangle is . . . ," "*democracy* is most commonly defined as . . . ," "Freud defined the ego as . . ."—but it plays a role in many other jobs as well. A librarian would need to define an "online database" for someone new to the world of electronic research; a physician's assistant might need to explain "complete workup" to an anxious patient; an employee training a new hire would have to define the jargon of the particular business. Similarly, the kind of definition that clarifies a decision, position, or policy is a part of most jobs: for example, a government official might state the technical definition of an "assembly" in discussing the need for a license for a planned public meeting while a restaurant server might have to clearly define the "early bird special" to avoid an argument with eager customers.

RESUMÉ BUILDER

Before you go for an interview, research the language that you will need to use to converse with your future employer. Make a list of the essential words you need to understand in your current job. Why are they important?

At a Glance

A good definition paragraph should not only define a term, phrase, or concept but also illustrate or demonstrate its meaning. For example, a construction trades instructor might ask you to write a paragraph defining the term *flush*. A simple answer is that flush is achieved by creating a continuous plane with two adjacent objects. However, to help someone understand that simple definition, you might describe how important creating flush walls is to the construction of a house, or you might explain the process of building a flush wall. Either of these approaches will more specifically define *flush*.

Generally, definition paragraphs are short and specific. The topic sentence states the term to be defined and possibly gives a general definition. The sentence that follows may state a reason for defining the term. The supporting details describe, explain, or illustrate the definition using specific examples or facts. The concluding sentence restates the definition in simple terms.

For some assignments, students must research something unfamiliar to them and then define some terms found in the readings. In such an assignment, you might need to identify the source(s) for your definition: "SOURCE defines (term) as _____" or "According to SOURCE, (term) is. . . ." Then, you will state explanations or examples to support this definition. Sometimes, different sources define a term differently, so you will need to determine which definition will suit your purpose. To make sure your reader understands your term, include the source of the definition you use ("According to X's definition of 'term'. . .").

The Definition Paragraph at a Glance

ASSIGNMENT   Write a paragraph that defines the term *work ethic*.

TOPIC SENTENCE
The writer repeats the definition term from the assignment and defines *work ethic* as an attitude.

SUPPORTING DETAILS
The writer cites examples of two different attitudes to work, positive and negative, to provide a definition of the term *work ethic*.

A work ethic is a person's attitude about work. **For example**, some people believe work is valuable and necessary for a good life. These people work for pay, but they also work for the satisfaction work brings them. Because of this positive work ethic, they feel that when they are working, they are using their time productively. They are making something of their lives. A negative attitude about work is **also** a work ethic. **In contrast** to those who embrace work, there are people who avoid work at all costs. They feel work takes something from them. They work for money because they want the money, not because they like or love the work. There is little or no satisfaction for them from a job well done. **Those with a positive work ethic** are probably more inclined to work for the fun of it. In their homes, they are cleaners and fixers and organizers. They have hobbies. They are perpetual activity machines. **Those people with a negative work ethic** might be less inclined to do work like this. They can walk around a mess, ignore it, and go sit on the couch. They can see a sink full of dishes and look the other way. In other areas of life, they may be happy people, but work is not one of their sources of happiness. <u>Positive or negative, a work ethic is about attitude and the effect of that attitude on what people do with their lives.</u>

ORDER AND TRANSITIONS
The writer uses transition words as he alternates between his two examples. He also uses repeating terms, "those with a . . . work ethic," to structure his discussion.

DISCUSSION QUESTIONS

1. Does this definition seem accurate? Discuss people you know who have either a positive or a negative attitude about work.

2. Do you agree or disagree with this definition of *work ethic*? What does it overlook? What would you add to it?

Thinking
DEFINITION THINKING

Sometimes a one-sentence definition for a term is sufficient. You open a dictionary, copy a phrase or two, and away you go. In academic writing, however, you may need to provide more detailed definitions of terms and concepts so that you and your reader have a shared understanding of their meanings. Clear, shared definitions help to prevent possible misunderstandings. Additionally, providing clear definitions forces you to clarify your own thinking about a topic and allows you to discuss complex issues intelligently.

Elements of Definition

An effective definition paragraph contains some basic elements that enable you to focus and elaborate on a useful definition.

- *Group or category:* In a topic sentence, associating the term, concept, or idea you want to define within a larger group or category gives it the proper context. A work ethic is an *attitude*. Placing *work ethic* in this category or group enables you to talk about positive and negative feelings and how they translate into actual behaviours or attitudes. For this reason, definition writing is often used in classification writing. (See Chapter 8 for more about classification.)

- *Examples:* A good definition often makes use of examples. Once a work ethic is defined as an attitude, you can cite examples of attitude, positive and negative, and in doing so, you add useful detail to your unique definition of *work ethic*.

- *Negatives:* When you define a term using negatives, you focus on misconceptions—what people erroneously think about your subject. Often this form of definition is a two-statement manoeuvre. You state what your subject is not; then you state what it is. *A work ethic is not simply a desire to make a lot of money; it is an attitude about work.*

Get Started

Good definitions begin with general statements. To make a general statement about the term you are defining, connect it to a group or category, which will then provide you with new ways of thinking in detail about examples and specific details that will illustrate your definition.

There may be several categories into which you can fit your term. Clustering can help to start your definition thinking. In this example, the student identifies ways of thinking about a hobby.

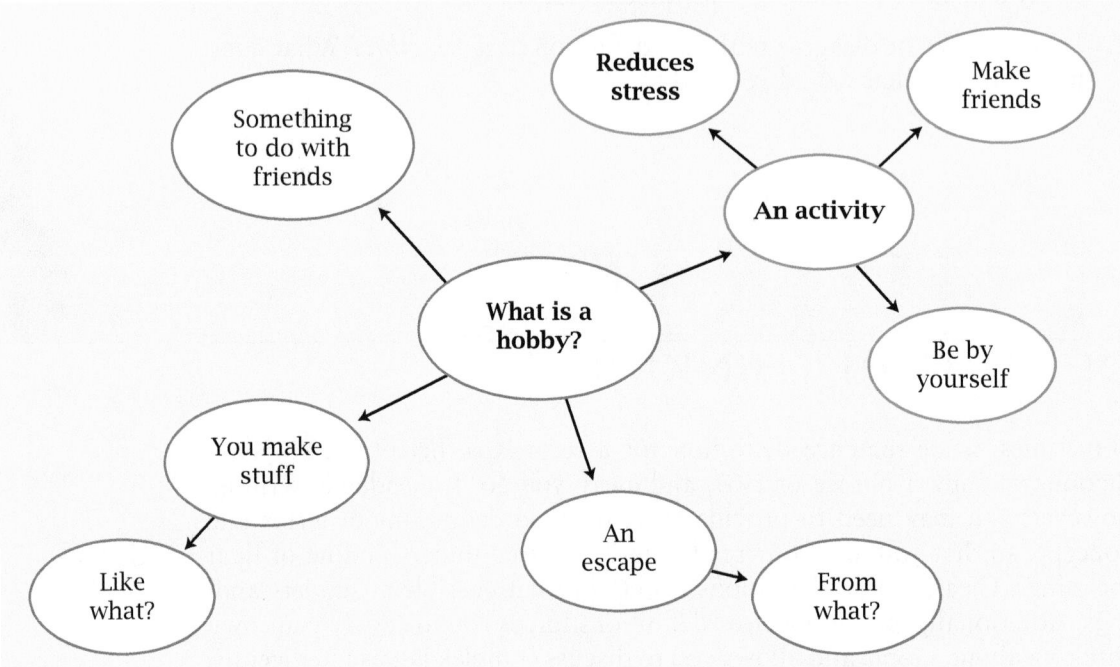

This student's clustering can be summarized as follows:

Term	*Category/Contextual Grouping*
A hobby is	an escape.
A hobby is	something you do.
A hobby is	something you do to make stuff.
A hobby is	something to do with friends.
A hobby is	**an activity that reduces stress.**

The sentence in bold type indicates the sentence this student liked best from his clustering ideas because it provides a focused direction to develop his personal definition for *hobby*. The other categories could lead to different definitions that might also be interesting, but "an activity that reduces stress" suited this student's purpose.

EXERCISE 11-1 **Definitions and Categories or Larger Groups**

Directions: *Pick three terms from the list of terms below. Write a sentence that associates the term to be defined with a group or category. To look for possible categories, do some clustering. From your clustering ideas, compose your definition sentence in the space provided. Also, try defining your term using negatives or stating what your subject is not. You will use this information in Exercise 11-3.*

Terms: *comfort food, a budget, music, responsibility, courage, religion, team player, accountability, opportunity*

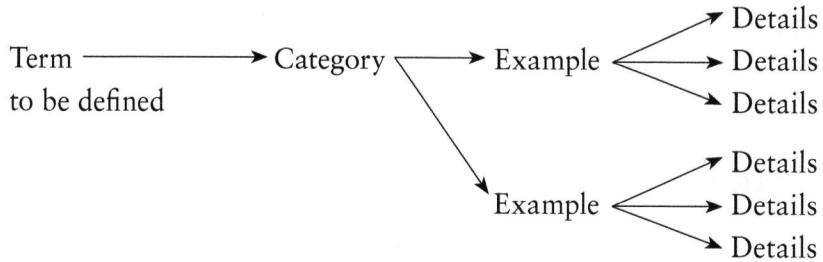

    Term   *Category/Group*

1. _____ is _____; is not _____.

2. _____ is _____; is not _____.

3. _____ is _____; is not _____.

Examples and Details

As you think further about the term you are defining, consider examples of the term. Examples lead you to details; details force you to consider whether your definition actually fits the facts.

Term ——————→ Category ⟨ → Example ⟨ → Details
to be defined   → Details
                                          → Details

                                 → Details
                           Example ⟨ → Details
                                     → Details

In the case of the student defining hobbies, he decides on a category—a stress-reduction activity—and then lists examples, as shown here.

Term		Category
A hobby	is a	stress-reduction activity.

Examples	Details
1. woodworking	done in a relaxing setting
	physical work
	complex—varieties of woods, tools
	no deadlines
	beautiful products of the work
2. skateboarding	done alone or with friends
	visible outcomes (better tricks, improved muscle tone)
	strenuous physical work

These examples and details elaborate on the student's definition sentence. Both woodworking and skateboarding are examples of hobbies, and the details he uses relate to the category of stress reduction, especially "relaxing setting," "no deadlines," and "visible outcomes." Based on this preliminary exploration, his definition appears to fit the facts. Now, the student freewrites about the thinking behind his definition of the term *hobby*:

> In both these examples, I note stress is reduced by physical activity. Stress is a mental thing. Physical activity is like stress medicine. A hobby is stress medicine! Also, in both examples, the individual has control over the activity. He can decide if he wants to do it or not. He is in control. He is the boss. A hobby is not something you do because you have to do it. It is something you do because you want to do it.

EXERCISE 11-2 **Definitions, Examples, and Details**

Directions: *Select two topics from Exercise 11-1 and write your definition sentences for them using the format presented below. Then cite two or three examples for each definition and two or three details for each example. When you finish working on the examples, write a few notes to comment on the accuracy of your definition.*

Term   *Category*

1. _____ is _____.

Examples   *Details*

_____

_____

Notes on My Definition: _____

_____

_____

Term   *Category*

2. _____ is _____.

Examples   *Details*

_____

_____

Notes on My Definition: _____

_____

_____

Negatives

Often, there can be disagreement on a key definition. In fact, disagreement can be the starting point of a protracted discussion. For this reason, it can be useful to think of negative definitions. Doing so says to an academic reader, "I am not talking about *that*. I am talking about *this*."

Higher education *is not* training that enables a person to make a living. Higher education is enrichment that enables a person to make a life.

Rock music *is not* just three chords played at high volume. Rock music is three chords and in-your-face lyrics.

These definition statements are argumentative. They prepare a writer to write *against* another person's point of view. What is the difference between making a living and making a life? The definition promises to explore that distinction. To say rock music is about in-your-face lyrics establishes the definition as defiantly confrontational. The sentence defining rock music promises to say both what the music is and what it says.

In the student sample on hobbies, he formulates both a positive and a negative definition:

> A hobby *is not* something you do because you have to do it. It is something you do because you want to do it.

A sentence like this establishes your territory. It sets your view apart from competing views. In fact, definition writing is connected to argumentative writing.

EXERCISE 11-3 **Establishing Your Territory**

Directions: *Choose the topic from Exercises 11-1 and 11-2 that appeals to you the most. Write a negative and a positive definition statement about your subject.*

Topic: _____

_____ is not _____.

It is _____.

Process

DEFINITION IN PROCESS

Definition writing begins with the exploration of a single word or phrase. As you move through the writing process, you develop your ideas, testing and refining your definition.

Select an Assignment

In college and university writing, definition is a basic writing task that often is used to demonstrate your understanding of course content. In the workplace, definition provides the basis for a common understanding of terms in reports you may have to write. It is also the starting point for more ambitious thinking and writing.

Selecting an Assignment for a Definition Paragraph

Directions: *Review the assignments listed below. Choose the one you know the most about and think is best suited to an effective definition paragraph.*

1. Provide a definition of a good job.

2. Define an operation or process that is important in the work you do.

3. Define a term you use at work that is essential to success.

4. Describe a personal value that is important to you, such as loyalty, consideration, responsibility, compassion, dedication, respect, or acceptance.

5. Define a social problem you have witnessed, such as discrimination, homelessness, physical or mental abuse, apathy, negligence, or poverty.

6. Define a word or phrase from your favourite subject that means more to you as you study the subject, such as environmental protection, patient-community, open dialogue, naturalization, or the lens of popular media.

7. Define a key phrase or slang term that describes an activity you love that others may not understand.

8. Give a definition of a food you love that might be unusual or unique.

9. Define overprotective or helicopter parents.

10. Provide a definition of a topic of your own choosing.

Prewrite: Write Before You Write

PREWRITE
- Talk
- Think
- Cluster
- Brainstorm
- Question
- Freewrite

Use prewriting to explore your topic. While it helps to start with a clear destination in mind, by following the writing process you may discover points of view you didn't anticipate when you first began your assignment.

Be open to new ways of understanding your subject. Trust the writing process to help you find something important to say. For definition, try clustering and freewriting to explore what you know about your word and subject.

Talk about it

Which combination of prewriting strategies is most effective for you? Why does this combination work so well?

EXERCISE 11-5 **Clustering**

Directions: *Cluster on your assignment for ten minutes. Try to include examples and details to explain important ideas in your definition, and think about the order in which you should present your ideas.*

EXERCISE 11-6 **Freewriting**

Directions: *Write for ten minutes on your subject. Because this is definition, think about the class or category your subject fits into, as well as examples and details that will help you write a good definition. You can also write what your definition is not about, i.e., use a negative definition.*

Draft: Focus and Organize

DRAFT
- Consider your audience
- Formulate your topic sentence
- Outline for unity and coherence
- Write a concluding sentence
- Compose your first draft

In definition thinking, it helps to keep in mind who your definition is for—i.e., your audience—and why the definition matters to them. In an English class, for example, a student's definition of *attendance* might be "coming to class regularly." To the instructor, in contrast, attendance might involve coming to class, participating in discussions, and coming for conferences during office hours. If part of the student's grade is based on participation, the precise definition of *attendance* would matter a great deal.

CONSIDER YOUR AUDIENCE

More often than not, the main reader of your writing in college or university is your instructor, who is interested in clarity and detail. You need to convince this particular reader that your definition is important and that it fits the facts. That means your main idea and supporting details have to work together. Use the following questions to consider how to explain your approach to your reader:

- Why is this subject important?
- What point do I want the reader to understand about my term?
- What details will make my definition more persuasive?

EXERCISE 11-7 **Considering Your Audience**

Directions: *Use the questions above to think critically about the subject you are defining from the previous exercises and the details you will use to develop your ideas. Talk with a classmate to clarify your thinking; take notes and add them to your prewriting.*

FORMULATE YOUR TOPIC SENTENCE

At this point in the writing process, think of your topic sentence as a work in progress. As you write, your understanding of your assignment and what you have to say about it may change. For now, a clear topic sentence should echo the assignment, state the term you are defining, and possibly connect the term to a category or group.

OUTLINE FOR UNITY AND COHERENCE

Your task as a writer is to produce a coherent paragraph that is unified around a single controlling idea. As you draft, watch for details and ideas that go off the subject. A unified paragraph contains only those details relevant to the point your paragraph makes. The coherence of your paragraph will be enhanced by appropriate transition words and phrases. Because you rely on examples and details to elaborate your definition, use transitions related to example.

TRANSITIONS BASED ON EXAMPLE		
for example	for instance	in this case
to illustrate	in addition	moreover
on the other hand		

If the order of your examples is based on importance, think about transitions related to priority and impact.

TRANSITIONS BASED ON PRIORITY OR IMPORTANCE		
however	more important	equally important
better	worse	in particular
specifically	of course	certainly
in fact		

WRITE A CONCLUDING SENTENCE

Plan your concluding sentence, which restates or rephrases the definition and the point of the paragraph. See "Supporting Details" in Chapter 3 for a detailed explanation of outlining.

EXERCISE 11-8 **Planning Your First Draft**

Directions: *Write a topic sentence that echoes the key words from the assignment. Then organize and outline your details.*

COMPOSE YOUR FIRST DRAFT

So far, you have chosen your term and selected the ideas and details you will use to define it. Now that you have decided on your approach to organize your material, you can write your paragraph's first draft. Make sure your paragraph has sufficient detail and explanation so a reader understands why your definition of this word or phrase is important.

EXERCISE 11-9 **Writing Your First Draft**

Directions: *Write a draft of your paragraph. Be sure you have included examples and details to fully explain the definition in the paragraph. Your concluding sentence should also summarize the definition in your paragraph.*

A PROFESSIONAL'S TAKE

Here is Thomas Moore's use of definition, from his book *Care of the Soul:*

Care of the soul is a fundamentally different way of regarding daily life and the quest for happiness. The emphasis may not be on problems at all. One person might care for the soul by buying or renting a good piece of land, another by selecting an appropriate school or program of study, another by painting his house or his bedroom. Care of the soul is a continuous process that concerns itself not so much with "fixing" a central flaw as with attending to the small details of everyday life, as well as to major decisions and changes. Care of the soul may not focus on the personality or on relationships at all, and therefore it is not psychological in the usual sense. Tending to things around us and becoming sensitive to the importance of home, daily schedule, and maybe even the clothes we wear, are ways of caring for the soul. When Marsilio Ficino wrote his self-help book, *The Book of Life,* five hundred years ago, he placed emphasis on choosing colors, spices, oils, places to walk, countries to visit—all very concrete decisions of everyday life that day by day either support or disturb the soul. We think of the psyche, if we think of it at all, as a cousin to the brain and therefore something essentially internal. But ancient psychologists taught that our own souls are inseparable from the world's soul, and that both are found in all the many things that make up nature and culture.

Directions: *Using the first draft checklist on the inside back cover as your guide, identify elements of an effective definition paragraph in A Professional's Take. Next, compare the elements the author used with the ones that you used in your first draft. Did you include enough effective examples and details in your paragraph to support your definition?*

Revise: Read Critically, then Rewrite

Revision gives you a chance to rethink. In definition writing, rethinking is key to clarifying your definition for your reader. A first draft gets just one angle on your term and subject. You might find that another angle is more effective. Be open to new thinking as you proceed with this step in the process. You may have to revise your first draft extensively.

REVISION IN ACTION

As previously mentioned, revision involves rethinking a draft in order to improve the quality of your writing: you read critically, plan your revision, and revise your writing. Quality revision will also improve your future writing. Here is an example of revision by a student named Taryn.

> **Assignment:** To finish our unit on history and government, pick a term used commonly by a subgroup and explain what it means.

REVISE
- Read critically
- Develop a revision plan

Taryn's First Draft

Aboriginal is a commonly used term by historians to describe people who are descended from the original groups living in North America before the first recorded arrival of Europeans around the 1500s. In Canada, the term includes the First Nations, Inuit, and Métis; *Indigenous peoples* is **another** term used to describe the pre-Columbian inhabitants of both North and South America while those in the United States are called Native Americans. When looking for new trade routes in the late 1400s, European explorers thought they had arrived at the East Indies and applied the term *Indians* to the people they encountered. Historically, *Indian* was the commonly used term for First Nations people. Many First Nations people in Canada prefer not to describe themselves as Indians, but this word has a legal meaning in the Indian Act and is used by the Federal Government of Canada for its laws and regulations. *Inuit* **also** describes the Aboriginal people of Arctic Canada. In the Inuit language, Inuktitut, *Inuit* means "the people," and this is the term that they use to refer to themselves. European explorers originally called the people in Canada's north "Eskimos," but this term is now not considered politically correct. Curiously, in 1939, the Supreme Court of Canada decided that Eskimos could be defined as Indians and would be represented by the Indian Act. Métis are the offspring of Indian

---

TOPIC SENTENCE
In her topic sentence, Taryn defines *Aboriginal* as a commonly used term and identifies a subgroup.

SUPPORTING DETAILS
She uses three examples of groups that are defined as Aboriginal. All of her details focus on these groups. Taryn includes reference to one of her sources of information. She eliminates redundancy.

ORDER AND TRANSITIONS
Taryn uses *another* and *also* as transitions. Her supporting points indicate chronological order.

women and European fur traders, and they developed distinct Métis communities along the trade routes of what are now Manitoba, Saskatchewan, and Alberta. Through treaties, the Government of Canada has obligations and commitments to First Nations, Inuit, and Métis. Each of these groups has distinct culture, history, traditions, language, geographical location, and lifestyle, and there is also rich diversity within these three groups. Lumping such diverse groups together into the confusing term *Indian* or *Aboriginal* creates difficulties for the government to fulfill its responsibilities.

CONCLUDING SENTENCE
Taryn concludes with several sentences to explore the complexity and suitability of sharing the term *Aboriginal* with three diverse groups.

Revision Plan: Change the order of the sentences to improve coherence. Add transitions. Add source information. Keep the academic tone that also helps define *Aboriginal*.

Taryn's Revised Draft

Today, *Aboriginal* is a term used to describe three groups of descendants from the original people living in North America before the first recorded arrival of Europeans. While looking for new trade routes in the late 1400s, European explorers thought they had arrived at the East Indies and applied the term *Indians* to the people they encountered. **Thus, historically,** *Indian* was a commonly used term that has now been replaced by a reference to First Nations people. Many First Nations people in Canada prefer not to describe themselves as Indians. **However,** this word has a legal meaning in the 1876 Indian Act and is used by the Federal Government of Canada for its laws and regulations. In Canada, the term *Aboriginal* includes not only the many First Nations tribes, but also Inuit and Métis. **Thus,** in addition to the First Nations, *Aboriginal* describes the people of Arctic Canada, or the Inuit. In the Inuit language, Inuktitut, *Inuit* means "the people" and this is what they call themselves. European explorers originally called the people in Canada's north "Eskimos," but this term is now not considered politically correct. According to Richard Diubaldo in the *Journal of Canadian Studies* (1981), the Supreme Court of Canada **curiously** decided in 1939 that Eskimos were Indians and would be represented by the Indian Act. **Finally,** the third group of Aboriginals includes the Métis, who are the offspring of Indian women and European fur traders. They developed distinct Métis communities along the trade routes of what are now the provinces of Manitoba, Saskatchewan, and Alberta. Through treaties, the Government of Canada has obligations and commitments to

TOPIC SENTENCE
Taryn keeps her original topic sentence but adds the word *today* to focus it.

ORDER AND TRANSITIONS
Taryn changes the order of the sentences to reflect the chronological development of the word *Aboriginal*. This improves the coherence or flow of ideas. She adds transition terms such as *however* and *thus* to connect the examples of Aboriginals.

SUPPORTING DETAILS
She defines *Aboriginal* by describing the groups included in the term. She then adds details like the 1876 Indian Act, in addition to the adverbs *historically* and *curiously* to show a more sophisticated explanation of her definition. Each sentence adds to the reader's understanding of *Aboriginal*. She eliminates the sentences that are not focused on Canadian Aboriginals.

First Nations, Inuit, and Métis. While all three Aboriginal groups have distinct culture, history, traditions, language, geographical location, and lifestyle from each other, there is also diversity within each group. <u>Lumping such diverse groups together into the confusing term *Indian* or *Aboriginal*</u> may create difficulties for the government to fulfill its responsibilities.

CONCLUDING SENTENCE
The concluding sentences show Taryn has understood the complexities of defining *Aboriginal*.

DISCUSSION QUESTIONS Identify two or three details that make Taryn's revised paragraph a more effective definition of *Aboriginal*.

READ CRITICALLY

When you are a critical reader for a classmate, you are also getting ideas about how you might improve your own paragraph. Critical reading is a search for the characteristics of effective writing: topic sentence, supporting examples and details, transitions, and concluding sentence. Being a peer reader can benefit you as you can study how classmates organize their thinking and the types of supporting details that they use to define a subject. Paying attention to how other writers write their definitions may help you write yours.

EXERCISE 11-11 **Reading Peer Papers**

Directions: *Exchange papers with another student. Keeping in mind the significant changes that Taryn made between writing her first draft and her revision, be a critical reader and make suggestions to improve your peer's first draft. Also, identify what your classmate did well. Make notes in the margin to remember your thoughts and suggestions. After you read, you will discuss your suggestions with each other. Use the guidelines from the revision checklist on the inside back cover.*

REVISE WITH A PLAN

Always reread your assignment instructions before revising to make sure the paragraph you have written relates directly to your assignment. Look back at all your prewriting for ideas and details you may have missed when you wrote your first draft. Think about cutting ideas and details to make room for more relevant material. Finally, consider rearranging the ideas and details in your paragraph to improve the coherence.

EXERCISE 11-12 **Revising Your Draft**

Directions: *Develop a revision plan and revise the paragraph you wrote for Exercise 11-9.*

Edit

The small things make all the difference in the quality of your writing. A misspelled word or an incorrect capitalization can instantly change your reader's view of your work—for the worse. You cannot afford to take that chance. In all your classes, not just English, you should get your writing as close to perfect as you can. If possible, read your work out loud. Look for the errors you know you make. Focus your editing using a personalized checklist or the editing checklist on the inside back cover. Remember to write for an academic audience by minimizing first- and second-person pronoun use; use third-person pronouns (*he, she, it, they*).

EDIT
• Search and correct
• Self-edit

Revising and Editing Practice

Directions: *Read the following paragraph that was written in response to the assignment below; it contains errors that require revising and editing. Then answer the questions that follow.*

Assignment: Define an activity, a job, an attitude, or a perspective that might be misunderstood.

(1) Waste management may be the most undervalued municipal service. (2) Most residents simply define waste management as garbage pickup. (3) _____, every urban area administration is committed to providing curbside pickup and environmentally sound waste management. (4) It might even be said that administrators embrace preservation of the environment through their waste reduction efforts. (5) For many years, recycling has been mandatory for house and apartment dwellers. (6) Diverting as much garbage as possible from landfill sites is important. (7) When we separate recyclables from our garbage, we stop re-usable materials from going to a landfill. (8) By recycling paper, cardboard, glass, and aluminum, energy use is reduced through reprocessing rather than producing new products from natural resources. (9) which can cut down on harmful emissions and water pollution. (10) Everyone must sort their waste as garbage, recyclable, compostable, or hazardous material. (11) Most municipalities use colour-coded bins or bags for the garbage collection. (12) Revenue collected from selling recyclable materials helps offset the high costs of collecting and sorting garbage. (13) Furthermore, organic waste is processed into clean, nutrient-rich compost that can be used in flowerbeds in community parks. (14) Household hazardous materials like paint, batteries, and some light bulbs need extra care when they are disposed of, so that they do not do harm to people, animals, or the environment. (15) Moreover, waste reduction saves consumers money and conserves resources. (16) _____. (17) _____.

REVISING

_____ 1. Which word or phrase should be inserted in blank 3? The word or phrase should focus the first point the writer is making to define *waste management*.

    a. First   c. In brief

    b. Most importantly   d. Similarly

_____ 2. To arrange the details of this paragraph in a logical order, select the change that is most logical.

    a. Move sentence 5 to follow 9, and sentence 15 so it follows sentence 11.

    b. Reverse the order of sentences 1 and 2.

c. Begin the paragraph with sentence 3.

d. No change is necessary.

_____ 3. Which sentence should be inserted in blank 16? The sentence should provide specific support details for sentence 7.

a. Garbage collection is about more than keeping litter off the streets.

b. The success of waste reduction relies on everyone's participation in the recycling program.

c. Waste management reduces the amount of garbage produced.

d. No change is necessary.

_____ 4. Which sentence should be inserted in blank 17? The sentence should provide a conclusion that restates the definition.

a. Recycling should be easy and convenient for you.

b. Garbage and waste generation rates have been steadily increasing in Canadian cities.

c. In summary, waste management is waste minimization, resource diversion, and environmentally friendly disposal.

d. Sorting garbage is too complicated.

EDITING

_____ 1. Choose the option that corrects the error in sentence 9.

a. Which can cut down on harmful emissions and water pollution.

b. Furthermore, recycling can cut down on harmful emissions and water pollution.

c. This can cut down on harmful emissions and water pollution.

d. No change is necessary.

_____ 2. Choose the option that corrects the error(s) in sentence 10.

a. The public must sort their waste into garbage, recyclables, compostable, or hazardous materials.

b. Everyone must sort his/her waste as garbage, recyclable, compostable, or hazardous materials.

c. All people must sort his/her waste as garbage, recyclable, compostable, or hazardous material.

d. No change is necessary.

_____ 3. Proofread the paragraph for spelling errors.

EXERCISE 11-14 **Searching and Correcting**

Directions: *Exchange papers with a peer and proofread each other's work. In addition to spelling, punctuation, and capitalization, find out what other errors your classmate has made; tell your classmate what errors you often make. Devise a personal editing checklist to help you focus on correcting your most common errors.*

Directions: *Carefully rewrite your paper, correcting errors you and your classmate found. Set aside the finished paper for a short time. Then come back to it, and read your final draft one last time, using the editing checklist on the inside back cover as a guide.*

REFLECT
- Identify strengths
- Set goals

Reflect

Definition writing puts you to the test. You made sophisticated decisions to apply your previous learning to the paragraph you wrote in the exercises in this chapter. Take a moment and reflect on what you have learned about writing definition paragraphs.

EXERCISE 11-16 **Identifying Strengths and Setting Goals**

Directions: *Review your writing and your writing process. Answer these questions:*

- *What did you do well in the paragraph you wrote?*
- *What did you enjoy working on in this chapter?*
- *What have you learned that you will apply in future writing assignments?*

Your answers to these questions will increase your awareness of your particular strengths and weaknesses. For your next writing assignment, you can focus on reaching your writing goals.

CHAPTER REVIEW

Recall what you have learned about definition writing.

■ DEFINITION THINKING

☐ Elements of definition

- *Group or category*

☐ Examples and details: examples elaborate on definition; details show accuracy of definition

☐ Negatives: define what you are *not* talking about

■ DEFINITION IN PROCESS

☐ Prewrite

- *Clustering and freewriting*

☐ Draft

- *Focus and organization; audience; topic sentence; unity and coherence; draft*

☐ Revise

- *Critical reading; revision plan; rewrite*

☐ Edit

- *Peer editing; self-editing*

☐ Reflect

- *Personal editing checklist: correct common errors*

Argument

THINK FIRST

Surveillance cameras are an invasion of privacy. Surveillance cameras are necessary for public safety. Which statement is correct? Write a paragraph in which you persuade the reader that one or the other viewpoint is accurate. Explain your reasons.

That Is Your Opinion

Much language activity is neutral. Casual conversation at home, classroom discussion, talk about a new person at work—in these contexts we are showing interest in each other, sharing information, or just passing the time of day. Then again, even casual conversation can have an edge. The give-and-take of talk can also become a contest. For example, one person says the best pizza in town is at Paisano's; the other makes a strong case for Milano Pizzeria. At first, there is a difference of opinion, and suddenly there is an argument. The focus of the argument is about crust, sauce, toppings, atmosphere, service, and prices. The argument about where to find the best pizza involves a careful (and passionate) analysis of what pizza is, how and where it is eaten, and why we like what we like. Such things are a matter of opinion, but from this argument comes a more detailed understanding of our subject—in this case, pizza.

BRAINSTORM

Do you have opinions? Sure you do. Make a list of your opinions on big issues and small issues. Then select three and write a sentence or two about each one.

Make Your Case

The academic writing you do will frequently be persuasive because it will ask you to evaluate: "most," "best," "least," "worst." When you write in college or university courses, you need to make a case for your reader. Why do students drop out of school? *The most common reason is . . .* This approach to the subject suggests that there are many reasons, that they are not all equal, and that the writer is going to make a case for what she feels is the most common. What if there is a difference of opinion? Then the writer has to dig down and present evidence for her opinion. She has to use information to convince her reader that her view is reasonable. Persuasion often involves finding facts that fit your point of view and then presenting those facts to win over your reader.

DISCUSSION

Talk with a classmate to answer the following questions: What is the most pressing problem facing your neighbourhood, your city, or your province? How can this problem be solved? What evidence, facts, statistics, or examples do you have to support your solution? Do you agree on how to solve this problem?

Sounds Like a Plan

On the job, you may have ideas about how to fine-tune processes and procedures. You assess the situation, think critically, and propose a plan of action. Often, however, it is not that easy. You have to persuade your co-workers and your boss that your plan makes sense. This requires careful observation and evidence and knowing how to appeal to others for support. If you convince co-workers that your plan reduces stress and reduces their workload, then you will have them on board, and they will probably agree to your idea. If you can convince your boss that your plan allows for greater efficiency and higher profits, then you will have a greater chance of seeing your plan taken seriously.

RESUMÉ BUILDER

There are many processes and procedures at work that you know well. Maybe you have a faster or better way to do something. Maybe you have a suggestion for handling customers. In what ways could your job be made more efficient or effective? What facts or details can you use to support your idea for change?

At a Glance

THE ARGUMENT PARAGRAPH AT A GLANCE

Argument begins with a difference of opinion. There may be two or more competing viewpoints on an issue, problem, or situation; as a writer, you need to take a stand. An effective argument paragraph will first crisply define the issue, problem, or situation, and then provide reasons and evidence for the stand, or point of view, taken.

Argument works best when the writer provides convincing information and compelling reasons for his/her point of view. The paragraph begins with your topic sentence, which clearly states your position or the claim of your argument. This opener is followed by details that explain the reasons for the argument. These details are usually ordered by importance, starting or ending with the most important details. Your final sentence clinches the argument, sums it up, and makes a powerful appeal to your reader to agree with your point of view.

The Argument Paragraph at a Glance

ASSIGNMENT   What is the best lifestyle choice a person can make to increase mental and physical health?

The best lifestyle choice a person can make to increase his or her mental and physical health is to decrease stress. Stress has been shown to have a negative impact on both mental and physical health. **For example**, people often deal with stress in one of two ways: they act out, which involves arguing, yelling, directing physical violence at others, and behaving self-destructively; or they withdraw inwardly, becoming depressed and isolated. **Those who deal with stress by** arguing or hurting others merely add to the stress in their lives. How can they possibly be happy when they hurt those they love? **Those who turn to** self-destructive behaviours, such as alcohol or drug use, are likely to do physical harm to themselves. **In contrast, those who turn inward** shut themselves away from people and experiences that might actually help them deal with the source of their stress. They concentrate on their own troubles, which only compounds their stress. People who decrease their stress can take pleasure in family and friends. **In addition**, an individual's health is enhanced when he or she is less stressed. **To the extent that** stress causes a person to direct negative energy both outward and inward, mental and physical health are going to be compromised. Live well. Minimize stress.

TOPIC SENTENCE
The student echoes the key words in the assignment and focuses on a health issue.

SUPPORTING DETAILS
The student discusses the consequences of stress, presenting them as reasons why stress has a negative effect on health.

ORDER AND TRANSITIONS
The student begins with the most important reason stress is negative: it hurts both the individual and other people. Then she shifts to the effects of stress on the individual alone.

CONCLUDING SENTENCES
In her last two sentences, the student emphasizes the point of her argument. Notice how short the two ending sentences are. This makes them stand out, reinforcing the writer's main idea.

1. What would be the effect of reversing the order of evidence in this paragraph?

2. What other lifestyle choices affect mental and physical health?

3. In your opinion, which of these other choices is the most important? Why?

Thinking

ARGUMENT THINKING

Argument is a special form of problem solving. You begin with a problem or issue. Should the government increase corporate taxes? What is your view? You have to settle matters in your own mind first. Then you have to anticipate the views of an audience. What do others think? Then you turn to reasons—why you think you are correct and what you believe to be the basis for opposing views. Finally, you present the evidence to support your position and explain your reasoning. If you want your argument to prevail, you need to be focused and logical.

Elements of Argument

These are the basic elements of argument thinking.

- *A claim:* Your topic sentence states a position or claim you are promoting.
- *Reasons, evidence, or details:* The body of your paragraph proves your claim with supporting details or evidence. Argument paragraphs use both personal and expert evidence. This evidence can be facts, examples, narrative, or compelling testimony. For example, you can use analogies where you point out the similarities of features in two items you are comparing (The heart works like a pump.) Alternatively, you can point out the assumptions or things your reader may take for granted. Yet another tool to support an argument is to explore the possible positive or negative outcomes or consequences of the event or issue under discussion.
- *Conceding other viewpoints:* Argument involves topics about which there are differences of opinion. It is common to acknowledge other viewpoints in your argument paragraph. In the sample above, for instance, the writer concedes that diet and sleep can both contribute to physical and mental health.

Get Started

In academic argument writing, you have to take a stand. Readers do not want to see, "In the end every person has to make up his or her own mind." No, your reader wants *you* to *make up your mind* and present detailed reasoning to make a case for your point of view. Doing so shows the reader that you can think critically and that you are well informed about your subject and confident about your point of view.

Suppose you are presented with a question like this: Should students be able to use smart phones in their classes? Maybe you take the stand expressed in the following topic sentence. Then you list reasons to support your claim.

Writer's Response ❯❯

When you argue, how do you support a claim you make? What kind of evidence is most effective?

Topic Sentence: Students should definitely be able to use smart phones in their classes.

Reasons

A. Technology makes the job of accessing Internet information easier. Why not use it?

B. Technology is widely used in other classes: word processors with spell-check, for example.

C. Technology helps students find relevant reference material faster.

This topic sentence and these reasons are just the start. You are not committed to this stand; you are exploring it. Your exploration might be based on an assumption (technology is good). It might be based on an analogy (technology is used in other classes). It might be based on consequences (easier and faster to access Internet resources).

EXERCISE 12-1 **Taking a Stand**

Directions: *Write a sentence that states your position on each of the following issues in the spaces provided. Then briefly list two or three reasons or details to support your view. Indicate whether your reasons are based on assumption, on analogy, or on consequences.*

1. Is it a good idea to give money to a homeless person standing on a street corner?

Topic Sentence: _____

_____

Reasons

A. _____

B. _____

C. _____

Reasons based on assumption/analogy/consequences: _____

2. Should servers in restaurants be required to pool or share the tips they receive?

Topic Sentence: _____

_____

Reasons

A. _____

B. _____

C. _____

Reasons based on assumption/analogy/consequences: _____

3. Should juvenile offenders who commit violent crimes be tried as adults?

Topic Sentence: _____

_____

Reasons

A. _____

B. _____

C. _____

Reasons based on assumption/analogy/consequences: _____

Review Evidence

Once you identify reasons for your position on a topic, you need to provide evidence. Your argument is only as good as your evidence, which might consist of personal narrative, observation and example, or expert opinion and data that show the validity of your reasons. To strengthen your argument, make use of other rhetorical modes such as example or cause/effect. Personal narrative is often a starting point for the writer, but academic writing is strengthened by using expert opinions, data, or examples to support your claim.

In the example that follows, the student argues for the use of smart phones in the classroom using all three forms of evidence to support his argument.

This evidence supports the student's first reason: "Technology makes some tasks easier."

Personal Narrative

Technology makes some tasks easier. Many years ago in elementary-school math classes, pupils did long-division problems for weeks at a time. The work was tedious and took forever. Everyone hated it. The only thing it taught some students was to hate math. Long division with a calculator on a smart phone takes only seconds. By hand, it takes a very long time.

Personal Observation and Example

My math class this semester, science class last semester; friends' classes where they go to college. Smart phones okay.

Expert Opinion

Patricia Campbell, a math professor at the University of Maryland, states in *The Washington Post,* "I would want a child to know how to add and subtract two and three digit numbers. However, I do not want to spend class time adding and subtracting five and six digit numbers. I would rather spend class time doing other math" (www.education-world.com/a_curr/curr072.shtml).

Expert opinion and data can be particularly useful in argument paragraphs. For a detailed explanation of how to go about finding expert opinion and data, see Chapter 16, "The Documented Essay."

Directions: *Select a topic that interests you from Exercise 12-1. Write your topic sentence in the space provided and list evidence, such as personal narrative, examples, or expert opinion, that supports your argument.*

Topic Sentence: _____

_____

_____

Evidence: _____

_____

_____

_____

Acknowledge Another Viewpoint

Argument involves the explanation of reasons that support a viewpoint. Your viewpoint must fit the facts. As you formulate opinions and review evidence, you will become aware of opposing views. What makes your viewpoint preferable? Is it more reasonable? Does it fit the facts better?

You may initially avoid thinking about views that are contrary to your own. Taking them into consideration, however, may actually help you better understand the basis of your viewpoint and strengthen your position. Acknowledging opposing viewpoints can be tricky, so it's important to acknowledge them during your prewriting activities by using T-charts or Venn diagrams to see where there might be common ground. The graphic organizers can help you evaluate which side of the argument has the strongest support. However, be sure that you show how the counterargument is weaker or not as valid as your own point of view.

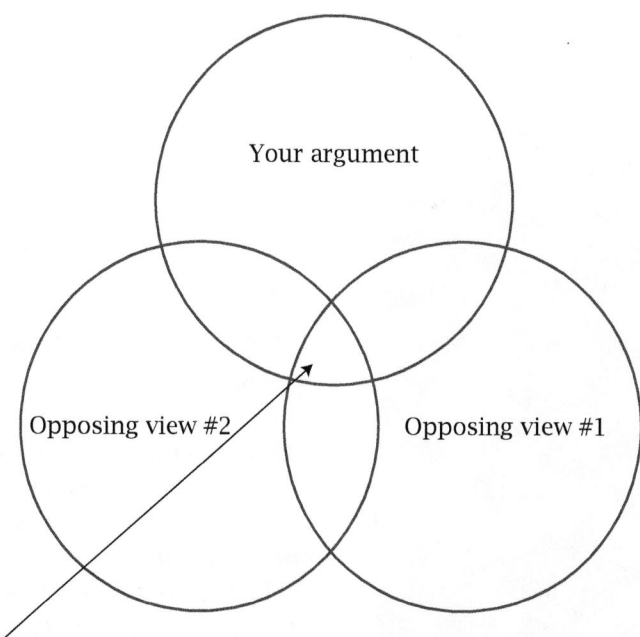

Look at the opposing viewpoints for where you can make concessions to your argument.

In the case of using smart phones in math classes, the student examines the opposing view and a few reasons to support it.

Opposing View: Smart phones should not be used in elementary math classes.

A. Students might not learn fundamentals of math.

B. Students become dependent on machines and technology and cannot think without their help.

These reasons seem valid. Learning the fundamentals is important. Being able to think without the help of machines is important. Simply to dismiss these reasons would actually hurt this student's argument for the use of smart phones in the classroom. His task then is to acknowledge these opposing reasons, to concede them, and in so doing, qualify his position. Another way of thinking of this is that the writer gives a little ground. He admits the value of another way of looking at the issues.

Topic Sentence: Students should definitely be able to use smart phones in their math classes.

concede opposing reasons

A. It is true that students might not learn fundamentals.

B. It is true that students might become dependent on machines and technology and be unable to think without their help.

qualifier

C. For this reason, students should not use smart phones until they have mastered the fundamentals.

D. After that, if technology makes the task easier, why not use it?

supporting reasons

E. Technology is widely used in other classes: word processors with spell-check, for example.

F. Technology helps math students get to higher-level math ideas faster.

Because he has acknowledged opposing reasons, the student's argument is now stronger. A reader cannot object, saying, "Wait, what about students who do not know how to multiply?" In his qualifier, he has answered this objection. When you qualify your position on an issue, you soften it slightly. You move from saying something is *always* true to saying something is *frequently* true or true *under certain conditions*.

The steps a student makes when framing an argument can be pictured as follows.

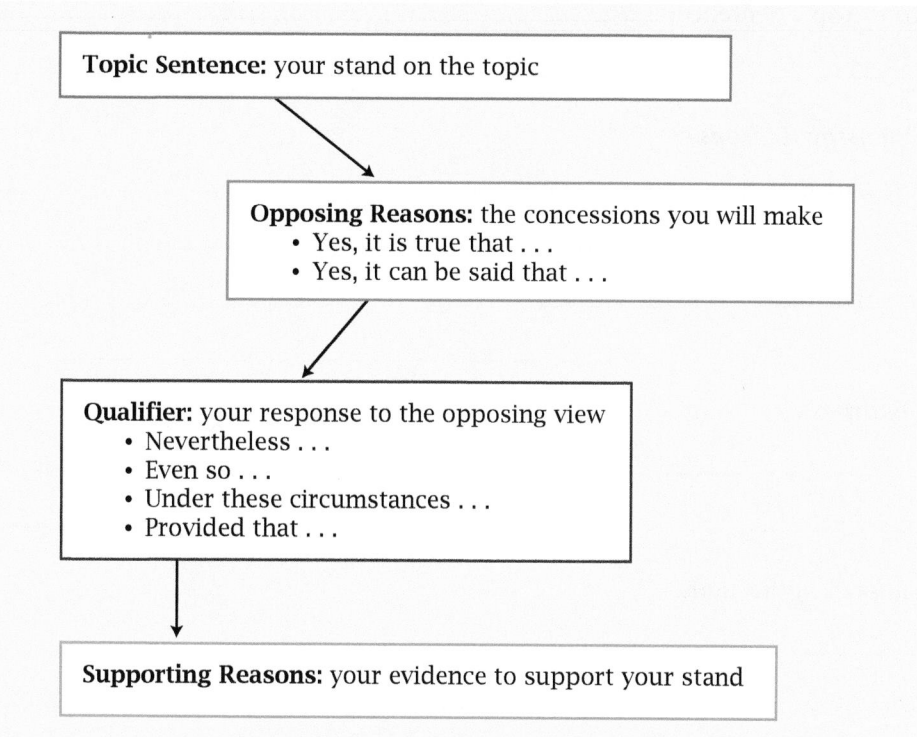

Topic Sentence: your stand on the topic

Opposing Reasons: the concessions you will make
• Yes, it is true that . . .
• Yes, it can be said that . . .

Qualifier: your response to the opposing view
• Nevertheless . . .
• Even so . . .
• Under these circumstances . . .
• Provided that . . .

Supporting Reasons: your evidence to support your stand

EXERCISE 12-3 **Acknowledging an Opposing Viewpoint**

Directions: *Review the topic you worked on in Exercises 12-1 and 12-2. You have taken a stand on an issue and reviewed evidence that supports your position. Now consider the opposing viewpoint. Using the outline that follows, list two or three reasons that support the opposing viewpoint and then qualify your position on the issue to reflect those reasons.*

EXAMPLE

Assignment: State your opinion on mothers working outside the home and the possible impact on their children.

Topic Sentence: It is often necessary for the well-being of the family for mothers to work outside the home, and this is ultimately good for their children.

Opposing Reasons

It is true that   A. Small children may be looked after in daycare rather than in the home, which is not optimal.

It is true that   B. Older children can be unsupervised after school, which has risks.

Qualifier

C. Nevertheless, <u>in cases where these supervision issues are addressed properly</u>, having women in the workplace can be a good thing.

Supporting Reasons

D. Working mothers contribute significantly to family income.

E. Working mothers provide positive role models for both their female and male children.

Your Topic Sentence: _____

_____

Opposing Reasons

It is true that   A. _____

                                        _____

It is true that   B. _____

                                        _____

Qualifier

C. _____

_____

Supporting Reasons

D. _____

_____

E. _____

_____

Process

ARGUMENT IN PROCESS

Argument often begins with something you read or hear. You think, *Wait a minute. That is not right.* This reaction triggers an investigation of your position on the subject, on the opposing viewpoints, and on the evidence you gather. Argument is about examining your beliefs and opinions, determining their foundations, and squaring them with the facts.

Select an Assignment

In academic courses, students need to persuade the reader that they are informed and that they have mastered the content. They also need to demonstrate fairness and openness to other viewpoints. Therefore, when you take a position on a subject, you must include the evidence to the contrary in your discussion.

EXERCISE 12-4   **Selecting an Assignment for an Argument Paragraph**

Directions: *Review the assignments listed below. Choose the one you know the most about and think is best suited to an effective argument paragraph.*

1. Should seniors over the age of 80 still be allowed to drive?

2. Should minimum age limits be considered when issuing credit cards?

3. Should voting in provincial and federal elections be made mandatory?

4. Should students caught cheating be kicked out of school?

5. Should smokers have to pay for their own health treatments?

6. Are the salaries of professional athletes reasonable?

7. Should people elected as Members of Parliament receive better pensions that the average person?

8. Should employers be allowed access to their employees' email accounts?

9. Discuss a current rule or law that needs to be changed.

10. Select a subject from a current course or a subject of your choice.

Talk about it

Making a strong argument is easier if you really care about the topic. Which topic interests you most?

Prewrite: Write Before You Write

Argument pushes you to examine your beliefs and opinions. It requires you to explore a subject from multiple viewpoints. We often have arguments in casual conversation. For that reason, after your initial exploration of your topic, square off with classmates to test your ideas and help you ascertain what particular point of view you wish to defend and write about.

PREWRITE
- Talk
- Think
- Cluster
- Brainstorm
- Question
- Freewrite

EXERCISE 12-5 Freewriting

Directions: *Freewrite on your subject for ten minutes. Take a stand and examine any facts, examples, and reasons related to your viewpoint. As well, explore opposing points of view. Be open to new thinking. You may find that a new claim will emerge. Graphic organizers can help you organize your ideas.*

EXERCISE 12-6 Talking about It

Directions: *Turn to your neighbour in class. Tell this person about your subject and state the opinion you explored in your freewriting. Explain both sides of the argument as you see it. Then listen to your classmate's viewpoint. Take notes to capture his or her views. Then be a critical listener of your partner's argument for his/her subject.*

Draft: Focus and Organize

When writing an argument, you must be clear about your viewpoint. What is your position on your topic? What examples and reasons can you cite to support your position? What facts support your position? What facts go against your position?

CONSIDER YOUR AUDIENCE

In argument writing, considering your audience will strengthen your argument and your paragraph. Identifying their counterarguments can be helpful. Review your prewriting to find the important ideas you want to use in your paragraph. Use the following questions to consider your audience.

- Why is this topic important?
- What do I want my reader to understand about my topic?

DRAFT
- Consider your audience
- Formulate your topic sentence
- Outline for unity and coherence
- Write a concluding sentence
- Compose your first draft

- What objections would a reader have to my position on this subject?
- What is my response to those objections?

EXERCISE 12-7 **Considering Your Audience**

Directions: *Use the questions above to think critically about your topic, opinion, and reasons. Talk with a classmate to clarify your thinking. Take notes on this conversation and add them to your prewriting.*

FORMULATE YOUR TOPIC SENTENCE

In an argument paragraph, your topic sentence establishes your topic and states your viewpoint. Write a topic sentence that clearly states your position.

OUTLINE FOR UNITY AND COHERENCE

Staying on topic is important in argument. If you go off topic, your reader loses your argument's train of thought. A unified argument paragraph focuses on ideas and details related to supporting the paragraph's main idea.

In addition to unity, coherence will add strength to your argument. Think ahead about your transitions, which make the relationships among ideas, details, and reasons visible for the reader. Consider using appropriate transitions related to evidence and conclusions in your argument paragraph.

WRITE A CONCLUDING SENTENCE

When writers place the topic sentence at the beginning of a paragraph, the concluding sentence generally restates the claim in different words and emphasizes the writer's viewpoint.

EXERCISE 12-8 **Planning Your First Draft**

See "Supporting Details" in Chapter 3 for a detailed explanation of outlining.

Directions: *Write a topic sentence that states your claim and connects to your assignment. Then use the topic sentence to outline your supporting details. Although your transitions may change in your first draft, include them in your outline to plan how the forms of proof will support your argument.*

COMPOSE YOUR FIRST DRAFT

As you write a first draft, remember that it is better to write too much than too little. Put all the evidence you have in your first draft. In a second draft, you can cut what a reader does not find convincing. Also, be sure you explain your ideas and reasons.

EXERCISE 12-9 **Writing Your First Draft**

Directions: *Write a draft of your paragraph. Include multiple forms of proof (facts, examples, or testimony) to convince your reader. Ask yourself if you have included reasons that explain the evidence. Refer to the first draft checklist on the inside back cover as a guide.*

A PROFESSIONAL'S TAKE

The use of argument from *The Economist*

The two main arguments against being helped into death are both of the "slippery slope" sort. The first is that it is hard to know where the boundary lies. Should a patient be three days, three months or three years away from death when the help is given? If the criterion is that a patient should be terminally ill, how should "terminally" be defined? Is it logical to distinguish between terminally ill and chronically ill, if a chronically ill person wants to die but may have years to live? Should people in good physical health but emotional distress be allowed help in dying? This is a matter of where to draw the line. The even tougher counter argument is that the whole process is dangerously open to abuse. To many, legal doctor-assisted suicide is a harbinger of evil, the start of a slide into a time of state-condoned euthanasia when the frail and the handicapped will be bullied into dying prematurely, doctors will become executioners, and the terminally ill will be offered the "treatment" of death instead of relief from pain. Death, after all, is cheaper than treatment. It is not hard to imagine health-insurance companies and managed-care organizations agreeing to pay for barbiturates that kill rather than pills that merely reduce pain. The strongest practical argument the defenders of a ban on doctor-assisted suicide can make is that, though some people would benefit from help in dying, a greater number are vulnerable to potential abuse from such a system; therefore, society has an interest in asking the state to protect their lives. The trouble is that this argument leaves dying people preserved in a state of suffering without any chance to choose oblivion instead. Even more important, it assumes that a law for doctor-assisted suicide cannot be drafted in a way that would prevent its abuse.

EXERCISE 12-10   **A PROFESSIONAL'S TAKE**

Directions: *Using the first draft checklist on the inside back cover as your guide, identify elements of an effective argument paragraph in A Professional's Take. Next, compare the elements the author used with the ones that you used in your first draft. Did you include enough effective examples and details in your paragraph to persuade your reader of your point of view?*

Revise: Read Critically, Then Rewrite

Before you revise your paragraph, examine the strengths in a classmate's argument paragraph. Then look at your argument paragraph with fresh eyes. Revision gives you a chance to rethink and improve your writing.

REVISION IN ACTION

Revision is rethinking a draft to improve the quality of your writing: read critically, plan revision, and revise the writing. As you plan your

> **REVISE**
> - Read critically
> - Develop a revision plan

revisions, you need to ensure that you are using enough reasons, evidence, or details to make your argument convincing. Rather than use only their own ideas, academic writers draw on the ideas of other writers to add strength to their arguments, but be sure to distinguish between your ideas and those of someone else. You must give credit to these outside ideas so that your reader knows you have researched more than one point of view for your argument and that you are not plagiarizing, or stealing, another person's ideas. When you refer to outside sources, document where you found the information by using in-text reference to the material and then adding a list at the end of the piece of writing where your reader can find the original sources that you used. There are several ways to format both the in-text citations and the list at the end, using bibliographies, Works Cited, or References. You will learn more about how to do this in Chapter 16.

Quality revision will also improve your writing by including sufficient, convincing supporting facts and details. Here is an example of revision by a student named Diana. Notice how she refers to two authorities to add details and strength to her argument.

Assignment: What can the informed individual do to make a difference on an environmental issue today? Be specific and use references to support your argument.

Diana's First Draft

A small thing consumers can do that would have a big environmental impact is to stop using plastic water bottles. **On the one hand**, plastic water bottles are convenient. They are light and easy to carry. They don't need to be filled up before leaving home and there's no need to wash them out after using them. Cases of water bottles are very cheap to buy at the grocery store. **However**, according to research done by Toxic Free Canada, the manufacturing process for a single plastic water bottle generates almost four times its weight in greenhouse gases and releases at least two potential cancer-causing chemicals. **Furthermore**, hundreds of millions of beverage bottles are dumped in Canadian landfills each year. With that volume of plastic waste, single-use plastic bottles are creating a big environmental footprint. Some European studies report that chemicals from the plastic can leach into the water people are drinking, with unknown health effects. **How about drinking tap water?** A report by the C.D. Howe Institute reports that ever since the 2000 Walkerton, Ontario, drinking water outbreaks, people in most urban areas of Canada worry about the quality of their public water supply. Water is one of the cheapest beverages available at the turn of the kitchen sink tap, and in all the provinces, municipalities do monitor and provide safe drinking water. **The best solution**, it turns out, is to take reusable water bottles filled with tap water with you to school, work, or the gym. This will save you money

TOPIC SENTENCE
Diana uses key words from the assignment and states a specific action an individual can take.

SUPPORTING DETAILS
Diana provides details about using plastic water bottles. Then she explores two ways a person can stop using them. She provides facts, details, and reasons to support her argument.

ORDER AND TRANSITIONS
She uses a variety of transitions to connect major and minor points in her paragraph. She clearly indicates the key point in her argument ("best solution")..

because you only need to buy a container once. Using fewer single-use plastic water bottles is one of the easiest changes we can make to protect the environment from plastic waste and to reduce greenhouse gases that cause global warming.

CONCLUDING SENTENCE
Diana uses one sentence to conclude and makes two comments about reusable drink containers.

Revision Plan: Remove the informal language and use third person rather than *you*. Work on adding more supporting details. Check sentence structures and transitions.

Diana's Revised Draft

A small step every consumer can take to have a positive environmental impact is to stop using plastic water bottles. Plastic water bottles are truly convenient. They are lighter and easier to carry than a Thermos bottle or a metal water bottle. They don't need to be filled up before leaving home, and there's no need to wash them out after using them. Cases of water bottles are economical to purchase at the grocery store. **However**, according to research done by Toxic Free Canada, the manufacturing process for a single plastic water bottle generates almost four times its weight in greenhouse gases and releases at least two potential cancer-causing chemicals. **Furthermore**, hundreds of millions of beverage bottles are dumped in Canadian landfills each year. With that volume of plastic waste, single-use plastic bottles are creating a staggering environmental footprint. **Additionally**, some European studies report that chemicals from the plastic can leach into the water in the plastic bottle with unknown health effects. **Could drinking tap water be a better option?** A report by the C.D. Howe Institute reports that ever since the 2000 Walkerton drinking water outbreaks, people in most urban areas of Canada began to worry about the quality of their public water supply. **Nevertheless**, water is one of the cheapest beverages available at the turn of the kitchen sink tap, and in all the provinces, municipalities are monitoring and providing Canadians with safe drinking water. **The best solution**, it turns out, is to take along reusable water bottles, like stainless steel containers, filled with tap water to school, work, or the gym. This will save money because a reusable container only needs to be purchased once. Using fewer single-use plastic water bottles is one of the easiest changes a Canadian consumer can make to protect the environment from plastic waste and to reduce greenhouse gases that cause global warming.

TOPIC SENTENCE
Diana revises her topic sentence.

SUPPORTING DETAILS
Diana concedes that plastic bottles are convenient and inexpensive. She adds detail to explain convenience. Diana also adds detail on the landfill impact in this draft. She uses third person.

ORDER AND TRANSITIONS
She moves the argument from plastic to reusable containers. Her transitions connect facts, details, and reasons in each major point.

CONCLUDING SENTENCE
Diana revises her concluding sentence, focusing responsibility on the individual.

References

Griffin, S. (2009). The toxic footprint of PET bottled water in British Columbia. Retrieved from http://toxicfreecanada.ca

Hrudey, S.E. (2011). Safe drinking water policy for Canada—Turning hindsight into foresight. Retrieved from http://www.cdhowe.org/safe-drinking-water-policy-for-canada-%E2%80%93-turning-hindsight-into-foresight/8585

DISCUSSION QUESTIONS What changes affect the tone of Diana's paragraph? Cite and discuss two or three specific examples. Examine the function of including the rhetorical question, "Could drinking tap water be a better option?"

READ CRITICALLY

When you read a peer's paper, you will gain skill at reading your own writing more critically. You learn to read systematically. Think about difficulties you had when you wrote your own paragraph. Look for ways your classmate handled similar difficulties in his or her writing. Peer reading gives you insight into what your reader will experience when reading your writing.

EXERCISE 12-11 **Reading Peer Papers**

Directions: *Exchange papers with another student. Keeping in mind the strengths and weaknesses of Diana's argument paragraph, be a systematic reader of your peer's work and identify the claim, points, evidence, and explanation. Also identify what you each did well in your writing. Make notes in the margin to remember your suggestions. After you read, discuss your suggestions with each other. Use the revision checklist guidelines found on the inside back cover to guide you.*

REVISE WITH A PLAN

Reread your assignment before revising. Be sure your focus matches the assignment. In addition, review the elements of argument and look for them in your paragraph. Do you take a clear position? Do you provide reasons and explain them? Do you take opposing viewpoints into account? Do you qualify your argument based on them? Reread your paragraph and the notes from your peer conference. Make changes accordingly as you rewrite the assignment.

EXERCISE 12-12 **Revising Your Draft**

Directions: *Develop a revision plan and revise the paragraph you wrote for Exercise 12-9.*

EDIT
- Search and correct
- Self-edit

Edit

In argument writing, facts matter. However, nothing is more persuasive than carefully edited writing. If your reader is distracted by careless errors, your argument is in trouble. This is true in English class and in all classes you take during your post-secondary studies. Focus your editing using the editing checklist on the inside back cover of the text.

Revising and Editing Practice

Directions: *Read the following paragraph that was written in response to the assignment below; it contains errors that require revising and editing. Then answer the questions that follow.*

Assignment: Select a topic about which you have a strong opinion. Write an argument paragraph stating your position on the topic. Use specific facts, details, and examples to argue and support your position, taking into account how others may disagree with your point of view.

(1) Animal rights groups argue that there is no reason to hunt animals, that it is inhumane, and that the animals are little more than target practice for the hunters. (2) Hunters argue otherwise they insist that hunting is much more than simply pointing a gun or a bow in the direction of game animals and taking close aim. (3) Ask bird hunters how often they miss or never even have a chance to take a shot at there prey. (4) They will describe the years of target practice, tracking, or dog training required to be a successful bird hunter. (5) No, hunting is not about killing. (6) _____. (7) A family-oriented tradition passed from father to son, hunting provides an excellent opportunity for bonding between parents and children and can offer lots of time for personal reflection. (8) Some fathers and sons have quality time together fishing. (9) While they are hunting, they enjoy watching the sun come up, walking in silence and listening to the birds, and breathing the fresh air. (10) _____, hunters eat what they kill, and they respect the regulations and limits set by game management policies so game is not overhunted. (11) Actually, hunters play an important role in holding the ecosystem in balance. (12) Thinning the population of wildlife that is moving into urban areas. (13) Hunters also protect the food supply and the health of the remaining wildlife. (14) The positive effects of hunting far outweigh the negatives both for the hunter personally and for the ecosystem as a whole.

REVISING

_____ 1. Which sentence should be inserted in blank 6? The sentence should state the argument and serve as the topic sentence.

   a. Hunting should be valued by nonhunters.

   b. Hunting is a tradition that requires skill and adherence to a code of ethics.

   c. Animal rights groups are wrong about hunting.

   d. People have their own points of view about hunting: some like it; some do not.

_____ 2. Select the order of sentences 2, 3, 4, and 5 to provide the most logical sequence of details to present the position of the paragraph and support the topic sentence.

a. 5, 2, 3, 4   c. 2, 3, 5, 4

b. 2, 5, 3, 4   d. No change is necessary.

_____ 3. Which word or phrase should be inserted in blank 10?

a. Second   c. In addition

b. As a result   d. In any case

_____ 4. Which sentence should be cut to improve the unity of the paragraph?

a. Sentence 1   c. Sentence 13

b. Sentence 8   d. No change is necessary.

EDITING

_____ 1. Choose the option that corrects the error in sentence 1.

a. Animal rights groups argue, that there is no reason to hunt animals; it is inhumane the animals are little more than target practice for the hunters.

b. Animal rights groups argue that there is no reason to hunt animals; that it is inhumane; and that the animals are little more than target practice for the hunters.

c. Animal rights groups argue that there is no reason to hunt animals. That it is inhumane, and that the animals are little more than target practice for the hunters.

d. No change is necessary.

Ask Yourself

Which revision strategy do you prefer: adding, cutting, or rearranging details?

_____ 2. Choose the option that corrects the spelling error in sentence 3.

a. Ask bird hunters how often they miss or never even have a chance to take a shot at there pray.

b. Ask bird hunters how often they miss or never even have a chance to take a shot at their prey.

c. Ask bird hunters how often they miss or never even have a chance to take a shoot at there prey.

d. No change is necessary.

_____ 3. Sentence 12 is a fragment. Choose the option to correct this sentence error.

a. Combine sentence 11 and 12.

b. Combine sentence 12 and 13.

c. Cut sentence 11.

d. Cut sentence 12.

4. Proofread the paragraph for a run-on sentence and correct the error.

Searching and Correcting

Directions: *Exchange papers with a peer and proofread each other's work. In addition to spelling, punctuation, and capitalization, find out what other errors your classmate often makes; tell your classmate what errors you usually make.*

EXERCISE 12-15 **Self-Editing**

Directions: *Rewrite your paper, correcting errors you and your classmate found. Set aside the finished paper. Then come back to it and read your final draft one last time, using the editing checklist on the inside back cover as a guide.*

Reflect

Take a moment and reflect on what you have learned about writing argument paragraphs.

EXERCISE 12-16 **Identifying Strengths and Setting Goals**

Directions: *Review your writing and your writing process. Answer these questions:*

- *What did you do well in the paragraph you wrote?*
- *What did you enjoy working on in this chapter?*
- *What have you learned that you will apply in future writing assignments?*

Your answers to these questions will increase your awareness of your particular strengths and weaknesses. For your next writing assignment, focus on improving your weaknesses.

REFLECT
- Identify strengths
- Set goals

CHAPTER REVIEW

Take a moment and reflect on what you have learned about argument writing.

■ ARGUMENT THINKING

☐ Elements of argument

- *A claim; reasons, evidence, or details; conceding other viewpoints; conclusion*

☐ Review evidence

- *Personal narrative, observation, example, expert opinion, data, cause and effect*

☐ Acknowledge another viewpoint

- *Give a little ground: strengthen your position*

■ ARGUMENT IN PROCESS

☐ Select an assignment

☐ Prewrite

- *Freewrite; talk*

☐ Draft

- *Focus and organize; audience; unity; transitions: coherence; concluding sentence: writer's viewpoint*

☐ Revise

- *Critical reading; revision plan; revision checklist and rewrite*

☐ Edit

- *Peer editing and self-editing; editing checklist*

☐ Reflect

- *Strengths; writing goals*

Essay Structure

THINK FIRST

Writing an essay can be a process of discovery. You go places you did not know were on the map. To start thinking about essay writing, write a paragraph about a time when you made a surprising discovery that would take longer than a paragraph to explain. What did you think you were going to find? What did you find instead? How do you account for the gap between your expectations and your actual experience? The answer to each of these questions would be explained in its own paragraph, but since the ideas are related, the paragraphs could be put together to form an essay.

Exchanging Ideas: Thinking in Expository Mode

If you find yourself disagreeing with someone about an issue, think about how and why you disagree. Supporting your beliefs with details and examples and conveying them in a civil, respectful tone will contribute to the strength and coherence of your message. By exchanging ideas, you will come to a better understanding of others' opinions as well as your own.

BRAINSTORM

Make a list of two or three hot topics you often argue about with others. Divide a sheet of paper in half. Choose one topic, and on one side write "My view"; on the other side, write "Their view." Make a list of opinions, reasons, and beliefs on both sides. Which ones are based on facts? Do the facts make you more inclined to agree with a particular point of view?

Assignment Techniques

An important part of writing is knowing what the assignment is asking you to do. When writing for an assignment or an exam, be sure to consider what the format of the answer should be—essay, paragraph, short answer, or something else. If the assignment includes an essay component, ask yourself about the key points in the material the exam covers, list these points, and make a note of examples and details that support them. Concentrate on including facts, such as dates, formulas, or examples, that demonstrate you know the content of the material you are being tested on. Focus on material that was emphasized in class by checking your notes or following the instructions given by your instructor.

DISCUSSION

Turn and talk to a classmate about the kinds of tests you like and dislike. What are the reasons for your respective positions? Do you agree or disagree with your classmate?

Multitasking: Staying Organized

At work, it is not unusual to be faced with several tasks simultaneously. This is where your organizational and outlining skills come into play. Many people find it helpful to write out a to-do list that outlines what needs to be done and in what order. Planning and structuring will make the tasks less daunting. Organizing will help you get the job done quickly and effectively.

RESUMÉ BUILDER

Recall a time when your organization skills paid off. What were the circumstances? Who else was involved? What did you do? Why did it matter? Write a paragraph that captures the important dimensions of this incident. As you write, think of your audience as a prospective employer since this is often a question asked at job interviews.

At a Glance

Readers of college and university writing have definite expectations when they see an essay. They expect multiple paragraphs. They expect a beginning, a middle, and an end. They expect the writer to explain how the ideas and details all fit together and make sense. The best students know that good ideas alone are not enough. They have to know their readers' expectations and give them something that looks and reads like an essay.

The Essay at a Glance

ASSIGNMENT Write an essay about a common problem in contemporary life.

The essay's title is a preview of the content.

The student begins with a captivating story.

THESIS STATEMENT

TOPIC SENTENCE

Threat on the Road

As she reached the intersection, a car was coming toward her at high speed. It looked like it would run the light. She swerved to avoid hitting the car. Then she rolled down her window and was ready to give the driver a piece of her mind. However, he slammed on his brakes, got out of his car, and began shouting obscenities at her. He was at fault, yet he was shouting at the blameless driver! She hit the gas pedal and got out of there, fast. There is much anger on the road these days. Anger is understandable, but sane people should not give in to road rage. Road rage incidents stem from aggressive driving, responses to careless driving, or frustrations from traffic and road conditions.

Anger and aggression on the road, or "road rage," can lead drivers to carry out violent acts against other drivers. People become so angry

that they overreact, drive aggressively, and cause accidents. They resort to physical violence, attacking cars or assaulting their drivers with weapons. Recently a mother of two was involved in a road rage episode. She was on her way to work when an SUV began tailgating her. In an attempt to get away from the SUV, the woman began speeding. The SUV changed lanes, passed her, and then crossed over in front of her. The SUV slammed on its brakes, causing the woman to turn sharply and crash into a guardrail. She worried that her automobile insurance rates would go up. **In another case**, a 20-year-old man was furious after a fender bender with a 33-year-old woman. He was so infuriated that he dragged her out of her vehicle and forced her to jump from a bridge into the river, where she nearly drowned. **Finally**, a young man suffered recently from a beating he received after a minor car accident. The 26-year-old had gotten out of his vehicle to see the damage to his car. The other driver became so enraged that he beat him with a baseball bat. Is it necessary to resort to violence to prove a point?

CONCLUDING SENTENCE

TOPIC SENTENCE

When a driver experiences a close call from someone else's careless driving, he or she, too, may give in to road rage. Careless drivers exude the attitude that they alone own the road. **For example**, they run stoplights intentionally, they make inappropriate lane changes, they tailgate, and they speed in and out of traffic, shouting, cursing, and making offensive hand gestures. **Probably** everyone has witnessed some of these things, but some drivers react to these careless driving incidents by trying to get even. They retaliate with aggressive driving. Race, gender, and age do not play a role in these road rage incidents. The problem is that some people go too far to prove the point that the other driver was at fault.

EXAMPLES
The student provides vivid examples of what drivers do when they act on road rage.

Drivers need to get from point A to point B within a certain time frame. Heavy traffic during rush hour may cause delays, which means a driver will be late for work. **Consequently**, the driver takes out his/her frustration on the car in front. Driving cars causes some people to lose control of their emotions. People standing in line do not assault each other. In a traffic jam, they sometimes do. Construction work on highways can also reduce traffic flow, causing drivers to become angry. **Additionally**, Canadian winter weather conditions often make roads hazardous, requiring drivers to slow down. This means reaching their destinations will take longer and the drivers become impatient. Thus, traffic, construction, and weather conditions can trigger road rage incidents.

CONCLUDING SENTENCE

CONCLUSION
The student asks an important question in her conclusion and includes some suggestions in the concluding paragraph of the essay.

Where does all this rage come from? What can be done about it? Many kinds of stress make people a little crazy, especially when they are in a hurry and driving a car. Others say there is something about the car, the power it has, and the impersonal space between the driver and other people. There has to be a limit to aggressive driving and road rage. Give yourself plenty of time to reach your destination. Slow down. Stay calm. Stay alive.

1. It can be difficult to think of good titles. Suggest two or three more titles for this essay.

2. The student makes use of examples to develop the ideas in this essay. Is the essay also about definition? Cause or effect? Explain.

3. Suppose the student were going to revise this essay. What would you like to know more about? Make two suggestions.

ELEMENTS OF ESSAY STRUCTURE

Here are the basic elements of an effective essay.

- *Introduction:* When you write an essay, you present information, but you also present yourself to the reader. For this reason, the introduction is like an invitation. It draws the reader into the essay, states and focuses the topic, and conveys the topic's importance. ". . . a car was coming toward her at high speed" is an interesting opening. The reader wants to know what happens next.

- *Body:* The paragraphs of the body of the essay provide the content and the support for the main idea. You examine and develop related ideas, making connections and explaining how the pieces fit together. Your job in the body of the paper is to control the communication.

- *Conclusion:* Finally, the conclusion signals a release. It says to the reader, "I'm finishing up. Here is something to think about."

The relationship of the essay to the paragraph is shown in the box. Note that the paragraph—with its topic sentence, supporting details, and concluding sentence—is the basis for the body paragraphs in the essay.

RELATIONSHIP OF PARAGRAPH TO ESSAY

Paragraph	Essay
Topic sentence states the main idea of a focused paragraph.	**Introduction:** The beginning sentences introduce the context of the topic and narrow the topic, and the thesis statement establishes the essay's focus.
Supporting details explore the main idea of the paragraph. The writer elaborates and explains, maintaining the unity and coherence of paragraph content.	**Body paragraphs** explore the main idea of the thesis. The writer provides supporting details in each paragraph, maintaining the unity and coherence of the essay content. Each paragraph covers one topic presented in the thesis statement.
Conclusion sentence restates the paragraph's main idea.	**Conclusion paragraph** sums up the essay's content, restating the thesis using different words with additional sentences that offer advice, a prediction, a suggestion, or a solution that relate to the thesis statement.

ESSAY STRUCTURE IN OUTLINE FORM

A convenient way to visualize your essay's structure is to use a formal outline that consists of your thesis statement and the topic sentences and supporting details for each paragraph. Many students outline repeatedly during the writing process. To begin, they use an outline after they prewrite to provide structure to their ideas. While they draft, they may go back to their outline to alter the structure. They revisit their outline when they prepare to revise. Here is a formal outline, also known as the *alphanumeric outline*. This outline form is only a guide and you may adjust your outlines to suit your purposes; for example, you may include fewer major details but more examples. An essay can have more or fewer paragraphs than this five-paragraph model outline.

Thesis statement: _____

I. Topic sentence: _____

   A. Major detail

      1.

      2.

      3.

   B. Major detail

      1.

      2.

      3.

   C. Major detail

      1.

      2.

      3.

II. Topic sentence: _____

   A. Major detail

      1.

      2.

      3.

   B. Major detail

      1.

      2.

      3.

See "Supporting Details" in Chapter 3 for a detailed explanation of outlining.

C. Major detail

    1.

    2.

    3.

III. Topic sentence: _____

  A. Major detail

    1.

    2.

    3.

  B. Major detail

    1.

    2.

    3.

  C. Major detail

    1.

    2.

    3.

IV. Conclusion

  A. Reworded thesis statement: _____

  B. Advice, a prediction, a suggestion, or a solution that relates to the thesis statement: _____

Here is a formal outline of the at-a-glance essay at the beginning of this chapter:

Thesis: Road rage incidents stem from aggressive driving, responses to careless driving, or frustrations from traffic and road conditions.

I. Anger or road rage leads drivers to carry out violent acts against other drivers.

  A. Overreactions, driving aggressively, causing accidents

    1. Drivers can resort to physical violence.

    2. They attack cars or assault other drivers.

  B. Mother of two rattled by driver of SUV tailgating her car.

  C. 20-year old man in a fender-bender accident accosts other driver.

  D. After minor car accident, one driver uses baseball bat to beat other driver.

II. When drivers experience a close call from someone else's careless driving, they, too, may give in to road rage.

    A. Careless drivers have bad attitudes.

        1. They run stoplights intentionally, they make inappropriate lane changes, they tailgate, and they speed in and out of traffic, shouting, cursing, and making offensive hand gestures.

    B. Some drivers react to these careless driving incidents by trying to get even.

        1. They retaliate with aggressive driving.

    C. Race, gender, and age do not play a role in these road rage incidents.

III. Drivers need to get from point A to point B within a certain time frame.

    A. Heavy traffic during rush hour may cause delays.

        1. The driver takes out his/her frustration on the car in front.

    B. Driving cars causes some people to lose control of their emotions.

    C. Construction work on highways can also reduce traffic flow.

    D. Canadian winter weather conditions often make roads hazardous.

IV. Conclusion:

    A. Many kinds of stress make people a little crazy, especially when they are in a hurry and driving a car.

    B. Give yourself plenty of time to reach your destination. Slow down. Stay calm. Stay alive.

GET STARTED

An essay assignment is an invitation for you to show what you know about a subject. Because it is a form of writing with multiple paragraphs, the essay challenges you to assert relationships among many ideas and details. You give your audience a big picture, but that picture has to be in focus.

Assignments and Topics

Essay assignments in courses other than English will frequently focus on specific content. For example, in an economics class, you may be asked to explain the multiple causes of job losses, or in a psychology class, you will be asked to define and illustrate common defense mechanisms. In these cases, your task is to read your assignments carefully, identify key terms, and organize your writing accordingly.

When you are given a more general assignment, your job will be to identify a topic and break it down into subtopics you can treat in each of the body paragraphs of your essay. Remember that each body paragraph develops only one topic. This keeps unity in your writing. Look at the following diagrams that show how one student broke down both a specific assignment and a general assignment into topics and subtopics. You can either write down your ideas for topics as phrases or write full sentences; do what works for you.

Specific History Assignment: Discuss the decline of bison in Western Canada as covered in our readings and course lectures.

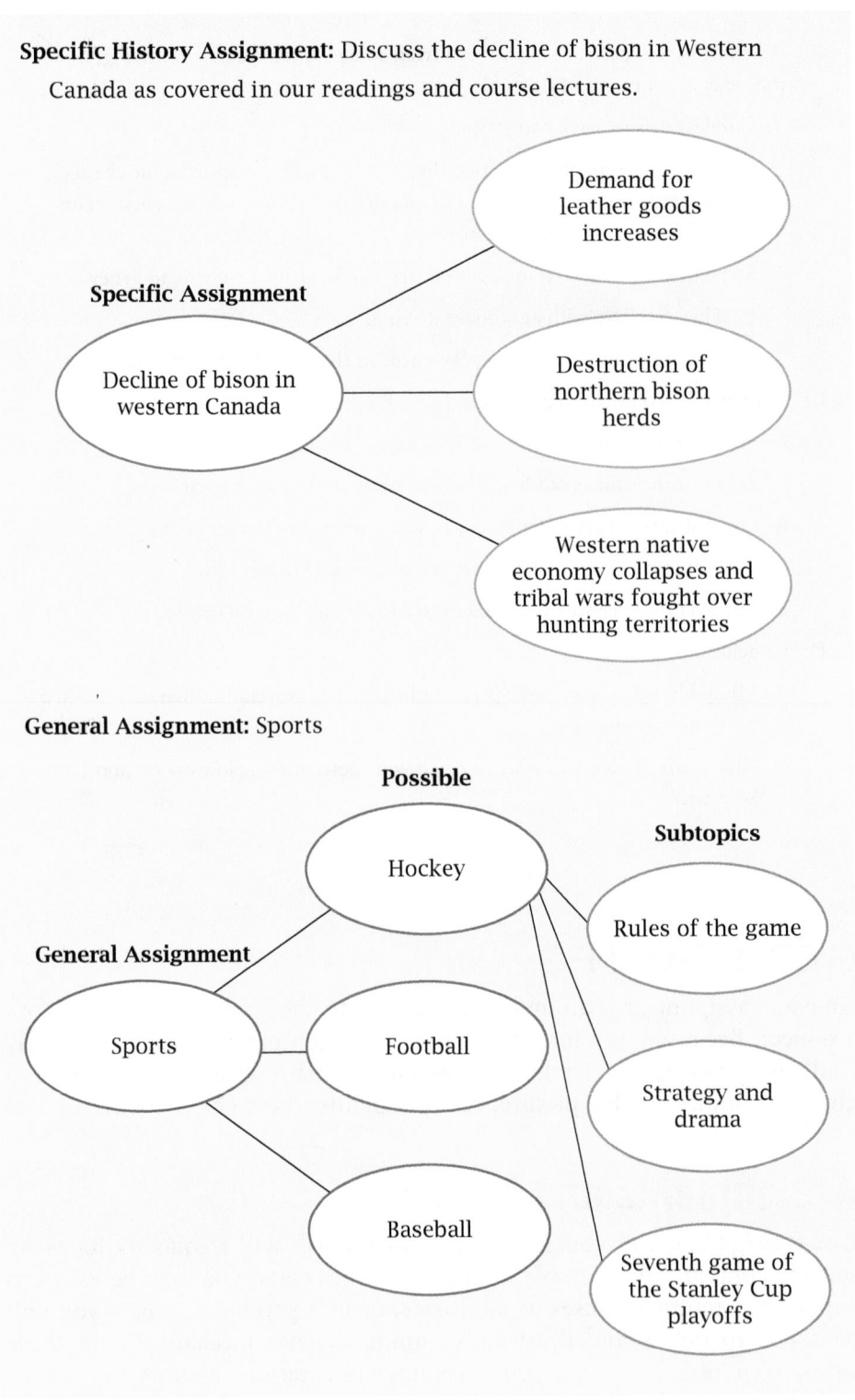

The illustrations show the writer's process with two assignments: one specific and one general. The writer begins by narrowing the assignments to identify possible topics, then narrowing the topics further to find subtopics. Effective writers often think in groups of three. They break down a main topic into three manageable subtopics that can be explored in individual paragraphs in the body of the essay. This idea of three items helps you with creating effective thesis statements. When you list the three points in your

PART 3 Going to the Next Level: Essay Writing and Patterns of Thinking

thesis statement, be sure to put them in parallel form. This means you use the same grammatical structure to list them, such as three adjectives, three nouns, or three phrases. A thesis statement using parallel structure is easier for the reader to understand.

EXERCISE 13-1 **Selecting an Assignment**

Directions: *Review the following assignments. Choose the one you think could be the basis for an effective essay.*

1. Describe an attitude or value of some people your age that you object to. How is their attitude or value expressed? Be specific about how you see it, hear it, and know it. Then explain your main reasons for objecting to it.

2. In our culture of celebrity, we see and hear about famous people all the time. Some celebrities use fame for good causes. Cite and discuss a few examples.

3. Nature can be a source of both calm and terror. Recall an experience you had in nature or one you heard about on the news that was very positive or frightening. Be specific about when and where the experience took place, as well as its outcome.

4. Technology has made new forms of communication possible. Discuss the safety issues involved in online communication and what precautionary steps people can take to ensure their safety.

5. The best way to save money is to have a budget that helps you keep track of cash flow. How would you classify expenses? Which type of expense could most easily be controlled and help you spend money wisely?

6. Discuss a popular form of entertainment—for example, action movies or a particular singing group. What makes it so entertaining? Be specific about the reasons.

7. Learning requires maturity, preparation, and readiness. Not everyone is ready to learn at the same time. Compare and contrast two learning experiences involving a particular subject in school that yielded very different results. In your discussion, consider reasons for the different results.

8. People demonstrate strength in different ways. Discuss two or three different kinds of strength and what their effects are.

9. Have you thought much about where your food comes from? What is the ecological consequence of having so many food products delivered year round from all over the world? Should people eat only what is produced from farms within a 100-kilometre radius of their communities? What is your view on this issue? Discuss reasons for or against bringing out-of-season food into our grocery stores.

10. Choose your own topic.

> **Writer's Response**
>
> Have you had a personal experience related to one of the topics that is common to what many other people have experienced? In other words, is your experience a typical one or an exception?

Prewrite

When you write an essay, you follow the steps of the writing process: prewriting, drafting, revising, editing, and reflecting. Prewriting gives you a chance to explore what you know about your subject. You probably already have a preferred type of prewriting—talking, thinking, clustering, brainstorming, questioning, or freewriting—that you automatically turn to when you start the writing process. You can refer back to Chapter Two to remind yourself about each of these techniques.

EXERCISE 13-2 **Prewriting**

Directions: *Carefully read the assignment you selected in Exercise 13-1. Do some prewriting to explore what you know about it and identify subtopics you could discuss in individual paragraphs. Begin with the type of prewriting you like best. Then use one of the other types of prewriting, too. This will help you determine which type of prewriting generates the most ideas for you.*

Introductions

Introductions should grab the reader's attention and set the tone of the essay. They should also establish the importance of the topic and focus the essay with a thesis statement.

The approach you choose for your introduction will vary according to the form of writing you do. Usually, you will be asked to write formal essays, but sometimes an assignment will ask for your response to something. In that case, you can write a personal essay. A personal essay might have an informal tone, whereas a report you write for a science class will be more formal. Here are two introductions for an essay on keeping a house clean.

> **Unfocused Introduction for Personal Essay**
>
> In our world today, people have to do things they do not want to do. These things are called jobs or maybe even chores. There are jobs one does at home, jobs one does at work, and jobs one does at school. One of the chores a person has to do around the house is vacuum the rug.
>
> **Focused Introduction for Personal Essay**
>
> Every morning I wake up and find dog hair all over the house. It is on the area rug in the living room, the carpet in my room, and the stairs that lead to the basement and upstairs. My dog is a golden retriever. Her very thick hair sheds a lot in the summer. I hate seeing dog hair in the house, but I do not like leaving her outside on hot summer days. That is why I depend on my vacuum cleaner. If I did not have a vacuum cleaner, the carpet and the rugs in the house would always be covered with dog hair. The vacuum is just one convenient device I use on a regular basis. It is useful for special jobs, regular cleaning, and even for some jobs outside the house.

The unfocused introduction states the obvious, and then states the obvious again. It reads as if anyone could have written it. In the focused introduction, on the other hand, the writer does not sound like anyone; she sounds like herself. What she has to say about keeping her house clean is interesting because of the detail she provides. You sense her attitude and her personality in the writing. Here are some guidelines for learning how to write a focused and interesting introduction.

GUIDELINES FOR WRITING AN EFFECTIVE INTRODUCTION

Start with a Snappy First Sentence to Grab Reader's Attention

My hard drive crashed.

She washed my mouth out with soap; then smacked my face.

Macbeth was a fool.

Spare change?

Tell a Captivating Story

She washed my mouth out with soap; then smacked my face. Then she made me run out to the apple tree in our yard to pick a switch. Grandma explained to me that she was going to whip my bottom with the switch that I brought back. She also told me that if the switch was not just right, I would be punished even more. To hear her say this to me was unbelievable. That was how she punished. In the process, she taught obedience, respect, and responsibility.

Cite and Explain Two or Three Specific Details

Macbeth was a fool. To begin with, he was a superstitious fool who listened to witches and allowed himself to be seduced by prophecy. He was also an ambitious fool. He was one of Duncan's favourites. If he had not been so ambitious, Macbeth would have lived a happy life and enjoyed power and wealth. To make matters worse, he allowed himself to be shamed into action by his wife. Shakespeare's play shows us a fool brought to ruin by superstition, ambition, and a foolish desire to "be a man."

Refer to Something You Have Read

Spare change? In the essay "On Compassion," Barbara Ascher asks why people feel compelled to give gifts to homeless people. She comes to the conclusion that they do it out of compassion. Compassion, she says, "is a feeling of pity or empathy." Those who give are not homeless, nor do they know how it feels to be homeless, but somehow they can relate. They probably have been in a situation that required someone else's help. Helping a homeless person makes them feel better about themselves. Nevertheless, many people will not give anything to the homeless, for what they claim to be very good reasons.

Offer a Concession

A gap year? Who could possibly be in favour of such a thing? Two young people finish high school. He has made plans to work part-time and go to school part-time, while she has been accepted as a full-time student to an excellent university out of province. Neither of them wants to set aside those plans for a year of travel, work abroad, or volunteering in community development. Deferring admission to post-secondary study, it seems clear, would be a setback, a long and needless delay to their plans for starting their lives. That argument may have merit. However, there are some very good reasons to consider exactly just such a delay.

Begin with a Compelling Fact or Statistic

"Well I thought that was what you meant!" Does this statement sound familiar? Miscommunication happens all the time. According to Deborah Tannen, 93 percent of communication is expressed nonverbally (129). Maybe that explains why communication breaks down so often. To communicate effectively, it is necessary to both listen and look.

Begin with an Analogy or Comparison

Living together is like pulling through the drive-through at McDonald's. It does not cost much. You get what everyone else has. You expect little from it. In contrast, marriage is like cooking a gourmet meal at home. It takes time. There is a lot of preparation and cleanup. However, in the end, you have something filling and wonderful. You have something that lasts. Marriage is hard work, but in the end, its benefits outweigh those of just living together.

Include a Focused Thesis Statement

After your opening sentences, you transition to the most important sentence of your essay: the thesis statement. The thesis states the point you want to make in your essay. It sums up the paper. It can appear at the beginning,

Remember, anytime you borrow a quotation, fact, or statistic from another writer, you need to identify your source as an in-text citation. Here the author is using a style called MLA. The number in parenthesis (129) indicates the page to find the information from the source, which would be listed after the essay in a Works Cited. See Chapter 16 for help on documenting your sources.

middle, or end of the introductory paragraph. However, for your English writing assignments, unless your instructor tells you otherwise, it's best to put your thesis statement at the end of your introduction paragraph since that is where your reader expects it to be.

As we discussed earlier, use three items or points in your thesis statement, making sure to put them in parallel form. This means you use the same grammatical structure to list them, such as three adjectives, three nouns, or three phrases. A thesis statement using parallel structure is easier for the reader to understand.

EXERCISE 13-3 **Your Introduction**

Directions: *(a) Review your prewriting to identify ideas for writing your introduction. Now write the first two or three sentences of your introduction.*

_____

_____

_____

(b) Now underline the guidelines listed below that helped you focus your thinking for writing an effective introduction.

GUIDELINES

Snappy first sentence

Captivating story

Two or three specific details

A reference to something you have read

A concession

Begin with a compelling fact or statistic

Begin with an analogy

(c) Next, circle the three points you are developing in your thesis statement. Check that these three points are in parallel form.

Develop a Thesis

Your thesis puts your particular fingerprint on your topic. It sums up the content of your essay, and it states the main point or idea you will explore. It answers your reader's question, *What is this essay really about?* Typically, readers look for your thesis statement at the end of your introduction paragraph. An effective thesis is specific, has edge, and states the divisions of your topic.

GUIDELINES FOR WRITING AN EFFECTIVE THESIS

Include a Specific Controlling Idea

Like the topic sentence in a paragraph, the thesis statement lets the audience know there is a plan behind the writing. However, the thesis statement promises more than the topic sentence. Because of its complexity, a thesis leads to multiple paragraphs of discussion. The differences between a topic sentence and a thesis statement are illustrated in these examples.

In academic writing, readers appreciate a direct approach. State your thesis early in the essay, preferably in your introduction.

This topic sentence limits the discussion to one cause of an epidemic.

This thesis statement states the main idea of the essay and the topics of each body paragraph (global mobility, agricultural practices, and bites from infected insects).

Assignment: Discuss some of the causes of massive outbreaks of disease covered in our reading and course lectures.

Topic Sentence: An important cause of epidemics is lack of inoculation.

Thesis Statement: Some important causes of recent outbreaks of diseases in Canada are the population's global mobility, unsafe practices in animal agriculture, and insect-borne viral infections.

In the case of a general assignment, the writer narrows her main point and thinks of three topics, breaking her thesis into ideas that can be explored in separate body paragraphs.

Assignment: Sports

Topic Sentence: Something that makes field hockey challenging are the rules of the game.

Thesis Statement: Because of the rigid rules of the game, field hockey often involves strategy, stamina, and skill.

Notice the key words in the topic sentence, *challenging* and *rules,* as opposed to those in the thesis statement, *rigid rules, strategy, stamina,* and *skill.* In a single paragraph, the writer might explore two or three examples of rules that make field hockey challenging. In an essay, on the other hand, the writer can do much more. She can explore two or three examples of rules and then explain how those rules enable managers and players to make strategy and add to the dramatic tension of a good game.

Like a topic sentence, a thesis statement is most effective when it is specific and focused, and in parallel form. The reader should be able to read a thesis statement and predict what the body of the essay will explore.

Vague Thesis Statement: Some people are terrified of flying.

Focused Thesis Statement: Because of their terrible fear of flying, some travellers have special rituals they follow both before and while they fly to minimize their anxiety.

The focused thesis statement enables the reader to predict the writer will discuss these questions: Why is the writer so afraid of flying? What is her before-flying ritual? What is her in-air ritual that minimizes anxiety?

State How the Topic Will Be Divided into Subtopics

A good thesis ensures that the content will be organized and specific. It indicates what subtopics you will address in the paragraphs in the body of your paper.

Vague Thesis Statement: The art fair is <u>enjoyable</u> for a variety of reasons.

Specific Thesis Statement: An art fair is enjoyable because of the <u>ambiance in the park</u>, <u>tasty local food</u>, and the <u>good deals</u> on ceramics and paintings.

The first thesis does not provide the reader with a preview of the essay's content because it is not specific about why the art fair is enjoyable. The second thesis divides the topic into three subtopics: ambiance, local food, and good deals. The reader can look forward to a discussion of these subtopics in the body of the essay in the same order they are presented in the thesis.

Avoid Making a Big Announcement, Such as "In This Paper, I Will Tell You about . . ."

A common problem students have is making a ponderous statement, such as "In this essay, I will talk about . . ." Usually a heavy-handed thesis like this can be revised by cutting the "I will talk about" and working with what comes next.

Heavy-Handed Thesis: ~~In this essay I will write about~~ <u>the problems students face in the financial aid office at this college.</u>

Revised Thesis: <u>Students face major problems at the financial aid office: long waits to get information, delays before funds are released, and rare referrals to scholarship opportunities at the institution.</u>

A focused thesis shows that you have done your prewriting and thinking before writing the first draft. The heavy-handed thesis is too general. You want to narrow down broad topics into manageable and more specific subtopics. The revised thesis focuses the essay on three specific problems. Writing a specific thesis makes your work as a writer much easier since you can focus on the three points identified in the thesis statement.

EXERCISE 13-4 **Vague Versus Focused Thesis Statements**

Directions: *Read the following thesis statements. Place* V *next to those that are vague,* F *next to those that are focused, and* A *next to those that make an announcement. For those that are focused, jot down two or three questions you think the writer promises to explore in the body of the essay. Rewrite those that are not focused, using parallelism. The first example is done for you.*

_F_ 1. Since Saturday morning television is designed to sell small children a lot of worthless junk, parents need to monitor what their children watch for three reasons.

1. What kind of worthless junk? _____

2. What is a good process for monitoring TV watching? _____

_____ 2. The wood bison is an endangered species in Alberta.

_____

_____

_____ 3. Older siblings either make life easier or a living hell for their brothers and sisters.

_____

_____

_____ 4. I am going to tell you why hockey is the greatest sport on earth.

_____

_____

_____ 5. Advances in technology are visible in a number of new films coming out of Hollywood.

_____

_____

EXERCISE 13-5 **Formulating Your Thesis**

Directions: *Review your prewriting and thoughts about your introduction. Then write a tentative thesis for your essay in the space provided. Check that you are using parallel forms for the points you plan to write about.*

_____

_____

The Body of the Essay

Explain. Academic writing requires detailed explanation. Your audience wants information: evidence that you have mastered course content as well as details from your personal observation, experience, or research that indicate careful thinking. In response to an assignment, you formulate a focused thesis statement in parallel form that says something substantive about the topic. That thesis statement is then explained by focused topic sentences.

FORMULATE A THESIS AND TOPIC SENTENCES

A focused thesis statement narrows your topic and identifies those ideas you plan to discuss in the body of the essay. From your thesis come your topic sentences. In a good essay, that connection is both necessary and obvious.

Some assignments are formulated so you can easily extract key terms and write a focused thesis statement. In your thesis, in turn, are the key terms that become part of your topic sentences.

> Assignment: Discuss a technological device in your home that has changed your family dynamics or caused significant differences of opinion between family members.

In this assignment, the key terms are *technological device*, *family dynamics*, and *significant differences of opinion*. A thesis statement, along with topic sentences related to it, might look like this:

> **Thesis Statement:** The voice mail feature on our phone has changed the family dynamics in our house, eliminating one source of conflict while creating new ones.
>
> **Topic Sentence 1:** The voice mail feature has eliminated a continuous source of conflict: lost or undelivered phone messages.
>
> **Topic Sentence 2:** A new source of conflict, however, is how long messages are left (or are not left) recorded.
>
> **Topic Sentence 3:** While message management is still a problem, an even more bothersome problem is that a general voice mail inbox means less privacy in phone communication.

In this illustration, the student's thesis statement leads to precise topic sentences. From each topic sentence, the student would write a detailed paragraph developing the idea with specific details.

In the case of general assignments, you need to limit and narrow the topic as shown below. The illustration, beginning with "Cathedral" on the left, shows a student narrowing an assignment to write on the short story "Cathedral," by Raymond Carver. He moves from assignment to topic and from topic to subtopics.

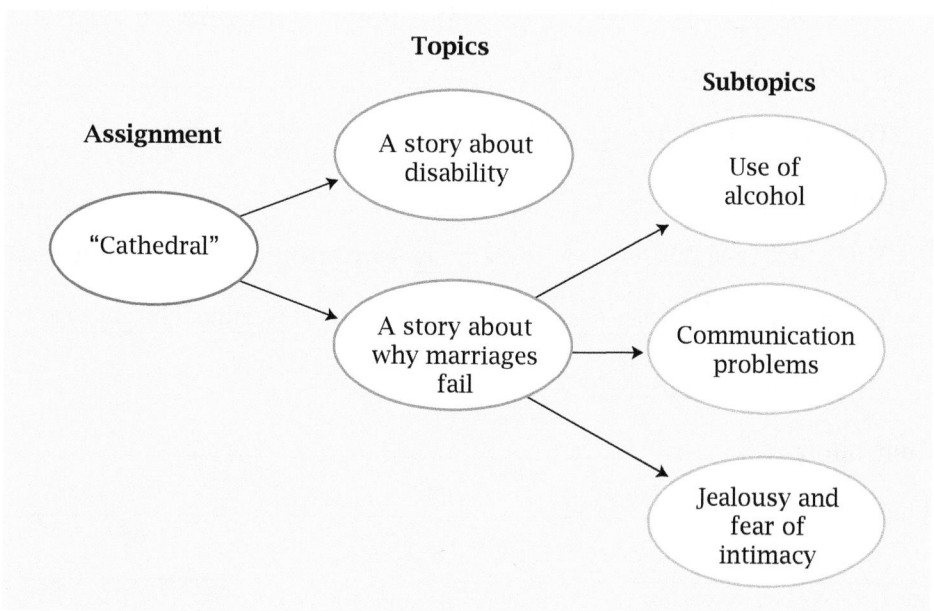

Assignment: Write an essay on the short story "Cathedral" by Raymond Carver.

Thesis Statement: Raymond Carver's short story "Cathedral" explores a troubled marriage, in particular, the impact of alcohol, poor communication, and jealousy on the narrator's marriage.

Topic Sentence 1: The narrator's marriage is in trouble because of alcohol abuse.

Topic Sentence 2: Communication problems plague the failing marriage and complicate the conflicts.

Topic Sentence 3: Jealousy causes the narrator to fear intimacy, creating more conflicts.

Thesis statements and topic sentences tell readers where they are, what is being discussed, and what connections are being made between ideas. These guiding sentences also establish the logic of your writing. There should be a reason for visiting the ideas and details of each subtopic in the order you have chosen.

EXERCISE 13-6 **Writing Focused Thesis and Topic Sentences**

Directions: *For each of the following general assignments, use an outline or a graphic chart similar to the one on the previous page to narrow the assignment and write a focused thesis statement. Then write two or three topic sentences that echo key terms from the thesis. The first one has been done for you.*

EXAMPLE

Topic: Health care

Controlling Idea: alternative medicines

Thesis: Using the Internet as a source of information, many young people take control of their health care, using alternative medications and dietary supplements to treat themselves.

Topic Sentence 1: The Internet has expanded people's access to information about health.

Topic Sentence 2: Alternative medications are effective for some ailments.

Topic Sentence 3: Dietary supplements are a useful treatment in some cases.

1. **Topic:** Transportation

Controlling Idea: _____

Thesis: _____

_____

Topic Sentence 1: _____

Topic Sentence 2: _____

Topic Sentence 3: _____

2. **Topic:** Recycling Programs

Controlling Idea: _____

Thesis: _____

_____

Topic Sentence 1: _____

Topic Sentence 2: _____

Topic Sentence 3: _____

3. **Topic:** Childhood

Controlling Idea: _____

Thesis: _____

_____

Topic Sentence 1: _____

Topic Sentence 2: _____

Topic Sentence 3: _____

Talk about it

No two people have the same view of a topic. Discuss someone who might disagree with you, and why. Discuss why it's important to present more than one point of view.

EXERCISE 13-7 **Your Thesis and Topic Sentences**

Directions: *Review your prewriting, ideas about an introduction, and tentative thesis. Compose your thesis and two to four topic sentences in the space below. Revise your thesis as needed, ensuring that it is written in parallel form.*

Thesis: _____

Topic Sentence 1: _____

Topic Sentence 2: _____

Topic Sentence 3: _____

Topic Sentence 4: _____

PROVIDE SUPPORTING DETAILS

The ultimate goal of an essay is to deliver the content. Readers of academic writing look for specific detail. Your movement toward greater specificity can be pictured as a stairway, with the most general content at the top, becoming increasingly more specific as you move downward.

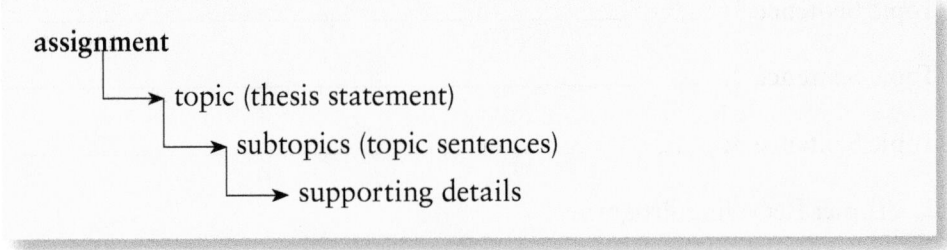

assignment
→ topic (thesis statement)
→ subtopics (topic sentences)
→ supporting details

This pattern of relationships can also be pictured in outline form.

Assignment: Discuss a technological device in your home that has changed your family dynamics or caused significant differences of opinion between family members.

Thesis Statement: The voice mail feature on our telephone has changed the family dynamics, eliminating one source of conflict while creating new ones.

Topic Sentence 1: Voice mail has eliminated a continuous source of conflict: lost or undelivered phone messages.

→ **Detail A:** Lost messages from friends
→ **Detail B:** Lost messages from family members
→ **Detail C:** Lost work-related messages

Topic Sentence 2: A new source of conflict, however, is how long messages are left (or are not left) on voice mail.

→ **Detail A:** Some people never even listen to their messages
→ **Detail B:** Some people never delete their messages
→ **Detail C:** Some people delete theirs and others' messages

Topic Sentence 3: While message management is still a problem, an even more bothersome problem is that voice mail means less privacy in phone communication.

→ **Detail A:** No control over who listens to private messages

THESIS STATEMENT
The student's thesis statement echoes key terms from the assignment.

TOPIC SENTENCE
This topic sentence echoes "source of conflict" from the thesis. The student will use examples to develop the main idea of this paragraph.

The student's topic sentence makes a direct reference to the thesis of the essay.

The student will use examples to develop the main idea of the paragraph.

The topic sentence refers back to the thesis.

The student will use narration to develop the main idea of this paragraph.

This outline shows a pattern of support at each level: thesis, topic sentence, supporting details. Your ultimate destination is specific detail: facts, statistics, description, and examples that support, explain, and illustrate your thesis. Typically, the content of body paragraphs is organized in one or more of the organizational patterns shown in the following chart.

Pattern	Description
Description	Provides precise sensory detail
Example and Illustration	Explores ideas in greater degrees of specificity
Narration	Examines an incident or experience, focusing on specific place, time, people, events, and outcomes
Process	Explains a procedure by describing steps involved, props and equipment used, and people involved
Classification	Sorts content into three or more types, detailing similarities and differences
Cause and Effect	Explores "symptoms" of a problem, prior conditions or reasons, solutions to or consequences of the problem
Comparison or Contrast	Examines similarities or differences in point-by-point or subject-by-subject organization
Definition	Specifies meaning of terms or important ideas: component parts, function or purpose, origins, illustrations
Argument	Explains opinions, examining their reasons and foundations

See Chapter 14 for detailed examples of essays written using these different patterns.

DEVELOP AN ESSAY PLAN

To plan your essay, make a tentative outline, beginning with your thesis, followed by each topic sentence and the details that support the main ideas stated in those topic sentences. Then stand back and look at your outline. Next, think about a logical order for your ideas. You should decide which of the following orders is the best way to present your information:

- *Spatial:* Organize by location, direction, or arrangement, whole to parts
- *Chronological or time order:* Beginning to end or reverse order
- *Order of importance:* Least to most important (ascending) or most to least important (descending)
- *Order of generality:* General to specific (deductive reasoning) or specific to general (inductive reasoning)
- *Order of complexity:* Simple to complex or familiar to unfamiliar
- *Order of materiality:* From concrete to abstract or vice versa

Directions: *Review the thesis and topic sentences that follow. Indicate the order of topic sentences that seems most logical to you. Write a sentence justifying your thinking. The first one is done for you.*

EXAMPLE

Thesis: Travel is valuable to young people because it helps them learn about different ways of life, shows them different geographic regions, and makes them appreciate home.

___3___ **Topic Sentence:** Travel is valuable because it makes young people appreciate home.

___2___ **Topic Sentence:** Travel helps young people learn about other people.

___1___ **Topic Sentence:** Travel shows young people different geographic regions.

Explanation: Begin with the body paragraph on different regions because young

people have to get someplace before they encounter different ways of life. The

paragraph about appreciating home makes sense last because young people feel

this appreciation after the trip is over.

1. **Thesis:** Students face major problems in the financial aid office: long waits to get information, delays before funds are released, and only rare referrals to scholarship opportunities at the institution.

_____ **Topic Sentence:** The financial aid office would do students a service by posting current information about scholarship opportunities.

_____ **Topic Sentence:** Perhaps the biggest headache about the office is the long wait and lack of organization when students arrive at the beginning of a semester.

_____ **Topic Sentence:** Many students complain about delays in fund release once financial aid is approved.

Explanation: _____

_____

2. **Thesis:** The local art fair is enjoyable because of the ambiance in the park, the tasty local food, and the good deals on ceramics and paintings.

_____ **Topic Sentence:** New painters and ceramic artists emerge every year selling their work at reasonable prices.

_____ **Topic Sentence:** Local restaurants set up booths offering taste treats and local specialties.

_____ **Topic Sentence:** A park setting offers the perfect atmosphere for an art fair.

Explanation: _____

_____

3. **Thesis:** Canada has made contributions to communications technology, enabling people to connect all over the world.

   _____ **Topic Sentence:** Today, a Waterloo, Ontario–based company, Research in Motion (RIM), produces the BlackBerry, a popular wireless phone noted for its email capabilities.

   _____ **Topic Sentence:** In 1876, Alexander Graham Bell conceived and developed the telephone at his parents' home in Brantford, Ontario.

   _____ **Topic Sentence:** Guglielmo Marconi sent the first transatlantic radio transmission from Cornwall, England, to St. John's, Newfoundland, in 1901.

Explanation: _____

_____

EXERCISE 13-9 **Developing Your Essay Plan**

Directions: *Write a detailed plan for your essay. Include your thesis, topic sentences, and supporting details. Depending on the complexity of your topic, you might plan on two, three, four, or more body paragraphs to develop your ideas. Organize your ideas and details in a logical order.*

CREATE UNITY AND COHERENCE

A reader should be able to look up from an essay and then look back without losing track of what the writer is saying. To create coherent text that a reader can easily follow, the connections of ideas within and across paragraphs need to be made explicit, using transitional words or phrases.

In the paragraphs you wrote in Part 2 of this book, you used transition words to make your writing coherent and connected. In the essay, your job is essentially the same. A web of connections is created when you repeat key terms and write transitional sentences between paragraphs. Some of the transitions signal a particular kind of writing; refer to the transitions charts in Part 2 to make sure you select appropriate transitional words.

Repeat Key Terms in Some or Most of Your Paragraphs

Key terms remind the reader of the essay's focus and give the writer a chance to explain how the discussion in a given paragraph relates to the main idea of the essay.

Write Transition Sentences Between Paragraphs

Paragraphs frequently end with transition sentences. A transition sentence points both backward and forward. It restates the idea of the current paragraph and it points to the main idea of the next paragraph.

The web of connections created by key terms and transition sentences is visible in this box:

> **Thesis:** In order to be a responsible pet owner, you should determine what size pet will be suitable for your living environment, figure out how much time and care you can give your pet, and understand that pets become part of the family.
>
> **Topic Sentence:** To be a responsible pet owner, you must determine what size animal is suitable in your environment. *[transition sentence]* Before acquiring a pet, family members can learn how to take care of one.
>
> **Topic Sentence:** In order to have a happy, healthy pet, you must provide it with care. *[transition sentence]* In short, a pet owner should know about its upkeep.
>
> **Topic Sentence:** Raising an animal is just like raising a child. It becomes part of your family unit.
>
> **Conclusion:** By addressing these three areas you can be a responsible pet owner.

Here is the complete essay with the thesis, topic, and transition sentences shown above.

> ### Sweet Little Pup
>
> *Oh my goodness! Someone hit that poor dog.* You see it sometimes on the city streets and highways, and you wonder, "How could this happen? Where are the owners of the pet?" The truth is that a lot of people who own pets should not. In order to be a **responsible dog owner**, you should determine what size pet will suit your living **environment**, figure out how much time and care you can give your pet, and understand that pets become **part of the family**.
>
> A **responsible dog owner** looks for an animal that fits his or her environment. One cannot keep a Great Dane in a studio apartment. When a family with two boys decided they wanted a pet, they looked for just the right fit. They had two turtles already, but they wanted something more affectionate. They had a long talk about their living arrangements, a three-bedroom townhouse with a small yard. Even though they lacked a lot of **outdoor space**, they decided to purchase a dog. They searched on the Internet for local dog breeders and found a cute Jack Russell Terrier puppy that they named Bruno. He was a frisky little devil and fit their **space** just about right. In the next year or so, the boys learned about how to take care of a pet.

THESIS STATEMENT

TOPIC SENTENCE

TRANSITION SENTENCE

In order to have a happy, healthy pet, you must provide it with care. Dogs cannot explain that they are sick. They have to be watched closely during the first few years. They need to be given two sets of innoculations. Some dogs are given additional medication to treat them for worms. If its physical needs are met, it does not take long for a dog to adjust to its new home, but that is when the **socializing and training** begins. An obedient dog learns to heel and to sit. The dog owner has to teach him to stay out of traffic, which can be very time-consuming. A good dog learns not to jump on people, not to chew things like shoes and furniture, and not to beg for food. In short, much like a child, a dog needs to be **brought up right**.

Raising an animal is just like raising a child. It becomes part of the family unit. It feels lonely when the owners are gone, and it loves the owners unconditionally. In addition to love, a dog needs plenty of exercise. It needs to be walked. It loves fresh air. Like a child, it loves to run, and it needs to eat right. Part of caring for a dog is also taking on a long-term commitment. Once again, like children, a dog joins a family for a long time, usually its whole life. That means the dog owner has to organize her life accordingly. She has to find someone to look after the animal when she goes out of town. She has to take care of it if it gets hurt or sick. A pet is not a machine. It goes through stages of life, just like a person does.

Someone hit that poor dog. There is really no excuse for it. Being a responsible pet owner means looking after the animal's physical, social, and emotional needs. In fact, that is what being a responsible pet owner is all about.

TOPIC SENTENCE
"Care" is the main idea of this paragraph.

SUPPORTING DETAILS
The student elaborates on two types of needs: physical and social.

TRANSITION SENTENCE

TOPIC SENTENCE
In this paragraph the student compares raising a dog to raising a child.

CONCLUSION
The writer repeats the first sentence of her introduction

DISCUSSION QUESTIONS

1. What is your opinion of the title of this essay?

2. What part or parts of the essay do you find particularly effective? Why?

3. Did the writer overlook anything? If so, would you put this additional detail in an existing paragraph or add a new paragraph? Explain.

Conclusions

While introductions prepare the reader for what is to come, conclusions help the reader see how the individual parts of the essay add up. How you finish depends on the form of writing. In a research paper, you might focus on solutions to an important problem. In an essay, you might tell an engaging story so the reader grasps the significance of your thesis. Whenever possible, try to match your conclusion with your introduction. Think of your concluding paragraph as a mirror image of the introduction. You can begin your conclusion by rephrasing your thesis statement and then transitioning to a more general, but related parting thought, advice, or prediction as the last sentence.

GUIDELINES FOR WRITING AN EFFECTIVE CONCLUSION

Retrieve a Specific Detail

Reread your introduction or the body of your essay and identify an interesting, important, or engaging fact or detail. This detail will emphasize the main point of your paper.

Introduction

Every morning I wake up and find dog hair all over the house. It is on the area rug in the living room, the carpet in my room, and the stairs that lead to the basement and upstairs. My dog Cheyenne is a golden retriever. . . .

Repeated Detail Conclusion

Cheyenne sheds. There is just no way around it. Nevertheless, I have found ways of keeping up with dog hair and most of the other problems associated with keeping my house clean. . . .

Ask and Answer a Question to Repeat and Reinforce Your Thesis

Introduction

Macbeth was a fool. To begin with, he was a superstitious fool who listened to witches and allowed himself to be seduced by prophecy. He was also an ambitious fool. He was one of Duncan's favourites. If he had not been so ambitious, Macbeth would have lived a happy life and enjoyed power and wealth.

Conclusion Question

Could Macbeth's fate have been different? If he had been a different kind of man, yes, his fate would have been different. As it is, his flaws eventually led to his destruction.

Select a Related Quotation from a Source Mentioned Earlier in the Essay

Use that quotation to explore the important message your essay imparts.

Introduction

Spare change? In the essay "On Compassion," Barbara Ascher talks about feeding the homeless. The writer asks why people feel compelled to give gifts to the homeless. She comes to the conclusion that people do it out of compassion. What does she mean by compassion? Compassion, she says, "is not a character trait like a sunny disposition" (37). These people are not homeless. . . .

Quotation Conclusion

Ascher says that compassion "is learned by having adversity at our windows" (37). Unfortunately, we do not all look out our windows. We are busy. We walk with our heads down. We are in our own world. . . .

Avoid Conclusion Missteps

Writers sometimes make specific mistakes in their conclusions. Avoid these missteps:

- Do not introduce new ideas in your conclusion that you have not discussed in the body of your essay as this may distract from the unity of your writing.
- It's not always necessary to use overly obvious language like "in conclusion," "in summary," or "to sum up."
- Do not simply summarize what you wrote in the body of the paper. Indicate why your topic is important or how your topic applies in a broader context. Alternatively, you can make a prediction or suggestion about the topic to leave your reader with a final impression of the ideas in your thesis statement.

EXERCISE 13-10 **Matching Introductions and Conclusions**

Directions: *Read the following introductions and conclusions. In the space provided, indicate what the writers have done to match their introduction and conclusion paragraphs.*

1.

Introduction

James Gleick notes in his essay that stress is an "ill defined term." Maybe that is the case because there are many types of stress in our lives. We stress about work, about education, and about political issues that concern us. Perhaps even more than these, we stress about family. What is family stress and where does it come from?

Conclusion

Stress can affect us physiologically, according to Gleick, sometimes in the form of heart ailments. Ironically, family can be both a source and a solution to stress. By being open, honest, and loving with those in our families we find troublesome, we can resolve stressful differences or misunderstandings.

Strategy: _____

2.   **Introduction**

A gentleman came to the drive-through on my shift and ordered 17 cheeseburgers. After he paid, I told him we would bring his order out to him, then politely asked him to pull into a parking space. "Why do I have to wait," he said. I responded, "Sir, this is fast food, not instant food." When people think of fast-food jobs, they think "easy work." In fact, it is quite the opposite. Managers constantly harass employees, and customers complain about service being slow. This is just part of the joy of Burger King. Fast food may be mindless and repetitive, but easy it is not.

Conclusion

Not all customers think we have it made. Some show a little appreciation, which makes the job tolerable. There is an elderly man who comes in singing every morning. He says, "G'morning beautiful!" every time. I look forward to his visit. The next time you visit your local fast-food joint, a smile and hello would make us grill jockeys feel appreciated.

Strategy: _____

3.   **Introduction**

It was the weekend. I was shopping and checking things off my list. At my last stop, when I reached for my wallet, it was gone. The panic was overwhelming. I rushed out and backtracked to the last store. Luck was on my side because there was my wallet, safely in the hands of the salesclerk. Many people are not as lucky. Identity theft has become a costly problem in our society today. It occurs when someone obtains and uses your personal information such as your social insurance number, bank and credit card accounts, and birth dates. There are simple, preventative steps a person can take that will keep their personal information safe.

Conclusion

It is the unknown crooks who steal your identity, right? In fact, ID theft was brought to my attention in a personal way. My father suffered from Alzheimer's, and while in my sister's care, his good credit was misused. When he passed away last February, over $40 000 of debt had been charged in his name—by my sister. Statistics show that 47 percent of all ID theft is committed by friends, neighbours, or family members. On a positive note, the situation led me to learn how to protect my information. Knowing what I now know, especially how to take necessary precautions, I feel much safer.

Strategy: _____

Your Conclusion

Directions: *Review your prewriting, your essay plan, and the plans for the introduction of your essay you wrote in response to Exercise 13-3. In the space below, write the first two or three sentences of your introduction paragraph. Then write the first two or three sentences of your conclusion. Check off which of the guidelines for writing an effective conclusion helped you focus your thinking.*

Introduction: _____

_____

_____

Conclusion: _____

_____

_____

Guidelines

_____ Retrieve a specific detail.

_____ Ask and answer a question that reinforces your thesis.

_____ Select another quotation from a source mentioned earlier in the essay. Remember to identify the source of quotation.

Drafting Your Essay

Directions: *Write a first draft of an essay that responds to the assignment you selected. Be sure the essay has an introduction, body, and conclusion; thesis and topic sentences; and supporting details that are logical and connected.*

Revise and Edit Your Essay

The difference between a pretty good essay and an excellent essay is in the revisions a writer makes. After drafting, many writers simply stop thinking. There is more you can do with your rough draft—much more. As you write an essay, you can use the editing checklist on the inside back cover of the text.

GUIDELINES FOR REVISING AND EDITING YOUR ESSAY

General Guidelines

- Allow yourself enough time to set aside your work so you can come back to it and see it with fresh eyes.

- Always read your essays out loud. Let your ears be your editor.

- Ask someone in your class who knows the assignment to read and comment on your essay.

- Revising involves cutting and adding words, phrases, and sentences, as well as moving sentences and whole paragraphs around to improve coherence.

- *The parts of the essay—introduction, body, and conclusion:* Your essay should have a clear beginning, middle, and end. Be sure your essay consists of multiple paragraphs, at least four or five, possibly more. Check the assignment's instructions regarding word length or word count. In addition, be sure that the paragraphs are similar in length. This adds balance to the points in your essay. The outline of your essay should indicate how long each paragraph will be. Finally, your conclusion should clearly signal the end is coming, reinforce the essay's main idea, and give the reader something to think about.

- *Focus—thesis and topic sentences:* Your thesis and topic sentences should include key words that indicate your essay's main ideas. Moreover, the key words may be repeated in transition sentences to help the reader make connections between paragraphs.

- *Supporting details:* Readers of academic writing look for specific details. In every paragraph, your essay will be more effective if you have fresh, vivid detail to go with your ideas. Review supporting details in Chapter 2, and patterns of organization and paragraph writing in Part 2.

- *Connections:* Transition words in your body paragraphs help the reader see connections. A web of connections is created by thesis, topic, and transition sentences.

- *Proofreading:* Check for spelling and capitalization errors. Proofread for those errors you know you are inclined to make. Readers lose patience with writers who make the same mistakes repeatedly. Proofread for sentence variety.

Ask Yourself

What three key terms can you use in your thesis and topic sentences?

Titles

The title of your paper is the first thing your audience will see. For many students, it is the last thing they think of. Although it does not matter when you put a title on your essay, be sure that it reflects the essay's content.

A little thought goes a long way with a title. Suppose you were asked to write an essay about a role model who has had an impact on your life. What would be the most predictable title for such an essay?

My Role Model

When you decide on a title, try to do the opposite of what your audience expects. Here are less predictable titles for essays on an important role model:

Always Ask Questions

We Will Always Have Pickles

Pass the Scissors

The title of your essay should arouse the reader's curiosity. Make your title an invitation that your audience wants to accept. Be sure to observe rules for capitalization of titles: first word, last word, all other words except articles, conjunctions, and prepositions. Do not underline your title. If you write your essay on a word processor, use the same font size for the title as for the rest of your essay.

The Essay Process Checklist

As you write your essays, you can refer to this Essay Process Checklist.

ESSAY PROCESS CHECKLIST

Prewriting Approaches

_____ Talking with classmates and people knowledgeable about my subject

_____ Thinking about my approach to the subject

_____ Clustering

_____ Brainstorming

_____ Questioning

_____ Free writing

Drafting Considerations

_____ Consider the audience, purpose, and form.

_____ Write a thesis statement using parallelism.

_____ Write topic sentences for each paragraph.

_____ Use an outline.

_____ Use transitions within paragraphs and transitional sentences between paragraphs.

_____ Revise and improve on early ideas.

_____ Write a conclusion.

Revision Strategies

_____ Double-check the assignment instructions and expectations.

_____ Read critically.

_____ Ask questions.

_____ Connect ideas logically.

_____ Get input from peers.

_____ Develop a revision plan.

_____ Add, cut, and reorganize.

Editing Activities

_____ Search for and correct errors you know you make.

_____ Eliminate one error at a time.

_____ Read your writing aloud.

_____ Find a peer to proofread.

_____ Use editing checklist found on the inside back cover.

_____ Identify strengths & weaknesses and set writing goals.

_____ Reflect on what you have learned and how to apply it to future writing.

CHAPTER REVIEW

Take a moment and reflect on what you have learned about essay structure and the writing process.

■ ELEMENTS OF ESSAY STRUCTURE
  • _Introduction, thesis statement, body, conclusion_

■ ESSAY STRUCTURE IN OUTLINE FORM
  • _Organize your thoughts: formal alphanumeric outline_

☐ Assignments and topics
  • _Identify key terms; focus on specific content_

☐ Prewrite
  • _Follow steps of writing process_

☐ Introductions
  • _Snappy, captivating, specific details, outside reference, concession, compelling fact/ statistic, analogy_

☐ Develop a thesis
  • _Specific controlling idea: states divisions of topic_

☐ The body of the essay
  • _Connections, logic: order, transitions; patterns of organization; key terms_

☐ Conclusions
  • _Match introduction; no new ideas; do not simply summarize_

☐ Revise and edit your essay
  • _Read aloud; cut, add, or move; proofread_

☐ Titles
  • _Arouse curiosity; reflect content; capitalization rules_

☐ The Essay Process Checklist

CHAPTER 14

Types of Essays

CHAPTER OVERVIEW

- THE ESSAY AT A GLANCE
- ELEMENTS OF THE ESSAY
- THE WRITING PROCESS
- ESSAYS WITH ONE PATTERN OF ORGANIZATION
- ☐ Description
- ☐ Example
- ☐ Narration
- ☐ Process
- ☐ Classification
- ☐ Cause and Effect
- ☐ Comparison and Contrast
- ☐ Definition
- ☐ Argument
- ESSAYS WITH MULTIPLE PATTERNS OF ORGANIZATION

THINK FIRST

Think about the habits of mind that are essential to being successful in school and the workplace. Pick the area—work or school—that is most important to you right now. Who is your role model? Write a paragraph discussing this person's characteristics and what he or she has done that you find inspiring and worthy of imitation.

Got a Minute?

In many cases, a short answer just will not do. For this reason, you need time to think through complex issues, analyze them, and discover relationships and connections in order to explain what they mean. For instance, it is said that people spend their entire adult lives figuring out their childhood: relationships with parents, siblings, and friends; decisions made, accidents and opportunities that happened. What does it all mean? How did everything happen so fast? How much control did they actually have over what went on around them?

BRAINSTORM

Brainstorm a list of important events, good or bad, that happened in your family life. Then focus on one. List all the people and places connected to the event. What circumstances or conditions led up to it? What were the consequences? How were you personally affected? How were others affected?

Not That Again . . .

Life is defined by repetition, especially in school. How often have you thought, sitting in class or working on an assignment, *Haven't I seen this before?* Yet there are benefits to repeated exercise. You build skills. You develop habits of mind. Sometimes you have breakthroughs that make all the difference in the world. Time, place, and people matter in this respect. What you did not understand about math at one place and time, from one particular instructor, suddenly becomes clear to you at another place and time, from a different instructor. Maybe the difference is the person sitting next to you in class. Then again, maybe you are different—more ready to learn, more capable of understanding connections and applications.

DISCUSSION

Turn and talk to a classmate about a class you like or dislike. Why do you feel the way you do? What prior experiences did you have with the class? Were they similar or different?

We Can Work It Out

Mature people learn how to adjust to circumstances. They listen, learn, and adapt. In the workplace, this kind of agility is highly valued. You work in teams of diverse individuals with a shared goal—to get the job done. When a job is completed, teams dissolve and form again: different people, new adjustments. Then there is the boss. Some make work wonderful; some do not. Either way, as an employee your abilities to adjust and to fit in are tested. In the process, you acquire both marketable and social skills.

RESUMÉ BUILDER

Turn and talk to a classmate about a job you really enjoyed. What made it satisfying? What were your co-workers like? Were there any challenges that required you to learn on the job?

At a Glance

In this chapter you will learn more about writing different types of essays. An essay is a multiple-paragraph assignment. At the very least, your readers will expect to see four or five paragraphs in your essays. They will read for both structure and content. In Chapter 13, you learned that an essay includes an introduction, body paragraphs, and a conclusion. You will also use the forms of thinking and writing you learned for paragraph writing in Part 2 of this text so that your essay can convey information in an organized fashion. The content of your essay may be personal observation or information you get from assigned reading. Unless the assignment specifically asks for it, refer to personal experience only when it supports the development of the points in your essay. Academic writing requires that you provide support based on evidence you will find by doing assigned readings or relevant research.

For all of the patterns of essays, depending on your purpose and your audience, you can choose between subjective or objective writing. Subjective writing communicates the writer's feelings, observations, or opinion and often uses first person. Examples of subjective writing include journal writing or blogs. Objective writing is more common in academic settings and in the workplace. It conveys information and facts in a logical, balanced, organized manner, and uses third person. The writer of objective writing wants to present unbiased facts so that readers can make their own conclusions. Examples of objective writing include reports and articles found in academic databases. Employees sometimes need to use objective writing to complete incident reports explaining what happened in a nonjudgmental way.

To be totally objective is quite difficult because each writer does indeed have opinions. You should think of writing as a continuum with subjective writing at one end and objective writing at the other. In between both of these extremes are degrees of writing that contain language that can subtly or overtly convey the writer's attitudes or emotions through the use of words with positive or negative connotations. Skilled writers carefully select words to influence their readers' interpretations. For more information about connotation and word choice, refer to Chapter 1.

The Essay at a Glance

`ASSIGNMENT`   Use classification to explore one of the following topics: types of injuries, jobs, learning experiences, parents, or homes.

Making Sense of Falling Numbers

The writer begins with a context to frame the topic of the essay and engage the reader.

When medical professionals diagnose their patients, they can classify the patients' injuries, diseases, or symptoms into broad categories. Canada uses the International Statistical Classification of Diseases and Related

Health Problems (ICD), whereby every health condition receives a unique code. Collecting and classifying this information provides Health Canada with data and statistics to make recommendations regarding the well-being of Canadians. Based on the information collected over time, analysis shows that unintentional falls are the leading trauma-related reason why over 5000 Canadians go to hospital emergency departments each year. Under the ICD system, unintentional falls can be broadly classified as falls from or out of something, falls after a collision, or falls by slipping, tripping, or stumbling.

The first category includes injuries as a result of falls from something such as buildings, ladders, play equipment, chairs, beds, or stairs. For example, construction or maintenance workers need special equipment, like ladders and scaffolding, to reach the outside of multi-leveled buildings. When these workers are not tethered or safely harnessed, they can fall from significant heights and seriously injure themselves. Window washers who work on scaffolding outside high-rise office towers, suspended many floors above the ground, wear harnesses and their equipment is securely fastened with ropes to the scaffolding. Developing industrial safety standards and ensuring workers adhere to them can prevent accidental falls as workers carry out their tasks. **Another example** from this category concerns children who frequently fall from outdoor play equipment, resulting in injuries requiring medical treatment. The injuries may depend on how far the child falls and on how resilient the ground surface is under the playground equipment, but often well-designed equipment can prevent certain injuries from happening. Occasionally, the news media report incidents of people falling from balconies, windows, trees, or roofs. **Also**, babies and toddlers are frequently reported to have fallen from change tables, cribs, or high chairs. Gathering and reporting the statistics of accidents from these kinds of falls increases public awareness, which can lead to effective preventative measures such as increased parental or caregiver supervision.

The second category includes the thousands of Canadians who are injured every year while participating in sports or exercise. **Examples** of these sports include winter activities such as skiing, snowboarding, tobogganing, skating, or playing hockey. Skiers, snowboarders, skaters, and children on sleds or toboggans can fall after colliding with others, with fences, or with trees on the hills. According to the Canadian Institute for Health Information (CIHI), many people with injuries from these seasonal activities are admitted to hospital for treatment of fractures. This number increases if visits to doctors' offices or treatments at hospital that do not result in hospital stays are included. **A further example**

THESIS STATEMENT
She ends her introduction with a sentence that establishes the focus of the essay.

TOPIC SENTENCE
She identifies the first type of accident.

SUPPORTING DETAILS
The writer's details, in this paragraph and those that follow, explain the various types of falls.

TOPIC SENTENCE

EXAMPLES
The writer cites instances of each category of injuries from falls, using transition phrases to connect them.

from this category includes hockey players in minor recreational leagues and professional leagues who often fall after colliding with each other or the boards on the sides of the rinks. The outcomes from falls in hockey are most commonly head trauma, like concussions, or musculo-skeletal injuries. Many of the injuries from falls of this nature may require longer treatment plans and rehabilitation to prevent future disability, so it's important for parents and coaches to regulate safe conditions for doing sports and to insist children and players wear protective equipment like helmets or wrist guards for sports activities year round.

CONCLUDING SENTENCE

TOPIC SENTENCE

The writer's use of "the last category" is an effective transition.

The writer introduces a third type of fall.

The last category includes injuries when people slip and fall, trip over something and fall, or just stumble and fall. During Canada's long winters, anyone can slip and fall on a patch of ice. Responsible homeowners and businesses can spread sand on icy sidewalks to prevent people from slipping, falling, and injuring themselves. Many pet owners have tripped over their own cats and dogs, so learning how to control an excited animal is part of the duty of caring for an animal, which can help reduce these kinds of falls. In an industrial setting, knowing about the hazards of tripping will encourage employees to keep aisles or pathways clear of any obstacles that could cause someone to trip and fall. The data gathered about injuries from falls can also be further divided by gender and ages. For example, as Canada's population ages, the number of seniors who become less agile will increase. When an elderly person loses his or her footing, a fall can result in a hip fracture. Additionally, the effects of certain widely prescribed medications can cause people to more easily lose their balance, possibly resulting in falls and injuries. Knowing accurate data about these kinds of falls enables practitioners to give seniors appropriate advice along with their prescriptions. Some recommendations about preventing falls for seniors include relaying the importance of wearing properly fitted shoes. Seniors can also be encouraged to arrange furniture strategically and remove loose rugs in their homes to help to reduce falls and the related injuries.

SUPPORTING DETAILS

The writer uses examples in this paragraph, too.

CONCLUDING SENTENCE

CONCLUSION

The shift in focus here tells the reader the essay is moving toward closing. The body paragraphs tell the reader how falls are categorized; the conclusion explains how collecting this information can be used to prevent falls in the future.

Using a systematic method to code, gather, and tabulate statistics related to injuries from falls can provide information about the factors that contribute to risk of falling. Once the reasons or conditions leading to these falls are understood, each province and territory and community can use the information to develop safety strategies and regulations appropriate to their jurisdictions that help prevent falls, reduce the burden on the health-care system, and lessen human suffering. Luckily, falls are a public health problem that is largely preventable.

1. What is your opinion of the title of the essay? Is it a good title? Why or why not?

2. What is the purpose of this essay? What kind of essay is this?

3. Do you agree with the order in which the writer presents different types of falls? Why or why not?

ELEMENTS OF THE ESSAY

As you write essays in response to the assignments in this chapter, keep in mind that you will need to include all the important elements of the essay as described in Chapter 13. Refer to the guidelines there for writing each part of your essay. Your thesis statement should be clear, focused, and use parallelism. You should avoid heavy-handed announcements or vague statements. Also, each topic sentence of the body paragraphs refers back to a point in the thesis statement. Furthermore, developing an essay plan or outline helps you decide on the logical order to present your supporting points, along with transitions. Finally, select an appropriate approach to build your concluding paragraph. Each pattern of essay has its own characteristic organization, yet it still includes all the elements of the essay.

THE WRITING PROCESS

When you wrote paragraphs, you learned about the writing process: prewriting, drafting, revising, editing, and reflecting. When you write essays, you examine more complex topics, so you have more ideas and details to monitor. The writing process you learned in Chapter 2 can also help you to organize and improve your essay. To become a more efficient and effective writer, spend enough time on each step of the process.

In this chapter, we present several kinds of writing, or rhetorical modes. You need to be able to recognize rhetorical modes in your readings and you will want to learn how and when to use each rhetorical mode in your own writing. Some essays will use only one pattern, but others will combine the patterns of organization. For example, many essays include descriptive details and persuasive language, combined with another pattern of organization.

ESSAYS WITH ONE PATTERN OF ORGANIZATION

In the following assignments, you revisit what you learned about writing paragraphs using a pattern of organization, such as description, example, and narration. In these assignments, however, you take your treatment of your topic to the next level.

In an essay, you delve deeper into your subject, offering a more detailed picture. You structure your essay to write multiple paragraphs with a thesis in the introduction and a topic sentence for each body paragraph. Finally, you bring your discussion to a close with a conclusion that emphasizes the point you have made and leaves your reader with something to think about.

Description

Remember that conveying a dominant impression is essential in effective description writing. Good description depends on sensory detail and frequently uses comparison. For a reminder of these elements of description writing, see these sections of Chapter 4: "Elements of Description," "Get Started," "Organize Your Thinking," and "Comparisons and Description Thinking."

Writing a description paragraph provides readers with a concrete, up-close look at the subject in a way that appeals to their senses. An essay can cover more territory than a paragraph can. As mentioned, often in an essay, you will use description along with other patterns of organization. Students often write description essays in the first person, especially for journal writing or reflective pieces. However, description is also effective when used in the third person. Here is a sample description essay.

ASSIGNMENT   Write a descriptive essay about a place that was important in your childhood.

The Oldest of Five

This is where I got my first kiss, smoked my first cigarette, and buried my first pet. This is where I grew up, the oldest of five, the only girl. All adventures took place in our big backyard. It was heavily wooded with tall birch trees. Three paths led to our favourite places on earth.

The first path led to the "mud hole." It was shaped like a saucer, shallow on the edges, deeper in the centre. If we got a good rain, it filled with the blackest, slipperiest, softest mud. **One day we were playing** in the woods when it began to rain. I started to run toward home. We never wore shoes in the summer, and **as I rounded the corner**, I slipped and fell on my side, sliding right through the mud. My brothers rounded the corner just behind me, and down they went, one after the other. **Soon** we had a contest to see who could slide the farthest. Seeing my brothers covered with mud was so funny; I started laughing. **When I did**, my brother John threw a pile of mud at me, which hit me in the back of the head. Naturally, I picked up some mud and threw it at him. **Soon** we were all throwing mud until my little brother Nick got mud in his mouth. He ran home crying, and we all followed. I will never forget the look on my mother's face when she saw us, covered in mud with only the whites of our eyes showing. It was a great day.

The second path led to the tree fort. It was in an old pine tree, about four metres up. It leaned on other trees for support. The fort was not properly constructed, to say the least. **One humid summer day** we had friends visiting. We were all in the tree fort when my little brothers, Gabe and Nick, started jumping. When my friend Lynn and I screamed, they jumped harder. **The next thing** we knew, the entire fort came crashing to the

---

The student begins with an inviting sentence.

THESIS STATEMENT
"Three paths" suggests the structure of the paper to come.

TOPIC SENTENCE
In her description of this place, the student tells a story.

ORDER AND TRANSITIONS
The writer uses transition words and phrases common to the narration pattern of organization, such as "One day," "Soon," and "When I did," which relate to time order.

TOPIC SENTENCE
The student tells a story as she describes the place.

ORDER AND TRANSITIONS
Transition words and phrases are commonly used for narration.

ground with us in it. John was the only one hurt; he was leaning against the pine tree with no shirt on. He had the biggest scratches down his back, but that did not stop any of us from rebuilding the fort the next day.

The third path led to the railroad tracks at the back of our property. We loved to walk the tracks. Sometimes my brothers would attempt to stop the train by stacking rocks on the track. **One day** when a train came by, we jumped across the water-filled ditch, only to find a fence at the top of the hill. Trapped, we decided to lie on the hillside and wait it out. **As the train sped by,** the wind pushed me onto the ground and I could not lift my head. I worried one of us would fall down toward the tracks. The train went on **forever**, blowing dirt into my eyes and onto my skin. When it **finally passed**, I hugged my brothers in relief. They laughed and said, "That was dangerous!"

E.B. White wrote, "It is strange how much you can remember about a place like that once you allow your mind to return into the grooves that lead back" **(121)**. This truly was a special place in my life, and there were many good times my brothers and I shared. I actually discovered my childhood again, simply by remembering instead of trying to forget.

Works Cited

White, E.B. "Once More to the Lake." *The Bedford Reader.* Ed. X. J. Kennedy, Dorothy M. Kennedy, and Jane E. Aaron. 6th ed. New York: St. Martin's Press, 1994: 120–26. Print.

TOPIC SENTENCE

NARRATION

ORDER AND TRANSITIONS

Notice the writer uses the author's name in the sentence and MLA-style in-text citation after the quote to show the page number where that quote is found. The Works Cited page after the end of the essay gives additional information for the source of the quotation.

DISCUSSION QUESTIONS

1. Is the introduction effective? Why or why not?

2. What description detail do you like best in the essay? Why?

3. In addition to description, what does the writer do to get her point across?

EXERCISE 14-1 **Outlining and Writing a Description Essay**

Directions: *Choose one of the following assignments for a description essay. Use the two forms of prewriting you like best to explore two possible topics related to the assignment. Next, narrow down one of the topics and develop a thesis and subtopics. When you complete your prewriting, use an outline form like the one provided in Chapter 13 to formulate your thesis and topic sentences and to plan your essay. Then write your essay, focusing on descriptive details that appeal to your readers' five senses.*

IMITATION ASSIGNMENT

1. Write a description essay using the previous essay as your guide. Describe a place that is important to you. Give the reader a sense of the place's spatial organization. Provide sensory details describing some important events that happened there or experiences you had.

Ask Yourself

Description calls for details. What kinds of details grab your attention when you read? What makes them interesting?

1. If you could create a time capsule to be opened after 100 years, what would you put inside? Describe the contents. Where would the items come from? Why are they important to you? Is the meaning of this content personal, or is there a public dimension to its value?

2. Pick a stereotype that is common in our society. Describe the stereotype as people commonly think of it, focusing on appearance, actions, and attitudes.

3. Describe an attitude or value of a particular age group with which you take issue. How is it expressed? Describe how you see it, hear it, and know it. Explain your main reasons for objecting to it.

GENERAL ASSIGNMENTS

1. Describe a difficult class.

2. Describe the ideal job for a post-secondary student.

3. Describe the qualities that make a good (or a bad) parent.

4. Describe a fear or phobia that is common to many people.

Example

Remember that effective example writing depends on including specific details. You present details to make your point. For a reminder of the elements of example writing, see these sections of Chapter 5: "Elements of Example," "Get Started," and "Types of Examples." For a reminder of how to organize example writing, see "Elaborate on Examples."

At the paragraph level, you briefly elaborate on examples. In an essay, however, you can go into much more detail, using similar, contrasting, and extended examples to make your point. Here is an example essay.

ASSIGNMENT   Discuss the benefits and challenges facing a young person who works.

The essay begins with an extended example.

Overtime

She still gets a call from an elderly man she made friends with when she worked at the retirement home. He says in his deep voice, "Hello, Leah. When are my two girlfriends coming over?" He means Leah and her two-year-old daughter, Natalie. Five years after working at the rest home, Leah still gets calls from Hershel, whom she refers to as "the gentle giant." When they are together, he and Leah talk about their families, school, and about his life "back in the day." He also gives Leah advice when she is having a tough time. There are many benefits and challenges to being a working high school student.

THESIS STATEMENT
The writer identifies advantages and disadvantages to working while in school as the focus of the essay.

To begin with, it is fun to meet people from different walks of life. Like Leah, Keianna was in high school when she got a job at The Village, a rest

TOPIC SENTENCE

home near campus. "I had never seen so many old people in my life," she says. They zipped past her on their motorized wheelchairs, called "hover rounds." Some almost ran over her. She worked in the dining room serving food. "Most of the dining room employees were high school students," Keianna notes, "so I met young and old alike." She grew to love the old people, who liked to see young faces. They liked to see energetic young people running around the room, serving the seniors their food quickly, and brightening the room.

There are other important benefits to being a working student. In addition to the pay, some employers offer tuition assistance and scholarship funds. If a student works 500 hours her last years of high school, she can save $4000 for post-secondary studies. A second benefit is learning responsibility. Being on time is a big priority at any job. When teenagers have jobs, they are responsible for their own actions. They also earn their own money and have to manage it. Presentation is also important at work. Knowing how to dress properly and speak confidently is a key factor in any work environment. These benefits can make a big difference to a young person's becoming more responsible.

TOPIC SENTENCE
"Other important benefits" provides a transition. The previous paragraph was about a benefit; the current paragraph will also be about benefits.

Then again, there are challenges to working and taking classes. **First and foremost** is fatigue. Working students only have so much energy. Some students work long hours after school, get home late, and have to study despite being tired. They also go to school tired. **A second challenge** is limiting their hours of work. It is tempting to add on, to take more work, and make more money. Even though it is against the law for high school students to work too many hours, employers will break the law if they have a good employee. Young people like to feel needed. They want to be important. It is difficult to turn down a boss who says, "You are my best worker." Finally, working students are not studying enough. **In many cases**, the good work they do for an employer is traded for good work they could be doing for a teacher.

TOPIC SENTENCE
"Then again" indicates a reversal of focus. Now the writer talks about the challenges of being a working student. These challenges contrast with the benefits. This presents a balanced point of view.

ORDER AND TRANSITIONS
The writer uses enumeration to connect details.

Every job has its satisfactions. In every situation, there are trade-offs. Leah does not regret working as a high school student. In fact, she says it was an excellent experience that prepared her for the adult world. However, Leah is only one person. There are others who go overboard, working too many hours. They need to be pulled back. They need to be teenagers.

The essay ends on a balanced note, reminding the reader there are benefits and challenges to being a working student.

DISCUSSION QUESTIONS

1. Is the introduction effective? Why or why not?

2. Does the writer reveal her point of view in this essay?

3. In addition to examples, what other patterns of organization do you see in the essay?

Directions: *Choose one of the following assignments for an example essay, using the previous example essay as your guide. On a separate sheet of paper, use the form of prewriting you like best to explore two possible topics related to the assignment. Next, narrow down one of the topics and develop a thesis and subtopics. When you complete your prewriting, use an outline form like the one provided in Chapter 13 to formulate your thesis and topic sentences and to plan your essay. Then write your essay. Be sure you elaborate on your examples.*

IMITATION ASSIGNMENT

1. Write an example essay using the example essay as your guide. Cite examples of a social behaviour you approve of or object to. Be sure to cite a number of examples, varying the length of the examples you use.

FOCUSED ASSIGNMENTS

1. It is said that adversity builds character. Write an essay in which you agree or disagree with this claim, or discuss how responding to challenges can make someone a better person. Consider using contrasting examples in your discussion to avoid a one-sided point of view.

2. Modern life is all about technological devices. Do they improve or complicate our lives? Write an essay in which you examine this question. Cite and discuss a number of examples of technological devices.

3. In a culture of celebrity, such as our own, we see and hear from famous people all the time. Some celebrities use fame for good causes. Cite and discuss a few examples.

GENERAL ASSIGNMENTS

1. Give examples of a positive and/or negative role model.

2. Provide examples of abilities you bring to the workplace.

3. Cite the qualities of an ideal job.

4. Give examples of fads you find amusing or annoying.

Narration

Effective narration depends on using specific details. Your reader needs to know about what happened, when and where, who was involved, and what the outcome was. For a refresher, see these sections of Chapter 6: "Elements of Narration," "Get Started," "Narration and Specific Details," and "Make Connections."

The narration paragraph illustrates that a well-told story provides the reader with specific details. In an essay, you can tell one long story, zeroing in on the details that are most significant, or you can tell multiple stories to make a point. Here is a narration essay.

ASSIGNMENT Write a narration essay about a phobia you have. A peer discussion of phobias can give you ideas to draw upon.

No Bones about It

"A dinner party? Great! What time? What should I bring?" I was invited to a dinner party at a new friend's house. It never occurred to me to ask what kind of meat would be served. They were serving chicken and ribs. Most people would be happy with this menu, but not me. Since the age of ten I have been unable to eat meat with bones in it or any meat that looks the way it did when it was alive: I have bonephobia.

The student begins with a captivating story.

THESIS STATEMENT

TOPIC SENTENCE

One of the funniest memories of my bonephobia is when I was in Orlando, Florida, during March Break. My friends and I went to Medieval Times. We were supposed to have dinner during a horse riding and jousting show. The show started, and they began serving dinner, that is, if you consider people wearing rags and throwing food on your plate "serving dinner." There was no silverware. Everything was to be eaten with your hands. We drank our soup out of dented metal bowls. It was all in fun, so I did not mind, until a man came by and threw an entire Cornish hen on my plate. I still remember how it jiggled as it hit the plate. I screamed with surprise and started yelling, "Get it off! Get it off!" I was so upset. I did not know what to do. My friend reached over, picked up the hen, and put it on his plate. I could not calm down at first. When I did, I was very embarrassed. I could not believe the way I reacted. The man sitting next to me, a complete stranger, laughed and said, "Can I have yours?"

In the body of the paper, the student starts right in with a narration to explain what bonephobia is.

She provides specific detail about place, actors, and actions.

Here she gives the outcome of the narration.

There are many people who actually enjoy eating meat off the bone. I go to the Renaissance Festival in Langley, B.C., every year, and I see many people buying huge turkey legs. They walk around eating them and seem to enjoy it. It is difficult for me to watch. I am also taken aback by some places that serve seafood. The fish come out cooked with heads still on them. **One year** my friends took me to a seafood restaurant for my birthday. Someone ordered lobster tail. To my surprise they brought the entire lobster. It sat across the table staring at me. I tried to ignore it at first. Then I asked them to put a napkin over it. Everyone thought it was funny that it bothered me. They had lots of fun tormenting me with it for the rest of the evening.

TRANSITION SENTENCE

TOPIC SENTENCE
The writer suggests she will look at contrasting examples.

A second narration begins here.

Here is the outcome of the narration.

Some doctors claim they can cure any phobia. In his book *Psychology, an Introduction,* Benjamin B. Lahey, the author, discusses a widely known study published in 1920 by Dr. John B. Watson on classical conditioning. Watson believed that many of our fears are acquired and taught to us. He did a study on counterconditioning. This is a way to reverse what we were taught to fear. For a situation like mine, a therapist would probably introduce the feared element (chicken bones) gradually. First, a plate of clean chicken bones would be placed in front of me. As I became more comfortable, the

TOPIC SENTENCE

Here the student uses an extended example.

therapist might leave small pieces of meat on the bone and have me pick it off and so on. I have heard of experts who try an approach different from Watson's. They claim to help a person overcome a phobia in 24 hours without having that person repeatedly exposed to the feared item(s).

I know a few other people who cannot eat meat off the bone. We all agree that it reminds us that we are eating an animal, which was killed simply for us to eat. If we think about it while eating, the meal is over. On the other hand, I was just talking to my nephew who stated, "Boned chicken is my favourite meat." He thinks that all of the vegetables I eat are gross. When he starts picking on my fear of bones, I just offer him some broccoli.

The student finishes her essay with a small comparison and contrast example.

DISCUSSION QUESTIONS

1. How many stories does the writer tell in the essay?

2. What is the effect of referring to her textbook in the essay?

3. Compose what you think would be a good thesis for this paper. Then look for a similar statement in the essay itself.

4. Describe what the writer does in her conclusion.

EXERCISE 14-3 Outlining and Writing a Narration Essay

Directions: *Choose one of the following assignments for a narration essay. Use the form of prewriting you like best to explore two possible topics related to the assignment. Next, narrow down one of the topics and develop a thesis and subtopics. When you complete your prewriting, use an outline form like the one provided in Chapter 13 to formulate your thesis and topic sentences and use it to plan and then write your narration essay.*

IMITATION ASSIGNMENT

1. Write a narration essay using the previous essay as your guide. Describe a phobia you have and, in the process, recall two or three incidents in which you were keenly aware of this phobia.

FOCUSED ASSIGNMENTS

1. Discuss a person, place, or thing you changed your mind about. Talk about how your attitude was formed. Then tell a story or stories exploring your change of attitude. Be sure to be specific about time, place, people, and events in the stories you tell.

2. We often celebrate our triumphs and our skills, dwelling on the positive. Write an essay about something you are not very good at and wish you were. Tell a story about a specific time you realized your lack of this skill, and consider what difference it makes in your life that you are not good at it.

3. Discuss the relative importance of health in your life. Recall a time when you or someone you know was injured or got sick. Be specific about what happened, including details of time and place. What was the outcome of this experience?

1. Cite a disappointing experience.

2. Give specific details about a technological device.

3. Recall a time when you had amazingly good luck.

4. Tell a story about a challenge many young people face in school or on the job.

Process

Process analysis is common in academic writing and writing in the workplace. You will frequently be asked to explain how something works, such as a piece of machinery or cell division. Remember that effective process writing depends on including specific details about the process. These details include when and where the process takes place, what materials are necessary, the people or steps involved in the process, and its key details. For a reminder on the elements of process writing, see these sections of Chapter 7: "Elements of Process," "Get Started," "Organize Your Details," and "Key Details."

In the process paragraph you wrote, you saw that a process usually has a key detail that requires explanation. In an essay, you have much more room to focus on one or more of the important components of a process. Here is a process essay.

ASSIGNMENT   Using process analysis, describe a security issue people should be aware of and how to protect themselves.

Identity Theft: Everyone's Problem

It was the weekend. He was shopping and checking things off his list. At his last stop, when he reached for his wallet, it was gone. He rushed out and backtracked to the last store. Luck was on his side because there was his wallet, safely in the hands of the salesclerk. Many people are not as lucky as this gentleman. Identity theft has become a costly problem in our society today. It occurs when someone obtains and uses an individual's personal information such as social insurance numbers, bank and credit card accounts, and birth dates. A few simple, preventative steps can keep an individual's personal information safe.

The first step in securing records begins at home. Instead of throwing receipts or pay stubs on the counter, it is wise to purchase a small filing cabinet. This cabinet keeps records neatly organized. At the end of the year, it is possible to sort and keep important papers for future use,

The student begins his essay with a captivating story.

THESIS STATEMENT
The writer clearly indicates this is a process essay.

TOPIC SENTENCE
The student identifies important materials needed for this process.

discard all unnecessary papers, and start the New Year right. This cabinet keeps personal information in one location, safely under lock and key. **However, all this organizational effort will not work without a paper shredder.** Shred all discarded documents. Catalogues with preprinted order forms inside can contain a person's name and credit card information. Shred the form first before throwing it away. If it is in the garbage, it is public property for anyone to use.

A second step is to take precautions with computer, telephone, and mail communication. Passwords are better than using your mother's maiden name; ensure Web sites have secure firewalls. **Once your password is established, be on the lookout for irregular requests.** These days it is not uncommon to receive an email from a financial institution requesting a social insurance number and password. A call to that institution invariably proves the request is a hoax. **The same goes for telephone calls.** Do not assume that the person on the other end is legitimate. Postal mail is **equally** important. Preapproved credit card applications are sent to households every day. They should be shredded and thrown away. Once more, shredding is the best defense against identity theft.

TOPIC SENTENCE

This conclusion paragraph covers the last step of the process.

Finally, individuals should consider asking for a credit report every year. Credit reports identify all open and closed credit accounts, balances on these accounts, and a person's credit rating. This rating can be the difference between purchasing that first home or having doors slammed in one's face. If there is suspicious activity on the report, the following credit reporting agencies can help: Equifax or TransUnion. They flag accounts and monitor any subsequent activity. By utilizing these steps, you can effectively prevent identity theft.

DISCUSSION QUESTIONS

1. What does the writer do to capture the reader's attention in his introduction?

2. What tool or device is important for identity theft protection?

3. Does the order of the paragraphs make sense? What do you think the writer's reasons were for placing the paragraphs in this order? Did the writer leave out any important information?

EXERCISE 14-4 **Outlining and Writing a Process Essay**

Directions: *Choose one of the following assignments for a process essay. Use the form of prewriting you like best to explore two possible topics related to the assignment. Next, narrow down one of the topics and develop a thesis and subtopics. When you complete your prewriting, use an outline form like the one provided in Chapter 13 to plan and then write your process essay.*

IMITATION ASSIGNMENT

1. Write a process essay using the previous essay as your guide. Explain the steps involved in becoming a good student. Consider materials, times, places, and people involved in the process. Be sure to identify a key detail.

FOCUSED ASSIGNMENTS

1. Every so often, people in a household are caught unprepared when they lose power in a storm. What is the best way to prepare for such an inconvenience? Once the power goes out, what steps can be taken to maintain a relatively normal way of life?

2. Complex skills call for smart learning processes. Discuss a complex skill you have, such as playing a musical instrument or speaking a foreign language. Describe the most effective process for acquiring such a skill.

3. Technology has made new forms of communication possible. Discuss the safety issues involved in online communication, such as chat rooms, and what precautionary steps a person can take to ensure safety.

Talk about it »»»

How do you select a writing assignment? Is your approach effective?

GENERAL ASSIGNMENTS

1. Explain the process of global warming.

2. Describe how avalanches occur.

3. Explain how to overcome a prejudice.

4. What are the steps involved in getting a promotion at work?

Classification

You saw in your classification paragraph that sorting detail into categories or types enables you to explain ideas more precisely. In an essay, you can say more about your categories and why they are important. Classification makes more exact thinking possible.

Classification writing involves sorting: dividing an undifferentiated topic into subtopics and categories. Your categories depend on the basis for classification and the inclusion of good details if they are to make sense to the reader. You also want to guard against thinking in stereotypes when you classify. For a reminder, see these sections of Chapter 8: "Elements of Classification," "Get Started," "Provide Examples of Categories," and "Avoid Stereotyping." Here is a classification essay.

ASSIGNMENT   Write a classification essay in which you discuss different types of people who use the Internet.

Internet Users

At one time, parents worried about how much television their children watched. Every day, a new report came out with alarming statistics: children were watching four, five, even six hours of television a day. Then came video games. Children sat in front of television screens, joysticks

The student begins with a general observation—appealing to a common fear.

He cites three examples of addiction, leading to the focus of the essay—types of Internet users.

THESIS STATEMENT

TOPIC SENTENCE
The writer identifies the first type of user.

ORDER AND TRANSITIONS
Repeating the term "average-type user" adds to the coherence of the details in this paragraph.

TOPIC SENTENCE
The writer identifies the second type of user.

After identifying the category, the student cites an example.

ORDER AND TRANSITIONS
Transition words and repetition enhance the coherence of this paragraph.

TOPIC SENTENCE

He identifies the type, then illustrates it with a specific example.

in hand, completely absorbed by their games. Add the Internet to TV and video games, and the population of the addicted increases significantly. However, many Internet users are not children. They are adult users, and they come in three recognizable types.

Less and less often do you see the average-type Internet user. He comes home from work about 5:00 p.m. He strolls up to his computer and checks his email. He finds an email for a bill he was expecting. He pays with his credit card and closes his email. He smiles, knowing he does not have to write a cheque and that this particular bill is taken care of until next month. That is the last time he is on the computer that day. **The average type** uses the Internet to save time. **The average-type user** takes advantage of the Internet when he can, but he has never depended on the Internet and probably never will.

Another type is the Web junk user. These users enjoy being on the Internet and exploring different areas of the Web. They are the window shoppers of the Internet world. They forward messages to bring themselves good fortune. Many seniors **used to be** the average-type user. One gentleman lives in Calgary. He would email his grandchildren just to say hello or see how they were doing. **That all changed.** He started emailing them ridiculous emails about having good luck. **At first** his family members were his only recipients. **After** a couple of months, the list was enormous. The letter carrier, his bingo buddies, and almost all of his other friends are now on his mailing list. He has met thousands of people on the Internet. **Web junk users** spend much of their spare time browsing the Internet. **They** are infatuated with the power and size of the Web. **They** enjoy knowing an article they found will travel around the world. These are the users who congest all of our email boxes.

The third type is the chat-room user. These users love being on the Internet. **They** would rather be on the Internet than pick up the phone and call someone. **They** have more fun in a chat room or on a social media Web site than at an amusement park. **They** love meeting people on the Internet. **They** love designing their profiles, which change on a daily basis. Many teenagers are this type. They buy, sell, email, download, bank, and check the weather. Chat-room users often talk to friends on the computer, i.e., they can literally talk through the Internet, and not just type the message. For some reason, they prefer to talk through the computer rather than use a cellphone. Chat-room users spend all of their spare time on the Internet. Many stay up all night online. They need it. It is an addiction.

Many average users spend much of their time on the Internet deleting their junk email. The junk users and chat-room addicts really bother them. Average users can enjoy the benefits of the Internet without relying on it too much. Even with the Internet, they still have a social life, actually meeting friends in person.

In this conclusion the student emphasizes the importance of the topic by discussing an effect: too much unwanted email.

DISCUSSION QUESTIONS

1. State the point of this essay in your own words.

2. For each type of user, the writer provides an example. What is the effect of doing so?

3. Which type of user is the writer?

EXERCISE 14-5 Outlining and Writing a Classification Essay

Directions: *Choose one of the following assignments for a classification essay. Use the form of prewriting you like best to explore possible topics related to the assignment. Select an appropriate basis for classification. Next, narrow down one of the topics and develop a thesis and subtopics. When you complete your prewriting, use an outline form like the one provided in Chapter 13 to formulate your thesis and topic sentences, plan, and then write your classification essay.*

IMITATION ASSIGNMENT

1. Write a classification essay using the previous essay as your guide. Classify different kinds of animal lovers. For each type, cite an example or two to elaborate and explain.

FOCUSED ASSIGNMENTS

1. Not everyone agrees on the proper approach to disciplining children. Talk about three different approaches and what they teach children.

2. Discuss different types of jobs available to young people today. Consider what these types of jobs offer and what kind of young person they would benefit.

3. The best way to save money is to have a budget that helps to keep track of cash flow. How could students classify their expenses? Which type of expense could most easily be controlled and enable them to spend money more wisely?

GENERAL ASSIGNMENTS

1. Classify your friends into different types.

2. Use classification to provide excuses for not getting homework done.

3. There are probably specific kinds of movies you prefer to watch. Use classification to categorize these movies.

4. Classify different types of sports fans.

Writer's Response >>>

When have you used classification effectively? For what purpose? Why?

Cause and Effect

In a cause or effect paragraph, you saw the importance of focusing on causes or effects. The cause and effect essay provides you with greater latitude, inviting you to think critically about both causes and effects.

Focus is essential in cause/effect writing. You must distinguish between causes and effects so your reader understands which you are explaining. In a shorter essay, focus either on causes or effects, rather than both. For a reminder, see these sections of Chapter 9: "Elements of Cause and Effect," "Get Started," "Cause and Effect Details," and "Organizing Your Thinking." Cause and effect details are not necessarily of equal importance, so you need to decide on a logical way to organize the events. Here is a cause and effect essay.

ASSIGNMENT   Select a common problem people face and consider causes or effects.

Sweet Dreams

This first sentence goes with the title. It invites the reader in.

Have a good sleep. That is the wish of just about every individual. Good sleep is tied to emotional, mental, and physical health. Good sleep, for many, is elusive. What should happen easily and naturally happens only with the help of medications, or it happens not at all. Sleep deprivation affects millions of people a year, possibly every night. Medical literature devotes increasingly more space and discussion to a range of new problems, such as sleep apnea, as well as to old problems, such as insomnia. Why do we have difficulty sleeping, and what are the effects of sleeplessness?

THESIS QUESTION
The student uses a question to indicate this is a cause and effect analysis.

TOPIC SENTENCE

ORDER AND TRANSITIONS

For each cause, the student provides details and explanation.

One reason people cannot sleep is conditions in the sleep environment. Their sleep is disturbed by **sound**. A barking dog will keep some people awake. The **sound** of blasting music from an upstairs apartment or in a car that drives by is enough to prevent sleep. **Such people** often go into "listening mode." They lie awake waiting for another car to go by. They listen for voices upstairs. **Still** others are kept awake by someone close by. Snoring is a big joke, but not to those whom it keeps awake. Now physicians talk about "restless leg syndrome," a neurological disorder that seems to activate when a person lies down. **Consequently**, the afflicted individual is unable to sleep, as is the person sharing his or her bed.

TOPIC SENTENCE

Another reason people cannot sleep is worry. They lie awake at night worrying about work, children, or the future. Work is often a culprit. Work is tied in with livelihood. Someone whose work changes or whose income is threatened is likely to lie awake at night, preoccupied with what is happening or about to happen, unable to sleep as a result. **Similarly**, parents may have trouble sleeping if they have a child who is in distress. Parents stay up at night waiting for their teenagers to come home. This wakefulness in fact begins early in their lives as parents. New parents listen for a baby's cry, for the slightest sound. They learn to sleep lightly. **Finally**, people may suffer sleep deprivation because they worry about the future. Asked why he did not sleep well at night, one patient in a sleep clinic said he lies awake at night worrying about death.

We need sleep to rest our minds. We also need sleep to be healthy. People who sleep poorly are more likely to get sick than those who sleep well because lack of sleep affects the immune system. People who are tired also are less able to perform at optimum levels and cannot concentrate as well. Their reflexes and mental agility are affected. Poor performance causes stress. That in turn may affect sleep. It is a vicious cycle.

In the conclusion, the student briefly examines the effects of poor sleep.

DISCUSSION QUESTIONS

1. This is cause and effect analysis. What pattern of organization does the writer use in the third paragraph?

2. The essay is written mostly in the third person. Where does the writer shift out of third person? Why does she make these shifts?

3. How would you describe the tone of this essay?

Tone can be formal or informal, positive or negative. Chapter 1 provides more information about tone.

EXERCISE 14-6 **Outlining and Writing a Cause/Effect Essay**

Directions: *Choose one of the following assignments for a cause/effect essay. Use the form of prewriting you like best to explore two possible topics related to the assignment. Next, narrow down one of the topics and develop a thesis and subtopics. When you complete your prewriting, use an outline form like the one provided in Chapter 13 to formulate your thesis and topic sentences. Plan and then write your cause/effect essay. Indicate whether your focus is primarily on causes or effects.*

IMITATION ASSIGNMENT

1. Write a cause and effect essay using the previous essay as your guide. Discuss something you changed your mind about. Be specific about what you liked or disliked about it initially as well as your reasons for changing your mind.

FOCUSED ASSIGNMENTS

1. Discuss a physical characteristic of fashion models and the effect it has had on teenagers' views of themselves. Examine that effect in three specific situations.

2. We say sometimes that experience is the best teacher. Write about an experience that taught you a valuable lesson. Be specific about the reasons why the lesson was valuable.

3. Discuss a popular entertainer in the music industry. What makes this person so entertaining? Be specific about the reasons.

GENERAL ASSIGNMENTS

1. Discuss reasons why students drop out of school.

2. Give the causes or the effects of being good at sports.

3. Discuss a bad habit and the consequences of it.

4. Write about having a special skill or lacking a specific skill at work.

Comparison and Contrast

Like classification, comparison and contrast focus on similarities and differences. We use comparison to show what two different things have in common; we use contrast to show the differences in what appear to be two similar things. Examining similarities and differences is a basic form of inquiry, useful in school, in the workplace, and at home.

In comparison and contrast writing, you explore similarities and differences, presenting supporting details to illustrate and explain your point. This form of writing poses unique organizational challenges. You should first pick three points of comparison for the two items being compared or contrasted. There are two methods you can use for this rhetorical mode and both provide the same information, just organized differently. In fact, the introductory and concluding paragraphs can be the same; it's in the body paragraphs where you notice the different organizational pattern.

Subject-by-subject (or block) format

You may choose to organize your essay in subject-by-subject (or block) format. In this case, you will have an introductory paragraph followed by one paragraph that discusses the three points of comparison for the first item. The next paragraph will discuss the same points of comparison, in the same order, for the second item. Then you reach a conclusion in the last paragraph. In this subject-by-subject pattern of organization, you will have only four paragraphs (introduction, body paragraph about first item, body paragraph about second item, and a concluding paragraph).

Point-by-point organization

Alternatively, it may be more effective to use point-by-point organization. In this method, you start with an introductory paragraph where you introduce the three points of comparison for two items. The first body paragraph discusses the first point of comparison for the first item and then the first point of comparison for the second item. The second body paragraph discusses the second point of comparison for the first item, followed by the second point of comparison for the second item. Likewise, the third body paragraph discusses the third point of comparison, beginning with the first item and then the second item. You finish your essay with a concluding paragraph. In a point-by-point organizational pattern, you have five paragraphs (introduction, body paragraph about the first point of comparison for both items, body paragraph about the second point of comparison for both items, body paragraph about the third point of comparison for both items, and the concluding paragraph).

For a reminder, see these sections of Chapter 10: "Elements of Comparison and Contrast," "Get Started," "Points of Comparison and Contrast," and "Select and Elaborate on Details." Here is a comparison and contrast essay.

ASSIGNMENT   Using Charles Dickens's *Hard Times* as your starting point, discuss differing views of education.

Possible Minds

The use of education, according to Thomas Gradgrind, a teacher in Charles Dickens's *Hard Times,* is to fill our heads with facts. There is no room for nonsense, play, or wonder. Gradgrind is a "cannon loaded to the muzzle with facts," (4) and he opens fire on the children before him, murdering their imaginations in the process. What is a horse? Bitzer, a Gradgrind success story, answers: "Quadruped. Graminivorous. Forty teeth. . . . Sheds coat in the spring. . . . Hoofs hard. . . . Age known by marks in mouth." (5) In a technical sense, Bitzer's right. That is a horse. Nevertheless, he has missed something. He has missed the majestic animal that excites awe. Education ought to be about awesome possibilities.

This is a reference to a classic Charles Dickens novel describing conditions of the working poor during Victorian times in England.

The student begins with a specific reference to something he has read.

In the school, Mr. Henke prowled the hallways and cafeteria on stubby legs. He had a hogshead chest and a flat face with a look of total certainty on it. Before becoming a principal, he had been a builder. He had measured and sawed lumber to fit, then bashed it into place with his roughing hammer. If it did not fit, he bashed harder. This was also his approach to education. His construction tongue often got the best of him. When riled, he called some students jerks and fools and was not above using tame four-letter words. In the cafeteria, where we inevitably saw him, he pulled lovers apart. "Hey, you should not be doing that here!" He stopped at tables of grade 9 students, shooting the breeze. He joked, laughing quickly and without reserve. We liked him. Like us, he was rough around the edges. I do not think he understood kids or that he was even very interested in them. To Mr. Henke, school was a place to keep order. What we learned from him was: Do not neck in the cafeteria. Do not question authority.

SUPPORTING DETAILS
This paragraph begins with a statement of fact. Much of the detail in the paragraph is description detail.

This view of school was consistent with the one I learned at home. My father was a businessman. In every interaction, he was selling himself. When I rode with him on his calls, he constantly waved to people he did not know. "You can wave," he said. "It does not cost anything." He had to sell himself before he could sell anything else. As parents will, he made me in his image. I learned to wave. I learned what he called "presentation skills": **how to** talk on the phone, **how to** deal with strangers, **how to** use language to get what I wanted. In school, I had to acquire **useful** learning. **Useful** meant math. My father was **a man of projects**. He drew pictures. He measured and cut. I needed math to size up the world and do **my own projects**. He kept accounts. I needed math to look after my money. Useful also meant reading. I had to learn to read well so I could become an independent learner, like my father.

TOPIC SENTENCE
The student states his main idea at the end of this paragraph.
TOPIC SENTENCE

TRANSITIONS
The writer uses repetition to make his paragraph coherent.

Then I got my hands on literature. **One fall**, I read poetry from an anthology. I also read *Death of a Salesman* and *Othello.* It was not my first

The student uses inductive order in this paragraph, too. It is "details first."

encounter with literature. **Up to that time**, reading had not affected me much. It was an information transfer system, a form of work. **That fall**, the terrible longings of Willie Loman, his massive dreams of success and his tragic inability to enjoy simple pleasures, affected me profoundly. At the end of the play, Linda stood over his grave, saying, "We're free, Willie. We're free"(139). It was more than I could stand. Then there was the majestic language of *Othello*. It was beautiful and dramatic. Reading was fun. In those weeks, education suddenly took on a new meaning.

TOPIC SENTENCE
The topic sentence comes at the end of the paragraph.

In his conclusion, the student refers to something read in class.

He also retrieves a detail from the beginning of the essay.

After that, to me, school became a place where a few thoughtful young people congregated, seeking contact with even more thoughtful older people. It became a place of awesome possibilities. I was still an obedient student, bent upon being useful somehow or other. However, **a little of the Bitzer** in me had died.

Works Cited

Dickens, Charles. *Hard Times*. 1907. Toronto: Random House, 1992. Print.
Miller, Arthur. *Death of a Salesman*. 1949. New York: Penguin Group, 1976. Print.

DISCUSSION QUESTIONS

1. Describe the different types of education the writer compares and contrasts in this essay.

2. Titles of essays are supposed to reflect content of the essay. What does the title of this essay mean?

3. What does the writer mean when he says "a little of the Bitzer in me had died"?

EXERCISE 14-7 **Outlining and Writing a Comparison/Contrast Essay**

Directions: *Choose one of the following assignments for a comparison and contrast essay. Use the form of prewriting you like best to explore two possible topics related to the assignment. Next, narrow down one of the topics and develop a thesis and subtopics. Comparison/contrast essays can use two different organization patterns so you should try to use both of the outlines that follow to formulate your thesis and topic sentences and to plan whether your essay will be organized as subject-by-subject (block) or in a point-by-point format. Choose the approach that works best for your topic. Then write your essay.*

SUBJECT-BY-SUBJECT OR BLOCK COMPARISON

Topic: _____

Thesis: _____

_____

Topic Sentence (Subject 1): _____

_____

   A. Point of comparison/contrast #1 _____

   B. Point of comparison/contrast #2 _____

   C. Point of comparison/contrast #3 _____

Topic Sentence (Subject 2): _____

_____

   A. Point of comparison/contrast #1 _____

   B. Point of comparison/contrast #2 _____

   C. Point of comparison/contrast #3 _____

Concluding Paragraph: _____

_____

_____

_____

POINT-BY-POINT COMPARISON

Topic: _____

Thesis: _____

_____

Topic Sentence (Point of comparison/contrast #1): _____

_____

   Subject 1: _____

   Subject 2: _____

Topic Sentence (Point of comparison/contrast #2): _____

_____

   Subject 1: _____

   Subject 2: _____

Topic Sentence (Point of comparison/contrast #3): _____

_____

   Subject 1: _____

   Subject 2: _____

Concluding Paragraph: _____

_____

_____

_____

Ask Yourself

Why imitate the example essay? What do you admire in the writing?

IMITATION ASSIGNMENT

1. Write a comparison and contrast essay using the example essay as your guide. Why do we work? What is it for? What does it do for us? Explain two different views of work and its purpose. In your essay, connect those views with specific people you know. Be sure to indicate the view you find most compelling.

FOCUSED ASSIGNMENTS

1. Change is the law of the universe. Write an essay about a change you have seen in a person or place. Provide specific descriptions both before and after the change.

2. Discuss two different job positions in your workplace. How are they similar or different in terms of responsibility, relationship to co-workers, and stress levels?

3. Learning requires maturity, preparation, and readiness. Not everyone is ready to learn at the same time. Compare and contrast two learning experiences involving a particular subject in school that yielded very different results. In your discussion, consider reasons for the different results.

GENERAL ASSIGNMENTS

1. Compare and contrast a book and a movie made from the book.

2. Compare and contrast two friends you enjoy being with.

3. Compare and contrast views of marriage from the perspective of two different generations.

4. Compare and contrast practical knowledge versus school knowledge.

Definition

Definition can be especially important in academic writing, where differences of opinion often rest on different understandings of what something is, where it came from, and how it has changed over time.

The definition essay provides the writer with room to be specific and examine important consequences of a particular definition. Definition writing enables you to clarify your terms. Often a definition begins with the writer placing the subject in a category, followed by examples to explain the definition further. For a reminder, see these sections of Chapter 11: "Elements of Definition," "Get Started," "Examples and Details," and "Negatives." Here is a definition essay.

ASSIGNMENT   Write an essay in which you explore James Gleick's assertion that stress is an "ill-defined term."

Family Stress

James Gleick notes in his essay that stress is an "ill defined term."

Maybe that is the case because there are many types of stress in our lives.

We stress about work, about education, and about political issues that

The student leads off with a short quote from a reading in class.

concern us. Perhaps even more than these, we stress about family. <u>What is family stress and where does it come from?</u>

<u>In the immediate family—husband, wife, and children—stress begins with the energy and time required to provide for and support a family.</u> **As soon as** your first child is born and you hold it in your arms, you begin a stressful journey. You are the life support system for this helpless infant. **Our first day** home with our first child, we kept her fed, dry, and content. **As the evening progressed**, so did our baby's unhappiness. This escalated into an unceasing crying spell. My wife racked her brain while I pored over our child-care books looking for causes and solutions to this situation, which was making us both feel helpless and stressed. We had been told at the hospital that our child did not receive a nightly feeding. Through trial and error, we finally realized our daughter was hungry.

<u>Family stress comes also from worry about the physical and emotional health of your family.</u> As children grow and the number of children in the family increases, you worry about their health, safety, and emotional states. They grow older, they spread their wings, they begin to push, bend, and break all the rules you have put in place to keep them safe and on the right track. Our oldest two children, 20 and 17, have both taken up smoking cigarettes. The oldest drinks as if she's 21 and the 17-year-old has imbibed more times than he should have. The youngest, at 13, is constantly on the computer chatting with her friends. She's interested in boys already. A fear of ours is the potential online "admirer" she may encounter. Family stress grows with the family.

<u>Extended family can also be a source of stress: while you love, stick up for, and grow on each other, you also get on each other's nerves.</u> It is just a matter of time before you get caught up in a stressful situation. Holidays provide added stress on the family front. Perhaps it is the coming together of family members who have conflicting personalities or the chaotic activity of hosting the whole family for a meal while surrounded by overactive children. If these holiday gatherings are not equally hosted by all the family members, you have yet another stressful point of contention. In my family the celebration of major holidays has fallen upon three out of six siblings since the passing of our parents. This has caused resentment, primarily between the wives of the siblings who have the gatherings and the spouses of those who will not. Arguing about who hosts the gathering adds to the stress of the holiday season.

Stress can affect us physiologically, according to Gleick, sometimes in the form of heart ailments. Ironically, family can be both a source and

THESIS STATEMENT

TOPIC SENTENCE

SUPPORTING DETAILS
The student tells a story to develop the main idea of this paragraph. He uses transitions related to time.

TOPIC SENTENCE
To define stress, this student focuses on its sources.

SUPPORTING DETAILS
The student uses both description and illustrations to develop the ideas in this paragraph.

TOPIC SENTENCE
The student introduces yet another source of stress.

SUPPORTING DETAILS
The student provides an illustration of stress related to extended family.

To further illustrate, he again refers to his own family as an example.

In his conclusion, the student refers again to the reading from class.

He ends with an ironic solution to the problem of stress.

a solution to stress. By being open, honest, and loving with those in our families we find troublesome, we can resolve stressful differences or mis-understandings. Knowing our limitations in providing for the needs of those dependent upon us, we can minimize daily stress. We can also help alleviate family stress by realizing our contribution to it. Love is the best antidote for family stress. By loving our family members, we can try to understand and overlook differences that cause family stress throughout the years.

DISCUSSION QUESTIONS

1. What organization pattern does the writer use in paragraph two for defining family stress?

2. What impact does the writer's use of personal details have in the essay?

3. Where and why does the writer refer to James Gleick?

EXERCISE 14-8 Outlining and Writing a Definition Essay

Directions: *Choose one of the following assignments for a definition essay. Use the form of prewriting you like best to explore two possible topics related to the assignment. Next, narrow down one of the topics and develop a thesis and subtopics. When you complete your pre-writing, use an outline form like the one provided in Chapter 13 and use it to formulate your thesis and topic sentences. Plan and then write your definition essay.*

IMITATION ASSIGNMENT

1. Write a definition essay using the previous essay as your guide. Define a form of stress you deal with in your life. When and where does it occur? What are its causes?

FOCUSED ASSIGNMENTS

1. Young parents with children often disagree on how to discipline their children. What is good discipline? What does it consist of? When does discipline become abuse?

2. Some people in the media and in our lives have charisma. What is char-isma? Where does it come from? What are its consequences? Is every-one charismatic in the same way?

3. People demonstrate strength in different ways. Discuss two or three dif-ferent kinds of strength and what their definitions are.

GENERAL ASSIGNMENTS

1. Write a definition essay on planning a budget.

2. Define *friendship*, using specific details.

3. Write an essay defining *imagination*.

4. Define *motivation* and give examples and details explaining it.

Argument

Argument is a common writing mode in many disciplines. The argument paragraph supports your viewpoint with reasons. In argument essays, you explore multiple viewpoints, examining their reasons, and how they fit the facts.

In argument writing, you make a claim that you believe is true; then offer reasons and evidence to support your claim. Argument may also involve a concession: you take another viewpoint into account, but you offer a rebuttal to convince your reader that your point of view is more compelling. For a reminder, see these sections of Chapter 12: "Elements of Argument," "Get Started," "Review Evidence," and "Acknowledge Another Viewpoint." Here is an argument essay.

ASSIGNMENT   Discuss a viewpoint that you find inaccurate. Identify where the view is in error and argue for a more accurate way of seeing your subject.

Would You Like Fries with That?

A gentleman came to the drive-through on my shift and ordered 17 cheeseburgers. After he paid I told him we would bring his order out to him, then politely asked him to pull into a parking space. "Why do I have to wait?" he said. I responded, "Sir, this is fast food, not instant food." When people think of fast-food jobs, they think "easy work." In fact, it is quite the opposite. Managers constantly harassing employees, customers complaining about service being slow—this is just part of the joy of Burger King. Fast food may be mindless and repetitive, but easy it is not.

I hear it said that the hours in fast-food work are great. This is not true. Burger King opens its doors at 6:00 a.m. Eight people on **weekdays** and four people on **weekends**, including me, come in at **5:00 a.m.** to stock the store and prep food. **From 7:00 a.m. till 2:00 in the afternoon** there is a constant stream of hungry people. **Between noon and 2:00 p.m.** the mid-shifters come in and usually work till 7:00 or 8:00 p.m. **The closing shift** graces us with their presence at about the same time the mid-shifters are leaving. Things get cleaned and stocked when the store closes between 1:00 and 3:00 a.m. On any of these shifts, if someone shows up late, or not at all, the entire system is thrown off, and there is utter chaos. Whatever job position the missing person was supposed to have must be covered by another. Doing the work of two or three people is obscenely difficult!

Some say it is an easy job. That depends on your definition of *easy*. The endless repetition of easy jobs is awful. My duties consist of drive-through cash, expediting (the handing out of food), counter cash, kitchen worker, or "whipping boy," which is doing all the nasty jobs no one else will. Whipping boy duties include cleaning under the grease vats where congealed

The student begins with a captivating story.

THESIS STATEMENT

TOPIC SENTENCE
The student begins by stating a common view of fast-food work.

ORDER AND TRANSITIONS
She uses time to organize the details of this paragraph, going through the daily schedule and explaining what work gets done on each shift.

TOPIC SENTENCE

Her descriptive detail here, even though positive in tone, reinforces the impression that fast-food work is demanding.

TOPIC SENTENCE
She identifies yet another misperception about fast-food work.

SUPPORTING DETAILS
These description details show the other point of view: that fast-food work is not clean, that in fact it can be very dirty work.

In her conclusion, the student restates the thesis of the essay: that fast-food workers do not have an easy job. She also provides an example that contrasts with the one in the introduction.

grease collects, scrubbing the freezer and "walk-in" fridge, putting away truck shipments, and doing other odd jobs. I started out on cash, and I trained myself on other jobs, so I would not be stuck doing the same thing every day. I love working in the kitchen the best. There is nothing like jumping around a kitchen, making at least five different sandwiches at once, and still getting the food out on time. The adrenaline starts rushing, and I feel like I can do anything. It really is a wonderful feeling.

People think fast-food work is relatively clean. Think again. The big problem at Burger King is grease. There is a pan in the top part of the broiler that holds the grease that evaporates off the burgers and turns back into liquid. This pan must be emptied every other day. I have yet to see anyone get it out without spilling it all over himself or herself. I find it quite entertaining to watch, but only because I have never had to do it. The grease vats are a real treat. They each hold a 23 kilogram block of solid shortening that reaches temperatures of 71 degrees Celsius when heated. With every basket of fries, chicken, fish, or "o-rings," the vat gets dirtier. The vats are drained through a tube every few days, and new shortening is put in. Grease spills, leaks, and takes a solid form after a few hours. It looks like a mixture of mashed potatoes and butterscotch pudding. To clean the vats, I use paper towels, degreaser, and a Brillo pad. It takes about one to two hours to do, and I look like I have not showered in weeks when I am done.

Not all customers think we have it made. Some show a little appreciation, which makes the job tolerable. There is an elderly man who comes in singing every morning. He says, "G'morning, beautiful!" every time. I look forward to his visit. The next time you visit your local fast-food joint, a smile and hello would make us grill jockeys feel appreciated.

DISCUSSION QUESTIONS

1. In arguments, writers take issue with viewpoints that are different from theirs. What views does the writer take issue with in this essay?

2. What pattern of organization does the writer use in the body of the paper?

3. Does the writer concede any points in her essay?

4. The essay provides a vivid picture of work in fast food. What detail did you find surprising or effective?

EXERCISE 14-9 **Outlining and Writing an Argument Essay**

Directions: *Choose one of the following assignments for an argument essay. Use the form of prewriting you like best to explore two possible topics related to the assignment. Next, narrow down one of the topics and develop a thesis and subtopics. When you complete your prewriting, use an outline form like the one provided in Chapter 13 to formulate your thesis and topic sentences. Plan and then write your argument essay.*

1. Write an argument essay using the previous essay as your guide. Focus on common misperceptions of a group of people, presenting evidence to show why these views are inaccurate.

FOCUSED ASSIGNMENTS

1. Parents often counsel their children not to take time off between high school and further studies. State your position on this issue. Then discuss the pros and cons of waiting a year or more before starting post-secondary studies right after high school.

2. Is it important to have a Canadian perspective on domestic and international news? Who should control and fund the media: government or privately run businesses? What is your view on this issue? Discuss reasons for or against providing Canadians with their own sources of news and events.

3. Canadians are very aware of American music bands and Hollywood movies. Do we need Canadian-made entertainment to preserve Canadian culture? How much Canadian content should the media provide? In your opinion, what is the best course of action to decide what content is broadcast through Canadian radios, televisions, and digital media?

GENERAL ASSIGNMENTS

1. Present an argument for (or against) restricting international shipping through Canada's northern waters.

2. Argue for (or against) whether employers have the right to ask a worker to allow them to access personal postings on social networking sites like Facebook or Twitter.

3. Present an argument for (or against) requiring all citizens to vote in municipal, provincial, and federal elections.

4. Argue for (or against) providing required classes in personal finances and money management in high school.

ESSAYS WITH MULTIPLE PATTERNS OF ORGANIZATION

Like paragraphs, essays often have a singular purpose: to explain a process, to classify information, or to compare and contrast ideas. Unlike paragraphs, however, which generally use one pattern of organization, such as description or argument, essays may require more than one pattern of organization. In an essay you write for a psychology class, for example, you might both define and illustrate the defense mechanisms you learned about. In a lab report, you might explain the process involved in an experiment, then consider a cause and effect analysis of the results. Usually, each paragraph will have a single, dominant, or identifiable pattern of organization. As an essay writer, you select the pattern of organization to best suit your purpose and to best present your supporting points.

In the workplace, a writer might also need to use multiple patterns of organization. Writing up a report on a domestic abuse call, a police officer uses narration to tell exactly what happened at the scene, but the narration will also include important description details such as the bruises on the victim's face and neck.

At a Glance

THE MIXED-PATTERN ESSAY AT A GLANCE

ASSIGNMENT Write an essay about the experience of growing older in today's society.

The essay's title tells the reader what the essay is about.

The writer uses a short personal narration to draw the reader in and make the essay interesting.

THESIS STATEMENT
The sentence clearly identifies the thesis.

TOPIC SENTENCE
The writer defines advertising as the focus in the first paragraph.

TRANSISTIONS
The writer transitions between one example and the next.

TOPIC SENTENCE
The writer's topic sentence indicates this will be a paragraph of classification.

TRANSITION
The writer moves from one type to the next.

Youth Rules the World

Our society is obsessed with youth, and I am no exception. I recently started wearing makeup for the first time in my 32 years. I never thought I needed it until I saw the old lady in my mirror. *Who is that?* I thought. I am far too young to have permanent lines between my eyebrows. Although I am not self-conscious enough for surgical correction, I did immediately go makeup shopping. Age matters in advertising and in the workplace, sometimes leading people to desperate measures to look young. This is something Natalie Angier addresses in her essay "The Cute Factor." According to Angier, humans are drawn to anything representing youth. Simply put, youth rules our world (1).

Advertising is saturated with images of youth. Look at the billboards on your way home from work or school. You will not see many older people up there trying to get you to go to a certain casino. Television commercials are **also** full of young people. **For example**, there is a new Band-Aid commercial. It features two children who are the very definition of the word *cute.* Even the little girl's voice is cute. They sing the Band-Aid jingle, and I want to go buy some even though I already have bandages in my medicine cabinet. Advertisers understand our obsession with youth, and they use it to draw us in.

Measures to keep us young come in two types. Women use creams and makeup to keep themselves looking young. Men and women colour their hair when it starts to show signs of gray. Women even wear push-up bras as a way to deny what time and gravity have done. **These are superficial and harmless measures enabling people to hold onto their youth. There are more extreme measures.** Men get hair implants when their hairline starts to recede. Plastic surgery slows the aging process. A facelift smoothes the skin of a woman's face and neck to recapture youth. Eyelid procedures counteract the sagging that comes with age. Doctors can get rid of age spots and spider veins, as well as lift breasts and buttocks when gravity starts to take its toll. This type of age-defying plastic surgery is a multi-million-dollar industry.

The writer cites and discusses two different approaches to looking young.

When competing in the workplace, age is a definite factor. For customer service jobs, the employer's preference is young beautiful people. Sales are better and business is increased when there are young, attractive people at the counter. I used to work at a chain pet store. The managers there made it clear that they only wanted pretty young girls at the checkout. They thought it made a bad impression to have older or average-looking people working at the registers. It is not that they refused to hire older people. They simply would not put them on the registers. It is not an uncommon practice.

EXAMPLES
The writer cites different examples to support the main idea of the paragraph.

TOPIC SENTENCE

The writer uses an extended example to illustrate the importance of looking youthful in the workplace.

Youth sells. Since we all crave youth, we all respond better to young people or at least to the appearance of youth. We see it in advertising, in customer service, and in all the products and services sold to keep us young. Angier touches on the causes in her essay. She believes that we are biologically programmed to respond to youth, babies, mainly, but this response has expanded to include youth in general. We cannot help ourselves. We love youth. We want to stay young.

The writer restates the important points of the essay and touches on the reading mentioned in the introduction.

Works Cited

Angier, Natalie. "The Cute Factor." *New York Times* 3 Jan. 2006: F1. Print.

DISCUSSION QUESTIONS

1. Does it matter that the thesis of this essay is not the last sentence of the introduction?

2. What patterns of organization does this writer use?

3. The writer mentions two types of measures people use to stay young. Can you think of a third?

4. Which supporting detail in the essay do you find the most effective? Why?

5. What specific details in the conclusion tell you the writer is finishing her essay?

EXERCISE 14-10 **Writing a Mixed-Pattern Essay**

Directions: *Choose one of the following assignments for a mixed-pattern essay. Use Exercise 14-11 to help you determine your approach.*

IMITATION ASSIGNMENT

1. Write an argument essay using the previous essay as your guide. Focus on views of some older people and the aging process. Provide evidence to show why these views are accurate and/or inaccurate.

FOCUSED ASSIGNMENTS

1. Pick a misconception that is common in our society. Describe the misconception as people commonly think of it, focusing on its causes or effects.

2. In a culture of consumption, such as our own, advertisers encourage us to buy the latest product. Most Canadians buy more than they really need. Discuss a few examples of things consumers buy but do not really need.

3. We often celebrate our triumphs and our skills, dwelling on the positive. Write an essay about something you are not very good at but wish you were, referring to a specific time you realized your lack of this skill. Consider what difference it makes in your life that you are not good at it.

4. Complex skills call for smart learning processes. Discuss a complex skill you have, such as playing a musical instrument or speaking a foreign language. Describe the most effective process for acquiring such a skill.

5. Not everyone agrees on the proper way to study. Discuss two different approaches and what their merits are.

GENERAL ASSIGNMENTS

1. Discuss the pros and cons of borrowing money for post-secondary studies.

2. Describe the importance of self-discipline.

3. Describe a prejudice that is overlooked in our society.

EXERCISE 14-11 Determining Your Approach

Directions: *Before you prewrite on your topic, respond to the questions below that will help you discover various approaches to thinking and writing about your topic. This will help you decide if you will use a single pattern or a mixed pattern of writing.*

1. What people, places, things, or ideas can you describe that are important to your topic? Why? What is your dominant impression?

_____

2. What important idea can you illustrate and explain with examples? Why is it important?

_____

3. Can you tell a story that relates to your topic in an important way?

_____

4. Is there a process that is relevant to this topic? What is it? Why is it important?

_____

5. Does classification thinking help you make a point about your topic? How so? What categories or types come to mind? Why are they important?

_____

6. Is it useful to think about causes in connection to your topic? What about effects? What will this kind of thinking enable you to explain?

_____

7. Can you use comparison and contrast to explore your topic? Are similarities and differences important in your topic? With respect to what points in particular would one of the comparison/contrast patterns be effective?

8. What issue or idea is important in this topic? Can you define the idea or issue for your reader?

9. Suppose you decide to change your reader's mind about your topic. What reasons would you need to explain to prove your point or points?

The Essay Checklist

Once you have revised and edited your essay, use this Essay Checklist to determine if your essay is ready for an academic reader.

ESSAY CHECKLIST

_____ The essay has an introduction, body, and conclusion.

_____ The introduction invites the reader into the essay.

_____ The thesis is focused, effective, develops three ideas, and uses parallel structure.

_____ Each body paragraph has focused topic sentences that point back to the thesis. The paragraphs have unity; they each develop only one topic.

_____ The sentences within each paragraph and the body paragraphs are arranged logically and coherently.

_____ The paragraphs have specific supporting details and follow one of the writing patterns.

_____ Facts and statistics, cases and examples, and quotations from research support the topic sentences. Any information borrowed or quoted from another source is properly cited and referenced.

_____ Key words from the assignment are repeated; transition words are used appropriately throughout the essay.

_____ Through critical reading and revision, relevant material has been added, deleted, or reorganized.

_____ The conclusion brings the essay to a close by restating the thesis, giving a reason or purpose for the essay or explaining how the readers can use what they have learned in the essay.

_____ The conclusion does not introduce new ideas that were not already discussed in the body of the essay.

_____ A list of Works Cited or References, following MLA or APA guidelines, is included.

_____ The essay has an appropriate and interesting title.

_____ The essay has been proofread for spelling, capitalization, common errors, and sentence variety.

CHAPTER REVIEW

Take a moment and reflect on what you have learned about the types of essays.

■ ELEMENTS OF THE ESSAY

- *Thesis statement in introduction; body paragraphs to support thesis; conclusion that mirrors thesis; multiple-paragraph assignment; structure, content important; academic setting: objective writing*

■ THE WRITING PROCESS

■ ESSAYS WITH ONE PATTERN OF ORGANIZATION

☐ Description

☐ Example

☐ Narration

☐ Process

☐ Classification

☐ Cause and Effect

☐ Comparison/Contrast

☐ Definition

☐ Argument

■ ESSAYS WITH MULTIPLE PATTERNS OF ORGANIZATION

15

Paraphrase, Summary, and Quotation

CHAPTER OVERVIEW

- [ ] Use Sources Correctly
- [ ] Paraphrase
- [ ] Plagiarism
- [ ] Summary
- [ ] Quotation
- [ ] Suggestions for Daily Practice

THINK FIRST

Think about the last documentary or newscast you saw. Write a paragraph summarizing what it was about. Who was in it? Where did it take place? What was happening? Why was it important?

In Other Words: The Art of Paraphrasing

At some jobs, you will be given instructions that you may not entirely understand. Asking a question by paraphrasing or summarizing what your supervisor has just said is sometimes helpful. For example, instead of asking for a re-explanation, say, "So I need to make two photocopies: one for the office, and one for the client. Correct?" By paraphrasing instructions, you can quickly pinpoint whether you have correctly understood your task.

BRAINSTORM

In a conversation, the ability to paraphrase what others tell you—or to repeat something in your own words—depends on your ability to listen well. Brainstorm about a few situations where you need to listen carefully. What are they? With whom do you interact? What are the consequences of listening well or poorly? In writing, you can paraphrase by taking information you have read, putting it into your own words, and weaving it into your sentences.

Summary: A Key to Understanding

Summarizing is a valuable skill in and out of the classroom. The plot summary of a movie, say, or the summary of an interesting magazine article you read could come in handy in a casual conversation. If you encounter something you know you will want to explain later, in writing or in person, you can enhance your memory by consciously identifying and reviewing main ideas, key details, and impressions. This works for anything from a news item to a long, involved novel.

DISCUSSION

Talk to a classmate about a movie you saw recently. Who were the main characters? What happened? Where did the action take place? What was the point of the movie?

Avoid Plagiarism: Document, Attribute, and Reference!

The process of finding and correctly documenting and attributing quotations and other information is necessary to avoid plagiarism. Plagiarism, which has serious ethical and legal repercussions, means you present someone else's work as your original writing. Using someone else's exact language without giving that person credit is considered plagiarism, but so is paraphrasing—putting their thoughts in your own words—if it is not properly attributed. When you document your sources with citations within your sentences and put together a "Works Cited" or "References" page, you give credit to the original author(s) and inform your reader that specific material in your paper belongs to outside sources.

BRAINSTORM

Make a list of instances when you did not get proper credit for something you said or did. Then focus on one. List all the people and places connected to the event. What circumstances or conditions were involved? What other people were involved? What happened? What were the consequences?

Use Sources Correctly

How do I write about what I've read without just repeating what the author says? As a college or university student, you will often be asked to write about what you read in order to demonstrate comprehension, recall, and critical thinking. You form connections between what you already know and new information; in the process, you acquire new knowledge.

Two basic forms of writing about what you have read are paraphrase and summary. Paraphrasing means capturing a writer's ideas in different words. You paraphrase to write a summary or to include ideas as supporting points in your own writing, but you must reference where you found the ideas. Using references to other writers' work makes the points in your writing more convincing. There are two steps to paraphrasing. First, you correctly put another's ideas into your own words. Second, you properly cite and reference the source of your paraphrase. There are several different ways, or styles, to cite and reference the sources of your information; each style includes the same information but formats it differently. This text will give examples of MLA and APA styles.

A summary is a shortened version of a reading that includes only the main points that you have restated in a different way from the original. It is an objective and accurate paraphrase and does not include your opinion. A summary excludes details, but reports the key ideas in a balanced way. In a summary, you state what you have read using your own words, capturing the most important points and providing the reader with an overview of the passage, article, or chapter. Again, you must cite your sources. You will find more information about writing summaries later in this chapter.

Occasionally, you might want to include a partial or complete quotation that captures a writer's idea or point of view in your essay. Just as you must do when you paraphrase, when you quote an author, you must also cite your sources in order to avoid plagiarism (discussed later in this chapter).

Paraphrase

College and university work involves reading a variety of materials—such as textbooks, news stories, and professional journal articles—when you do research. You can use highlighting to identify important ideas and details in your readings. Taking notes and outlining as you read can help you capture key content and the relationship of ideas and details.

Paraphrase goes a step further. When you paraphrase, you condense and restate an author's ideas using your own words. Paraphrasing what you have just read is a good study technique as it helps you to fully understand the ideas in the material, and you can remember them more easily. Therefore, learning how to accurately paraphrase will help you in all areas of your academic studies.

Paraphrasing is also used to summarize, which is a difficult skill to master. For this reason, it deserves continuous practice. Try the following guidelines to learn how to paraphrase accurately. It's important to record information about your source along with your notes and outlining as you need to document where you found your ideas. As mentioned, you must include the source information for your paraphrase and your quotes. Chapter 16 provides more information about proper formatting for APA and MLA citation styles.

Guidelines for Paraphrasing Accurately

1. Read the original passage. Circle or underline the main ideas and key supporting details.

2. Write a sentence that sums up the passage's main idea.

3. Set aside the text and, using the sentence you just wrote, restate what the author said in your own words. You want to keep the author's intent but write it differently. Use synonyms (words that are similar in meaning) to replace the key words that you circled or underlined. Break long sentences into shorter ones, and reword sentences so that you are expressing the author's ideas in a different way.

4. Include the author's name and/or the title of the source at the beginning of your paraphrase.

5. Read your paraphrase and compare it to the original.

6. Underline any of the author's words that you have used. Avoid using more than three consecutive words from the original sentence.

7. Revise your paraphrase to eliminate the author's exact words. Replacing the author's original words with your own paraphrase is usually better than quoting the original words. If you cannot avoid repeating the original work, then put quotation marks around the author's words, followed by source information. For both paraphrasing and quoting, you provide enough information within your essay so that your reader can find that source in the complete list of sources at the end of your essay. Please refer to Chapter 16 for examples of citation and referencing.

When you paraphrase, a short sentence is almost always better than a long one. Also, a good summary reports what an author says; it does not express your own opinions on those ideas. In other words, both paraphrasing and summary writing are objective writing. Recall the difference between objective and subjective writing by reviewing The Essay at a Glance in Chapter 14.

If you use the author's exact words without quotation marks, or the author's paraphrased ideas without proper citations, you are committing plagiarism, a serious act of academic dishonesty (see the section on plagiarism). To avoid charges of plagiarism, be sure to cite your sources in the text of your essay and also at the end in a References list or Works Cited list for both quotations and paraphrases.

Here are some additional strategies to help you paraphrase; you will need to use more than one strategy to effectively paraphrase a sentence.

1. Replace some key words in the sentence with synonyms or synonymous phrases.

2. Select a key word and change the word form, for example, change a noun to verb.

3. After changing a word form, you may have to change the order of words in the sentence.

4. Change a long sentence into two shorter ones.

5. Consider using opposite or negative forms, or antonyms, if appropriate.

6. Change from passive to active tense or vice versa.

The following original sentences come from Richard Sennett's *The Corrosion of Character*. For the purpose of focusing on learning and practising paraphrasing, no page numbers are given in these examples, but for paraphrasing in your own research and writing, you must supply source information to avoid plagiarism.

ORIGINAL

The bakery was filled with noise; the smell of yeast mingled with human sweat in the hot rooms; the bakers' hands were constantly plunged into flour and water.

PARAPHRASE

This paraphrase is short and to the point. The writer captures the main idea of Sennett's description.

> Sennett reports that it was noisy, hot, and smelly in the bakery, and the work was constant.

ORIGINAL

The bakers needed to cooperate intimately in order to coordinate the varied tasks of the bakery.

PARAPHRASE

In her phrase "working together," the writer captures Sennett's idea.

> Working together was important.

ORIGINAL

The bakery no longer smells of sweat and is startlingly cool, whereas workers used to throw up from the heat. Under the soothing fluorescent lights, all is now strangely silent.

PARAPHRASE

The writer's sentence both sums up Sennett's description and eliminates detail. Note that the writer is objectively paraphrasing Sennett's original and she does not include her own opinions.

> The bakery is now a cool, quiet place to work.

In these paraphrases, the student captures the essence of Sennett's ideas. She restates the ideas in her own words and eliminates the very specific details. Notice, too, that the student merely reports on what Sennett wrote. She does not express an opinion or make a judgment about it since paraphrasing is objective writing.

EXERCISE 15-1 **Recognizing Effective Paraphrase**

Directions: *Following are some sentences from Mary Sherry's essay "In Praise of the F Word." (You can read the full essay in Chapter 27.) For each sentence, select the paraphrase that most effectively states the main idea of the original sentence. To focus on learning and practising paraphrasing, no page numbers are given, but for paraphrasing in your research and writing, you will have to supply source information to avoid plagiarism.*

_____ 1. Tens of thousands of eighteen-year-olds will graduate this year and be handed meaningless diplomas.

    a. Lots of high school students graduate without full degrees.

    b. Many high school graduates will receive meaningless diplomas this year.

    c. Tens of thousands of high school graduates will be handed meaningless diplomas this year.

_____ 2. These diplomas won't look any different from those awarded their luckier classmates.

    a. Their diplomas will look like everyone else's diplomas.

    b. These kids ought to be really angry.

    c. These diplomas aren't worth the paper they are printed on.

_____ 3. Their validity will be questioned only when their employers discover that these graduates are semiliterate.

    a. These kids won't know how to do anything on the job.

    b. The meaning of their diplomas won't be questioned until they go to work.

    c. These students won't know their diplomas are worthless until they get a job.

_____ 4. Eventually a fortunate few will find their way into educational-repair shops—adult-literacy programs, such as the one where I teach basic grammar and writing.

    a. Educational-repair shops, such as adult-literacy programs, will eventually save a fortunate few.

    b. Some of these graduates will eventually go back to school.

    c. Naturally these unfortunate individuals will lose their jobs and go back for more education.

_____ 5. There, high school graduates and high school dropouts pursuing graduate equivalency certificates will learn the skills they should have learned in school.

    a. They will have to hit the books again, in hopes of eventually making some big bucks.

    b. They will pick up basic skills in these programs.

    c. Here, high school graduates and high school dropouts pursuing graduate equivalency certificates will make up for lost time.

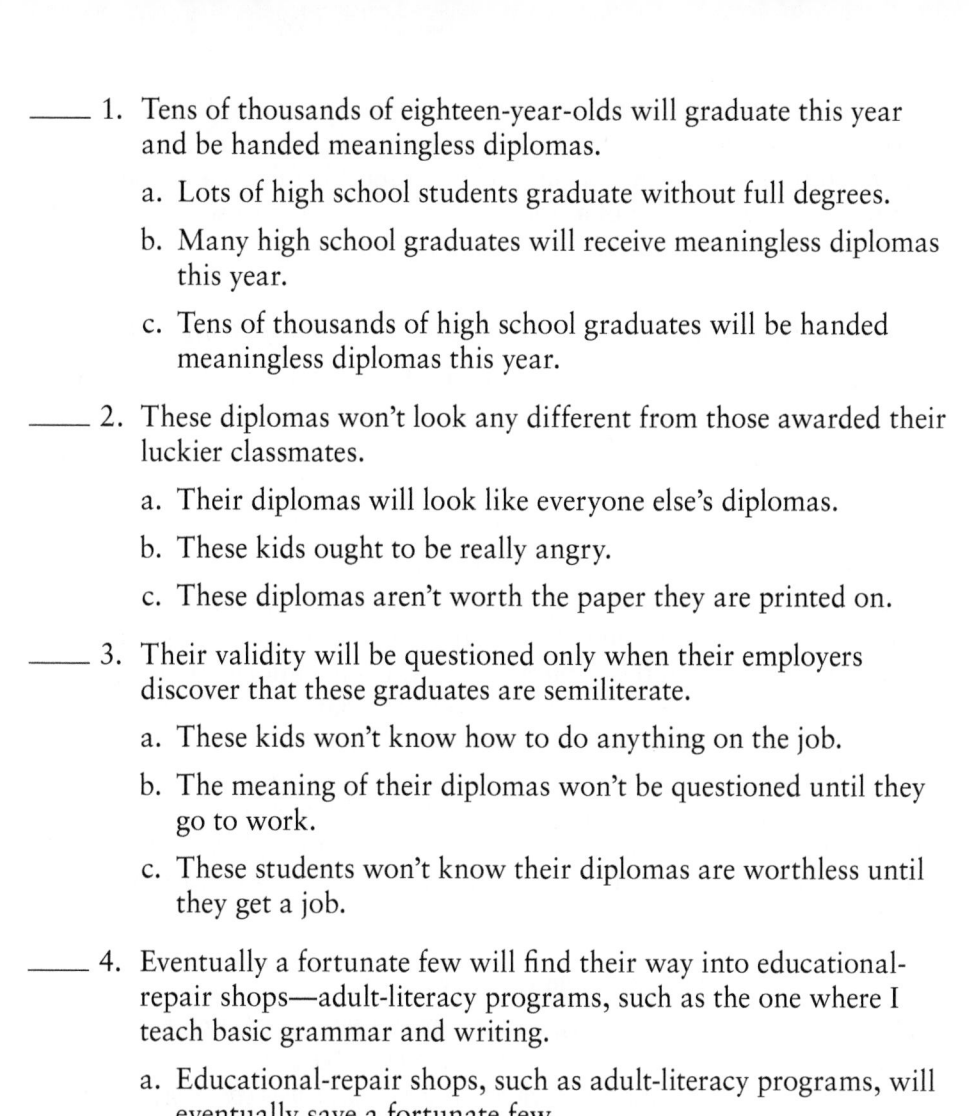

Talk about it

Name two things a writer can do to improve the accuracy and quality of a paraphrase.

ACKNOWLEDGE SOURCES

Because paraphrase involves writing about something you have read that was written by others, you must acknowledge your sources. In a phrase or sentence before the paraphrase, you should mention the author's name, the organization the author is associated with, or the name of the publication from which the information is taken. Use a parenthetical citation with the author's name if you do not cite the writer's name in your text. To make your writing more coherent, you must also weave this information into one of your sentences by using reporting verbs, such as *advises, mentions, explains, recommends*. "According to" is the most common and useful way to set up an in-text citation of a source. Notice the writer's use of a reporting verb from this example: "Richard Sennett points out that . . ."

> In his description of bakery work in his book *Corrosion of Character,* Richard Sennett points out that at one time it was noisy, hot, and smelly in the bakery, and the work was constant. Working together was important. Twenty-five years later, the bakery is a cool, quiet place to work.

You should acknowledge your source as soon as you begin to paraphrase, and use the author's full name in your first reference. After the first reference, use the author's last name only. If you do not know the author's name, mention instead the name of the publication in which the information appeared.

In addition to protecting yourself from the charge of plagiarism, citing an author's name (and the publication in which the piece appeared) indicates that you have done some research, enhancing your credibility.

Once more, no page numbers are given in the next examples, but for paraphrasing in your research and writing, you must supply source information, including page numbers, to avoid plagiarism. For more information on documentation and citation styles, refer to Chapter 16.

EXERCISE 15-2 Paraphrasing Practice

Directions: *Paraphrase the ideas in each of the following original sentences. Begin your paraphrase by acknowledging the source, which is provided. Your paraphrase sentences should be short, simple, and to the point. Avoid using more than three consecutive words from the original sentence.*

EXAMPLE

We may have come a long way baby, but the latest Voices of Women opinion poll suggests we still have a long way to go. (United Press International)

Paraphrase: A story published in United Press International suggests women have made a lot of progress, but more work lies ahead.

1. The survey found men are beginning to share the same attitudes toward work as women—with like percentages seeking flexible work hours and the ability to work from home. (United Press International)

Paraphrase: _____

_____

2. Health Canada's drug abuse prevention program, the Drug Strategy Community Initiatives Fund, announced on Thursday that they were changing their approach, admitting that the vastly expensive program appears to be ineffective. (Leona Aglukkaq, Minister of Health)

Paraphrase: _____

_____

3. A report on the Government of Canada's National Anti-Drug Strategy was issued this week, about the progress in reducing illicit drug use among youth through health promotion and prevention projects. (Sharon Blanchard, a consultant for the Drug Strategy Community Initiatives Fund)

Paraphrase: _____

_____

4. Checking players' weight after practice and the following day to monitor excessive weight loss, and taking mandatory rest breaks in the shade and water breaks during practice and at needed intervals, are essential to help prevent heatstroke. (Carl Stevens, sportswriter for the *Edmonton Sun*)

Paraphrase: _____

_____

5. Few, if any, countries have adapted notions like automation and virtual reality so widely or embraced them so fully as Japan, where animated films, for example, are consistently the biggest hits. (Howard W. French)

Paraphrase: _____

_____

Plagiarism

Borrowing another person's writing without acknowledging the source is called **plagiarism**. In some classes, you will use ideas, facts, and details from your readings—for example, when you write a research paper. You will acquire information from books, journals, magazines, newspapers, and the Internet. Some students succumb to the temptation of copying and pasting other people's writing into their papers as if it were their own. To do so is dishonest. It is plagiarism. Plagiarism occurs whenever you

- use another writer's ideas without giving that person credit, even if you do not use the other writer's exact words.
- paraphrase and/or summarize another person's words without acknowledging your source.
- cite facts or statistics without stating your source.
- use a quotation by an authority without saying who it is.
- fail to use quotation marks around someone else's original words, even if the original author has been identified.

Copying another person's words in your writing may result in your receiving a failing grade for the assignment or possibly even the course. Plagiarism can be avoided by careful use of paraphrase, by use of quotation marks

WRITING TIP

Written texts are considered the "intellectual property" of the authors so you cannot use their ideas without acknowledging that you are referring to their works. Therefore, if you do use others' ideas to support points in your essays, be sure to properly cite and reference the sources; your writing will be considered more academic and you won't be plagiarizing.

if you do borrow someone's writing word-for-word, and by acknowledging your source. There are several different ways of acknowledging your sources, but they all contain information about the source, including the author(s)' names, title, year of publication, publisher, and so on. Your source documents can be almost anything, including chapters from books, print articles from journals or a library database, and information from the Internet and other media.

The source information is organized in certain styles and there are guides available to show you how to format your information according to a particular style. Two common styles are MLA (Modern Languages Association), which is used in liberal arts and the humanities, and APA (American Psychological Association), which is used in the social sciences. Check to find out which style your instructor wants you to use in your assignments.

COPY AND PASTE

The most flagrant instance of plagiarism is simply copying and pasting another person's writing into your assignment. Here is an example of this type of plagiarism. The original text is from a Web site published by the National Stepfamily Resource Center, which published an article called "Democratic Discipline for Stepteens," by Sharon Hanna.

ORIGINAL

Authoritarian style, the preference of yesteryear, puts the parent/stepparent in total power as the "boss." As such, he or she is dictatorial, strict, and inflexible. The parent or stepparent/child relationship is characterized by fear, distance, coldness, and rigidity.

PLAGIARISM

This student copies word for word from what he read. Doing so says to the reader, "I wrote this." For stealing another person's words like this, the student could be failed for the assignment.

The dominant parent's word is the law and puts the parent/stepparent in total power as the "boss." As such, he or she is dictatorial, strict, and inflexible. The parent/child relationship is characterized by fear, distance, coldness, and rigidity. In my experience, this type of relationship began early and lasted a long time. It resulted in depressed and rebellious children with low self-esteem.

This student has copied several sentences from the original text into his paragraph without using quotation marks and without acknowledging his source. To avoid plagiarism, the student should acknowledge his source, then either paraphrase the passage or present it as a quotation. You should practise all four techniques, shown below, in order to use information effectively and avoid plagiarism.

1. Include the Source in the Paraphrase, with an In-Text Citation

This example uses MLA style. APA citation would look like this: According to Sharon Hanna (1990) . . .

The dominant stepparent's word is the law. According to Sharon Hanna, writing for the National Stepfamily Resource Center, this stepparent wants total control. There is little warmth or closeness in the relationship. It is about giving orders and obedience. In my experience, this type of relationship began early and lasted a long time. It resulted in depressed and rebellious children with low self-esteem.

2. Include the Source in the Paraphrase as a Parenthetical Citation

The dominant stepparent's word is the law. This stepparent wants total control. There is little warmth or closeness in the relationship. It is about giving orders and obedience (Hanna). In my experience, this type of relationship began early and lasted a long time. It resulted in depressed and rebellious children with low self-esteem.

This example uses MLA style citation. APA would look like this: (Hanna, 1990).

3. Include the Source as a Quotation, with an In-Text Citation

The dominant parent's word is the law. This "authoritarian style," according to Sharon Hanna, writing for the National Stepfamily Resource Center, "puts the parent/stepparent in total power as the 'boss.' As such, he or she is dictatorial, strict, and inflexible. The parent or stepparent/child relationship is characterized by fear, distance, coldness, and rigidity." In my experience, this type of relationship began early and lasted a long time. It resulted in depressed and rebellious children with low self-esteem.

This example uses MLA style. In APA style, you would format like this: . . . according to Sharon Hanna (1990), writing for the National Stepfamily Resource Center . . .

4. Include the Source as a Quotation, with a Parenthetical Citation

The dominant parent's word is the law since "[t]his authoritarian style, the preference of yesteryear, puts the parent/stepparent in total power as the 'boss.' As such, he or she is dictatorial, strict, and inflexible. The parent or stepparent/child relationship is characterized by fear, distance, coldness, and rigidity" (Hanna). In my experience, this type of relationship began early and lasted a long time. It resulted in depressed and rebellious children with low self-esteem.

This example uses MLA style. In APA style, the parenthetical citation would be (Hanna, 1990). Notice that the quotation is "framed" within the writer's own sentence and is not just pasted into the paragraph to stand alone.

CLOSE PARAPHRASE

In **close paraphrase** the writer changes a few words here and there, possibly rearranging the order of the original, without acknowledging his or her source. Here is an example of close paraphrase. The original text is from an article written by Abraham Thiombiano for the *Dixie Sun Online Edition*, a publication of Dixie State College of Utah.

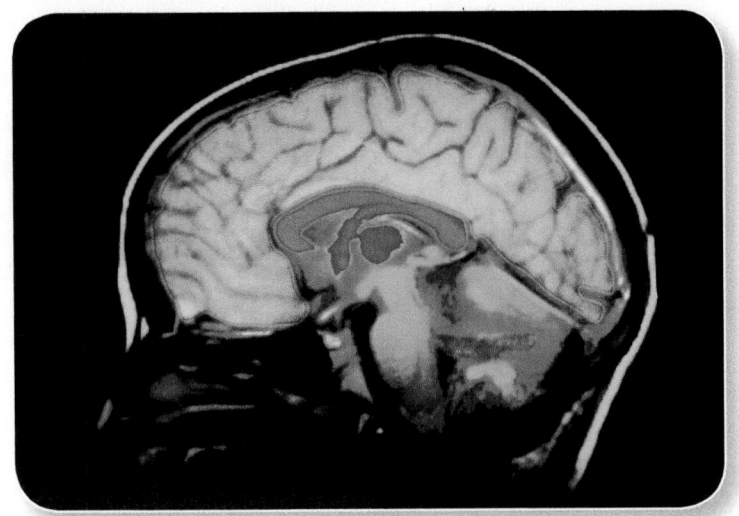

ORIGINAL

Scientists have come to accept that a few fundamental differences between men and women are biological. It turns out that men's and women's brains, for example, are not only different, but the way we use them differs too. Women have larger connections and more frequent interaction between their brains' left and right hemispheres. This accounts for women's ability to have better verbal skills and intuition. Men, on the other hand, have greater brain hemisphere separation, which explains their skills for abstract reasoning and visual-spatial intelligence.

PLAGIARISM

In this student's close paraphrase, he makes small changes in phrasing and vocabulary, while retaining the exact order of the sentences in the passage.

This use of source material would also be considered plagiarism and might result in failure of the assignment or the course.

Men and women do communicate in different ways. I can tell this from what I have experienced in life so far, and also from the research I have done. Scientists now believe that the basic differences between men and women are a result of biology. They have concluded that men's and women's brains are not only different, but we use them differently too. In women's brains, the left and right hemispheres interact more due to larger connections. This fact explains why women have better verbal skills and intuition. In men's brains, the hemispheres are separated more, a fact that accounts for better ability to reason abstractly and use their visual-spatial intelligence.

This student's close paraphrase is considered to be plagiarism. He does not acknowledge his source. Moreover, he makes only minimal changes to the original text. To avoid plagiarism, this student should paraphrase more carefully or paraphrase and quote some of the original text. He should also acknowledge the source either with an in-text or parenthetical citation as shown below.

PARAPHRASE WITH IN-TEXT CITATION

This in-text citation is in MLA style. APA style would look like this: According to Abraham Thiombiano (2006), writing for the *Dixie Sun* . . .

Men and women do communicate in different ways. I can tell this from what I have experienced in life so far. Recent brain research also explains why. According to Abraham Thiombiano, writing for the *Dixie Sun,* the brains of women and men are slightly different, particularly with respect to connections between hemispheres. These differences explain difference in form of intelligence: women are more given to intuitive thought, men to abstract reasoning.

Men and women do communicate in different ways. I can tell this from
what I have experienced in life so far. Recent brain research also explains:
"Women have larger connections and more frequent interaction between
their brain's left and right hemispheres. This accounts for women's ability to have better verbal skills and intuition. Men, on the other hand,
have greater brain hemisphere separation, which explains their skills for
abstract reasoning and visual-spatial intelligence" (Thiombiano).

Here MLA style is used. APA
style would be (Thiombiano,
2006).

Summary

As mentioned earlier in the chapter, a **summary** is a snapshot of what you
have read. You summarize to capture the key details of a story, the main ideas
of an article, or the important ideas from a textbook reading assignment.

The same basic rules apply in both paraphrase and summary: acknowledge your source, use your own words, and keep it short. Generally, a summary is significantly shorter than the material it summarizes. Here are some
guidelines for writing an accurate summary.

Guidelines for Summarizing Accurately

1. Read the original text. Look for the main ideas and key supporting details.
2. Write a sentence that sums up the main point, or thesis, of the author's
   writing.
3. Use your own words to state the main points the author makes and
   include them in the same order in which the author presents them. Use
   the paraphrasing tips from earlier in the chapter to put the author's
   ideas into different words.
4. Include information about any important concepts, definitions,
   procedures, or rules the author discusses. Again, use your own words.
5. Include the author's name and the title of the source in your first sentence.
6. Read your summary and compare it to the original.
7. Underline any of the author's words you have used. Avoid using more
   than three consecutive words from the original sentence in your
   paraphrase, and revise your summary to eliminate them. Alternatively,
   to indicate you are using the author's exact words, use quotation marks
   followed by in-text citation to show where the quotation comes from.
8. Include the author's opinion, if it is clearly stated. Avoid stating your
   own opinion or making a judgment of the author in your summary.
   A summary should be written objectively.

Ask Yourself

Which courses require you to
summarize the original text? What
kinds of papers or assignments
require you to summarize?

Summary is an important skill if you are doing research on a subject. For
example, if you are writing about the impact of moulds on people with allergies, you might (1) read about people with allergies in a newspaper or magazine; (2) read about competing medical treatments in magazines or journals
written for doctors and nurses; and (3) read about the science of mould and its
relationship to the environment in your science textbook. In all three instances,

summary would be an essential skill for capturing what you read and preparing it for use in your writing. Whether you are reading a newspaper, magazine journal, or a textbook, the same reading and writing skills apply.

CAPTURE THE MAIN IDEA OF A STORY

Stories are central to many areas of academic education. In an investigation of Canadian medical discoveries, a student might encounter the story of Dr. Frederick Banting's discovery of insulin as a treatment for diabetes. In an investigation of the history of the Red River Settlement region, a student might encounter stories that explain the course of events during the Riel Rebellions. To summarize these stories, you identify the main idea and important details: what happened; where, when, and why it happened; and who was involved. You avoid providing minute detail. Instead, you give an overview.

Here is an op-ed article about immigrants looking for work in a new country in their trained professions. As suggested above, the main points and proper names have been underlined, and annotations that will serve as the basis of the summary have been made in the margin. A model summary follows.

from "Treating Canada's Case of 'Taxi, M.D.'" by ALI OKHOWAT

WHO
John Zhang and other foreign-trained immigrants to Canada

WHAT
He couldn't find a job. It wasn't what he expected.

"Chief of General Surgery at the largest hospital," he said. "From appendicitis to gallstones, I treated them all." He turned to me with furrowed brow: "Here's my card. Please, let me know if you find out anything else about how I can get in here." John Zhang—not his real name—had immigrated to Canada six years ago from China and was still navigating his province's labyrinthine system of medical re-accreditation. I meet people like John every day and in all walks of life. Whatever their training and education, the common denominator is that they came to Canada with the promise of finding work in their profession yet remain struggling to find work in any field. Immigrating to Canada, it seems, can be a bad career move.

WHAT HAPPENED
His foreign credentials were not recognized by the Canadian workforce.

WHEN AND WHERE
Currently, all across Canada

WHAT
New immigrants to Canada have a difficult time finding jobs. This article is about what happened to one immigrant. It is also about other immigrants with the same difficulties finding jobs in their fields.

Accepting more immigrants per capita than almost any other country in the world, Canada welcomed more than 2.2 million immigrants between 1991 and 2000, and even more this past decade. Yet 60% of immigrants work in fields other than the ones they worked in at home and get paid on average $2.28 less per hour than Canadian-born employees, or about $3 billion dollars less per year. Moreover, 42% between the ages of 25 and 54 have a higher education than their job requires; that number is just 28% for those born in Canada. In medicine, 90% of physicians trained in Canada work here while that number is only 55% for foreign-trained physicians and, of the remaining, 33% work in a non-healthcare related field.

WHY
The federal government accepts immigrants based, in part, on their education, but the provincial regulatory organizations determine who can become licensed to work in their jurisdictions.

Some are encouraged that the federal government has promised $50 million for a new framework to reduce wait times for foreign credential recognition to less than one year. Starting with eight professions at the beginning of 2011 and another six (including medicine) at the beginning of 2013, this program serves to accelerate evaluating credentials. Yet this is akin to strengthening just one link within an entire chain that is in dire need of repair. Without an all-inclusive plan, we are just shortsightedly patching one broken link while ignoring the others.

What Canada needs is a comprehensive strategy involving the federal government working with provinces and their professional regulatory associations to give immigrants a detailed understanding of the steps required to practice their profession in Canada. Maximum wait times should be negotiated for every step of the process and protectionist policies should be set aside in favour of increased recognition of the education and experiences of immigrants. If these wait times are breached, a Fairness Commission or similar body, as has recently been established in Ontario and Alberta, could mediate disputes. At the same time, employers must be consulted to ensure that their definition of what it means to have "Canadian experience" is incorporated in this framework.

Lastly, a cultural shift has to occur in the workplace to value the expertise of immigrant workers and compensate them on par with their Canadian-born peers. While there are criteria that must be met to guarantee a standard level of performance and care, there's a world of difference between ensuring effective standards versus effectively ensuring discrimination. Far too often foreign-trained professionals find their knowledge and skills underutilized or deemed substandard, all in the name of quality assurance or the Catch-22 of Canadian experience.

Our system for integrating foreign-trained professionals into the Canadian workforce is broken and the time to fix it is now. With more people immigrating to Canada than ever before, we have to design a system that is streamlined, responsive and just, from embassy evaluation to professional recertification to employment interview. In our competitive world, talent will be rewarded—and if not in Canada, then elsewhere.

I called John the other day to tell him about the new program for physicians that starts in 2013, excited about his future here and the possibilities that might open up for him. I reached him in New York. "I just got a job here," he said. "I start in a month."

Summary

The article "Treating Canada's Case of 'Taxi, M.D.'" describes the difficulties that new foreign-trained immigrants to Canada have getting jobs in their professional fields. John Zhang is a medical doctor and he arrived in Canada with the expectation of continuing his medical career, but he could neither work as a doctor nor find any kind of job in the medical field because he encountered bureaucratic obstacles to get his credentials recognized here. Other professionals who immigrate to Canada share his experience. Ali Okhowat suggests a compromise must be found between the government that accepts immigrants, the groups that determine professional standards, and the employers that look for workers in order to better utilize the talents of these newcomers to Canada. When immigrants cannot find work here in Canada, they leave.

CAPTURE THE KEY DETAILS OF A STORY

Summary is effective both for what it includes and what it leaves out. The summary of "Treating Canada's Case of 'Taxi, M.D.'" does not include details about the employment statistics of immigrants to Canada. These details are interesting but too detailed to include in a summary. When you summarize a story, stick to the main ideas and key points.

EXERCISE 15-3 **Capturing the Main Idea and Key Details of a News Story**

Directions: *Read the following news story. Underline the main ideas and the key details that support them. Make notes in the margin to provide a basis for your summary. In the space provided, write a short summary.*

from "Should Bodychecking Be Banned?" by KOLBY SOLINSKY

This article was originally posted on White Cover Magazine.

We know we're at a scary moment in the history of minor hockey when a local Canadian association has banned bodychecking according to the *Peace Arch News,* a paper based in a suburb of B.C.

The article says, "It's just for the house leagues," but that makes no sense. "Just for the house leagues" doesn't mean a lot, especially in B.C., where house leagues are far more competitive than they are in the rest of Canada. In B.C. house leagues, many players bring insane skill and can compete with their "enlightened" brethren in the B and A leagues.

To take bodychecking out of the sport doesn't make it safer. Players will still hit, because boys will be boys. And, it will still be hard for girls to play and fit in, if that's your goal, because boys will be boys.

I was the smallest, shortest, most frail player in my house league for my entire playing "career," and I couldn't wait for bodychecking. *You know why?* Because, like I said, it was happening anyway, and I was sick and tired of being run on every play and not being able to legally hit or fight back. I wanted to learn to protect myself, for my own survival and for my pride. It wasn't that these other players were dirty . . . it's that I was small. I wouldn't blame them for going after someone my size, because it must have been fun. I understood that.

Bodychecking helped me. It helped me develop as a player, and as a person. I learned to hit and I learned to play. Without contact—*without hitting and being hit*—I wouldn't have been a real hockey player.

These kids that are coming into your sterilized version of hockey won't be real hockey players either.

It didn't strip me of my safety. Quite the opposite. It let me grow up. It's part of the sport. I belonged, and I felt I thrived. I could be proud of the game I played, not ashamed. I would have always felt cheated if I wasn't able to really play the sport as it was meant to be played. I love the game too much, and I wanted to play it so bad. I didn't want to play some half-assed version that pandered to other kids that wanted to play shinny hockey or touch football.

If I was never allowed to bodycheck, I would have been embarrassed to tell my friends what league I played in. I never was. But, somewhere in the Pacific Coast Association, some kid is feeling cheated right now. He's feeling slighted.

Come on, guys. You're not helping your sons (or daughters) with this initiative. You're only trapping them by stripping the game they love of one of its most essential assets. You're not letting them play their game, and you're not letting them live their passion and their dream. Because, let's face it: Nobody from house league is going to the NHL. Neither are those kids in B. It's a hard show to make. The auditions are tough, and they last for life. These kids only have a few years left of playing the game they love, every night of every week. Don't steal it from them now just because you decided to go on a crusade against "concussions," that unholy C-word you know nothing about.

Don't steal this from them. Don't steal this from us. Congratulations. You've flicked the first domino in a movement that could ruin Canada's only national pastime. I hope you're happy.

SUMMARY

_____

_____

_____

_____

_____

_____

PROVIDE AN OVERVIEW OF A TEXTBOOK, MAGAZINE, OR JOURNAL ARTICLE

A summary of a magazine or journal article provides an overview. It states the writer's purpose, lists the main ideas, and mentions key details. To write such a summary, follow "Guidelines for Summarizing Accurately," found earlier in this chapter.

Following is a short magazine article on the equality of education. The student's notes are shown in the left margin. Notice how, in these notes, the student is already beginning to paraphrase the article's content. His paraphrased notes serve as the basis for the summary he writes after reading.

from "We Can Make Education More Equal," By ADAM GOLDENBERG

Canada has one of the best education systems on the planet. So says the Conference Board, whose most recent report card gave us top marks for high school completion, college completion, math, science, and problem-solving skills. This is cause for pride—but not complacency. At best, statistics like these offer a bird's eye view of Canadian education. But this country is too big to be described by aggregates. Zoom in, and you see a different story—one of inequality, injustice, and unkept promises.

One in five Canadian teenagers, aged 15 to 19, didn't go back to school last fall. On Aboriginal reserves, nearly 60 percent of young people don't finish high school. In rural Canada, dropout rates are twice the national average. In minority francophone communities, high-school students have weaker literacy skills than their majority-language counterparts. And in some of Canada's biggest cities, young people from low-income backgrounds are falling behind their better-off peers, as the gap between rich and poor neighbourhoods widens. These facts are surprising. They contradict the comfortable assumptions that we often make about education in Canada. Canada's education system is, in fact, unfair; we are failing to honour the basic conviction that every Canadian student deserves an equal shot at a world-class education.

This is an issue of fairness, but it's also a matter of progress and prosperity. Brainpower is an increasingly valuable commodity in the global economy. Education and skills training will be indispensible to Canada's success in a competitive world. We can't afford to waste an ounce of talent. We can't afford to leave out any Canadian.

We must make education more equal—but how? Raise the issue with experts and they respond with exasperation. Governments resist change. So do teachers' unions. School principals need more resources. School boards are hamstrung by conflicting priorities. Canada doesn't actually have one education system, we have 14; 10 provinces and three territories, plus the federal government, which is responsible for Aboriginal education. This division of responsibilities cannot be dismissed in the name of expediency. Any effort to improve education will falter if we do not respect provincial jurisdictions. But in describing the web of interests that is Canada's education system, one group is too often forgotten: students. The young people who have the most to gain—or lose—from any reform don't figure in the conversation. Instead, they are reduced to pie charts, percentages and bird's eye statistics.

Canada is a big country. Hadn't really thought about how education can be different depending on where one lives.

20% of older teenagers don't finish school and 80% of Aboriginal youth drop out. Double the number of students living outside large urban areas drop out compared to city students. These dropout rates are shocking. Finishing high school is a minimum requirement for almost every job. I wonder why kids drop out.

There must be a way to make finishing high school education possible for every Canadian.

We can make education more equal if we start with students—if we inspire them, motivate them, and give them role models in whom they can recognize their own potential. We can change the system—one pupil at a time. What if we recruited top university graduates—the best and brightest—to teach in schools where students struggle to achieve? We could create a national youth teaching corps, adapting a model that has worked successfully in the United States ("Teach For America"), the United Kingdom ("TeachFirst"), and a dozen other countries. A new Canadian program—call it "Teach For Canada"—could recruit a diverse cohort of university and college graduates, give them an intensive course in teacher training, and send them into schools where, for at least two years, they would share their talent and energy with young people. In one shot, we could invest in two groups of young Canadians—those about to enter the workforce, and those who might not otherwise get the opportunity to be inspired by committed role models. Many of the top graduates who join Teach For Canada would leave after their two years of service, to attend graduate school or begin their careers. But many others would stay in education—in the US, more than 60 percent of Teach For America teachers stay in the teaching profession beyond their initial two-year commitment. Those who leave Teach For Canada would remain part of an expanding network of alumni, committed to improving education, and capable of making a difference in the long term.

We won't solve the shortcomings of Canadian education all at once. One initiative alone cannot make our school system match our ideals, but we can begin. Classroom by classroom, student by student, we can make education more equal.

Summary

Compared to other countries, Canadian schools rank highly. In his article, *We Can Make Education More Equal,* Adam Goldenberg reports that given our country's large size, there are many schools that don't meet these high standards. This leaves some students with inferior education. He finds the discrepancies in the quality of education unfair to young Aboriginals, students from rural communities, and students living in low-income neighbourhoods of large cities. Since education is the basis for future success and prosperity, Goldenberg feels the inequity must be addressed, but he notes that there are government, financial, and bureaucratic obstacles preventing a quick and easy solution. He proposes setting up a system where recent college and university graduates are recruited to go teach in schools where students are struggling. The recruits would act as role models and inspiration to small groups of students, slowly reducing the dropout rates.

Effective summary gets at the main ideas of a source. The more specific detail you provide, the more you risk plagiarizing. Reporting general information and only key details makes your job easier. Remember to report objectively on what someone else says and thinks, not your opinions on the subject.

EXERCISE 15-4 **Summary and Overview**

Directions: *Read the following article. Underline the main ideas and key details, such as proper names, make notes in the margin to provide a basis for your summary, and then write a summary in the space provided.*

from "Seduce Me With Soap and Water" by SCOTT ROBERTSON

The advances in modern medicine are astounding: heart transplants from one human to another, stunning three-dimensional imaging of the body, sexy helicopters to rescue trauma victims. Yet science has yet to find a solution to one of the most baffling health challenges: how to get people to wash their hands. The introduction of basic hygiene is probably the biggest life-saving technology ever invented. Compare the leading causes of death worldwide and there is a dramatic divide between developing and developed nations. Millions of people in developing nations die every year from poor sanitation. Hand washing wouldn't solve all of them, but it would make a big difference.

A study done in the slums of Kirachi several years ago proved the stunning effectiveness of this basic practice. Households where hand washing was taught saw an immediate reduction in respiratory and gastrointestinal infections in children by 50% compared to other households with a corresponding decrease in hospitalizations. Reducing childhood illness and hospitalization is a goal of most governments and many international development organizations, and as far as effort is concerned, soap is cheap.

Similar studies have been conducted in schools, and even in the US military. The effects of hand washing have not always been as dramatic, but even studies with modest results showed respiratory infections fall by at least 20% and lost time at work and school by 40%. The average Canadian is away from work about nine days a year due to personal illness or injury or to care for a sick family member. This costs employers over $10 billion annually, so even modest reductions in these rates could have a big impact on productivity.

One of the lessons for healthcare workers is the importance of washing hands. Hand washing, or the more contemporary term "hand hygiene," is something that we actually do, apparently just not often enough. In Canada almost 700 patients a day receive a serious infection while in a hospital—one they didn't arrive with. Twenty of these patients will die, and the leading reason is dirty hands. The irony is that most of these people will require expensive antibiotics to combat the infections they received because of a lack of the simple process of hand hygiene. The actual costs to the healthcare system as well as to the patient and family are difficult to calculate but are estimated to be in the billions of dollars. Did I mention that soap is cheap? So why isn't more effort put into getting people to wash their hands? Perhaps because we just can't see the millions of bacteria and germs that are everywhere, and we don't realize how many we pick up even when we touch "clean" parts of other patients, or even just the side of the bed. Despite public education campaigns it seems we aren't getting the message. Virtually every healthcare facility has signs posted reminding us of the importance of this basic infection control step, particularly with the sharp increase in resistant organisms. To complicate matters further, the more specialized the work environment is, the worse we become. Intensive care units looking after patients who are already the most vulnerable are in fact the places where hand hygiene by staff is among the worst.

Time is often a factor. To properly lather, scrub, rinse, and dry a pair of hands takes about 45 seconds. Having to walk to the nearest sink adds even more time. Hand-sanitizer solutions have been found to be as effective as soap and water in many cases, are more convenient, and only take about 15 seconds to use properly.

One of the best motivators might be from patients themselves. The Canadian Patient Safety Institute recognizes that both patients and their families have an active role to play in preventing errors and improving safety in health care. During a recent tour of a Vancouver emergency department, a bright yellow sign in the staff area warned: "if I don't see you wash your hands, I'm going to ask you to do it." This is the type of empowerment that needs to get into the hands of patients who should be encouraged to ask their healthcare professional if he or she has washed their hands.

The cultural shift to being a nation of conscientious hand washers is slowly taking hold, helped from time-to-time by the publicity of a pandemic. It's not quite at the point where it is embraced as being a cool piece of medical technology, but healthcare workers and patients can play an important role reducing infections and saving lives by simply asking "did you wash your hands?"

_____

_____

_____

_____

_____

_____

_____

_____

Quotation

A well-chosen quotation can add both authority and colour to your writing, but it must be both skilfully introduced and properly integrated in order to be a real asset.

CHOOSE QUOTATIONS

Choose your quotations carefully. A poorly chosen quotation indicates a lack of critical thought. Any quotation will not do. Choose a quotation that has one or more of the following qualities:

- It sums up a point of view.
- It illustrates or supports an important point in your summary.
- It has colourful language and is therefore memorable.
- It adds authority to your writing.

Choose a quotation after you have read carefully, absorbed the meaning of what you have read, and summarized the reading. For example, here are quotations from "Treating Canada's Case of 'Taxi, M.D.'" and "Seduce Me with Soap and Water." These quotations sum up the main idea of each article:

> "Whatever their training and education, the common denominator is that they came to Canada with the promise of finding work in their profession yet remain struggling to find work in any field. Immigrating to Canada, it seems, can be a bad career move."

> "Hand washing, or the more contemporary term 'hand hygiene,' is something that we actually do, apparently just not often enough."

You would, of course, include the name of the author and the title of the article along with the quotation.

EXERCISE 15-5 Choosing Quotations

Directions: *Reread the two articles you summarized, "Should Bodychecking Be Banned?" and "Seduce Me with Soap and Water." Select a one-sentence quotation from each article that sums up a point of view, has colourful language, or illustrates an important point from each article. Write the sentences below and put quotation marks around them and explain why you chose them. In an actual assignment, you would need to provide the source information for in-text citations.*

1. From "Should Bodychecking Be Banned?":

   _____

   _____

2. From "Seduce Me with Soap and Water":

   _____

   _____

INTRODUCE QUOTATIONS

For the sake of variety, learn to use both partial and complete quotations. A partial quotation is a phrase you build a sentence around; a complete quotation is a grammatical sentence that begins with a capital letter and ends with a period. If you are writing a paragraph, use a partial quotation or a very short complete quotation as support for a point you are making. If you are writing an essay, use both partial and complete quotations.

Introducing your quotation has two functions. First, you acknowledge your source and protect yourself from charges of plagiarism. Second, having good sources enhances your credibility and persuades the reader you know what you are talking about. Here are illustrations of language taken from a reputable source—the first, a partial quotation; the second, a complete quotation.

ORIGINAL

from Rick Weiss, "For First Time, Chimps Seen Making Weapons for Hunting," washingtonpost.com

Chimpanzees living in the West African savannah have been observed fashioning deadly spears from sticks and using the tools to hunt small mammals—the first routine production of deadly weapons ever observed in animals other than humans. The multistep spearmaking practice, documented by researchers in Senegal who spent years gaining the chimpanzees' trust, adds credence to the idea that human forebears fashioned similar tools millions of years ago. The landmark observation also supports the long-debated proposition that females—the main makers and users of spears among the Senegalese chimps—tend to be the innovators and creative problem solvers in primate culture.

PARTIAL QUOTATION

MLA:
The Washington Post reports chimpanzees have been observed making and using weapons, which suggests that "human forebears fashioned similar tools millions of years ago" (Weiss).

APA:
The Washington Post reports chimpanzees have been observed making and using weapons, which suggests that "human forebears fashioned similar tools millions of years ago" (Weiss, 2007).

COMPLETE QUOTATION

MLA:

Chimpanzees have been observed making weapons. According to *The Washington Post*, "The multistep spearmaking practice, documented by researchers in Senegal who spent years gaining the chimpanzees' trust, adds credence to the idea that human forebears fashioned similar tools millions of years ago" (Weiss).

APA:

Chimpanzees have been observed making weapons. According to *The Washington Post*, "The multistep spearmaking practice, documented by researchers in Senegal who spent years gaining the chimpanzees' trust, adds credence to the idea that human forebears fashioned similar tools millions of years ago" (Weiss, 2007).

To protect yourself from a charge of plagiarism, all quotations should be associated with their source. In addition, when you associate your ideas with a source that has name recognition, such as the scholarly journals in your academic field, you enhance the credibility of your writing.

Guidelines for Acknowledging Sources

1. If you are quoting from a magazine or newspaper article, identify the name of the publication. Place your acknowledgment at the beginning of your paraphrase or quotation.

Here is a reference to an article published online by *The Washington Post* in MLA style.

APA would look like this: (Etzioni , 1986).

The Washington Post reports that a large number of high school students work at fast-food restaurants and that McDonald's serves as "the pioneer, trend-setter and symbol" (Etzioni).

2. When you cite a source by the author's name, use the full name and, if possible, include a phrase describing the author's credentials.

Here is a reference to an article by Bernard P. Horn published online by *Frontline* in MLA style.

APA style would include the date after the author's name: Bernard P. Horn (1997), a political director . . .

Bernard P. Horn, political director for the National Coalition Against Legalized Gambling, observes, "The American Psychiatric Association and the American Medical Association recognize pathological gambling as a diagnosable mental disorder."

If you include a second quotation by the same author or speaker, use that person's last name only.

Horn adds that gambling problems in the United States are reaching "epidemic proportions."

3. When you quote from a textbook, article, essay, or book, identify the author, or authors, by name and refer to the article, essay, or book you are quoting from.

> Frances Mayes says of her home in *Under the Tuscan Sun,* "Much of the restoration we did ourselves, an accomplishment, as my grandfather would say, out of the fullness of our ignorance."
>
> In *Dakota: A Spiritual Biography,* Kathleen Norris appreciates "the harsh beauty of a land that rolls like the ocean floor it once was, where dry winds scour out buttes, and the temperature can reach 110 degrees or plunge to 30 degrees below zero for a week or more" (26).

APA would include the date: Frances Mayes (1997) . . .

APA: Kathleen Norris (2001) . . . (p. 26).

Quotations that are longer than four lines or over 40 words are inserted in your writing as block quotations. Rather than use quotation marks, the material is inserted as a block with a left-indented margin (in APA, half an inch; in MLA, one inch). The parenthetical reference or in-text citation is placed after the punctuation following the quotation.

It is best to avoid providing too much information, such as Web addresses, in the in-text citations. It is usually sufficient to introduce and acknowledge your source by stating the name of the author(s) and the title of the source. More details are provided in the Works Cited (MLA) or References (APA) page at the end of your essay.

EXERCISE 15-6 **Introducing Partial and Complete Quotations**

Directions: *Read the following short excerpts. Write a short paraphrase of each passage. In the first paraphrase select and include a partial quotation. In the second paraphrase, select and include a complete quotation. Write paraphrases with quotations and acknowledge your source in each paraphrase.*

EXAMPLE

from *Walrus Magazine:* "Road Rage" by John Lorinc—a book review of Taras Grescoe's *Straphanger*

In Bogotá, Grescoe documents the remarkable story of how a pair of forward-thinking mayors not only created one of the world's busiest bus rapid transit networks, but also triggered something of an urban cycling renaissance by adding hundreds of kilometres of bike paths. Sundays are car-free on Bogotá's major arteries. For Grescoe, this is about taking back the streets from the gangster-owned vehicles that roared through the city as if they owned the place (a dynamic he also observes in Moscow). Revealing an urban-minded populism, Mayor Enrique Peñalosa explains that Bogotá's bike paths "showed that a cyclist on a $30 bike was equally important as a citizen in a $30,000 car." Those, surely, are the words of a politician who knows how to count votes.

PARTIAL QUOTATION IN MLA STYLE

In his review of Taras Grescoe's book, *Straphanger,* John Lorinc relates how the city of Bogotá has embraced cycling as a mode of transportation and "also triggered something of an urban cycling renaissance by adding hundreds of kilometres of bike paths" (2).

In APA style: John Lorinc (2012) . . . (p. 2).

COMPLETE QUOTATION

To describe his city's solution to improving transit woes, Bogotá's mayor

Enrique Peñalosa built new bicycle lanes that "showed that a cyclist on a

$30 bike was equally important as a citizen in a $30,000 car" (Grescoe 2).

1. from "I Was a Plagiarist" by Emma Teitel in *Maclean's* magazine

Plagiarism as defined by my alma mater is "the submission or presentation of the work of another as if it were one's own." In other words, plagiarism is meant to be an inherently moral error, not a technical one. It should be full of intent. But on university campuses today it's morphed into a dishonesty policy that you can violate in an honest way. Which means it regularly paints honest (if careless or ignorant) people (like me) as dishonest ones, liars and cheats.

PARTIAL QUOTATION

_____

COMPLETE QUOTATION

_____

2. from "Rise of Electronic Media and Readers Putting a Damper on Paper Products Industry," The Conference Board of Canada online

The steady shift in consumer preferences toward electronic information sources has gone beyond print media and is now taking its toll on demand for paper to produce books. As a result of this waning demand in North America—combined with ongoing turmoil in the world economy—Canada's paper products industry faces a weak outlook in the next few years, according to The Conference Board of Canada's Spring 2012 outlook for the industry.

PARTIAL QUOTATION

_____

COMPLETE QUOTATION

_____

3. from John Gormley, "Tear Down the Stigma Around Depression" in the Saskatoon *StarPhoenix*

During our lifetimes, however, as many as 20 to 25 per cent of adults may encounter at least one episode of major depression, which can affect sleep, eating, work, study and the enjoyment of friends and activities. Sometimes triggered by a major stress event, but not necessarily, depression's symptoms differ and are as prone to run in families as they are to affect someone with no family history of the illness. Depression is not a character flaw. It is not a weakness. It is no one's fault. It is a disorder brought on by a chemical imbalance in the brain.

PARTIAL QUOTATION

COMPLETE QUOTATION

EXERCISE 15-7 **Finding Quotations in Your Reading**

Directions: *Read several articles from a newspaper or a news magazine. Find at least five examples each of partial quotations and complete quotations. Copy them exactly as they appear in the article you select, and cite the source.*

EXAMPLE

Source: Natalie Stechyson. "War on Drugs Behind Spread of Disease, Global Report Says." *Vancouver Sun* 26 June 2012. Web. 27 June 2012.

Canada must embrace a public health approach to drug addiction rather than treating it as a criminal justice issue in order to curb the spread of HIV/AIDS among drug users, says a Canadian adviser for a new global report.

The report, released Monday by the Global Commission on Drug Policy, condemned the worldwide war on drugs as a "remarkable failure" and claimed it is driving the rapid spread of HIV/AIDS among drug users and their sexual partners. The emphasis on law enforcement has not achieved its stated objectives in terms of reducing the availability or rates of drug use, said B.C.'s Dr. Evan Wood, founder of the International Centre for Science in Drug Policy and an adviser on the report.

Partial Quotation: Dr. Evan Wood claims the current approach to consider drug addiction as a criminal activity rather than a health condition has been a "remarkable failure."

Complete Quotation: A speaker for the International Centre for Science in Drug Policy, Dr. Evan Wood, reports that, "The emphasis on law enforcement has not achieved its stated objectives in terms of reducing the availability or rates of drug use."

1. Source: _____

Partial Quotation: _____

_____

Complete Quotation: _____

_____

2. Source: _____

Partial Quotation: _____

_____

Complete Quotation: _____

_____

3. Source: _____

Partial Quotation: _____

_____

Complete Quotation: _____

_____

4. Source: _____

Partial Quotation: _____

_____

Complete Quotation: _____

_____

5. Source: _____

Partial Quotation: _____

_____

Complete Quotation: _____

_____

Suggestions for Daily Practice

1. At the end of each of your classes, write short summaries of the main points discussed or activities covered.
2. Select a sentence from your textbook. Count the number of words. Write a paraphrase that restates the idea in half the number of words.

3. Select an interesting article from a newspaper and write a short summary of it.

4. Keep a journal. Make journal entries that summarize your daily activities.

5. Write summaries of movies or television programs you find entertaining.

6. Find a newspaper or magazine article on a subject that interests you. Copy the article's quotations. Count the number of partial and complete quotations.

CHAPTER REVIEW

Take a moment and reflect on what you have learned about paraphrasing, summarizing, and quoting.

☐ Use sources correctly
- *To support points in your writing*

☐ Paraphrase
- *Be accurate*

☐ Plagiarism
- *Acknowledge sources; choose a citation style*

☐ Summary
- *A shorter, paraphrased version; objective and balanced; cite the source*

☐ Quotation
- *Well-chosen, properly integrated; cite the source*

☐ Suggestions for daily practice
- *Paraphrasing and summarizing*

CHAPTER

16

The Documented Essay

THINK FIRST

Recall a project you did at school or work that involved finding information from various sources. Write a paragraph describing the project. What was it about? Who were you doing the project for? What kind of research did you do? Where did you search for your information? What were the strengths and weaknesses of the final project? What did you learn from doing the project?

Hungry for More?

Have you ever seen a movie and found yourself hungry for more information about who acted in it, who directed it, or what it was based on? To find out this information, it helps to know how to do research quickly and efficiently. Whether you want to know who played Frodo in *The Lord of the Rings* movies or what critics were saying about *The Fellowship of the Ring* book when it was first published in 1954, online and print sources offer more than facts; they are a great resource for reviews and conversations about the books, films, or music you enjoy.

DISCUSSION

Talk to a classmate about a subject you would like to know more about. How did you become interested in it? What do you currently know about it? Why is the subject important to you?

The Internet versus the Printed Page

The Internet offers a wealth of information that is literally at your fingertips; type a few key words into a search engine, and your computer will return hundreds of sites related to your chosen topic. Be warned, however! Many of these sites contain irrelevant, highly personal, or downright false information. Anyone with access to a computer and some basic tools can post to a site, so be sure to check a site's credibility before believing what is presented there and citing it as a reference. When you find a Web site with information you want to use, you need to know who wrote it, who sponsors the site, why it was written, and for what kinds of readers it is intended. Is it well written and carefully edited? Is the information complete or is only one point of view presented? Are the sources of information cited? Do the facts presented check out when you compare them to other sources? Evaluating all sources for credibility will ensure that you choose the right resources to cite.

BRAINSTORM

Make a list of Web sites you visit. How did you find out about these sites? What kind of information do they provide? Is the information reliable and true? How do you know?

Doing Research on the Job

The research skills you hone during your time in school will not simply gather dust after graduation. Finding and managing outside information is an important aspect of many jobs. You could be asked, for example, to locate reliable sales figures (internally) or news stories (externally) that relate to a project you are doing; you might be asked to design a field survey that will help your company determine whether or not to embark on a new venture. Whether you are plowing through years of sales receipts or surfing the Internet for new techniques for building a better mousetrap, research skills will aid you in almost any job.

DISCUSSION

Talk to a classmate about the work you expect to do. Take turns talking about the kind of research you might be expected to do in your potential future jobs.

At a Glance

A documented essay demonstrates your ability to (1) focus on a problem, (2) gather information while distinguishing between different viewpoints, and (3) present what you have learned in a specific format. You are showing your reader that you have digested the information you gathered and made judgments about its value by arriving at a reasonable conclusion about an important issue regarding the problem you are focusing on.

The documented essay also demonstrates your ability to manage this information and use your knowledge of the conventions of college or university writing. These conventions include the presentation of facts and statistics, quotations, or case studies as support for the points you are making. You paraphrase the information and weave it into your writing, as well as make specific references to the sources by using a certain conventional format. As mentioned in Chapter 15, there are two common styles or formats you may be asked to use. One is the MLA style (Modern Languages Association), which is used in liberal arts and the humanities; the other is APA style (American Psychological Association), which is used in the social sciences. Find out which style your instructor wants you to use in your assignments.

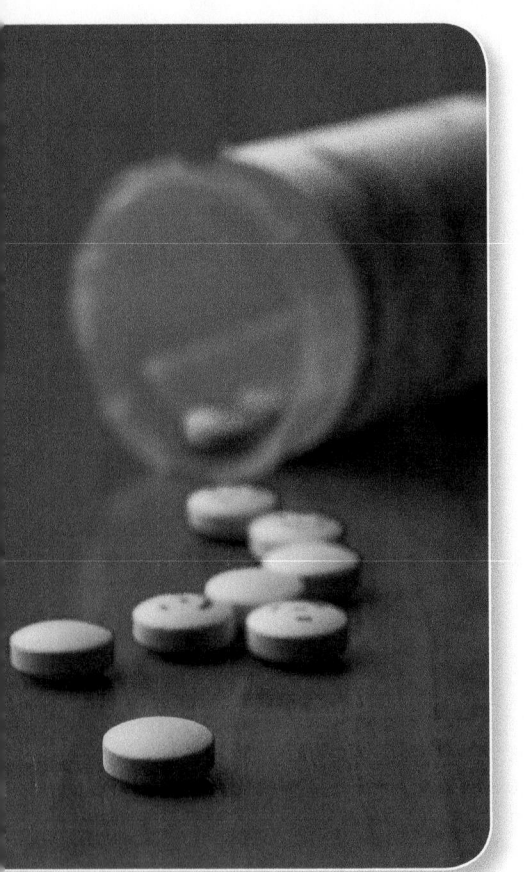

All citation styles include information about a source and tell your reader the form of the source, such as book, journal article, or Web site, with the purpose of enabling the reader to locate your sources. The formatting of the information is slightly different for each citation style and, at first, it can be confusing to learn how to properly cite and reference in your writing. However, most college and university libraries offer resources such as tutorials or Web sites with tips and support to help you master documentation in your essays. Some word-processing programs have built-in tools to help you keep track of your sources by automatically generating your citations. Additionally, there are many helpful scholarly Web sites. Nevertheless, not all Internet sites or software programs give you accurate citation formatting. You can check the accuracy of your citation in the *MLA Handbook for Writers of Research Papers,* 7th ed., or the *Publication Manual of the American Psychological Association,* 6th ed. Both are updated every few years to reflect new sources of information. Again, check with your instructor about which format and edition to follow.

The Documented Essay at a Glance

ASSIGNMENT   Discuss a societal issue, preferably a controversial one. Describe the problem and discuss some of the causes. Use MLA style to document any supporting information you provide.

Ron Fritz

Fritz 1

Professor Hathaway

English 150

November 21, 2012

Did You Take All Your Pills?

Canadians are lucky. Whenever they get sick, they can visit a doctor to get a prescription for medication to treat what ails them, and a short time later, they feel healthy again. Doctors have routinely prescribed a commonly used class of medicine, antibiotics, to treat bacterial infections. Recently, many medical professionals have become alarmed that previously curable diseases or injuries are becoming more difficult to treat because of the rise of drug-resistant bacteria due to overuse, misuse, and industrial use of antibiotics.

First of all, an increase of antibiotic resistant bacteria can be traced to the overuse of antibiotics. Many sick people want to feel better quickly and they expect their doctors to recommend some medication, even if it is not needed. For example, viruses cause some illnesses, such as the flu, and taking antibiotics for that will not speed up the cure. Nevertheless, patients still want their doctor to prescribe some medicine, in the mistaken belief they will get better sooner. According to the World Health Organization, taking an antibiotic when it is not warranted enables bacteria to develop a resistance mechanism to the antibiotic, resulting in that particular antibiotic no longer being effective ("Antimicrobial Resistance"). This means these former life-saving drugs will no longer work in curing some cases of bacterial infection. Medical professionals worry that for Canadians who get seemingly minor infections, such as sore throats or infected cuts on their skin, an antibiotic may not work to treat the infections caused by the drug-resistant bacteria.

In addition to the overuse of antibiotics, many people misuse the antibacterial medications prescribed by their doctors. As soon as a person's health begins to improve, he or she may stop taking the medication. The medication needs to be taken for the full length of time as prescribed; otherwise, bacteria will not be killed. Instead, it will be given an opportunity to develop the ability to fight the potency of the drugs. Bacteria survive the first antibiotic treatment and become more difficult to treat next time. The World Health Organization reports that "The more antibiotics are used, the higher the risk of resistance" in subsequent infections ("Antimicrobial"). In other words, when this person takes the same antibiotic at a later date, the less effective it will be at fighting the second bacterial infection. A professor of medicine from the University of Alberta,

The student begins with a problem that the reader can identify with.

THESIS STATEMENT
The writer states the main idea of the essay.

In APA, in-text citations would be formatted as (World Health Organization, 2012).

TOPIC SENTENCE
The student presents a second possible reason.

The information in the third paragraph, both informed opinions and quotations, enables the student to further discuss causes of the problem.

Using APA formatting, this would appear as (World Health Organization, 2011).

Lynora Saxinger, reveals that the noticeable rise of superbugs, more powerful than antibiotics, has become a huge challenge in the healthcare field ("Overuse"). Furthermore, with information readily available on the Internet, many patients self-diagnose their ailments, and take over-the-counter medications without consulting doctors. In some countries where Canadians go on vacation, antibiotics do not need a prescription and are easily purchased; thus, some take antibiotics needlessly. Combined with the failure to complete all the treatment, taking antibiotics unnecessarily contributes to mounting misuse of an important cure for infections.

Not only are antibiotics used to fight human infections, but they are also used for animal and plant diseases. In fact, Michael Teuber reports that since the production of antibiotics began some 70 years ago, "more than 1 million metric tons of antibiotics have been introduced into the biosphere." Veterinarians prescribe the same antibiotics for our pets and farm animals. The agricultural industry uses antibiotics to prevent infections in herd animals and in some countries to promote growth of food animals (Teuber). The World Health Organization notes that this agricultural use of antibiotics "in food animals—for treatment, disease prevention or growth promotion—allows resistant bacteria . . . to spread from food animals to humans through the food-chain" and antibiotics have been found in the water supplies of some communities ("Tackling"). The use and misuse of antibiotics in animals speeds up the development of resistant bacteria that pose an ever-increasing risk to human health ("Antimicrobial Resistance").

Historically, many Canadians have benefited from antibiotics to cure bacterial infections. However, overuse and misuse of these beneficial drugs in both humans and animals will soon create fully drug-resistant bacteria. With ineffective antibiotics, in the near future, many people could succumb to infections that can no longer be treated. Canadians need to become more vigilant about following the instructions on their medicine bottles.

Works Cited

"Antimicrobial Resistance." Fact sheet No. 194. *WHO Media Centre*. World Health Organization, Mar. 2012. Web. 24 Apr. 2012.

"Overuse of Antibiotics Causing Resistance that Could Undermine Medical Advances." *Globe and Mail* 03 Apr. 2012. Web. 05 Apr. 2012.

"Tackling Antibiotic Resistance from a Food Safety Perspective in Europe." *World Health Organization*. 2011. Web. 25 Apr. 2012.

Teuber, Michael. "Veterinary Use and Antibiotic Resistance." *Current Opinion in Microbiology* 4.5 (2001). 493-499. Web. 10 Apr. 2012.

In APA style: ("Overuse of Antibiotics," 2012).

The concluding sentence of this paragraph restates the main idea.

TOPIC SENTENCE
The student presents a third cause and presents supporting explanations.

To support the observations in the fourth paragraph, she cites a statistic.

In APA style: (Teuber, 2003).

In her conclusion, the writer restates her argument.

The student's list of Works Cited tells the reader exactly where her information came from.

In APA your sources would be formatted like this:

Fritz 3

References

Overuse of antibiotics causing resistance that could undermine medical
advances. (2012, April 4). *The Globe and Mail.* Retrieved from http://
www.theglobeandmail.com/commentary/editorials/overuse-of-
antibiotics-causing-resistance-that-could-undermine-medical-advances/
article4098034

Teuber, M. (2003). Veterinary use and antibiotic resistance. *Current Opinion
in Microbiology* 4(5), 493-499. Retrieved from http://www.sciencedirect.
com/science/article/pii/S1369527400002411

World Health Organization. (2011). Tackling antibiotic resistance from
a food safety perspective in Europe. Retrieved from http://www.
euro.who.int/en/what-we-do/health-topics/disease-prevention/
antimicrobial-resistance

World Health Organization. (2012, March). Antimicrobial resistance.
Fact sheet no. 194. Retrieved from http://www.who.int/mediacentre/
factsheets/fs194/en/

DISCUSSION QUESTIONS

1. What is the function of the statistics and quotations used in this
   assignment?

2. How are these statistics and quotations introduced?

3. What do you think the three dots (ellipsis) in the quote in the fourth
   paragraph mean?

ELEMENTS OF THE DOCUMENTED ESSAY

Readers of academic writing have very definite expectations when they see
a documented essay. These expectations relate to both form and content.
Below is a brief description of the elements you should have in mind when
you write a documented essay.

- *The problem:* Your work usually begins with a problem or issue.
  Something is wrong, and there is a public discussion on Web sites, in
  newspapers, magazines, and journals about a reasonable approach to
  addressing this problem. For example, drug resistant infections are an
  increasingly common problem across Canada. What is to be done?

- *Locating information:* Readers of the documented essay look for
  quality information. You need to find good sources and read them with
  understanding. The evidence you borrow from your sources comes in
  three forms: facts and statistics, cases and studies, and authoritative
  opinion. In the at-a-glance essay, for example, the student cites her
  reading from sources specifically published to address this issue. Read
  critically the information you find. Be sure that it is up-to-date and
  comes from reliable sources.

- *Processing information:* Once you locate information, you need to
  process it. You read, take notes, select what is useful, and integrate

it into your essay. You should evaluate the information you find to determine the author's perspective and if there is bias.

- *Integrating information:* How you present information matters. If you present it effectively, your essay is more persuasive. Use signal phrases or reporting verbs ("according to . . .") in the paper, cite authors and publications by name, use parenthetical citations (also known as in-text citations) where necessary, and provide a list of Works Cited (MLA) or References (APA).

GET STARTED

Like most writing in college and university, documented essays often begin with an assignment. For example, during a unit of study, your instructor would like you to dig deeper into a specific problem, learn what authorities are saying about this problem, and state your opinion about it. Often students begin with an opinion, and in the process of doing their research, their opinions become more informed. An informed opinion is based on careful thought about reliable information. The goal of learning how to write documented essays is for you to become connected to the academic community by learning about researchers in your field and their work. You use your critical reading skills to determine if the information you find is complete, accurate, and reliable.

EXERCISE 16-1 **Problem and Opinion**

Directions: *Select one of the topics below. In a short paragraph, briefly state what you know about the problem and what should be done about it.*

EXAMPLE

Problem: Plastic bottles and the environment

Plastic bottles are everywhere, especially since bottled water has become so popular. Half the people walking down the street are holding onto bottles. What happens to those bottles? Don't they just get thrown away? In my opinion, using plastic bottles is bad and is creating an environmental disaster. Plastic drinking bottles should be outlawed.

1. The use of calculators in lower grades
2. Trying young offenders as adults
3. Regulating the use of genetically modified seeds
4. Openness in adoption records
5. Misleading labelling of consumer products
6. Home schooling
7. Free digital downloads of music
8. Digital privacy and controlling who collects one's personal information on the Internet

Locate Information

Your goal in the investigation process is to improve your information literacy. "Just Google it" is not the best formula for success. You need to be informed on a variety of sources of information, many of which are probably available through your college, university, or local public library.

INTERNET SOURCES

From any computer with an Internet connection, you have access to an abundance of information to get you started on your research. Internet searches are done with search engines.

> ## INTERNET SEARCH ENGINES
>
> - www.google.ca
> - www.yahoo.ca
> - www.wikipedia.com
> - www.canfind.ca

These powerful applications search literally hundreds of thousands of sites for key words that you supply. Because search engines can find thousands of Web sites that relate to your topic, you must be as specific as possible in your searches. Then you need to quickly survey a site and decide whether the information you find there will be valuable to you.

Search Hints

After choosing a search engine, enter key words that relate to your topic. To avoid an unreasonably large number of "hits," use as many terms in a single search as you think apply to your topic. Google is one of the largest databases of Web pages and has become one of the most popular search engines, but there is much scholarly information available in other databases, so you might want to learn to search those as well. Scholarly database articles are peer-reviewed, which acts as a quality control for the information you are looking for.

> ## SEARCH TIP
>
> If you precede each of your terms with a "+" sign, a search engine like Google will return only sites that contain *all* of the specified terms (as opposed to one of the terms or a combination of them). Adding quotation marks to a phrase (say, "effects of television") will return only sites with that exact phrase:
>
> + "effects of television" + children + research

For further information on how to search sites for information, look for the "advanced search" link on the home page of the search engine you want to use. There you will find helpful tips on how to search most effectively.

Evaluating Sites

Scan the list of sites your search engine returns. Look at the Internet addresses (URLs, or universal resource locators) of the Web sites to determine whether they are sponsored by a commercial group (.com or .ca), an educational institution (.edu), a government organization (.gov), or a nonprofit organization (.org). Since .com/.ca sites are selling something, you should be wary of the information they provide.

Go to specific sites and continue your evaluation. Scroll from the top to the bottom of the site. Check for dates to see if the information is current because information gets outdated very quickly. Look for "About Us" or "Who We Are" links to learn more about the source of the information. These links will provide information on the organization's background, authors' credentials, and their affiliation with institutions, such as government agencies and universities, or with mainstream publications. This will help you determine if there is any bias in the information presented. Get an idea about the completeness of the information provided.

If the site passes these initial tests, you should bookmark it using the "Favourites" or "Bookmarks" function of your Internet browser so that you can find the site again. Then, either on a note card or in a computer file, record the source and title information, a description of the information you found, and the date you accessed it. Repeat this process for other sites that are likely to have useful information. By methodically keeping track of the information as you come across it, you will find it easier to properly cite and reference your sources.

PERIODICAL LITERATURE

College, university, and public libraries subscribe to a variety of online periodical databases to help writers search for quality print sources of information more efficiently. Many professional journals now publish electronically, and their articles are available only digitally on these periodical databases. Of course, you can search all or as many of the databases as you wish, but you can search more efficiently within the database most likely to contain information related to your research. Alternatively, you can conduct a search for a particular journal or magazine.

Using key words, you can search for articles in a database much as you do on the Internet. Among the databases with Canadian content, you might want to use the following:

- *Canadian Business and Current Affairs (CBCA):* Full-text business and general interest articles from popular, academic, and business periodicals
- *Canadian Periodical Index (CPI.Q):* Articles from general, academic, and business magazines. Index from 1988, full text from 1995
- *CANSIM:* A database updated daily by Statistics Canada providing key socio-economic statistics
- *EBSCO Canadian Literary Centre:* Information provided for Canadian and international magazines, newspapers, newswires, reference books, and company information

Talk about it ▷▷▷

Discuss two or three tips in this chapter that you will use to make your research both efficient and effective.

Searching Databases

Key word searches may lead to subtopics, enabling you to narrow your search and be more specific. Follow this four-step process when you do a database search.

1. **Enter terms into the database's search window.** Narrow your search as much as possible at this stage. Most periodicals databases allow for "Subject," "Author," "Title," and "Key Word" searches, among other options. Check the "Help" section of the database to see how to narrow your searches most efficiently—for example, whether it accepts signs, quotation marks, and/or Boolean operators like AND, OR, NOT, and so on. Boolean operators define the relationships between words or groups of words in your search term and refine your search.

2. **Make a quick evaluation of the results of your search.** Most results include a brief summary of the article in an "abstract." Along with content descriptions (if any), titles, length, and authorship, consider the types of periodicals in which articles appear and where they are published. Depending on your topic, consider popular sources, such as *Maclean's,* or more academic or professional publications, such as *Journal of Clinical Nursing.*

3. **If an article is available online, skim it.** Scan the article top to bottom, reading headings and the first sentence of each paragraph. Check for dates to see if the information is current. If the article seems useful, print it out, save an electronic copy, or email a copy of it to yourself (if possible). If you cannot print or email it, record the author's name, the name of the publication, the article's title, a description of the information, the date, and page number(s) on a note card or in a notebook you can use for your research information. Also record the database where you found the article.

4. **If the full text of an article is not available, print or write down the publication information.** Sometimes, only the name and publication information, rather than the full content, are available in a search. When that happens, record the publication information for articles that look useful and consult the library for a print (or microfilm) copy.

5. **If you find an article that is suitable for your research topic, look at the Works Cited or References list at the end of the article.** There you might find leads to other relevant articles.

LIBRARY CATALOGUE AND REFERENCE BOOKS

Library catalogues can be searched by "Subject," "Author," "Title," and "Key Word." Be specific and include as many search terms as are relevant to your topic. Evaluate catalogue sources (that is, the actual books or periodicals) for relevance, trustworthiness, authorship, publication information, and dates. Once you have found a book or periodical that passes these tests, consult the table of contents and index to find sections and pages that address your topic.

Libraries provide access to reference books and online materials, such as dictionaries, biography resources, handbooks, maps and atlases. They also have many sources on geography, politics, and populations, as well as information on countries, provinces and territories, cities, and businesses.

Directions: *For each of the sources of information described on the previous page, write down some key words you would use to search for information on the topic you chose in Exercise 16-1. Refer back to the Search Tips in the previous section to make your search as specific and efficient as possible through the use of quotations or symbols.*

EXAMPLE

Topic: Plastic bottles and the environment

Internet Search Key Words: "plastic water bottles" + environment

Periodical Search Key Words: plastic bottles, plastic bottles AND environment, plastic beverage containers AND pollution

Your Topic: _____

Internet Search Key Words: _____

Periodical Search Key Words: _____

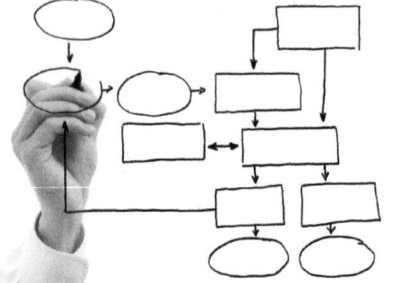

Process

PROCESS INFORMATION

When you write a documented essay, you must work efficiently and effectively. You need to locate useful information, process it, and integrate it into your writing. Find information from a number of sources to provide a balanced approach to your topic. Usually, the latest information might appear first in newspapers or magazines, which are intended for a general audience. Scholarly articles in journals or trade magazines often report original research or current trends and are intended for researchers, professionals, or specialists in the field. These different sources will provide you with a variety of information and differing points of view about the same topic.

Types of Information

You will work more efficiently if, after making an outline for your essay, you have clearly defined types of information in mind when you start your search. Here are three of the most common types of information that academic writers should use.

FACTS AND STATISTICS

Facts and statistics are numerical data you can use to dramatize a problem and convey the size and dimensions of an issue to a reader. In these examples, MLA-style formatting is used.

- According to the journal *Environment,* recent data show 23.4 billion plastic bottles of soda were sold in the U.S. in 2000 (Nicholson 6). [The large number of bottles accentuates how large the problem is.]
- In Japan, the use of plastic is expanding at 10 percent a year. Of that production, 413 000 tons of plastic are used for beverages (Yoshihiro 24). [This statistic helps your reader visualize the magnitude of material involved.]
- *Environment* reports that from 1996 to 2000 recycling rates have fallen from 48 percent to 35 percent (Nicholson 6). [Noting that recycling rates are significantly declining makes your argument more convincing.]

Facts and statistics also provide support for a viewpoint.

- *Waste News* suggests that consumers lose $26 million a year on unredeemed plastic bottles. That is, the consumer pays the deposit and the bottle is never returned (Johnson 1). [This reference puts a dollar figure on the problem.]

Where in your essay assignment will you use an example of facts or statistics?

AUTHORITATIVE OPINION

Authoritative opinion comes from experts whose credentials invite us to believe what they say.

- Researchers from the School of Public Health at the University of Alberta note that "waterborne disease outbreaks in affluent countries almost universally demonstrate that the outbreaks were eminently preventable" (Rizak and Hrudey 170).

Where in your essay assignments could you use an example of an authoritative opinion?

In addition to experts with credentials, authoritative opinion can come from journals and respected publications. A student writing on plastic bottles could refer to *Environment, Waste News,* and *Chemical Week.*

CASES AND EXAMPLES

Cases and examples are likely to provide you with both factual information and a basis for informed opinion. If you are writing on the topic of misleading labelling of consumer products, for example, you can find detailed reports at Industry Canada's Office of Consumer Affairs, where specific legislative and judicial actions have addressed this issue. Reading about these cases will give you factual information on the specific requirements to comply with the guidelines and regulations. Learning about specific cases will also give you access to informed opinion on the issue.

Take Notes

Once you identify sources you would like to use, you need to process them. Use specific parts of the sources to support points you are making in your essay, and organize your notes so you can easily find what you have researched.

Plagiarism is a critical issue at this point. Some students copy large passages from sources into their notes, then copy from their notes to their paper. This is plagiarism. Other students email themselves a full copy of the source, then copy and paste from the source straight into their papers. This also is plagiarism and will likely result in a failing grade on the assignment, and possibly the course, because you have not written the work yourself and have not indicated where the information came from.

See Chapter 15 for a more detailed discussion of plagiarism.

To prevent plagiarizing, begin with a tentative outline for your paper. What is the problem or issue you are addressing? What questions will you explore in your reading? What is your viewpoint? Your outline will help you focus your reading and research and provide you with a system for organizing your notes. This student's very simple outline creates a structure for organized reading and thinking.

Antibiotics and drug-resistant bacteria

   I.   How big of a problem is this?

   II. Why are antibiotics not always effective?

   III. What can be done?

As you read, take careful notes on note cards, on your computer, or in a notebook. Here are some tips for recording information.

Take Notes Using Your Computer

Some journal articles you find online have now been assigned a DOI number (Digital Object Identifier). Since Web sites change over time, the DOI is intended to help with retrieving the sources in a digital environment. The DOI number acts as a persistent link to the item's online form. Record this in your notes because in APA style, you will include the DOI at the end of the entry in your references. If the document has been assigned a DOI number, it is usually listed on the first page of the article.

When you find information electronically, MLA style requires both the date of publication and the date you accessed the material. Although not required by MLA style, some instructors also want you to include the URL of your sources, so include this information in your notes. When you must add a URL, provide it at the end of the citation within angle brackets followed by a period, like this: <www. . . .>. For APA style, you do need to provide the URL, so be sure to record this in your notes as well.

As you can see, taking accurate notes as you do your research is very important. If you cannot provide accurate citation or references, you cannot use the information in your essay. Make good use of your time and record all the information you might need in your research notes by following these steps:

1. **Create an electronic folder on your computer dedicated to your assignment.** In this folder, keep notes, publication information for your sources, and drafts of the paper you are writing. You must document *where* you find your information, as well as *the date* you accessed it, since you will need to include that information in the Works Cited or References list at the end of your essay.

2. **Use a new word-processing file for each source.** When you take notes on your reading, put these notes in the dedicated file. Save the file either by the author's last name or by the first two or three words of the title (for example, Nicholson or "A Billion Bottles").

3. **Follow steps 2–5 in "Take Notes Using Note Cards," discussed below.**

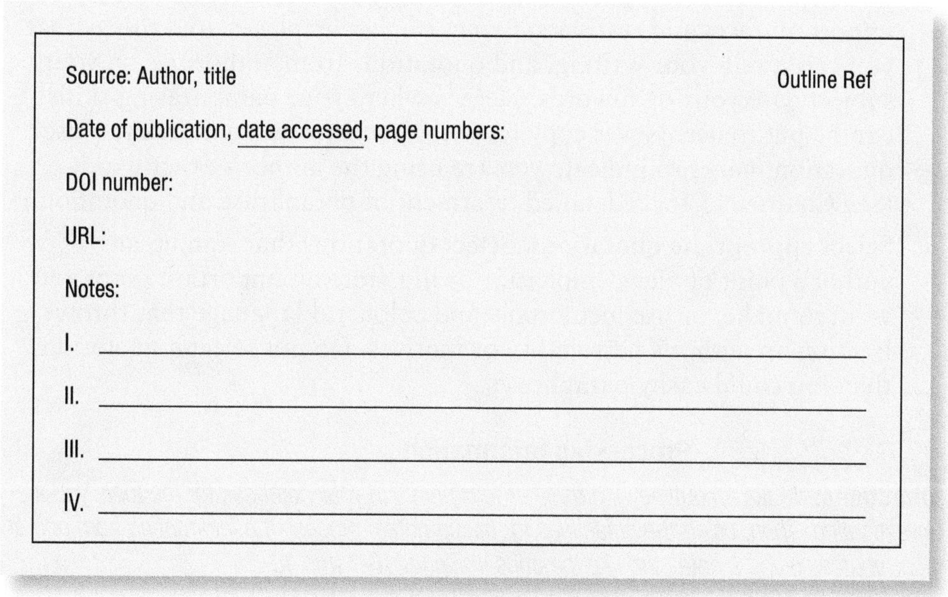

FIGURE 16-1 Example Note Card

Take Notes Using Note Cards

1. **Use a separate note card for each source.** If you find an informative source, use a note card for each separate item on your outline.

2. **Record publication information.** For each source of information, record information that answers these questions: *Who* created the information? *When* was it written and published? *What* is the source called and what is the format (article, Web site, film, etc.)? *Where* can your reader find this reference? Each citation style will format this information a bit differently, but you only need to follow a kind of "formula" to provide the information in the proper order and format. For example, for an Internet source, write down the name of the author(s), the title of the article, the title of the Web site, the version or edition used, the publisher or sponsor of the site, the DOI number (if there is one), the date of publication (day, month, year), and the date you accessed the site. Also record the URL. If you have accessed an article via the Internet or an online database that also appears in print, try to obtain the information listed for print sources as well. For books, newspapers, magazines, and periodicals, write down the name of the author(s); the title of the article, periodical, book, newspaper, or magazine; the date and place of publication; the publisher; and the page numbers where the information can be found. (See Figure 16-1 for an example note card.) It is always better to record as much information as you can when you first find your source.

3. **Use a number or Roman numeral on the card to refer to your outline** (see Figure 16-1) and indicate the connection between the notes you take and your essay's structure or outline. This will help keep your notes organized so you can find the information as you write your assignment. It will also help you be accurate with your citations.

4. **Take brief point-form notes that paraphrase or summarize information.** Most students take too many notes. Write down only important facts and statistics; names of people, places, and things that you can use in your writing; and quotations from authorities on your subject. Use your own words. Here is where your paraphrasing skills can be put to use. Never copy material word-for-word unless you use quotation marks to indicate you are using the author's exact words. (See Chapter 15 for a detailed treatment of paraphrase and quotation.)

5. **Select appropriate quotations.** Select quotations that sum up an author's point of view, emphasize or illustrate an important point you want to make, or use memorable and colourful language that throws light on an author's personality or motives. Do not select a quotation that you could easily paraphrase.

EXERCISE 16-3 **Processing Information**

Directions: *Make an outline with three or four points in your notebook for the topic you are investigating. Then, using the guidelines for taking notes, process the information from one of your sources using a note card like the ones in Figure 16-1 and 16-2.*

The student uses separate cards for these notes because they provide facts and statistics related to different points on his outline.

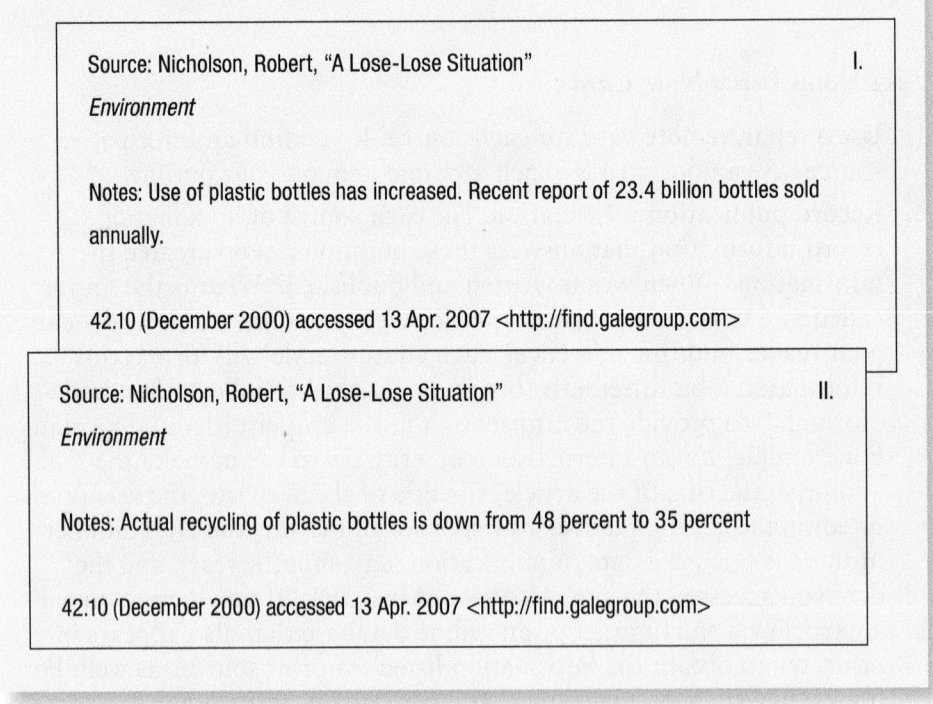

Source: Nicholson, Robert, "A Lose-Lose Situation"   I.

Environment

Notes: Use of plastic bottles has increased. Recent report of 23.4 billion bottles sold annually.

42.10 (December 2000) accessed 13 Apr. 2007 <http://find.galegroup.com>

Source: Nicholson, Robert, "A Lose-Lose Situation"   II.

Environment

Notes: Actual recycling of plastic bottles is down from 48 percent to 35 percent

42.10 (December 2000) accessed 13 Apr. 2007 <http://find.galegroup.com>

FIGURE 16-2 Numbered Note Cards for Different Outline Points

Integrate Sources

To integrate your reading into your work, cite your sources by name in your paper and, when appropriate, include parenthetical references or in-text citations.

PARENTHETICAL REFERENCES/IN-TEXT CITATIONS

An **in-text citation** provides information about your source. By accurately providing this information, you show that you have researched your topic and that you are not plagiarizing. You should provide an in-text citation for information in these situations:

- When you use a complete or partial quotation from a source
- When you refer to facts, statistics, or paraphrased information that can only be found in one specific source

For information that is widely known—thought of as common knowledge—there is no need for an in-text citation. For example, it is widely known that plastic water bottles have replaced glass for many beverages and that bottled water consumption has increased dramatically in the past ten years. There is no need to use an in-text citation to acknowledge a source that mentions these facts. In contrast, the fact that consumers lose $26 million a year on unredeemed plastic bottles is information you might find in only one source; consequently, you need an in-text citation to tell your reader where you found that information. If you have any doubt about whether information is common knowledge, use an in-text citation to indicate where you found it.

Ask Yourself

How do you decide which information is common knowledge and which information requires a citation?

Provide an in-text citation immediately after any quotation, fact, or statistic in your paper. The citation should be placed in parentheses at the end of the sentence where the information appears. Place the period *after* the in-text citation. The information you include in your citation depends on the type of publication you cite and on how you identify the source in your writing.

Following are a few examples of paraphrasing information showing both MLA and APA style guidelines. There are many sources and formats of information, such as interviews, pamphlets, films, lectures, or even Twitter messages. For all sources, record the *who? when? what? where?* information. Then check with your instructor or library to ensure you use the correct style and format in your assignment.

Author name(s). For both traditional and electronic sources for which you have the author's name, include the last name in the in-text citation *unless* you refer to the author by name prior to the information you are citing (in which case include only the page number/s for MLA). Note that APA format also includes the date of publication and abbreviation for page(s).

MLA: *Waste News* suggests that consumers lose $26 million a year on unredeemed plastic bottles. That is, the consumer pays the deposit and the bottle is never returned (Johnson 1).

APA: *Waste News* suggests that consumers lose $26 million a year on unredeemed plastic bottles. That is, the consumer pays the deposit and the bottle is never returned (Johnson, 2003, p.1).

The student integrates an important statistic into her essay.

She cites the author's last name and the relevant page number in her in-text citation.

Titles. If no author is listed for a source, include the entire title (if it is short) or a shortened version before the page number in your in-text citation, *unless* you have already mentioned it in the sentence (in which case only include the page number/s). Note that APA format also includes the date of publication and abbreviation for page(s).

> MLA: In Mexico, polyethylene terephthalate (PET) plastic bottles are fast replacing glass and metal. Producers hope the technology is soon available for packaging beer in plastic ("Resins" 40).
>
> APA: In Mexico, polyethylene terephthalate (PET) plastic bottles are fast replacing glass and metal. Producers hope the technology is soon available for packaging beer in plastic ("Resins," 2006, p. 40).

Page numbers. For traditional print sources, such as books and magazines, that have page numbers, include the specific page number(s) where the information (fact, statistic, quotation) you are citing can be found. If the author and title of the work being cited are both included in the sentence, for MLA style, only the page number(s) should be included in the citation. APA format also includes the date of publication as well as the abbreviation for page(s).

The student integrates a complete quotation into her essay. Longer quotations use a slightly different format.

On first reference to this source, the student uses the author's full name; therefore, she includes only the page number in parentheses. If she refers to the same author again, she only uses the last name. In APA, the year and page number are included.

> MLA: In his article in *Environment* magazine, Robert Nicholson reports, "Plastic bottles have to be sorted by color and type of resin, and all extraneous materials have to be removed; in many cases, these processes have to be done by hand" (6).
>
> APA: In his article in *Environment* magazine, Robert Nicholson reports, "Plastic bottles have to be sorted by color and type of resin, and all extraneous materials have to be removed; in many cases, these processes have to be done by hand" (2000, p. 6).

INTRODUCING QUOTATIONS

Practise using a variety of verbs or signal phrases to introduce your sources: *says, reports, states, explains, argues, observes*. The more variation you use when you set up your quotations, the smoother the integration process. This is called "framing" your sources, which means you place the quote or paraphrase within your own sentence. Make a list of the verbs you can use, noting that some of the verbs can be neutral, have doubt, or have connotations such as *analyzed, questions, believes, doubts, denies, suggests, interpreted*.

The student integrates a partial quotation into her essay. In MLA style, she uses the authority's full name; "qtd. in Johnson" in the in-text citation indicates Johnson used this quotation in his article. In APA style, use "as cited in."

> MLA: Darryl Young, from the California Department of Conservation, <u>notes</u> that plastic beverage bottles have become "as common as a cell phone" (qtd. in Johnson 1).
>
> APA: Darryl Young, from the California Department of Conservation, <u>notes</u> that plastic beverage bottles have become "as common as a cell phone" (as cited in Johnson, 2003, p. 1).

Here are other ways she could integrate the quotation:

MLA: Darryl Young, from the California Department of Conservation, points out that plastic beverage bottles have become "as common as a cell phone" (qtd. in Johnson 1).

APA: Darryl Young, from the California Department of Conservation, points out that plastic beverage bottles have become "as common as a cell phone" (as cited in Johnson, 2003, p. 1).

MLA: Darryl Young, from the California Department of Conservation, indicates that plastic beverage bottles have become "as common as a cell phone" (qtd. in Johnson 1).

APA: Darryl Young, from the California Department of Conservation, indicates that plastic beverage bottles have become "as common as a cell phone" (as cited in Johnson, 2003, p. 1).

Be sure to distinguish between partial and complete quotations, observing the rules for capitalization and punctuation. (See Chapter 15 for additional information on quotations.)

Complete Quotation

MLA: Nicholson points out, "Plastic bottles have to be sorted by color and type of resin, and all extraneous materials have to be removed; in many cases, these processes have to be done by hand" (6).

APA: Nicholson points out, "Plastic bottles have to be sorted by color and type of resin, and all extraneous materials have to be removed; in many cases, these processes have to be done by hand" (2000, p. 6).

The student uses only the author's last name because she has already referred to him earlier in her paper.

Partial Quotation

MLA: Moreover, according to *Look Japan,* we are now at a point where PET bottles can be made from recycled plastic, which "will decrease waste volume and reduce consumption of the petroleum resources used to make PET plastic" (Yoshihiro 24).

APA: Moreover, according to *Look Japan,* we are now at a point where PET bottles can be made from recycled plastic, which "will decrease waste volume and reduce consumption of the petroleum resources used to make PET plastic" (Yoshihiro, 2004, p. 24).

The student refers to the name of the magazine to set up this quotation. In parentheses, she cites the last name of the author.

In your in-text citations, provide only enough information to help your reader clearly identify your source. Do not include the names of publishing companies or Internet addresses. Save this information for your list of Works Cited or References.

DOCUMENT SOURCES

Once known as the bibliography, the Works Cited section of your paper in MLA style provides the reader with publication information on your sources. APA style calls this section References. Listing your sources is a matter of academic honesty. When you process information, you must take care not to plagiarize. Since you integrate sources into your essay to make stronger arguments, you should tell your reader about those sources. Include only those sources you actually use for facts and statistics, details on people and places related to your topic, and quotations. Of course, how you document your sources depends on the academic discipline of the course for which you write the paper. Some citation styles use footnotes or endnotes, but in MLA and APA the citations immediately follow what you are including in your text.

Citation styles also standardize your text, such as which typeface or font to use, the font size, the margins, the spacing, and the headings. Different citation styles also give guidelines about whether to include a cover page or where to place your name, the date, the course number, the assignment title, or the instructor's name. No matter which citation style you use, follow the formatting instructions and the correct style of documentation given by your instructor for your course or assignment.

In humanities courses, including English, you will often use guidelines published by the Modern Language Association (MLA). The Modern Language Association's *MLA Handbook for Writers of Research Papers,* seventh edition, is a comprehensive treatment of documentation issues. To check how to format a particular source document, you might find the answer at the MLA Web site: www.mla.org/handbook_faq.

As already mentioned, in social science courses you are most likely to use guidelines published by the American Psychological Association (APA) in the *Publication Manual of the American Psychological Association,* sixth edition. You can also find information and tutorials on APA style at the APA Web site: www.apastyle.org/learn/

Check if your own college or university library has text copies of the *MLA Handbook* and the *Publication Manual of the APA.* Make sure you are using the latest edition, since every few years, a new edition is released with up-to-date changes, such as how to document new electronic documents.

GENERAL GUIDELINES FOR CITING SOURCES

According to MLA and APA guidelines, your Works Cited or References list should be organized in the following way:

- Start on a new page and at the top of the page; centre the title (Works Cited or References).
- List sources in alphabetical order by author's last name; or, if there is no author given, list alphabetically by the first word of the title. List the government agency name first for government publications when no author is given.
- Double-space within and between all entries.
- Indent the second line and all subsequent lines for each entry (a hanging indent).
- Include specific publication information according to the type of source you have used (format).

Cite Different Types of Sources

How you cite a source depends on the kind of document it is. There are traditional print sources, such as newspaper articles, magazine articles, professional journal articles, and books. These print sources can also be delivered through electronic sources like Web sites and databases. There are also documents that are only available electronically, such as emails or Web sites, and these can also be formatted according to your citation style.

Following are examples of a few of the most common document sources in MLA and APA style. Your library will provide you with resources to learn how to format other kinds of documents. Notice that each type of document provides information that enables a reader to easily locate the same source you used. However, each style puts the information in a different order and in a slightly different format (e.g., use of capitals, italics, quotation marks, commas, or periods).

NEWSPAPER

Author(s). "Title of Article." *Name of newspaper* Date: Section page. Medium of publication.

Rickwood, Lee. "Calgary Transit Gets High Tech Boost for Bus Schedules, Timetables." *Calgary Herald* 30 April 2012: A3. Print.

MLA example

Who? (author) When? (date) What? (title) Where? (newspaper)

Rickwood, L. (2012, April 30). Calgary transit gets high tech boost for bus schedules, timetables. *The Calgary Herald,* p. A3.

APA example

MAGAZINE

Author(s). "Title of Article." *Title of Source* Date: Pages. Medium of publication.

Coates, Ken, and Bill Morrison. "The Uses and Abuses of University." *The Walrus* Oct. 2012: 34-39. Print.

MLA example: Titles of articles are surrounded by quotation marks; names of magazines are in italics.

Who? (author) When? (date) What? (title) Where? (magazine)

Coates, K., & Morrison, B. (2012, October). The uses and abuses of university. *The Walrus, 9*(8), 34-39.

APA example: Titles of articles are not surrounded by quotation marks.

BOOK BY ONE AUTHOR

Author. *Title of Book.* City: Publisher, date of publication. Medium of publication.

Friedman, Thomas. *The World Is Flat: A Brief History of the Twenty-First Century.* New York: Farrar, Straus and Giroux, 2006. Print.

MLA example

Author. (Date). *Title of book.* City, Province/State: Publisher.

Friedman, T. (2006). *The world is flat: A brief history of the twenty-first century.* New York, NY: Farrar, Straus and Giroux.

BOOKS BY TWO OR THREE AUTHORS

MLA example: For sources with more than one author, the source is alphabetized by the last name of the first author; all other authors are first name first.

Authors. *Title of Book.* City: Publisher, date of publication. Medium of publication.

Levitt, Stephen D., and Steven J. Dubner. *Freakonomics: A Rogue Economist Explores the Hidden Side of Everything.* New York: HarperCollins, 2005. Print.

APA example: When there are two or more authors, list the first author's last name, followed by a comma, and then the first name initial. Use the ampersand (&) and commas between the names.

Authors. (Date). *Title of book.* City, Province/State: Publisher.

Levitt, S., & Dubner, S. (2005). *Freakonomics: A rogue economist explores the hidden side of everything.* New York, NY: HarperCollins.

BOOK BY MORE THAN THREE AUTHORS

MLA example

First authors, et al. *Title of Book.* City: Publisher, Date of Publication. Medium of Publication.

Belenky, Mary Field, et al. *Women's Ways of Knowing.* New York: Basic Books, 1996. Print.

APA example

All authors. (Date). Title of book. City, Province/State: Publisher.

Belenky, M. F., McVicker, B. M., Goldberger, N. R., & Tarule, J. M. (1996). *Women's ways of knowing.* New York, NY: Basic Books.

TWO OR MORE BOOKS BY THE SAME AUTHOR

MLA example: Three typed hyphens are used to replace the same author's name in the second citation.

Friedman, Thomas. *The World Is Flat: A Brief History of the Twenty-first Century.* New York: Farrar, Straus and Giroux. 2006. Print.

---. *Hot, Flat, and Crowded: Why We Need a Green Revolution—And How It Can Renew America.* New York: Farrar, Straus and Giroux. 2008. Print.

APA example: One-author entries by the same author are arranged by putting the earliest publication first.

Friedman, T. (2006). *The world is flat: A brief history of the twenty-first century.* New York, NY: Farrar, Straus and Giroux.

Friedman, T. (2008). *Hot, flat, and crowded: Why we need a green revolution—And how it can renew America.* New York, NY: Farrar, Straus and Giroux.

ARTICLE FROM ANTHOLOGY

Author. "Title of Article." *Title of Anthology.* Ed. Name of editor. Edition number. City: Publisher, date of publication. Page(s). Medium of publication.

White, E. B. "Once More to the Lake." *The Bedford Reader.* Eds. X. J. Kennedy, Dorothy M. Kennedy, and Jane E. Aaron. 11th ed. New York: St. Martin's, 1994. 120-126. Print.

Author, A. A. (Year). Title of chapter. In B. B. Editor (Ed.), *Title of book (Edition number)* (pp. xxx-xxx). City, Province/State: Publisher.

White, E. B. (1994). Once more to the lake. In X. J. Kennedy, D. M. Kennedy, & J. E. Aaron (Eds.), *The Bedford reader* (11th ed.) (pp. 120-126). New York, NY: St. Martin's.

An anthology is a collection of articles by different authors or a collection of writings by the same author. An anthology usually lists the editor(s) who put the collection together.

MLA example

APA example

WEB SITE ARTICLE THAT ONLY APPEARS ONLINE

Author(s). "Title of Article." *Title of Web site.* Name of publisher. Date of publication. Medium of publication. Date of access.

"'It's Just Harmless Entertainment.' Oh Really?" *Parents Television Council.* Parents Television Council. n.d. Web. 3 May 2012.

Author, A. (date). Title of document. Retrieved from http://xxxxxxxxx

"It's just harmless entertainment." Oh really? (n.d.). Retrieved from http://www.parentstv.org/ptc/flyers/factsheet.htm

MLA example: An article for which no author is given is alphabetized by the first word of the title. Use *N.p.* if no information on publisher and *n.d.* if there is no date of publication.

APA example: In reference citations with no author, APA moves the content's title into the author position (with no quotation marks around it). This most commonly occurs for wiki entries, dictionary entries, and unattributed Web site content. If no date is available, use (n.d.).

ONLINE PERIODICAL ARTICLE

Author(s). "Title of the Article." *Journal Title* Date of Publication: page number(s). Medium of publication. Date of access.

Stirling, Ian, and Andrew E. Derocher. "Effects of Climate Warming on Polar Bears: A Review of the Evidence." *Global Change Biology* 18.9 (2012): 2694-706. *Biological Sciences; Environmental Sciences and Pollution Management.* Web. 3 Oct. 2012.

Author, A. (date). Title of article. *Journal Title, Volume*(Issue), page number(s). Retrieved from http://xxxxxxxxx

Stirling, I., & Derocher, A. E. (2012). Effects of climate warming on polar bears: A review of the evidence. *Global Change Biology, 18*(9), 2694-2706. doi: 10.1111/j.1365-2486.2012.02753.x

MLA example

APA example

ARTICLE FROM A DATABASE

Cuvelier, Monique. "Does the Sun Skew Your Judgment?" *Psychology Today* (Nov.-Dec. 2001): 24+. *Academic Search Premier.* Web. 15 Nov. 2011.

MLA example: Both the title of the journal and the database name are italicized. When the article does not appear on consecutive pages, write the first page number followed by a plus sign.

Bryan, B. A., Ward, J., & Hobbs, T. (2008). An assessment of the economic and environmental potential of biomass production in an agricultural region. *Land Use Policy, 25,* 533–549. doi:10.1016/j.landusepol.2007.11.003

APA example: Notice that the DOI number is included after the page numbers.

ONLINE VIDEO

MLA example

Creator's name + Title of video + title of website + date of video + medium + access date

Harvard. "The Many Faces of Chocolate, Lecture 3." *YouTube.* 21 Sept. 2011. Web. 23 May 2012.

APA example

Creator's name + Date video was posted + file type + URL

Harvard. (2011, September 21). The many faces of chocolate, lecture 3 [video file]. Video posted to http://www.youtube.com/watch?v=HS263kc m8Jc&feature=edu&list=PL546CD09EA2399DAB

EXERCISE 16-4 **Integrating and Documenting Sources**

Directions: *Read the following essay written in APA style and identify the student's use of source material in the essay. Then respond to the questions that follow.*

ASSIGNMENT Does TV pose a real threat to young people? Drawing upon research, defend your viewpoint on this issue.

Randy Pothin   Pothin 1
Prof Toma
Soc 188
November 16, 2012

Trouble with the Tube

The student begins with specific details.

They watch in the morning. Then they come home and watch after school. Don't forget every single night. Some children even watch TV in bed. All this television cannot be good for children. They could be reading or playing outside, exercising their imaginations, doing anything besides sitting there like zombies or couch potatoes watching a show they have already seen 25 times. Nevertheless, that's the way it is nowadays. TV is a negative fact of life, impacting education, health, and behaviour.

THESIS STATEMENT
The writer puts the thesis statement at the end of the introduction.

TOPIC SENTENCE
The student begins with a focused topic sentence.

He cites statistical information from a Web site.

One problem with TV is how much time it takes away from schoolwork. According to the Parents Television Council (n.d.), a group of over 800 000 parents who would like to improve the quality of television, the average North American child watches 25 hours of television a week and plays video games for 7 hours. It is hard to see how young people can find time to do any schoolwork. Consider the average high school student who is having a hard time in her classes. She does all of her homework sitting in front of the TV. Some nights she may not do any homework at all because she is watching reruns of her favourite shows. There is only one solution: turn off the TV.

Another problem with TV is its impact on children's health. The physical ramifications of a sedentary lifestyle are enormous and not always obvious until a health crisis occurs. Type II diabetes in children, caused by poor eating habits, too much fast food, and too little physical activity, is at an all-time high. High-blood pressure is also on the rise in children, teenagers, and young adults. According to *Pediatric News,* "Adolescents who had television sets in their bedrooms had less physical activity, poorer dietary habits, and worse school performance than did adolescents without bedroom TVs" (Walsh, 2008, p. 24). As little as an hour each day of moderate physical activity reduces the risk of these health issues substantially. However, many young people do not find time for even this small amount of exercise.

Yet another problem with TV is sex and violence. Sex sells. Evidently, so does violence. That's what people want to see. The Parents Television Council (n.d.) reports that by 18 years of age, the average North American child has seen over 10 000 murders and 200 000 acts of violence on TV. Not all acts of violence kids see on TV are imaginary. Some are real, too real, and must have an impact. Surely, if children see violence, they become violent. Jib Fowles (2001), writing for *Reason* magazine, points out that television's "sinister reputation lives on," even though there is no evidence that it actually causes children to be aggressive (p. 27). He may be right, but what about copy-cat crime? The most horrific examples are the massacres at high schools. After one incident, there are more school shootings. Where do kids get these ideas from if not from television? Then there are young people dealing drugs and shooting each other up in the streets. That probably wouldn't be happening if it weren't for TV. TV glamorizes violence. Turn it off.

One thing is true: North American children are fatter now than they have ever been before, and it is partially the fault of TV. Most of us may be dumber than we used to be, again, the fault of TV. And we are more violent, probably at least partially the fault of TV. There is a bumper sticker going around on some cars. "Kill your TV," it says. It's a violent solution, but maybe that is exactly what we should do. We would be better off without TV, or at least with less of it. Turn it off.

References

Fowles, J. (2011, March). The whipping boy. *Reason,* 27–28.

Grossman, D. & DeGaetano, G. (1999). *Stop teaching our kids to kill: A call to action against TV, movie, and video game violence.* New York, NY: Crown Publishers.

Parents Television Council. (n.d.). "It's just harmless entertainment." Oh really? Retrieved from http://www.parentstv.org/ptc/facts/mediafacts.asp

Walsh, N. (2008). Teens' bedroom TVs may hurt activity level, diet, grades. *Pediatric News. 42*(5), 24. doi: 10.1016/S0031-398X(08)70220-0

He ends his paragraph with an emphatic plea.

TOPIC SENTENCE
Use of the transition term *another* moves the reader smoothly to the next major point of the essay.

He presents more statistical information.

"One thing is true" signals the paper is coming to a close. The conclusion paragraph summarizes content from the essay.

The student repeats "turn it off," echoing the solution posed at the end of the preceding paragraph.

APA EXAMPLE

Works Cited

Fowles, Jib. "The Whipping Boy." *Reason* Mar. 2001: 27–28. Print.

Grossman, Dave, and Gloria DeGaetano. *Stop Teaching Our Kids to Kill: A Call to Action Against TV, Movie, and Video Game Violence.* New York: Crown, 1999. Print.

"'It's Just Harmless Entertainment.' Oh Really?" *Parents Television Council.* Parents Television Council. n.d. Web. 21 Oct. 2008.

Walsh, Nancy. "Teens' Bedroom TVs May Hurt Activity Level, Diet, Grades." *Pediatric News.* 42.5 (2008): 24. *Academic OneFile.* Web. 31 Oct. 2008. <doi:10.1016/S0031-398X(08)70220-0>.

MLA example: MLA does not require a DOI or URL unless your instructor requests it. If you are providing a DOI or URL, place it after the date of access and enclose in angle brackets.

DISCUSSION QUESTIONS

1. What purpose does the student's source material serve in this paper?

_____

2. Do the in-text citations effectively support the author's points?

_____

3. Does the list of Works Cited or References accurately reflect the sources cited in the essay?

_____

EXERCISE 16-5 **Drafting and Revising Your Documented Essay**

Directions: *Using your tentative outline as a guide (Exercise 16-3), write a draft of your documented essay. Integrate information from your research into the essay, including in-text citations as needed to document your sources. Provide a list of Works Cited (MLA) or References (APA). When you finish your draft, use the checklist below to focus your work, revising and editing your essay.*

DOCUMENTED ESSAY CHECKLIST

_____ The essay has an introduction, body, and conclusion.

_____ The introduction invites the reader into the essay.

_____ The thesis is focused, effective, develops three ideas, and uses parallel structure.

_____ Each body paragraph has a focused topic sentence that points back to the thesis. The paragraphs have unity; they each develop only one topic.

_____ The sentences within each paragraph and the body paragraphs are arranged logically and coherently.

_____ The paragraphs have specific supporting details and follow one of the writing patterns.

_____ Facts and statistics, cases and examples, and quotations from research support the topic sentences. Any information borrowed or quoted from another source is properly cited and referenced.

_____ Key words from the assignment are repeated; transition words are used appropriately throughout the essay.

_____ Through critical reading and revision, relevant material has been added, deleted, or reorganized.

_____ The conclusion brings the essay to a close by restating the thesis, giving a reason or purpose for the essay, or explaining how the readers can use what they have learned in the essay.

_____ The conclusion does not introduce new ideas that were not already discussed in the body of the essay.

_____ A list of Works Cited or References, following MLA or APA guidelines, is included.

_____ The essay has an appropriate and interesting title.

_____ The essay has been proofread for spelling, capitalization, common errors, and sentence variety.

CHAPTER REVIEW

Take a moment and reflect on what you have learned about the documented essay.

■ ELEMENTS OF THE DOCUMENTED ESSAY

- *Focus on problem or issue*
- *Locate or gather information*
- *Process information*
- *Integrate what you have learned into your essay using a proper citation style*

■ GET STARTED

☐ Locate information

- *Use key words in search for appropriate academic material*
- *Internet, databases, periodical literature, reference books*

■ PROCESS INFORMATION

☐ Type of information

- *Facts and statistics, authoritative opinion, cases and examples*

☐ Take notes

- *All source information for Works Cited or References; match source information to points in outline; be selective and brief*

☐ Integrate sources

- *In-text citation; frame source information into your own sentences*

■ DOCUMENT SOURCE

☐ Cite different types of sources

- *Use variety of sources for balanced approach*

THINK FIRST

Write a paragraph discussing what you know about studying for and writing in-class exams. Cite and discuss specific classes and the instructors who provided you with this instruction. Organize your paragraph by looking first at those ideas and strategies that are not as useful and then move to more useful ones.

The Heat Is On

Pressure. We have all felt it: the intensity in the air, the sense of urgency, and the lump in your throat. In an academic setting, the greatest pressure arrives at exam time, although regular quizzes and in-class writing may constantly keep you on your toes. This stress does not end with graduation. Throughout life, you will face high-stakes, time-sensitive situations, and the sooner you learn to cope with them, the better. If you can write a well-crafted essay in the pressure cooker of a classroom, you will find it that much easier to deal with "pressurized" situations in your nonacademic life. It is almost midnight on April 30, and you suddenly realize you forgot to file your taxes—no problem, right?

DISCUSSION

Turn and talk to a classmate about writing under pressure—a specific time when you performed (or did not perform) well under pressure. When and where? What subject? How did you prepare for the writing?

Working Against the Deadline

The working world is filled with deadlines. Clients need answers, projects must be submitted, bosses demand reports . . . and all this work must be completed by a specific time on a particular day. Even the best-prepared professionals sometimes find themselves in the deadline crunch, with work that needs to be done yesterday. Unfortunately, time pressure is never an excuse for lack of quality. Mastering the ability to work well in a limited amount of time will make you a valuable contributor to whatever field you work in.

DISCUSSION

Turn and talk to a classmate about working under pressure on the job. How do you maintain your composure to guarantee you do your best work?

Showing What You Know

Instructors cannot grade you on what you know; what you can *show* you know is what counts. No matter how well prepared you are, if you write an incoherent, threadbare essay exam, your instructor will likely assume that your knowledge and ideas are just as incoherent and threadbare. Bridging the gap between what you have learned and what you can write is an essential academic skill. Learning to write an effective exam essay is an important step toward closing this gap. The techniques you use to master the essay exam will help you surmount other academic tasks as well.

BRAINSTORM

Brainstorm a list of steps to prepare for writing under pressure. What can you do at home to prepare in advance? What can you do in the classroom, as you write, that will help you be successful?

At a Glance

THE IN-CLASS ESSAY AT A GLANCE

Like the paragraphs and essays you have practised writing in this text, effective in-class writing includes topic sentences, supporting details, and transitions to make connections within and across paragraphs. You do not have a lot of time, so in-class writing assignments must get to the point. Introductions and conclusions are held to a minimum. To persuade your instructor that you know the content, in your answer you must make detailed references to the course material. Details matter. Finally, in-class writing is usually not personal in focus. Unless you are specifically asked to talk about yourself, you should maintain a steady focus on the question and how it relates to course content by using third person (i.e., *it, they*) in your writing, rather than first person (*I, me*).

The In-Class Essay at a Glance

When you are writing an in-class assignment and do not have access to the details of your sources of research, check to see how your instructor would like you to do in-text citations.

ASSIGNMENT   Discuss the research we have reviewed on doing homework in this unit of study. What is the connection between doing homework and learning and academic achievement? How important are age and grade level? Please relate your answer to your own preparation for post-secondary studies. You may use notes during the exam period.

THESIS STATEMENT
The writer provides a general overview of her response to the assignment.

TOPIC SENTENCE
The writer echoes key terms from the essay question.

SUPPORTING DETAILS
The student refers to specific articles by title. The articles describe research on her subject. She reports what they say.

ORDER AND TRANSITIONS
She uses a transition phrase to show she is shifting to a contrasting view of homework.

The research on the role of homework in academic achievement has been contradictory; some studies say homework improves learning and achievement; others caution against assigning too much homework, especially drills.

Studies support two conflicting views of homework's role in learning and academic achievement. **Some of the most interesting research** comes from two Penn State researchers. In the article "Too Much Homework" the researchers state that many instructors use homework as a drill for memorization. Homework should be used for helping students understand and comprehend course content. Making homework all about drill and repetition is not a good way to increase a student's understanding of the material. **On the other hand,** in the *Atlantic Monthly* study, Jonathon Rauch argues that homework is the best way of increasing "time on task." According to his research, North American students spend far less time doing homework than students in other countries. Rauch cites the National Assessment of Educational Progress, which indicates that American

17-year-olds do less than one hour of homework each night. Those students who do have homework learn more and achieve more. Harris Cooper, an educational psychologist says, "The effect of homework can be impressive." Homework, according to these experts, is valuable, but there are limits.

Studies also show that age or grade level should be taken into consideration when homework is assigned. In the article "Yes, Johnny, Homework Is Important" researchers from the American Psychological Association mention that doing homework in lower grades is important for helping students develop study skills, even though the benefits of study at home might not show immediately. **However**, homework can also have a negative effect on younger students. Too much homework can result in unfavourable attitudes toward school in lower grades. Rauch also points out this negative effect. He writes, "For young children homework appears not to be particularly helpful." It can turn off young kids to learning. The problem is worse in homes in which parents cannot or do not help young children with homework. If parents do not make homework come first, students may think that it is not that important and not complete their assignments. Worse, in those homes where parents cannot help, children may associate homework with frustration and anger. For homework to be effective, teachers have to assign the right amount. Further, if they communicate well with parents, homework is more likely to improve academic achievement.

Evidently, the National Assessment of Educational Progress did not talk to my school; at my high school, homework was a given, and there was a lot of it. The school offered advanced placement courses, which always had college and university levels of homework. On a regular basis, I would come home with about four to five hours a night needed for studying and doing homework. It was a stressful time then, but I learned about time management. Now I am in college, and I see that I was well prepared by my high school for the demands of post-secondary studies.

In addition to summarizing major points, the student uses a short quotation to demonstrate her knowledge of the material.

TOPIC SENTENCE
The student goes immediately to the next major point in the assignment.

TRANSITION
The sentence beginning "However" allows the student to switch to a contrasting view.

SUPPORTING DETAILS
The student draws on other research the class has covered, demonstrating she has mastered the content.

In addition to summarizing major points, the student uses a short quotation to demonstrate her knowledge of the material.

TOPIC SENTENCE
In this part of her answer, the student shifts to first person, talking about herself. This paragraph addresses the third part of the essay question.

DISCUSSION QUESTIONS

1. How would you describe the introduction of this essay?

2. This essay is a mixture of fact and opinion. Where do you see the student expressing her opinion? Why has the student not used in-text citation?

3. Reread the assignment. How is the organization of the essay based on the assignment?

ELEMENTS OF IN-CLASS WRITING

Because in-class writing is timed, you must quickly determine the assignment's focus and how much detail to provide in your answer.

- *The assignment:* An assignment may be a question, a series of questions, or a series of statements directing your attention to the focus of your writing. In the at-a-glance example in this chapter, the student responds to some questions and statements in the assignment instructions. You must be certain that you are answering the question and not going off on a tangent or giving an unrelated answer. Read the instructions twice to make sure you understand what is expected of you.
- *Topic sentences:* Topic sentences echo key terms from the assignment. Assignment instructions written as a series of questions or statements usually take multiple paragraphs to answer. In the at-a-glance example, the student writes a paragraph focusing on each specific part or sentence of the assignment instructions.
- *Specific details:* An essay exam demonstrates how much you know about the subject matter in question. The answer you formulate refers to facts, examples, proper names and dates, and important concepts covered by in-class learning and the textbook.

TYPES OF IN-CLASS WRITING

In-class writing is widely used to evaluate learning in college and university classes. While the content may vary from class to class, most instructors have similar expectations. First of all, you need to demonstrate that you have met the course learning outcomes. Instructors look for answers written in complete sentences. They also look for detailed answers that show you have paid attention in class and retained important course content. You will encounter in-class writing that falls into three categories:

- Sentence-length short answers
- Paragraph-length short answers
- Essay-length answers

Be aware of the evaluation criteria that your instructor will use to grade your assignments.

Sentence-Length Short Answers

You will often use sentence-length short answers for definitions. Answers should be formulated in complete sentences. An effective sentence-length definition begins with the term to be defined, contains a present-tense linking verb (for example, *is* and *are*), and ends with an elaborated idea. Here are two responses in which a student is asked to define the term *precipitation*.

Inadequate Definition

Precipitation—rain.

Satisfactory Definition

> Precipitation *is* any form of water or moisture that condenses in the
> upper atmosphere and falls to earth, including snow, sleet, rain, mist,
> and dew.

The first definition is incomplete—both in what it says about precipitation and how it is formulated. In contrast, the second definition is detailed and specific. It is also a complete sentence. The second definition would receive full marks while the first definition would not.

The form of an effective short-answer definition varies. For the sake of practice, use this template, which shows you how to elaborate on a this-is-that statement:

This-Is-That Statement

> Alliteration is a literary device.
>
> Education is a process.

This-Is-That Statement + Elaboration

> Alliteration is a literary device in which two or more consecutive words
> begin with the same consonant.
>
> Education is a process that imparts a body of knowledge and trains the
> minds of students.

EXERCISE 17-1 **Sentence-Length Short Answers**

Directions: *Write definitions for the following terms using the examples above as templates. Consult a dictionary if necessary, but paraphrase rather than copy the definitions you find. Be sure to write in complete sentences.*

1. ethics _____

2. mitochondria _____

3. collaboration _____

4. activist _____

5. latitude _____

EXERCISE 17-2 **Defining Key Terms in Your Courses**

Directions: *Select important terms from another course (or courses) you are taking and define them. If necessary, use study guides as well as textbooks from your courses to find relevant ideas and details to help you formulate your definitions. Use the same sentence structure you practised in Exercise 17-1.*

Paragraph-Length Short Essay Answers

Paragraph-length short essay answers will usually be evaluated on three qualities: (1) focus, (2) number and relevance of supporting details, and (3) grammatical and mechanical correctness. To focus your paragraph-length answer, identify the key terms in the question by underlining, circling, or highlighting them to make sure you are answering the question correctly. Make those terms part of your paragraph's topic sentence. Try to repeat the terms at least once in the paragraph-length answer.

> **Short Essay Question:** State one drawback or problem with using the philosophy of utilitarianism.

> **Key Terms:** one drawback, problem, philosophy of utilitarianism
>
> **Topic Sentence:** <u>One drawback</u> to using the <u>philosophy of utilitarianism</u> is that actions or ways of life that have no observable use or effect cannot be evaluated as good.

In Part 2, you learned about the different patterns of organization and how to write effective paragraphs using them. Read questions carefully to see if they ask for answers related to a specific pattern—for instance, examples, causes or effects, or a comparison of two ideas. (See Table 17-1 for language that indicates which pattern of organization you should use when answering a specific question. If your instructors have used additional terms in their assignments, you can add them to the table.) For example, if the question asks you to discuss the three main consequences of the Canadian Charter of

TABLE 17.1

PATTERNS OF ORGANIZATION AND TEST QUESTIONS	
Pattern of Organization	**Test Question Language to Notice**
Description	*Describe . . .*
Example	*Discuss the two (three, four . . .) main . . .*
Narration	*Tell what happened when . . .*
Process	*Explain how . . .*
Classification	*What types of . . .*
Cause and effect	*Explain why . . .* *What were the consequences of . . .*
Comparison and contrast	*How is . . . similar to . . .* *How does . . . differ from . . .* *How has . . . changed . . .*
Definition	*Define . . .*
Argument	*Make a case for . . .* *State your opinion . . .*

Rights and Freedoms, you should provide an answer with three main points. Moreover, your discussion of the three points should have roughly equal emphasis. For a 15-point question, you can assume that each of the main points in your answer is worth 5 points.

Short Essay Question: Explain three ways in which mass media act as agents of gender socialization during childhood.

Key Terms: three ways, mass media, gender socialization, childhood

Topic Sentence: The <u>mass media</u> act as agents of <u>gender socialization</u> during <u>childhood</u> in <u>three important ways</u>.

Pattern of Organization: illustration and example

Finally, always use proper grammar and mechanics in any writing you do in college or university or at work. Although you may think, "Well, this is not an English class, so *how* I write is not as important as *what* I write," nothing could be further from the truth. All your instructors care about the way you write. Using proper grammar and mechanics will add points to your score, while poorly edited writing will lead to points being deducted.

EXERCISE 17-3 Short Essay Answers

Directions: *Underline the key terms in the following short essay questions and indicate what pattern of organization you would use in your answers to them.*

1. What were some of the events that Pierre Berton reconstructs in his book *The Last Spike*?

Pattern of Organization: _____

2. What is DNA (deoxyribonucleic acid)? What information is stored in DNA?

Pattern of Organization: _____

3. Explain how Steinbeck did both primary and secondary research as he prepared to write *The Grapes of Wrath*. Why would an author research information before writing a book?

Pattern of Organization: _____

4. Describe two general differences between visual merchandising in a retail establishment and an online marketing Web site.

Pattern of Organization: _____

5. Explain the principles of child development in the Montessori theory.

Pattern of Organization: _____

Essay-Length Answers

On an essay test, you will be evaluated on your essay's focus, inclusion of supporting details, and mechanical and grammatical correctness. You may use more than one pattern of organization as you formulate your answer. If you do not know what the essay question will be in advance, prepare for the test by anticipating possible questions. (See the list of tips for test preparation at the end of this chapter.)

Here are some suggestions for what to do at the beginning of and during an essay exam to provide the best possible answers.

At the Beginning of an Essay Test

1. Underline key terms in the essay question.
2. Drawing on your memory of the material you have studied, or of a pretest outline you made, list key terms, concepts, and details from the course content that you must mention in your essay.
3. Identify patterns of organization that will help you organize and focus your answers.

Talk about it ▶▶▶

In which courses do you write essay-length answers? Do you write in-class or at home? How do you prepare for this writing?

While Writing Your Essay Answer

1. Include key terms from the test question in your first sentence. Double-space your answer to allow room for revisions and for editing your writing.
2. Get to the point. Avoid long introduction paragraphs and wordy preludes.
3. When ideas occur to you as you write, make quick changes and jot down additions to your outline.
4. Place check marks in the margin of your paper to signal those areas that require attention during the editing phase of your writing.
5. Use the pattern of organization called for in the question. If you are asked to cite examples, be sure to explain each example using relevant details. If you are asked to discuss causes and effects, be sure to use those key terms and provide sufficient elaboration.
6. Keep an eye on your outline. Check off key details as you integrate them into your essay; make a point of mentioning additional key terms, concepts, and details from the course in your answer.
7. Leave enough time at the end of the exam period for proofreading. Look for check marks you have made in the margin. Erase or lightly cross out misspelled words or grammatical errors and make corrections. Unless you are told otherwise, do not copy your paper over.

EXERCISE 17-4 **Essay-Length Answers**

Directions: *Read the following essay questions and underline the key terms in each. Indicate what pattern of organization you would use in answering each question and how many paragraphs you would need for a detailed answer. (*Suggestion: *Plan to write one or two paragraphs for each key term in the test question.)*

EXAMPLE

Canadian History Test Question: Explain how the clash of the English and French empires affected the settlement of what is now Canada.

Pattern(s) of Organization: <u>definition, cause and effect</u>

Number of Paragraphs: <u>one on English objectives, one on French objectives,</u>
<u>one on conflict between England and France, one on consequences for North</u>
<u>America</u>

1. What were your perceptions of geography before signing up for this class? Has your initial view of geography changed? If so, how and why? What do you see as the value of utilizing geography's approach to address contemporary problems and issues?

Pattern(s) of Organization: _____

Number of Paragraphs: _____

_____

2. Define the "shadow" side of the personality. Use Goffman's ideas on the "presentation of self" to explain how the shadow side develops. Discuss one of your shadow traits and use Goffman's ideas to explain how it developed.

Pattern(s) of Organization: _____

Number of Paragraphs: _____

_____

3. Describe a set of symptoms that characterize one kind of mental disorder. Include how a person affected would think, feel, and behave. What, in your opinion, would be the best support to give a person with the symptoms you describe? In your answer, refer to at least three symptoms in detail.

Pattern(s) of Organization: _____

Number of Paragraphs: _____

_____

EXERCISE 17-5 **In-Class Writing in Your Courses**

Directions: *Survey members of your class for the types of writing they have done on tests. If possible, collect specific questions for four or five tests. Analyze the language of each test question and circle the type of answer required (sentence, paragraph, or essay), list the key terms, recommend the best thinking and writing strategies for answering the question, and estimate the number of paragraphs (if an essay) required to answer it.*

How to Prepare for In-Class Writing

Students who perform well during an in-class writing assignment have a reliable preparation process. Preparation consists of both general and specific actions. On the day of the test, you should be physically and mentally ready to do your best work. Here are some tips for general preparation. Use these for any test situation.

As you look over your test or exam, use the back of the exam booklet or the inside cover to jot down ideas that come to you. If you experience "writer's block," begin by brainstorming and outlining to get you started.

- Get a good night's rest.
- Eat a good breakfast and, if you have more than one exam in one day, pack snacks to eat between exams. Also, be sure to take a bathroom break before you enter the exam room. It's probably not a good idea to drink several cups of coffee just before your exam since the exam monitors won't want to let you leave the exam room during the exam.
- Find out when and where the exam is, how long it will be, and what its value is in your overall grade in the class.
- Arrive early, with the necessary materials (identification, pencil, pen, paper, dictionary). Leave cell phones off and do not take other electronic devices with you.
- Read all the directions carefully. Look through the entire test before you begin and check the value allotted to each question. This way you can plan to spend more time on the questions worth the most marks.
- Budget your time properly based on the number of questions and the point values of questions.

CHAPTER REVIEW

Take a moment and reflect on what you have learned about writing in class.

■ ELEMENTS OF IN-CLASS WRITING

- *Read and follow instructions; determine type of writing expected; in topic sentence, echo key terms from instructions*

■ TYPES OF IN-CLASS WRITING

□ Sentence-length short answers

- *This-is-that statement; this-is-that statement + elaboration*

□ Paragraph-length short essay answers

- *Focus,/supporting details, grammatical/mechanical correctness*

□ Essay-length answers

- *Outline, pattern of organization*

□ How to prepare for in-class writing

- *Prepare before class*
- *Refer to Tips for Test tables*

Of course, along with being physically and mentally ready, you must study the material you will be tested on to the best of your ability. Most instructors indicate what will be emphasized in their exams. As they lecture, they may explicitly state, "this material will be on the exam," or they may underscore important themes through repetition, notes and outlines on the board, and the use of PowerPoint presentations. Take full advantage of all these clues to what will be on the exam. There are also a number of specific actions you can take to get ready for a test.

SPECIFIC TIPS FOR TEST PREPARATION

- Review all notes you took during lectures and class discussions.
- Review the course syllabus and outline, circling unit titles and themes. Get as much information about the exam or test in advance, such as the type of test it will be and how long you have to finish it.
- Review reading material, particularly any study guides provided by the textbook. Check if your instructor can give you practice tests or exams.
- Review previous quizzes and tests. Examine the kinds of errors you made and try to figure out how you can avoid these.
- Review any annotations you made when you read the textbook.
- Generate possible questions based on the themes and topics your instructor most emphasized in class and lectures.
- Formulate answers to possible questions. Think of a thesis statement, identify the main points that support it, write an outline, and practise drafting an answer. Doing so will help you remember information and make it easier for you to write under pressure.

The Simple Sentence

The simple sentence is a building block for more sophisticated thinking and writing. Learning the grammar and mechanics of the simple sentence will enable you to write more complicated and effective sentences. All good writing begins with the simple sentence structure.

An Introduction to the Simple Sentence

A simple sentence expresses a complete thought or idea. It makes a meaningful statement that another person can process and respond to. A simple sentence, or independent clause, is a sentence with one subject-verb pair.

> Awakened by the sound of gunfire in the distance.
> A park with a playground is two blocks from our house.

The first example does not express a complete idea. There is reference to gunfire, but nothing definitive is said about it. *Who was awakened? What happened?* The second example, in contrast, expresses a complete idea. The reader can process and respond to the statement. *That's interesting. Do you ever go to this park?*

EXERCISE 18-1 The Sentence as Complete Idea

Directions: *Write CI next to each of the following items that expresses a complete idea.*

_____ 1. Sparkling blue eyes with a dash of gold in the middle.

_____ 2. A look of pure distrust enveloped their cola-stained faces.

_____ 3. Girls and boys holding hands, most of them dancing, swaying back and forth to the music as if they were hypnotized.

_____ 4. The students met back in November of 2011.

_____ 5. The employee was living life day by day, wondering what tomorrow would bring.

_____ 6. A normal day with many phases and challenges that await.

_____ 7. Every Friday, on the eve of graduation day, as we called it.

_____ 8. The workers would go to Autozone to get materials for the job.

_____ 9. As the college students sit thinking back a couple years to their childhood days.

_____10. It seems like yesterday that the two entrepreneurs met.

Find Subjects and Predicates

Typical simple sentence word order in English is subject, verb, object: S + V + O.

In a simple sentence, the subject usually comes before the predicate.

A sentence contains two parts: a subject and a predicate. The **subject** is who or what a sentence is about, and can be singular, plural, or compound. The **predicate** contains the verb and related words and phrases to express the subject's action or state of being. More than one verb may appear in a simple sentence, which is called a compound verb. In the example below, the sentence's subject is underlined; the predicate is double-underlined.

The entire Wilson **family** *drove* to the seashore on Sunday.

Usually a sentence's subject and predicate can be reduced to one word each: the simple subject and the simple verb. The simple subject of this sentence is *family,* and the simple verb, or action, of the sentence is *drove.*

In the next example, the subject is underlined, the predicate double-underlined. The sentence's simple subject is *hair,* and the simple verb, or action, is *blew.*

Alice's long dark **hair** *blew* in the salty ocean breeze.

Hint: To find the verb in a sentence, look for the word that expresses action and has tense (places the sentence in the past, present, or future). In the preceding example, the verb *blew* can be written in different tenses: *blow, will blow, had blown.*

EXERCISE 18-2 **Identifying the Complete Subject and Predicate**

Directions: *Identify the subject and predicate in each of the following sentences. To find the verb, look for the word that expresses action or can be written in different tenses. Underline the complete subject; double-underline the complete predicate.*

1. The elderly woman with the funny hat walked her dog around the subdivision every morning.

2. Robert caught two salmon after getting skunked on his first day of fishing.

3. The ladies in the neighbourhood swap ideas about gardening every year in April.

4. The regional health department declared the food supply to be safe.

5. Scientists who study outer space no longer consider Pluto to be a planet.

6. Each student sketches the parts of the cell before writing a description of the lab activity.

7. Computer technology, more than any other consumer product, gets better and cheaper with every passing year.

8. Years ago auto manufacturers worried very little about alternative fuels and their possible use in the near future.

9. Dutch elm disease totally wiped out most of the trees in our community.

10. Ms. Howard will join the departmental meeting later this afternoon.

The Subject

A sentence's subject is usually found near the beginning of the sentence. The subject performs the action or is the main focus of the sentence. The most common simple subjects to look for in a simple sentence are nouns, pronouns, and gerunds.

TYPES OF SUBJECTS		
Noun	person, place, thing, or idea	<u>Unemployment</u> is on everyone's mind these days.
Pronoun	a word taking the place of a noun	<u>It</u> has increased in the past 16 months.
Gerund	a word for an activity, ending in -ing	<u>Finding a good job</u> is easier for those with a post-secondary degree.

NOUNS

A **noun** names a person, place, thing, or idea, and it can be the subject of a sentence.

> The little **girl** on the plane *cried* through much of the flight.

This sentence has three nouns: *girl, plane,* and *flight.* The noun acting as subject comes near the beginning of the sentence. This sentence is primarily about the girl. She performed the action in the sentence. She cried. *Girl* is the simple subject of the sentence.

PRONOUNS

Pronouns take the place of nouns or other pronouns.

Do not use subject and pronoun for the same grammatical function: "The little girl ~~she~~ cried through much of the flight."

TYPES OF PRONOUNS		
Personal Pronouns	**Indefinite Pronouns**	
I you she he we they	it all each few none any either neither something	everything several somebody someone anybody anyone everyone one

Pronouns eliminate endless repetition in our speaking and writing. Just as nouns can be the subject of a sentence, a pronoun replacing a noun can also be the subject of a sentence.

> The little <u>girl</u> on the plane cried through much of the flight.
> <u>She</u> finally went to sleep near the end of the flight.

In this example, the pronoun *she* substitutes for "the little girl" and acts as the subject of the second sentence. The little girl did something: she went to sleep. *She* is the subject of the second sentence.

GERUNDS

A **gerund**, the -ing form of a verb, is the name of an activity. Activities such as running, reading, thinking, or stopping can also be the subject of a sentence.

> The little <u>girl</u> on the plane cried through much of the flight.
> <u>She</u> finally went to sleep near the end of the flight.

Flying can be very difficult for small children.

It can also be hard on people around them.

In the third sentence, the gerund *flying* acts as the subject. In that sentence, flying is what is being talked about.

HOW TO FIND THE SIMPLE SUBJECT

The simple subject is the most important part of the complete subject. To identify a sentence's simple subject, ask the following questions:

1. Who or what did the action?
2. What is being described?

The simple subject is usually a noun or pronoun. It is the doer of the action or the thing being described. The answers to these questions will be the simple subject of the sentence.

> The supervisor's **statements** about female employees *got him in a lot of trouble.*

Who or what did the action? Who or what is being described? The supervisor's *statements* did the action. They got the supervisor in trouble.

> The underground parking **structure** was *crammed* with construction equipment.

Who or what did the action? Who or what is being described? The underground parking structure is described as crammed. Therefore, the *structure* is the simple subject of the sentence.

EXERCISE 18-3   **Identifying the Simple Subject**

Directions: *Find the simple subjects in the following sentences. (a) Write the one-word simple subject in the space provided. (b) Then indicate whether it is a noun, pronoun, or gerund by circling the correct answer.*

1. a) Offenders of whatever age and social class are promptly arrested and put in jail.

   _____ are promptly arrested and put in jail.

   b) noun   pronoun   gerund

2. a) They then pay a significant fine and are asked to attend classes designed to improve their behaviour.

   _____ pay a significant fine and are asked to attend classes designed to improve their behaviour.

   b) noun   pronoun   gerund

3. a) Finding just the right electronic toys on the market today is a big headache for parents of small children.

   _____ is a big headache for parents of small children.

   b) noun   pronoun   gerund

4. a) It takes hours of time and commitment.

    _____ takes hours of time and commitment.

    b) noun   pronoun   gerund

5. a) Swimming across Lake Ontario was Annaleise Carr's goal in August 2012.

    _____ was Annaleise Carr's goal from a very early age.

    b) noun   pronoun   gerund

6. a) Hovering over the city, the storm clouds dumped five inches of rain on a community already suffering the effects of inclement weather.

    _____ dumped five inches of rain on a community already suffering the effects of inclement weather.

    b) noun   pronoun   gerund

7. a) Nobody at the meeting expected things to end with a resolution to change school policy in such a drastic way.

    _____ expected things to end with a resolution to change school policy in such a drastic way.

    b) noun   pronoun   gerund

8. a) The eccentric old gentleman living above the barber shop, a decorated World War II veteran and a gifted photographer, will exhibit his photos and talk about his life in the next community cultural activities event.

    _____ will exhibit his photos and talk about his life in the next community cultural activities event.

    b) noun   pronoun   gerund

9. a) The living will, a document that expresses an individual's end-of-life wishes, can make a family's and a physician's decisions easier at difficult times.

    _____ can make a family's and a physician's decisions easier at difficult times.

    b) noun   pronoun   gerund

10. a) Sitting around swapping stories and generally taking it easy is many people's idea of well-spent holiday time.

    _____ is many people's idea of well-spent holiday time.

    b) noun   pronoun   gerund

SUBJECTS AND PREPOSITIONAL PHRASES

A prepositional phrase consists of a preposition and an object. The phrase provides information about time and place, stating the relationships between one noun and another. A list of common prepositions used at the beginning of prepositional phrases can be found in the box on the following page.

The object of a preposition will never be the subject of a sentence. Place the prepositional phrase in brackets so that you know it is not the subject of the sentence.

The **singer** (*in the band*) is still unavailable.

Here the prepositional phrase is "in the band": *in* is the preposition, "band" is the object. Ask, *Who or what did the action? Who or what is being described?* "Singer" is what is being described; "in the band" describes the simple subject "singer."

The sentence states that the singer is unavailable, not that the band is unavailable. "Band" is part of the complete subject, but it is not the simple subject of the sentence. Here is another example:

The **owner** (*of the professional football team*) will sell his interest to the highest bidder.

"Owner" is the subject. The owner will sell his interest. The prepositional phrase "of the professional football team" describes "owner." "Team" is not the subject. The team is not selling; the owner is selling.

COMMON PREPOSITIONS

about	above	across	after	against
along	among	around	at	before
behind	below	beneath	beside	between
beyond	but	by	despite	during
except	for	from	in	inside
into	like	near	of	off
on	onto	out	outside	over
past	since	through	throughout	till
to	toward	under	underneath	until
up	upon	with	within	without

EXERCISE 18-4 **Simple Subjects and Prepositional Phrases**

Directions: *Cross out the prepositional phrases and circle the simple subject in each of the following sentences.*

1. For the next three weeks, science classes will meet in temporary classrooms.

2. The piping plover population, along with other beach-nesting birds, has been threatened by cats and dogs.

3. The largest organ in the body is the skin.

4. Most salespeople in the organization go on calls with their computers under their arms.

5. All rescue operations except those involving the military have been halted until further notice.

Talk about it

Check your last assignment. How many prepositional phrases did you use? What do you notice about prepositional phrases and punctuation?

6. The impact of poor nutrition on health deserves greater emphasis in medical education.

7. Alcohol consumption among high school students is on the rise.

8. In the opinion of most health care professionals, a sedentary lifestyle is more dangerous than smoking for students' health.

9. Investors, in a state of shock over recent revelations, scrambled for their cellphones.

10. Readers of detective fiction, along with assorted film buffs, showed up for the book signing early Saturday evening.

SUBJECTS IN QUESTIONS AND COMMANDS

To find the simple subject in a question, turn the question into a statement.

Question: Why can't Bill stop smoking?
Statement: Bill can't stop smoking because he is nervous.
Simple Subject: Bill

Question: When will classes begin?
Statement: Classes will begin on August 23.
Simple Subject: Classes

In commands, the simple subject is always "you." It is understood that "you" is the subject, so it is not necessary to write "you" as the subject.

Look for the lost keys.

This is a command, also known as an imperative. *Who should look for the keys? You should look for them.*

EXERCISE 18-5 **Simple Subjects, Questions, and Commands**

Directions: *Find the simple subjects in the following sentences. Rewrite each question as a statement that answers a question, and circle the simple subject of the statement. For commands, rewrite the sentence using "you" for the subject.*

1. When did the student's mother get out of the hospital?

_____

2. At the beginning of class, open your books and take out your homework.

_____

3. What is the most important idea about being a Canadian?

_____

4. Before the plane pushes back from the runway, be sure to fasten your seat belt.

_____

5. Never underestimate the power of a good idea whose time has come.

_____

6. When did the black mould first appear to affect the atmosphere in the classroom portable?

_____

7. In the interest of maintaining a quality work environment, please refrain from smoking on the premises.

_____

8. How does a university or college athlete attend hours of practices every week and also maintain good grades?

_____

9. Where is the best pizza in town?

_____

10. Divide and conquer.

_____

EXERCISE 18-6 **Additional Practice Finding Simple Subjects**

Directions: *Apply what you have learned in Exercises 18-2, 18-3, and 18-4 to find the simple subjects of the following sentences. Write the simple subjects in the space provided. For sentences written as commands, write* you *in the space provided.*

1. Before buying a dog, the Corwins visited an animal shelter located in their city.

_____

2. For information on budgeting and saving money, listen to "Money Talks" on CBC Radio One.

_____

3. He will never steer his employees wrong.

_____

4. Don't leave home without your credit card.

_____

5. Arriving late is never a good idea.

_____

6. What is the worst thing that can happen in a national election?

_____

7. Flying over the devastation left by the floods, rescue workers and journalists alike watched intently for survivors.

_____

8. Many students never have quite enough time to finish their homework.

_____

9. Open your test booklets and begin work.

_____

10. The best math teacher in the college was recognized with an award.

The Predicate

All sentences have a predicate. The **predicate** consists of the verb, as well as words and/or phrases that modify the verb. A verb can express an action (physical or mental). Linking verbs connect the subject to a description in the predicate. A state-of-being verb establishes a fact or condition about the subject. Verbs can be in the past, present, or future.

ACTION VERBS

Your writing often focuses on a series of events or actions. In these instances, you rely heavily on **action verbs**, which express the action of the subject. When you analyze a sentence, use the subject to help identify the action verb. Ask these questions:

What did the subject do?

What action took place?

Also, you will know you have found the action verb if you can write it in different tenses.

The oldest **sister** always *worked* harder than the rest of the family.

The subject of this sentence is "sister." What did the sister do? What action took place? The action verb is *worked*. It states what action the subject ("sister") did. The complete predicate, *always worked harder than the rest of the family,* describes how the sister worked. Note that the verb can be written in different tenses: *my sister worked, my sister works, my sister will work.*

EXERCISE 18-7 **Identifying Action Verbs**

Directions: *Underline the simple subjects and double-underline the action verbs in the following sentences. To be sure you have found the action verbs, write each one in the past, present, and future tense in the space provided.*

1. For the next three weeks, sciences classes will meet in temporary classrooms.

Action Verb: _____

2. Dogs threatened the piping plover population and other beach-nesting birds.

Action Verb: _____

3. The number of cosmetic surgeries increased dramatically.

Action Verb: _____

4. Most salespeople in the organization go on calls with their computers under their arms.

Action Verb: _____

5. All rescue operations except those involving the military have been halted until further notice.

Action Verb: _____

6. The study of nutrition and its impact on health deserves greater emphasis in medical education.

Action Verb: _____

7. Alcohol consumption among high school students reached alarming new levels.

Action Verb: _____

8. In the opinion of most health care professionals, a sedentary lifestyle poses almost as much danger to a person's health as smoking.

Action Verb: _____

9. Investors felt in a state of shock over recent revelations and scrambled for their cellphones.

Action Verb: _____

10. Readers of detective fiction, along with assorted film buffs, showed up for the book signing early Saturday evening.

Action Verb: _____

Ask Yourself

Check your last assignment for the verbs you use. Are there more action verbs or linking verbs? Which do you think is better? Why?

LINKING AND STATE-OF-BEING VERBS

A linking verb connects a subject to the words that explain or describe it. (See the box below for a list of linking verbs.) These explanatory, descriptive words follow the verb and are called the **subject complement**.

All the **paintings** *looked* beautiful.

The linking verb *looked* connects the subject "paintings" to the word that describes them. The subject complement "beautiful" describes the paintings.

The oldest **sister** *is* the hardest worker of the family.

The linking verb *is* connects the subject "sister" to the word that describes her. The subject complement "worker" describes the sister.

COMMON LINKING VERBS	
am	shall be
are	could have been
is	will be
can be	would be
was being	have been
has been	may have been
may be	must have been
were	

STATE-OF-BEING VERBS	
appear	become
feel	grow
look	seem
smell	sound
taste	remain

Identifying Linking and State-of-Being Verbs

Directions: *Underline the simple subjects, circle the linking verbs, and double-underline the subject complements in the following sentences. To be sure you have found the linking verbs, write each one in the past, present, and future tense in the spaces provided.*

1. Taking a few days off work seemed like a good idea.

Linking Verb: _____

_____

2. The colour of the gourds grew faint in the weeks after harvest.

Linking Verb: _____

_____

3. Being a smoker in a federal government building is not easy.

Linking Verb: _____

_____

4. The geriatric patient felt like a teenager again.

Linking Verb: _____

_____

5. Some parents' disciplining styles seem aggressive.

Linking Verb: _____

_____

6. Some distractions may be for the better.

Linking Verb: _____

_____

7. The main problem many adult students face is financial.

Linking Verb: _____

_____

8. Vanessa's battle would be very difficult one minute, hardly noticeable the next.

Linking Verb: _____

_____

9. The children feel betrayed, unloved, and angry.

Linking Verb: _____

_____

10. The professor was an interesting person.

Linking Verb: _____

_____

HELPING VERBS AND VERB PHRASES

A **verb phrase** contains a helping verb and a main verb. **Helping verbs** may be used with either action verbs or linking verbs to convey when something happened and to form questions. (A list of common helping verbs can be found in the box earlier in this chapter.) Verb phrases are used to express the tense of actions with greater precision.

The **female students** *are sitting* on the left side of the classroom.

The helping verb *are* locates this action in the present tense. Joined with *sitting,* the verb phrase describes a continuous action, possibly an action that is not generally the case. (Compare this with "The female students *sit* on the left side of the room," suggesting that the girls *usually* or *always* sit on the left side of the room.) The complete verb phrase "are sitting" is the current action of the subject "female students."

Canada *has been* a good <u>friend</u> to Haiti.

The verb phrase *has been* links the subject "Canada" to the subject complement "friend." The sentence suggests Canada was and continues to be a friend. (Compare "Canada was a good friend to Haiti," which suggests the friendship no longer exists.)

COMMON HELPING VERBS

am	are	is	was
were	do	did	can
may	must	has	have
had	be	been	shall
will	could	would	should

EXERCISE 18-9 **Identifying Helping Verbs and Verb Phrases**

Directions: *Underline the simple subjects and double-underline the helping verbs in the verb phrases in the sentences that follow.*

EXAMPLE

Young <u>drivers</u> <u>have been known</u> to drive with their radios on and their cellphones pressed to their ears while eating fast food.

1. Under other circumstances, Darrell would have gone to the University of Saskatchewan on a scholarship.

2. Friday night the team will eat with their coaches at the Adobe Grill downtown.

3. That summer all the team members were working on basic skills.

4. To get your student ID, you should go to the Registrar's Office in the Hallisey Building.

5. The student's amazing skill with high-level math would have been noticed in her high school years.

6. The drama coach is often seen sitting in his office, wearing a white scarf and reading a script.

7. Rogers had been pulled aside from surgical procedures a number of times because of his poor attendance and tardiness.

8. Telling a child no, without any real explanation, will sometimes cause a rebellious attitude to develop.

9. Some people can't imagine doing anything without modern technological devices.

10. The other students would make fun of the new student's clothes and accent.

EXERCISE 18-10 **Putting It All Together**

Directions: *Underline the simple subject and double-underline the verb and any helping verbs in the sentences that follow.*

EXAMPLE:

My friend took me to a fast-food restaurant for dinner a few weeks ago.

1. The experience was terrible.

2. The lines extended to the door.

3. I did not want to stay.

4. We actually stood in line for 45 minutes.

5. She entertained me the whole time.

6. Even in a bad experience like this, we always have fun.

7. We were having so much fun, some of the other customers gave us dirty looks.

8. In the end, the manager offered everyone coupons as an apology for the wait.

9. I will never go back to that place again.

10. My friend knows many other good places to eat.

EXERCISE 18-11 **Observing Your Verbs**

Directions: *Go to a public place on campus and observe events taking place around you. Write a paragraph-length description of the scene and the action. When you finish, double-underline all verbs and helping verbs in your sentences. Count the number of linking verbs and action verbs. Compare your writing and your use of verbs to the work of two or three classmates.*

CHAPTER OVERVIEW

Take a moment and reflect on what you have learned about the simple sentence.

☐ An introduction to the simple sentence: a complete thought or idea with a subject and a verb

☐ Find subjects and predicates

☐ The subject: noun, pronoun, or gerund

- *Nouns: a person, place, or thing*

- *Pronouns: take the place of nouns; personal, indefinite pronouns*

- *Gerunds: the name of an activity, a word ending in –ing*

- *How to find the simple subject: who performed the action, or what is being described?*

- *Subjects and prepositional phrases: preposition + object; never the subject*

- *Subjects in questions and commands: commands have understood "you" as subject*

☐ The predicate: verb + words or phrases to modify verb

- *Action verbs: express action of subject*

- *Linking or state-of-being verbs: explain or describe subject; often used with adjectives*

- *Helping verbs and verb phrases: helping verb + main verb; express tense; used for questions*

SIMPLE SENTENCE STRUCTURE REVIEW

SUBJECT +	VERB (Predicate) – present, past, future tenses
noun(s)	action verbs
gerunds	state-of-being verbs
personal pronouns	linking verbs
indefinite pronouns	helping verbs

Beyond the Simple Sentence: Compounds, Coordination, and Subordination

As you read in the previous chapter, the simple sentence is the building block for richer, more complex sentence structures. There are a variety of ways to expand the simple sentence using compound forms and complex forms.

Build on the Simple Sentence

The simple sentence contains one subject and one predicate and is useful for making simple, straightforward statements. However, what if the details and ideas you write about are not simple? Compound forms enable you to talk about more than one subject and action in a single sentence. The most common compound forms are compound subjects and compound predicates.

COMPOUND SUBJECTS

In a **compound subject**, two or more subjects are connected by a conjunction or joining word—usually *and* or *or*.

> Simple Sentence: On Friday, **Bob** *drove* to the seashore alone. *Who else drove to the shore?*
>
> Simple Sentence: **Alice** drove to the seashore.
>
> Compound Subject: On Friday, **Bob and Alice** *drove* to the seashore together.

Note: No punctuation is used before or after the conjunction when the compound consists of two subjects.

> Simple Sentence: **Irish setters** *make* good hunting dogs. *What other breeds make good hunting dogs?*
>
> Simple Sentence: **Brittany spaniels** *make* good hunting dogs.
>
> Simple Sentence: **Beagles** *make* good hunting dogs.
>
> Compound Subject: **Irish setters, Brittany spaniels, and beagles** *make* good hunting dogs.

EXERCISE 19-1 **Identifying Compound Subjects**

Directions: *Underline the compound subjects in the following sentences. Circle the coordinating conjunctions.*

EXAMPLE

Snow, ice, (and) rain made it impossible for people to travel far at Thanksgiving this year.

1. A bouquet of flowers and a box of candy are popular gifts on Valentine's Day.

2. Mustard and onions on hot dogs are a favourite ballgame food.

3. Angelica or I will be at the concert early enough to get front-row seats.

4. The windows in the house, the roof on the barn, and the car's windshield were all damaged in Saturday's hailstorm.

5. Bicycle racing and volleyball are two exciting, but frequently overlooked, sports.

EXERCISE 19-2 **Adding Compound Subjects**

Directions: *Rewrite each of the following sentences so that it has a compound subject. For help creating the compound subject, respond to the question provided. Be sure to change verbs so they agree with your compound subject.*

EXAMPLE

A bowl of vegetable soup makes a great lunch.

What else makes a great lunch?

A bowl of vegetable soup, a sandwich on rye bread, and a slice of cheese

make a great lunch.

1. Less exposure to sunlight in the winter months causes a form of depression called "seasonal affective disorder."

What else causes a form of depression called "seasonal affective disorder"?

_____

2. Not washing their hands frequently enough is a common reason why children catch the common cold.

What are other reasons that children catch the common cold?

_____

3. A trip to the Atlantic seashore can be a very restful vacation.

What else can be a very restful vacation?

_____

4. Being on time for work enhances an employee's possibilities for getting a raise.

What else enhances an employee's possibilities for getting a raise?

_____

5. The patriating of the British North America Act in 1982 to become the Constitution of Canada was an important event in Canadian history.

What were some other great events in Canadian history?

_____

COMPOUND PREDICATES

A sentence with a **compound predicate** has two or more verbs that share the same subject. Like the compound subject, the compound predicate enables you to express more complex details and ideas.

> **Simple Sentence:** The **telephone** *rang* in the middle of the night.
> *What else did the telephone do?*
> **Simple Sentence:** The **telephone** *woke* up the baby.
> **Compound Predicate:** The **telephone** *rang* in the middle of the night and *woke* up the baby.

Note: No punctuation is used before or after the conjunction when the compound predicate consists of two verbs (see example above).

> **Simple Sentence:** Computers *distract* employees from their work.
> *What else do computers do?*
> **Simple Sentence:** Computers *diminish* production.
> **Simple Sentence:** Computers *increase* costs.
> **Compound Predicate:** Computers *distract* employees from their work, *diminish* production, and *increase* costs.

Look at the following chart to see how you can combine single subjects and compound subjects with single verbs and compound verbs.

SIMPLE SENTENCE STRUCTURE VARIATIONS

one subject + one verb	S	+	V
compound subject + one verb	S + S	+	V
	S + S + S	+	V
one subject + compound verb	S	+	V + V
			V + V + V
compound subject + compound verb	S + S	+	V + V
	S + S + S	+	V + V + V

EXERCISE 19-3 **Identifying Compound Predicates**

Directions: *Underline the compound predicates in the following sentences. Circle the coordinating conjunctions.*

1. The financial advisor invested his client's money but made very poor choices.

2. The tourists sat on the dock, watched the blue water glisten in the sun, and talked about old times.

3. The plumber sent a bill and charged the customer for two visits instead of one.

4. Conway wants a raise and has complained about his job assignment.

5. The student complains about her boyfriend constantly but still dates him.

Directions: *Rewrite each of the following sentences so that it has a compound predicate. For help creating the compound predicate, respond to the question provided by writing one or two new sentences. Then combine the sentences by putting the predicates together. Circle the verbs in each predicate.*

EXAMPLE

Squirrels built a nest in the apple tree.

What else did the squirrels do?

Squirrels built a nest in the apple tree, jumped onto the bird feeders, and ate every scrap of food they could find.

1. Thomas moved out of his parents' house.

What else did Thomas do?

_____

2. After the storm, the search and rescue unit came to town.

What else did the search and rescue unit do?

_____

3. On July 1, the children watched the Canada Day parade.

What else did the children do?

_____

4. For a healthy diet, consumers should avoid transfats.

What else should consumers do?

_____

5. The artist took out his sketch book.

What else did the artist do?

_____

The Compound Sentence and Coordination

Two simple sentences, or two independent clauses, that are connected form a **compound sentence**. Making use of **coordination**, the compound sentence comes in three forms that enable you to express the logical relationships between details and ideas:

1. Coordination using a comma and a conjunction
2. Coordination using a semicolon and a conjunctive adverb, followed by a comma
3. Coordination using a semicolon

USING A COMMA AND A CONJUNCTION

You can combine two related simple sentences by replacing the period after the first sentence with a comma and a coordinating conjunction.

Simple Sentence: Gordon's sister got married at a young age.

Simple Sentence: She has been happy ever since.

Compound Sentence: Gordon's sister got married at a young age, and she has been happy ever since.

The conjunction you use establishes a logical connection between the two sentences. Here is a list of common coordinating conjunctions and the logical connections they imply.

COORDINATING CONJUNCTIONS AND THEIR LOGICAL CONNECTION		
and	*means*	in addition
but, yet	*means*	exception or contrast
or, nor	*means*	options or alternatives
so, for	*means*	logical conclusion

Here are some examples of compound sentences that illustrate the logical connections that can be made by using coordinating conjunctions:

Simple Sentence: She says good things about marriage.

Simple Sentence: Not every young married person does.

Compound Sentence: She says good things about marriage, but not every young married person does.

The coordinating conjunction but *suggests contrast or an exception.*

Simple Sentence: Some young people took full-time work right away.

Simple Sentence: They became parents too soon.

Compound Sentence: Some young people took full-time work right away, or they became parents too soon.

The coordinating conjunction or *suggests options or alternatives.*

Simple Sentence: Getting married is a big responsibility.

Simple Sentence: You want to be sure you have chosen the right partner.

Compound Sentence: Getting married is a big responsibility, so you want to be sure you have chosen the right partner.

The coordinating conjunction so *expresses a logical conclusion.*

Note: In a compound sentence, a comma is placed before the conjunction. In the case of very short sentences—such as "I sat and I waited"—a comma is unnecessary.

EXERCISE 19-5 **Choosing Coordinating Conjunctions**

Directions: *Choose a coordinating conjunction to connect each of the following sentences to make it into a compound sentence. Write the conjunction in the space provided. When you insert a conjunction in place of a period, put a comma before the conjunction.*

EXAMPLE

His car stalled this morning. It was inexpensive to repair.

, but _____

His car stalled this morning, but it was inexpensive to repair.

1. Janice will bring the desserts. Nancy can bring the drinks.

   _____

2. Britta and Clem wanted to know how to salsa. They took ballroom dancing lessons.

   _____

3. Erica did not apply to the nursing program this semester. She did not even sign up for classes.

   _____

4. Latasha was unwilling to go to the football game. She was willing to go the movie.

   _____

5. Jake's worst subject in high school was geometry. He also was also terrible in physics.

   _____

EXERCISE 19-6 **Commas and Compound Forms**

Directions: _Some of the sentences below are simple sentences with compound subjects or predicates. Others are compound sentences._

- _Circle the conjunctions in all the sentences._
- _Add commas to the compound sentences. Do not add commas to compound subjects or compound predicates. Some of the sentences are correct as written._

EXAMPLE

Email is now used by nearly everyone, (and) many businesses have Web sites to advertise their products and services. (Insert comma after _everyone._)

1. The tow-truck driver saw a car standing by the side of the road this morning and the tire was flat.

2. Most people hate doing the dishes and detest taking out the garbage but those are the jobs they have to do.

3. A student delegation went to France last year and this summer another group wants to go.

4. Jessica and Gregory work afternoons and don't really have time to cook dinner.

5. The roommates went to the grocery store and bought the ingredients for the meal they decided to make.

6. Vegetarians like to make salads a lot so they always buy some kind of vegetables to go with the meal.

7. Students usually make something that is simple and doesn't require a whole lot of cooking time.

8. They often make spaghetti or fruit salad.

9. Others like refried beans and guacamole.

10. One person can cut up the vegetables and cook the meat and the other can set the table and do the dishes afterward.

EXERCISE 19-7 **Compound Sentences in Your Writing**

Directions: *For each of the following subjects, write a compound sentence. Use a variety of conjunctions.*

EXAMPLE

horses

In the nineteenth century city horses generated huge amounts of manure, so a large segment of the population found work transporting manure out of the city every day.

1. sleep

_____

2. assignments

_____

3. health care

_____

USING A SEMICOLON AND A CONJUNCTIVE ADVERB

You can combine two simple sentences by replacing the period with a semicolon and a conjunctive adverb followed by a comma. A **conjunctive adverb** is a connecting word, like a conjunction, that makes a logical connection between two ideas.

Simple Sentence: One of my co-workers came late today.

Simple Sentence: He was completely distracted and unable to do his job properly.

Compound Sentence: One of my co-workers came late today; furthermore, he was completely distracted and unable to do his job properly.

Furthermore expresses the logical connection between these two simple sentences. Like coordinating conjunctions, conjunctive adverbs express the logical connection between two related sentences. They also function as transition words.

The semicolon is a strong mark of punctuation, almost as strong as a period. For this reason, it replaces the period after *today* in the preceding example; the comma after *furthermore*, in contrast, marks the pause of an introductory modifier.

The following box shows a list of conjunctive adverbs.

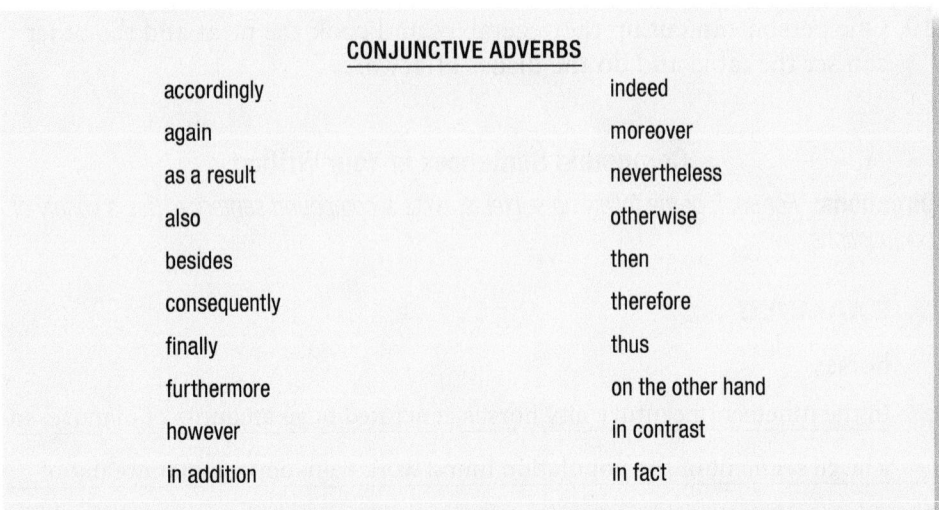

CONJUNCTIVE ADVERBS	
accordingly	indeed
again	moreover
as a result	nevertheless
also	otherwise
besides	then
consequently	therefore
finally	thus
furthermore	on the other hand
however	in contrast
in addition	in fact

Simple Sentence: Digital photography is becoming more popular all the time.

Simple Sentence: All of my friends now have digital cameras.

Compound Sentence: Digital photography is becoming more popular all the time; indeed, all of my friends now have digital cameras.

Here, *indeed* expresses the logical connection between these two simple sentences.

USING A SEMICOLON

In cases where you are expressing clearly related or contrasting ideas, consider using a semicolon alone.

Simple Sentence: Life in the country tended to be dull.

Simple Sentence: Life in the city provided too much stimulation.

Compound Sentence: Life in the country tended to be dull; life in the city provided too much stimulation.

Simple Sentence: My father is pretty quiet in social gatherings.

Simple Sentence: My mother will talk your ear off.

Compound Sentence: My father is pretty quiet in social gatherings; my mother will talk your ear off.

Compound Sentences, Conjunctive Adverbs, and the Semicolon

Directions: *Referring to the list of conjunctive adverbs found earlier in the chapter, combine the following sentences using a semicolon and a conjunctive adverb that expresses the logical relationship between the two sentences. For contrasting sentences, just use a semicolon.*

1. The team lost five consecutive games. The coach continued to practise basic skills and work toward their first victory.

   _____

2. Mutual funds offer better growth over time than savings accounts. Most young investors choose the mutual fund option.

   _____

3. Fast foods typically have high calorie counts. They have high salt and fat contents.

   _____

4. One of the brothers went to medical school. The other brother went to law school.

   _____

5. Having drunk so much coffee, Parker was in an agitated state when he arrived at the doctor's office. His blood pressure was much higher than usual.

   _____

6. The store-bought pumpkin pies did not sell well at the bake sale. The home-baked pies practically flew out the door.

   _____

7. Trish scored very high on her entrance exams and interviewed very well. She was offered a generous scholarship.

   _____

8. Michelle and Agnes attended the same university, took the same classes, and were guided by a stern, yet caring advisor. She provided them an introduction into the real world of the hospital operating room.

   _____

9. According to the Centers for Disease Control and Prevention, around 63 percent of all adults consume alcohol. Around 32 percent of those consume five or more drinks a day.

   _____

10. Many people initially purchase technological gadgets to make their lives easier. Those good intentions erode over time and become something else.

   _____

COORDINATION SUMMARY

To review compound sentences, look at the sample sentences below. Then refer to the tables that follow to help you build your own compound sentences. The second independent clause does not begin with a capital letter.

Comma and Coordinating Conjunction

- Traffic stopped in the tunnel for 45 minutes, but no one in the subway car seemed to mind.

	Independent Clause	Punctuation	Coordinating Conjunction	Independent Clause	End Punctuation
1	simple sentence	, (comma)	and but, yet or, nor so, for	simple sentence	. (period)

Semicolon, Conjunctive Adverb, and Comma

- The neighbours on our right are enthusiastic about gardening and yard work; in contrast, those on the left work on the inside of their house.

	Independent Clause	Punctuation	Conjunctive Adverb*	Punctuation	Independent Clause	End Punctuation
2	simple sentence	; (semicolon)	again also besides finally then thus	, (comma)	simple sentence	. (period)

*See Conjunctive Adverb chart earlier in the chapter for more examples.

Semicolon

- A small car is purchased for economy; a large car is bought for space and convenience.

	Independent Clause	Punctuation	Independent Clause	End Punctuation
3	simple sentence	; (semicolon)	simple sentence	. (period)

EXERCISE 19-9 **Putting It All Together**

Directions: *The following paragraphs consist of simple sentences. On a separate sheet of paper, use all three approaches to coordination—(a) comma and conjunction; (b) semicolon, conjunctive adverb, and comma; or (c) semicolon—to create three compound sentences within each paragraph.*

1. We met in high school. We were both first-year students. He was very focused and spontaneous. He would make anyone laugh. He was a very good friend. He always helped me out. I really needed the help then. We played football together all four years of high school. During football he would push others to do their best. Chris was an amazing individual. After school he volunteered to do landscaping for our town parks on the weekends and during the summer. This saved the town a lot of money. He even won an achievement award for this. He was always helping out others.

2. Soon Vanessa felt a little better. She found herself still in pain at times. This didn't bother her though. She was determined to get on with her life. She wanted to accomplish all the goals she had set for herself. First she returned to work. Then she went back to school. She started off taking one class a semester. She made sure she could handle the sickness, work, and the workload of college again. Soon she was taking two, then three classes. She was comfortable with this workload. It was difficult trying to manage working, going to school, and still cooking and cleaning her home. She was determined. She found the time and strength to get it done. She graduated with a bachelor's degree in business.

3. There are times when the parent and child are at an impasse. Both are speechless and storm away. There is nothing left to do but yell and scream at each other. One or the other decides to stop. Maybe the child takes something the parent says completely the wrong way. The child attacks with unkind words or insults. Maybe the parent fights back. The two will fight for hours on end. It is sad. These conflicts start with a miscommunication. Both individuals are too stubborn to give up the fight. Both truly want it all to end. There is a perfect balance of power in this communication between the parent and the child. Neither gives in. Neither actually achieves ultimate victory.

The Complex Sentence and Subordination

Subordination occurs when an independent clause (containing a subject and verb) is made into a dependent clause by joining it to another independent clause using a **subordinating conjunction**. Sentences making use of subordination are called **complex sentences**. If they are separated, the subordinate elements do not express a complete thought. The dependent clause can be added to the independent clause in two ways: before or after.

Notice the effect the subordinating conjunction has on an independent clause:

Riley mowed the lawn.

After Riley mowed the lawn.

The first statement is an **independent clause.** It states a complete idea. However, when the subordinating conjunction *after* is placed in front of the independent clause, it no longer expresses a complete idea: "After Riley mowed the lawn." What happened? By itself, the dependent clause does not make a statement.

Riley went swimming next door after she mowed the lawn. (no comma needed)

The added language completes the statement. Notice that "Riley went swimming next door" is an independent clause. It stands alone, whereas the second part has to be added to the whole sentence to make sense. Here is a chart to show you one possible structure of a complex sentence where the dependent clause is added *after* the independent clause.

Independent Clause	Subordinating Conjunction*	Dependent Clause	End Punctuation
simple sentence	after since when while	simple sentence	. (period)

See Subordinating Conjunctions chart that follows for other subordinating conjunctions.

The following box is a list of subordinating conjunctions.

Do not use *because* or *although* with conjunctions that mean the same thing: "Although a good-looking guy asked her to dance, ~~yet~~ she turned him down.

SUBORDINATING CONJUNCTIONS

after	so that
although	though
as	unless
as long as	until
because	when
before	whenever
even though	whereas
if	wherever
in order that	whether
provided that	while
since	

In the following example, notice the effect a subordinating conjunction has on two simple sentences that are combined to form a complex sentence:

Simple Sentence: A great-looking guy asked her to dance.

Simple Sentence: She turned him down.

Complex Sentence: <u>Although a great-looking guy asked her to dance,</u> she turned him down.

Although expresses the logical relationship between these two simple sentences. The underlined section of the sentence has become a dependent clause. It can no longer stand alone as a complete sentence. It "depends" on the rest of the sentence, "she turned him down."

When the dependent clause of a complex sentence comes first, you must use a comma to attach it to the rest of the sentence. Here is a chart to show you a second possible structure of a complex sentence where the dependent clause is added *before* the independent clause.

Subordinating Conjunction*	Dependent Clause	Punctuation	Independent Clause	End Punctuation
as long as whenever whether	simple sentence	**,** (comma)	simple sentence	**.** (period)

See Subordinating Conjunctions chart that appears earlier for a longer list.

Use a comma to set off a dependent clause at the end of a sentence only if the dependent clause reads like an afterthought, adding *nonessential information*. Afterthoughts often begin with the subordinating conjunctions *although, though,* and *whereas.*

1. Salespeople need a comfortable car because they spend a lot of time on the road.

In this first sentence, the subordinate section, beginning with *because,* adds essential information. The sentence expresses a cause and effect relationship so no comma is used.

2. Because they spend a lot of time on the road, salespeople need a comfortable car.

In contrast, the subordinate clause in the second sentence comes first and a comma is used to attach it to the rest of the sentence.

3. She turned down a great-looking guy who asked her to dance, <u>although she regretted it later.</u>

In the third sentence, the subordinate clause, beginning with *although,* adds nonessential information. It reads like an afterthought so a comma is used. Here is a chart to show you another possible structure of a complex sentence where the dependent clause is added as an afterthought with nonessential information *after* the independent clause.

Independent Clause	Punctuation	Subordinating Conjunction	Dependent Clause (afterthought)	End Punctuation
simple sentence	**,** (comma)	although though whereas	simple sentence	**.** (period)

Selecting the Right Subordinating Conjunction

Directions: *Review the list of subordinating conjunctions from the table earlier in the chapter. Then read the following simple sentences and select a subordinating conjunction that can be used to express the logical relationship between the ideas in each one. Add commas as needed.*

EXAMPLE

While Matthew barely opened a book and did poorly, Andrew studied hard for the exam and did well. (Insert comma after *poorly*.)

1. _____ I am not winning I like playing the game.

2. _____ Richard played in the game he went to the dance at the youth centre.

3. Ling studies every night from 7:00 p.m. until midnight _____ she can get a scholarship for college.

4. _____ you go or not I plan to see the Degas art exhibit on dance.

5. The boss requires all his employees to submit vacation requests six months in advance _____ he wants to accommodate as many as possible.

6. Stephen King is a very popular novelist _____ most literary critics do not think of him as a "serious" writer.

7. I do not want to go to the movies _____ you might persuade me to change my mind.

8. _____ I always wanted a dog my brother's allergies kept us from having one.

9. Mark broke his hand _____ he was moving scenery around the stage.

10. _____ you decide to quit your job let me know so that I can apply for it.

EXERCISE 19-11 **Dependent Clauses and the Comma**

Directions: *For each of the following pairs of sentences, select a subordinating conjunction from the list earlier in the chapter and use it to combine the sentences. Write the subordinating conjunction you choose with punctuation as needed.*

Ask Yourself

Do you insert too many commas or too few commas? What do you see in this exercise that applies to your writing?

EXAMPLE

Sarah cooked on a gas range at work. At home she used an electric range.

Although Sarah . . . , at home. . . .

1. Early tools used in logging were the axe and the chainsaw. Now tractors and helicopters make heavy work lighter.

2. CEOs want the public to see them as dedicated entrepreneurs. They want their shareholders to know they will do anything to make a profit.

_____

3. Most of the family was very supportive during this time. No one suffered too much.

_____

4. Another big draw, "the summer blockbuster," comes along. Movie executives bank their futures on it.

_____

5. "Be cool, stay in school" was always the motto of schools when I was growing up. Not everyone stayed in school.

_____

6. Ron started working at Wilson's Leather in Southland Mall. I stumbled in there looking for a present for my boyfriend.

_____

7. Throngs of window shoppers descend upon the local malls and shopping centres. There has been a media blitz announcing big sales and huge savings on consumer goods.

_____

8. Students and teachers work together and show mutual respect. The classroom is a welcoming place.

_____

9. The government has increased the tax on tobacco. Being a smoker is not easy.

_____

10. This is a day everyone is excited about. We're going back to Vancouver for our family reunion.

_____

SUBORDINATION AND THE RELATIVE CLAUSE

A **relative clause** begins with one of the relative pronouns: *that, which,* or *who.* A relative clause can appear at the beginning, in the middle, or at the end of a sentence. In the following examples the relative pronouns are in bold and the relative clauses are underlined.

Who and *that* replace a person; *that* and *which* replace a thing.

Which <u>guitar player they would choose</u> was not immediately clear.

The band members **who** <u>heard Phil first</u> immediately asked him to join the band.

Then Phil completely took over a band **that** <u>had been struggling for quite some time.</u>

When you combine sentences using a relative clause, you add information about a person or a thing. Usually the relative pronoun comes immediately after the person or thing being modified. Which band members? *The band members who Phil heard first.* Which band? *A band that had been struggling for quite some time.* A relative clause adds the detail needed to specify a person or thing. *We're talking about that one,* the clause says. In the following examples, the relative clauses are in bold.

A news journalist covered the story. *Which news journalist?*

A news journalist **who happened to be on the scene** covered the story.

A car can be expensive to operate. *Which car?*

A car **that requires a lot of repairs** can be expensive to operate.

Punctuation can be required for some relative clauses. When the information is an afterthought, or when it is not essential information, add commas. When this nonessential information comes at the end of the sentence, use a comma before the relative pronoun. In the following examples, the relative clauses are in bold.

Gretzky signed autographs for the youth **who were working at the arena.**

In this sentence, the relative clause "who were working at the arena" provides essential information: it tells which youth got autographs, so a comma is not used.

Both that man and my father come from Moose Jaw, **which is a city in south-central Saskatchewan.**

Here the relative clause provides nonessential information because the city is named and specified. Therefore, the relative clause is set off with a comma.

If the nonessential clause is in the middle of a sentence, you need a pair of commas. Look at the following examples.

Martin Brodeur, **a Canadian-American hockey goaltender who has played his entire National Hockey League (NHL) career with the New Jersey Devils,** has now hired an agent to negotiate his next contract.

In this sentence, because the subject of the sentence is named, the relative clause is considered nonessential information and is therefore placed between a pair of commas.

A man **who was a childhood friend of my father's** invented superglue.

In this example, "a man" is neither named nor specified, so the relative clause provides essential information for determining who the man is, and no commas are necessary.

EXERCISE 19-12 **Adding Relative Clauses**

Directions: *Add a relative clause to each of the following sentences and rewrite them. Use commas as needed.*

EXAMPLE

Mark Messier who _____ switched to play centre position in the 1984 playoff games.

Mark Messier, who was initially a left winger, switched to play centre position in the 1984 playoff games.

1. Taking a psychology class which _____ can completely change your mind about human nature.

_____

2. The clothes that _____ will be ready by 4:00 p.m. tomorrow.

_____

3. Their family ended up going for a short vacation in August which _____.

_____

4. The flowers that _____ are now on sale at the local market for half what they cost last week.

_____

5. When we were children, we always waited for the crash and flash of thunderstorms which _____.

_____

6. The country's dependence upon oil which _____ leads to continuing vulnerability.

_____

7. School lunch programs that _____ actually contribute to problems with obesity in this country.

_____

8. Be sure to buy a computer that _____.

_____

9. Train travel which _____ hardly exists in many North American cities now.

_____

10. Most zoo animals that _____ are probably quite happy in their confinement.

_____

Combining Sentences Using Relative Clauses

Directions: *Use relative clauses to combine the following sentences. Add commas as needed.*

Talk about it

Short sentences are easy to write and punctuate. How do you usually combine sentences to make your writing more sophisticated?

EXAMPLE

The Arrow was a Canadian-designed aircraft. We saw it at the Canadian Air and Space Museum.

The Arrow was a Canadian-designed aircraft that we saw at the Canadian Air and Space Museum.

1. The construction trades once provided thousands of secure jobs in many large cities. The construction trades are now booming only in certain parts of the country.

_____

_____

2. There is an antique market at the edge of town every second Saturday. That is not often enough for some enthusiasts.

_____

_____

3. Scuba diving is a popular sport in the Caribbean. It appeals to the brave-at-heart tourists.

_____

_____

4. The ferry boats used to run between the city and the island every 20 minutes. They were replaced by a four-lane bridge five years ago.

_____

_____

5. Some elective surgeries are not covered by most health insurance policies. These surgeries are primarily cosmetic in nature.

_____

_____

6. Methane gas is used by some municipalities. The gas is generated at landfills.

_____

_____

7. Charles Dickens's *David Copperfield* is still one of my favourite novels. I first read it when I was in high school.

_____

_____

8. Burning leaves has been banned in many parts of the country. The smell of burning leaves is intoxicating.

_____

_____

9. During my time as a camp counsellor, I gave speeches on a regular basis. Giving speeches never bothered me in the least.

_____

_____

10. Most people sleep better at night if the temperature in the house is lowered. Lowering the temperature is made easy by a programmable thermostat.

_____

_____

EXERCISE 19-14 | **Editing and Subordination**

Directions: *The following paragraphs consist entirely of simple sentences. On a separate sheet of paper, combine the sentences using subordinating conjunctions and relative pronouns. Use commas as needed.*

1. I quit smoking for a variety of reasons. The first reason was inconvenience. I did not enjoy carrying my pack of cigarettes everywhere. It took up space in my pocket. It was just one more thing to worry about. There was another reason I quit smoking. The worst part about smoking was the smell. Smoke got on my clothes. That was bad enough. The smell got in my hair and on my breath. It was hard to get rid of the smell. I smoked for seven years. At first, the price was not that bad. Then the taxes on tobacco started increasing. Next thing I knew, it was eight, nine, then ten dollars a pack. That was another reason to quit. I woke up and looked at my bank account. It was pretty pathetic. I realized how much money I could save if I quit smoking. So I quit. I quit cold turkey. The nicotine craving never got that bad. My hands needed to be doing something. I ended up chewing on coffee straws every time I had a craving for a cigarette. I needed to do that for a couple of weeks. Now I never think of having a cigarette. I am much better off.

2. Consider the young male student and his computer use. His parents buy him a computer to help with his homework. He uses it only for school. One day in his room he logs into a chat room to talk about the local

Ask Yourself

What punctuation will you try to use in your writing? In what kinds of sentences?

football team. He begins to lose track of time. He chats with friends from various messaging services. The Internet becomes a secondary social environment. He tries to do his homework. His friends distract him. This causes him to fall behind in his responsibilities. In his free time he explores other uses for his computer. Soon he downloads illegal music, chats with friends at all hours, and looks for ways to access age-restricted sites. The line blurs between responsible use of technology and letting technology have far too much of a place in his life.

3. Some people can be cruel. The classroom can be a very unwelcoming place. I was in elementary school. There was a foreign student named Katya. She had not been in Toronto very long. She had a thick Polish accent. The other students made fun of her clothes and the way she spoke. She became socially withdrawn, had few friends, and ended up changing schools. This is a perfect example of cruelty in the classroom. This cruelty is often directed at new students. That is so unfortunate. If schoolchildren were more accepting of different types of people and cultures, it would help newcomers feel welcome.

CHAPTER REVIEW

Take a moment and reflect on what you have learned about compounds, coordination, and subordination.

☐ Build on the simple sentence

- *Compound subjects:* no punctuation before or after the conjunction when there are two subjects

- *Compound predicates:* no punctuation before or after the conjunction with two verbs

☐ The compound sentence and coordination

- *Using a comma and a conjunction:* (s + predicate), + coordinating conjunction + (s + predicate)

- *Using a semicolon and a conjunctive adverb:* (s + predicate) ; conjunctive adverb, (s + predicate)

- *Using a semicolon:* (s + predicate) ; (s + predicate)

☐ The complex sentence and subordination

- *Complex sentence:* uses independent clause + subordinating conjunction + subordinate clause

- *Subordination and the relative clause:* begins with *that, which,* or *who;* can appear at beginning, middle, or end of sentence

The Sentence Fragment

Readers of academic writing expect you to write in complete sentences. You learned in the previous two chapters that there are several kinds of sentences and that a **complete sentence** always contains a subject and a verb or predicate; additionally, it also must state a complete idea that a reader can understand and respond to. A complete sentence can also be identified by the use of a capital letter at the beginning and punctuation (a period, question mark, or exclamation point) at the end. A **sentence fragment** does not contain either a subject or a verb, and it does not express a complete thought.

Types of Fragments

A fragment is not a complete sentence. Most fragments are phrases or dependent clauses that are detached from a complete sentence. While most fragments can be corrected by changing a period to a comma, at times it is preferable to add words so the fragment becomes a complete sentence.

NOUN PHRASES

Noun phrases are modifiers at the beginning or end of a sentence. Watch for phrases that sound like an afterthought.

> The construction project downtown was a regular danger zone. A disaster waiting to happen.

The first sentence is a complete sentence. The fragment, "a disaster waiting to happen," is a noun phrase that describes "danger zone." It sounds like an afterthought, an additional descriptive detail the writer has added. By itself, it does not express a complete idea. Correct the fragment by attaching it to the complete sentence or by adding words to make the fragment a complete sentence.

> The construction project downtown was a regular danger <u>zone, a</u> disaster waiting to happen.

> The construction project downtown was a regular danger <u>zone. It was</u> a disaster waiting to happen.

ADJECTIVE PHRASES

Adjective phrase fragments also become detached at the beginning or end of complete sentences. Watch for a phrase that sounds introductory.

> Way too smart and generous for his own good. The technician invented programs that were sold by his company with little compensation in return.

Common sentence errors include the following:

- Using commas instead of periods to link complete thoughts
- Omitting subjects and/or verbs
- Using a subordinate clause as a complete sentence

Talk about it

Have you found fragments in your writing? Look at a few examples with your classmates.

The second sentence is a complete sentence. The fragment, "way too smart and generous for his own good," is an adjective phrase that describes "the technician." It does not express a complete idea on its own. It sounds like introductory information, which should be connected to the main sentence with a comma, not a period. Correct the fragment by attaching it to the complete sentence or by adding words to make the fragment a complete sentence.

> Way too smart and generous for his own good, the technician invented programs that were sold by his company with little compensation in return.

> The technician was way too smart and generous for his own good. He invented programs that were sold by his company with little compensation in return.

PREPOSITIONAL PHRASES

Prepositional phrases occasionally become loose threads the writer needs to tie up in editing. Watch for afterthoughts.

> The nursing students' real stress is felt once they begin their clinical rotations. Usually in the third semester of the program.

The first sentence is a complete sentence. The fragment, "usually in the third semester of the program," is a prepositional phrase that modifies *begin* in the complete sentence. It sounds like an afterthought, a descriptive detail the writer has added. By itself, it does not state a complete idea. Correct the fragment by attaching it to the complete sentence or by adding words to make the fragment a complete sentence.

> The nursing students' real stress is felt once they begin their clinical rotations, usually in the third semester of the program.

> The nursing students' real stress is felt once they begin their clinical rotations. This usually happens in the third semester of the program.

VERBAL PHRASES

Verbal phrase fragments contain either *-ing* forms (participles) or "to" forms (infinitives). They become sentence fragments when they are detached from the beginning or end of a complete sentence. Watch for *-ing* forms and "to" forms coming at the beginning of a sentence.

> Robert put off his homework all weekend. Waiting until late Sunday night to start it.

> To the surprise of his physics teacher. Robert, a natural born genius, scored 100 percent on the test, even without studying.

These fragments can be corrected by attaching them to the complete sentence (the first sentence in the first example, the second sentence in the second example) or by adding words to make the fragments complete sentences.

> Robert put off his homework all weekend, waiting until late Sunday night to start it.

> Robert put off his homework all weekend. He waited until late Sunday night to start it.

To the surprise of his physics <u>teacher</u>, Robert, a natural born genius, scored 100 percent on the test, even without studying.

He surprised his physics <u>teacher</u>. Robert, a natural born genius, scored 100 percent on the test, even without studying.

Learn to listen for sentence completeness. When you read your work out loud, give periods a good long pause, as you listen for complete ideas. In addition, look for noun, adjective, prepositional, and verbal phrases and make sure they are attached to a complete sentence. You can also add words to make the phrases a complete sentence.

EXERCISE 20-1 Noun, Adjective, Prepositional, and Verbal Phrase Fragments

Directions: *Underline the phrases in the following items. Correct the fragments by connecting them to a complete sentence or by adding words to make them complete sentences.*

1. How do you use math in your life now? Here is just one important example. Cutting coupons for shopping and knowing how much you are actually saving. It's the best way to save money.

   _____

   _____

2. There's no better feeling than driving a shiny red car, with the top down and the hum of the large motor under the hood. The feeling of power and control, sheer excitement. The driver can't help thinking, "Don't I look cool?"

   _____

   _____

3. As a child, there were many things I did to pass the time. Everything from playing video games, to riding bikes, to playing sports. What made it even better was the fact that I was surrounded by really good friends.

   _____

   _____

4. With a stern voice, my mother told me to get in the car. And to get ready to go home. I knew then I was in big trouble.

   _____

   _____

5. From helping my little brothers with homework to taking the garbage out every Monday. I really had a lot of responsibilities. A kid's work was never done.

   _____

   _____

6. Working under extremely hot conditions. Chasing golf balls, cleaning golf balls, and cleaning golf clubs after every use. This was an ideal job for the teens. They got lots of sun, and every once in a while they played some free golf.

_____

_____

7. The counsellor taught the campers how to blow bubbles with their fingers when they washed their hands. It gave her a feeling she will never forget. Just to see their smiling faces every time she taught them something new or just played with them.

_____

_____

8. The job he has now has some good and bad qualities. He is a food server, which gives him excellent experience with people. All types of people. Which also helps him develop patience.

_____

_____

9. Some teens start working when they are 15 years old. They work at grocery stores. They are too young to be cashiers. They work as baggers, which is more than just bagging groceries. Their job includes cleaning the entranceways. Getting change for the cashiers. Finding items that customers forgot and putting back items that customers did not want. It isn't the world's greatest job, but it gets teens started earning money.

_____

_____

10. Then came high school. It started out just like elementary school. The teachers calling students by their first names and friends calling each other by nicknames. Some things never change.

_____

_____

DEPENDENT CLAUSES

A dependent clause fragment can occur either before or after the independent clause to which it belongs. Watch for subordinating conjunctions at the beginning of a sentence. (See Chapter 19 for a list of subordinating conjunctions.)

I was asked to submit transcripts for the committee to review. As soon as I possibly could.

The first sentence is a complete sentence. The fragment, "as soon as I possibly could," can be joined to the complete sentence or made into a complete sentence.

> I was asked to submit transcripts for the committee to <u>review</u> as soon as I possibly could.

> I was asked to submit transcripts for the committee to <u>review. They</u> wanted them as soon as possible.

Watch also for sentences beginning with one of the relative pronouns, such as *that, which, who,* and *whoever.* Fragments with relative clauses often sound like afterthoughts.

> The argument then turned violent. Which didn't change anyone's mind.

The first sentence is a complete sentence. The fragment, "which didn't change anyone's mind," can be corrected by joining it to the independent clause or by making it into a complete sentence.

> The argument then turned <u>violent, which</u> didn't change anyone's mind.

> The argument then turned <u>violent. The fighting</u> didn't change anyone's mind.

When you read your work out loud, give periods a good long pause as you listen for complete ideas; watch for subordinating conjunctions. Read and listen carefully to all sentences that begin with a subordinating conjunction.

EXERCISE 20-2 Fragments and Dependent Clauses

Directions: *Circle subordinating conjunctions and relative pronouns in the following sentences. Underline any sentence fragments you find. Correct the fragments by connecting them to a complete sentence or by adding words to make them complete sentences. Some are correct as written.*

1. When will I ever have to know how many degrees are in an octagon? The answer is never, unless I become an engineer. Which I choose not to be. So all those engineers can just enjoy their math. I'm doing fine without it.

_____

_____

2. When we first moved to this country, I would help my dad balance his chequebook. Usually after he had mailed out all of his bills. Some math knowledge came in handy then.

_____

_____

3. I currently work as a waiter. More than likely, technology will not take my job. Unless they build robots to serve people, I'm going to be all right. Although not too many people are in my shoes. At least I can say for the time being that I'm not worried about new technology.

_____

_____

Ask Yourself

Subordinating conjunctions and relative pronouns can help you find fragments. Do those words occur in fragments you have written this semester?

4. Spitting should be banned in public. Because some people are sick, and their spit in public places can spread germs and make others sick. That's just the simple fact of the matter.

5. Once, without permission, I gave a lot of my mother's things to charity, Which made her pretty angry. When we sat down and talked about it, my mother didn't look angry anymore. For the next few years after that, my mom designated a charity box for everyone in the family to contribute to.

6. When people ask questions about my name, it gives me a story to tell. About my father, how I was named after him, and how he got his name. No one believes it, but it's true.

7. There are some famous people who have the same name I do, for instance, Pierre Berton. Another is Pierre Trudeau. Who was a prime minister.

8. When I was nine years old, my brother, my friend, and his brother. We used to collect chestnuts. We had buckets full of chestnuts. We polished them and put them in our rooms on display. Eventually I heard someone refer to them as "buckeyes."

9. I played a lot of sports when I was a child. On some teams I became a leader, which I valued a lot because it gave me important experience working with people.

10. I worked in customer service. That meant all the upset people came to me. I handled all the Better Business Bureau complaints. Which meant talking to some irate people and getting them results. Sometimes I really wanted to quit.

Directions: *Underline each fragment in the following sentences. Correct the error by joining the fragment to the appropriate sentence or by making it a complete sentence. Some of the sentences may be correct.*

1. Every day I used to kick the fence and throw rocks and sticks at the neighbours' dogs, hoping they would get hurt. I was only four years old. I didn't care about those dogs.

   _____

   _____

2. One day on our way to the store. My dad and I had an incident with an angry dog. It was a warm Friday afternoon.

   _____

   _____

3. The thought of safety didn't enter my mind. I stared in awe at this beast charging in my direction, ready to devour me. Just as it closed in, my guardian angel scooped me up from behind and placed me on top of the car.

   _____

   _____

4. As I look back on it now, I really don't think the dog was going to hurt me. Because it didn't bite my dad or even really bark. But ever since then, I have been scared of my neighbours' dogs.

   _____

   _____

5. Melissa really learned her lesson in a summer job. Which was to keep an eye on infants and what they have in their mouths. She also learned to help an infant when its life is in danger.

   _____

   _____

6. When the group of friends found the perfect spot for the prank, they unloaded their gear. The most important of which were the digital camera, a recorder, and a flashlight. One teen's duty was lookout. He had to let the other boys know if the security guard was around.

   _____

   _____

7. I never saw a real moose until I was ten years old. When my family was driving along the highway and a moose began crossing in front of our car. I was never so scared in my life because of the animal's enormous size.

   _____

   _____

8. We played "jailbreak" when we were children. The bad guy would be thrown into our makeshift jail, and moments later, he or she would break out. Repeating the same cycle of running, hopping fences, and eventually getting caught. We had fun like this the entire summer.

_____

_____

9. The woman wasn't afraid of crossing the bridge itself. She was just afraid of falling into the water below. The bridge seemed like it was a million kilometres long, and time seemed to slow down. The guide thought she would never get to the other side.

_____

_____

10. The sun had gone down. It was a cool night. Sitting by the riverbank, smoking their first cigarettes. The teens felt like the coolest guys alive.

_____

_____

EXERCISE 20-4 **Editing Fragments in Paragraphs**

Directions: *Read the following paragraphs and underline the fragments. On a separate sheet of paper, correct the fragments by altering the punctuation or revising the wording.*

1.

I had been driving for only a couple of months. My father had just purchased a brand-new Ford F-150 pickup truck. I was taking a music class at night. While en route to my instructor's home. I was headed westbound on West Road, crossing Allen Road. Out of nowhere, I got broadsided by another car. He took out the whole side of the truck. From the front bumper to the tailgate. Try to explain this to your dad right after he told you to be extra careful with the car. Something that he had worked so hard for. It was the worst feeling of my life. I had destroyed his car in a matter of minutes. There was no escaping his wrath. I had no control of the situation.

2.

Math can be very difficult. Maybe it is all the numbers, the formulas, and the boring work. Nowadays there are cheap calculators that pretty much do the work for you. Some people are opposed to using calculators in class. It makes sense not using them in grade school, when students are just learning the basics. For example, addition and subtraction and then the multiplication and division tables. Children should not need help from calculators to do things like that. They should not be allowed to use calculators. Until around grade 6. At that point calculators should be permitted. Because most students will have a good understanding of basic math. In addition, they will need to become familiar with calculators for the coming years. For example, the high school classes that require use of a calculator. In high school, calculators become essential for math and other subjects.

3.

Looking at me and my two grandmothers just proves how much the times have changed. Each of us has had a very good life. Yet one thing separates me from my grandmothers. I had options. I was a typical college student. At school full-time and working only part-time as a waitress. My grandma Lynn chose to get a job straight out of high school. She was a full-blown workaholic. Finally, there is Nana Marisa. Who had a child right out of high school. She managed a full-time job and a child all on her own. Now which one of us has worked the hardest? The answer is that we all worked equally hard. They chose their own paths. Because they had few options available.

Sometimes, academic writers, aiming for long sentences, overlook the most basic rule in writing: put a period at the end of a sentence. This chapter looks at long sentences gone wrong, sentences that can be easily fixed with end punctuation, or by using what you have learned about coordination and subordination in the previous chapters.

Comma Splices

A **comma splice** occurs when two complete sentences are wrongly connected with a comma. Correct a comma splice by replacing the comma with a period or by forming a compound or complex sentence.

IDENTIFYING COMMA SPLICES

If you can substitute a period for a comma in a sentence and make two separate, complete sentences, then you have a comma splice. Consider this example:

> Robert's first job ever was a paper route, it was easy, all he had to do was get up early on Sundays and get home early from school on Wednesdays to deliver the local newspaper to 75 homes.

There are three complete sentences in this example. Each sentence expresses a complete idea and can be written as a separate sentence:

1. Robert's first job ever was a paper route.
2. It was easy.
3. All he had to do was get up early on Sundays and get home early from school on Wednesdays to deliver the paper to 75 homes.

Putting a period at the end of each complete sentence corrects these comma splices.

> Robert's first job ever was a paper route. It was easy. All he had to do was get up early on Sundays and get home early from school on Wednesdays to deliver the paper to 75 homes.

EXERCISE 21-1 Comma Splices and Simple Sentences

Directions: *Read the following sentences and circle the commas. Identify the simple sentences. Where you see a comma splice, change the comma to a period.*

1. Everyone is intelligent in at least one field, take my brother John, for instance. He's a businessman.

2. Year after year he would save up his money for his big break, finally it happened. He opened up a restaurant with his friend. A couple of years passed, he was constantly fighting with his friend because they both wanted to do different things.

3. I never lie to my parents about anything major. I'd rather have them know what I'm doing, they were kids once too.

4. Most single mothers do good jobs keeping their households together, Even though they are single parents, they take care of their responsibilities and make sure the children are taken care of.

5. The customer came in for his car. The boss said, "You don't owe us anything, it's on us." The customer just stood there with an unforgettable look on his face, he was extremely happy.

Writer's Response

Search your papers for comma splices. Then describe what a comma splice is, using the example from your own writing.

CORRECTING COMMA SPLICES

When you find a comma splice, you can make a decision about sentence variety. If you put a period at the end of a sentence, you will never be wrong. You will have concise, emphatic sentence structure.

However, there are more options available to you when you edit comma splices. For example, you can replace a comma with a comma and a coordinating conjunction; replace a comma with a semicolon, conjunctive adverb, and a comma; or replace a comma with a subordinating conjunction. (See Chapter 19 for additional information and practice on coordination and subordination.)

Add a Coordinating Conjunction after the Comma

Here's a comma splice:

I've been going to school for 13 years, I'm beginning to realize how important it is.

This comma splice can be corrected by adding an appropriate conjunction after the comma:

I've been going to school for 13 years, and I'm beginning to realize how important it is.

See Chapter 19 for a list of coordinating conjunctions.

Substitute a Semicolon for the Comma and Add a Conjunctive Adverb Followed by a Comma

Here is another comma splice:

College is simply a lot harder than high school was, I have a lot more homework to do every day.

To correct this comma splice, replace the comma with a semicolon and add a conjunctive adverb, followed by a comma:

College is simply a lot harder than high school was; moreover, I have a lot more homework to do every day.

See Chapter 19 for a list of conjunctive adverbs.

Use the comma–conjunction and semicolon–conjunctive adverb–comma options when they are appropriate.

EXERCISE 21-2 **Correcting Comma Splices Using Conjunctions and Conjunctive Adverbs**

Directions: *Underline the comma splices in each of the following items. Then correct them, using one of these three options: (a) replace the comma with a period, (b) add a coordinating conjunction after the comma, or (c) replace the comma with a semicolon and a conjunctive adverb followed by a comma.*

1. The first time I ever saw a real celebrity I was ten years old. A TV personality named William Shatner walked out of a restaurant, he looked just like he did on TV, only smaller.

_____

2. When I was a child, I was very curious about puzzles. I often took apart toys, I sometimes dismantled clocks.

_____

3. The doctor said everything he tested the child for was positive. The parent couldn't believe it, his daughter was allergic to 82 things.

_____

4. The students are glad the final exams are over with. Now their instructors and families won't bug them about studying, that will be a great relief.

_____

Ask Yourself

Which five conjunctive adverbs are you most likely to use? Can you write a sentence for each?

5. Ah, the last days of summer. It was a cool night, the sun had just gone down.

_____

6. When children are young, they always love to own dogs. Some are lucky to have pets of their own, to name and train, they can provide the care to the animal.

_____

7. It was a hot June morning, I was coming back from McDonald's when I saw one of my neighbours, Mark, playing with a neighbour's dog.

_____

8. This dog was horrible, it would not stop barking, it kept slobbering on my new shoes, and it would not listen to anything I said.

_____

9. The wasps were crazy, they tried attacking me every time I cut the grass or cleaned my swimming pool.

_____

10. One afternoon I got annoyed at the squirrel eating from the bird feeder, I started yelling at it, from that time on it has stayed away.

_____

Add an Appropriate Subordinating Conjunction

Like coordinating conjunctions and conjunctive adverbs, subordinating conjunctions establish a logical relationship between consecutive ideas. Look at the following example:

> Some of the problems you have are brought on by yourself, others are caused by your friends. The important thing is recognizing what needs to be fixed and taking care of business.

The comma splice can be corrected and the relationship between the two statements indicated through the addition of a subordinating conjunction in place of the comma.

> Some of the problems you have are brought on by <u>yourself **while**</u> others are caused by your friends.

Here is another example:

> I worked hard to change things in my life, everything seemed to remain the same. It was easy to get discouraged, but I didn't lose hope. In the end, everything came out okay.

Once again, the comma splice occurs at the beginning of the short paragraph. The logical relationship between the two statements here can be indicated through the addition of a subordinating conjunction at the beginning of the first sentence and a comma to join it with the next sentence.

> **Even though** I worked hard to change things in my life, everything seemed to remain the same.

See Chapter 19 for a list of subordinating conjunctions.

EXERCISE 21-3 Correcting Comma Splices Using Subordinating Conjunctions

Directions: *Underline the comma splices in each of the following items. Then correct them either by using a subordinating conjunction with a comma or by using a period at the end of the sentence. Some items may have more than one comma splice.*

1. When we have company over, I don't have to worry about putting the cat in a different room, she won't come out from her hiding spot.

   _____

2. Our cat is also an indoor cat, she rarely wants to go outside, I am happy about that.

   _____

3. The math teacher started solving a problem on the board I studied every step, she asked me to do the same problem on the board. I did the problem, and I got it right. I was so happy. From that day I started liking math, that was six years ago.

   _____

4. When I was in grade 7, I was at a school dance, a girl approached me and asked me to dance, but I turned her down.

   _____

5. Then came time to enter high school it was a brand-new experience.

   _____

6. I see people smoking, I have the urge to ask them if I can have one, I just turn away my head instead.

   _____

7. Most teenagers want to smoke because they think it makes them look cool. Some smoke because parents tell them not to, they are rebellious and do it just to disobey.

_____

8. There is too much homework, children are losing out on fun after school, parents can help, they can monitor their children's homework, they can meet with teachers and discuss the amount of homework that students receive.

_____

9. That woman is a calm person, she just loves to chat and laugh with her children, occasionally she gets a little excited. She can lose her temper then.

_____

10. The two friends went to the same school, they went everywhere together, they often spent the night at each other's houses on the weekend.

_____

EXERCISE 21-4 Putting It All Together

Directions: *Find the comma splices in the following paragraphs. Rewrite the paragraphs and underline your corrections. Try to use all of the methods listed for correcting comma splices: (a) replace the comma with a period; (b) add a comma and a coordinating conjunction; (c) replace the comma with a semicolon, a conjunctive adverb, and a comma; or (d) add a subordinating conjunction.*

1.   Violence has become the answer to many teenagers' frustrations in life. The introduction to violence starts when they are very young. Television dramas show everything from guns to blood and death, media glamorizes the violent behaviour. Teens relate to these dramas and feel violence is the way to end their depression. Another important cause of violence is a lack of family structure. Those teens lacking love and family structure often are in trouble, they all too often take out their troubles through violent actions. Finally, violence may be seen as a cry for help or a way to get attention for some adolescents. Teens see that the only time they are noticed is when they become violent, hurt others, or cause trouble, sometimes they are scared or confused and do not know how to properly express or release those emotions, then violence becomes the vent through which they release steam.

2.   Some men think the women's movement has made it difficult for men and women to enjoy an old-fashioned relationship. This is true to the point that some men have to watch practically everything they say and do. It bothers them that they can't compliment a woman on how she looks, it's not sexist, it is just appreciation. Some men still like to open the door for a woman and pay for dinner, most men do so with the hope that she won't consider it sexual harassment. At one time these kinds of things were just simple manners. Take a look at the previous generations, they treated each other with respect, sometimes some men wish they lived in the olden days. Today it is important for women to be treated as equals, in the workplace. Nevertheless, everyone needs to understand that being

courteous is sometimes just that, being courteous. Being equal is important, that does not mean people cannot just be nice to each other.

3.   Attitudes about credit cards can vary a great deal, depending on when a person is born. My grandfather is old school, he purchased his last truck with $15 000 in $20 bills he had been socking away for years. Then there are people like my parents, who prefer to make their purchases without the long savings period. They got their first taste of plastic in the mid-1980s and never looked back, they enjoy the ability to spend what they want, when they want it, and simply make their planned monthly payments to eliminate debt. If for some reason their cards are lost or stolen, the bank replaces them in 7 to 10 days, forgiving any unauthorized purchases. These days my parents are educated on the dangers and benefits of a credit lifestyle. They believe that plastic makes their lives easier. Being a Generation Xer, on one hand, I am terrified of identity theft, I prefer to carry cash. On the other hand, the reality is that I cannot make a hotel reservation, rent a car, or take advantage of shopping online without a credit card. Our society is a credit culture, there are purchases that cannot be made without a credit card. I have learned to walk a fine line between cash and credit, I am both old school and new school.

Run-Ons

Like a comma splice, a **run-on** is an error involving two complete sentences. Whereas a comma splice occurs when two complete sentences are joined by a comma, a run-on sentence has no connecting punctuation. The sentences simply run together.

IDENTIFYING RUN-ONS

Consider this example:

> I remember the day we met I was swimming to the raft in the lake. This guy went speeding by on a wave runner he was so close I could almost reach out and touch him later that day I ran into him in town.

There are five complete sentences in this example. Each sentence expresses a complete idea and can be written as a separate sentence:

1. I remember the day we met.
2. I was swimming to the raft in the lake.
3. This guy went speeding by on a wave runner.
4. He was so close I could almost reach out and touch him.
5. Later that day I ran into him in town.

This series of consecutive actions can be expressed in concise simple sentences:

> I remember the day we met. I was swimming to the raft in the lake. This guy went speeding by on a wave runner. He was so close I could almost reach out and touch him. Later that day I ran into him in town.

End punctuation brings your writing into focus. It helps you see your ideas clearly, giving you an opportunity to edit, combine sentences, and vary sentence length and structure.

EXERCISE 21-5 Run-Ons and the Simple Sentence

Directions: *Underline the run-ons in the following sentences. Insert a period at the end of each complete sentence.*

1. Don't get me wrong I enjoyed where I worked and what I was doing, but it was not enough I wanted more challenges.

2. After thinking about my employment prospects, I came to a decision I decided I do not want to be a secretary for the rest of my life I want to be a registered nurse.

3. I tried skipping class while in grade 8 my friends didn't that is when my trouble with school began I spent some time in detention after school I met a couple of bad characters there.

4. I think I watched too much TV when I was a child it must have had some effect on me I didn't spend enough time on schoolwork even now I watch too much TV, and it affects my grades.

5. I guess it wasn't the type of work that was important to me it was the place I work that led me to a change of attitude that was my value system then that's my value system now.

CORRECTING RUN-ONS

You can correct a run-on in much the same way you would a comma splice. Because you are joining two simple sentences, you can use the options for coordination and subordination that you learned in Chapter 19. These include adding a comma and a coordinating conjunction; adding a semicolon, conjunctive adverb, and a comma; or adding an appropriate subordinating conjunction.

Note: You do not correct a run-on by placing a comma between the two simple sentences. Doing so turns a run-on into a comma splice.

Talk about it »»»

Are your sentences long or short? Are you more inclined to write comma splices or run-ons?

Add a Comma and a Coordinating Conjunction

Here is a run-on sentence:

My son tries hard in <u>school it</u> takes him a little longer to get good grades.

The error can be corrected by the addition of a comma and an appropriate conjunction.

My son tries hard in <u>school, **but** it</u> takes him a little longer to get good grades.

Add a Semicolon, a Conjunctive Adverb, and a Comma

Here is a run-on sentence:

I had five hard classes last <u>semester my</u> hardest class was economics.

The error can be corrected by adding a semicolon and a conjunctive adverb followed by a comma.

I had five hard classes last <u>semester; **however,** my</u> hardest class was economics.

Use the comma–coordinating conjunction and semicolon options when they make sense and sound right.

Correcting Run-Ons with Coordinating Conjunctions and Conjunctive Adverbs

Directions: *Underline the run-ons in the following sentences. Then correct the errors using one of these three options: (a) add a period at the end of the sentence; (b) add a comma followed by a coordinating conjunction; or (c) add a semicolon and a conjunctive adverb followed by a comma. Some items may not need correction.*

1. Usually the drive down to Florida would take about nine hours if my mom was driving, it would take twelve.

   _____

2. He purposely mixed his languages together to make me confused it took years for me to catch on to this.

   _____

3. My aunt is a very important person in my life she is my great-aunt, my grandmother's baby sister. She's my mother's favourite aunt, that is why we are so close.

   _____

4. Peter enjoys playing golf two or three times a week during golf season in the off-season he bowls.

   _____

5. Janice's favourite knick-knack is a jade elephant it was given to her as a gift.

   _____

6. The ceramic egg has green and gold designs all over it and around the rim of the egg itself. This egg opens up, and it has a working clock inside.

   _____

7. My sister is a friend to everyone she is more than a friend to me she is my best friend she is the person I confide in the most.

   _____

8. It's hard enough just being in high school my friend turned high school into a roller coaster of love-hate situations our first year was great we would spend the weekend at each other's houses and study together we sang a duet in our choir's spring festival. Then things changed.

   _____

9. I thought about the decision for quite a while I decided that I did not care. She had her turn now I would get mine.

   _____

10. He is using basketball as a tool to reach his goal of becoming an engineer it is not just a game to him it is a way to balance his life.

___

Add an Appropriate Subordinating Conjunction

The two simple sentences in a run-on can also be joined using a subordinating conjunction. (See the list of subordinating conjunctions in Chapter 19.) The connecting words establish a logical relationship between the two sentences in the run-on.

> The trash collectors come every morning at 7:30 I usually take out the garbage the night before.

The logical relationship in the first sentence is cause and effect. This relationship can be indicated by using a subordinating conjunction and a comma to join the simple sentences.

> **Because** the trash collectors come every morning at 7:30, I usually take out the garbage the night before.

To develop a feel for sentence variety, use both coordination and subordination when you proofread for and correct run-on sentences.

EXERCISE 21-7 **Correcting Run-Ons Using Subordinating Conjunctions**

Directions: *Underline the run-ons in the following sentences. Then correct them either by inserting a comma with a subordinating conjunction or by using a period at the end of the sentence.*

1. Some people still do not use seat belts when they drive seat belts save lives.

___

2. The time and place were set all he had to do was complete the task.

___

3. I turned to say goodbye to my cousin and his friends they were gone seconds later I realized why their bus had actually arrived five minutes early.

___

4. He had to use a lot of heavy machinery it was hard work somehow he managed and actually began to like what he was doing.

___

5. When she was young, she was somewhat of a collector all she collected was dolls her friends would ask her if they could hold one of her dolls she just said no.

___

6. The men are twins they are the bosses of their catering company they prepare food for any kind of occasion they say they like wedding receptions the best it looks like a cool job.

___

7. Everyone has problems some people just have more than others that is the way it is.

_____

8. Jim and his friend Joe stopped at the fireworks store they spent a couple hundred dollars each Jack went inside and decided to buy some he only had about 20 dollars to spend.

_____

9. All of a sudden Emily wanted to leave we started walking out the alarm went off. The manager came out and asked us if we had stolen anything. Never in my life had I stolen anything Emily was another story.

_____

10. I misbehaved the teacher told me to get out and go home I was excluded from the play I figured if I went back the next day and apologized maybe she would let me back in the play that didn't work she told me she already had someone else to play my part.

_____

EXERCISE 21-8 **Proofreading for Comma Splices and Run-Ons**

Directions: _Read the following sentences. Mark those that are comma splices CS and those that are run-ons RO. Some sentences may have more than one error. Correct the errors using one of these four options: (a) add a period at the end of the sentence; (b) add a comma and a coordinating conjunction; (c) add a semicolon and a conjunctive adverb; or (d) add a subordinating conjunction._

_____ 1. His first job was at Franklin Wright Settlements. He started that job the summer of 2004, he was 14 years old. He was really excited the whole summer about that job. So he did his best.

_____

_____ 2. Even strangers teach you things. Sometimes it doesn't matter who it is if it means something to you or relates to you, somehow you never forget it.

_____

_____ 3. It's not his fault he was born with a birthmark on his face what can he do about that?

_____

_____ 4. He operates a forklift, it is hard to drive, but at the end of the day he feels like he did something. The thing he finds challenging about his job is his boss, she always tries to do things too fast and always wants to be right.

_____

_____ 5. Greta drinks orange juice it prevents her from catching colds, she really likes the taste of it.

_____

Ask Yourself

Which errors are easier to identify and correct, comma splices or run-ons? Why?

☐ Comma splices

- *Identifying comma splices: replace comma with period*

- *Correcting comma splices: use coordinating conjunctions, subordinating conjunctions, and conjunctive adverbs*

☐ Run-Ons

- *Identifying run-ons: use correct punctuation*

- *Correcting run-ons: use a period; a comma and an appropriate coordinating conjunction; a semicolon, conjunctive adverb, and a comma; or an appropriate subordinating conjunction*

_____ 6. When you're 16 or 17, you don't think about the value of your job you just want to work so you can earn money to go shopping with friends and blow your money on whatever grabs your attention.

_____

_____ 7. When he was trying to quit smoking, he never wore the patch it is not that he didn't want to put one on it is just that he always forgot.

_____

_____ 8. It was very interesting to meet the travellers who had no knowledge of Quebec, to them it was just another place to have a business meeting.

_____

_____ 9. Then one day she started doing time cards, making beds, and working overtime while still getting paid only eight dollars an hour, she tried to talk to her boss but it wasn't any help, so she finally said goodbye to that job. She really did enjoy that job it was fun and diverse every day.

_____

_____ 10. How she got her name is very simple, she was born, her parents looked in the phone book and selected the first name they liked.

_____

The English you are accustomed to hearing and speaking every day in an informal setting with friends may differ from the English used in the classroom or in the workplace. If this is the case, you need to make a *code shift*, a term used to define speaking more formally and avoiding use of slang. Academic writing assignments require more formal English, which requires paying close attention to verbs.

Verbs and Verb Agreement

VERBS

In Chapter 18 you learned that **verbs** express physical or mental actions, or link subjects to their modifiers, or establish a fact or condition about the subject. Verbs also state *when* something happens—in the past, the present, or the future. In other words, verbs also reveal the tense of the action in the sentence.

1. Most college and university <u>instructors</u> <u>assign</u> homework every day.

This sentence is about college and university instructors and homework, but the heart of the sentence is the verb, *assign*. The verb expresses present action, what college instructors *do* habitually.

2. Most college and university <u>instructors</u> <u>assigned</u> homework every day.
3. Most college and university <u>instructors</u> <u>will assign</u> homework every day.

Verbs can also place the action in the past or in the future. In the second sentence, *assigned* indicates an action that took place in the past. In the third sentence, *will assign* indicates an action that will take place in the future.

> **A SIMPLE TEST FOR ACTION VERBS**
>
> To find the action verb in a sentence, ask these questions:
> - What is happening?
> - When is it happening?
>
> When you identify the word or words that answer these questions, you have found the verb in the sentence.

Verbs can also link subjects to modifiers. A modifier can be another noun or an adjective. A noun gives the subject another name, whereas an adjective ascribes a quality to the subject.

Verb Errors: Agreement, Irregular Verbs, and Consistency

1. The committee <u>chairperson</u> <u>is</u> a tyrant.
2. The committee <u>chairperson</u> <u>is</u> serious.
3. The committee <u>chairperson</u> <u>remains</u> for a two-year term.

In the first sentence the verb links the subject, "chairperson," to a noun, *tyrant;* in the second sentence, the subject is linked to an adjective, *serious.* The third sentence uses *remains* to point out a fact about the chairperson position. Like action verbs, linking verbs or state-of-being verbs can also express time: past, present, and future.

The hurricane <u>damage</u> <u>appeared</u> widespread. (past tense)

The hurricane <u>disaster</u> <u>will be</u> a wake-up call. (future tense)

In these examples the verb in past tense links the subject first to an adjective, *widespread,* then in the second sentence, to a noun, *a wake-up call,* in future tense.

COMMON LINKING OR STATE-OF-BEING VERBS		
is	feel	remain
are	get	seem
was	grow	smell
were	sit	sound
appear	look	taste
become	prove	turn

EXERCISE 22-1 **Identifying Verbs**

Directions: *Underline subjects once and verbs twice in the sentences below. Indicate in the space provided whether the verb is an action verb (A) or a linking verb (L).*

_____ 1. All the new employees wanted overtime.

_____ 2. The situation between the neighbours and the new resident turned out fine.

_____ 3. At first all the reading in psychology class seems excessive.

_____ 4. Work stoppages in the transportation sector will complicate people's travel plans this summer.

_____ 5. Efforts to beautify the state were vigorous and well funded.

_____ 6. The arguments against young people giving a year or two of national service are much less persuasive than those in favour of service.

_____ 7. New technologies emerge every day and transform the workplace practically overnight.

_____ 8. Opinions vary on the best networking activities for university graduates.

_____ 9. The cook will taste the sauce and pronounce it ready to serve.

_____ 10. Both the coach and the players remain confident in the team's prospects for the coming year.

SUBJECT AND VERB AGREEMENT

Subject and **verb agreement** occurs when the subject and verb of a sentence go together properly. Subjects of sentences can be singular or plural. For subject and verb to agree, singular subjects must have singular verbs and plural subjects must have plural verbs. Here are some guidelines for editing subject and verb agreement.

Regular Verbs in Present Tense

Most verbs in English are regular. That means you apply the same conjugation rules to them. With regular verbs in present tense, third-person singular has an -s ending. The table shows the present tense forms of the regular verb *to like*.

In present tense, third-person singular verbs end in *s* or *es*. Do not confuse this ending with the plural of nouns, *s* or *es*. He likes to read novels.

to like	Singular	Plural
First person	I *like*	we *like*
Second person	you *like*	you *like*
Third person	he/she/it *likes*	they *like*

Notice that verbs following he/she/it or third person nouns have the *s* ending.

I start school in September.

Football practice starts early in August.

My cousin plans to go out for football this year.

The first game of the season falls on a Saturday this year.

EXERCISE 22-2 **Verb Agreement and Regular Verbs**

Directions: *Underline subjects and double underline the correct verbs for each of the sentences below.*

1. The crazy bus driver on Yonge Street (sing/sings) out each bus stop when he (feel/feels) happy.

2. Passengers (like/likes) to ride his bus for that reason.

3. We usually (sit/sits) halfway back on the bus and (wait/waits) for him to start singing.

4. Sometimes he (drive/drives) one-handed and (play/plays) the harmonica.

5. Company regulations (require/requires) drivers to minimize interaction with passengers.

6. I (know/knows) this because my uncle (drive/drives) the bus on Kipling Avenue.

7. You just never (know/knows) what surprises (await/awaits) you on a city bus.

8. Afternoon traffic (get/gets) heavy.

9. Passengers (appreciate/appreciates) his singing.

10. It (make/makes) time pass a little faster.

Verb Agreement and Regular Verbs

Directions: *Read the following paragraph. Correct the verb agreement errors you find.*

My mother is a great role model for me and my brother. She works, goes to school, clean the house, cooks, and still finds time to help us out when she can. She reads to my little brother, explains things, and breaks words down to their simplest meanings. She is a role model because she cares about whether my brother understand things and how he behaves in school. She is also a very good cook. We don't go out to eat as much as I would like to. I tell her that food in restaurants smell good. Not only that, but the food always taste good too. She agrees with me, but then she help me understand that food cost less when we cook it at home. Finally, my mother is an outgoing woman. She will help anyone who need help. If someone ask her for some spare change, she will dig down deep in her purse and find a little something. Then she say to us, "Help others. Work hard so you don't find yourself in a bad situation, but always remember the poor." My mother work hard and tries her best to raise us well.

Irregular Verbs in Present Tense: *Be, Have, Do*

Irregular verbs are those that do not follow the pattern shown above. Notice, however, that the third-person singular retains the *s* on the end of the verb.

to be	Singular	Plural
First person	I *am*	we *are*
Second person	you *are*	you *are*
Third person	he/she/it *is*	they *are*
to have	**Singular**	**Plural**
First person	I *have*	we *have*
Second person	you *have*	you *have*
Third person	he/she/it *has*	they *have*
to do	**Singular**	**Plural**
First person	I *do*	we *do*
Second person	you *do*	you *do*
Third person	he/she/it *does*	they *do*

Agreement and Irregular Verbs

Directions: *Underline subjects and choose the correct verbs for each of the sentences below. Be sure to choose present tense forms of* to be, to have, *and* to do.

1. After my two best friends, I _____ the third-best basketball player on the team.

2. They _____ not practice very much, but somehow they _____ better skills.

3. Some people say basketball _____ a waste of time.

4. It _____ take up a lot of time, if you let it.

5. My friends and I _____ careful not to get carried away.

6. Homework _____ important.

7. Jobs _____ important, too.

8. I _____ a job, and one of my friends _____ a job.

9. We _____ very busy people.

10. Still, if we _____ not play some ball at least once a week, we _____ a tendency to get a little nervous.

Agreement and Irregular Verbs in Past Tense

In the simple past tense, agreement problems may occur with the irregular verb *to be*.

to be	Singular	Plural
First person	I *was*	we *were*
Second person	you *were*	you *were*
Third person	he/she/it *was*	they *were*

The neighbourhood school grounds <u>are</u> always open for public use.
The neighbourhood school grounds <u>were</u> always open for public use.
The neighbourhood school <u>is</u> fully Internet accessible.
The neighbourhood school <u>was</u> fully Internet accessible.

EXERCISE 22-5 **Agreement and Irregular Verbs in Past Tense**

Directions: *Underline subjects and choose the correct past tense form of* to be *for each of the sentences below.*

1. There _____ never any doubt about who would move out of the house first.

2. People _____ talking a lot about organizing a ski trip, but no one _____ actually doing anything yet.

3. Students _____ not really independent if they _____ still living at home.

4. At the time, he _____ working 30 hours a week, and his parents _____ eager for him to live at home and go to school.

5. His friend, Tanya, on the other hand, _____ working 40 hours a week, and her mother _____ always giving her a hard time.

6. Some other good friends _____ not working at all.

7. One night there _____ an incident.

Talk about it

Who do you know who is good at grammar and finding verbs? Why is knowing about verbs important to your writing skills?

8. Something happened, and, at midnight, Tanya _____ on his front doorstep.

9. _____ there any good reasons for her to continue living at home?

10. They talked all night and saw that there _____ no good reasons, and the next day she _____ ready to pack up and leave.

EXERCISE 22-6 **Agreement and Irregular Verbs in Present and Past Tense**

Directions: *Read the following sentences and underline the subjects. Then double underline the verb that agrees with the subject of the sentence. Read the simple subject and verb together to watch for the single s ending.*

1. Before the Kyoto Summit, many fingers (was/were) pointed at assumed guilty parties.

2. The Great Bear Rainforest in British Columbia (contain/contains) 1000-year-old cedars.

3. When they went outside, a police officer (was/were) sitting right in front of the house.

4. Many fans (go/goes) to every sporting event they can think of.

5. Then one afternoon I (was/were) watching TV, and I heard the motorcycle start up.

6. We had lunch at the Olive Garden. The food (was/were) excellent.

7. Over time, graphing calculators (has/have) become standard equipment in the classroom.

8. Now, no smoking signs (is/are) visible everywhere in the workplace.

9. A second reason for battling against illegal drugs (has/have) to be their effects on babies born to addicts.

10. Almost all businesses (do/does) at least some of their work on the Internet these days.

EXERCISE 22-7 **Missing Verb Endings**

Directions: *Read the following sentences and edit for missing verb endings. Add -d and -ed, -s, and -es endings as needed. Some items may have more than one verb error.*

1. For a number of reasons it is easy to understand why he feel the way that he do.

_____

2. My grandfather always made us do various chores around the house. From his favourite chair, he also watch everyone that came to the door.

_____

3. My aunt's complexion was dark brown. She had no wrinkles. She use moisturizer on her skin.

_____

4. This aunt still calls me Baby Bobby. How old do I have to be before she stop calling me that?

_____

5. She respect the person who live down the street. He has encourage her to work hard at everything she do and not to let anybody stop her.

_____

6. The first time I got into trouble with the law, my own family did not come to visit, but our pastor did, and I change because of him.

_____

7. The job he do make a difference to many young teens.

_____

8. He took one look at the new math teacher and judge his character wrong.

_____

9. My grandmother remembers a lottery number based on my birthday. She still remember the first time she play it, but she can't remember my name.

_____

10. In her spare time, she like to read and do crafts such as floral arrangements.

_____

ADDITIONAL VERB AGREEMENT PROBLEMS

In addition to knowing regular and irregular verbs, it helps to recognize sentence constructions in which verb agreement can be confusing.

Compound Subjects

In Chapter 19, you learned about compound subjects, which may be two subjects joined by *and* or three or more subjects in a series ending with *and*.

Simple Subject: The bicycle gets people around town in many European cities.

Compound Subject: Bicycles and motorcycles get people around town in many European cities.

Compound Subject: Bicycles, motorcycles, and cars get people around town in many European cities.

Hint: To check for the correct verb, substitute a singular pronoun for simple subjects and a plural pronoun for compound subjects.

Simple Subject: The bicycle gets people around town in many European cities.

Substitute Singular Pronoun: It gets people around town in many European cities.

Compound Subject: Motorcycles and cars get people around town in many European cities.

Substitute Plural Pronoun: They <u>get</u> people around town in many European cities.

Compound Subject: <u>Bicycles, motorcycles, and cars</u> <u>get</u> people around town in many European cities.

Substitute Plural Pronoun: They <u>get</u> people around town in many European cities.

EXERCISE 22-8 **Verb Agreement and Compound Subjects**

Directions: *Underline the simple or compound subject in each sentence below and choose the verb that agrees with it. Substitute a pronoun for the subject to test your answer and write the sentence, using the pronoun.*

1. Technology (is/are) essential in most lines of work.

_____

2. Clever use of language and creative graphics (keep/keeps) the child interested in reading.

_____

3. Music and painting (express/expresses) the way people feel.

_____

4. A good diet (is/are) essential to maintaining health.

_____

5. People's jobs (define/defines) who they are.

_____

6. If a longer school day and a program to get more parents involved in education (doesn't/don't) work, then what is the answer?

_____

7. Working in a pharmacy, taking care of his family, and going to school full time (was/were) all he could handle.

_____

Ask Yourself

Which part of verb agreement is difficult for you? Which part is easy?

8. In large group settings, her interests and the interests of others (is/are) completely different.

_____

9. Jacinthe usually got As and Bs. Class participation and attendance (was/were) not all that was needed to do well in the class.

_____

10. The number of healthy people (has/have) been increasing over the past few years.

_____

Verb-First Sentences

In sentences beginning with the words *here* and *there,* the subject comes after the verb. These are called inverted sentences because the word order in the sentence is different. Inverted sentences are often used to introduce a topic. To choose the verb that agrees with the subject, put the subject in front of the verb.

Here at last was the one perfect job for me to do.
The perfect job for me was here.

There/have been many fingers pointed at assumed guilty parties.
Many fingers have been pointed at assumed guilty parties.

In these sentences, "here" and "there" are not the subjects. The subjects come after the verbs—"the job *was*" and "many fingers *have*."

Sentences with Relative Pronouns

In Chapter 19 you learned about relative clauses. Recall that in complex sentences, relative pronouns "repeat" the subject and are either singular or plural.

The peaches that (fall/falls) to the ground (rot/rots) quickly.
Peaches fall.
Peaches rot.
The peaches that fall to the ground rot quickly.

The main part or independent clause of this sentence is "peaches rot quickly." The relative clause tells which peaches. The relative pronoun *that* echoes the plural subject "peaches" and consequently takes a plural verb.

The neighbourhood children who (stop/stops) by our house (is/are) always welcome.
Children stop.
Children are welcome.
The neighbourhood children who stop by our house are always welcome.

The main part of this sentence is "children are welcome." The relative clause "who stop by our house" specifies which children. *Who* echoes the plural subject "children" and therefore takes the plural verb.

EXERCISE 22-9 Editing for Subject and Verb Agreement

Directions: *Underline simple subjects and double underline verbs in the following sentences. Correct verb agreement errors. Some of the sentences may be correct as written.*

1. There are things a person can do to get better grades and improve himself as a student.

   _____

2. There has been many situations in which people recognized me from the competitions I entered.

   _____

3. The areas that I need to work on is attending classes, keeping up with material, and paying attention in class.

   _____

4. These are a few strategies that has worked for me and is bound to make you a successful student.

_____

5. Some people have to work at their talents; then again there is some who just has them naturally.

_____

6. The strong family values that influence his work habits makes this person stand out above the rest.

_____

7. We know there is many distractions while you are driving.

_____

8. That is his suggestions on how to become a more alert and safe driver.

_____

9. Common team injuries include pulled muscles, which is usually a result of not stretching before exercising.

_____

10. You can imagine the looks that was on their faces when they saw me.

_____

EXERCISE 22-10 **Additional Practice Editing for Subject and Verb Agreement**

Directions: *Underline simple subjects and double underline verbs in the following sentences. Correct verb agreement errors.*

1. He didn't know anyone who worked in the store, but when he started, there was interesting people.

_____

2. This experience taught me that there is many great people out in the world.

_____

3. She rode her bike around town, trying to find someone who would be generous enough to keep a few little kittens. She didn't get home until late. There was no kittens left in her backpack.

_____

4. Her favourite comedy show was *Corner Gas,* which aired once a week and stars Gabrielle Miller.

_____

5. His skills working with animals gets better all the time.

_____

6. She did not like working at the optical company. The people who worked there was older than she was and not very friendly.

_____

7. Statutory holidays are any holidays established by a society or government that has no religious bearing.

_____

8. There has been times growing up when he would have enjoyed having a different name.

_____

9. Upkeep or maintenance of bicycles is relatively inexpensive.

_____

10. There is all kinds of different exercises a person can do to improve muscle mass.

_____

Irregular Verbs

You make most past tense verbs in English by adding -ed. In addition, the -ed past tense form also serves as the past participle, a form preceded by a helping verb.

To look is a regular verb. Here is its present, past, and participle forms:

Present: I <u>look</u> for my keys every time I leave the house.
Past: I <u>looked</u> for my keys this morning.
Past Participle: Often I <u>have looked</u> for my keys without finding them.

Now consider the irregular verb *to find*.

Present: I <u>find</u> my keys in the most unlikely places.
Past: This morning I <u>found</u> them under the couch.
Past Participle: Often I <u>have found</u> them in the kitchen.

If you know your irregular verbs, you know not to write "I finded them under the couch." There are plenty of irregular forms that are less obvious. For this reason, you may be inclined to make mistakes like these:

I <u>seen</u> a good movie last night (should be *saw*)
My prized possession got <u>broke</u> last night. (should be *broken*)
The major most often <u>chose</u> by first year students is psychology. (should be *chosen*)

At the end of this chapter are some tables of irregular verbs to help you avoid possible mistakes.

Writer's Response

Sometimes verb agreement errors are hard to "hear." Why is that? What can you do if you don't hear them?

IRREGULAR PAST TENSE VERBS

There are four types of irregular past tense forms, shown in the following tables.

1.

PAST AND PAST PARTICIPLE ARE THE SAME		
Present	**Past**	**Past Participle**
bring	brought	brought
build	built	built
buy	bought	bought

Students bring pens and paper to class with them.
Students brought paper and pens to class with them.
Students should have brought paper and pens to class with them.

2.

PRESENT, PAST, AND PAST PARTICIPLE ARE ALL DIFFERENT		
Present	**Past**	**Past Participle**
forget	forgot	forgotten
forgive	forgave	forgiven
freeze	froze	frozen

The fruit crop freezes in December.
The fruit crop froze in December.
The fruit crop has frozen in December.

3.

PRESENT, PAST, AND PAST PARTICIPLE ARE ALL THE SAME		
Present	**Past**	**Past Participle**
cut	cut	cut
hurt	hurt	hurt

He hurts his wrist.
He hurt his wrist.
He has hurt his wrist.

4.

PRESENT AND PAST PARTICIPLE ARE THE SAME		
Present	**Past**	**Past Participle**
run	ran	run
become	became	become

The crowd becomes unruly.

The crowd became unruly.

The crowd has become unruly.

Refer to the tables of irregular verbs at the end of the chapter when you do exercises in this book. You can also use them as a reference as you learn to use these irregular verbs.

EXERCISE 22-11 **Proofreading for Irregular Verbs**

Directions: *Read the following sentences and underline the verbs. Using the tables at the end of the chapter as your guide, substitute corrected verb forms as needed. Some sentences may be correct as written.*

1. The recent slowdown in economic activity has hurt the housing industry. Lawmakers have rose to the challenge in the past and provided tax incentives to stimulate demand; the premier, however, has forbade his advisors to consider such a stimulus at this time.

2. Athletes at Seneca College has always rose to the challenge when they needed to. Now that the basketball team has lost three consecutive games, the coach has spoke forcefully to the players about the importance of spirit, dedication, and perseverance.

3. The candidate has ran a good campaign. She stands an excellent chance of being elected to the student council.

4. The children had hid for so long in the woods that they no longer remembered the way back to their campsite.

5. After Cleary had drunk so much, he ventured out on the road, which had froze to glare ice and was perilous for even the best of drivers.

6. She has taught me how great a slow cooker is, and I use mine all the time. She has also gave me many tips on cleaning and cooking.

7. In the morning it was a clear day, and the sun shone on everything.

8. The problem with late-night pizza parties is that after you have ate all that food and went to bed, you have no desire to get up and exercise the next morning.

9. After Suzanne was thrown from her horse, she was taken to the hospital, treated for broken ribs, then sent home. She rode again as soon as her ribs started to feel better.

10. For as long as I can remember, we have flew Air Canada to go to Winnipeg to visit my grandparents, and we have come to trust them to get us to our destination on time.

Consistent Verb Tense

In academic writing, readers look for a consistent use of the present or past tense. The agreement of one verb tense with another is called *consistency*.

> **Inconsistent:** It <u>was</u> a beautiful summer day. My brother and I <u>had found</u> ourselves sitting on our rusty swing set with nothing to do.

In the example above, the student uses two different forms of the past tense: *was* and *had found*. To be consistent, the student should use one form: *was* and *found*.

> **Consistent:** It <u>was</u> a beautiful summer day. My brother and I <u>found</u> ourselves sitting on our rusty swing set with nothing to do.

Watch out for auxiliary verbs—such as *can/could, will/would,* and *may/might*—and keep them consistent with the tense you establish.

> **Inconsistent:** This time we <u>agreed</u> that we <u>will study</u> together.
> **Consistent:** This time we <u>agreed</u> that we <u>would study</u> together.

More often than not, consistency errors occur because of inattention. Be alert when you check your writing for these (and other) common errors.

EXERCISE 22-12   Proofreading for Inconsistent Verb Tense

Directions: *Read the following sentences and underline the verbs. Then correct errors in verb tense consistency. Some may be correct as written.*

1. She believe that if people are dependable, it helps a great deal. They could make a positive contribution to the world.

2. She would always be the cop, which means catching and arresting her brother. When she catches him, he would always cry, stomp his feet, and say she was cheating.

3. My stepfather came to me first and asks who drove his truck without permission.

4. His parents always used to brag about how he is the perfect child.

5. The few times my friend tried to make dinner, she could not make it taste as good as her mother's cooking.

_____

6. As soon as the firecracker exploded, they all take off running.

_____

7. One morning my sister and I were walking to school, and we meet up with some of our friends.

_____

8. A lot of people play their music loudly just to get attention. For example, Moe had a system in his car, and he always turns up the sound.

_____

9. One time when I was eight or nine years old, I asked my mother if I can go outside and play with friends.

_____

10. When I was a child, most of the kids pass their time collecting hockey cards, basketball cards, and baseball cards.

_____

IRREGULAR VERBS: PAST AND PAST PARTICIPLE ARE THE SAME					
Present	**Past**	**Past Participle**	**Present**	**Past**	**Past Participle**
bring	brought	brought	deal	dealt	dealt
build	built	built	feed	fed	fed
buy	bought	bought	feel	felt	felt
catch	caught	caught	fight	fought	fought
find	found	found	sell	sold	sold
have	had	had	send	sent	sent
hear	heard	heard	shine	shone	shone
hold	held	held	sit	sat	sat
keep	kept	kept	sleep	slept	slept
lay	laid	laid	spend	spent	spent
lead	led	led	stand	stood	stood
leave	left	left	swing	swung	swung
lose	lost	lost	teach	taught	taught
make	made	made	tell	told	told

(continued)

IRREGULAR VERBS: PAST AND PAST PARTICIPLE ARE THE SAME

Present	Past	Past Participle	Present	Past	Past Participle
meet	met	met	think	thought	thought
pay	paid	paid	understand	understood	understood
say	said	said	win	won	won
seek	sought	sought			

IRREGULAR VERBS: PRESENT, PAST, AND PAST PARTICIPLE ARE ALL DIFFERENT

Present	Past	Past Participle	Present	Past	Past Participle
be	was/were	been	forgive	forgave	forgiven
begin	began	begun	freeze	froze	frozen
blow	blew	blown	get	got	gotten
break	broke	broken	give	gave	given
choose	chose	chosen	go	went	gone
do	did	done	grow	grew	grown
drink	drank	drunk	hide	hid	hidden
drive	drove	driven	know	knew	known
eat	ate	eaten	lie	lay	lain
fall	fell	fallen	ride	rode	ridden
fly	flew	flown	ring	rang	rung
forbid	forbade	forbidden	rise	rose	risen
forget	forgot	forgotten	see	saw	seen
shake	shook	shaken	take	took	taken
sing	sang	sung	tear	tore	torn
speak	spoke	spoken	throw	threw	thrown
spring	sprang	sprung	wake	woke/waked	woken/waken or waked
steal	stole	stolen	wear	wore	worn
swim	swam	swum	written	wrote	written

IRREGULAR VERBS: PRESENT, PAST, AND PAST PARTICIPLE ARE ALL THE SAME

Present	Past	Past Participle
burst	burst	burst
cut	cut	cut
hurt	hurt	hurt
let	let	let
quit	quit	quit
read	read	read

IRREGULAR VERBS: PRESENT AND PAST PARTICIPLE ARE THE SAME

Present	Past	Past Participle
become	became	become
come	came	come
run	ran	run

CHAPTER REVIEW

Take a moment and reflect on what you have learned about verb errors.

☐ Verbs and verb agreement

- *Verbs: express actions; link subject to modifiers; indicate when something happens (past, present, future)*

- *Subject and verb agreement: singular subjects take singular verbs; plural subjects take plural verbs*

- *Additional verb agreement problems*

☐ Irregular verbs: *be, have, do;* check table for other verbs

- *Irregular past tense verbs; third person singular s*

☐ Consistent verb tense: do not switch verb tenses in a sentence or paragraph unless a time change must be shown

Pronoun Agreement, Case, and Consistency

People constantly slip up grammatically when speaking, and no one corrects them. The error either goes unnoticed, or no comment is made because it is considered slightly bad manners to correct another person's speech. Even more than mistakes made with verb tenses, people get pronouns wrong when they speak. The pronoun errors to look for in your own writing involve agreement, case, and consistency.

Pronoun Agreement

Pronouns are words that take the place of nouns. They eliminate repetition and enable you to manage more information when you speak and write.

> Last night, after soccer practice, I ate pizza with all my buddies. The pizza was delicious. My friend Phil paid for the pizza. Phil likes pizza, too, but Phil prefers that someone else pay for the pizza next time.

Notice the repetition of the words *pizza* and *Phil*. In the following sentences, this repetition is eliminated by the use of pronouns.

> Last night, after soccer practice, I ate pizza with all my buddies. It was delicious. My friend Phil paid for it. He likes pizza, too, but he prefers that someone else pay for it next time.

Table 23-1 shows a list of commonly used pronouns.

Agreement occurs when a pronoun agrees in number with the noun to which it refers, called the **antecedent.** Singular antecedents take singular pronouns. Plural antecedents take plural pronouns.

> Smoking stinks. It also poses terrible health risks. I just don't understand why people would want to pollute the air and risk their health at the same time.

In these sentences, *it* is a singular pronoun that refers to "smoking," a singular antecedent. *Their* is a plural pronoun that refers to "people," a plural antecedent. In both cases, the pronouns and antecedents agree in number.

> My sister was very athletic when she was a child. She could do just about anything. Her favourite sport was gymnastics. It appealed to her because it was a performance, almost like dance.

The antecedent "sister" is followed by a number of singular pronouns: *she, she, her,* and *her.* The singular pronoun *it* refers to the singular antecedent "gymnastics." **Note:** Some nouns in English are singular in meaning even though they end in *s. Economics, ethics,* and *mathematics* are other examples.

Table 23-1

COMMON PRONOUNS			
Subjective	**Objective**	**Possessive**	**Reflexive**
I	me	my	myself
you	you	your	yourself
it	it	its	itself
she	her	her	herself
he	him	his	himself
we	us	our	ourselves
they	them	their	themselves

EXERCISE 23-1 **Identifying Pronouns and Their Antecedents**

Directions: *Underline the pronouns and circle the antecedents in the following sentences. Write them in the space provided and indicate whether they are singular or plural.*

1. Some parents today neglect teaching their children the importance of saving money.

_____

2. Street drugs can be a huge problem. They can even destroy a person's life.

_____

3. One time, I was watching *Oprah,* and she asked members of the audience to raise their hands to show if they would have preferred being raised at a daycare centre rather than at home.

_____

4. A teacher definitely affects learning. Her voice, attitude, personality, and even her penmanship create this unique feeling of character one cannot get from staring at a computer screen.

_____

5. The novel describes a boy who was so full of life. He was also full of surprises.

_____

6. An angry neighbour called my parents. He told them that he had caught everything my friend and I did to his car on video. We got in a lot of trouble.

_____

7. It was a beautiful summer day, yet my brother and I found ourselves sitting on our rusty swing set with nothing to do.

_____

8. I bought a new sound system for my car. It was so loud that people ran for cover every time they heard it.

_____

A pronoun does not change to agree with the noun it modifies: "Marie showed me her rings."

9. It is amazing how many people are working out of their homes these days.

_____

10. People who cannot manage time properly can lose the most important thing in their lives, and that's the love of their families.

_____

DETECTING ERRORS IN PRONOUN AGREEMENT

One of the most common errors in spoken English involves pronoun agreement. In fact, this grammatical misstep is so common that even radio and television professionals frequently make statements like this:

> **Incorrect:** If an older person (*singular*) applies for a job, they (*plural*) will probably be overlooked.

They is a plural pronoun that refers to a singular antecedent, "person." The pronoun and antecedent do not agree in number.

In formal English, it would be preferable to say and write one of the following:

> If older people (*plural*) apply for a job, they (*plural*) will probably be overlooked.

Solution: Make the antecedent plural to agree with the plural pronoun.

> If an older person (*singular*) applies for a job, he or she (*singular*) will probably be overlooked.

Solution: Make the pronoun singular to agree with the singular antecedent.

> An older person who applies for a job will probably be overlooked.

Solution: Revise the sentence to eliminate the pronoun in question.

Because of the gap between what you hear in spoken English and what is required in academic writing, agreement errors can be difficult to detect and correct. It is good practice to examine plural pronouns every time they occur.

> **Incorrect:** Every person (*singular*) has talents and special abilities. Their (*plural*) talents and abilities make them (*plural*) who they (*plural*) are and determine the impression they (*plural*) make on other people.

The pronouns here are all plural: *their, them, they,* and *they.* The antecedent is singular: "person." (Think every single person.) The pronouns in this sentence, then, are not in agreement with their antecedent. Because there are four pronouns for one antecedent, it makes sense to make the antecedent plural. However, there are two other options as well:

> People (*plural*) have talents and special abilities. Their (*plural*) talents and abilities make them (*plural*) who they are and determine the impression they (*plural*) make on other people.

Solution: Make the antecedent plural to agree with the plural pronouns.

Writer's Response

What is an antecedent? What is its relationship to a pronoun?

Every person (*singular*) has talents and special abilities. His or her (*singular*) talents and abilities make that person who he or she (*singular*) is and determine the impression he or she (*singular*) makes on other people.

Solution: Make the pronouns singular to agree with the singular antecedent.

Every person has unique talents and abilities that make an impression on other people.

Solution: Revise the sentence to eliminate the pronouns in question.

Your goal when correcting these errors is to produce a sentence that is grammatically correct and that retains the meaning of the original sentence. In the preceding examples, the first revision sounds the best and expresses the same idea as the original sentence.

EXERCISE 23-2 **Editing Pronoun Agreement Errors**

Directions: *Underline the pronouns and circle the antecedents in the following sentences. Then determine whether the antecedents and the pronouns agree. Use one of these three solutions to correct any errors and write the corrected sentences in the space provided:*

- *Make an antecedent plural to agree with a plural pronoun.*
- *Make a pronoun singular to agree with a singular antecedent.*
- *Revise the sentence and eliminate the pronoun in question.*

1. When a person is under the influence of a drug, they are less inhibited and do things that they normally would not do.

   _____

2. There are many ways a person can protect themselves from other drivers on the road. One is defensive driving. The person driving next to you might not realize they are crossing into your lane.

   _____

3. Not every driver is as good as they should be, but that does not mean we are all doomed.

   _____

4. This person has gone through many hardships in their life.

   _____

5. The strengths of this course would be that the student can work at their own pace and set their work schedule around the rest of their life.

   _____

6. A good server should make it her duty to satisfy the customer, regardless of their ethnic or financial background.

_____

7. A child has a vivid imagination, the ability to create things that do not exist, before the cruel adult world gets hold of them.

_____

8. Whether it is a nine-to-five office job or shift work, every person has something that they are committed to every day.

_____

9. If a teacher pronounces my name right after the first try, I give them a lot of respect.

_____

10. When I meet a new employee for the first time, they always ask my name.

_____

INDEFINITE PRONOUNS AND AGREEMENT

In spoken English, speakers frequently use plural pronouns with indefinite pronouns (see box). Although these indefinite pronouns sound plural, they are clearly singular in meaning.

INDEFINITE PRONOUNS	
one	everyone
nobody	everybody
anyone	someone
anybody	somebody

Incorrect: Someone (*singular*) always parks their (*plural*) car too close to mine.

Incorrect: Everyone (*singular*) brought their (*plural*) own lunch on the trip to the museum.

There are three solutions (the same ones discussed earlier) to correct agreement errors involving these indefinite pronouns:

1. Make the antecedent plural.
2. Make the pronoun singular.
3. Revise the sentence to eliminate the pronoun in question.

Ask Yourself

Proofread your papers for indefinite pronouns. Do you use the correct pronouns? Check your work.

People (*plural*) always park their (*plural*) cars too close to mine.

Someone (*singular*) always parks his or her (*singular*) car too close to mine.

Someone always parks too close to my car.

All the visitors (*plural*) brought their (*plural*) own lunches on the trip to the museum.

Everyone (*singular*) brought his or her (*singular*) own lunch on the trip to the museum.

Everyone brought a lunch on the trip to the museum.

As always, your goal is to choose the revision that sounds the best and retains the meaning of the original sentence.

EXERCISE 23-3 Indefinite Pronouns and Pronoun Agreement

Directions: *Underline the pronouns and circle the antecedents in the following sentences. Use the space provided to rewrite the sentences so that the pronouns and antecedents agree. Use one of these three solutions to correct the errors:*

- *Make an antecedent plural to agree with a plural pronoun.*
- *Make a pronoun singular to agree with a singular antecedent.*
- *Revise the sentence and eliminate the pronoun in question.*

1. When somebody is addicted, they will want to try stronger and more dangerous drugs.

_____

2. Happiness is something everyone needs in their life.

_____

3. When someone has a good attitude, they bring everyone else's spirit up.

_____

4. No matter what occupation one has or how large their income is, if they are happy with their lives, that is the best fortune they could ask for.

_____

5. Sometimes, one's ignorance can get the best of their principles.

_____

6. Anybody can succeed. They just have to try hard enough to get what they want.

_____

7. I need someone who will not turn their back on me.

_____

8. My manager does a good job of keeping the office running. Even though she is young and inexperienced, she makes sure that everyone is taken care of and that their needs are met.

_____

9. Each person is smart in their own way.

---

10. I hope everyone has someone in their lives that they can truly respect as much as I do my neighbour.

Pronoun Case

Pronouns can have a variety of functions in a sentence. Pronouns can act as the subject of a sentence or as the object of a preposition or verb. They can also indicate possession. Table 23-2 presents these three types of pronouns.

1. **Subjective pronouns** are used as the subject of a sentence:

   We foreign language students are a competitive bunch.

   She called home on her new cellphone and said hello to her sister.

   After waking up late, he skipped breakfast and went directly to work.

2. **Objective pronouns** are used as the objects of verbs and prepositions:

   The principal called us down to the office.

   My father gave me some good advice.

   Robert went with me to Florida last spring.

3. **Possessive pronouns** are used to indicate possession:

   Young people spend much of their time online these days.

   Their shopping online is a particularly interesting development.

If the subject of the sentence is an *-ing* word preceded by a personal pronoun, the pronoun should be possessive case:

Daniel decided to join the Canadian Forces. His *going* into the military was a very big decision.

Incorrect: Him/He *going* into the military was a very big decision.

We all went to the Parliament Buildings in Ottawa. Our *being* there on Canada Day was important to everyone.

Incorrect: Us/We *being* there on Canada Day was important to everyone.

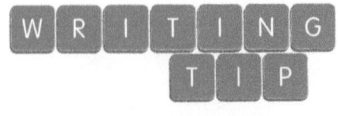

Avoid confusion between *your/yours, her/hers, our/ours, their/theirs.*

Table 23-2

THREE TYPES OF PRONOUNS		
Subjective	**Objective**	**Possessive**
I	me	my/mine
you	you	your/yours
it	it	its
he	him	his
she	her	her/hers
we	us	our/ours
they	them	their/theirs
who	who/whom	whose

Directions: *Underline the pronouns in the following sentences, write them in the space provided, and indicate whether they are subjective, objective, or possessive pronouns. Some sentences will have both subjective and objective pronouns.*

1. This student I met on vacation is the same age as I am.

   _____

2. When my parents got home, they found me sitting in the kitchen reading the newspaper.

   _____

3. After a while, he opened up a business. It was rough in the beginning, but now his business is doing extremely well.

   _____

4. Every day after school, I used to play baseball with my friends.

   _____

5. My parents thought my going to Whistler on spring break was a mistake.

   _____

6. For the past three years I have gone to the finals, but I haven't been able to win.

   _____

7. He attended the same school my sister did.

   _____

8. He was younger than she was, but he was also the boss.

   _____

9. Her brothers all have their own cars, whereas she still takes the bus.

   _____

10. I followed her to an empty office, where she did the paperwork and called the cops. She left as I waited for what seemed a half an hour. Then she came back with the security guard, who began to interrogate me.

    _____

> **Talk about it**
>
> With a classmate, identify the types of pronouns you used in your last paper. Are there any pronoun choices you question?

COMPOUND SUBJECTS AND OBJECTS, SENTENCES WITH *THAN* AND *AS*

Subjective and objective pronoun errors occur frequently in sentences with compound subjects and objects and in sentences with *than* and *as*.

Compound Subjects and Objects

Compound subjects and objects put two pronouns together with the conjunction *and*.

   Compound Subject: Me *and* Bill got scholarships. (**incorrect**)
   Compound Object: The boss gave Bill *and* I a bonus. (**incorrect**)

Because pronoun errors commonly occur in spoken English, to some people the previous sentences might sound correct. The best way to detect incorrect pronoun usage is to make a compound sentence into two separate sentences and then put them back together:

It is preferable to make *I* the second of two subjects in sentences with two compound subjects. In sentences with three subjects, make *I* last, as in, "Professor Janes, Mr. Hacker, and *I* attended the council meeting last Tuesday."

Incorrect: <u>Me</u> got a scholarship. Bill got a scholarship.
Correct: <u>I</u> got a scholarship. Bill got a scholarship.
Correct: Bill *and* <u>I</u> got a scholarship.

Incorrect: The boss gave Bill a bonus. The boss gave <u>I</u> a bonus.
Correct: The boss gave Bill a bonus. The boss gave <u>me</u> a bonus.
Correct: The boss gave Bill *and* <u>me</u> a bonus.

Do not use reflexive pronouns in place of subjective or objective pronouns:

Incorrect: Bill and <u>myself</u> got a scholarship.
Correct: Bill *and* <u>I</u> got a scholarship.

Incorrect: The boss gave Bill *and* <u>myself</u> a bonus.
Correct: The boss gave Bill *and* <u>me</u> a bonus.

Sentences with *Than* and *As*

Sentences that express comparisons are formed with *than* and *as*. These sentences actually combine two ideas.

<u>I</u> finished the test early.
<u>You</u> finished the test earlier.
<u>You</u> finished the test earlier *than* <u>I</u> did.

Speakers and writers frequently choose the wrong pronoun in these sentences.

Incorrect: <u>She</u> grew so much faster than <u>me</u>.
Incorrect: <u>He</u> played tennis well, but not as well as <u>me</u>.

To detect pronoun errors in comparative forms, make the sentence two separate sentences and then put them back together:

Incorrect: <u>She</u> worked faster *than* <u>me</u>.
Correct: <u>She</u> worked fast. <u>I</u> worked fast.
Correct: <u>She</u> worked faster *than* <u>I</u> (worked).

Incorrect: <u>He</u> played tennis too, only not *as* well as <u>me</u>.
Correct: <u>He</u> played tennis well. <u>I</u> played tennis well.
Correct: <u>He</u> played tennis well, only not *as* well as <u>I</u> (played).

Talk about it

Read the examples under "Sentences with *Than* and *As*." Which sentences sound right to you? What clue helps you choose the right pronoun?

EXERCISE 23-5 **Proofreading for Errors in Pronoun Case**

Directions: *Read the following sentences and underline the subjective and objective pronouns. In the space provided, replace incorrect pronouns as needed.*

1. Most of the people I met on vacation were older than me.

_____

2. When they got home, they found Rachel and I in the kitchen reading the newspaper.

_____

3. After a while, my sister and him opened up a business. It was rough in the beginning, but now the business is doing extremely well.

_____

4. Every day after school, me, Dan, and Ron used to play baseball with some friends.

_____

5. Rhonda and myself were selected to chair the orientation meeting at the college.

_____

6. For the past three years, Cheryl and me have made it to the dance contest finals, but we have not been able to win.

_____

7. He attended the same school as me.

_____

8. She was as young as him, but she was also his boss.

_____

9. Her brothers all have their own cars, whereas her and her sisters still take the bus.

_____

10. At the end of the unit of study, the instructor asked Janet and me to act as tutors. We agreed to it.

_____

Pronoun Consistency

Depending on your subject matter, one pronoun will be more appropriate to use than another. If you write about yourself, you will probably use the first person: *I, me, my.* If you write about a social issue or problem, you may choose the pronoun *it* to refer to the problem—racism, for example—and the pronoun *they* to refer those who are affected by the problem. It is difficult to avoid some shifting from one pronoun to another, but be aware of these shifts and try to be consistent.

Inconsistent

I had a great experience in high school band class. I learned to play an instrument and went to competitions with the band. I had a great time at these competitions. The director was great. He always pushed you to do your best.

The first-person pronoun is appropriate when you write about yourself.

In this example the writer shifts from first person (*I, me, my*) to second person (*you, your*).

I is first person. The shift to second person—*you* and *your*—is conversational but inconsistent. For formal or academic writing try to minimize the use of *you*.

Consistent

I had a great experience in high school band class. I learned to play an instrument and went to competitions with the band. I had a great time at these competitions. The director was great. He always pushed me and my fellow band players to do our best.

The use of *me* and *our* is more consistent than *you* and *your*.

Here's another example:

The student begins with first-person plural (*we, us, our*).

Here she shifts to second person (*you*).

Inconsistent

Our class took part in a "city beautiful" program. We were assigned to groups and took responsibility for keeping a section of the city clean. This is a good program. It taught you to take pride in where you live. Once you finished, you sort of wanted to show off your city.

The shift from *we* to *you* is inconsistent pronoun use.

Consistent

Our class took part in a "city beautiful" program. We were assigned to groups and took responsibility for keeping a section of the city clean. This is a good program. It taught us to take pride in where we live. Once we finished, we sort of wanted to show off our city.

Consistent pronoun use, like consistent verb tense, is an important characteristic of academic writing. Consistent pronoun use makes your writing more coherent and connected. Practise consistently avoiding first- and second-person pronouns, when it is possible and appropriate to do so. Writing in third person is less personal and considered more academic.

EXERCISE 23-6 **Proofreading for Consistent Pronoun Use**

Directions: *Read the following sentences and underline the pronouns. Cross out incorrect pronouns and write your corrections to make the pronoun use consistent in the space provided.*

1. We have a tendency to pick up something quick for dinner on your way home, instead of going home and taking time to cook dinner. It's convenient. However, eating takeout on a regular basis can get costly.

---

2. A person doesn't always have to be happy all the time. There are many different emotions we go through. You simply have to expect that.

_____

3. The most important thing an employer looks for is trust. You don't want an employee to cheat you when the employer turns his or her back.

_____

4. I took the test and waited nervously for the results. The level of your score would give you the opportunity to go further.

_____

5. Collecting rocks was easier than collecting seashells because you could find them everywhere. I made use of the rocks I found. I painted them, decorated them, or decorated with them. But mostly I collected them and kept them in my room.

_____

6. I also learned that by helping people in need you can really make a difference.

_____

7. With a cat, you set out her food and she's happy. I don't have to walk her every day or let her outside to use the bathroom.

_____

8. Having a cold is dreadful to me because you feel horrible and just wish it would go away.

_____

9. The cellphone has had a big impact on my life. You can reach anyone, anywhere, at any time.

_____

10. I tried to drive and use my cellphone a couple of times. I was so distracted it was horrifying. I became unaware of my surroundings to such a great degree. It was like driving in a dream, and nothing around you was real.

_____

CHAPTER REVIEW

Take a moment and reflect on what you have learned about pronoun agreement, case, and consistency.

☐ Pronoun agreement

- *Detecting errors in pronoun agreement: plural antecedents agree with plural pronouns; singular antecedents agree with singular pronouns*

- *Indefinite pronouns and agreement: pronouns ending in -one or -body are singular*

☐ Pronoun case

- *Compound subjects and objects, sentences with than and as: to choose correct pronoun, make two separate sentences and then put them back together with the right pronoun*

☐ Pronoun consistency: do not shift from one pronoun to another unless there is a reason

CHAPTER 24

Adjectives and Adverbs

If you want to write well in the academic or business worlds, you need to know how to use adjectives and adverbs properly. Although in casual conversation, there is a high tolerance for adjective and adverb error, in writing nothing distracts an academic reader from your message as quickly as one of these slips. If you want to do *well* (not *good*), you must learn the difference between an adjective and an adverb.

Adjectives

Adjectives modify or describe nouns and pronouns. They provide information about quantity and quality. In most cases, adjectives are found right next to the noun they modify, usually directly *before* the noun.

> The team's **last** game was its **best** game. (adjectives *last* and *best* modify noun *game*)
>
> The **visiting** artist changed his **preferred working** hours soon after arriving on campus. (adjectives *visiting* and *preferred working* modify nouns *artist* and *hours*)

In some sentences with linking verbs—such as *is/are, was/were, seem/seems*—adjectives come after the verb.

> We are **vulnerable**.
>
> Mrs. Kraft seems **happy**.

Also, in the case of indefinite pronouns—such as *someone, something,* or *anything*—the adjective comes after the pronoun.

> Someone **special** called me last night.
>
> Anything **good** to read will be on his desk sooner or later.

EXERCISE 24-1 Identifying Adjectives

Directions: *Underline adjectives in the sentences below. Circle the noun each adjective modifies.*

1. There were three steps leading to the porch of the brick bungalow.

2. When the horse and buggy arrive, you sit on the comfortable bench seat and take a long ride. You feel great.

3. His pants were faded and threadbare.

4. Toward the end of the school year, she threw a tea party and told all of the students they had to bring bone china cups to drink out of.

5. This classic sandwich, a club pita, contains sliced ham, turkey, lean bacon, and crispy lettuce.

CHAPTER OVERVIEW

- ☐ Adjectives
- ☐ Adverbs and the *-ly* Ending
- ☐ *Good/Well, Bad/Badly, Real/Really*
- ☐ Adjectives: Comparatives and Superlatives
- ☐ Adverbs: Comparatives and Superlatives
- ☐ Hyphenated Adjectives

6. Cooking is therapeutic, an enjoyable activity. Mozart had his piano. I have my gleaming cleavers and trusty skillets. I am always happy in the kitchen. Anything complex is what I like to cook.

7. Outdoor work is annoying. In winter, the weather is freezing cold. Shovelling heavy snow can be a health risk.

8. A good reason to not live in the city is endless traffic. It can be bad. Imagine living in the middle of rush hour in Toronto.

9. Organization is an important skill needed for online education. Even if adequate time is allotted, success requires time management and the ability to meet deadlines.

10. I was on my high school swim team, and every day I dreaded the long practice hours and endless drills.

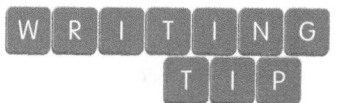

Learn to distinguish between past participles (-ed) and present participles (-ing) used as adjectives.

Adjectives ending in *–ed* describe a feeling someone or something feels (a tired child); adjectives ending in *–ing* describe the effect someone or something causes (a boring movie).

EXERCISE 24-2 **Choosing Adjectives**

Directions: *Fill in the blank and provide an adjective for each of the nouns below.*

1. the _____ question

2. a(n) _____ opportunity

3. these _____ interruptions

4. my _____ phobia

5. a(n) _____ friend

6. the _____ mail delivery

7. her _____ objection

8. your _____ responsibility

9. a(n) _____ need

10. our _____ co-workers

Unlike some other languages, the adjective usually appears *before* the word it modifies in English. It does not change form to agree in number or gender with the noun it modifies.

In English we often like to use more than one adjective to describe something or to give specific instructions. Normally, you would not use more than three adjectives in a row. If you want to describe something with more than three words, then use another sentence.

However, there is a specific order to placing adjectives before a noun so that the description "sounds" right. These are known as *cumulative adjectives* since they build their meaning in a particular order. If placed out of order, the sentence does not make sense. Table 24-1 shows you how to sequence adjectives. You will sometimes find a slightly different order for adjectives giving a physical description, but in general you should follow the order in the table. You do not need to use commas to separate cumulative adjectives.

Adjectives in the "opinion" category are words that not everyone would agree with, such as *boring, fantastic,* or *difficult.* In the "origin" category are adjectives that describe the geographical area where something comes from, such as *Atlantic* or *Italian.* The "material" category contains adjectives that refer to what something is made of, such as aluminum or silk.

TABLE 24-1

ROYAL ORDER OF ADJECTIVES*

#	Category		a	his	those	that	some	the
1	Determiner/pronoun		a	his	those	that	some	the
2	Number			two				
3	Opinion/observation/evaluation		practical			modern	useless	
4	Size	Physical Description						
5	Age/condition				new		old	antique
6	Shape		rectangular					
7	Colours/patterns			blue				
8	Origin							French
9	Material			suede		glass		
10	Purpose				electric	office	gardening	flower
	Noun		table	shoes	cars	tower	tools	vase

*Please read table from top to bottom.

Adjectives used for purpose often end in -*ing*, such as *cooking* tools or *writing* paper.

If you choose several adjectives from only one category, then the words carry equal value and can appear in any order. These are called *coordinate adjectives,* and you must use a comma between them. Look at this example:

The horse had a beautiful, long tail.

The horse had a long, beautiful tail.

Both sentences make sense, but you need to use a comma between the two adjectives.

EXERCISE 24-3 Order of Adjectives

Directions: *First, decide which category each of the words from the blue box below belongs in. Then, in the proper order, according to the Royal Order of Adjectives, choose adjectives from three different categories to combine with each of the five nouns that appear after the box.*

WRITING TIP

If you can put an *and* or a *but* between the adjectives, a comma will probably belong there.

a tall, stately tree = a tall and stately tree (use a comma)

a little old lady = a little ~~and~~ old lady (no comma)

Canadian	boring	red	interesting	wooden	woollen
octagonal	wireless	sandy	plastic	eight	designed
wavy	sewing	square	French	yellow	polka-dot
camping	young	three	repulsive	a dozen	graceful

Example: (opinion + age + purpose) + noun: useless old gardening tools

1. sign

2. bags

3. machine

4. socks

5. lumber

Adverbs and the -ly Ending

Adverbs modify or describe verbs, adjectives, and other adverbs. They provide information about how or when an action occurs. Most adverbs can be easily spotted because of their -ly ending. In fact, many adverbs are merely adjectives with -ly endings. (**Note:** In the case of adjectives ending in y, remember to change the y to i.)

Note that not all words ending in -ly are adverbs, such as belly, bully, reply, folly, fly, and others.

> Saturday's game was an **easy** <u>victory</u> over the other team. (adjective modifies noun *victory*)
>
> Our team **easily** <u>beat</u> the other team. (adverb modifies verb *beat*)

Along with the -ly ending, you can tell if a word is an adverb if you can move it around in a sentence and place it before or after the verb or at the beginning or end of the sentence and the sentence still makes sense.

> Our team **easily** <u>beat</u> them.
> Our team <u>beat</u> them **easily**.

> James **gradually** <u>came</u> to his senses.
> **Gradually**, James <u>came</u> to his senses.

EXERCISE 24-4 | **Adverbs and the -ly Ending**

Directions: *Complete the sentences below by selecting adverbs from the following list. In cases where an adjective is needed, remove the -ly ending.*

consistently	immediately
continuously	initially
diligently	instantly
eventually	quickly
frequently	seriously
greatly	superbly

1. Marisa _____ considered going away to school.

2. She _____ considered the alternative option of staying home.

3. Once she started, she _____ saw that she had made the right decision.

4. In high school, Marisa was not a _____ student.

5. She preferred _____ gratification to the _____ drudgery of homework.

6. As a college student, she decided to take things _____.

7. She studied _____ and _____.

8. She _____ saw the results of her _____ efforts.

9. Her grades were _____ improved.

10. Her new approach produced _____ better grades than those she had earned in high school.

Directions: *Proofread the sentences below for adverbs missing -ly endings. Underline the error and add -ly where needed.*

1. The failure rate in new marriages in this country is frightening. People get married, try it for a while, and then when the real work starts, they just give up. The problem is that not everyone takes marriage serious. Like everything in modern life, marriage is temporary.

2. His new car is a full-size vehicle, great for transportation. It has four doors, and automatic windows and locks. The colour is tan, which is a very neutral colour. It runs smooth and floats like a boat.

3. Not punishing a person can have long-term effects. An individual needs to see there are consequences for his actions. If there is no follow-through after someone does something wrong, he might think he can commit a crime easy. The next thing you know, he is in real trouble.

4. There have been lots of studies of how men and women are alike and different. Mostly they are different. The writer Deborah Tannen has written extensively about how men and women think and speak different. Her goal is to help people get along better.

5. Since starting school, I have been working in the social science department of the college. I work close with a lot of people who are educated. I listen to them speak. I try to imitate their vocabulary.

Good/Well, Bad/Badly, Real/Really

Common slips in conversation sometimes find their way into college writing. *Good, bad,* and *real* are adjectives; they modify nouns and pronouns. *Well, badly,* and *really* are adverbs; they modify verbs, adjectives, and other adverbs.

Ask Yourself

Do you know the difference between *good* and *well?* Write a few sentences using the words correctly.

The members of the study group did **good** work. (adjective-noun)

Their work was **good**. (noun-adjective)

They worked **well** together. (verb-adverb)

Their study time was **well** worth the effort. (adverb-adjective)

The ski instructor regretted the **bad** weather. (adjective-noun)

The ski conditions were **bad**. (noun-adjective)

Many of her pupils skied **badly** as a result. (verb-adverb)

The **badly** conceived idea did not receive funding from the developers. (adverb-adjective)

Marie's mother makes **real** mayonnaise. (adjective-noun)

It **really** makes a difference in some of her sandwiches. (adverb-verb)

Her vegetable roll-up tastes **really** good. (adverb-adjective)

Directions: *Underline the correct modifiers in the sentences below. For each choice, circle the words that are modified.*

1. Our family vehicle is a (real/really) (good/well) car. It is very spacious. It has many miles on it, but the engine still runs pretty (good/well).

2. A (bad/badly) organized store means the flow of traffic on the floor is (bad/badly) and individual workers co-operate (bad/badly).

3. I am (real/really) motivated right now to get my work done and do (good/well) in school. Sometimes older students have to wait a (good/well) long time to come back to school.

4. We all agreed that Cooper's (bad/badly) reputation was (good/well) earned. He ran the meetings (bad/badly), as he tended to be overbearing and not (good/well) suited to getting people to work (good/well) together.

5. The coach was an all-around (good/well) guy. He taught us (real/really) discipline. He always pushed players to study hard, to make (good/well) decisions in their personal lives, and to do (good/well) on the field.

6. As far as future work is concerned, Willis is in a (good/well) position. In fact, he is (good/well) positioned to take a (good/well) entry-level job and run with it (good/well) into the future.

7. I think Henderson writes (good/well) books. Nevertheless, his first few publications were (bad/badly) received. Some critics object to his confrontational style. He handles their criticisms (good/well). When they criticize him, he attacks them in return.

8. My child was (real/really) ill for a number of years. Now, after medical treatment, he is doing (good/well). We can thank the hospital staff for their (good/well) work.

9. After the argument, everyone felt (bad/badly). It was agreed that a (real/really) long cooling-off period would be helpful.

10. Hallie's job with the advertising company worked out really (good/well). It was a (bad/badly) needed jumpstart to her career in marketing.

States-of-being verbs describe emotions or feelings, and you use adjectives with these verbs since they link to the subject. Action verbs are described with adverbs.

Adjectives: Comparatives and Superlatives

An adjective assigns a quality to the noun it modifies. There are degrees of modification, as shown in the following examples. Comparative adjectives are used in comparison and contrast writing. Superlative adjectives are often used in classification.

A statement

A **sad** statement (adjective)

A **sadder** statement (comparative)

The **saddest** statement (superlative)

In most cases the degree of modification is indicated by suffixes, or endings on the adjective.

1. For one-syllable adjectives and two-syllable adjectives ending in *y*, add the -*er* suffix to comparative adjectives; add the -*est* suffix for the superlative.

close	closer	closest
jolly	jollier	jolliest

TABLE 24-2

IRREGULAR ADJECTIVES		
Adjective	**Comparative**	**Superlative**
good	better	best
bad	worse	worst
little	less	least
much many some	more	most
far	further	furthest

2. For all other adjectives, use *more* and *most* to indicate degree.

   controversial   more controversial   most controversial

3. Learn to recognize the irregular comparatives and superlatives shown in Table 24-2.

   Note: Use *little, less,* and *least* for indefinite amounts; use *few, fewer,* and *fewest* for things that can be counted.

4. Do not use *more* and *most* with the *-er* and *-est* suffixes:

   Incorrect: hard   more harder   most hardest
   Correct: hard   harder   hardest

   Note: Be sure to use *than* (not *then*) in sentences expressing a comparison.

   Economics was a harder course **than** sociology.

5. Use the comparative when talking about two things; use the superlative when talking about more than two things.

   Jordan was the **taller** of the two boys. (*not* "the tallest")
   Of all the jobs James worked, the one that paid **best** was the warehouse job. (*not* "that paid better" since James had several different jobs, more than two)

EXERCISE 24-7 **Adjectives: Comparatives and Superlatives**

Directions: *Underline the correct adjectives in the following sentences.*

1. The success of a product will be enhanced if the marketing is (more broad/broader).

2. Everyone has had a teacher who preferred some students over others. This is the (most common/commonest) grievance students have.

3. In my computer class the teacher would always send me on the (craziest/most crazy) errands.

4. After taking both pre-calculus and first semester calculus, Jane decided pre-calculus was (the more difficult/the most difficult) of the two.

5. One time our class was being a little loud. When the teacher first asked us to quiet down, we did not listen. The second time he asked us, we still did not hear him. The third time he threw the (most awful/awfulest) fit.

6. You can meet the (shyest/most shy) person at a party. Get that person away from the crowd, and he or she will open up and be the (most outgoing/outgoingest) individual you have ever met.

7. This particular breed of dog is the (most calm/calmest), (most friendly/friendliest) animal you could ever hope to find.

Writer's Response »»

Write three sentences about movies using *good, better,* and *best.*

8. Maybe because my father was (less talkative/less talkativer) than my mother was, there was a fair amount of conflict in our family.

9. It is common to find large numbers of seniors walking in malls for exercise. They like malls because weather is not a factor. They like mornings because (less/fewer) teens are there at that time.

10. If we were more accepting of different types of people and cultures, it would help people feel (welcomer/more welcome).

Adverbs: Comparatives and Superlatives

Like nouns, verbs can also be modified in degrees. That is, you can express not only how an action takes place—*fast*—but differences in how it takes place: *fast, faster, fastest* or *slow, slower, slowest.* Degrees can be positive, negative, comparative, and superlative.

1. Add *-er* and *-est* to one-syllable adverbs, such as *fast, close, near, slow,* and *late.*

   The semester went by **fast.**
   The semester went by **faster** than I expected.
   The semester goes by **fastest** when you are very busy.

2. Use *more* and *most* to form the comparatives and superlatives in longer adverbs.

   One tutor **quickly** answers questions.
   This tutor answers questions **more quickly** than the others.
   The tutor who answers questions **most quickly** is the most popular tutor.

Talk about it »»

Comparatives and superlatives define quality. Discuss the places in your day where defining quality is important.

EXERCISE 24-8 **Adverbs: Comparatives and Superlatives**

Directions: *Insert the correct comparative or superlative adverb form of the adjective in parentheses.*

1. (quick) I am meeting and getting to know people _____ this year than I did last year.

2. (close) Out of all the debate teams in the competition, our team came _____ to getting a perfect score.

3. (serious) The current crop of new employees takes the job _____ than the previous one and earns as much as possible.

4. (discreet) The professor could not have asked for the class's attention _____.

5. (tactful) The morning bus driver handles disturbances and angry riders _____ than the afternoon driver.

6. (smooth) Out of the two landings observed, it was agreed the aircraft touched down _____ the first time.

7. (fierce) The battles fought _____ were those in which the combatants defended against invaders on their own soil.

8. (clear) Once the smoke cleared, I saw my situation _____ than I had in a long time.

9. (efficient) The operation that is run _____ is most likely to realize the best profit.

10. (rapid) Out of all the sectors of the economy, the one that has recovered _____ is information technology.

Hyphenated Adjectives

A hyphenated adjective uses several words as a single descriptor in front of a noun, such as *an easy-to-remember rule, an 80-year-old man.* Here are more examples:

> If you have a question about refunds, the **go-to** <u>person</u> is the registrar.
>
> After the patient comes home from the hospital, a visiting nurse comes on an **as-needed** <u>basis</u>.

Hyphenated adjectives precede the nouns they modify. *Go-to* is a hyphenated adjective that modifies the word *person. As-needed* modifies the word *basis.* Try to avoid hyphenated adjectives that are longer than three or four words by changing the order of the words in the sentence.

> Your exam will consist of ten **fill-in-the-blank** questions.
>
> The group of **18-year-old** volunteers have transformed the department.

Unusually long hyphenated adjectives can usually be written as straight-forward sentences:

> When we first met, she was definitely a **you-will-not-dance-with-me-tonight-or-probably-ever-for-that-matter** kind of girl.
>
> When we first met, she had a look on her face that said, "You will not dance with me tonight or probably ever, for that matter."

EXERCISE 24-9 Hyphenated Adjectives

Directions: *Find strings of words that function as adjectives in the following sentences. Add hyphens as needed. Write the hyphenated adjectives and nouns they modify in the space provided.*

1. To get an up to date source, I went to a CBC News article to research this topic a little further.

   _____

2. Parents should be explaining to their children that the happily ever after movies are just pretend, and nobody's life is actually like that.

   _____

3. My neighbour, wanting a life altering change, went back to school to study for a second career.

_____

4. It did not take him long to realize that he was in a no win situation and that he could not do this alone.

_____

5. Parents must do their homework when searching for a child care provider. They should ask questions about daily events. One of the most important factors is the staff to student ratio.

_____

6. The government debated the need for national regulatory standards regarding child care needs. Currently, the responsibility is a city by city matter, with each province handling its own standards.

_____

7. Every day, she wore long dresses that came down to her sock and sandal covered feet.

_____

8. As I came upon the reduce your speed sign, I took my foot off the gas.

_____

9. I purchased a beautiful white sleeveless dress with a split up the front right leg to wear to the gala event.

_____

10. I attended an all girls school, which by definition eliminated the potential for too much interaction with boys.

_____

EXERCISE 24-10 **Proofreading Practice**

Directions: *Proofread the paragraphs below for adjective and adverb errors. Underline the seven errors and write your corrections in the margin.*

Blizzards are one of the extremest weather conditions that can make driving a dangerous task. There are several conditions created by a blizzard that can impair one's ability to drive. An obvious factor is that heavy snow decreases visibility. The driver becomes almost blind. Then heavy amounts of snow pile up on the road, creating slick conditions that cause vehicles to lose traction. After snow accumulates, cars driving over the road warm the pavement enough to melt the snow, which then freezes into ice. This is especially hazardous in the evening and nighttime when the patches of ice cannot be seen as easy. Snow is not the only weather condition that is dangerous. Rain is very unsafe to drive in as well.

Take a moment and reflect on what you have learned about adjectives and adverbs.

- ☐ Adjectives: modify or describe nouns or pronouns; placed before the noun; cumulative and coordinate; order of adjectives

- ☐ Adverbs and the *-ly* ending: modify verbs, adjectives, and other adverbs

- ☐ *Good/well, bad/badly, real/really:* adjective/adverb

- ☐ Adjectives: comparatives and superlatives: degrees of modification

- ☐ Adverbs: comparatives and superlatives: degrees of describing verb; positive, negative, comparative or superlative

- ☐ Hyphenated adjectives: two or more words used as a single adjective

Driving in a thunderstorm can be real dangerous. Like snow, rain can decrease visibility to zero. Along with affecting visibility, a downpour can render windshield wipers ineffective at clearing the windshield. The rain can also cause the road to become slickly and dangerous. Slippery roads like this increase the braking time needed to stop. If a person slams on the brakes, the car can skid out of control. Hydroplaning can occur if water has collected on the road and if a person drives careless. The car literally floats across the road. On side streets water can accumulate near the curb causing the vehicle to pull into the curb.

Both types of weather conditions can be treacherous. Most people would agree that snow is the worst. This fact is evident because less drivers venture out in a blizzard.

Punctuation

If I get all my commas in the right place, my writing will be okay. Right? Not exactly. Punctuation matters, but the content of your writing matters more. Your task is to minimize punctuation errors because they distract the reader from the content of your writing and the message you are trying to make. In earlier chapters, you saw that punctuation goes along with good sentence structure. In this chapter, you revisit how to use commas, semicolons, and colons. You also practise using quotation marks and apostrophes properly.

Commas

Most student writers use too many commas. They think, "I'm pausing in this sentence, so I must need a comma." While it is true that the comma signals a pause, correct usage relies on understanding the role of the comma: it joins related parts of a sentence to one another.

COMMAS AND CONJUNCTIONS

The conjunctions *and, but,* and *or* often link pairs of terms in compound subjects or compound verbs that do not require commas. One of the most common punctuation errors is placing a comma before a conjunction when it is not needed.

> **Incorrect:** My mother, and my sisters explained to me that lying will get me nowhere in life.
>
> **Correct:** My mother and my sisters explained to me that lying will get me nowhere in life.

> **Incorrect:** My father loves to chat, and laugh with his children.
>
> **Correct:** My father loves to chat and laugh with his children.

In these examples, the conjunction *and* joins the two nouns of the compound subject, *mother* and *sisters,* and the two verbs of the compound predicate, *chat* and *laugh.* Generally, for the subject or predicate of a sentence, when you put two things together with *and* or *or,* you do not use a comma. In Chapter 19, you learned about the structure of a compound sentence. In that case, a comma is required before a coordinating conjunction that joins two complete sentences (or independent clauses):

> **Comma Required:** I agree that discipline is needed, but I don't think corporal punishment is the answer.
>
> **Comma Required:** I wasn't making very much money, and my social life was beginning to suffer.

The comma and conjunction in these two examples are equivalent to a period.

> I agree that discipline is needed. I don't think corporal punishment is the answer.
>
> I wasn't making very much money. My social life was beginning to suffer.

For more explanation of punctuation and independent clauses, see the section on coordination in Chapter 19.

Whenever you want to use a comma with a conjunction, ask yourself, "Could I put a period here instead? Is what comes before and after the conjunction a complete sentence?" If the answer is yes, the comma is probably needed.

EXERCISE 25-1 Commas and Conjunctions

Directions: *Circle all conjunctions in the following sentences and if any commas are needed, indicate where you would put them in the space provided. Some sentences may be correct as written.*

1. I got into trouble often and for the stupidest reasons and a lot of the time it was at the dinner table.

   _____

2. I tried not to make trouble or be a burden to anyone but I was human.

   _____

3. It was morning and I was alone with some matches and my curiosity.

   _____

4. At first, it was a small fire but it increased quickly because it was summer and very dry.

   _____

5. I tried to put out the fire with some water but it was futile and the flames rose higher and higher.

   _____

6. I worked frantically to put out the fire but sometimes foolishness and bad luck conspire against a person.

   _____

7. I shouted at my little sister to help and she did her best. We worked together at it but it did not help and soon the fire was out of control.

   _____

8. The fire trucks came wailing and shrieking and the firefighters put out the fire.

   _____

9. The damage was minimal but having the water and smoke in the house meant big trouble.

   _____

10. It was a difficult time when my father got home that night and saw everything that had happened.

    _____

Writer's Response

Commas and conjunctions connect items in lists. Write two sentences: 1) list subjects you study; 2) list activities you enjoy.

COMMAS AND INTRODUCTORY MODIFIERS

Introductory words, phrases, or clauses at the beginning of a sentence are called **introductory modifiers.** Sentences starting with introductory modifiers include a natural pause. The pause occurs where the intonation falls, and this is where the comma should be placed.

As I sat alone at the picnic table, Joanna and her boyfriend began to dance.

The box that follows provides a list of two kinds of words that signal an introductory modifier.

SIGNAL WORDS FOR INTRODUCTORY MODIFIERS

Subordinating Conjunctions

after	if	until
although	in order that	when
as	provided that	whenever
as long as	since	whereas
because	so that	wherever
before	though	whether
even though	unless	while

Conjunctive Adverbs

accordingly	furthermore	otherwise
again	however	then
as a result	in addition	therefore
also	indeed	thus
besides	moreover	on the other hand
consequently	nevertheless	in fact
finally		

These words all signal an introductory pause, which is marked by a comma. The same pause comes after a prepositional phrase that precedes an independent clause.

> *Since there were a number of short-answer questions on the sociology exam*, students were provided with exam booklets.   **SUBORDINATING CONJUNCTION**

> *Moreover*, a multiple-choice section of the test called for a Scantron card for answers.   **CONJUNCTIVE ADVERB**

> *At the end of the exam period*, students were also given a chance to have a short conference with the professor.   **PREPOSITIONAL PHRASE**

In all of these examples, the comma marks the dividing line between the main sentence and the modifier that introduces it.

EXERCISE 25-2 **Commas and Introductory Words, Phrases, and Clauses**

Directions: *Look for introductory words, phrases, and clauses in the following sentences. Read each of the sentences out loud. Listen for the natural pause where the intonation falls. Using the space provided, indicate where the commas should be placed.*

1. When I have worries on my mind my grandmother is always there to let me know that everything will be just fine.

2. Money also causes great debate between both groups. Indeed it is a primary cause of conflict.

_____

3. Even after I began high school I still had chores to do at home.

_____

4. She was the nicest woman in the whole world, and she loved me a lot. Although we were best friends we were very different, and we would fight a lot. She was such a perfectionist.

_____

5. When I was in grade 6 a French teacher told me my name was French, and when I was in grade 7 a Spanish teacher told me my name was Spanish.

_____

6. When I was in college some of my friends and I used our "soap opera" names. A soap opera name was your middle name and the name of the street you lived on. My name was Dawn Orchard.

_____

7. After a short time the officer let us go, and when we went into the house Derrick's dad started to yell at us.

_____

8. After five minutes or so my dad would come out just as angry as my mom, and she would say, "I already reprimanded him."

_____

9. If you were not good you knew what would happen to you, and the punishment would not be a time-out.

_____

10. In most cases an adult tone of voice gave the impression of authority, and the children knew who was in charge.

_____

COMMAS AND INTERRUPTERS

Use a pair of commas to insert a parenthetical word, phrase, or clause into the middle of a sentence. **Parenthetical modifiers,** as they are sometimes called, interrupt the natural flow of the sentence. The commas act like parentheses and thus are used in pairs. For example:

> The teacher would say our first and last names when he called on one of us. His name was Mr. Cowell.
>
> The teacher, Mr. Cowell, would say our first and last names when he called on one of us.

> Eric was the first name my parents chose for me. It means a powerful leader or king.
>
> Eric, which means a powerful leader or king, was the first name my parents chose for me.

My sister is always picky about where she eats. She is picky for a variety of reasons.

My sister, for a variety of reasons, is always picky about where she eats.

When an interrupter comes at the end of a sentence, it sounds like an afterthought. The parentheses are formed by the comma and the period at the end of the sentence:

I was in grade 8. That made me 14 years old.

I was in grade 8, which made me 14 years old.

It was starting to get late in the evening. It was maybe around midnight.

It was starting to get late in the evening, maybe around midnight.

EXERCISE 25-3 **Commas and Interrupters**

Directions: *Read the following sentences and identify the parenthetical modifiers. Those coming in the middle of a sentence will need two commas; those coming at the end will need one comma. Indicate where commas are needed by using the space provided.*

1. My friend with his chiselled good looks and quick wit couldn't master the task of inserting an IV in a patient while in the back of a speeding ambulance.

   _____

2. Japan host of the environmental conference proposes to reduce global warming despite the country's weakened domestic economy.

   _____

Ask Yourself

Does an interrupter contain essential information or nonessential information?

3. Failure to take action to reverse this cycle however would mean a world in peril.

   _____

4. My friend always went to the mall with her friends. Every time she went, her mother gave her a curfew time to be back which was 10:00 p.m.

   _____

5. I choose to be honest even if the truth hurts someone.

   _____

6. A couple of weeks later after days and nights of terrible arguments he filed for divorce.

   _____

7. In the summer of 1996 the year my father passed away my brothers and I all began to receive the Canada Pension Plan children's benefit.

   _____

8. At the present time the rule is that a dependent child receives the payments until he or she reaches 18 years of age or is between the ages of 18 and 25 and in full-time attendance at a post-secondary school.

   _____

9. We had a long talk which consisted mostly of her telling me what she'd been up to for the last ten years.

_____

10. The only downside to memory enhancement for humans is that they will remember everything such as annoying songs on the radio.

_____

COMMAS IN A SERIES

Use commas in a list of three or more items. Lists can consist of nouns, verbs, adjectives, phrases, or clauses. You will use this structure of a series of three items, called parallelism, when you write a thesis statement for an essay.

1. **Series of Nouns:** At the shop, I pushed the cart while he picked up the items we needed, such as wet and dry towels, wheel cleaner, car wash detergent, car wax, a buffer, and tire gloss.

2. **Series of Adjectives:** Todd was a cool name. It sounded tough, mean, and just plain cool.

3. **Series of Clauses:** Once you lose control of a child, he will end up doing what he wants, what his friends want, but definitely not what you want him to do.

4. **Series of Verb Phrases:** When I came back outside, the ball wasn't on the porch. It had rolled off the porch, hit the hood of my dad's car, and put a huge dent in it.

In academic writing, readers expect you to use a comma before the conjunction and the last item in a series:

I read the newspaper, a few magazines, and an occasional novel.

EXERCISE 25-4 **Commas in a Series**

Directions: _Identify items in a series in the following sentences. Using the space provided, indicate where you would add commas as needed. Refer to the table in Chapter 24 to guide you with cumulative adjectives._

1. My friends live for clubs. They go to clubs every weekend stay up all night and sleep all day.

_____

2. There's no need to run around with your feathers all up your chest sticking out and a nasty look on your face. Nobody is impressed with that kind of attitude.

_____

3. You don't need to dress like a man cut your hair like a man and act like a jerk to let people know you're equal to a man.

_____

4. People do goofy things when they use drugs. These can include saying inappropriate things acting crazy and committing crimes.

_____

5. Every day computers become more outdated complex and confusing. System conflicts and programming errors hinder access to the Internet and cause delays and downtime.

_____

6. I was waiting for my nephew to come around the corner with his hair sticking up from his nap. I thought we would get into his secret cupboard and have a snack. He never came. I walked over to the cupboard opened it and had some crackers. That's how I said good-bye.

_____

7. One task I despise is cleaning out my locker. It takes up too much time. My friends have a different point of view. They enjoy cleaning their lockers because they find old assignments listen to music and get organized for the next semester at the same time. I sometimes wonder if they enjoy the stale sandwiches and dust.

_____

8. She's a young intelligent beautiful classy woman. She's also bright and friendly.

_____

9. We had a black BMW 760i Series with black-tinted windows large 20-inch light-alloy wheels and a bad-boy aura. We nicknamed it the Baron.

_____

10. My nephew is eight years old. His poor bicycle is covered with dust. You can hardly tell what colour it is. Jim would rather spend hours on the couch watching TV eating chips and playing his video games.

_____

EXERCISE 25-5 **Putting It All Together**

Directions: *Identify and punctuate items in a series in the following sentences. Rewrite the sentences in the space provided, inserting commas as necessary to set off introductory and parenthetical modifiers and before conjunctions introducing independent clauses.*

1. After I finish school I go home do my homework and then go out to have fun.

_____

2. Learning to take on responsibility is important. If you are a responsible young adult when you want to go away to university get a job or move away from home your mom and dad won't have second thoughts.

_____

3. The other night my friend came over to my house intoxicated got sick and then passed out.

---

4. When it comes to art history I can remember the artist's daily routine his or her relatives and in most cases what medium he or she used but I forget the title of his or her most famous piece of art.

---

5. Jake and I love to play watch and just talk about soccer. Unfortunately not all the other friends we play soccer with share our enthusiasm. If it were up to me and Jake we would have everyone play the game every day.

Talk about it

With a classmate, compose a sentence about music with items in a series.

6. The summer season seems to sneak up on us and then all of a sudden it is 32 degrees in the shade and the heat is scorching the grass baking the earth and turning everything to dust.

---

7. Where I work sometimes a car is parted out which means the parts are sold the proceeds go to charity and someone's life is made a little easier.

---

8. The principal wanted to send me home because of my tank top short skirt and slingback sandals. Honestly I was very angry and did not agree with his decision. As a matter of fact I had a big argument with him.

---

9. The artist still puts on his best clothes and goes for a stroll around the village every night. If someone recognizes him and asks him about a painting he smiles stops and gives generous explanations of his work.

---

10. After an hour of lecturing my children about the television their future and the importance of education I cool off for a while give them some breathing room and then look in on them to see if they have started their homework.

Semicolons and Colons

Semicolons and colons are strong marks of punctuation, almost as strong as periods. Used correctly, they express the relationship of ideas within sentences.

SEMICOLONS

1. Use a semicolon between two complete sentences that express closely related or contrasting ideas.

These nicknames did not say anything meaningful about my <u>personality; they</u> just made fun of my name.

Charity is not doing something you have to <u>do; it is</u> doing something that you want to do.

2. Use a semicolon with a conjunctive adverb to link two related sentences.

Big cars have a lot of <u>room; consequently,</u> people who carry around a lot of stuff are likely to buy them.

My grandfather is in a nursing <u>home; however,</u> he is in control of all his faculties.

3. Use a semicolon for items in a series that need internal punctuation.

When I was younger, I mowed lawns, a job I <u>liked; weeded</u> the flower beds, which I liked less than <u>mowing; and</u> washed windows, a job I totally hated.

Refer to chapters 19 and 21 for additional examples of using semicolons correctly.

COLONS

1. Use a colon to connect a list to a complete sentence. The list can come either before or after the complete sentence.

That was our idea of <u>fun: running</u>, hopping fences, and screaming like maniacs.

Building hot rods, fixing a leaking water pump, or fixing a flat <u>tire: it's</u> all fun to me.

2. Use a colon between two complete sentences when the second sentence explains the first or when one is general and the other is specific. **Note:** The second sentence can begin with either a lowercase letter or a capital letter.

My mother was <u>sad: she</u> was mourning the loss of her mother.

To be successful today, young people need to learn a valuable <u>lesson: Get</u> the best education you can.

3. Other situations for using colons are before a quotation or to separate titles and subtitles:

After a long pause, the judge lifted her eyes from her desk and <u>spoke:</u> "The court has decided to rule in favour of the defendant."

The title of her paper was "*West Side Story:* Romeo and Juliet Made Modern."

EXERCISE 25-6 **Using Semicolons and Colons**

Directions: *Insert semicolons and colons in the following sentences as needed. In the space provided, briefly explain your reason for using the punctuation mark you chose.*

CHAPTER 25 Punctuation

The food there was amazing. They had everything, duck, steak, and roast beef.

The food there was amazing. They had everything: duck, steak, and roast

beef. (Chose a colon because it is used to connect a list to a complete sentence.)

1. The police academy allowed us to handle two types of guns. Machine guns and hand pistols.

2. Although we had the same name, we were different in every other way. She was the oldest child in her family. I was the middle. She was chubby. I was thin. She had two brothers. I had three.

3. At first I had doubts about police work. However, I changed my mind when the recruiter started telling me about the benefits. Pay for post-secondary tuition, self-discipline, or even better a motorcycle.

4. For youth who play in the street, there are two significant things to be aware of. Motor vehicles and human nature.

Talk about it

With a classmate, compose a sentence that uses a semicolon properly.

5. A dog owner has to walk his dog every day or let it outside to relieve itself. In contrast, I simply set out food for my cat and keep her litter box clean.

6. I hoped I would never see this customer again. I didn't get angry because she didn't tip me. I was annoyed at the fact that she was so rude.

7. I learned a lot from this experience. Don't be greedy and take what you're given.

8. I learned that flunking a course does not indicate failure. It can be a necessary measure that teaches students right priorities from wrong ones. Students should learn from their mistakes.

9. Most educators say teach real math basics first. Allow pupils to use calculators once they have the basics in place.

10. I will name my son one of three names. It could be Richard because that is the name of his grandfather. It could be Mick for a friend of mine. Then again, it could be Justin for Justin Bieber, my favourite singer.

Quotation Marks

A **quotation** is language you borrow from someone else. Place quotation marks around words that are clearly not your own. These words might be in the form of dialogue, or they might be a phrase, sentence, or multi-sentence passage you borrow word for word from a newspaper, a magazine, or a book.

Always use a pair of quotation marks, one where the quotation begins and one where it ends. When you write quotations, observe punctuation conventions both before and after the quote.

COMPLETE-SENTENCE QUOTATIONS

A complete-sentence quotation is preceded by a comma or a colon and begins with a quotation mark and a capital letter. It ends with a period, question mark, or exclamation mark, which goes inside the closing quotation mark.

> My father looked up from his work. He said, "Hand me that end wrench."

> Every so often, the thoughtful citizen should look up from her personal pursuits and ask, "Where is this country going?"

PARTIAL QUOTATIONS

A quotation that is less than a complete sentence, such as a word or phrase, is not preceded by a comma and does not begin with a capital letter (unless the first word is a proper noun). Periods always go inside quotation marks.

> My name means "dark-skinned" in Arabic.

> The brochure refers to Sanibel Island as "Florida at its best."

> It says right on the side of the cigarette pack that smoking can cause "fetal injury, premature birth, and low birth weight."

EXERCISE 25-7 **Using Quotation Marks**

Directions: *Using the space provided, correct errors in the use of quotation marks, correcting the punctuation and capitalization as necessary.*

1. I learned very little in grade 6. Consequently, I was held back. Teachers said I had a very difficult time "Concentrating and absorbing the information" that was needed in order to pass that grade.

   _____

2. I ran home screaming "It's alive"!

   _____

3. One thing I recall from my younger days is when we played "spy".

   _____

4. I was afraid for my sister that night. I told my mom "Please don't let her go because the weather is really bad out there".

   _____

5. The next day I woke up to the phone ringing, and I heard my aunt talking to somebody. I heard her say What happened? Right there and then I started crying because I knew something had happened to my sister.

   _____

6. When we finally got to the hospital, we had to wait in the emergency room. I was sitting with my head down when my uncle said there's your dad.

_____

7. Come on, man. Try it. It won't hurt. It makes you feel good. These are just some of the temptations teens have to deal with these days. Words such as these can affect a teen's life greatly.

_____

8. Every time I introduce myself to people, and I tell them my name is Val, they always respond by saying "what, short for Valerie?" Sometimes they say "let me guess. You were born on Valentine's Day!"

_____

9. The doctor looked up at the mother and said she was going to have "A little princess".

_____

10. "Here" Steve said. Then he handed me the keys to the car.

_____

INDIRECT QUOTATIONS

Indirect quotations paraphrase what someone said. They do not require quotation marks. Indirect and direct quotations differ in their use of pronouns and verb tense:

> **Direct:** My father looked up from his work and said, "Hand me an end wrench."
>
> **Indirect:** My father looked up from his work and told me to hand him an end wrench.
>
> **Direct:** A friend saw me walking back to the locker room, so he pulled up and asked, "Do you want a ride home?"
>
> **Indirect:** A friend saw me walking back to the locker room, so he pulled up and asked me if I wanted a ride home.

EXERCISE 25-8 **Indirect Quotations**

Directions: *Using the space provided, rewrite the following quotations as indirect quotations. See examples above.*

1. When I asked the teacher if I could make up the assignment, she said, "I don't think so."

_____

2. My son is always telling me, "I hope my comic book collection is worth something someday."

_____

3. When I stepped in the house, my mother asked me, "What's wrong?"

_____

Writer's Response

Tell about an important conversation with a family member. Use both direct and indirect quotes to tell who said what.

4. I asked my uncle, "Do you know anything about constellations, and if you do, can you help me?"

_____

5. Our neighbour's son grew up saying, "I will never do drugs."

_____

6. I stopped, got out of my car, and asked him, "What is going on?"

_____

7. Being in a hurry I thought, "I won't forget."

_____

8. I asked her if she gets bored reading all these books. She said, "No, I love reading them."

_____

9. With suspicious looks on their faces, they politely asked us, "Where did you get the money?"

_____

10. When he asked about the spelling of my name, I said, "My parents could not spell."

_____

INTERNAL QUOTATIONS AND TITLES

A special use of quotation marks is required when you have an internal quotation. In these cases, the quotation within the quotation is surrounded by single quotation marks.

> One official was quoted as saying, "When we are faced with 'the lesser of two evils,' when we make a choice, we are still choosing an evil."

'The lesser of two evils' is the quote within the quote.

Use quotation marks around the titles of newspaper articles, essays, short stories, poems, and songs. (Note, however, that italics are usually used for titles of movies, books, TV series, or works of art.)

> A newspaper article titled "Cruising Alaska, This Time on Land" describes the amazing sights to be seen from an automobile.

> The only Walt Whitman poem I remember from high school is "When Lilacs Last in the Dooryard Bloom'd."

EXERCISE 25-9 Internal Quotations and Titles

Directions: _Edit the following sentences, adding quotation marks as needed._

1. Perhaps because it is written in two languages, many people have difficulty remembering the words to O Canada.

_____

2. The instructor asked who has memorized the words of the poem In Flanders Fields written by John McCrae?

_____

3. Because of his temperamental moods, Frederick Horsman Varley was difficult to get along with. He was once commissioned to paint the portrait of an important rich businessman. After the client arrived one hour late, Varley said to him You sit there now. I'll be going out for an hour while you wait.

_____

4. In 1986, Tomson Highway's play The Rez Sisters was published.

_____

5. An exasperated linguist remarked, "One problem with young people's speech today is their overuse of "you know."

_____

Apostrophes
POSSESSIVE FORMS

Apostrophes are used to indicate possession or ownership. In the case of singular nouns, including those ending in *s,* and plural nouns not ending in *s,* add an apostrophe and an *s* (*'s*) to indicate possession: for example, *the store manager's attention, Chris's book, the children's toys.* In the case of plural nouns ending in *s,* simply add the apostrophe: for example, *so many mammals' habitats.*

EXERCISE 25-10 **Possessive Forms and Apostrophes**

Directions: *Complete the table below. Put together the possessors and objects listed.*
(a) Add apostrophe plus s *to those possessors that do not end in* s:

EXAMPLE

my brother + Ford Mustang = my brother's Ford Mustang
_____

most women + career plans = most women's career plans
_____

(b) Add just an apostrophe to possessors that end in s:

EXAMPLE

the delegates + conference = the delegates' conference
_____

1. a child   first role model
_____

2. children   first role models
_____

3. the book   last chapter
_____

4. most books   last chapters
_____

5. the student   good fortune
_____

6. students   good fortune
_____

7. the airlines   responsibility
_____

8. my job   biggest drawbacks
_____

9. the boss   pet peeves
_____

10. that employee   bad attitude
_____

11. most movies   earnings
_____

12. the idea   power
_____

13. modern music   audience
_____

14. a performer   time to act
_____

15. my neighbours   French poodle
_____

CONTRACTIONS

An apostrophe can be used to replace a missing letter in **contractions**—words that have been created by dropping letters or combining some of the sounds from two or more words:

As you edit your writing, remember to remove unnecessary contractions.

cannot	can't
have not	haven't
it is	it's

Note: The words *its* is the possessive form of the pronoun *it*. Writers often accidentally interchange *it's* ("it is") and *its* ("belonging to it"). Be on the lookout for this common mistake when proofreading your work. Also, bear in mind that contractions are considered informal, more appropriate to use in conversation than in writing. For that reason, many academic writers prefer to minimize their use of contractions.

PLURALS

A frequent error made by writers is the addition of apostrophes to simple plurals, as illustrated in the following example:

Incorrect: I didn't like dog's when I was a child.

Correct: I did not like dogs when I was a child.

Here, the word *dogs* is a simple plural; it means "more than one dog." The inclusion of the apostrophe indicates the possessive, belonging to the dog, rather than the fact that there is more than one dog. Therefore, the apostrophe is not needed. Be aware of this common pitfall when proofreading your writing.

EXERCISE 25-11   **Proofreading for Apostrophes**

Directions: *Edit the following sentences. Delete apostrophes from plurals. Proofread for its/ it's errors. Eliminate unnecessary contractions. In the space provided, write corrections of the errors you find.*

1. Television has made many advances since it's debut.

_____

2. The news let's you know what's happening around your city, province, and country right away.

_____

3. There were five of us: one sister, three brother's, and me.

_____

4. It's Thanksgiving weekend, always a good time for us to catch up on the latest news in the family.

_____

5. When I first get to work, I don't do anything except check inventory. It doesn't matter what else is happening. That's my first responsibility.

_____

6. It makes sense to society that mother's carry a child for nine months, care for it when it is born, listen and meet it's needs, feed it when it is hungry, and reassure it that it is going to be safe and happy all it's life.

_____

7. Let's say things have improved somewhat. We are in the twenty-first century, and women are playing role's that were once dreamt about but have now become reality.

_____

8. Every morning the cat will sit with me as I'm having my coffee. At night, I know when it's time for bed because that's when she comes out of her hiding spot.

_____

9. I don't want to take the chance of having too many friend's that might hurt me one day. It's hard to trust anyone.

_____

10. The age of electronic education is here, and like everything it has it's advantages and it's disadvantages.

_____

EXERCISE 25-12 **Editing for Apostrophe Errors**

Directions: _Read the following sentences to determine whether the correct possessive form is being used. Correct any errors you find in the space provided. Some sentences are correct as written._

1. Every childs' idea of fun is different.

_____

2. My mother read every novel by Charles Dickens. She says the book's portraits of miserable children interested her.

_____

3. I used to work in the childrens' department.

_____

Ask Yourself

What type of apostrophe error are you most likely to make?

4. The airline's pilots refused to cross the picket lines that day.

_____

5. My job's benefit package includes dental insurance.

6. His cousins' real trouble began when their stepfather lost his job.

7. I read in this mornings' paper about a mans' journey around the globe in a hot air balloon.

8. This movies' content is too violent for young children to see.

9. He was obsessed with time travel. The ideas appeal was both complete freedom and the chance to meet historical people.

10. My sisters workplace closed suddenly. Now they are unemployed.

CHAPTER REVIEW

Take a moment and reflect on what you have learned about punctuation.

☐ Commas

- *Commas and coordinating conjunctions: compound sentences*

- *Commas and introductory modifiers: subordinating conjunctions; conjunctive adverbs*

- *Commas and interrupters: parenthetical word, phrase, or clause; afterthought*

- *Commas in a series: in a list of three or more*

☐ Semicolons and colons

- *Semicolons (;): between closely related complete sentences; with a conjunctive adverb; for items in a series*

- *Colons (:): to connect a list to a complete sentence*

☐ Quotation marks

- *Complete sentence quotations: preceded by comma; end punctuation inside closing quotation marks*

- *Partial quotations: not preceded by comma; end punctuation inside closing quotation marks*

- *Indirect quotations: no quotation marks; check pronouns and verb tenses*

- *Internal quotations (single quotation marks) and titles: newspaper articles, etc.*

☐ Apostrophes

- *Possessive forms: singular nouns, add 's; plurals ending in s, add only apostrophe*

- *Contractions: informal, minimize use; its = possessive; it's = it is*

- *Plurals: no apostrophe*

Mechanics

Everyone misspells words occasionally, omits a capital letter, forgets to write out numbers from one to ten, or uses an incorrect abbreviation. This chapter provides a few strategies to identify and correct errors in spelling, capitalization, numbers, abbreviations, and confusing words that sound alike. You can use the information in this chapter to help you make a personalized editing checklist for errors you frequently make in your writing.

Spelling

To ensure you spell correctly, use a dictionary (including a misspeller's dictionary) and a thesaurus when you write. Learn to use spell-check on your computer. Finding a reliable proofreading partner can also help you eliminate recurring mechanical errors.

Spelling Tips

1. **Keep a vocabulary or word log.** Make a list of words you frequently misspell. Then study these words and write them multiple times.
2. **Be vigilant while writing and proofreading.** As you draft a paper, underline words that look misspelled. Check these words as you proofread your paper.
3. **Use a dictionary.** Don't wait until you proofread. Use your dictionary as you draft. In addition to definitions, a dictionary will help you with prefixes, suffixes, word combination, and word splits.
4. **Use a misspeller's dictionary.** Organized in alphabetical order, a misspeller's dictionary is a quick reference to find the correct spelling of a word. You can also identify the common errors you make. Here is a sample from *The McGraw-Hill Dictionary of Misspelled and Easily Confused Words.*

Wrong	*Correct*
buleten	bul • le • tin
evassion	eva • sion
particepant	par • tic • i • pant

5. **Use spell-check.** Computer spell-checks underline and correct words you misspell. Unfortunately, spell-check has limitations and is no substitute for a good proofreading partner.

BASIC SPELLING RULES

Memorizing a few basic rules will help you spell correctly. These rules pertain to vowel combinations, suffixes, and plural spellings.

Rule 1: *ie* and *ei*

Words with the letters *ie* and *ei* are frequently misspelled. To avoid these spelling errors, remember this saying: *i* before *e* except after *c* or when sounding like *a* as in ne<u>ig</u>hbour or we<u>ig</u>h.

Examples

i **before** *e*: ch<u>ie</u>f, f<u>ie</u>ld, bel<u>ie</u>ve, or n<u>ie</u>ce

except after *c*: dec<u>ei</u>ve, rec<u>ei</u>ve, or c<u>ei</u>ling

sounding like *a*: fr<u>ei</u>ght or v<u>ei</u>n

There are always exceptions to a rule. When in doubt, consult a dictionary.

Exceptions

their	seize
science	counterfeit

EXERCISE 26-1 **Using *ie* or *ei***

Directions: *Insert* ie *or* ei *in the blanks to correctly spell the following words.*

1. for ____gn
2. br ____f
3. y____ld
4. pr____st
5. suffic____nt

6. gr____f
7. rel____ve
8. w____ght
9. fr____nd
10. handkerch____f

Rule 2: Suffixes

Suffixes are endings that are added to words. Suffixes change the word form—for example, from adjective to adverb. Remember the following rules to avoid misspelling words when you add suffixes to them.

1. Words ending in *e*.
   - **Drop the final *e* in a word if the suffix begins with a vowel, such as *-ed* or *-ing*.**
     rake + <u>e</u>d = raked
     care + <u>i</u>ng = caring
   - **Drop the final *e* in a word when it is preceded by a vowel.**
     tr<u>ue</u> + ly = truly
     arg<u>ue</u> + ment = argument
   - **Drop the final *e* in a word when you add the suffixes *-able* or *-ous*.**
     advise + able = advisable
     ridicule + ous = ridiculous
     Exception: If eliminating a silent *e* creates confusion, keep it.
     mile + age = mileage
   - **Keep the final *e* in a word if the suffix begins with a consonant.**
     home + less = homeless
     care + ful = careful

- **Keep the final _e_ in a word if it follows a soft _c_ or _g_.**

    trace + able = traceable

    outrage + ous = outrageous

2. Words ending in _y_.
   - **Change the _y_ to an _i_ at the end of a word when it follows a consonant.**

     happy + ness = happiness

     ready + ly = readily

   - **Keep the _y_ at the end of a word if it follows a vowel.**

     portray + ed = portrayed

     habitual + ly = habitually

   - **Keep the _y_ at the end of a word if you are adding the suffix _-ing_.**

     play + ing = playing

     copy + ing = copying

3. Words ending in a consonant.
   - **Double the final consonant in a single syllable word when it follows a single vowel.**

     wet + er = wetter

     trap + ing = trapping

   - **Do not double the final consonant in a single syllable word when it does not follow a single vowel. For a word that ends with _w, x, y,_ or _z_, just add the suffix.**

     mark + er = marker

     crow + ing = crowing

   - **Double the final consonant when the word has more than one syllable, the end consonant follows a single vowel, and the last syllable of the word will be stressed once the ending is added.**

     forget + ing = forgetting

EXERCISE 26-2 **Adding Suffixes**

Directions: _Combine each word and suffix. Spell the new word correctly._

1. stubborn + ness   _____

2. appoint + ment   _____

3. control + er   _____

4. run + ing   _____

5. propel + ed   _____

6. benefit + ed   _____

7. move + er   _____

8. remove + able   _____

9. write + ing   _____

10. fame + ous   _____

Rule 3: Plurals

To improve your spelling, remember these rules for making nouns plural.

1. **Add *s* to most singular nouns to make them plural.**

   frog + s = frogs

   lemon + s = lemons

2. **Add -*es* to singular nouns ending in *s, ss, z, zz, x, sh, ch,* or *tch*.**

   bus + es = buses

   buzz + es = buzzes

   sex + es = sexes

   wish + es = wishes

   church + es = churches

   watch + es = watches

3. **Add -*ies* to singular nouns ending in a consonant plus *y*. Change the *y* to *i* and add -*es*.**

   baby + es = babies

   party + es = parties

   Exception: Add *s* to proper nouns that end in *y*.

   Mondays

   Kennedys

   Wendys

   Will all the Wendys in the senior class report to the office?

4. **Words ending in *o*.**
   - **Add *s* when the word ends in a vowel plus *o* combination.**

     studio + s = studios

     rodeo + s = rodeos
   - **Add -*es* when the word ends in a consonant plus *o* combination.**

     mosquito + es = mosquitoes

     potato + es = potatoes
   - **Some words that end in *o* can be made plural by adding *s* or *es*.**

     avocado + s = avocados

     avocado + es = avocadoes

5. **Irregular nouns are made plural in different ways. Memorize the nouns that are irregular.**

   child = children

   mouse = mice

   woman = women

   goose = geese

   ox = oxen

   person = people

   tooth = teeth

EXERCISE 26-3 **Creating Plural Nouns**

Directions: *Make the nouns plural and spell them correctly.*

1. rodeo   _____

2. lady   _____

3. donkey   _____

4. hero   _____

5. comedy   _____

6. goose   _____

7. fox   _____

8. class   _____

9. chief   _____

10. bench   _____

11. ghetto   _____

12. zoo   _____

13. radio   _____

14. kiss   _____

15. foot   _____

COMMONLY MISSPELLED WORDS

Learn to edit for commonly misspelled words, such as *always* (allways), *parallel* (paralel), *special* (specal), and *surprise* (suprize). Table 26-1 shows a list of the words most commonly misspelled by writers of all ages.

Keep a list of words you misspell. Use memory aids to help you remember correct spelling. For example, underline or circle the misspelled part of the word:

Misspelled	Correctly Spelled
usualy	usual<u>l</u>y
definate	defin<u>it</u>e
u	<u>you</u>

You can use common memory aids like "remember that skiing uses two poles so you spell *skiing* by doubling the *i* in the middle," or make up your own aid. Here are memory strategies for *a lot* and *argument*, which are frequently misspelled.

Misspelling	Correct Spelling	Memory Strategy
alot	a lot	*A lot* is two words because it is not just one thing. It is a lot of things.
arguement	argument	To win an argument you must have an idea that sticks in someone's head. The correct spelling of *argument* has the word *gum* in it.

Directions: *On a sheet of paper, make a list of ten words you frequently misspell. Select these words from your papers or review the table of commonly misspelled words (Table 26-1). Create a chart like the one for* a lot *and* argument *to study the words. Write the misspelled words, then the correct spellings. Underline the letters where the errors occur. Write a strategy or memory aid you can use to remember the correct spelling of each word.*

COMMONLY MISUSED WORDS

Spelling is often complicated by the fact that some words sound alike, look alike, or both. For example, the words *knew* and *new* look and sound alike but have different spellings and different meanings. They are also different parts of speech.

Knew and New

knew: (verb) to know or to understand

Ricardo **knew** how to operate the forklift.

new: (adjective) just created or unfamiliar

A **new** minister is sworn into office.

Develop a system to help you master these words. Some commonly confused words have a unique feature that helps you remember how to spell them and how to use them.

PARTS OF SPEECH

All words serve a specific purpose or function in a sentence. The part of speech is the name of that purpose or function.

There are eight parts of speech: noun, pronoun, adjective, verb, adverb, preposition, conjunction, and interjection.

TABLE 26-1

COMMONLY MISSPELLED WORDS

a lot	dining	licence	psychology
absence	disappoint	lightning	receiving
ache	dying	loneliness	recognize
across	eighth	manoeuvre	relevant
address	embarrassing	marriage	restaurant
aisle	environment	mathematics	rhythm
always	equivalent	meant	roommate
among	especially	minimum	schedule
analyze	familiar	missile	seize
appearance	fascinate	mortgage	secretary
argument	flexible	mysterious	separate
attendance	foreign	necessary	sincerely
believe	formerly	noticeable	skiing
business	friend	ninety	sophomore
beautiful	fulfill	occurrence	special
beginning	generally	opinion	subtle
calendar	gesture	parallel	succeed
campaign	grammar	paralysis	surprise
career	government	paralyze	technique
category	grief	particular	therefore
cemetery	height	peculiar	transferred
changeable	humorous	perceive	truly
compelled	illegal	perform	until
conscientious	immediately	physically	usually
convenient	independent	preference	valuable
defendant	intelligence	prejudice	weight
definite	interrupt	probably	weird
description	irrelevant	procedure	woman
desperate	knowledge	proceed	women
dilemma	leisure	profession	written

principle   principal (the principal is the head of a school and your *pal*)

incite   insight (insight provides the <u>sight</u> to understand something)

However, not all words with different meanings have unique spellings that allow you to distinguish between them, so having a reference book handy or using the reference tools on your computer will help.

Ask Yourself

Which of the words in Set 1 do you generally use correctly? Commonly misuse?

Commonly Misused Words—Set 1

accept—except

- **accept:** (verb) to receive, to understand, to allow in

  I was pleased to **accept** the nomination for class secretary.

- **except:** (preposition) otherwise, than, to the exclusion of; (conjunction) unless; or (verb) to take out

  Everyone **except** five new students attended the rally.

advice—advise

- **advice:** (noun) opinion given as to what to do

  The physicist provided **advice** on how to understand the problem.

- **advise:** (verb) to give advice

  Wilson would **advise** the prime minister to amend the tax bill, but the prime minister would not listen.

all ready—already

- **all ready:** (adjective or adverb/verb or noun) everyone or everything is ready to go or prepared

  The judges were **all ready** to begin the barbecue taste test.

- **already:** (adverb) previously

  The engineers had **already** triple-checked the missile prior to blast-off.

all right—alright

- **all right:** (adverb or adjective) satisfactory; adequate, safe

  The outfielders were **all right** after lightning hit left field.

- **alright:** (adjective or adverb) disputed spelling of *all right*

all together—altogether

- **all together:** (adjective) gathered; united

  When the children were finally found, they were **all together.**

- **altogether:** (adverb) completely; thoroughly

  It was a completely different situation **altogether.**

choose—chose

- **choose:** (present tense verb) to select or decide

  The committee must **choose** the theme for the festival.

- **chose:** (past tense verb) to select or decide

  After the meeting, the committee **chose** the theme for the festival.

conscious—conscience

- **conscious:** (adjective) having awareness; being mentally awake
  Conscious of the traffic problems, the bus driver chose another route.
- **conscience:** (noun) having a sense of morality and choosing to do good
  My **conscience** guides me to make good choices in my life.

hear—here

- **hear:** (verb) to perceive sound; to listen
  The audience could **hear** the violins echo the main melody.
- **here:** (adverb) a place or location
  We decided to camp **here** because the trees would shade our tent.

its—it's

- **its:** (pronoun) possessive form of *it*
  The starving dog ate **its** food quickly.
- **it's:** (pronoun/verb) the contraction for *it is*
  It's easy to find a phone number using yellowpages.ca.

knew—new

- **knew:** (verb) past tense of *know*; understood
  Denise **knew** how to drive a motorcycle.
- **new:** (adjective) just created or unfamiliar
  A **new** store opened at the mall recently.

leave—let

- **leave:** (verb) to depart a place or to allow a person or thing to remain
  Please **leave** the papers on the kitchen table so I can mail them.
- **let:** (verb) to give an opportunity; assign; allow
  Let me mail the letters when I go to the store.

lay—lie

- **lay:** (verb) to place a thing onto something
  Lay the books on the book cart, and the librarian will put them on the shelf.
- **lie:** (verb) to rest in a horizontal position
  Lie on the couch and relax before dinner.

loose—lose—loss

- **loose:** (adjective) not fastened; detached
  Tightening the **loose** wires repaired the faulty light.
- **lose:** (verb) not able to keep or find something
  More people will **lose** jobs with a weak economy.
- **loss:** (noun) the result of losing a person or thing; failing to gain or win
  The financial **loss** was too large to ignore, and the company closed its doors.

raise—rise

- **raise:** (verb) to lift a person or thing; to increase the amount; to grow
  The farmer will **raise** a variety of crops: corn, wheat, and alfalfa.
- **rise:** (verb) to move upward; ascend; respond
  The team will **rise** to the challenge to beat their opponents.

set—sit

- **set:** (verb) to place a thing down or onto something
  He **set** the basket on top of the picnic table.
- **sit:** (verb) to rest in a sitting position
  Please **sit** in the lobby and wait for the next available agent.

than—then

- **than:** (conjunction) used to make a comparison between two things
  I am taller **than** the doorway, so I always duck when I enter the house.
- **then:** (adverb) indicating a time period or a future time period
  First, I picked up my laundry, and **then** I went to the post office.

Writer's Response

What words that sound alike do you often confuse? Explain how to solve that confusion.

their—there—they're

- **their:** (pronoun) possessive pronoun of *they;* to show possession of a person, place, or thing
  The travellers checked into **their** suites at the ski resort.
- **there:** indicating a place or position or point
  There are three reasons that I cannot go to the party.
- **they're:** (pronoun and verb) the contraction for *they are*
  The bridesmaids are late for the wedding. **They're** caught in traffic.

to—too—two

- **to:** (preposition) indicating action toward a person, place, or thing
  Robert mailed the package **to** his sister in Newfoundland.
- **too:** (adverb) also; very; excessive amount
  I wanted to go, **too.**
  I ate **too** many calories at lunch so dinner has to be mostly vegetables.
- **two:** (adjective) the number 2
  I read **two** chapters before class this morning.

whose—who's

- **whose:** (pronoun) inquiring about ownership of a person, place, or thing
  Whose tennis shoes are sitting in the hallway?
- **who's:** (pronoun and verb) the contraction for *who is*
  Who's going to buy the tickets for the hockey game next month?

your—you're

- **your:** (pronoun) indicating ownership by a specific person
  Your son causes frequent disruptions and may be suspended.

- **you're:** (pronoun and verb) the contraction for *you are*

  You're causing frequent disruptions in class, and you may be suspended.

Self-Assessment of Commonly Misused Words—Set 1

Directions: *Read the following sentences and underline the correct word in the parentheses for each one. Use the definitions above to help you select the correct word.*

1. I have (all ready/already) packed the children's books in those boxes so they are (all ready/already) to go.

2. I (hear/here) there is a (knew/new) restaurant downtown, but anyplace you choose is (all right/alright) with me.

3. (Their/There/They're) is more to eat at the party (than/then) you imagine.

4. If you have to (leave/let) early, please (leave/let) the instructor know at the beginning of the class.

5. I never give (advice/advise) to friends, but (your/you're) an exception (to/too/two) my rule.

6. If we go (all together/altogether), (whose/who's) driving to the game?

7. I will (choose/chose) a new course for my schedule, so I can (raise/rise) my grades.

8. I am (conscious/conscience) of the confusion between the (to/too/two) political groups, but I (accept/except) your facts and will reconsider.

9. If you let the rope (loose/lose/loss), I can (lay/lie) it flat on the ground.

10. Before (its/it's) too late, (sit/set) down and talk about your decision.

Spelling Challenges from Set 1

Directions: *Score Exercise 26-5 to identify words you need to add to your spelling log. Create a memory aid like the one in the box below for each word or pair of words that gave you difficulty. Then write a sentence for each word and study the words before you test yourself again.*

EXAMPLE: *WHOSE* AND *WHO'S*

Whose is a pronoun used to ask who owns a person, place, or thing.

Who's is the contraction of *who is*.

- **Whose** backpack was left on the front porch?
- **Who's** going to wash the dishes after dinner?

Commonly Misused Words—Set 2

allowed—aloud

- **allowed:** (verb) past tense of *allow;* to permit

  The professor **allowed** his students to turn in their assignments late.

- **aloud:** (adverb) loudly

  The whole congregation heard the little boy talking **aloud** during the sermon.

behalf—behave

- **behalf:** (noun) in the interest of, in support of, or for the benefit of a person or group

  The daughter spoke on **behalf** of her extremely ill father.

- **behave:** (verb) to act in a certain way

  Please **behave** properly while we wait for our food to come.

breath—breathe

- **breath:** (noun) air inhaled or exhaled

  Take a **breath** before you talk to calm yourself.

- **breathe:** (verb) to inhale and exhale

  Back up and give him room to **breathe.**

capital—capitol

- **capital:** (adjective and noun) primary or main; a punishment requiring the death penalty; an accumulation of money

  The owner had enough **capital** that he was able to expand his store.

- **capitol:** (noun) a building in which governments of states or nations meet; a city where a state locates its government

  The legislature will meet in the **capitol** to discuss immigration laws.

clothes—cloths

- **clothes:** (noun) clothing

  I bought new **clothes** with my birthday money.

- **cloths:** (noun) fabric or material

  The mechanic used some old **cloths** to clean the windows and instrument panels of the car.

complement—compliment

- **complement:** (noun) something that improves or enhances a person, place, or thing

  Creamy coleslaw is a **complement** to the sharp taste of barbecue ribs.

- **compliment:** (verb) to express respect or praise

  The senators **complimented** the committee on a thoughtful review of educational policies.

hole—whole

- **hole:** (noun) an opening; a flaw

  A gaping **hole** was left after the car crashed into the building.

- **whole:** (adjective) an entire thing; a system or group working together

  The **whole** office attended the retirement party.

know—no

- **know:** (verb) to understand or have knowledge of

  First-year students **know** they must learn to study and manage their time effectively.

- **no:** (adjective or adverb) not any; used to express a negative choice

  There are **no** carrots left in the refrigerator.

lead—led

- **lead:** (verb) present tense; to guide or show

  The conductor is going to **lead** the orchestra to success.

- **led:** (verb) the past tense of *lead;* to guide or show

  The team captain cheered his teammates as he **led** them to a victory last week.

passed—past

Talk about it

Discuss with a classmate which words you most often mistake. How can you avoid making that mistake in the future?

- **passed:** (verb) past tense of *pass;* to give or transfer an object or person from one place to another; to act in order to gain credit, certification, or permission

  The legislature **passed** a law to restrict dumping chemicals into rivers.

- **past:** (adjective, adverb, or noun) a time period that has already occurred

  In the **past** months, an infestation of grasshoppers ate my crops.

  In the **past,** women were unable to vote.

propose—purpose

- **propose:** (verb) to suggest an idea or action

  I **propose** we do not consider cutting costs by reducing medical care.

- **purpose:** (noun) a reason to do or have a person, place, or thing

  Aesthetic beauty is the primary **purpose** for planting flowers and shrubs.

safe—save

- **safe:** (noun) a place to keep valuable things; (adjective) protected from harm or worry

  I put my diamond necklace in the **safe** in the hotel lobby.

  The basement is a **safe** place during a tornado.

- **save:** (verb) to keep; to rescue from danger

  You can **save** lives by telling people about the dangers of smoking.

scared—scarred

- **scared:** (verb) past tense of *scare;* to be frightened

  The small boy was **scared** by the trick-or-treaters.

- **scarred:** (noun) having a scar or a feeling of being damaged

  The small boy's face was **scarred** after the dog bit him.

scene—seen

- **scene:** (noun) a place; a view or stage setting; a sequence of action

  The third **scene** in the play portrays the fears of new parents.

- **seen:** (verb) past participle of *see;* to have the experience of seeing; to come to know

  Bystanders were frightened by the accident they had just **seen.**

threw—through

- **threw:** (verb) past tense of *throw;* to toss

  The pitcher **threw** three straight fastballs to strike out the batter.

- **through:** (preposition) to go from one place to another; to complete a direct passage

  The needle went **through** the thick carpet with ease.

were—where

- **were:** (verb) past tense of *to be;* to be in a place; to be doing an action

  You **were** at the market all afternoon.

- **where:** (conjunction, adverb, and noun) at or in a place or position

  Where are you going after class?

EXERCISE 26-7 **Self-Assessment of Commonly Misused Words—Set 2**

Directions: *Read the following sentences and underline the correct word in the parentheses for each one. Use the definitions above to help you select the correct word.*

1. My brother's face was (scared/scarred) when another child (threw/through) a rock at him.

2. My cousin often created a huge (seen/scene) at home; he would (behalf/behave) better at school.

3. My yoga instructor reminds us to (breath/breathe) deeply as we stretch.

4. Since I gained weight, I am always hunting through my (clothes/cloths) trying to find an outfit that is (loose/lose) enough to wear.

5. There is no talking (allowed/aloud) in my sign language class.

6. (Threw/Through) the (passed/past) few months, gas prices have doubled.

7. My (hole/whole) family loves bargain shopping, and my sister will drive 15 kilometres to (safe/save) even a single dollar.

8. (Know/No) matter how unpleasant a summer job might be, you have to remember that the primary (propose/purpose) is to make money.

9. I always wanted to (lead/led) a tour of the (capitol/capital).

10. She (complemented/complimented) her employee for a job well done.

EXERCISE 26-8 **Spelling Challenges from Set 2**

Directions: *Score Exercise 26-7 to identify the words you need to add to your spelling log. Create a memory aid like the one in the box below for each word or pair of words that gave you difficulty. Then write a sentence for each word and study the words before you test yourself again.*

EXAMPLE: *PASSED* AND *PAST*

Passed is a verb used to state an action that has already occurred.

Past is a noun used to indicate a past time or experience.

- Greg **passed** the store and had to turn around and go back.

- The argument was in the **past** and not worth talking about.

---

altar—alter

- **altar:** (noun) a table or platform used for worship
  The priest stepped up to the **altar** in the church.
- **alter:** (verb) to change
  Your comments did not **alter** my opinion of the movie.

affect—effect

- **affect:** (verb) to influence or to make an impression on
  Carbon monoxide **affects** the quality of the air.
- **effect:** (noun) the result of an action or event
  The **effects** of carbon monoxide are a concern for environmentalists.

Writer's Response

Write a short paragraph about the environment. Use *affect* or *effect* in your paragraph.

brake—break

- **brake:** (noun) a device used to stop a vehicle; (verb) to stop a vehicle
  I stepped on the **brake** to miss the dog running in front of my car.
  To avoid swerving, truck drivers **brake** hundreds of feet before a stop.
- **break:** (noun) an intermission in a show, game, or event; (verb) to damage something; to separate into parts
  There will be a 15-minute **break** in the middle of the show.
  My sons **break** their toys because they throw them around.

council—counsel

- **council:** (noun) a group of people who meet to provide advice
  The teacher's **council** recommends reading nightly to your children.
- **counsel:** (noun) advice, a person hired to provide advice
  The company hired legal **counsel.**
  My best **counsel** for new parents is to worry less and laugh more.

cite—site—sight

- **cite:** (verb) to state facts or information
  Three coaches **cite** injuries as the biggest challenge for high school football teams.
- **site:** (noun) location of a building, park, or monument
  I walked the **site** with the architect to understand the future building.
- **sight:** (noun) a thing that is seen; the ability to see something
  Margaret's furniture in her new house is a **sight** to behold.
  The blind man miraculously regained his **sight.**

coarse—course

- **coarse:** (adjective) rough or harsh; poor quality
  The ground salt has a **coarse** texture.
- **course:** (noun) class or lecture series; a way to act
  I signed up for a cooking **course** on pasta and sauces.

desert—dessert

- **desert:** (noun) a geographic location that is hot, dry, and sandy; (verb) to leave or abandon a person or thing

  The **desert** blooms in the spring each year.

  Soldiers who **desert** their posts are severely punished.

- **dessert:** (noun) the last course in a meal, usually sweet

  Dessert is my favourite part of the meal so I always eat it first.

discreet—discrete

- **discreet:** (adjective) respecting privacy; keeping quiet about personal issues

  A **discreet** nurse avoids discussing a patient's health in front of visitors.

- **discrete:** (adjective) distinct part of something

  Reading requires a child to learn a series of **discrete** skills in order to recognize known and unknown words.

do—due

- **do:** (verb) to act; to accomplish a task

  I **do** five sets of crunches every morning to strengthen my abdominal muscles.

- **due:** (adjective) when a debt is owed; a date required to pay a debt or obligation

  I sent my payment after the bill's **due** date.

fourth—forth

- **fourth:** (noun) one-quarter of a whole; related to the number 4

  Give me a **fourth** of the pie to take home.

- **forth:** (adverb) moving forward

  The driver rocked his car back and **forth** to get out of the snow bank.

moral—morale

- **moral:** (adjective or noun) the significance of a lesson; the point of a story

  The **moral** of the story is simple: trying and failing is better than giving up.

- **morale:** (noun) mental or emotional attitude

  The commander works to keep up the army's **morale.**

principal—principle

- **principal:** (noun) a person in charge of a school; the sum of a loan that is being repaid; (adjective) a primary influence or person

  The **principal** called five boys to his office for causing a food fight.

  The **principal** investor vetoed the decision to raise employee salaries.

- **principle:** (noun) a rule, law, or code; the essential nature or concept

  There are five **principles** for a successful work ethic.

quiet—quite

- **quiet:** (adjective or noun) a state of peace and rest; (adjective) being free from noise; gentle

  My vacation in the woods gave me the **quiet** and calm that I needed.

- **quite:** (adverb) wholly, completely

  I am **quite** sure the man on the left stole my purse.

real—really

- **real:** (adjective) not false; actual

  The blonde's hair colour was **real.**

- **really:** (adverb) truly; unquestionably; very

  The race was loaded with **really** dangerous curves.

stationary—stationery

- stationary: (adjective) not moving, not changing place or position

  I ride a **stationary** bike every night as I watch television.

- stationery: (noun) paper or materials to write notes or letters

  The company's **stationery** has a letterhead featuring the president's photograph.

Ask Yourself

Which of the words in Set 3 do you generally use correctly? Commonly misuse? Why?

EXERCISE 26-9 Self-Assessment of Commonly Misused Words—Set 3

Directions: *Read the following sentences and underline the correct word in the parentheses for each one. Use the definitions to help you select the correct word.*

1. I was (real/really) hungry, so I ate an appetizer, salad, entrée, and two (deserts/desserts).

2. The (council/counsel) voted on a noise abatement law to create a (quite/quiet) and serene environment for our town.

3. The (coarse/course) requires you to (cite/site/sight) specific examples of (moral/morale) (principles/principals).

4. William has difficulty keeping secrets: he has never been very (discreet/discrete).

5. I purchased new (stationary/stationery) for the office.

6. The doctor told Bill that although he did not (brake/break) any bones, any further (affects/effects) from the accident would take months to appear.

7. The (principal/principle) brought (fourth/forth) a new set of rules to be approved by the Board of Education.

8. It is illegal to (altar/alter) your driver's licence.

9. Students knew work was (do/due) at the beginning of the week.

10. A good speller must learn dozens of (discreet/discrete) rules.

EXERCISE 26-10 Spelling Challenges from Set 3

Directions: *Score Exercise 26-9 to identify the words you need to add to your spelling log. Create a memory aid like the one in the box that follows for each word or pair of words that gave you difficulty. Then write a sentence for each word and study the words before you test yourself again.*

Capitalization

Capitalization is used to distinguish between **proper nouns**—words that are the specific names of people, places, and things—and **common nouns**—words that refer to general categories or types of people, places, and things.

WRITING TIP

Remember to capitalize the names of days, months, and holidays.

Common Nouns	Proper Nouns
woman	Adrienne Clarkson
day	Tuesday
month	July
city	Charlottetown
country	England

Capitalization is also used to indicate the first word of a sentence, the titles of books and newspapers, and job titles. Here are some guidelines for capitalization.

1. **Capitalize the first word of a sentence.**

   Don't drop out of high school if you want a good job.

   Machines replace people in more and more unskilled jobs each year.

2. **Capitalize proper nouns (specific people, places, and things).**
   - **Specific people (including the pronoun *I*)**

Sarah McLachlan	Sting
David Suzuki	I
Margaret Laurence	Terry Fox

   - **Nationalities, cultures, and languages**

Japanese	Hispanic
African American	Portuguese

   - **Religions, religious followers, and religious/sacred texts**

Baptist	Bible
Semitic	Torah
Jesuit priests	Quran

   - **Governmental organizations, company names, other institutions, or brand names**

World Wildlife Fund	Consumers Gas
Niagara Regional Police	Phi Kappa Delta
Tim Hortons	Tostito

- Social, political, sports, and other organizations

YMCA	Student Activities Safety Association
Clutterers Anonymous	Loyal Order of the Moose
FactCheck.Org	Toronto Maple Leafs

- Specific places (continents, countries, regions, counties, cities, towns, addresses, and so on)

Avonlea	Miramichi
Newfoundland	Quebec City
the Arctic Circle	Kicking Horse Pass
Portage Avenue	Moose Jaw, Saskatchewan

- Specific things (buildings, monuments, famous objects, titles of works, and so on)

CN Tower	Canadian Museum of Civilization
Saddledome	*The Jack Pine*
Rogers Centre	"O Canada"
Beaver Crest Pole	The Big Nickel

- Days of the weeks, months, holidays, and religious holidays (Note: Seasons are not capitalized.)

Thursday	Yom Kippur
December	Eid al-Fitr
Labour Day	Mardi Gras

- Historical time periods, events, movements, and documents

Renaissance	Expressionist movement
Industrial Revolution	Constitution
World War II	*Brown v. Board of Education*

3. **Capitalize formal and informal titles.**
   - **Capitalize job titles or positions** when the title appears before the name, but **not** when it comes afterward or separately from a name.

chairperson	Chairperson Benger
senator	Senator Dallaire
doctor	Doctor Franklin

     The patient looked frantically for **Doctor Franklin.**

     He could not find the **doctor** anywhere.

4. **Capitalize the titles of relatives when they are used to replace proper names or appear immediately before proper names.**

   After my parent's divorce, **Mother** kept in close contact with **Aunt** Maria.

5. **Capitalize the following words when they serve as proper nouns:**
   - **Directions** such as north, south, east, or west when they refer to a geographic region: the Southwest, the Northeast.
   - **Course titles** only when they name a specific course: Introduction to Anthropology, Apprentice Drafting, Calculus 101.

EXERCISE 26-11 **Proper Nouns**

Directions: *Select the sentence that uses the correct form of capitalization from each of the following pairs.*

_____ 1.

    a. Yosemite national park is nearly 1200 square miles of mountains, valleys, and spectacular waterfalls.

    b. Yosemite National Park is nearly 1200 square miles of mountains, valleys, and spectacular waterfalls.

_____ 2.

    a. Thousands of teens head south to Florida for March break.

    b. Thousands of teens head South to Florida for March break.

_____ 3.

    a. The Ministers from Ottawa will arrive shortly.

    b. The ministers from Ottawa will arrive shortly.

_____ 4.

    a. Technological weapons used in the Gulf War changed warfare.

    b. Technological weapons used in the Gulf war changed warfare.

_____ 5.

    a. I'm taking English 101 and archeology 232 this semester.

    b. I'm taking English 101 and Archeology 232 this semester.

_____ 6.

    a. the southwest is facing a dire water shortage (Severe water shortages affect 400 million people).

    b. The Southwest is facing a dire water shortage (severe water shortages affect 400 million people).

Talk about it

What is the difference between common and proper nouns?

_____ 7.

    a. Learning spanish on DVD is easier than I thought.

    b. Learning Spanish on DVD is easier than I thought.

_____ 8.

    a. I had an interview with the Advisory Council on Historic Preservation.

    b. I had an interview with the Advisory Council on historic preservation.

_____ 9.

    a. Tell the cab driver to drop you off at 34667 N. Wilshire Boulevard.

    b. Tell the cab driver to drop you off at 34667 N. Wilshire boulevard.

_____ 10.

    a. After the surgery, the surgeons and Doctor Moss spoke with the family.

    b. After the surgery, the Surgeons and Doctor Moss spoke with the family.

Another rule for capitalization is that the titles of publications should be capitalized. Titles of books, newspapers, magazines, poems, articles, stories, documents, films, TV shows, plays, tapes, and works of art all have a single rule for capitalization: **Capitalize the first word, last word, and all other words except articles, conjunctions, and prepositions.** Prepositions of five letters or longer may be capitalized.

Book: *Obasan* by Joy Kogawa

Newspaper: *The Globe and Mail*

Magazine: *The Walrus*

Poem: "We Are More" by Shane Koyczan

Article: "New Fossil Site Found at Prehistoric Burgess Shale" by Colette Derworiz

Story: "The Hockey Sweater" by Roch Carrier

Work of Art: *The Old Stump* by Lawren Harris

TV show: *Corner Gas*

Song: "I'm Like a Bird" by Nelly Furtado

EXERCISE 26-12 **Titles of Publications**

Directions: *Underline the words that should be capitalized in the following titles.*

1. "the road not taken"
2. *the freedom writers diary: how a teacher and 150 teens used writing to change themselves and the world around them*
3. "seventeen hits and a sigh of relief for the yankees"
4. *the mona lisa*
5. *black and decker: the complete guide to home masonry*
6. *maclean's*
7. "new pacman xbox is swan song for founder"
8. *harry potter and the goblet of fire*
9. "you give love a bad name"
10. "stem cell industry set to break out"

Numbers

Here are the basic rules for writing numbers.

1. **Spell out numbers that start a sentence.**
   Two Russian spacewalkers attached a micrometeorite shield to the space station.
2. **Spell out numbers one to ten.** Use figures for numbers 11 and over.
   - I had **eight** jobs before I found one I really liked.
   - The local food store has **27** employees.
   - I love music and have **325** CDs in my collection.
3. **Hyphenate all compound numbers.**
   Seventy-five top companies were cited for creating a quality work environment.

PUNCTUATION ALERT
1. Italicize titles of books, newspapers, magazines, works of art, and TV series.
2. Use quotation marks for titles of poems, articles, stories, TV programs that are not continuing series, and songs.

4. **Use figures for most dates, addresses, percentages, fractions, decimals, scores, statistics, pages, and time.**
   - **Dates:** One of the most famous dates in Canadian history is **July 1, 1867.**
   - **Addresses:** My new address is **87 George Street.**
   - **Percentages:** I always wait for the ultimate price of **75 percent** off the original price.
   - **Scores:** The Blue Jays won with a final score of **7 to 5.**
   - **Statistics:** In 2009 over **250 000** immigrants entered Canada.
   - **Surveys:** Recent surveys indicate **9 out of 10** dentists recommend fluoride.
   - **Divisions in Books:** I am currently reading the *Complete Letters and Speeches of Charles Dickens,* and I am on **page 358 in Chapter 5 of Volume 2.**
   - **Time:** I have a meeting at **9:37 a.m.** exactly to discuss the budget.

5. **Spell out simple fractions and use hyphens.** Use figures for mixed fractions.
   - **One-fourth** of new employees doubt their ability to be successful.
   - I anticipate my salary will increase by **3½ percent** next year.

6. **Spell out decades (eighties) or use complete numerals (1980s).** Do not use an apostrophe between the year and the *s* (1980s). Choose one approach and be consistent.

   I love the early rock and roll music of the **1960s,** even though I was a teenager during the disco era of the **1980s.**

7. **Spell out noon, midnight, and time when using *o'clock*.**

   We work eight-hour shifts at the hospital. We change shifts at **eight o'clock, four o'clock, and midnight.**

EXERCISE 26-13 **Numbers**

Directions: *Determine if the numbers underlined below are written correctly. Write a C at the beginning of an item if the number is written correctly. If it is not, write the corrected version in the space provided below.*

_____ 1. 25 drivers qualified in the first round of the Indianapolis 500.

_____

_____ 2. The Toronto Stock Exchange fell 100 points in the last week.

_____

_____ 3. Five men were stranded in a snowstorm for two days in Nova Scotia.

_____

_____ 4. The band Great Big Sea has produced 9 studio albums.

_____

_____ 5. In a single year 16 coral reefs were destroyed by changes in the environment.

_____

_____ 6. <u>10</u> years ago the Species at Risk Act began protecting wildlife.

_____ 7. Can a dog that loses <u>0.25</u> percent of its body weight in a week be healthy?

_____ 8. Just over <u>100</u> volunteers looked for the lost dog in the neighbourhood.

_____ 9. Like the droughts experienced in the <u>2000s</u>, the <u>2010s</u> will probably include more severe and extended droughts because of global warming.

_____ 10. The new store hours will be <u>one o'clock</u> to <u>10 o'clock</u> on Saturday.

Abbreviations

Use an abbreviation, such as CSIS or YMCA, only when you are sure a reader will understand it. Here are the basic rules for writing abbreviations.

1. **Write the full title the first time you use it, followed by the abbreviation in parentheses.** Then use the abbreviation throughout the rest of the paper.

   Due to the controversy surrounding euthanasia at **the Society for the Prevention of Cruelty to Animals (SPCA), donations to the SPCA have dropped.**

2. **Use standard abbreviations for titles used before or after a proper name.** Do not abbreviate a title if it is not used with a proper name.

   Mr. William McDougal   Ms. Shree Zabawa

   George P. Wilson Sr.   George P. Wilson Jr.

   Dr. Rachel Russio   David White MD

   Prof. Michael Bates   Michelle Anderson PhD

   Zavira Cussins DDS

3. **Capitalize abbreviations of agencies of government, corporations, and call letters of radio and television stations.**

   NASA   IBM

   CRA   102.1 The Edge

   ROM   CBC

4. **Use BC, AD, CE, a.m., p.m., No., and $ with specific dates, times, numbers, and amounts only.**

   510 BC   7:35 a.m.

   AD 476   No. 3

   3:15 p.m. $100

5. Avoid using overused or inappropriate abbreviations.

Avoid	Use
i.e.	that is
e.g.	for example
etc.	and so forth, and so on
lb.	pound
Mon.	Monday
Xmas	Christmas
Jan.	January
Am Lit.	American Literature
ON	Ontario

EXERCISE 26-14 **Abbreviations**

Directions: *Determine if the underlined abbreviations are written correctly. Write a C above abbreviations that are correct. Correct errors by writing the corrections on the lines provided.*

1. The <u>prof.</u> in my <u>poli. sci.</u> 327 course required we visit the ACLU Web site.

_____

2. Ben Farmer <u>Sr.</u> visits the <u>YMCA</u> daily to work out, meet friends, drink coffee, <u>etc.</u>

_____

3. On Tuesday and <u>Thurs.</u>, it costs only <u>$15.00</u> for walk-ins at the barbershop.

_____

4. <u>ON, QC, NB, and NS</u> are the four provinces that first entered Canadian Confederation in 1867.

_____

5. The Canadian Space Agency <u>(CSA)</u> designed and built the Canadarm, a famous robotic and technological achievement, which made its space debut on the Space Shuttle in 1981.

_____

CHAPTER OVERVIEW

Take a moment and reflect on what you have learned about mechanics.

☐ Spelling: Use a dictionary and thesaurus; spell-check; proofread
   • *Basic spelling rules*
   • *Commonly misspelled words: different spellings, different meanings; different parts of speech*
   • *Commonly misused words: create a memory aid*

☐ Capitalization: used for proper nouns

☐ Numbers: seven rules

☐ Abbreviations: five rules

Critical Reading, Thinking, and Writing

THINK FIRST

Suppose you could change jobs right now. What would you do? Write a paragraph in which you describe the new job and what it would involve. To what extent would critical reading, thinking, and writing be important in this job?

The Critical Citizen

All of us are bombarded with information—online, on television, in print, in the classroom, and on the street. To function effectively, you must hone your critical thinking skills. In other words, you need to learn to reject what is false or inaccurate and to accept what is trustworthy and reliable. You undoubtedly do this already, to some extent. After all, do you really trust a tabloid newspaper as much as *The Globe and Mail* or CBC? Nonetheless, practice is necessary for finer distinctions: Which op-ed piece makes more sense on the issues of the upcoming election? Which candidate should you vote for and why? Consider the ways in which this sort of thinking occurs in other aspects of your life, and ask yourself how you can become a more "critical citizen."

DISCUSSION

Talk to a classmate about what it means to you to be a citizen. What are your responsibilities? Is a citizen the same as a resident? In this context how does being a citizen differ from one's nationality? What does the term "critical citizen" mean to you?

The Academic Reader

One of the differences between high school and college or university is the amount of reading required. You have to process a great deal of information. Furthermore, the reading demands vary, from multiple chapter assignments in textbooks to short essays and articles. When you read for college and university, you need to be aware of what you are reading and what the goal of the reading assignment is. Does the reading provide background? Does it prepare you for a lecture? Does it reflect and reinforce content your instructor presents in class? Does the reading ask you to use classroom knowledge to think critically about a specific case or problem? You do not want to read everything the same way.

BRAINSTORM

Think about the kind of reading you have done so far in college or university. In what courses was the reading heavy? In what courses was it light? What was the purpose of the reading?

The Critical Worker

All the critical thinking skills covered in this book can be applied directly to the working world. For example, you might be asked to write reports in a business office, document patient progress in a hospital or outpatient setting, analyze client records and draw conclusions, problem-solve technological problems, and research information on the Internet. The more skills you acquire in school about learning how to approach situations critically, the more valuable you will be as a good decision-maker on the job.

RESUMÉ BUILDER

Talk to a classmate about decisions you make (or have made) on a job that require critical thinking. What kind of information do you use to make your decisions? What are the consequences of the decisions you make?

Critical Reading

What is your approach to reading? If you do not have an answer to this question, then you need to develop an academic approach. Critical reading is one of the most important skills you develop as a college or university student. It is a skill that is not limited to written texts: it extends to visual images, graphs, maps, and tables. Whether you are reading an article, thinking about it, or writing critically about it, your understanding of the content will be improved if you have a strategic approach to reading.

Five Strategies for Effective Reading

Effective readers are active and critical readers. They set a purpose for reading before they begin and monitor their understanding as they read. During and after reading, they ask questions to understand the author's purpose. Here are five strategies for active reading that will help you understand what you read, think critically about the material, and draw conclusions about the author's ideas or arguments.

PREVIEW

Previewing a reading allows you to get a general idea of the topic being discussed, how the material is organized, what the author's main points are, and what you already know about the subject. First, ask yourself these questions:

1. What kind of text am I about to read (narrative, essay, nonfiction article, or textbook)?

2. What do I know about the subject that I can use to help me understand it?

3. How is the text organized? Are there subtitles, sections, illustrations, and so on that will help me understand the content?

4. How difficult is the selection? Does it contain technical vocabulary? Will I need to use a dictionary?

If the reading looks challenging, you may prefer to read it in a quiet room so you can concentrate and have a dictionary nearby for difficult words. Find out where you can study best and go there regularly. The following steps will help you to get an overview of a text you need to read.

How to Preview

*   *Read the title.* This will give you an idea of the general topic of the selection.

*   *Read the introduction or first few paragraphs.* Authors usually provide a brief overview of their subject and the main points they plan to make at the beginning of a reading or chapter.

*   *Read any headings.* Particularly in textbooks or longer articles, subheadings provide an outline of the main points of a chapter or section.

*   *Read the first sentence of each paragraph (or the first sentence under each heading).* These are often topic sentences and will provide information about what is going to be discussed in a paragraph or section of text.

- *Look for boxes, visuals, and boldfaced or italicized print.* All these features are used to highlight important information. For example, in textbooks key words and terms are often in boldface font and are followed by definitions.
- *Read the final paragraph.* Usually authors will summarize their main points at the end of an article or essay. In textbooks you will often find a heading like "Chapter Summary" where the main points are clearly stated.

EXERCISE 27-1 Previewing

Directions: *Preview the following excerpt from a textbook, highlighting the title, headings, introduction, and the first sentence of each paragraph. Then use the highlighted material to answer the questions that follow.*

EDISON AND THE KINETOSCOPE

from *American Cinema, American Culture* by JOHN BELTON

CAPTURING TIME

The origins of the cinema lie in the development of mass communication technology. The cinema serves as the culmination of an age that saw the invention of the telegraph (1837), photography (1826–1839), the typewriter (1873), the telephone (1876), the phonograph (1878), roll film (1880), the Kodak camera (1888), George Eastman's motion picture film (1889), Thomas Edison's motion picture camera (1891–1893), Marconi's wireless telegraph (1895), and the motion picture projector (1895–1896).

QUESTION
What does this writer mean by "mass communication"?

Interior view of Kinetoscope with peephole viewer at top of cabinet.

Edison, who had played a role in the development of the telegraph, the phonograph, and electricity, used the phonograph as a model for his "invention" of the motion picture. Actually, Edison did not so much invent as produce the first motion picture camera, the Kinetoscope. The actual execution of Edison's goal of creating an "instrument which [did] for the eye what the phonograph [did] for the ear" was accomplished through the effort of Edison's assistant, W. K. L. Dickson, which was itself based on earlier work by Étienne-Jules Marey.

PEEPSHOWS VERSUS PROJECTORS

The cinema did not emerge as a form of mass consumption, however, until its technology evolved from its initial format of peepshow into its final form as images projected on a screen in a darkened theater. Edison's Kinetoscope was designed for use in Kinetoscope parlors, which contained only a few individual machines and permitted only one customer to view a short, 50-foot film at any one time. The first Kinetoscope parlors contained five machines. For the price of 25 cents (or 5 cents per machine), customers moved from machine to machine to watch five different films (or, in the case of famous prizefights, successive rounds of a single fight).

These Kinetoscope arcades were modeled on phonograph parlors that had proved successful for Edison several years earlier. In the phonograph parlors, customers listened to recordings through individual ear tubes, moving from one machine to the next to hear different recorded speeches or pieces of music. The Kinetoscope parlors functioned in a similar way. More interested in the sale of Kinetoscopes (for roughly $250 apiece) to these parlors than in the films (which cost approximately $10 to $15 each) that would be run in them, Edison refused to develop projection technology, reasoning (quite correctly) that if he made and sold projectors, then exhibitors would purchase only one machine—a projector—from him instead of several Kinetoscopes.

1. What are the origins of the cinema?

   _____

2. Who "invented" the motion picture?

   _____

3. What was the initial format of the cinema?

   _____

4. What were the Kinetoscope parlours modelled on?

   _____

ASK QUESTIONS

Effective readers ask questions before, during, and after reading. For example, the title of the essay "Money Is Not Wealth" generates a question: how can anyone argue that having money won't make you wealthy? The minute you ask that question, you start to focus your reading to find, understand, and evaluate the evidence the author uses to support his point. You might ask yourself other questions that focus your reading: Why is money so important to many people? Can I trust the author's point of view?

Questions create active engagement with the text and call to mind your prior knowledge about a topic, helping you understand new ideas and arguments. Every question you ask begs for an answer. Every answer requires you to think and read more carefully.

EXERCISE 27-2 **Asking Questions**

Directions: *Reread the first paragraph of "Edison and the Kinetoscope" from earlier in this chapter, and answer the question in the margin. Then, as you read, ask at least two additional questions and write them in the margin. Underline words or phrases that answer your questions and comment on them. Remember you can use the same questioning techniques you learned in Chapter 2 (Who? What? Why? When? Where? How?).*

CONNECT TO PRIOR KNOWLEDGE

Try to connect the topic of a new reading to information you have previously learned or read. Even challenging texts can be mastered if you already know something about the subject. For instance, while reading about the Kinetoscope you might be reminded of an article you have read about the production of the latest movies in 3-D or Blu-ray. As you read, you can use your prior knowledge of a subject to help you understand an author's points and to remember new information by connecting it to what you already know.

Connecting Prior Knowledge

Directions: *Reread the rest of "Edison and the Kinetoscope." As you read, keep track of what you already know about the subject by writing notes in the margin or on sticky notes. Underline the words or phrases that prompt your note taking.*

IDENTIFY IMPORTANT INFORMATION

Different types of texts use different techniques to highlight important information. Textbooks use headings, bold and italic fonts, bulleted or numbered lists, colour, and icons to announce that important ideas are being discussed. Essays contain a thesis statement that states the essay's purpose, topic sentences that outline paragraphs' main ideas, and concluding sentences that emphasize or comment on the essay's purpose. Transition words are used to emphasize important connections between details.

EXERCISE 27-4 **Identifying Important Information**

Directions: *In "Edison and the Kinetoscope," the thesis is stated in the first sentence. Identify and underline important facts, details, or examples that support the thesis. Place numbers and brief labels in the margin beside each major point. You can develop your own symbols to indicate important information.*

REREAD

Plan to reread. Every reader's mind wanders. If you are just reading words and not thinking about what you are reading, or you lose your concentration, stop! Then back up and reread. Reading something once is rarely enough. Here are three reasons to reread:

- *Improved comprehension:* As you read, monitor your understanding. At the first sign of confusion, stop reading. You may need to reread a sentence or two or even an entire paragraph or essay in order to figure out what is being said. Be vigilant and continually ask yourself: *Does this make sense? Do I know what is happening? Do I understand what the author is explaining?* If the answer is no to these questions, then stop and reread until you are sure you understand what the author is saying. Do the following things to clarify your comprehension of the material:
  1. Summarize the section of the reading that seems confusing.
  2. Connect what you are reading to what you know, to what you read earlier in the text, or to what was discussed in class.
  3. Highlight key words or phrases and write notes in the margin. Some students use their computers to take notes as they read.
  4. Ask questions in the margins to set a purpose for further reading.
- *Improved recall:* To make sure you have understood what you have read and to help you remember new information, pause occasionally to check your comprehension. Then review sections of the text, words and phrases you highlighted, your margin notes, or the questions you wrote in the margins. Take a moment and answer your questions. If you cannot answer a question, go back and reread the relevant section of text. Doing this will improve your recall of the material.

- *Expanded vocabulary:* Academic readings often contain discipline-specific vocabulary. These words slow down your reading and make it harder to understand what an author is saying until you know the meaning of the vocabulary. To deal with challenging vocabulary, you can use resources in the text or context clues.

Resources

Some texts define difficult vocabulary in the margin or at the bottom of the page. Many provide a glossary of technical terms at the back of the book. You should keep a dictionary by your side as you read. Be sure you are familiar with all the additional information that a dictionary can provide, such as pronunciation and other word forms. Write down the meanings for specific vocabulary so you can go back and make sure that you understand the words in the context they are used. Over time, you will want to be able to integrate this new vocabulary into your conversations when you are speaking to your instructor or when you are on the job.

Context Clues

Use the context in which a word appears to infer or guess what it means. Context clues—hints in the text—can often help you figure out the meaning of unfamiliar words without having to turn to a dictionary. There are five types of context clues:

- *Definition clues:* The word or phrase is defined immediately after it appears. Definitions can be preceded by terms like "means," "refers to," or "can be defined as." In textbooks, words to be defined are often in **bold** or *italic*. Punctuation—such as commas, dashes, colons, or parentheses—is often used to indicate a definition is about to be provided by setting the explanation off from the word being defined, as in this example:

   > **Calligraphy,** the art of beautiful writing, has gained popularity with brides who want handwritten place cards for their wedding receptions.

- *Synonym clues:* The word or phrase is restated using a different word or phrase that has the same or a similar meaning. Synonym clues may be preceded by phrases like "in other words," "also known as," "sometimes called," and "that is."

   > The lawyer declined filing a lawsuit at this **juncture** in the case. In other words, without more specific information, he had no choice, and at this point in the lawsuit he had to wait.

- *Antonym clues:* The word or phrase is explained through the use of words that mean the opposite to it. Antonym clues may be followed by terms like "but," "in contrast," "although," "on the contrary," "instead of," "unlike," "yet," and "however."

   > The artist created a series of **melodramatic** conflicts to resolve problems with clients, *unlike* his calm and matter-of-fact business partner who resolved problems with ease.

- *General meaning clues:* The clues to the meaning of the word are found in the sentences immediately before or after the unfamiliar word. The reader may need to reread these sentences in order to infer the meaning of the word.

Writer's Response »»

Describe how you read. Are you easily distracted? How do you stay connected to a reading?

Provincial governments are playing a major role in identifying the key **sectors** responsible for global warming. By analyzing the role of small businesses and local governments, the provincial governments are implementing strategies to reduce greenhouse gases, improve air quality, and create jobs that are cost-effective.

EXERCISE 27-5 | **Rereading**

Directions: *Choose one of the readings in this chapter. Read the title and write a note in the margin stating what you imagine the reading will be about. Put a star in the margin at each place you decide to stop, write a question, and reread looking for the answer. As you reread, underline words or phrases that clarify your thinking and answer your question.*

Read with a Pen

A critical reader is an active reader. Your mind is one of the tools you use; a pen or pencil is the other. Always read with a pen or pencil in hand. Apply the strategies of effective readers by interacting with the text. As you read, underline, highlight, circle, or annotate the following information:

- The thesis statement (which states the main idea of the article or selection)
- Topic sentences that state the main ideas of paragraphs
- Key terms and definitions
- Unfamiliar vocabulary (look up new words in your dictionary and write definitions in the margin of the selection or in your notebook)
- Examples and important supporting details or ideas

Then write notes in the margin to explain your underlining or highlighting. Ask questions; indicate important information; make connections with prior learning; and note difficult vocabulary or concepts you find challenging to understand.

Following is an essay annotated by a student named George. George's text markings and notes show that he is practising all five strategies for active reading. Prior to reading, George previewed the text. As he read, he also underlined important information and wrote notes in the margin to make connections between his prior knowledge and what he read. Finally, he asked questions, sought answers to those questions, and noted what he did not understand.

A SIMPLE GLASS OF WATER

by TED FISHMAN

CONNECT TO PRIOR KNOWLEDGE
I have read about cities in Ontario and Alberta that have intolerable heat waves in the summer. People working outside can have heat strokes, and everyone worries about older people without air conditioning. Plus, the cities ask people to stop watering their lawns.

Recently, on a day so blistering in Chicago that authorities issued a heat warning, telling people to stay inside when possible, I was out early with my wife and 10-year-old son, hoping to run errands before the temperature topped 90. Alas, at 9:45 a.m., we were too late, and the heat hit. We wanted water. We went into a coffee shop and ordered a latte for my wife, an iced coffee for my son, and please, a glass of water for me. "I can only give you a small cup," the clerk told me. That would be fine, I told him. He came back with a thimble-sized cup with roughly one ounce of liquid in it. Was it possible to get more? I asked. "No," said the clerk. "That's all we can give out. We do sell water, though."

ASK QUESTIONS
Is this essay going to be about the dangers of heat?

90°F = 32°C

<table>
</table>

These days it seems that providing a simple drink of water is not so much an exercise in quenching the thirsty as in soaking them. Worldwide, bottled water is a $35 billion business. Over the next four years, the bottled water market is expected to grow 15 percent annually. That dwarfs the growth rates for fruit beverages, beer and soft drinks, all under 2 percent. Of course, sometimes, bottled water does taste better or is more convenient or safer than tap water—and is worth paying for. That's nothing new. More novel is the pervasive push by businesses to sell bottled water by depriving customers of tap water.

For the past few years, the movie theaters I frequent have been declining requests for water, pushing—at $2.50 each—the bottled product instead. Seen a water fountain at a gasoline station lately? Not likely. Bottled water is one of the highest selling items—after cigarettes—in the stations' convenience stores. In restaurants, waiters now frequently ask for your drink order before they bring you tap water, in the hope that you can be talked into buying bottled water. A waitress I asked called this the "beverage greeting" that her manager required her to say before bringing a glass of water.

During my travels nearly 20 years ago through Indonesia's coffee-growing regions, I would often stop by a bamboo-thatched lean-to for a drink. Water in the land of the coffee bean rarely comes from a tap; it has to be hauled from wells, strained and boiled. Often I was served by rail-thin old men or women in fraying sarongs who subsisted on a few dollars a week. Yet, ask for water and they brought it. At first I asked to pay, not for the water, but for the work behind it. They'd refuse even the smallest coin. The custom of sharing water was too elemental to gum up with finagling.

In India, the Sarai Act mandates that an innkeeper give a free glass of drinking water to any passerby. Indeed, in most places around the world, giving strangers water is the bare minimum of humane behavior. Why is that not so here?

Notice that George uses his prior knowledge of the topic to connect to the reading and to understand the author's point. George underlines the thesis sentence, topic sentences that state main ideas, and important examples, details, and ideas in the selection. As he reads he also asks questions and underlines details that help him answer those questions. As a result, his questions focus his reading and help him understand the author's purpose. In addition, George uses questions to monitor his comprehension. He asks a question when he is confused about what the author is doing. He asks, "Why is the author changing the subject and talking about Indonesia now?" and then he reads on to understand the purpose for that shift.

ADDITIONAL READINGS

This section contains readings on a variety of subjects. Each reading is followed by a few comprehension questions, discussion questions, and writing assignments.

The readings are a valuable way for you to build your vocabulary.

- *Before you read*, skim the reading and underline any words that are unfamiliar to you.
- *As you read*, use context (clues in the reading) to help you figure out the meanings of these words.
- *After reading*, use a dictionary to find definitions of the words for which you could not determine the meaning by using context. Write the definitions in the margin beside the words.

WORDS THAT WOUND

by EMIL SHER

1   I lived in an African village for two years. As I search for the words that are faithful to what I experienced, words that capture the poetry of rural Botswana, there is one I won't use. On the printed page, it's an irritant to my eyes, a thorn that pricks at my skin. Spoken, it leaves a bitter taste in my mouth. The word is "primitive."

2   Bobonong is a sprawling village nestled between the borders of Zimbabwe and South Africa. It's blessed with the most beautiful sunsets this side of heaven, and has all the characteristics many Canadians would call primitive. The Batswana build their traditional homes as they have for centuries, with round walls moulded from mud and **thatch**. With few exceptions there is no indoor plumbing or electricity. Villagers **fetch** water from communal taps. Women with perfect posture balance buckets on their heads in **regal** processions that wind through a maze of huts. Tired donkeys pull carts along unpaved roads as rough as the washboards used to scrub laundry. Meals are prepared over hot coals that flicker in the night like fireflies.

thatch: dried straw, reeds

fetch: to go get something and bring it back

regal: majestic

3   It could all look so "primitive." But I've learned that there are different ways of seeing. Life in industrialized countries comes with a risk: a severe case of **myopia**. We gaze at the Bobonongs scattered around the world through lenses framed in rigid assumptions. We see a way of life "less developed" than ours. We see people eating with their hands and **smugly** wave our forks. We see people walking comfortably in barefeet and tap our leather shoes.

myopia: unable to clearly see far away things

smugly: complacently

4   As we look on in judgement of others, we lose sight of ourselves. I don't know how the Batswana would say "**appalled**," but I do know that's how many would feel if they saw how we treat the elderly amongst us. They don't ship the older ones in their communities to homes for the aged; there aren't any. In Botswana, the word "nuclear" had only one meaning for me: communal families of three generations, tightly bound by the spirit of collective care. Back home, where technology thrived, I knew that nuclear referred not only to families, but to weapons of destruction that could tear them apart. Mothers in Botswana would surely be puzzled and amused to learn that public breastfeeding is still taboo in Canada. They nurse their babies wherever they happen to be—on buses, in shops, in the comfort of a neighbour's yard. And no one bats an eye.

appalled: horrified

5   At the end of a long day, teenagers often gather in school yards. They meet not to sniff and smoke but to sing and dance. Some keep the rhythm on a goatskin stretched over an oil can.

Others wear traditional rattles around their ankles. A shoeless train of feet rumbles along tracks of dry soil, and clouds of dust mingle with voices sweet and pure. Few of their younger sisters or brothers have the electronic toys sold here in suburban malls. Resourceful village children twist wire and empty beer cans into toy cars with waist-high steering mechanisms that actually work.

6   The word "primitive" doesn't sit well with me anymore. I need to find one that does justice to the way others live. For the pen is mightier than the sword, and words have the power to wound.

COMPREHENSION QUESTIONS

1. Did the author like living in rural Botswana? Cite two to three examples of word choices Sher uses to indicate his attitude about Botswana.

2. What do Botswana teenagers do at the end of the day?

3. What does the author mean by the last sentence?

DISCUSSION QUESTIONS

1. Have you ever travelled to another country and been surprised by the different way that people lived there? What differences did you notice between life here and life in the place where you travelled to?

2. Who has a "better" life: people in Canada or the people described in the essay?

3. The author writes that he has "learned that there are different ways of seeing." In what ways can you "see," and in what circumstances do you see differently?

WRITING ASSIGNMENTS

1. Look at the vivid descriptions that Sher uses in the first and third paragraphs. Use description to write a paragraph in which you describe people in a specific community group. What are the most outstanding characteristics of that group? What are the key details that support your view?

2. Write an essay in which you agree or disagree with Sher's argument about the word *primitive*. State your position, and support it with facts, examples, and reasons from research or from your own experience.

3. Most people would say that Canada provides very good lifestyles for its residents. However, the author questions whether life in other places is undesirable. Write an essay where you describe and explain the expectations you have for the community that you live in. Consider what you contribute to your community. Who is responsible for providing a good life to people in a community? Can you supply examples of people in Canada who do not have good lives? Why not?

MONEY IS NOT WEALTH

by PAUL GRAHAM

1   If you want to create wealth, it will help to understand what it is. Wealth is not the same thing as money. Wealth is as old as human history. Far older, in fact; ants have wealth. Money is a comparatively recent invention.

2   Wealth is the fundamental thing. Wealth is stuff we want: food, clothes, houses, cars, gadgets, travel to interesting places, and so on. You can have wealth without having money. If you had a magic machine that could on command make you a car or cook you dinner or do your laundry, or do anything else you wanted, you wouldn't need money. Whereas if you were in the middle of Antarctica, where there is nothing to buy, it wouldn't matter how much money you had.

3   Wealth is what you want, not money. But if wealth is the important thing, why does everyone talk about making money? It is a kind of **shorthand**: money is a way of moving wealth, and in practice they are usually interchangeable. But they are not the same thing, and unless you plan to get rich by counterfeiting, talking about *making money* can make it harder to understand how to make money.

4   Money is a side effect of specialization. In a specialized society, most of the things you need, you can't make for yourself. If you want a potato or a pencil or a place to live, you have to get it from someone else.

5   How do you get the person who grows the potatoes to give you some? By giving him something he wants in return. But you can't get very far by trading things directly with the people who need them. If you make violins, and none of the local farmers wants one, how will you eat?

6   The solution societies find, as they get more specialized, is to make the trade into a two-step process. Instead of trading violins directly for potatoes, you trade violins for, say, silver, which you can then trade again for anything else you need. The intermediate stuff—the *medium of exchange*—can be anything that's rare and portable. Historically metals have been the most common, but recently we've been using a medium of exchange, called the *dollar,* that doesn't physically exist. It works as a medium of exchange, however, because its rarity is guaranteed by the U.S. Government.

7   The advantage of a medium of exchange is that it makes trade work. The disadvantage is that it tends to **obscure** what trade really means. People think that what a business does is make money. But money is just the intermediate stage—just a shorthand—for whatever people want. What most businesses really do is make wealth. They do something people want.

The Pie Fallacy

8   A surprising number of people retain from childhood the idea that there is a **fixed** amount of wealth in the world. There is, in any normal family, a fixed amount of *money* at any moment. But that's not the same thing.

9   When wealth is talked about in this context, it is often described as a pie. "You can't make the pie larger," say politicians. When you're talking about the amount of money in one family's bank account, or the amount available to a government from one year's tax revenue, this is true. If one person gets more, someone else has to get less.

10   I can remember believing, as a child, that if a few rich people had all the money, it left less for everyone else. Many people seem to continue to believe something like this well into adulthood. This **fallacy** is usually there in the background when you hear someone talking about how x percent of the population have y percent of the wealth. If you plan to start a startup, then whether you realize it or not, you're planning to disprove the Pie Fallacy.

11   What leads people **astray** here is the **abstraction** of money. Money is not wealth. It's just something we use to move wealth around. So although there may be, in certain specific moments (like your family, this month) a fixed amount of money available to trade with other people for things you want, there is not a fixed amount of wealth in the world. *You can make more wealth.* Wealth has been getting created and destroyed (but on balance, created) for all of human history.

12   Suppose you own a beat-up old car. Instead of sitting on your butt next summer, you could spend the time restoring your car to **pristine** condition. In doing so you create wealth. The world is—and you specifically are—one pristine old car the richer. And not just in some **metaphorical** way. If you sell your car, you'll get more for it.

13   In restoring your old car you have made yourself richer. You haven't made anyone else poorer. So there is obviously not a fixed pie. And in fact, when you look at it this way, you wonder why anyone would think there was.

14   Kids know, without knowing they know, that they can create wealth. If you need to give someone a present and don't have any money, you make one. But kids are so bad at making things that they consider home-made presents to be a distinct, **inferior**, sort of thing to store-bought ones—a mere expression of the proverbial thought that counts. And indeed, the lumpy ashtrays we made for our parents did not have much of a resale market.

[. . .]

Wealth and Power

15   Making wealth is not the only way to get rich. For most of human history it has not even been the most common. Until a few centuries ago, the main sources of wealth were mines, slaves and serfs, land, and cattle, and the only ways to acquire these rapidly were by inheritance, marriage, conquest, or confiscation. Naturally wealth had a bad reputation.

16   Two things changed. The first was the rule of law. For most of the world's history, if you did somehow accumulate a fortune, the ruler or his **henchmen** would find a way to steal it. But in medieval Europe something new happened. A new class of merchants and manufacturers began to collect in towns. Together they were able to withstand the local feudal lord. So for the first time in our history, the bullies stopped stealing the nerds' lunch money. This was naturally a great **incentive**, and possibly indeed the main cause of the second big change, industrialization.

17   A great deal has been written about the causes of the Industrial Revolution. But surely a necessary, if not sufficient, condition was that people who made fortunes be able to enjoy them in peace. One piece of evidence is what happened to countries that tried to return to the old model, like the Soviet Union, and to a lesser extent Britain under the labor governments of the 1960s and early 1970s. Take away the incentive of wealth, and technical innovation **grinds** to a halt.

[. . .]

18   . . . Without the incentive of wealth, no one wants to do it. Engineers will work on sexy projects like fighter planes and moon rockets for ordinary salaries, but more **mundane** technologies like light bulbs or semiconductors have to be developed by entrepreneurs.

[. . .]

19   . . . Europeans rode on the crest of a powerful new idea: allowing those who made a lot of money to keep it.

20   Once you're allowed to do that, people who want to get rich can do it by generating wealth instead of stealing it. The resulting technological growth translates not only into wealth but into military power. The theory that led to the stealth plane was developed by a Soviet mathematician. But because the Soviet Union didn't have a computer industry, it remained for them a theory; they didn't have hardware capable of executing the calculations fast enough to design an actual airplane.

21   In that respect the Cold War teaches the same lesson as World War II and, for that matter, most wars in recent history. Don't let a ruling class of warriors and politicians squash the entrepreneurs. The same recipe that makes individuals rich makes countries powerful. Let the nerds keep their lunch money, and you rule the world.

COMPREHENSION QUESTIONS

1. What are some roles that Graham gives for the use of money?

2. Does Graham believe there is a fixed amount of wealth in the world that is controlled by only a few? How does he support his point of view?

3. How does the author explain how children are able to create wealth?

DISCUSSION QUESTIONS

1. Graham suggests one way an adult can create wealth. What specific example does he use? Identify the general point that the author is suggesting through the use of this example. Do you agree with his position?

2. Have you ever received a homemade or hand-made gift from someone? Did you like it? Did you think that gift was more or less valuable than a store-bought gift?

3. There are many online sites where one can buy, sell, and trade items. Have you ever bought or sold something online? Why would you decide to use an online site to get something you need? Can you trade or barter rather than use money? Explain your answer.

WRITING ASSIGNMENTS

1. Graham writes that wealth is what people want and it can be created without being bought. Yet most people want money to buy things that they think they need or just want to own. If someone, for example, a scientist, created new medicines or a cure for a deadly disease, should that person give away the cure for free to help many people or sell it to get lots of money for him- or herself? Write a paragraph stating your view. Provide examples to support your view.

2. How do most people measure success? Write an essay where you define what success means.

3. Imagine you are a politician and you want to improve the country's finances. Write an essay where you describe what you would you do to create wealth for more Canadians. Alternatively, write an essay describing how Canadians can create wealth for themselves.

20s

by LAUREN KIRSHNER

1   My teenage years were so terrible that I dreamed constantly of my 20s, believing they would deliver me from pimples, hot solo dates at garage sales and weekends selling popcorn at the cinema. I held my breath, expecting a Cinderella-like transformation.

2   But it was my mistake to think my life would change as soon as I hit 20—**poof** would go the comparing myself to others, the wondering if I could make it as a writer, the insecurity. When I realized that building my confidence would take work, I felt just slightly **ripped off**. I thought other girls had it easier: when they looked in the mirror they saw perfection. When they wrote, they loved every word. When they shaved their legs, the hair didn't grow back for weeks.

3   It's not that I didn't like who I was. But I am part of the generation that grew up on makeovers on *Montel* and reality shows like *The Swan* where everyone is a cup size or a wax away from becoming their ideal self—an ideal that is mentioned only as a physical **entity**. In my early 20s I sought improvement in so many ways. I dyed my hair blonde, at home, to varying shades of orange. I counted calories, displaying math skills unseen before in the Kirshner family. I'm a **homebody**. But at home I sometimes wondered if I was wasting my youth by not **putting on the ritz** and going to the clubs, wearing lots of jewellery and buying fizzy drinks like Carrie Bradshaw.

4   Now, at the end of my 20s, I'm far from being an expert on myself and I still lie in bed at night with the questions. Should I have gone out more, in heels, at least to work out my calves? Why was I so shy? In a university class I sat beside a guy I liked for two months and the closest I got to grabbing his attention was once **coyly** dropping my pencil, then retrieving it like a panicked octopus. I should have talked more. I should have worn that bikini. I should have **clobbered** my anxiety with action. If I had a 20-year-old in front of me now, I'd say, Love yourself and take the chance of others not sharing your good taste.

5   I still think about improving my outer self, but I've learned to spend more time trying to understand what's behind the face in the mirror. It's a lot cheaper than getting manicures. And I keep reminding myself that instant transformation takes place only in reality TV and in fairy tales. Be a messy work-in-progress, I tell myself. It may be uncertain, but it's a lot more interesting than waiting for the pumpkin carriage.

poof: suddenly

ripped off: cheated

entity: individual thing, separate from others

homebody: person who prefers to stay at home

putting on the ritz: acting glamorously, elegantly

coyly: pretending to be shy or acting innocently

clobbered: defeated decisively

COMPREHENSION QUESTIONS

1. What problem did the author face in her teen years? What examples does she use to illustrate this?

2. What happened when the author reached her twenties?

3. What advice does Kirshner want young people to follow?

1. Kirshner gives a series of examples to illustrate how she felt at a certain age. Is she the only one who has felt like that or does she exemplify how most teenagers feel? Identify a sentence or two that clearly states how she felt. Then select the two most effective examples that illustrate her point of view. Who is the audience for this essay?

2. What do you think makes teenagers unhappy? What could help teenagers become more confident?

3. Kirshner mentions Cinderella transformations and makeover shows, but then decides not to wait for "the pumpkin carriage." What does she mean by that? What technique is she using?

1. Write a paragraph discussing the challenges that today's youth face compared to earlier generations.

2. Write an essay about the effects that advertising and the media have on people's perception of their own looks or appearances. Why do many young people idolize TV stars or musicians?

3. Discuss society's image of beauty. What is your definition of beauty? Write an essay that compares or contrasts your definition with what is generally accepted as beautiful. Are women the only ones with insecurities about their looks, or do men feel the same way?

LAST LECTURE

by IAN SPEARS

anti-apartheid: against racial separation of people through government policy, esp. in South Africa

culminated: ended or resulted in

haggled: argued

embodied: represented ideas or qualities

integrity: honesty; strong morals

1   In the days before the great African **anti-apartheid** leader Nelson Mandela was released from jail, the then-president of South Africa, F. W. de Klerk, paid him a visit. The president wanted to release Mandela and to begin the negotiations and reforms that ultimately **culminated** in the achievement of majority rule in South Africa. Mandela protested his sudden and very unexpected release, arguing that his people would not yet be ready to receive him. The South African president would have none of it and insisted that Mandela be released as soon as possible.

2   They **haggled** and eventually reached a compromise. But Mandela later noted in his memoirs the irony that it was the jailer who wanted to release the prisoner but could not, while the prisoner himself wanted to remain in jail but was, over his objections, being released!

3   What is remarkable about Mandela's story, though, is what happened after he was released. He was the man everybody watched; the role model on whose shoulders were the hopes and aspirations of so many other people. **Embodied** in him were all the great things the world could be. After so many years in jail, Mandela still demonstrated **integrity**, forgiveness, and a sense of

justice. Mandela was unique for his lack of bitterness towards his former oppressors. And yet, surprisingly, his were values that we all share and aspire to. They are his **legacy**.

4   Canadian Supreme Court Justice Frank Iacobucci has said that a university should not be measured in terms of the number of publications from its faculty, or the size of its library, or the grade point average of its students; rather it should be measured in terms of what the students take to the community once they leave the university. What will people notice when you leave this place? What will be your legacy?

legacy: something left by an earlier generation

- They will notice you taking the high road and standing up for what is right.

- They will notice your individuality, your willingness to differentiate yourself, your determination to **defy** the fashions and trends of the day and leave your own mark or make your own statement.

defy: refuse to obey; openly oppose

- They will notice your humbleness when you succeed and your strength and perseverance when you do not; your "courage" in times of hardship, ill-health and uncertainty.

- They will notice your patience and your sense of empathy, your ability to forgive others, to learn from others, and to inspire others.

5   I have asked student leaders who and what has inspired them. It turns out that the small acts were as important as the big ones. In my world, every person brings something to the table. Shy or bold, sciences or the arts, aggies or engineering, man or woman, each of us weaves threads into the personal fabric of others around us. Do not underestimate the many and varied examples you set for others.

6   Maybe the most important gifts are those things we share with others. And the most important responsibility you have as graduates is to conduct yourselves with the knowledge that others are watching and learning from you. The hand of friendship that you extend, the ear you lend, the goodwill you demonstrate, the good deeds that you do, will be seen by others and appreciated. It will all go to make this world a much better place.

COMPREHENSION QUESTIONS

1. What does the lecturer say about the relationship between Mandela and then-president de Klerk?

2. Why was Mandela a role model for the whole world?

3. According to Canadian Supreme Court Justice Frank Iacobucci, what makes a great university? How does this apply to your school?

DISCUSSION QUESTIONS

1. Where and when have you had the opportunity to listen to an inspirational speech? Were you the intended audience? How long did you remember what was said?

2. Professor Spears asked student leaders for examples of what inspired them. Give examples of something or someone who has inspired you.

3. How did you react to reading this lecture? Are there other things you might want to add to the list? What legacy do you want to leave to your college or university?

1. Write a paragraph about a person who has acted as an inspiration to you. Describe the person and what that person does or did to inspire you. Is that person aware of his/her effect on you? Does this person also provide an inspiration to others?

2. Most parents have high expectations for their children studying in colleges or universities. What are some of these expectations? Are they realistic ones? What happens when there is a clash between what the parents or other family members want and what the graduating student wants to do? Write an essay discussing the positive and negative implications of family expectations for a student. Use examples of students you see around you or your own experiences. As you discuss these examples, analyze what makes them positive or negative.

3. Professor Spears writes that the most important gifts are those shared with others. Write a paragraph describing an unexpected experience where you shared something with someone or someone shared something with you that you still remember. Describe why that shared experience was important or memorable.

ALL KINDS OF FRIENDS

by JUDITH VIORST

1   Friends broaden our horizons. They serve as new models with whom we can identify. They allow us to be ourselves—and accept us that way. They enhance our self-esteem because they think we're okay, because we matter to them. And because they matter to us—for various reasons, at various levels of intensity—they enrich the quality of our emotional life.

2   In my discussions with several people about the people we call our friends, we established the following categories of friendship:

Convenience Friends

3   These are the neighbor or office mate or member of our car pool whose lives routinely intersect with ours. These are the people with whom we exchange small favors. They lend us their cups and silverware for a party. They drive our children to soccer when we are sick. They keep our cat for a week when we go on vacation. And, when we need a lift, they give us a ride to the garage to pick up the Honda. As we do for them.

4   But we don't, with convenience friends, ever come too close or tell too much: We maintain our public face and emotional distance. "Which means," says Elaine, "that I'll talk about being overweight but not about being depressed. Which means I'll admit being mad but not blind with rage. And which means I might say that we're **pinched** this month but never that I'm worried sick over money."

5   But which doesn't mean that there isn't sufficient value to be found in these friendships of mutual aid, in convenience friends.

pinched: distressed by lack of money

Special-Interest Friends

6   These friendships depend on the sharing of some activity or concern. These are sports friends, work friends, yoga friends, nuclear-freeze friends. We meet to participate jointly in knocking a ball across a net or saving the world.

7   "I'd say that what we're doing together is *doing* together, not being together," Suzanne says of their Tuesday-doubles friends. "It's mainly a tennis relationship but we play together well." And as with convenience friends, we can, with special-interest friends, be regularly involved without being intimate.

Historical Friends

8   With luck we also have a friend who knew us, as Grace's friend Bunny did, way back when . . . when her family lived in that three-room flat in Brooklyn, when her father was out of work for seven months, when her brother Allie got in that fight where they had to call the police, when her sister married the **endodontist** from Yonkers, and when, the morning after she lost her virginity, Bunny was the person she ran to tell.

endodontist: a dentist who treats diseased gums

9   The years have gone by, they have gone separate ways, they have little in common now, but they still are an intimate part of each other's past. And so, whenever Grace goes to Detroit, she always goes to visit this friend of her girlhood. Who knows how she looked before her teeth were straightened. Who knows how she talked before her voice got un-Brooklyned. Who knows what she ate before she learned about artichokes. Who knew her when.

Crossroads Friends

10   Like historical friends, our crossroads friends are important for what was—for the friendship we shared at a **crucial**, now past, time of life: a time, perhaps, when we roomed in college together; or served a **stint** in the U.S. Air Force together; or worked as eager young singles in Manhattan together; or went through pregnancy, child birth and those first difficult years of motherhood together.

crucial: very important

stint: a period of time

11   With historical friends and crossroads friends we **forge links** strong enough to **endure** with not much more contact than once-a-year letters at Christmas, maintaining a special intimacy— dormant but always ready to be revived—on those rare but tender occasions when we meet.

forge links: make friendships or connections despite difficulties

endure: last a long time

Cross-Generational Friends

12   Another tender intimacy—tender but unequal—exists in the friendships that form across generations, the friendships that one woman calls her daughter-mother and her mother-daughter relationships. Across the generations the younger enlivens the older, the older instructs the younger. Each role, as mentor or quester, as adult or child, offers gratifications of its own. And because we are unconnected by blood, our words of advice are accepted as wise, not intrusive, our childish **lapses** don't **summon up** warnings and groans. Without the risks, and without the **ferocious** investment, which are always a part of a real parent-child connection, we enjoy the rich **disparities** to be found among our cross-generational friends.

lapses: mistakes; misbehaviour

summon up: call for a specified action

ferocious: strong

disparities: differences

Close Friends

13   Emotionally and physically (by seeing each other, by mail, by talks on the phone) we maintain some ongoing friendships of deep intimacy. And although we may not expose as much—or the same kinds of things—to each of our closest friends, close friendships involve revealing aspects

of our private self—of our private feelings and thoughts, of our private wishes and fears and fantasies and dreams.

14   Close friends contribute to our personal growth. They also contribute to our personal pleasure, making the music sound sweeter, the wine taste richer, the laughter ring louder because they are there. Friends furthermore take care—they come if we call them at two in the morning; they lend us their car, their bed, their money, their ear; and although no contracts are written, it is clear that intimate friendships involve important rights and obligations. Indeed, we will frequently turn—for reassurance, for comfort, for come-and-save-me help—not to our blood relations but to friends.

COMPREHENSION QUESTIONS

1. What is the main point of the reading?

2. How many kinds of friendship does Viorst describe?

3. According to the author's classification, in which category would most people have the most friends? Why?

Talk about it

Do you agree or disagree with the classifications of friendship described in the article? How do you define friendship?

DISCUSSION QUESTIONS

1. Why would the author classify her friends into different groups? Would you classify your friends in the same way?

2. Is there a group or groups of friends that the author has left out?

3. Viorst supports her thesis with examples and details from her own life experiences. Would a male perspective be different? How would it differ and why?

WRITING ASSIGNMENTS

1. Write a paragraph in which you explain your definition of friendship. Cite examples to explore your definition in detail. Are friends more important than family?

2. Write an essay that categorizes friendships in another way. Provide specific examples to illustrate your categories.

3. How well can you judge a person's personality or intentions? Have you ever thought someone was a friend only to discover that person did not feel the same about you? Write an essay to compare and contrast the views two people have of each other and what the result of these different views has been.

ENGAGE IMMIGRANT COMMUNITIES

by Dr. ROMILA VERMA

1   Water issues are one of the most immediate challenges we face today because of their impact on food security, health and economic growth of countries. With booming populations and the dangers of climate-change, water is one of the most vulnerable resources on this planet.

For solutions, we need to look at change-makers. In a community as **vibrant** as The Regional Municipality of York, the **catalysts** in **propelling** change are the people, specifically, the considerable immigrant population*.

2   Like me, these immigrants come from some of the world's most water-deprived regions: South Asia, China and sub-Saharan Africa among them. They have first-hand experience in living with water scarcity. They have learned valuable lessons on how to be more efficient in using water. The real challenge is to figure out how to engage the skills and knowledge of this huge population. One big step in this direction is to identify and bring together the change-makers. Change-makers can be from any part of society: science, government, education, non government organizations and residents.

3   Incorporating cultural values and traditional knowledge about water into our policies can allow us to find comprehensive and **holistic** solutions, reaching a wider audience with the conservation and innovation message.

4   By studying the complex relationship between water and cultural diversity, there is an opportunity to gain case-specific insights and develop strategies to address expected and emerging challenges. For instance, on my recent trip to India, I was struck by the enormity of water challenges facing the South Asian countries, especially the dynamics between India, Pakistan and Bangladesh. The geopolitics of that area, such as who controls the headwaters in the Himalayan region and consequently, the entire river-system, play a significant role in water distribution and availability in that region. Understanding water-sharing between countries can be an asset to Canadians negotiating with the U.S. and other countries over the Great Lakes and the Arctic region.

5   Change-makers could also address the psychological impacts due to natural disasters such as the recent floods in Pakistan. How will people be impacted once the water recedes? How prepared are we for the increasing incidences of natural disaster in North America? These are **vital** questions to developing a **resilient** population.

6   In many parts of the world, frugal use of water is **ingrained**, because when you only get one bucket of water a day, it can lead to some wonderful conservation techniques, such as collecting rainwater to brush your teeth. Does this sound far-fetched for Canadians? Maybe, but every drop counts. In many parts of the world, this is the **mantra** people live by.

*Statistics Canada reports that in 2006, 43 per cent of York Region inhabitants were born outside of Canada. (York Region is north of Toronto.)

vibrant: lively, exciting

catalysts: people or things that cause change

propelling: pushing forward

holistic: considering the larger situation

vital: necessary; essential

resilient: able to quickly recover from an unpleasant situation

ingrained: describes a habit or attitude that has existed for a long time

mantra: a word or saying repeated in prayer or meditation

COMPREHENSION QUESTIONS

1. According to Verma, how does availability of water impact a country?

2. What is the connection between knowledge about water and cultural values?

3. What makes the writer think that immigrants should be consulted about Canadian water policies?

DISCUSSION QUESTIONS

1. What is the purpose of the essay? Who is the intended audience?

2. What countries in the world face the most challenges regarding their water supplies? Traditionally, a community evolved around a water supply. Does that still apply to communities in Canada? Where does the water you use come from?

3. How is water provided to your home? Do you pay for the water you use? Do you expect it to be clean and safe to drink? The author suggests brushing your teeth with rainwater. Would you do that? Why or why not? Explain your answer.

WRITING ASSIGNMENTS

1. Verma's essay explores the concept of change-makers. Using examples, write a paragraph in which you illustrate your point of view about one of the following: Do you agree that residents of an area should be consulted for any knowledge they may have about water policies in other jurisdictions? Or do you think politicians, local authorities, and corporations should decide how water is used in their area?

2. Do you think much about water conservation? Write an essay in which you discuss how individuals can make responsible decisions about how much water they and their families use. What issues are important in the decision? What steps should people take to ensure they make wise decisions about conserving water?

3. On the other side of the scale are floods. Certain areas in Canada have experienced devastating floods with much damage to the communities. Who is responsible for preventing such floods? Who is responsible for cleaning up the damage from floods? Write an essay where you make recommendations for preparing for or preventing flood damage to a community or for dealing with the aftermath of a flood.

BEGINNING OF A NEW ERA

by SHELAGH D. GRANT

sustained: continued for a long time without reduction or slowing down

mitigate: make less harmful

1   Amid the economic prosperity of the 1990s came the realization that the world might be encountering a **sustained** warming trend that could prove irreversible unless there was coordinated global action to **mitigate** unnatural causes. Initially the trend was considered part of a normal cycle, but at the turn of the century meteorologists and scientists began to warn of unusual acceleration of Arctic temperatures, in part caused by release of increasing amounts of carbon dioxide and other greenhouse gases into the atmosphere. Exactly what percentage of the causes was man-made is still under debate, but it was enough to create a "tipping point" in the Arctic, which resulted in a chain reaction that has accelerated the rate of ice melt and warming of the air. Most scientists concur that the rate might be slowed by new technologies and alternative energy sources but likely is not reversible in our lifetime, if ever. To do nothing will simply make the situation worse. Some alarmists warn of possible worldwide instability, local unrest, **insurrections** and perhaps even global war. Others claim that such concerns are exaggerated and there is no **impending** crisis. Exaggeration and misinformation from both sides have confused the debate as has the diversity of personal experience.

insurrections: acts of taking political control or revolting against the government

impending: about to happen

2   Effects of climate change have been experienced in varying degrees throughout the world but nowhere so dramatically as in the Arctic. Here, the permanently frozen ice cover is rapidly shrinking. Pack ice is fast disappearing, large blocks of the ice shelf are breaking off and huge

glaciers are melting faster than scientists had predicted only a few years ago. Of increasing concern is the amount of methane, twenty-five times more potent than carbon dioxide, which is being released into the atmosphere as a result of melting **permafrost**. Scientific studies are under way to determine how much of the accelerated ice melt is **attributable** to methane and what measures might be taken to prevent its release into the atmosphere. Other factors are also contributing to the warming Arctic air currents and waters, such as the unusually high winds associated with climate change driving the broken icepack into the Atlantic and Pacific Oceans and reducing the ice cover's normal cooling effect on the Arctic waters. As well, the thinning ozone layer around the North Pole has increased the intensity of the sun and in turn the rate of evaporation. As a result of the disappearing snow and ice cover, less of the sun's energy is reflected back into space, creating a spiral **domino effect** with no sign of reversal. Scientific studies now confirm that the surface air temperature over lands just north of the Arctic Circle trended upward for the last two decades, with the year 2007 marking a high at 2°C or 3.6°F above the average temperature at the turn of the twentieth century. This is occurring in spite of the fact that the present **tilt** of the earth's axis should have created a general cooling period.

permafrost: permanently frozen layer of soil

attributable: probably caused by

domino effect: a chain reaction

tilt: to turn slightly to one side

COMPREHENSION QUESTIONS

1. What is the author describing?

2. What does Grant mean by "tipping point"? Describe the chain reactions listed in this reading.

3. What are scientists increasingly concerned about? Why?

DISCUSSION QUESTIONS

1. Who is Grant's intended audience? What word choices does the author use to clearly explain the situation in Canada's polar region?

2. Most of Canada's land mass is in the north and contains many as yet undiscovered resources. Is it more important to preserve the north or more important to mine the resources?

3. If you know that driving an automobile contributes to the greenhouse effect, causing the polar ice to melt, how willing are you to give up driving your car? What would have to happen to change people's existing transportation habits?

WRITING ASSIGNMENTS

1. Write a paragraph in which you describe how global warming affects the Canadian environment and the consequences that has for Canadians.

2. How important is it to know about the history of Canada's north? How much do you know about the history of the Arctic? As global warming and technological advances make the Arctic more accessible, how should decisions be made about protecting the fragile Arctic environment? What role do the indigenous people play in the decision-making process? Write an essay that explores the effects of developing Canada's Arctic regions.

Talk about it

Self-monitoring is the key to comprehension. How do you ensure that you understand what you read?

3. How important is government policy in Canada's Arctic region? Write an essay defending why Canada should or should not exercise its sovereignty over the Arctic. Explore both sides in your essay.

CANADIANS: WHAT DO THEY WANT?

by MARGARET ATWOOD

jackboots: heavy military boots

1   Last month, during a poetry reading, I tried out a short prose poem called "How to Like Men." It began by suggesting that one start with the feet. Unfortunately, the question of **jackboots** soon arose, and things went on from there. After the reading I had a conversation with a young man who thought I had been unfair to men. He wanted men to be liked totally, not just from the heels to the knees, and not just as individuals but as a group; and he thought it negative and inegalitarian of me to have **alluded** to war and rape. I pointed out that as far as any of us knew these were two activities not widely engaged in by women, but he was still upset. "We're both in this together," he protested. I admitted that this was so; but could he, maybe, see that our relative positions might be a little different.

alluded: mentioned in an indirect way

2   This is the conversation one has with Americans, even, uh, *good* Americans, when the dinner-table conversation **veers** round to Canadian-American relations. "We're in this together," they like to say, especially when it comes to continental energy reserves. How do you *explain* to them, as delicately as possible, why they are not categorically beloved? It gets like the old Lifebuoy ads: even their best friends won't tell them. And Canadians are supposed to be their best friends, right? Members of the family?

veers: changes direction suddenly

3   Well, sort of. Across the river from Michigan, so near and yet so far, there I was at the age of eight, reading *their* Donald Duck comic books (originated, however, by one of *ours;* yes, Walt Disney's parents were Canadian) and coming at the end to Popsicle Pete, who promised me the earth if only I would save wrappers, but took it all away from me again with a single asterisk: Offer Good Only in the United States. Some cynical members of the world community may be forgiven for thinking that the same asterisk is there, in invisible ink, on the Constitution and the Bill of Rights.

quibbles: arguments over unimportant or small matters

4   But **quibbles** like that aside, and good will assumed, how does one go about liking Americans? Where does one begin? Or, to put it another way, why did the Canadian women lock themselves in **the john** during a '70s "international" feminist conference being held in Toronto? Because the American sisters were being "imperialist," that's why.

the john: bathroom

5   But then, it's always a little naive of Canadians to expect that Americans, of whatever political stamp, should stop being **imperious**. How can they? The fact is that the United States is an empire and Canada is to it as Gaul was to Rome.

imperious: expecting people to obey you

6   It's hard to explain to Americans what it feels like to be a Canadian. Pessimists among us would say that one has to translate the experience into their own terms and that this is necessary because Americans are incapable of thinking in any other terms—and this in itself is part of the problem. (Witness all those draft dodgers who went into culture shock when they discovered to their horror that Toronto was not Syracuse.)

7   Here is a translation: Picture a Mexico with a population ten times larger than that of the United States. That would put it at about two billion. Now suppose that the official American language is Spanish, that 75 percent of the books Americans buy and 90 percent of the movies they see are Mexican, and that the profits flow across the border to Mexico. If an American does scrape it together to make a movie, the Mexicans won't let him show it in the States, because they own the distribution outlets. If anyone tries to change this ratio, not only the Mexicans but many fellow Americans cry "**National chauvinism**," or, even more effectively, "National socialism." After all, the American public prefers the Mexican product. It's what they're used to.

8   Retranslate and you have the current American-Canadian picture. It's changed a little recently, not only on the cultural front. For instance, Canada, some think a trifle late, is attempting to regain control of its own petroleum industry. Americans are predictably angry. They think of Canadian oil as theirs.

9   "What's mine is yours," they have said for years, meaning exports; "What's yours is mine" meaning ownership and profits. Canadians are supposed to do retail buying, not controlling, or what's an empire for? One could always refer Americans to history, particularly that of their own revolution. They objected to the colonial situation when they themselves were a colony; but then, revolution is considered one of a very few home-grown American products that definitely are not for export.

10   Objectively, one cannot become too self-righteous about this state of affairs. Canadians owned lots of things, including their souls, before World War II. After that they sold, some say because they had put too much into financing the war, which created a capital vacuum (a position they would not have been forced into if the Americans hadn't kept out of the fighting for so long, say the sore losers). But for whatever reason, capital flowed across the border in the '50s, and Canadians, traditionally sock-under-the-mattress hoarders, were reluctant to invest in their own country. Americans did it for them and ended up with a large part of it, which they retain to this day. In every sellout there's a seller as well as a buyer, and the Canadians did a thorough job of trading their birthright for a mess.

11   That's on the capitalist end, but when you turn to the trade union side of things you find much the same story, except that the sellout happened in the '30s under the banner of the United Front. Now Canadian workers are finding that in any empire the colonial branch plants are the first to close, and what could be a truly progressive labor movement has been weakened by compromised bargains made in international union headquarters south of the border.

12   Canadians are sometimes **snippy** to Americans at cocktail parties. They don't like to feel owned and they don't like having been sold. But what really bothers them—and it's at this point that the United States and Rome part company—is the wide-eyed innocence with which their snippiness is greeted.

13   Innocence becomes ignorance when seen in the light of international affairs, and though ignorance is one of the spoils of conquest—the Gauls always knew more about the Romans than the Romans knew about them—the world can no longer afford America's ignorance. Its ignorance of Canada, though it makes Canadians **bristle**, is a minor and relatively harmless example. More dangerous is the fact that individual Americans seem not to know that the United States is an imperial power and is behaving like one. They don't want to admit that empires dominate, invade

National chauvinism: unreasonable belief that one country is superior to another

snippy: rude

bristle: to suddenly become annoyed or offended

and subjugate—and live on the proceeds—or, if they do admit it, they believe in their divine right to do so. The export of divine right is much more harmful than the export of Coca-Cola, though they may turn out to be much the same thing in the end.

14   Other empires have behaved similarly (the British somewhat better, Genghis Khan decidedly worse); but they have not expected to be *liked* for it. It's the final Americanism, this passion for being liked. Alas, many Americans are indeed likable; they are often more generous, more welcoming, more enthusiastic, less picky and **sardonic** than Canadians, and it's not enough to say it's only because they can afford it. Some of that revolutionary spirit still remains: the optimism, the 18th-century belief in the fixability of almost anything, the conviction of the possibility of change. However, at cocktail parties and elsewhere one must be able to tell the difference between an individual and a foreign policy. Canadians can no longer afford to think of Americans as only a spectator sport. If Reagan blows up the world, we will unfortunately be doing more than watching it on television. "No **annihilation** without representation" sounds good as a **slogan**, but if we run it up the flagpole, who's going to salute?

15   We *are* all in this together. For Canadians, the question is how to survive it. For Americans there is no question, because there does not have to be. Canada is just that vague, cold place where their uncle used to go fishing, before the lakes went dead from acid rain.

16   How do you like Americans? Individually, it's easier. Your average American is no more responsible for the state of affairs than your average man is for war and rape. Any Canadian who is so narrow-minded as to dislike Americans merely on principle is missing out on one of the good things in life. The same might be said, to women, of men. As a group, as a foreign policy, it's harder. But if you like men, you can like Americans. Cautiously. Selectively. Beginning with the feet. One at a time.

sardonic: mocking

annihilation: complete destruction

slogan: an easy-to-remember word or phrase

COMPREHENSION QUESTIONS

1. What is the main point (thesis) of this reading?

2. Reread Atwood's last paragraph. She claims it's easier to like Americans on an individual basis rather than lumping them all together into one country. What strategy does she use to convince her reader about her point of view? Is the author's argument convincing?

3. According to Atwood, who knows more about the other: Americans or Canadians? Give examples from the essay to support your answer.

DISCUSSION QUESTIONS

1. Does Atwood use a formal or informal tone in her essay? Give examples from the essay to support your answer. How effective is this strategy? Who is the intended audience?

2. What introductory strategy does Atwood use to begin the essay? How does her strategy introduce her subject?

3. Atwood's essay was first published in 1982 in *Mother Jones* (an American magazine) to explain why so many Canadians were anti-American. Is Atwood's view still current, or have Canadians' views of Americans changed?

1. Atwood uses irony in this essay. Write a paragraph where you explain how three of her examples use irony to develop her thesis.

2. Canadians and Americans have many things in common, yet there are differences between the two countries. Write an essay to compare or contrast the two, using specific examples for support.

3. How important is it to maintain a distinct Canadian identity? In today's global economy, is national identity still important? Think of the products you buy and the brands you use and where they are made. Write an essay where you argue for or against maintaining Canadian identity. Include specific examples to support your point of view.

THE METRIC SYSTEM (SORT OF)

by WAYNE GRADY

1   Canada was declared a metric nation in 1971, and after 2.8 decades, it's safe to say that we're as metric as we're going to get. At first the two systems, metric and imperial, battled it out—the metricists seized the road signs and thermostats, while the stubborn imperialists refused to buy anything that wasn't measured out according to some body part. You may recall extremists in Ottawa driving all the way to Carleton Place, a distance of sixty-three kilometres, to fill up at a service station that still sold gasoline in gallons. But that's all over now. Resistance and insistence proved equally **futile**.

futile: useless, no chance of success

2   Purists on both sides have **lamented** the resulting **mishmash**, failing to see that what we have now is a system that's uniquely Canadian. By combining the more sensible features of the metric system, or SI (for Systeme Internationale d'Unites), with some long-cherished aspects of the imperial system, we've come up with a seamless hybrid that makes perfect sense to us all. Let's call it sim-perial. Like franglais and "Progressive Conservative," simperial is the ideal Canadian compromise.

lamented: expressed sadness or disappointment over something

mishmash: a confusing mix

3   For example, the other day I asked directions to an auction sale: "Drive ten kilometres down this road," I was told, "and you'll see a barn about two hundred feet in from the highway." That's simperial. Only in Canada can a river be half a mile wide and thirty metres deep. At building supply yards, you can buy 100 square metres of shingles and a box of three-quarter inch roofing nails to hold them down. When I ask my daughter, who is fourteen and has been raised metric, how tall she is, she says "Five four." What's the temperature outside? "Plus three." Simperial.

4   In our quiet, peacekeeping way, we took the best features from each extreme and **consigned** the rest to **oblivion**. Simperial simply makes more sense than either of its two feeder systems. Nobody's feet should be size forty-two anything. But at the same time, zero degrees, not thirty-two, is obviously the temperature at which water should freeze; if anyone knows that, it's us.

consigned: put something somewhere to get rid of it

oblivion: the state of being forgotten

5   After the auction, I stopped at that gas station in Carleton Place. The pump registers gasoline by the litre now, of course, and when I went in to pay, the guy in the booth pointed his chin at my car.

6   "How is she on gas?" he asked.

7   "I get 100 kilometres on six litres," I said, quoting the manual; I had no idea what it meant.

8   He nodded appreciatively. "That's pretty good mileage."

COMPREHENSION QUESTIONS

1. What technique does Grady use to support his definition?

2. What examples does the author give of the hybrid measurement system that Canadians use?

3. Does the author believe that using two systems is confusing? What word choices does he use to support this?

DISCUSSION QUESTIONS

1. When you go shopping to buy food, do you buy items in grams or pounds? When you describe your height or weight, do you use the metric system or the imperial system?

2. Give examples from your experience where *simperial* is used.

3. In your field of study, what units of measurement do you use? How important is it that everyone uses the same?

WRITING ASSIGNMENTS

1. Think of something that is uniquely Canadian and write a definition paragraph where you explain what it means, using specific examples.

2. Think of a term that you use in your field of study or at work that has a specific meaning. Write a paragraph to compare or contrast the discipline-specific meaning with the general meaning. What does the term mean to you? What does it mean to the average person?

3. Europeans have adopted a common currency, the euro. Write an essay arguing for or against whether it would be beneficial to Canada to adopt a common North American currency. If so, what unit of currency should be used? Support your point of view with specific explanations.

IN PRAISE OF THE F WORD

by MARY SHERRY

validity: acceptance, logic, truth

1   Tens of thousands of 18-year-olds will graduate this year and be handed meaningless diplomas. These diplomas won't look any different from those awarded their luckier classmates. Their **validity** will be questioned only when their employers discover that these graduates are semiliterate.

2   Eventually a fortunate few will find their way into educational-repair shops—adult-literacy programs, such as the one where I teach basic grammar and writing. There, high-school graduates and high-school dropouts pursuing graduate-equivalency certificates will learn the skills they should have learned in school. They will also discover they have been cheated by our educational system.

3   As I teach, I learn a lot about our schools. Early in each session I ask my students to write about an unpleasant experience they had in school. No writers' block here! "I wish someone would have had made me stop doing drugs and made me study." "I liked to party and no one seemed to care." "I was a good kid and didn't cause any trouble, so they just passed me along even though I didn't read well and couldn't write." And so on.

4   I am your basic **do-gooder**, and prior to teaching this class I blamed the poor academic skills our kids have today on drugs, divorce and other **impediments** to concentration necessary for doing well in school. But, as I rediscover each time I walk into the classroom, before a teacher can expect students to concentrate, he has to get their attention, no matter what distractions may be at hand. There are many ways to do this, and they have much to do with teaching style. However, if style alone won't do it, there is another way to show who holds the winning hand in the class-room. That is to reveal the **trump card** of failure.

5   I will never forget a teacher who played that card to get the attention of one of my children. Our youngest, a world-class charmer, did little to develop his intellectual talents but always got by. Until Mrs. Stifter.

6   Our son was a high-school senior when he had her for English. "He sits in the back of the room talking to his friends," she told me. "Why don't you move him to the front row?" I urged, believing the embarrassment would get him to settle down. Mrs. Stifter looked at me steely-eyed over her glasses. "I don't move seniors," she said. "I flunk them." I was flustered. Our son's aca-demic life flashed before my eyes. No teacher had ever threatened him with that before. I regained my **composure** and managed to say that I thought she was right. By the time I got home I was feeling pretty good about this. It was a **radical** approach for these times, but, well, why not? "She's going to flunk you," I told my son. I did not discuss it any further. Suddenly English became a priority in his life. He finished out the semester with an A.

7   I know one example doesn't make a case, but at night I see a parade of students who are angry and resentful for having been passed along until they could no longer even pretend to keep up. Of average intelligence or better, they eventually quit school, concluding they were too dumb to finish. "I should have been held back," is a comment I hear frequently. Even sadder are those students who are high-school graduates who say to me after a few weeks of class, "I don't know how I ever got a high-school diploma."

8   Passing students who have not mastered the work cheats them and the employers who expect graduates to have basic skills. We excuse this dishonest behavior by saying kids can't learn if they come from terrible environments. No one seems to stop to think that—no matter what environments they come from—most kids don't put school first on their list unless they perceive something is **at stake**. They'd rather be sailing.

9   Many students I see at night could give expert testimony on unemployment, chemical depend-ency, abusive relationships. In spite of these difficulties, they have decided to make education a priority. They are motivated by the desire for a better job or the need to hang on to the one they've got. They have a healthy fear of failure.

10   People of all ages can rise above their problems, but they need to have a reason to do so. Young people generally don't have the maturity to value education in the same way my adult stu-dents value it. But fear of failure, whether economic or academic, can motivate both.

11   Flunking as a regular policy has just as much **merit** today as it did two generations ago. We must review the threat of flunking and see it as it really is—a positive teaching tool. It is an expression of confidence by both teachers and parents that the students have the ability to learn the material presented to them. However, making it work again would take a dedicated, caring **conspiracy** between teachers and parents. It would mean facing the tough reality that passing kids who haven't learned the material—while it might save them grief for the short term—dooms

do-gooder: a naive person with good intentions

impediments: obstacles; things that stop progress

trump card: something that gives one the advantage over the other

composure: being calm and in control of one's emotions

radical: unusual or different from the norm

at stake: at risk or what can be lost or won

merit: worth, value

conspiracy: a secret plan

them to long-term illiteracy. It would mean that teachers would have to follow through on their threats, and parents would have to stand behind them, knowing their children's best interests are indeed at stake. This means no more doing Scott's assignments for him because he might fail. No more passing Jodi because she's such a nice kid.

12   This is a policy that worked in the past and can work today. A wise teacher, with the support of his parents, gave our son the opportunity to succeed—or fail. It's time we return this choice to all students.

COMPREHENSION QUESTIONS

1. Who is Sherry's intended audience?

2. According to the author, do all high school diplomas have the same validity?

3. Does the author believe that all students should pass their courses? Why or why not?

DISCUSSION QUESTIONS

1. What is the purpose of this essay? Why aren't some students motivated to do well? Support your answer by citing evidence from the essay.

2. Many schools are rated provincially according to how many students pass or fail. School administrators want their schools to rank highly, and, therefore, teachers have great pressure from administrators (and parents) to pass undeserving students. What suggestions can you give to change this practice?

3. Why has the author chosen the title that she did? Is it an effective title? Were you drawn in to read the essay? What kind of titles do you give your own essays?

WRITING ASSIGNMENTS

1. Write a narrative paragraph about a positive or negative experience you have had in school. What made the experience positive or negative? Use a specific example to illustrate your point.

2. Should teachers be allowed to give students zero for a course assignment? Should teachers be able to flunk students so they have to repeat an entire year or semester? Write an essay in which you take a stand about passing or flunking students and indicate when failing a student is or is not appropriate. State your position, and support it with facts, examples, and reasons.

3. Colleges and universities decide what classes will prepare individuals for specific careers. What is your opinion of the required courses for your program? Should post-secondary institutes rethink required courses or even the methods they use to teach these courses? Write an essay where you analyze the courses in your program and rate their suitability to prepare students for the job market.

CREDITS

TEXT CREDITS

p. 16: Excerpt from "On Baking" by Richard Sennett, from *The Corrosion of Character: The Personal Consequences of Work in the New Capitalism*. Copyright © 1998 by Richard Sennett. Used by permission of W.W. Norton & Company, Inc.

p. 17: Excerpt from "Mother Tongue" by Amy Tan. Copyright © 1990 by Amy Tan. First appeared in *The Threepenny Review*. Reprinted by permission of the author and the Sandra Dijkstra Literary Agency.

p. 33: Excerpt from "Growing up Game" by Brenda Peterson, from *Living by Water: True Stories of Nature and Spirit* by Brenda Peterson.

p. 73: Sherwin Sully Tija, "Of Lemons and Lemonade" from *Adbusters* magazine. Reprinted by permission of the author.

p. 94: Excerpt from *Life of Pi* by Yann Martel. Copyright © 2001 Yann Martel. Reprinted by permission of Knopf Canada.

p. 113: *The Night Wanderer: A Native Gothic Novel* by Drew Hayden Taylor. Copyright © 2007 Drew Hayden Taylor, published by Annick Press Ltd. Reproduced by permission.

p. 131: Mark Caldwell, "Polly Want a PhD?" *Discover Magazine*, January 2000.

p. 150–151: "How Countries of the World Are Classified" adapted from *Classifications of Countries Based on Their Level of Development: How It Is Done and How It Could Be Done*, by Lynge Nielsen, IMF

p. 170: Laurence Steinberg, "Bound to Bicker," *Psychology Today*, December 1987. Reprinted with permission from *Psychology Today* magazine. Copyright © 1987 Sussex Publishers, LLC.

p. 190: "A Passion for the Environment: Two Accounts," by Monte Hummel. First appeared in *Queen's Quarterly* 107/1 (Spring 2000), pp. 66–67.

p. 208: Excerpt from *Care of the Soul* by Thomas Moore, pp. 3–4. Copyright © 1992 by Thomas Moore. Reprinted by permission of HarperCollins Publishers.

p. 227: Excerpt from "Last Rights" in *The Economist*, June 21, 1997, p. 21.

p. 312: Excerpt from "Treating Canada's Case of 'Taxi, M.D.'" by Ali Okhowat. Downloaded from: http://www.actioncanada.ca/en/2010 Fellows' Op-Ed, page 26.

p. 314: "Should Bodychecking be Banned?" by Kolby Solinsky. Originally posted on *White Cover Magazine*. Reprinted by permission of the author.

p. 315: Excerpt from "We Can Make Education More Equal," by Adam Goldberg, Co-Founder of Teach for Canada. Downloaded from: http://www.actioncanada.ca/en/2010 Fellows' Op-Ed Articles, page 17.

p. 317: Excerpt from "Seduce Me With Soap and Water," by Scott Robertson. Downloaded from: http://www.actioncanada.ca/en/2010 Fellows' Op-Ed Articles, page 36.

p. 319: Excerpt from "For First Time, Chimps Seen Making Weapons for Hunting," by Rick Weiss, washingtonpost.com

p. 321: Excerpt from "Road Rage: In Taras Grescoe's *Straphanger*, pitched battles over transit are about where and how we want to live," by John Lorinc. Originally published in *Walrus* magazine. John Lorinc is a Toronto journalist and author of *The New City* (Penguin 2006).

p. 322: "I Was a Plagiarist," by Emma Teitel, http://oncampus.macleans.ca/education/2011/11/08/i-was-a-plagiarist/

p. 322: Excerpt from "Rise of Electronic Media and Readers Putting Damper on Paper Products Industry" Conference Board of Canada.

p. 322: Excerpt from "Tear Down the Stigma around Depression," by John Gormley.

p. 323: Excerpt from "War on Drugs Behind Spread of Disease, Global Report Says," by Natalie Stechyson.

p. 500: Edison and the Kinetoscope from *American Cinema, American Culture* by John Belton.

p. 504: Ted Fishman, "A Simple Glass of Water" *New York Times*, August 23, 2001 issue. Copyright © 2001 New York Times. All rights reserved. Used by permission.

p. 506: "Words that Wound," by Emily Sher. Retrieved on January 28, 2011 from: http://www.emilsher.com/essays/words.htm

p. 508: "Money Is Not Wealth" by Paul Graham, *Hackers and Painters: Big Ideas from the Computer Age* (2004: O'Reilly Media, Inc.), pp. 90–91. Reproduced with permission.

p. 511: "20s," by Lauren Kirshner. *Chatelaine*, October 2010 issue. Reprinted by permission of the author.

p. 512: "Last Lecture," by Ian Spears. From the *Guelph Tribune*, Thursday, July 8, 2010 issue. Reprinted by permission of the author.

p. 514: "All Kinds of Friends," from *Necessary Losses* by Judith Viorst. Copyright © 1986 by Judith Viorst. Published by Simon & Schuster, Inc. Digital usage granted by permission of the Choate Agency, LLC.

p. 516: "Engage Immigrant Communities," by Dr. Romila Verma, from *Our Water Our Future* Spring 2011 publication.

p. 518: "Beginning of a New Era," from *Polar Imperative: A History of Arctic Sovereignty in North America*, © 2010 by Shelagh D. Grant. Published by Douglas & McIntyre, an imprint of D&M Publishers Inc. Reprinted with permission from the publisher.

p. 520: "Canadians: What Do They Want?" by Margaret Atwood. Mother Jones: San Francisco: Mother Jones, Inc. © 1982, Foundation for National Progress.

p. 523: "The Metric System (Sort Of)," by Wayne Grady. Originally appeared in *Saturday Night* magazine. Reprinted by permission of the author.

p. 524: "In Praise of the F Word," by Mary Sherry. May 6, 1991 edition of *Newsweek*.

Corrosion of Character (Sennett), 306
cumulative adjectives, 447

D

daily writing, 18
databases
    citing, 347–348
    searching, 334–335
deductive order, 55–56
definition essays, 290–292
    focused assignments, 292
    general assignment, 292
    imitation assignment, 292
    reminder of elements, 290
definition paragraph
    assignment selection, 205–206
    audience, 207
    category in, 201
    clustering, 206
    coherence of, 207
    concluding sentence, 208
    correcting, 213
    critical reading of, 211
    details in, 203–204
    editing, 211–213
    elements of, 201–202
    establishing territory in, 205
    examples in, 201, 203–204
    first draft, 208
    focus of, 206–208
    freewriting, 206
    getting started with, 202–203
    glance at, 200–201
    goals, 214
    group in, 201
    negatives, 202, 204–205
    organization of, 206–208
    prewriting, 206
    process of, 205–208
    reflecting on, 214
    revision, 209–213
    searching, 213
    self-editing, 214
    sources of, 200
    strengths in, identifying, 214
    thinking, 201–205
    topic sentence, 207
    unity of, 207
denotation, 11
dependent clauses, 390–391
    and commas, 390–391
    fragment, 400–402
description essay, 272–274
    focused assignments, 274
    general assignment, 274
    imitation assignment, 273
    reminder of elements, 272
description paragraph
    assignment selection, 69–70
    audience, 71
    brainstorming, 70

    coherence of, 71–72
    comparisons in, 65, 68–69
    concluding sentence, 72
    correcting, 78
    critical reading of, 75
    details in, 66–67
    dominant impression in, 65
    editing, 75–78
    elements of, 65–66
    first draft, 73
    focus, 71–72
    freewriting, 70–71
    getting started with, 66–67
    glance at, 64–65
    goals, 78
    organization of, 67–68, 71–72
    prewriting, 70
    process of, 69–73
    reflecting on, 78
    revision, 74–75
    searching, 78
    self-editing, 78
    sensory description in, 65
    strengths in, identifying, 78
    thinking, 65–69
    topic sentence, 71
    unity of, 71–72
details
    adding, 32
    argument paragraph, 218
    in cause and effect paragraph,
        163–164
    in comparison and contrast paragraph, 181,
        183–184, 185–187
    concrete, 67
    cutting, 32
    in description paragraph, 66–67
    in example paragraph, 83
    and examples, 203–204
    general to specific, 83–84
    key, identification of, 128
    minor, 51–52
    in narration paragraph, 106–107
    order of, 59
    organizing, 126–128, 166
    process paragraph, 123, 126–128
    selection and elaboration on, 185–187
    specific, 49, 52–53, 106–107
    vague, 52–53
details, supporting, 42
    elaboration of, 50–52
    essay, 253–255, 264
    in example paragraph, 83–84
    major details, 49–50
    in narration paragraph, 102
    outlines, 49
    specific details, 49, 52–53
diction, 9
Digital Object Identifier (DOI), 338
Dixie Sun Online Edition, 309, 310, 311
documented essay

    checklist, 350–351
    draft, 350
    elements of, 331–332
    getting started with, 332
    glance at, 328–331
    integrating information, 332
    locating information, 331, 332–336
    process of, 336–343
    processing information, 331–332, 340
    revision, 350
    types of information, 336–337
DOI. *See* Digital Object Identifier (DOI)
double-checking, 37
draft
    classification paragraph, 150, 153
    documented essay, 350
    narration paragraph, 112
    process paragraph, 131
    writing process, 21, 27–31

E

EBSCO Canadian Literary Centre, 334
The Economist, 227
editing
    See also self-editing
    for apostrophes, 472–473
    argument paragraph, 230–232
    cause and effect paragraph, 173–174
    checklist, 35–36
    classification paragraph, 153–156
    comparison and contrast paragraph,
        194–196
    definition paragraph, 211–213
    description paragraph, 75–78
    elimination of usual errors, 35
    essays, 263–264
    example paragraph, 97–99
    narration paragraph, 115–116
    process paragraph, 134–136
    for pronouns, consistency, 444–445
    strategies, 35–38
    subordination, 395–396
    writing process, 21
elaboration, 87–88
    major supporting details, 50–52
    narration paragraph, 106, 109
Engage Immigrant Communities (Verman),
    516–518
essay structure. *See* essays
essays
    See also specific types of essays
    assignments, 241–243
    body, 238, 250–253
    checklist, 265, 299
    coherence of, 257–259
    conclusion, 238, 259–263
    connections, 264
    editing, 263–264
    elements of, 238, 271
    first draft, 263
    glance at, 236–238, 268–271

NOTES

NOTES

NOTES

NOTES

NOTES

NOTES

NOTES

NOTES

NOTES